MW01193544

# The Practice of Lending

Terence M. Yhip • Bijan M. D. Alagheband

# The Practice
# of Lending

## A Guide to Credit Analysis
## and Credit Risk

Terence M. Yhip
University of the West Indies
Mississauga, ON, Canada

Bijan M. D. Alagheband
McMaster University and
Hydro One Networks Inc.
Toronto, ON, Canada

ISBN 978-3-030-32196-3      ISBN 978-3-030-32197-0   (eBook)
https://doi.org/10.1007/978-3-030-32197-0

This Palgrave Macmillan imprint is published by the registered company Springer Nature Switzerland AG.
The registered company address is: Gewerbestrasse 11, 6330 Cham, Switzerland

# Preface

The purpose of this book is to provide the reader a comprehensive guide to assessing creditworthiness, quantifying and rating credit risk, and modelling default likelihood. The emphasis is on the practical—techniques and tools. Credit is a highly inter-disciplinary subject, and whereas a background in business, accounting, economics, statistics, and mathematics is useful, this book attempts to present the material as non-technically as possible for those with only some exposure to these subjects, or may be studying related courses concurrently. We focus on the "how it is done", as much as the "why it is done". Another unique feature of the book is its presentation of diverse material in a cohesive and inclusive structure in order to lessen the search for supplementary readings.

This book presents both principles and practical applications, so it should be a valuable resource for beginners who are aiming for a career in credit, but lack the broad skill set for analysing financial statements, preparing a *pro forma* financial statement, projecting cash flows, analysing economic data, developing scorecards, and modelling loan default. For professional bankers, the book should serve as a refresher and a source of new material for bank professionals looking for techniques to develop the *Advanced Internal Ratings Based (AIRB)* approach outlined in the Basel II accord. And for those in research in economics and finance, the book should be a useful guide for developing and testing probability models.

Lending out money, regardless of whether it belongs to you or the institution you work for, requires a careful consideration of financial and nonfinancial factors. For credit analysts and credit risk managers, the ability to differentiate between acceptable and unacceptable credit risk is the ultimate test of professionalism. Further, a lender must be able to rank counterparty risk consistently to be able to price and capitalise the risk. This second point leads to the question of what tools are available in the risk assessor's analytical toolbox.

To begin let us introduce the criteria-based approach to credit risk rating. It conforms to the AIRB approach of a two-dimensional credit-rating system. The criteria-based method belongs to a class of models called expert-judgement and it amounts to constructing a scorecard of a borrower's risk profile. The advantage of such hybrid models, compared to purely statistical models (which we will also discuss), is their ability to process a large volume of quantitative *and* qualitative information in a structured format, namely, the scorecard. This book equips the reader with the principles and the techniques to build such a scorecard from scratch—information that is not available in books and articles in current circulation. We provide a practical application in rating a (fictional) passenger airline. To summarise the important features of the criteria-based approach are the following:

- Increased objectivity: *We cannot get away from the fact that credit risk assessment and risk rating are opinions.* Much of the information is qualitative, for example, management quality, so that subjectivity cannot be avoided. The challenge for the credit analyst is to minimise bias. We claim that the risk criteria approach will not eliminate subjectivity but it will reduce it because ultimately the selected criteria are subject to validation.
- Risk rating consistency and replicability: Within a portfolio, the ratings assigned by analysing the same set of borrower information should be the same, irrespective of who is performing the risk assessment. Across portfolios, all rated counterparties are subject to a single or standard rating scale.
- Flexibility and transparency: A model is a simplification of reality and therefore cannot capture every detail. Still, accuracy in the risk rating must take precedence because a risk rating is a principal component in credit decisions, pricing, and the capitalisation of risk. Therefore, there needs to be sufficient flexibility that allows the user to override or modify model results with the benefit of additional *material information*. In this book, we discuss the override functionality and the safeguards for risk rating integrity.
- Customisation: Every industry has its own set of risks and we show that the criteria-based approach is perfectly suited for customisation.

The other set of tools—probit, logit, and discriminant models—involve more formalisation and quantification, much less subjectivity, and they are well suited to modelling default risk. There are excellent statistics textbooks on these methods, but the challenge is to find one that shows step-by-step how to (a) test the theories on real data for companies and countries, (b) improve the fitted equations, and (c) interpret and apply the regression results. This book attempts to bridge this knowledge gap. Part II of this book presents material that makes it easier for beginners to gain proficiency in using these tools.

This book is organised in three parts. Part I, "The Criteria-Based Approach to Credit Assessment and Credit Risk Rating" presents the methodology, the techniques, and specific expert-judgement models. Our objective is that by the end of Part I, with all the practical examples, one would be able to apply the tools and the techniques to design a Borrower Risk Rating (BRR) scorecard for any industry that one examines.

Chapter 1, "Credit Analysis and Credit Management", is an overview of the big themes that readers can expect in the book. This chapter starts with a discussion on creditworthiness. We include a discussion on information asymmetry and the problems they cause in lending and credit rating. We outline the loan underwriting process, review "Five Cs" method of credit analysis, and introduce "The Criteria-Based Approach to Credit Analysis". This chapter discusses loan administration in the context of managing credit risk.

Chapter 2, "Financial Statements Analysis", introduces financial ratio analysis and reviews the important ratios used in credit analysis. This chapter serves as a refresher on how to read financial statements, calculate, and interpret financial ratios. It gives a detailed discussion on off-balance sheet liabilities and presents methods to capitalise such obligations in the section, "Off-balance Sheet Debt". The importance of accurate financial disclosures is discussed. Financial ratios by themselves are not a perfect tool, so we look into its limitations under "Uses and limitations of Ratio Analysis".

Chapter 3, "The Criteria-Based Approach to Credit Assessment and Credit Risk Rating", introduces the methodology for designing a consistent, transparent, and replicable risk rating system. We guide the reader through each step in the section, "The Framework of Credit Risk Assessment", thus laying the theoretical foundations of an industry-specific scorecard. In the section, "Assembling the Risk Criteria on a Scorecard", this chapter presents the framework of the criteria-based approach, and the building blocks consisting of Risk Criteria, Risk Factors, weights, and Descriptors. We show how to apply the principles and concepts in a computer spreadsheet.

Chapter 4, "The Building Blocks of Credit Analysis and Credit Risk Rating", takes the reader into the practical details of a credit risk scorecard. We achieve this result by applying the general principles outlined in Chap. 3 to each building block. We look at Country and Sovereign Risk, Industry

Risk Assessment, Business Risk Assessment, Management Risk Assessment, and Financial Risk Assessment. This chapter gives many examples.

Chapter 5, "How It All Fits", presents a "case study". We select the air transportation industry and analyse a fictional airline, *AY Intercontinental Airways*. The purpose of a case study is not only to apply techniques but also to demonstrate the kind of thinking that goes into the modelling process. This is not easy to explain but learning by doing gets around the abstraction and helps to achieve the aim.

Chapter 6, "Credit Risk Analysis and Credit Risk Rating of Commercial Real Estate", broadens the application of the criteria-based approach to commercial real estate (CRE) under the headings, "Application of the Criteria-Based Methodology to CRE". We develop a scorecard for assessing various types of CRE funded by a mortgage. This chapter compares techniques for valuing CRE assets and preparing necessary financial projections, namely, NOI (net operating income) statement and the balance sheet. This chapter examines the cap rate and quantifies the sensitivity of valuations to assumptions about the cap rate and the growth rate in income.

Chapter 7, "Bank Credit Risk Analysis and Bank Credit Rating", focuses on commercial banks. We show how to adapt the criteria-based methodology to the banking industry. Bank analysis is completely different from that of non-bank businesses on many levels: the assessment of capital strength or solvency, asset quality, management, profitability, and liquidity—commonly called CAMELS analysis. This chapter gives a comprehensive treatment of the CAMELS analysis, including Basel III rules on capitalisation. As in previous chapters, the main objective of this chapter is to develop a BRR scorecard for the banking industry and rate a bank.

Part II, "Statistical Methods on Credit Scoring", steps up the formalisation of credit risk analysis by introducing regression models for predicting defaults. By the end of Part II, the reader should be in a position to apply the models to corporate borrowers and country borrowers.

Chapter 8 of Part II, "Statistical Methods of Credit Risk Analysis", introduces linear probability, probit and logit models and the use of financial predictors of loan default. This chapter explains how to fit regression equations to actual company data in the sections, "Probability Models", "Case Study – Probit Model to Predict Default", and "Example of Linear Probability and Logit Models". This chapter extends the treatment of probability models to the development of *application scorecards* in the section, "Scaling the Log Odds Ratio". We examine the limitations of statistical models and credit rating scorecards used in personal lending.

Chapter 9, "Statistical Methods of Predicting Country Debt Crisis", focuses on country risk assessment. We briefly review expert opinion, hybrid models like the criteria-based approach, and logit and discriminant models. This chapter gives a rigorous but easy-to-follow presentation of discriminant analysis. The section, "Applying Discriminant Analysis to Predict Sovereign Debt Crisis", emphasises a real application where actual country data are used for the estimation.

Finally, Part III, "Credit Management", moves the spotlight from credit rating to credit management, thus completing the credit process. *The objective of Part III is to discuss loan administration and to show that although it is not as high profile as loan origination, it is an important back-office function supporting credit delivery by the front office (sales) and middle office (risk management) to ensure the full repayment of a loan.* Chapter 10, "Credit Monitoring and Compliance", examines the reasons as to why the process is so vital to lending and looks at best practices in the banking industry. We discuss the benefits of automating the credit monitoring process. Chapter 11, "Problem Loan Management", focuses on problem loans and its management structure within the enterprise-wide framework. We explain loan loss provisioning, and the strategies that banks use to recover impaired loans and overdue loans that are written off. This chapter examines the pros and cons of each recovery strategy.

Mississauga, ON, Canada                                     Terence M. Yhip
Toronto, ON, Canada                                    Bijan M. D. Alagheband

# Acknowledgements

Writing a book is just part of a long and demanding process of getting it to press, and this book is no exception; so we are indebted to many people who helped us reach the end. For reading earlier drafts and for consultation, we thank Brian Alagheband, Kenneth Clarke, Daniel Yhip, Celia Gibb, David McIntosh, and Bing Wang. The feedback from them was amazing. In order to work out practical examples, data are vital and for this, we thank S&P Global for their assistance by Saleem Daya, Tim Love, and Howard Bernheim. Thanks go to the experts in the field who gave us permission to quote their names as potential evaluators: Professor Jan Keil, Kurt von dem Hagen, Shamim Malik, Garbis Iradian, Professor Dean Mountain, Professor Victor Yu Sing, and Marla Dukharan. Just as importantly, deep thanks to our families, Martha, Gina, Can, and Brian for support and the encouragement throughout the length of the process. Despite the help provided by the people mentioned, errors may still remain for which we accept full responsibility. We welcome comments and ask that they be sent to the care of Palgrave Macmillan.

# Contents

# List of Figures

# List of Tables

# Part I

## The Criteria-Based Approach to Credit Assessment and Credit Rating

# 1

# Credit Analysis and Credit Management

**Learning Objectives**

1. Provide a general understanding of the various processes in lending and credit analysis
2. Review the "Five Cs" method of credit analysis
3. Introduce the Criteria-Based Approach to risk rating
4. Examine the reasons that asymmetrical information poses serious problems for lending and risk rating
5. Discuss credit culture and its influence on credit analysis and lending
6. Look at banking regulations and their relevance to credit analysis and lending

## 1.1 Introduction

**Historical and Philosophical Bases of Credit Analysis**
This chapter provides a broad discussion on lending, which consists of two connected activities: credit origination and credit administration. A basic understanding of the issues around them allows a deeper appreciation of the work of a credit professional and the philosophical approach the credit analyst brings to the task of assessing creditworthiness. Credit and the credit market are vital to the efficient functioning of a modern economy that is intrinsically

**Electronic Supplementary Material:** The online version of this chapter (https://doi.org/10.1007/978-3-030-32197-0_1) contains supplementary material, which is available to authorized users.

characterised by complexity across production, consumption, and financial intermediation. This third activity featuring a developed credit market is intrinsic to a modern economy. For example, we instinctively think of loans when we see a commercial bank, a credit union, or an investment bank, some of the principal institutions that deliver the full array of credit, including sophisticated financing products such as securitisations. Regardless of the complexity of the loan facility, lending in its simplest form is as old as civilisation going back thousands of years to agrarian societies. The oldest surviving codes governing lending date back to 2000 BC in Mesopotamia.[1] Not surprisingly, the fundamentals of lending have not changed over millennia. A lender still asks the same old question: *Should I lend to this person or firm?* So, in terms of the *modus operandi*, there is no essential difference between a moneylender in 2000 BC and the manager of your local bank, where you go to for a personal loan or a business loan.

The word "credit" comes from the Latin word *creditum*, something entrusted to another; or some would say, *credere* meaning to trust or believe. In the Western world, credit involves a contract, articulated in a legal document called the Loan Agreement or Credit Agreement, in which a borrower receives a sum of money, or anything of value, now, and promises to repay the lender, usually with interest, at some future date. By definition, a credit agreement is enforceable by law. In Islamic countries where Sharia law[2] rules, banks lend not on the basis of interest but on the principle of profit-and-loss sharing, through which the parties in the transaction agree to distribute profits according to an agreed ratio, and to absorb the loss in proportion to the capital invested by each partner. Regardless of the cultural difference in the approach to lending or, broadly speaking, investing, the universal and fundamental principle embodies two concepts: *willingness* and *ability* to repay. Islamic commercial lending practices do not eliminate risk and, thus, a financial assessment of creditworthiness is still necessary as in traditional Western banking. The models that we will be introducing in later chapters attempt to quantify directly the second concept. You will observe in later chapters that we are not ignoring willingness because we capture it in business risk and country/sovereign risk analysis.

Credit risk analysis is both art and science; how much of each depend on the problem in question. It is part art because it involves experience, practice, skill, and imagination; but it is also science in the narrow sense of credit risk analysis employing the essential methodology of natural science, which consists of the procedures and the practices of theorising, testing, and revising with new information. All this goes on with the awareness that even the reigning theory is always provisional.

The predictions of an economic model (of which financial and accounting models are a subset) will never be precise for many reasons, which is a subject all of its own. In physics, the king of all sciences, 100% model accuracy is an unrealistic expectation. The common expression "this or that method is not an exact science" is based on the fallacy that science is absolutely exact or accurate—a belief that was debunked long years ago by the nineteenth-century English economist and logician, Will Stanley Jevons.[3] Consider gravity. Isaac Newton described this force by the Inverse Square law, which explains and predicts the paths of planetary bodies "accurately" for all practical purposes, but more than one and a quarter century later Albert Einstein's General Theory of Relativity (1915) came along and proved more accurate. Many people have the false notion that science is "exact" and "certain" without stopping to think that science is essentially an endless series of refinements, and that the answers are never 100% certain. Consider the laws of motion in physics: the certainty or the determinism of the laws in classical or Newtonian mechanics has been supplanted by uncertainty in quantum mechanics, which teaches that the laws of physics would only allow one to calculate *relative probabilities* of various future outcomes.[4]

A related fallacy is the belief that the mathematisation of credit analysis makes it more accurate and objective. At best, mathematics and statistics are just *tools*, albeit indispensable, to detect, test, and quantify patterns in large datasets. Consider asset valuation models that we will examine in later chapters. For one thing, the inputs or assumptions used for valuation leave plenty of room for personal bias, but that does not mean valuation models are worthless. Used properly, they are powerful and useful tools for making informed investment decisions. Mathematical models, no matter how sophisticated or carefully constructed, will still be a limited although important tool in credit analysis because much of the information inputs is qualitative.

There is also a common fallacy to equate subjectivity with everything from guesses to personal prejudices. In Chaps. 4 and 5, we will be discussing the criteria approach to credit risk analyses, a hybrid model that combines features of qualitative/heuristic models and mathematical/causal models, which includes statistical models. In criteria-based modelling, we allocate weights to the criteria and the predictors judgementally. The weights come from expert judgement rather than from a statistical procedure. That said it would be a mistake to equate judgement with guesswork or bias.[5] Subjectivity ought to be grounded in observation, meaning both empirical data and interpretation borne out of experience (which, by definition, is not impersonal). As more information emerges, overall understanding of the issues improves, thus compelling the credit practitioner to review the thinking, the current model, the methodology, and the methods.

Updating the "priors" as in Bayesian analysis is a natural and essential way to approximate objectivity and to make more accurate decisions, which implies there is no escaping the fact that the model will still fall short of the ideal.[6] Expert judgement is both unavoidable and necessary. The good thing about the criteria-based approach is that the subjectivity is not buried deep within the analysis but is laid bare in the weights one assigns to the risk criteria and sub-factors, and the choice of predictors. In this way, one can go back and do over the analysis with revised weights in the light of better information. Other adjustments, such as adding or replacing variables, may also be made.

---

**Process**

You would be seeing the word process used numerous times in this book. The word comes up regularly in all activities that require a series of steps to transform inputs to outputs. Credit underwriting, credit structuring, credit analysis, loan monitoring, credit review, problem loans management, Watch List, and so on are quintessentially processes with defined aims (outputs). In the case of loan underwriting, the ultimate aim is to get the loan on the books with all the features of an appropriately structured loan. Related to *process* is *process mapping*, an important tool for not only operations but also risk management.

---

## 1.2    A Framework for Credit Operations

We may view the lending process as part of a much larger system characterised by linkages between decision-making units of an organisation, its internal credit policy and ERM (Enterprise Risk Management) framework, and the overarching economic and legal environment in which the organisation operates. Figure 1.1 explains the system. The ellipse in the centre is the credit process of originating and managing the exposure of individual borrowers and loan portfolios. The centre is where loan underwriting and approval processes occur, and where loans are booked, serviced, and managed. The rectangle nesting the ellipse depicts the organisation's lending policy, the ERM framework, and the related oversight by the board of directors. Credit policy determines single name limits, portfolio limits, and sector limits. The ERM framework of a bank (a) establishes risk tolerance and self-imposed risk limits by business type, (b) manages and monitors the risk categories, limits, and targets, and (c) prepares regular reports that at least address and document developments pertaining to (a) and (b). To give an example, the business unit (e.g., mortgage finance) might want to put more residential real estate loans on the books (because the demand is high), but due to risk appetite the total for the whole organisation cannot breach the limits, otherwise a formal approval process has to be followed to exceed the targets.

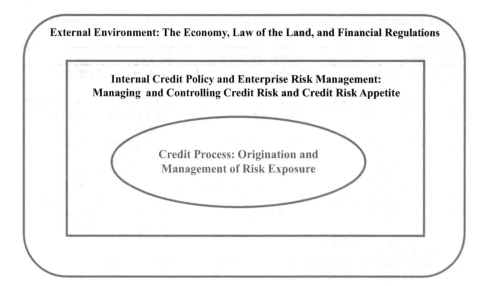

**Fig. 1.1**  A framework for credit operations

The external environment encompasses the economy, law of the land, and financial regulations. The economy includes business conditions, industry risks, and the business cycle. These limit the potential risk ratings of borrowers. In any given economic cycle, some industries will be highly risky and lenders would be unwise to ignore the trends. In a recession, lenders exercise more caution in lending. Law of the land is self-explanatory: a country's laws set the parameters for what a financial institution can and cannot do. Financial regulations come under various acts or laws governing domestic and international banking. In relatively developed financial markets, many regulators are responsible for supervising financial organisations. Table 1.1 gives a list of the independent regulatory bodies for the US, the UK, and Canada.

But in emerging financial markets, the responsibility for the day-to-day supervision is usually executed by the central bank that has the regulatory authority. Regardless of whether the economy is developed or developing, regulators are expected to be independent bodies because of their authorities. For example, they monitor compliance and enforce prudential regulations and lending practices. Financial institutions face heavy fines and penalties for not complying. The regulatory environment helps to shape a bank's lending policy and rating system.

**Table 1.1** National regulators of the financial system of the United States, the United Kingdom, and Canada

| United States | United Kingdom | Canada |
|---|---|---|
| Federal Reserve System ("Fed") | Bank of England (BoE) | Bank of Canada (BoC) |
| Office of the Comptroller of the Currency (OCC) | Prudential Regulation Authority (PRA) | Office of the Superintendent of Financial Institutions (OSFI) |
| Federal Deposit Insurance Corporation (FDIC) | Financial Services Compensation Scheme | Canada Deposit Insurance Corporation |
| Securities and Exchange Commission (SEC) | Financial Services Compensation Scheme | Canadian Securities Administrators (CSA) |
| Financial Crimes Enforcement Network (FinCEN) | Financial Conduct Authority | Financial Transactions and Reports Analysis Centre of Canada (FINTRAC) |
| Financial Industry Regulatory Authority (FINRA) | | |

## 1.3   The Credit Underwriting Process

For an individual borrower, the main source of financing is a loan from a financial institution (banks and credit unions). Businesses or commercial enterprises raise financing through various channels:

1. Bilateral borrowing from a bank or a syndicate of banks
2. Leasing (capital and operating leases)
3. Issuing secured and unsecured bonds (notes and bonds, respectively) directly in the fixed-income capital market
4. Issuing common shares/private placement (equity market)
5. Issuing hybrid instruments with bond and equity features
6. Securitising and factoring/forfaiting

In this book, we focus on credit or, more narrowly defined, balance sheet debt *and* off-balance sheet debt. This type of debt in the Western banking tradition is called *funded debt* because the debt is *funded* by the *interest payments*. The credit rating system that we will be looking at is a two-dimensional system proposed under Basel II and supervised by the regulators. The essential requirement of such a system is that borrower risk is separate and distinct from facility risk. Together, however, they determine the expected credit loss of a loan that is classified "impaired".

**Difference Between Funded and Unfunded Debt**

Liabilities consist of funded and unfunded obligations. A **funded debt** is a credit facility that is funded with actual cash and bears interest. It includes overdraft, loans, and bonds, so whether it gets reported on or off the balance sheet is irrelevant in credit analysis. *The debt is said to be funded by the interest payments to the lender.* In contrast, **unfunded debt** are contractual obligations for *future* lending, such as guarantees and documentary letters of credit. For such lending, the financial institution (FI) does not advance actual cash but only assumes the risk of non-payment. In return, the FI charges a commission (but not interest). These are *contingent or potential liabilities* that depend on an uncertain *future* event.

Determining the BRR (Borrower Risk Rating) and the Facility Risk Rating (FRR) are essentially the work involved in loan underwriting. In particular, *loan underwriting* is the process of a lender determining whether an obligor's loan application is a safe risk based on the entity's capacity to repay the loan primarily through cash generated from the business and secondarily through collateral. The loan can be the funds to buy a car for personal use and not commercial use, which makes it a personal credit; or the loan can be a term loan to acquire plant and equipment for the enterprise; hence, a business loan. For business or commercial loans, underwriting includes in this general definition the evaluation of the business owner *and* the business. Consequently, the underwriting process for business and corporate loans will be more complex and lengthier than for personal loans and residential mortgages.

A business usually needs more than one credit facility (or a loan product), the amounts would be larger than for personal loans, and altogether there is more documentation to complete. The customer provides some of the documents, but the lender does most of the "paper work" to support the loan application. They are the legal documents to close the transaction. One important document is the contract that binds the obligor and the lender, called the Loan Agreement or the Credit Agreement. Other important documentation would include business licences and registration, Articles of Incorporation, and various security agreements for secured loans. Regardless of the type of credit, credit underwriting involves the same process flow from start to finish and includes the following steps:

1. Credit Initiation
2. Credit Analysis
3. Loan Structuring

4. Credit Submission and Adjudication
5. Loan Documentation
6. Loan Closing and Disbursement
7. Loan Monitoring
8. Problem Loans Management

Although the focus of this book is credit analysis and credit risk rating, it is important for credit analysts to have a fundamental understanding of the lender's credit policies and the procedures. They are the controls that make the lending process systematic and methodical, but most of all minimise credit losses (e.g., due to poorly executed documentation) and enhance the likelihood of full repayment. Lending is a very risky business and creditors face the statistical certainty that a fraction of their loan portfolios will go bad, just like firms that sell products expect their accounts receivables will not all be paid. An essential part of the credit process is identifying and managing problem loans in order to prevent and recover losses. We provide an overview of each of the underwriting components listed above.

### 1.3.1 Credit Initiation

Either a borrower approaches a lender for a loan or a relationship manager (or account manager) finds a prospective loan customer as part of his sales effort. The credit initiation and analysis process ensures that loans made by a lending institution adhere to the lender's enterprise-wide credit policy, guidelines, credit procedures, and credit standards. The credit policy lays out the types of loans that are acceptable, the loan purposes, tenor, collateral, structure, and acceptable guarantees. Furthermore, the credit policy establishes that policy exceptions must have the explicit approval of the loan approval authority, which adjudicates credit transaction requests.

In banks, the authority rests in Risk Management that provides *independent* risk oversight across the enterprise. The credit policy sets the criteria that a prospective borrower must meet. Let us suppose that the preliminary client screening is completed, the customer meets the threshold requirements, the relationship manger has identified the customer's credit needs, based on which, the customer submits a loan application. What follows next in the underwriting process is a thorough analysis of the borrower's creditworthiness, which is the capacity and the willingness to repay the loan.

## 1.3.2  Credit Analysis

Loan underwriting is the process of determining if a loan application is an acceptable risk. An important objective of the process is to evaluate the credit risk, which has two components: the borrower's ability to repay the loan and collateral supporting the loan. The traditional "Five Cs" method is a good jumping-off point for a deeper dive into credit risk rating methodology. The credit analysis process begins with the collection, analysis, and evaluation of the information pertaining to the "Five Cs":

1. Capacity
2. Capital
3. Collateral
4. Condition
5. Character

**Capacity to Repay** The capacity to repay a loan is the borrower's *financial* ability to repay a loan with interest on schedule. In order to assess capacity, reliable and timely financial statements are required. In later chapters, you will learn how to interpret and use financial statements to calculate financial ratios and perform a forecast of cash flow.

**Capital**[7] Capital refers to shareholders' equity in the enterprise. It is what the owners of the firm have invested and what they have at risk if the business were to fail. In addition, we will be looking at two other types of capital in credit analysis: regulatory capital and economic capital. Regulatory capital, as the name suggests, is capital that banking authorities define for regulatory purposes, and the items in the definitions are balance sheet items. The economic capital of a bank is derived from an economic capital model that does not require assets as inputs. It is the difference between some given percentile of a loss distribution and the expected loss derived from combining the probability of default (PD) and the loss given default (LGD). Capital, as a factor of production, refers to physical assets that a business uses to produce goods and services.

**Collateral** The primary source of repayment is cash flow. The secondary source of repayment is collateral in case the borrower cannot repay the loan through cash flow. Personal assets, paper assets, physical assets, and even future income (such as customers' orders) are all considered collateral. A borrower would pledge these assets to *secure* a loan; hence, the phrase *secured loan*. In the event of default, the central concern of the lender of a secured loan is whether the realisable value of the collateral is sufficient to cover the expected loss. Since the quality of the asset is important, lenders usually keep current and accurate record of the realisable value of the collateral. Part of the exercise of updating collateral value is obtaining current evaluations of the assets such as property, inventory, and accounts receivable. An important function of loan administration is to ensure that collateral documentation held by the lender is in (legal) order to facilitate orderly sale of assets and orderly recovery of losses.

**Condition** The desire to grant a loan depends on certain conditions that are *external* to the lender. The relationship manager and the credit analyst must be aware of recent and emerging trends in the borrower's line of work, the borrower's industry, business conditions affecting sales, and economic forces such as inflation and interest rates that might affect the loan. Additionally, certain conditions *internal* to the lender are important to lending. Therefore, credit officers need to know the institution's lending policy and the guidelines. Consider, for example, the purpose of a loan for three different transactions: buy a house purchase, buy a car, and personal needs. The interest rate on a mortgage would be the lowest because the lender has a better chance of recovering the loan if the borrower were to default. In the case of personal needs, which are not specific, there is more risk or uncertainty of repayment and, thus, the interest rate would be the highest of the three.

**Character** An assessment of an obligor's credit history is necessary to determine willingness to repay a loan. A poor credit history is a good predictor of future repayment problems. Therefore, reputation for repaying debt is an essential part of character assessment. There is also *name lending*, which is lending based on a borrower's social standing rather than the capacity to repay. The practice exists in mature markets but is prevalent in emerging markets. This is not to deny the fact that in emerging markets, borrowers of high social status usually have stronger capacity to repay. For a corporate borrower, the character assessment will include an assessment of the competence, capability, and the integrity or honesty of management. The analysis of leadership and reputation is qualitative and subjective, but the qualitative nature of the analysis makes it no less reliable or rigorous than the more quantitative and objective financial analysis.

### How Important Is Character in Risk Rating?

Character assessment has been under closer scrutiny in the light of some recent financial scandals involving companies like Enron Corporation, WorldCom, Carillion Plc, and Nortel that made world headlines.[8] The list of reported accounting scandals in the 2000s is the longest, making this period the worst for the notoriety in the last century.

The ease of obtaining character-related information depends partly on the type of borrower. For a personal borrower, the lender has more readily available information from a variety of sources that include credit reports, collection agencies, and media reports. For a public corporation or private company, character valuation requires assessing management conduct and ethics. If the borrower is a current customer or is new, the bank's credit analyst obtains the information partly from call reports, face-to-face interviews with the principals of the company, meetings with lower level staff, and site visits. But in the absence of these means of gathering information, the analyst must rely on media reports and local market knowledge. For public companies listed on stock exchanges, character-type information is available from the Securities Commission of the country in question. In the United States, for example, the SEC (Securities Exchange Commission) Office of the Whistle-blower rewards eligible individuals for sharing original information that will lead to successful law enforcement actions.

Management can be a nebulous activity, with much of the information limited, qualitative, and hard to quantify, making Management Risk the most difficult of all Risk Criteria in a BRR (Borrower Risk Rating) scorecard to evaluate. A common remark that one hears is that evaluating management is a thankless job. Yet **Management Risk** cannot be swept under the rug because it subsequently surfaces in **Financial Risk** of the scorecard, but then it is too late because the lender had been making credit decisions based on an inflated Financial Risk rating and hence, an inflated BRR. The common thread in both risks is the problem of inadequate information, specifically the *information asymmetry* that occurs when the borrower possesses better information than the lender in a credit relationship. Thus, the fact that management can be vague is not a reason to ignore it in the scorecard. This book attempts to include information asymmetry explicitly in the BRR. The lender faces an information asymmetry problem stemming from the difficulty of performing an accurate assessment of the borrower's creditworthiness. If the bank has the ability to obtain full information when loan applications are accepted, the assigned BRR will be a more accurate measure of the default risk and the lender will be able to minimise default risk. We will examine information asymmetry and the resulting problems later in this chapter.

**Credit Risk**  What do we mean by credit risk? It is the potential for a borrower or counterparty to fail to make full and timely payments of interest and principal. Credit risk consists of these two components.

1. **Default risk:** measured by assessing the borrower's capacity and willingness to service the debt under the terms of the loan agreement; and
2. **Loan recovery prospects:** The lender determines the expected loss based on the default risk (as a separate factor) and the loan structure and the value of the collateral held (as a separate factor).

The expected credit loss is the probability of default multiplied by the exposure at default, times the fraction of loss given default. The expected loss has a direct bearing on economic capital, which we will examine in Chap. 7. To convert loss expectation in percentile to a dollar amount, an estimate of the exposure at risk is needed; hence, the following equation.

$$\textbf{Expected Loss} = \textbf{EAD} \times \textbf{LGD} \times \textbf{PD}$$

where·

EAD = Exposure at default
LGD = Fraction of the loan amount lost given default (%)
PD = Probability of default (%)

The EAD is an *estimate* of the drawn amount, or the amount expected to be owed by a borrower at the time of default; stated another way, the EAD estimate is based on past utilisation of the undrawn credit and the possible future changes in that exposure due to the nature of the credit commitment before default. The Facility Risk Rating (FRR) reflects information that is specific to the *transaction*, so it includes collateral, guarantees, seniority, and maturity for each transaction or credit facility, such as a short-term revolving loan, a term loan, and a lease. Each FRR has a LGD rate calibrated against each other. The BRR reflects the credit creditworthiness of the borrower and takes into account the attributes that are specific to the obligor (and sometimes the guarantor of a borrower). The combination of PD risk and LGD risk gives the *loan quality risk*. Figure 1.2 illustrates low PD risk combining with low LGD risk translates into acceptable loan quality risk, and vice versa in quadrant III. Quadrant II and quadrant IV involve trade-off between PD and LGD. When PD Risk > LGD Risk as in quadrant II, which often happens as the BRR deteriorates over time, prudent banks ensure that the collateral remains solid with low LGD and legal enforceability. Lenders encounter this situation for borrowers that are on the Watch List or are non-performing. When LGD Risk > PD Risk as in quadrant IV, prudent lenders will ensure that the BRR is accurate so that the implied PD is also accurate. Banks cannot avoid quadrant III and they have a specialised group that manages only non-performing loans.

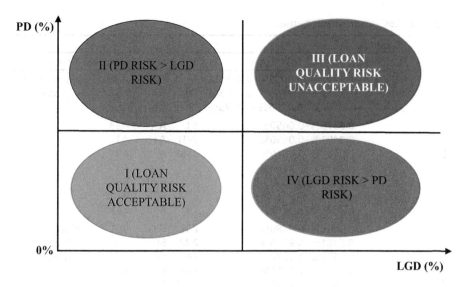

**Fig. 1.2**  Loan quality risk from combining PD and LGD

There are numerous studies on the negative relationship between credit ratings and probability of default, also known as the PD curve.[9] The findings show a reasonably close correlation between the BRR and PD. Following the Basel II accord, banking institutions that implement the AIRB (Advanced Internal Rating-Based) approach, calibrate the BRR and the PD against each other—a statistical procedure that entails as much art as it does science.[10] In general, the mapping depicts a common pattern: default rates start out low for the least risky grades and then rise rapidly as the grade worsens. This means that the PD increases *non-linearly* and *monotonically* as rating grades deteriorate from highest to lowest. For example, the average one-year default rate of say "AAA" (investment grade) may be 0%, compared to 20% for "CC" (non-investment grade).

Many banks report their PD-BRR mapping in their annual reports. Table 1.2 gives the PD-BRR calibration of the 22-point rating scale of Canada's largest Bank, Royal Bank of Canada. It is a detailed mapping and, for this reason, serves as a perfect illustration of the non-linearity and the monotonicity. The better is the rating, the lower the PD; the worse the rating, the higher the PD. The PD values range from 0% for the highest grade to 100% for the lowest grade and the range subdivides into *discrete* bands, as they should for a one-on-one correspondence. Banks align their scale to the ratings used by the ratings agencies. The RBC Internal Rating Map is one such example where the bank uses S&P and Moody's. The main reason they compare their internal ratings to external ratings is to determine whether they are too conservative or too liberal in their lending policy. If a bank is too conservative, it risks losing safe customers; if it is too liberal, it risks making loans to weak borrowers that are more likely to default.

**Table 1.2** RBC internal ratings map

| Ratings | PD bands Business and bank | Sovereign | BRR | S&P | Moody's | Description |
|---|---|---|---|---|---|---|
| 1 | 0.0000%–0.0300% | 0.0000%–0.0155% | 1+ | AAA | Aaa | Investment |
| 2 | 0.0000%–0.0300% | 0.0156%–0.0265% | 1H | AA+ | Aa1 | grade |
| 3 | 0.0301%–0.0375% | 0.0266%–0.0375% | 1 M | AA | Aa2 | |
| 4 | | 0.0376%–0.0490% | 1 L | AA– | Aa3 | |
| 5 | | 0.0491%–0.0650% | 2+H | A+ | A1 | |
| 6 | | 0.0651%–0.0810% | 2+M | A | A2 | |
| 7 | | 0.0811%–0.1120% | 2+L | A– | A3 | |
| 8 | | 0.1121%–0.1800% | 2H | BBB+ | Baa1 | |
| 9 | | 0.1801%–0.2620% | 2 M | BBB | Baa2 | |
| 10 | | 0.2621%–0.3845% | 2 L | BBB– | Baa3 | |
| 11 | | 0.3846%–0.6480% | 2-H | BB+ | Ba1 | Non- |
| 12 | | 0.6481%–0.9625% | 2-M | BB | Ba2 | investment |
| 13 | | 0.9626%–1.4070% | 2-L | BB– | Ba3 | grade |
| 14 | | 1.4071%–2.1785% | 3+H | B+ | B1 | |
| 15 | | 2.1786%–3.4210% | 3+M | B | B2 | |
| 16 | | 3.4211%–5.2775% | 3+L | B– | B3 | |
| | | 5.2776%–7.9410% | 3H | CCC+ | Caa1 | |
| 18 | | 7.9411%–11.4475% | 3 M | CCC | Caa2 | |
| 19 | | 11.4476%–19.6535% | 3 L | CCC– | Caa3 | |
| 20 | | 19.6536%–99.99990% | 4 | CC | Ca | |
| 21 | | 100% | 5 | C | C | Impaired |
| 22 | | 100% | 6 | D | C | |

Source: 2018 Annual Report

An illustration of the EL equation for a given transaction is the following. Consider a weak BRR (e.g., "CC"), a PD of 75%, and an LGD of 40%, the latter representing the average percentage loss rate over time. The product of PD and LGD is the *statistical or expected loss* of 30%, which translates to 30 cents/1 dollar EAD. Expected loss is an increasing function of each of the three variables. As you can see in this example, the LGD or the LIED (Loss in the Event of Default) is always transaction specific, whereas the PD is borrower specific and independent of the LGD rate. This is the essence of a two-dimensional rating system of the AIRB Approach that grades the borrower and the credit facility separately rather than mixing them together.

In this book, we are concerned with the PD component of credit risk, so our focus is on the methods that credit analysts use to assign BRRs. We look at four types of borrowers:

1. **Business/Commercial:** Commercial or business credit is used to fund capital expenditures and a firm's day-to-day operations. Commercial borrowers are companies operating in the non-financial sector, such as agriculture, fishing, mining, mineral exploration, manufacturing, and services.

2. **Banks:** Simply put, banks borrow money to make money in the form of loans. Thus, bank risk assessment adopts a different approach than the analysis of non-financial companies, though the basic mechanics of deriving a rating are the same for all borrowers. Spend a few minutes on a bank's financial statements and you will see how different the line items are from those of non-financial firms even though the common language is accounting and the terms are the same, such as revenue, expense, assets, liabilities, and capital. The risks are different. Banks receive deposits (essentially borrowing from depositors) or borrow in the wholesale capital market, and recycle money to make money (loans and advances) on which the bank expects to make a profit margin over its funding cost. This operation involves numerous risks (which we will discuss in detail later).

3. **Commercial real estate (CRE):** Commercial real estate comprises income-producing real estate (IPRE) assets used solely for business purposes, such as shopping centres, offices, apartments, motels, and hotels. The financing of these assets is CRE mortgages, which are loans secured by liens on the property. Thus, both the repayment and recovery of the loan depend primarily on the IPRE's cash flows and secondarily on the owner of the asset or guarantors of the mortgage.

4. **Sovereign states:** Cross-border lending has been a major activity by banks. Direct foreign investments by companies are essentially cross-border lending. Country risk analysis is used to assess the creditworthiness of sovereign or country debtors, and to obtain a more accurate BRR for private entities operating in the same jurisdiction. The country equivalents of a firm's audited financial statements are national accounts statistics (gross domestic product, gross national income, prices, production, balance of payments, and government finance).

---

### Monotonicity

The Basel 2 Accord makes the internal ratings a critical building block. Under the AIRB (Advanced Internal Rating Approach), both internal ratings and scores should map to a master scale of the default probability attached to each rating or score. The mapping implies that default probabilities of the master scale are monotonic functions of ratings. In general, a **monotonic function** is one that is consistently increasing and never decreasing, or consistently decreasing and never increasing in value. In the risk rating business, we call a forecast of grade-level default rates a PD (probability of default) curve. The reliability of the forecast requires monotonicity, which gives the rating system rank-ordering capability. If not we have a system that will forecast lower PD values as the BRR improves and reversions with even higher ratings.

Once the credit analysis of a borrower is complete, the rating model assigns a BRR based on the credit rating system. A credit rating system[11] must be capable of differentiating default risk effectively, a result achieved by the *granularity* of the rating scale (see Table 1.2). Insufficient grades in a rating scale severely limit a lender's ability to differentiate default risk, quantify the profitability of a loan, and determine the amount of capital for the exposure (see the applications of the BRR in Sect. 1.6). That said, there is no gain in striving for finer rating scale because the data would be unavailable and because of the increased likelihood that the relationship between the numerous rating grades and the default probabilities will fail the test of *monotonicity* (more on this in Chap. 3). The rating scale of S&P, Moody's, Fitch Group, and DBRS consists of 20 or more grades. As we noted earlier, banks align their internal BRRs to the credit ratings of the rating agencies for the loan portfolio of the firms that are externally rated. Both Risk Management and the business units use the information to determine whether the bank is losing creditworthy borrowers or encouraging and retaining less creditworthy borrower, or taking on excessive risk. One major criticism of rating comparison is that the external ratings used as a standard of sorts can be very unreliable in an *ex ante* or forward-looking sense. The most glaring example is the 2008 financial crisis where borrowers that were at the high end of the rating scale (even "AAA") were downgraded to non-investment grade in just a short period of time after actual results contradicted the expectations of the rating agencies.

### 1.3.3  Loan Structuring

We think of loan structuring as a process to achieve two main goals (outputs). The first is to preserve the borrower's ability to service the debt from a profitable operation. Repayments derive primarily from the cash flow and secondarily from collateral security. The second is to position the lender closer to the borrower's assets than other creditors in the event of a liquidation. Banks prefer to lend only in the first position so that they have first rights on the borrower's assets. Banks ensure or attempt to ensure that various payments (accrued expenses) are subordinated to bank debt. Hence, a lender must know a borrower's capital structure—referring to the asset and liability sides of the balance sheet—to determine where and how the company funds its operations, and the rights of other creditors to the company's cash flow and assets. Loan structuring is best understood as a *process* that involves all the following starting with the crucial ones.

- Determining the purpose of the loan
- Determining the amount of the loan
- Matching the repayment schedule to the cash flow of the borrower. (Note: profit is not cash flow, which is the primary source of loan repayment)
- Matching the term of the loan to the asset being financed (e.g., short-term funding for working capital; long-term loan for plant and equipment)
- Setting interest rates appropriate to the credit risk and setting fees.
- Drafting the Loan Agreement, the principal loan document
- Determine the covenants, which are intended to ensure a loan gets repaid and to protect the lender
- Deciding the need for a guarantor serving as a secondary or even tertiary repayment source (which means the lender must also perform a credit risk assessment on the guarantor to assign a guarantor BRR)
- Deciding whether to take collateral and if so, what collateral is appropriate. (Note: Collateral is a secondary source of loan repayment)
- Determining *structural subordination*. It refers to the positions of various creditors to the group's assets in an event of insolvency. In lending to a holding company (holdco) especially, understanding the holdco's structure is vital. A lender would want to ensure that in the event of a default, it has access to the cash flow and assets of the operating subsidiary or subsidiaries through *upstream* guarantees. In the absence of such guarantees, the claims of a lender of a holdco are structurally subordinated to the claims of the creditors of the operating companies (opcos) in the group. This is because the claim of the holdco, as a shareholder of the subsidiary, is subordinated to the claims of the other creditors of the opcos. In a bankruptcy scenario, a lender prefers to be at the top of the heap, or at least on an equal footing (*pari passu*) with other creditors for repayment. To ensure that lenders of the holdco rank equally with lenders of the opcos, the latter guarantee the liabilities of the holdco. The upstream guarantee offsets the structural subordination. (Note: In a downstream guarantee, the holdco guarantees the debts of the opcos.) There are other subordination mitigants like intercompany loans; however, this subject is outside the scope of this book.

**Structural Subordination: Don't Forget the Opco in the Credit Analysis**

Banks do not like the idea that opco creditors are paid before holdco creditors. Whist upstream guarantees from the opco to the holdco make for a tighter loan structure, the primary source of repayment on a loan is cash flow and collateral is only secondary, which comes into play only in a default situation. Moreover, if the opco files for bankruptcy protection, a bank cannot realise on the collateral. Credit analysts must always examine the holdco's assets and its ownership structure to ensure they include the opco in the credit analysis regardless of the upstream guarantees. *Advice: get an up-to-date org chart as part of due diligence.*

## The "Right" Credit Exposure

How does a lender know the size of the loan is too much or too little? Lenders consider many factors but the major one is whether the borrower has the repayment capacity. This entails analysing the borrower's capital structure, leverage ratios such as debt/capital, and debt-service ratios. We leave the details of this discussion for later chapters.

## Loan Pricing

The interest rate on a loan reflects creditworthiness. Consider a *ceteris paribus* scenario and two borrowers with the same amount of loan and the same maturity. In this example, the creditworthy borrower is less likely to default, so the interest rate on his loan is expected to be lower. Loan pricing involves establishing the interest rate on a loan, and the way a bank set a rate is far from being formulaic. For this reason, loan pricing is a mystery to the public. These are some of the questions usually asked: Why so many rates? Why are some rates higher for some customers and lower for others? Why are some rates higher for some types of credit and lower for others?

Banks use a combination of loan pricing models and practices to set loan rates. Whilst the macroeconomic environment sets the overall level and direction of interest rates, banks have hurdle rates or target RAROC (risk-adjusted return on capital)[12] as guidelines on a case-by-case basis. The target rates help decide which loans meet the threshold for consideration. That said, interbank competition often forces a lender to charge interest that is lower than the hurdle rate. In this case, the rate serves as a loss leader for higher future returns. Let us look at three pricing models to get a basic idea of the factors determining loan rates:

- Cost-plus loan pricing
- Price leadership
- Risk-based loan pricing

But let us first consider some common factors that determine loan pricing:

- **Relationship lending:** Banks look at the value of the total client relationship. Long-standing and valuable clients tend to get favourable loan rates and fees when they do most or all of their banking transaction with one. As mentioned earlier, a common practice by banks is to use the loan interest rate as a sweetener to secure long-term rents on the relationship business.

- **The borrower's size:** There is evidence that interest charged by commercial banks on small businesses varies inversely with the size of the loan and therefore the size of the borrower; however, the relationship may be capturing differential credit risk premium as much as differential costs of loan servicing.
- **Loan type and purpose:** There are different types of credit facilities: term loan, demand loan, revolving credit, standby letter of credit (LC), lease, and so on. The interest rates on these facilities are different reflecting the options available to the bank and the borrower for drawn down, payment, prepayment, and redrawing. There are also many loan purposes, including working capital, acquisition, debt repayment, stock buyback, confirmed LC (letter of credit) to support commercial paper (CP), leveraged buyout, and so on. The differences in the rates reflect default risks. For example, a loan for leveraged buyout raises the debt/equity ratio and makes the borrower riskier, although only for a time until the ratio returns to "normal". The LC, on the other hand, does not increase the borrower's debt/equity ratio, until and unless the borrower draws on the line, which could occur if the company cannot issue new CP.
- **Geographical location of the borrower:** The location in which a borrower is based or does most its business is an important factor. This risk is usually factored into credit risk (e.g., country and sovereign risk).

Clearly, the interplay of the numerous factors determines loan pricing. Borrowers who understand this reality are better informed to "shop" for the best rate. Let us examine these pricing models to see what the main determinants are.

### Cost-Based Loan Pricing
Cost-plus pricing involves four steps. First, the bank determines the average cost to attract deposits and to borrow. The funds could be retail deposits (e.g., individual savings accounts and time deposits, chequing accounts) and wholesale deposits, which are very large deposits made by a large business, another bank, and institutional investors. Second, the bank calculates the average cost of servicing the loan, which covers the fixed, administrative costs we discussed earlier. The administrative cost is expressed as a percentage of the loan. Finally, after the costs are covered, the bank adds a percentage figure representing compensation for risk taking. Fourth, the bank applies a profit margin. The pricing formula in percentage terms is:

$$\text{Lending Rate} = \text{Avg.Deposit Rate} + \text{Avg.Servicing Cost} + \text{Default Premium} + \text{Profit Margin}$$

**Price Leadership**

Recall that banks maximise not only profit but also growth, and in order to grow they must compete for market dominance; hence, there is a trade-off between maximising current profitability and maximising future growth. Competition in banking has always been intense and more so with non-bank entities encroaching on traditional banking turf. The intense competition has resulted in banks using a form of price leadership to establish the cost of credit. In many countries, a prime or base rate is set by the major banks and is the rate of interest charged to a bank's most creditworthy customers on short-term loans used for working capital. The base rate serves as an anchor for other types of loans. It is common for a major bank to announce its prime lending rate and the rest of the banks tend to follow. The interest rates on various loans are based on this rate, including variable-rate mortgages, car loans, lines of credit, and credit cards.

**Risk-Based Loan Pricing**

Risk-based loan pricing models focus on the credit risk, aligning the pricing of the loan to a borrower's probability of default. The credit rating is one of many inputs in the determination of the risk premium. The higher is the credit rating, the lower the risk premium. Risk-based models use as inputs various characteristics of the loan such as the size and the term. The shorter is the term, the less likely the ability of the borrower to repay the loan will change. Banks that use risk-based pricing models (which they can develop in-house or buy from a vendor) are able to set competitive lending rates for the strongest credits and reject or price at a premium those that represent the highest risks.

With risk-based pricing the borrower with a strong credit rating will get a lower rate on a loan than the borrower with a weak credit rating and vice versa. As a result, the lower risk borrowers do not end up subsidising the cost of credit for the high-risk borrowers. Simply put, risk-based pricing enables a bank whose portfolio has a high concentration of high-risk borrowers, to retain the low-risk borrowers. Without risk-based pricing, the bank must raise average rates, but, as rates rise, this will squeeze out creditworthy borrowers, increase the proportion of risky borrowers in banks' loan portfolios and cause the *probability* of defaults to rise, resulting in creditors' reluctant to lend even at the new higher rates. In Sect. 1.6, we will have more to say on how the problem of adverse selection, caused by information asymmetry, can lead to credit rationing through rising interest rates.

Other factors that affect the risk premium include the collateral pledged. Generally, a secured loan has lower interest rate than an unsecured loan. For example, a mortgage loan (secured by a commercial property) has a lower rate than an unsecured credit card debt. The lower is the loan-to-value (LTV) ratio of a secured loan, *ceteris paribus*; the lower is the interest rate.

Given the multiplicity of considerations in loan structuring and the fact that the lender and the borrower have different interests, defining a good loan structure is pointless. What may be "good" for the lender might be "bad" for the borrower and vice versa; however, if the procedures are followed diligently, the result would likely be a good loan structure satisfying both parties.

## 1.3.4 Credit Submission and Adjudication

The business unit prepares and submits a transaction request (TR) to Risk Management for adjudication. This document summarises the "deal" in a number of sections. A typical TR would likely include these sections as shown in Table 1.3.

- **Transaction Details:** This section documents important customer information:

    - Renewing date of the Risk Assessment (essentially the BRR)
    - Renewing date of the Transaction Request that documents the total exposure under the name of the borrower, the facilities requested, the type of facilities, facility risk ratings (FRRs), facility terms, the pricing (using the BRR), and various codes for portfolio monitoring. Renewing a credit achieves the objective of ensuring data integrity.
    - Structuring: The amount of loan requested, when the funds will be disbursed, and for how long the funds will be outstanding. Structuring includes whether the funds are committed or uncommitted. With a committed facility, the lender commits to advance money to the borrower when requested once it meets specific requirements stated in the loan agreement. With an uncommitted facility, there is no obligation to provide funds. A basic principle of loan structuring is matching the facility term with the life of the asset. For example, long-term loans are used to finance long-term assets like plant and equipment; short-term loans finance things like accounts receivables and inventory.

**Table 1.3** Transaction request template for commercial banking

| I: GENERAL INFORMATION | | | | | |
|---|---|---|---|---|---|
| **BRR/ Risk Assessment Dated:** | **Transaction Request Dated:** | **Banking Unit:** | | | |
| 27-Sep-19<br>BRR: "BBB+" | 27-Sep-19 | Address<br>Name/ID Number of Relationship Manager | | | |
| | **Codes:** | **Type of Request:** | **TR Revision Date:** | | |
| | Borrower Reference Number<br>SIC codes (3523)<br>Others | Annual Review | 27-Sep-20 | | |
| **Borrower/ Address** | **Primary Business:** | **Ownership:** | | | |
| Green's Farm Machinery Inc<br>200 Main St East<br>North Bay, Ontario. | Manufacture of ploughs<br>and harrows | Public | | | |

**II: CREDIT FACILITIES AND TRANSACTIONAL RISK**

| Facilities | FRR | C/U | Facility type and Term | Rate | Risk Prem. | Loan Ins. | Prev. Auth. | Net Inc. |
|---|---|---|---|---|---|---|---|---|
| 1) $100MM | BBB+ | U | Operating<br>Accepted: date<br>Matures: date | Prime | 1.75% | No | $100MM | Nil |
| 2) $300MM | BBB+ | C | Term<br>Accepted: date<br>Matures: date | Prime | 2.75% | No | $300MM | Nil |
| $400MM | | | Total Credit Exposure | | | | $400MM | Nil |

**Amount:**      **Transactional Risk:**
$500MM      Settlement

**Fees:**
List all fess: amounts and frequency of collection.

**Repayment Term and Sources:**
1) Revolving from collection of accounts receivable
2) Five-year term, interest payable monthly, with equal principal payments of $5MM beginning (state date), with final payment (state date). State the amount that was initially disbursed and the date if the term loan is a renewal.

**III: TRANSACTION OUTLINE**
**Reasons for Submission:**
Purpose of the transaction. E.g., renewal, request for exceptions to credit policy, increase in a facility,
Outline the reasons for proposing the transaction. If it is a renewal, include the proposed changes.

**Purpose of Facility:**
1) Working capital to finance accounts receivable and purchase inventory
2) Purchase machinery and equipment for plant at 200 Main St East, North Bay, Ontario, Canada

**Transaction Proposal:**
Outline the transaction: The details involve renewing, structuring, pricing, commitment of funds, repaying, and waivers, etc.
E.g. Recommend straight renewal of the facilities. Comment of the business, the covenants, the BRR and the FRR as may be pertinent to support the renewal request.

**Credit Policy and Exceptions:**
State the exceptions as applicable and reasons for requesting exception approval.

**IV: RISK ASSESSMENT:**
**Strengths of the Transaction:**
Identify the strengths

**Weaknesses of the Transactions**
Identify the weaknesses.

**How are the Risks Mitigated & Early Warning Signals:**
Outline how the identified risks are to be mitigated and managed.

**V: EXCEPTIONS TO POLICY & GUIDELINES**
List the exceptions and provide rationale for authorisation.

**VI: TRANSACTIONS MONITORING**

| | Frequency | Trigger | Covenant | Responsibility |
|---|---|---|---|---|
| Early Warning Signals<br>  Itemise EWSs. | mth/qtr/year | value | value | Department/ positions |
| Covenants<br>  Itemise covenants and define<br>  all formulas for calculations. | | | | |
| Margin Requirements<br>  Define margin requirements and<br>  all formulas for calculations. | | | | |
| Pre-disbursement conditions<br>  List the conditions. | | | | |
| Financial reports<br>  List all required reports. | | | | |

(continued)

**Table 1.3**  (continued)

| VII: COMPLIANCE STATUS | | | |
|---|---|---|---|
| | Compliance (Yes/No/NA) | Details and Amount | Date Non-compliance to be remedied. |
| Covenants | | | |
| Margins | | | |
| Security | | | |
| Environment | | | |
| Interest current | | | |
| Principal payments up-to-date | | | |
| Non-accrual | | | |
| Provision | | | |
| Overdue debts written off | | | |

| Monitor: | Date: | Sign off: |
|---|---|---|
| Name of banking officer | Write in date | Initial (manually or electronically) |

**VIII: COLLATERAL SECURITY SCHEDULE:**

| Security | Hdd/TBO | Book Value | - Adjustment | EMV | Margin (%) | Priority Claims | Realizable Value |
|---|---|---|---|---|---|---|---|
| List security with full description: amounts, dates, names, addresses, first/second/third lien, etc. | | | | | | | |
| 1) General Security Agreement: | | | | | | | |
| -Accounts Receivable | Held | $200MM | -$20MM | $180MM | 75% | $35MM | $100MM |
| -Inventory | TBO | $305MM | -$35MM | $270MM | 50% | Nil | $135MM |
| | | | | | | | |
| 2) First Mortgage for $1MM on property located on (address). Appraised at $1.5MM at September 27, 2019. Fire insurance on property and contents for $2.5MM. | Held | | | $500MM | 80% | Nil | $400MM |
| | | | | | | | |
| **TOTAL SECURITY** | | | | | | | **$635MM** |

Notes: C committed, U uncommitted, TBO to be obtained

- **Transaction Outline:** The section describes the rationale for the loan, exceptions to credit policy and request for waivers, the strengths and weaknesses of the transaction, and the means through which the lender will mitigate the identified risks. The Transaction Outline ends with the summary recommendation that includes the rationale for entering into the transaction, recaps the main strengths and weaknesses, and the key measures that the lender will adopt to mitigate the downside risks. For the most part, the mitigation of the risks will be reflected in the Loan Agreement and in the collateral security taken.
- **Transactions Monitoring and Reporting:** This section provides instructions on how the account will be monitored in order to detect and mitigate risk, and protect the interests of the lender. The instructions would include the following details:
  - Early Warning Signals, the accountabilities, and the responsible parties
  - Financial covenants and the calculation method

- Reporting covenants for financial statements, certificates, environmental reports, and many others as applicable
- The frequency and timing of reports, the accountabilities, and the responsible parties such as the business unit (front office) and the loan servicing unit (back office)
- Pre-disbursement conditions
- Margin calculations

**Collateral Security** This section lists and describes every collateral security—identified by a form number—the lender takes to back up the facility and shows the total realisable value of all security, thus ensuring the total credit exposure is fully covered. Collateral security includes many things such as real estate, bonds, stocks, precious metals, accounts receivable, and inventory. In banking, it is important to differentiate *lending value* from *realisable value*. The bank formula for the lending value (LV) of a collateral security is the following:

$$LV = (\text{Realisable value of Asset} - \text{Adjustments}) \\ \times \text{Margin}(\%) - \text{Priority Claims}$$

*Banks usually lend the lesser of the lending value of the collateral or the limit of the authorised credit facility.*

Realisable value is understood as a *net concept*. For example, accounts receivable in the financial statement is the debit balance of the asset account minus the credit balance in Allowance for Uncollectible Accounts in the contra asset account. Inventory is the lower of cost or net realisable value (NRV), an alternative term for "book value". The "adjustments" of the formula above include depreciation, which subtracts from NRV, as well as upgrades that add to NRV. Priority claims also reduce lending value. The margin is the percentage of the collateral, which a lender may define for its own purposes. Examples: for accounts receivable, only those that are 60 days old qualify; for inventory, only unencumbered inventory that are free of claims or liens qualify. The ageing of receivables is therefore crucial information in the margin formula. The margin gives the lender a cushion.

The realisable value of a collateral security, as you might have already observed, is essentially valuation or appraisal. Because assets vary in their cash-flow features, there is no single valuation formula. The main point to grasp, however, is that *NRV is the cash amount that the owner expects to receive*. If it is a property, NRV is the selling price minus the costs incurred in selling or disposing it. For inventory, NRV is the market value minus the recorded cost less other costs to dispose the asset. Accountants use the lower of cost or NRV (which means a write-down if recorded cost exceeds NRV). Note that a bank calculates realisable value differently from the practice used in accounting. For example, under Collateral Security Schedule of Table 1.3, the margin and priority claims reduce realisable value but, in accounting, these have no effect.

## 1.3.5 Loan Documentation

Proper loan documentation is a critical component of the underwriting process because loan documents serve as the lender's primary protection once it pays out the loan. If the documents are not in perfect order, there is potential for loan losses. The legal department of a bank, or outside counsel, prepares the necessary documentation for signing by all parties to the agreement. The signatures evidence the fact that all parties agree to the terms of the agreement. The documentation typically includes the Promissory Note, the Loan Agreement, Titles, Deeds, GSAs (General Security Agreements), and others. The documentation of a transaction serves three important functions:

1. Supports the completion of the life cycle of a transaction.
2. Helps ensure the proper recording of transactions and subsequent changes to the transaction.
3. Mitigates credit loss risk due to deficiencies in documentation, particularly loan documents and collateral. Accurate documentation enhances a lender's attempt to recover debt, or liquidate collateral securing the outstanding debt.

The Loan Agreement is the legal document that binds the lender and the borrower to the contract. It serves as the primary monitoring tool for the lender because it contains all of the requirements that the borrower must fulfil—including covenants—until the loan is fully repaid. The reasons that a lender uses loan covenants include the following:

• Protecting the lender's interests whilst providing the lender flexibility to manage the business effectively.

- Maintaining the quality of the borrower by identifying key operational risks.
- Raising timely red flags of potential problems the borrower might encounter.
- Bringing the borrower back to the negotiating table to restructure the loan should the borrower breach specific obligations.

Still, no matter how well loan covenants are crafted, only cash from operations repays loans. For this reason, the central concern of credit analysis is to determine whether a company can generate sufficient cash flow from the operations.

Debt covenants are either affirmative or negative. A negative covenant restrains the borrower from taking certain actions. Examples include:

- Compensate or increase salaries of certain employees
- Incur additional debt (or subordinate additional borrowing to the original loan agreement)
- Sell certain assets
- Merge with another firm or engage in any partnership

An affirmative covenant requires that a party comply with certain terms of the contract. Examples include:

- Providing financial statement at certain regular intervals
- Meeting clearly defined financial metric, such as interest coverage, minimum tangible net worth, debt to tangible net worth, and current ratio, in specific period of the fiscal year

In a typical loan structure, covenants serve many objectives of the lender. Table 1.4 presents a partial list of covenant protections.

## 1.3.6   Loan Closing and Credit Disbursement

The closing refers to the date and time that a loan becomes final and the lender pays out a loan. Take a mortgage loan for example. The closing date of the loan and the closing date of the home purchase usually coincide. At the closing, both the lender and the borrower sign numerous legal documents binding both parties to the loan agreement. The closing of a loan means that the borrower is legally required to repay the loan and the lender is legally committed to advance funds (or tranches of funds) subject to the loan conditions. Before the lender disburses funds into the borrower's

**Table 1.4** A checklist of covenants to protect the interests of the lender

| Objective | Covenant |
|---|---|
| Protection of cash flow | Debt service coverage |
| | Restrictions on capex (capital expenditures) and operating leases |
| | Restrictions on investments |
| | Restrictions on officers' salaries |
| | Maintenance of minimum level of cash flow |
| Protection of asset quality | Restrictions on sales of assets |
| | Maintenance of property insurance |
| | Maintenance of working capital and liquidity |
| Protection of net worth | Maintenance of minimum tangible net worth (TNW) |
| | Restrictions on additional borrowings |
| | Current settlement of taxes owed and other accrued liabilities. |
| Provision of full disclosure of information | Timely reporting of financial information |
| | Adherence to accounting standards |
| Control of growth | Maintenance of minimum tangible net worth (TNW) |
| | Restrictions on additional borrowings |
| | Restrictions on mergers and acquisitions or a transformation of the business. |
| Assurance of a legitimate business | Maintenance of corporate existence |
| | Restrictions on asset sale |
| | Restrictions on change in management or ownership |

account, the lending service unit of the financial institution ensures that pre-disbursement requirements in the approved TR are fulfilled. Additionally, loan disbursement occurs once the documents are in perfect order with all required signatures, and the lender or the law firm for the lending institution holds said documentation.

## 1.3.7 Loan Monitoring and Reporting

The monitoring process begins once the lender disburses the loan and the monitoring requirements that include the types of reports and the frequency of the reporting are outlined in the Loan Agreement. Banks have monitoring systems in place and the borrower is required to submit financial and other information on a regular basis, such as monthly, quarterly, and yearly. A breach of a loan covenant triggers a default of the loan. Usually, however, the lender would grant a waiver of the default and charge a fee. The lender also monitors EWSs reflecting the borrower's strengths and weaknesses outlined in the TR. The EWSs could be both financial and non-financial measures for which the information is relatively current, or continuously available. Creditor monitoring also involves regular site visits, and client meetings to see how the business is performing and to get a sense of the quality of the management.

## 1.3.8 Problem Loan Management

In general, a problem loan is one that cannot be repaid according to the original terms of the loan agreement. In the Basel Committee on Banking Supervision (BCBS) framework,[13] problem loans come under the rubric of non-performing loans. BCBS defines these as loans that "the bank considers the obligor is unlikely to pay its credit obligations to the banking group in full, without recourse by the bank to actions such as realising security (if held)". The definition includes loans that are 90 days past due (commercial loans) and loans that are up to 180 days delinquent (retail/consumer loans). Banks have different arrangements or structures for managing problem loans. In many banks, problem loan management is the responsibility of a special workout unit in the Risk Management structure.

Regardless of the method, the key to successful loan workouts is early identification of credit weaknesses and negative credit trends in the BRR. The mechanism for early detection is the Early Warning System and its "watch list". Under the Basel Accord, a BRR must be refreshed at least once a year and monitored continually for deteriorating trends. In nearly all cases, the borrowers that a lender places on the Watch List have BRRs that have fallen below a certain threshold. Once a bank decides to place a borrower on the Watch List, best practices call for a plan and specific timeframes to regularise the credit. The plan will normally include either a rehabilitation strategy or an exit strategy, including the realisation of collateral, subject to a thorough cost-benefit assessment by the Problem Loan Management group.

Banks are required to make provision for loan loss or write-offs. The three types of provisions are:

1. General provision. This loss is written off the income statement
2. Specific provision. This item is written off the income statement
3. Bad debt write-offs. This is a balance sheet item that is written off (the amount is debited to a contra-asset account called "Allowance for bad loans/debts" and credited to loans)

We defer the discussion on loan provisioning and the accounting to Chap. 11, which deals with problem loan management.

# 1.4  Credit Culture

The credit culture of a bank is the implicit understanding, the expected behaviours resulting from policies, practices, and experiences of the bank. Credit culture empowers bank personnel in the business units and in risk management to withstand the pressures to underwrite increasingly risky transactions to meet revenue and profitability targets for short-term gains at the expense of long-term growth and stability. Bankers balance risk against return in their dual roles of performing sound, conservative underwriting, and developing and promoting business to drive revenue. Every lending institution has a credit culture that may have evolved informally over time or may have been formally defined by management.

Credit decisions are *essentially* both rational and instinctual. John Maynard Keynes[14] coined the phrase "animal spirits" to describe the characteristics of human behaviour—the tendencies, and the spontaneous instincts and emotions—that influence economic activity. So, how do banks discipline their behaviour between the lending extremes of conservatism and aggressiveness? Credit culture is a top-down process starting with leadership, which is quintessentially "tone at the top". In the light of recent financial scandals, the leadership factor has been getting closer attention in credit risk assessment.

### The 2008 Irish Financial Crisis

At the heart of the systemic crisis in 2008 was the breakdown of a credit culture of sound policies and practices. The bank that was singled out for reckless lending that caused its demise was Anglo Irish Bank (AIB) whose principal franchise was property lending. At the time of AIB's liquidation, the bank had over €22 billion of assets. In 2010, the Irish Government asked the Finnish regulator Peter Nyberg to lead a Commission to make a thorough report on the Irish banking crisis. The Commission investigated the period between January 2003 and January 2009, when the Irish Government nationalised Anglo Irish Bank. The lessons drawn from the Nyberg report apply as much to Irish banking regulations as to the governance of Irish banks (See the full Nyberg report (2011), Report of the Commission of Investigation into the Banking Sector in Ireland).[15]

In terms of the execution, the commitment to managing credit risk goals include all the following attributes:

- An effective Risk Appetite Framework that (a) defines risk capacity, (b) establishes risk appetite, (c) translates risk appetite into limits and tolerances, (d) measures risk profile against the limits and tolerances for effective monitoring, and (e) takes actions before the business units breach their limits and tolerances.

- A coherent set of *written* internal controls—the policies and procedures to achieve the organisation's goals and objectives. (Note: written refers to a printed document or a digital document.)
- Written guidelines and a formal process for review and update.
- A dedicated (internal) web-based library housing the enterprise-wide Policies and Procedures (P&P) and informing users of amendments to the P&P Folios.
- Independence of risk rating and credit approval from credit marketing.
- Clearly defined, delegated approval authorities in Risk Management and in the Business.
- Accountability in credit adjudication evidenced by proper documentation.
- Integrated Enterprise Risk Management (ERM) framework involving the Board of Directors, the Business, Risk Management, and Internal Audit/ Compliance.
- Risk Management's monitoring of the credit quality and the exposure concentrations (by industrial sector) of the loan portfolios.
- Stress testing of loan portfolios.
- Periodic testing of the risk rating system's predictive accuracy, a procedure called validation.
- Comparative analysis of internal BRRs and external ratings.
- An enterprise-wide Watch List process to document and follow up problem loans.
- A promotion and compensation policy based on the execution of specific duties including credit risk management, if applicable.

## 1.5   The Criteria-Based Approach to Credit Analysis

The methodology of credit risk[16] rating covers a broad spectrum of methods or tools that vary in their degree of formalisation and quantification. In Sect. 1.3.2, we examined a traditional tool called the "Five Cs". This method is the least formalised and the least quantified. The drawback of the "Five Cs" method in the context of risk rating is that it mixes together borrower risk with facility or transaction risk; however, more and more banks are adopting a "dual risk ratings" process of the Basel AIRB approach. As we saw in the section, in a two-dimensional rating system, the probability of default (PD) is estimated separately from the loss given default (LGD). For this reason, more and more banks use what we label The Criteria-Based Approach to determine a borrower's creditworthiness. The Criteria-Based Approach may be viewed as a formalised or structured version of the "Five Cs" *sans* "collateral"; hence, the focus is only on the borrower.

Many considerations come into play in analysing credit risk but for simplicity, they may be grouped under five broad categories:

1. **Country and sovereign risk analysis:** Assesses the risks associated with the legal and regulatory system of a country, and political, financial, and economic conditions.
2. **Industry risk analysis:** Assesses the risks associated with the industrial sector's characteristics that include such things as barriers to entry, regulations, capital intensity, maturity of the industry, and environmental issues to list some.
3. **Business risk analysis:** Assesses the risks to profitability associated with competitive pressure and market share.
4. **Management risk analysis:** Assesses the risks associated with management strategy, management decisions, and management behaviour that are not in accordance with the interest of the company and shareholders. The notable examples of management failure leading to financial collapse include Enron Corporation (2001) and WorldCom (2008).
5. **Financial risk analysis:** Assesses the financial health of a borrower by analysing the financial statements to determine how a firm's profitability, efficiency, liquidity, and solvency. All these provide insights into whether the firm is able to service its debts. Financial risk analysis forms the core of credit analysis, and for this reason, it carries more weight than any other risk factor in the criteria-based model. In addition to financial performance, access to funds is part of a borrower's financial strength. The credit analyst assesses the *potential* or the *ability* of a borrower to obtain bank loans, issue bonds, or raise equity. With limited access to these sources of financing, a firm that is short of cash cannot pay its bills, including the interest on its outstanding loans.

These risk categories are not mutually exclusive but are related, as you might have correctly thought. Notice that management risk affects financial risk so that character in the "Five Cs" will have an important influence on the success of a business. You would have also noticed that weights assigned to each factor and their sub-factors are subjective, although they must be consistent across borrowers of the same industry. These are some of the distinctive features of expert-judgement models, and though they may not be appealing in a certain

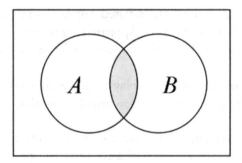

**Fig. 1.3**   Illustration of intersection

philosophical or epistemological sense, they do have their practical advantages over purely statistical models. So, this brings us to question that we have been leading up to: *Is credit analysis art or science, or both?* We say it is both. In the Venn diagram below, if A represents Art and its attributes and B represents Science and its attributes, then credit analysis belongs to the shaded area, which is the intersection of A and B (written A∩B). The answer to the fundamental question of credit analysis, "will you lend money to this person or firm?" must come from the judicious application of art (experience and practice) and science (the deductive process rather than trying to discover universal laws) (Fig. 1.3).

## 1.6   Information Asymmetry

The presentation to this point has largely ignored principal-agent problems and its cause, *information asymmetry.*[17] Principal-agent problems exist in varying degrees in all markets or transactions where one party possesses better information and thus more transaction power than the other party does. The *principal-agent problem* may be defined as the conflict between the actions of one party (the agent) and the interest of another (the principal). A widely held explanation or the cause of the problem is the asymmetry in information. In this section, we explain how these general concepts relate particularly to borrowing and lending money. Specifically, in the credit market, information asymmetry gives rise to two typical problems of "adverse selection" and "moral hazard".

> **Economic or Risk Capital**
>
> It is a *measure of risk* (a probability value) that is used to determine the *amount of capital* that a financial institution needs to ensure that it stays solvent given its risk profile, counting all the assets on the balance sheet and off the balance sheet.

Adverse selection in the credit market is a risk exposure that exists *before* all parties sign the loan contract, or the Loan Agreement, and before the money is lent out. The problem arises from the fact that the "borrower" (defined broadly to include corporate CFO and CEO) knows more about its financial condition and the future prospects of the firm than the lender does, but hides or even dupes the lender during the credit assessment process. Enron Corporation is the infamous example of the agent-principal problem where senior executives of the company (collectively, the agent) were not working in the best interest of the lenders and investors (collectively, the principal).

If financial institutions are unsure about the creditworthiness of their borrowers, they will charge a higher interest rate to compensate for the risk. If low-risk and high-risk prospective borrowers are indistinguishable *ex ante*, that is, before contracts are signed, low-risk borrowers are likely to quit the loan market leaving the unsafe borrowers who will gladly sign up for loans even at the higher interest rates. The resulting problem where the safe borrowers *self-select out of* the market, causing the average riskiness of loan portfolios to deteriorate, exemplifies the problem of adverse selection. In order to alleviate the adverse selection problem and reduce the average default risk of their loan portfolios, lenders will ration the supply of credit (Stiglitz and Weiss 1981).

Additionally, the *information asymmetry* causes inaccurate credit risk ratings, and the credit ratings of the rating agencies and the BRRs will be unreliable indicators of default risk. Simply put, a lender may still be uncertain about a borrower's creditworthiness or the default risk despite checking the boxes in the "Five Cs" or employing more structured and empirical methods. In Chap. 3, we will examine an approach to account for asymmetric information. The BRR is a key input in the credit process. These four BRR applications underscore the vital importance of the BRR in a bank's operations:

1. Approving or declining loan application
2. Pricing the credit facility
3. Requiring collateral security
4. Determining *economic or risk capital*

In contrast to the adverse selection problem, the moral hazard due to information asymmetry arises *after* the parties sign the Loan Agreement. The result is excessive risk taking. Let us examine how this may come about. First, the actions of managers (the agents) acting on behalf of shareholders may be harmful to lenders, a scenario that is likely for levered firms. Such companies are characterised by high debt/equity ratios. Because the downside risk of equity is limited, the managers of such firms have the incentive to substitute safe assets with risky assets to maximise shareholder value, although at the expense of lenders. If the risky investments succeed, the upside profit potential is *unlimited*, whereas if they fail, the downside loss is *limited*.[18]

Second, after the loan is advanced, the actions of the borrower may be unobservable or hidden. For example, it can be difficult for shareholders and lenders to ascribe weak operating results to incompetent management, who may in fact be incompetent and unethical, rather than to factors outside the firm's control, such as economic recessions. Moral hazard is the risk that a borrower will take excessive risk. A spectacular example is American International Group (AIG)[19] which went bankrupt and agreed to a "too big to fail" government bailout plan in 2008. AIG had been selling hundreds of billions of dollars' worth of credit protection on collateralised debt obligations (CDOs) without bearing any risk, such as posting collateral or increasing its capital base. With the collapse of the US real estate bubble in 2008, followed by the rapid deterioration in the credit ratings of the CDOs, AIG credit ratings plummeted, and the company was required to post additional collateral with its counterparties. This led to a liquidity crisis in the company and eventual bankruptcy in September 2008.

**Information Asymmetry**

Information asymmetry is present in all markets where one party to a transaction (the agent) has more information than the other (the principal). In lending, this can have severe consequences, one of which is creditors overrating a borrower based on incomplete and often false financial information. A properly designed BRR scorecard includes provision for BRR override to mitigate this ever-present risk. The case of Enron Corp. has been the most widely covered, but there are numerous other examples in recent history.

## 1.6.1  Minimising Adverse Selection and Moral Hazard Risk

As we discussed above, adverse selection and moral hazard are market failures due to the lack of information so that one party is at a transactional disadvantage. Obviously, the cure is more information about the borrower, but full information disclosure in a timely manner is virtually impossible before any transaction occurs. Best practices to reduce information asymmetry include the following:

1. Reporting of financial statements
2. Enforcing legal disclosure requirements. In the US the Sarbanes-Oxley Act[20] of 2002 came in response to major corporate financial scandals (e.g.,

Enron and WorldCom) earlier that decade. The act created stricter rules for accountants, auditors, and corporate officers, and tightened the requirements for recordkeeping by public companies.

3. Auditing
4. Monitoring
5. Checking the credit history of the loan applicant. For personal loans, lenders often check credit scores, the loan applicant's credit files, employment history, and the tax returns (provided voluntarily by the individual requesting a loan). For businesses, lenders look up credit ratings and reports issued by the rating agencies, government agency that oversees securities transactions, and various search engines like Google.
6. Requiring collateral security. Miskin (2005)[21] notes:

"Collateral reduces the consequences of adverse selection because even if the borrower turns out not to be a good credit risk and defaults on a loan, the lender can sell the collateral and use the proceeds to make up for the losses on the loan. Collateral also reduces moral hazard by reducing the incentives for borrowers to take on too much risk. When a borrower has pledged collateral on her loan, she has more to lose if she cannot pay it back and so she naturally is more reluctant to engage in risky activities that make it more likely she will default and lose the collateral. With collateral, even if the borrower defaults, the lender can recover losses by selling the collateral. Therefore, the asymmetric information about the borrower's default probability becomes less important."

To alleviate moral hazard, lenders use a variety of methods including the following:

1. Collateral (as noted earlier)
2. Restrictive and affirmative covenants that encourage desirable borrower behaviour, such as maintaining high net worth, providing financial information, reporting any changes in the company's operating and ownership structure (including mergers or sale of the company).

# 1.7 Regulatory Environment: Financial and Legal

The financial sector is amongst the most heavily regulated industry in all countries. The government regulates financial markets for two main reasons: to increase the information available to investors and consumers and to ensure soundness and stability of the financial system. One of the characteristics of a sound financial sector is the presence of independent government agencies whose responsibility is to ensure that financial institutions comply with the regulations.[22] The regulatory system affects all key aspects of banking: profitability, ownership structure, growth, asset quality, liquidity, and capital adequacy. The efficacy of financial regulations depends on a country's legal system and its ability to enforce laws.

It is worth noting that banking regulations are not limited to those of the domestic jurisdictions in question. Foreign banks that do business in the US or with US nationals in their own countries cannot escape the long arm of certain US banking regulations. For example, FACTA (The Foreign Account Tax Compliance Act) requires that foreign financial institutions and certain other non-financial foreign entities report on the foreign assets held by their US account holders to the IRS (Internal Revenue Service) or be subject to withholding on withholdable payments.

### 1.7.1 Banking Regulations

A sound and safe banking system is vital to the health of the economy. In general, the purpose of bank regulations is to foster a healthy banking industry, benefit the economy through financial intermediation, and to protect consumers. Broadly speaking, there are three types of banking regulations:

1. **Prudential regulations**: Broadly speaking, they govern the behaviour of permitted banks, and their sole purpose is to ensure that the banks are sound. The Basel III accord applies to capital adequacy thresholds defined in terms on *minimum* capital ratios, liquidity, and loan loss provisioning.

    i. CET1 Capital Ratio = Common Equity Tier 1/Credit risk-adjusted asset Value ≥ 4.5%
    ii. Tier 1 capital ratio = Tier 1 capital/Credit risk-adjusted assets value ≥ 6%
    iii. Total capital (Tier 1 and Tier 2) ratio = Total capital (Tier 1 + Tier 2)/Credit risk-adjusted assets ≥ 8%
    iv. Leverage Ratio = Tier 1 capital/Average total consolidated assets value ≥ 4% Tier I and Tier II capital, which includes *general* (as against *specific*) provision for loan loss. Two Liquidity ratios under Basel III: (1) The Liquidity Coverage Ratio (LCR) has been phased in, rising steadily increasing: 70% (2016), 80% (2017), 90% (2018), and 100% (2019), and (2) Net Stable Funding Ratio (NSFR) ≥ 100%

$$LCR = \frac{\text{High quality liquid asset amount} \left( \text{HQLA} \right)}{\text{Total net cash flow amount}}$$

$$\mathrm{NSFR} = \frac{\text{Available amount of stable funding}}{\text{Required amount of stable funding}}$$

v. Loan loss provisioning (LLP): Regulators and supervisors pay greater attention to LLP, in the aftermath of the 2008 financial crisis, which highlighted the systemic costs arising from banks and other lenders not responding fast enough to credit losses. Under Basel III capital accord, from the time a loan is originated, banks are expected to make forward looking, "through-the-cycle" loan loss provisioning based on an expected loss (EL) approach.[23] The EL approach is less pro-cyclical and recognises that (a) credit risk is not static but changes over the business cycle, and (b) banks cannot wait for "trigger events" to occur before provisioning for credit loss. Consistent with the EL approach, IFRS (International Financial Reporting Standards) 9 on provisioning for loans has replaced IFRS 39, and its requirements are intended to cause banks to increase provisions before default occurs.[24]

2. **Structural Regulations**: They are the rules for how the banks may carry on business. One of the purposes of the regulations is to ensure competition. Therefore, they include what products banks may sell, ownership structure, and bank mergers and acquisitions.
3. **Policy Regulations**: They include regulations encouraging or requiring banks act in certain ways for social welfare and national security goals. For example, banks may be required to provide loans to companies in certain sectors and to individuals (such as student loans). For monitoring, the government may require lenders meet some minimum percentages of such loans in the loan portfolio. Banks must have reliable MIS (Managements Information Systems) to report loans coded by their SICs (Standard Industrial Classification). Other examples are laws on money laundering and the financing of terrorism, known as AML/CFT.

---

**Key Principles of Basel III**

The Basel Accord is a series of regulations developed by The Basel Committee on Banking Supervision (BCBS). Under Basel III:

1. *Minimum* Capital Requirements. Tier 1 capital requirement increased to 6%.
2. Leverage Ratio. Leverage ratio in excess of 3% (Tier 1 capital as a percentage of average total consolidated assets)
3. Two new liquidity ratios. The Liquidity Coverage Ratio and Net Stable Funding Ratio.

## 1.7.2   AML (Anti-Money Laundering) and Anti-Terrorism

International regulators require commercial banks to combat money laundering and to counter the financing of terrorism, otherwise be subject to penalties. The last 15 years have seen many large domestic and foreign banks operating in the United States fined heavily for being in breach of AML and Anti-Terrorism regulations. Banks are exposed to compliance risk for failure to comply with financial regulations. The Basel Committee defines compliance risk as follows:

> The expression "compliance risk" is defined in this paper as the risk of legal or regulatory sanctions, material financial loss, or loss to reputation a bank may suffer as a result of its failure to comply with laws, regulations, rules, related self-regulatory organisation standards, and codes of conduct applicable to its banking activities (together, "compliance laws, rules and standards").[25]

As recommended by the Basel Committee, commercial banks must be able to manage compliance risk by establishing in their organisation a formal compliance function or a division to carry out compliance responsibilities under the supervision of the Board of Directors. Banking supervisors ensure that banks comply. Banks place heavy emphasis on KYC (know your customers) internal controls to ensure they are not conduits for money laundering and terrorist funding.

Basel Institute on Governance[26] is an international organisation against corruption, money laundering, and terrorism financing. On its website, it defines itself as "an independent not-for-profit competence centre, specialised in corruption prevention and public governance, corporate governance and compliance, Collective Action, anti-money laundering, criminal law enforcement and the recovery of stolen assets". Through its International Centre for Asset Recovery (ICAR), the organisation has developed the *Basel Anti-Money Laundering (AML) Index* available from the same website. The AML Index series start from 2012. The organisation provides support, technical assistance, and advice to governments and private corporations in four broad areas: asset recovery, public governance, corporate governance and compliance, and anti-corruption collective action.

## 1.7.3   The Importance of the Regulatory Environment to Credit Risk Assessment

The quality of banking supervisions, the adequacy of the regulations, and the enforcement capabilities all affect the credit quality of the banks that operate in the jurisdiction in question. Low ratings of the regulatory framework are a negative in assessing the BRRs for banks. This positive relationship between the rating of the regulatory environment and the overall BRR for lending institutions follows logically from the purposes of bank regulations, particularly in regard to banking safety and soundness. It is not difficult to see that if a country's legal framework is deficient, its financial system will also be deficient.

## Notes

1. Known as the Code of Hammurabi, discovered by archaeologists in 1901. Hammurabi was the sixth Babylonian king who ruled between 1792 and 1750.
2. Sharia law is the law of Islam, a comprehensive legal system, based strictly on the Quran.
3. Jevons, W. S., (1871), *The Theory of Political Economy*. In Chap. 1, the author writes under the heading, Confusion between Mathematical and Exact Sciences:

   > Many persons entertain a prejudice against mathematical language, arising out of a confusion between the ideas of a mathematical science and an exact science. They think that we must not pretend to calculate unless we have the precise data, which will enable us to obtain a precise answer to our calculations; ***but, in reality, there is no such thing as an exact science, except in a comparative sense.*** Astronomy is more exact than other sciences, because the various and often unknown contours of the seas do not admit of numerical verification. In this and many other cases we have mathematical theory without the data requisite for precise calculation.

4. In quantum mechanics the Schrödinger wave function tells you everything you can possibly know about a quantum system (any system based on quantum physics). The function tells you where a particle (like an electron) will probably be but not where it will be. It is only when you actually measure it that you know with 100% certainty. Furthermore, before measurement, the electron is in a *superposition* of all possible places at the same time; hence, the famous Schrödinger cat that is both dead and alive in a sealed radioactive box before the experimenter opens it to check. Only upon opening the box, you know the cat is either dead or alive. Contrast this with Newtonian mechanics for large visible objects, the second law gives you both the position and momentum of the object from an initial position to a final position for any moment in time, like a golf ball on a tee to where it lands after it is hit. Classical mechanics is a special case of quantum mechanics.
5. We read and hear often that the police profile suspects based on their race. An example: given that a person is a drug dealer, the probability that he is a black is high. The prejudice is to believe that if a person is black, then he's likely to be a drug dealer. The prejudice can then be stated as the equality of two conditional probabilities:

$$P(\text{drug dealer|black}) = P(\text{black|drug dealer})$$

The above statement is a fallacy because P(blacks) > P(drug dealers), so we need to be careful with conditional probability because it is generally not true that P(A|B) = P(B|A). Bayes' Theorem does this by the rule:

$$P(H|E) = \frac{P(H)P(E|H)}{P(E)}$$

The rule says that if we want to know the probability of some hypothesis H, given some evidence E which we just observed, we begin by asking what was the prior probability P(H) of the hypothesis before taking data. Then we ask what is the likelihood P(E|H), if the hypothesis H were true, we would see the evidence that we did. We multiply these two numbers together and divide the result by the probability P(E) of observing that evidence E. This is a normalising operation to ensure that the probabilities all add up to 1.

6. See the IEP (Interned Encyclopedia's of Philosophy) discussion under the title, **Objectivity.** IEP states, "Objective judgment or belief" refers to a judgment or belief based on objectively strong supporting evidence, the sort of evidence that would be compelling for any rational being. A subjective judgment would then seem to be a judgment or belief supported by evidence that is compelling for some rational beings (subjects) but not compelling for others. It could also refer to a judgment based on evidence that is of necessity available only to some subjects."

7. Capital often refers to physical capital (things like plant and equipment). In this book, capital is used in the financing sense and it refers to debt and equity of the balance sheet. Thus, capital structure refers to the composition of financing for the firm's operations and growth. Debt includes loans and bonds; equity consists of common stock, preferred stock, and retained earnings. Mezzanine financing is a hybrid of the two.

8. **Enron Corporation** was an American company based in Houston, Texas. Fortune magazine named Enron "America's Most Innovative Company" for six consecutive years. It was by far one of the largest American corporations. It's auditor was Arthur Anderson. At the end of 2001, it was revealed, not by the Auditor, that the company had been engaged in fraudulent accounting practices for many years. The scandal led to the enactment of the Sarbanes–Oxley Act of 2002, and the dissolution of Arthur Andersen. Enron filed for bankruptcy in late 2001. **WorldCom** was the United States' second largest long-distance telephone company for a time. WorldCom grew largely by acquiring other telecommunications companies. Its CEO (Chief Executive Officer) Bernard Ebbers became very wealthy from the increasing value of his holdings in WorldCom common stock as its price soared on the back of ficti-

tious accounting of assets and profitability. On July 21, 2002, WorldCom filed for bankruptcy. ***Carillion Plc*** was UK's second largest construction company. In January 2018, it was forced to file for bankruptcy after it failed to get government bailout. ***Nortel Networks*** was a Canadian telecommunication company. In March 2005, "the company said it would have to delay filing its audited financial statements for 2003 and will likely have to restate more of its earnings reports. Four days later, Nortel placed its chief financial officer and controller on paid leave pending completion of an independent review of the company's financial results (CBC News April 5, 2004)." The SEC launched formal investigation of Nortel earnings restatements in early April 2004.

9. There have been numerous studies over the last two decades. Basel Committee on Banking Supervision (August 2000), *Credit Ratings and Complementary Sources of Credit Quality Information*. The study notes, "This section looks at the power of external credit ratings to predict defaults. It draws on various sources, including reports of the rating agencies as well as academic studies of defaults. Some of the studies cited are quite recent, including articles published both by Moody's and S&P in 1999. In broad terms, the results of all these studies suggest that credit ratings constitute useful predictors of defaults at various time horizons, particularly for nonfinancial companies in the United States, for which the most extensive data are available." Moody's and S&P regularly publish their own studies on the predictive power of credit ratings and find that credit ratings and defaults tend to be highly correlated: the better the rating, the lower the PD; the worse the rating, the higher the PD.

10. Banks have developed models (proprietary), based on logistic and linear regression techniques to estimate PD and LGD. Obviously, their database is their own records on defaults by industry (for PD estimation) and by borrower (for PD estimation), and utilisation of undrawn credit limits prior to default (for the LGD rates). For most banks, the data go back only to the early 2000s. Before, banks did not keep such data. Other predictors used in these models include economic variables such as interest rates and the unemployment rate, and other macroeconomic variables that capture economic downturns through the business cycle. Banks use different FRR models depending on the industry and the obligor. Similarly, banks use different BRR models or scorecard based on the industry and the borrower. EAD estimates reflect the historically observed utilisation of undrawn credit limit prior to default.

A *minimum requirement* of a rating system is that it should be monotonic or consistent in its ranking, which means the estimated PDs should be increasing as the rating moves from higher to lower. The opposite of this condition is *inversion* of default rates, which means the default rate observed for a better rating grade is higher than the default rate of the adjacent worse rating grade. In any particular year, it is usual to find examples of the inversion. See S&P, *2018 Annual Global Corporate Default and Rating Transition Study* for the period 1993–2018. This does not mean there is a problem with the ordinal ranking capability of a risk rating system. For their PD mapping procedure, banks assume monotonicity of the estimated PD curve, based on the long-run average evidence, which the S&P article reports in Table 9. Otherwise, the assumption of monotonicity is invalid and the PDs will be inconsistent and unreliable for prudential, risk management, or pricing applications. The procedure involves smoothing of the observed default rates in order to create a positive and monotonic PD curve.

11. The other requirement of the AIRB approach is two-dimensionality of the rating system: one grade reflects PD and the other LGD. This procedure promotes precision and consistency by separately grading the borrower (PD) and the facility or transaction (LGD) rather than mixing them together. An effective rating system promotes consistency in the BRR by ensuring that with the same information about the borrower and using the same scorecard for a given industry, the BRR is expected to be the same regardless of the person who is performing the assessment. For example, rating an airline company using the Airline Transportation scorecard and the same financial and other data should yield the same BRR. Furthermore, an effective rating system promotes consistency across portfolios because a common enterprise-wide rating scale applies to all obligors.

12. RAROC = Expected Return/Economic Capital

    The economic capital of a bank is a measure of risk calculated *internally* with the use of a probability model whose output is a monetary level of capital necessary to adequately support specific risks or absorb unexpected loss. For example, for a given loan, the interest rate, the term of the loan, and the annual repayments, along with the Borrower Risk Rating, the bank's profitability model calculates the economic capital supporting the loan exposure. The expected return is a net figure. It includes the interest income from the loan less the bank's borrowing costs. Typically, a bank is more interested in the total relationship, so it will add in investment income from the customer's deposits, fees, and service charges and subtract out interest expense on the customer's deposits and the cost of activities to service the customer. The lender compares the computed RAROC with the target or hurdle RAROC to determine if the loan is worth pursuing.

13. Basel Committee on Banking Supervision Consultative Document Guidelines (2016), *Prudential treatment of problem assets – definitions of non-performing exposures and forbearance*, Issued for comment by July 15, 2016. See also Basel Committee on Banking Supervision (June 2006), Basel II: International Convergence of Capital Measurement and Capital Standards: A Revised Framework - Comprehensive Version. Refer to the paragraphs under Rating Systems Design.

14. Keynes, John Maynard (1936), *The General Theory of Employment, Interest and Money. London.* Macmillan (reprinted 2007). See Chapter 12: The State of Long-Term Expectations.

15. Report of the Commission of Investigation into the Banking Sector in Ireland (2011), *Misjudging Risk: Causes of the Systemic Banking Crisis in Ireland.*

16. Ganguin, Blaise & Bilardello, John (2005), *Standard & Poor's Fundamentals of Corporate Credit Analysis,* McGraw-Hill. This book provides a detailed treatment of five risk factors. See also bank annual reports. For example, see page 75 of the 2015, Annual Report of the Bank of Nova Scotia states: Credit adjudication units within Global Risk Management analyse and evaluate all significant credit requests for corporate and commercial credit exposures, to ensure that risks are adequately assessed, properly approved, continually monitored, and actively managed. The decision-making process begins with an assessment of the credit risk of the individual borrower or counterparty. Key factors considered in the assessment include:

   - The borrower's management;
   - The borrower's current and projected financial results and credit statistics;
   - The industry in which the borrower operates;
   - Economic trends; and
   - Geopolitical risk.

   Based on this assessment, a risk rating is assigned to the individual borrower or counterparty, using the bank's risk rating systems.

17. In 2001 George Akerlof, Michael Spence, and Joseph E. Stiglitz shared the Nobel Memorial Prize in Economics for their "analyses of markets with asymmetric information". This is in contrast with perfect information, a key assumption in neo-classical economics. See George A. Akerlof (1970), *The Market for 'Lemons': Quality Uncertainty and the Market Mechanism.* Quarterly Journal of Economics, 84 (3): 488–500; Michael Spence (1973), *Job Market Signaling,* Quarterly Journal of Economics, The MIT Press, 87 (3): 355–374; and Joseph Stiglitz & Andrew Weiss, (1981), *Credit Rationing in Markets with Imperfect Information,* American Economic Review, 71: 393–410.

18. A stockholder's claim on a company that is using debt to finance its investments (called a levered company) can be viewed as a call option on the firm's asset value, so in the case of the levered company, its managers (acting on behalf of stockholders) have unlimited upside but limited downside. In a call option, the option buyer (the investor) has an unlimited potential for the stock price to exceed the strike price, conferring potentially unlimited profit (buying the stock at the strike price and selling it at the higher spot price). Just as well, the stock price could have fallen below the strike price in which case it makes no economic sense for the buyer to exercise the option (buying high and selling low). However, the point worth stating is that the investor's loss is limited to the amount he paid for the option.

19. AIG was designated "too big to fail". It went bankrupt in September 2008 at the height of the US financial crisis, and agreed to US government bailout at the cost of $180 billion. It is the largest government rescue of a private com-

pany in US history. After several years of restructuring and selling off assets, AIG is back in the business of selling insurance. In 2017, nine years after the initial bailout, the U.S. Financial Stability Oversight Council removed AIG from its list of too-big-to-fail institutions. Now, AIG is rated "BBB+" (investment grade) by S&P but the Outlook rating is "negative".

20. Two main provisions of the Act in regard to the accuracy of financial information are the following:

   a. The CEO (Chief Executive Officer) and the CFO (Chief Financial Officer) are responsible for signing their firm's financial statements and indicating that the statements do not omit material information. Misrepresentation of the company's financial reports could mean many years in jail.
   b. The CEO and CFO must indicate they are responsible for the firm's system of internal controls over financial reporting and the firm's auditor must attest to management's assessment of internal controls. Good internal controls help to assure that financial records state transactions accurately and fairly.

21. Mishkin, Frederic. S. (2005), *Is financial globalization beneficial?* National Bureau of Economic Research, Working Paper 11891.
22. Basel Committee on Banking Supervision (2011), *Basel III: A global regulatory framework for more resilient banks and banking systems.*
23. Gea-Carrasco, Cayetano (2015), *FRS 9 Will Significantly Impact Banks' Provisions and Financial Statements*, Moody's Analytics, May 2015.
24. Basel Committee on Banking Supervision (June 2006), *Sound Credit Risk Assessment and Valuation for Loans.*
25. Basel Committee on Banking Supervision (April 2005), *Compliance and the Compliance Function in Banks.*
26. See website: https://index.baselgovernance.org/about_us

# 2

# Financial Statement Analysis

**Chapter Objectives**

1. Discuss financial disclosure and the importance of critical interpretation by the users of company financial reports
2. Calculate and analyse selected financial statements
3. Identify and discuss some of the key problems in measuring, comparing, and interpreting financial ratios
4. Distinguish between on-balance and off-balance sheet (OBS) liabilities
5. Explain methods to capitalise operating leases
6. Examine the effects of OBS adjustments on solvency and liquidity ratios
7. Review the useful applications and the limitations of financial ratios

## 2.1    Introduction

In order to perform a complete financial analysis, ratio analysis is essential. In this chapter, we lay the foundations of financial statement analysis by defining and examining a small set of commonly used financial ratios. There are, however, numerous financial ratios but the quality of financial analysis does not necessarily improve with the quantity of ratios; however, it is useful to familiarise yourself with them. For those who wish to explore this area further, they are many specialised books, amongst them Bernstein, Leopold and Wild (1998)

**Electronic Supplementary Material:** The online version of this chapter (https://doi.org/10.1007/978-3-030-32197-0_2) contains supplementary material, which is available to authorized users.

© The Author(s) 2020
T. M. Yhip, B. M. D. Alagheband, *The Practice of Lending*,
https://doi.org/10.1007/978-3-030-32197-0_2

and White, Sondhi and Fried (1997).[1] In this chapter, we focus on financial ratios of firms that sell products. For service companies and commercial banks, the credit analyst uses different ratios to tell the same story—a comprehensive profile of the firm's profitability, operating efficiency, liquidity, and solvency. We will have many opportunities to work with a variety of ratios for entities that are not in the business of manufacturing products or merchandising. In Chap. 5, we do a credit analysis for a passenger airline company. In Chap. 6, the analysis is for a borrower in commercial real estate, and in Chap. 7, we turn to a commercial bank.

Ratios by themselves are useless metrics, but with the correct interpretation and an understanding of their limitations, they are a powerful tool to explain the current financial performance of a company and to predict financial performance. This is the overarching objective of ratio analysis rather than just spreading financial statements and cranking out ratios mechanically according to some formula. Thus, it really comes down to the credit analyst's *modus operandi*. One of the more comprehensive discussions on this aspect of financial analysis is in Fridson and Alvarez (2011).[2] Here is a passage that sets the tone for this chapter on financial statement analysis.

> Financial statement analysis is an essential skill in a variety of occupations, including investment management, corporate finance, commercial lending, and the extension of credit. For individuals engaged in such activities, or who analyze financial data in connection with their personal investment decisions, there are two distinct approaches to the task.
>
> The first is to follow a prescribed routine, filling in the boxes with the standard financial ratios, calculated according to a precise and inflexible definitions. It may take little more effort or mental exertion than this to satisfy the formal requirements of many positions in the field of financial analysis. Operating in a purely mechanical manner, though, will not provide much of a professional challenge. Neither will a rote completion of all of the proper standard analytical steps ensure, or even a no harmful, result. Some individuals, however, will view such problems as only minor drawbacks.
>
> This book is aimed at the analyst who will adopt the second and more rewarding alternative, the relentless pursuit of accurate financial profiles of the entities being analysed. Tenacity is essential because financial statements often conceal more than they reveal. To the analyst who embraces this proactive approach, producing a standard spreadsheet on a company is a means rather an end. Investors derive but little satisfaction from the knowledge that an untimely stock purchase recommendation was supported by the longest row of figures available in the software package. Genuinely valuable analysis begins after all the usual questions have been answered. Indeed, a superior analyst adds value by raising questions that are not even on the checklist.

With these cautionary notes as a backdrop, let us review financial statements and some basic concepts of accounting.

## 2.2 Financial Reports and Reporting: A Quick Overview

A financial statement is a record of the financial activities and position of a person, a household, a business, or other entity. It could be formal or an informal record. Lenders prefer formal records that have been reviewed or audited by an independent third party, typically a certified accountant or an accounting firm. The purpose of this section is not about preparing financial statements nor is it about accounting *per se*. Rather, the goal is to familiarise you with the presentation of financial statements so that you can read them, interpret them, and look for the items that are critical to the analysis.

Financial reports for credit analysts come under the two broad types listed below. Our focus is on corporate borrowers so we will be analysing business financial statements.

1. **Financial Statements for Personal Lending**

    Consumer credit analysis and a substantial portion of commercial credit analysis are based on the Individual Income-tax Return of the borrower and the guarantor as applicable. Whether self-employed or working for a firm, the individual is required by law to report all income from all sources, domestically and internationally. Individuals are allowed certain deductions to arrive at a net income figure. The self-employed, like a business, reports all expenses to derive the net income or profit figure. Lenders often ask for Personal Statement of Affairs (PSOA).
2. **Financial Statements for Business/Corporate Lending**

    A typical commercial loan package submitted to a Credit Analyst would include these financial statements:

- Annual audited financial statements for the last three fiscal years,[3] current (unaudited financial statements, e.g., last quarter), and *pro forma* financial statements which are hypothetical statements as they would appear if some event were to happen, such as a merger, an acquisition, or a recession. *They are a financial forecast or projection—a set of hypothetical results based on the initial conditions and the assumptions.*
- Rent roll for commercial real estate (CRE) credit analysis
- CRE cash flow
- Any other financial record that is necessary for a complete analysis of a borrower's current and expected financial health.

## Principal Financial Statements for a Business

A company's Financial Statement consists of four records:

1. The income (or profit and loss) statement
2. The balance sheet
3. The statement of cash flows
4. The Statement of shareholders' equity

### Be Aware of the Abuse of *Pro Forma* Financial Statements

Credit analysts and investors need to be alert to false and misleading *pro forma* financial reports. On January 16, 2002, the SEC brought a landmark action against Trump Hotels and Casino Resorts. This was the SEC's first enforcement action involving the abuse of so-called *pro forma* accounting to mislead shareholders. In a press release of QIII: 1999, Trump Hotels & Casinos excluded an $81.4 million one-time charge, but included a one-time gain of $17 million in profit. The agency accused Trump Hotels of using "fraudulent" reporting to "tout purportedly positive results". The SEC found that Trump Hotels violated Section 10(b) Anti-fraud provision of the Exchange Act and Rule 10b-5 that prohibits the use of any "device, scheme, or artifice to defraud". Trump Hotels & Casinos consented to the SEC's cease-and-desist order, acknowledging its findings without admitting or denying them (see https://www.sec.gov/litigation/admin/34-45287.htm, and The New York Times report by Steve Lohr, "Trump Hotels Settles Case Accusing It of Misleading Investors." January 17, 2002.)

### Big Profits and Returns Can Be Deceiving

Profit hardly ever equals cash flow under accrual accounting. A company can show tremendous profits, whereas cash flow is negative. For example, highly profitable estate companies find they cannot refinance their debts because the market expects rents and cash flow to drop.

In this book, we approach financial statements from the perspective of a lender rather than an equity investor. In credit analysis, the overriding purpose of financial statement analysis is to get a good fix on the subject's creditworthiness. Before moving to actual ratio calculations, we examine the four statements to understand what each is reporting, what are some of the peculiarities that a credit analyst should be aware of in spreading the financial statements, and how the statements interrelate. A credit analyst is at liberty to define his or her own metrics to obtain the most reliable measurements of financial performance. Therefore, the analyst is primarily interested in informational value or content rather than whether a metric conforms to accounting principles per se.

### Income Statement and Statement of Comprehensive Income

Comprehensive income consists of net income and unrealized income, such as unrealized gains or losses on derivative financial instruments and foreign currency transaction gains or losses that caused stockholders' equity to change during the accounting period. The income statement reports a firm's overall performance resulting from both operating and regular activities and from certain gains and losses such as those realised from the disposal of non-current assets or long-term assets, for example, property, plant and equipment, and intangible assets. International Financial Reporting Standards (IFRS) require the preparation and reporting of another income statement called Statement of Comprehensive income.[4] The statement includes such things as unrealised gains or losses on derivatives used in hedging, unrealised gains, or losses on pension and post-retirement liabilities, and foreign currency translation adjustments. Publicly traded firms may report comprehensive income in a separate statement (as most do) or combine it with the income statement. The regular operating performance is measured by the revenues and expenses that a business incurs from producing and delivering products—defined as goods and services—from the entity's central operations. To drive home the point, the risk analyst adds value not by mechanically cranking out ratios from a spreadsheet but by ensuring the variables measure what they are supposed to measure and, at least, are not misleading. Non-recurrent transactions can mask the true profitability of a firm, as we pointed out earlier.

The income statement reports income and expenses on an *accrual accounting* basis, which means that a firm records revenues and expenses when they are incurred, regardless of when cash changes hands. Recording the revenue when it is earned is often different from when cash is received, and recording an expense when it occurs or expires is also often different when cash payment is made. Hence, bottom-line profit/loss will seldom match cash inflow/outflow from operations. Another important point to note is that the profit and profitability measures are sensitive to extraordinary and non-recurring items, choice of accounting methods, the underlying assumptions (e.g., estimated useful life of equipment), and other factors. As we stated earlier, credit analysts need to be particularly mindful of *pro forma* financial press releases that attempt to mislead investors and lenders.

## Balance Sheet

The balance sheet, referred to as the statement of financial position, reports the assets (resources owned and controlled by the firm), the liabilities (external claims on the assets), and stockholders' equity (owners' capital contributions and internally generated sources of capital). The balance sheet presents a firm's financial position or a snapshot at the end of a specified period of the fiscal year, such as October 31, 2015 and December 31, 2015. The accounting equation or identity below forms the basis for recording all transactions in financial reporting:

$$\text{Assets}(A) = \text{Liabilities}(L) + \text{Owner's Equity}(E)$$

The balance sheet must always balance and this is important to understand because, as simple as it looks, it means that changes in A accompany changes in L, E or both, or changes in L accompany changes in A or in E to bring the two sides into balance. Companies issue financial statements quarterly, semi-annually, and annually. They also issue *pro forma* financial statements in their press releases.

Assets are the things that a company owns. They are the resources like plant and equipment, inventory, receivables, securities, and loans that a company has acquired through transactions. The assets generate income and cash flow. The accounting tradition is to list assets in decreasing order of liquidity (starting with cash), and grouping them as either current or non-current. A current asset is expected to be sold and turned into cash within one year of the balance sheet date. Otherwise, it is a long-term asset like intangibles (patents, copyrights, goodwill), and fixed assets that vary in type across industries (banking, airline travel, entertainment, retail, hospitality, and manufacturing to name a few). Current assets are important line items in the calculation of liquidity strength. The book value of current assets like inventory and accounts receivable tends to be misleading because the company has not fully recognised impairment; otherwise, a write-down reduces the carrying amounts and shareholder's equity. A contra asset is an asset account with a credit balance, such as allowance for loan losses, which we will discuss in Chaps. 7 and 11. A *contra* asset account is by definition *contrary* to the usual debit balance of asset accounts.

### The Failure to Adjust for Impaired Assets Means

1. The book value of assets is inflated (the firm could even be bankrupt).
2. Debt/Equity is low when it should be higher.
3. The difference between reporting a profit and reporting a loss. The write-down is a loss in the income statement.

Liabilities are the things a company owes to creditors. The obligations along with shareholders' equity are the funding sources of the company's assets. The liabilities of non-financial enterprises are typically accounts payable, wages payable, taxes payable, and bank loans to name some. For a bank, the liabilities are customers' deposits and wholesale borrowings to fund loans. Liability accounts will normally have credit balances, except contra-liability accounts like discount on bonds payable. Contra-liability accounts are not used as often as contra asset accounts. Not all liabilities or obligations are debt for credit analysis purposes. A debt is a special type of liability with a repayment schedule, a fixed interest stream, and mandatory principal payments. Funded debt is essentially interest bearing liabilities. Analysts are expected to identify and estimate as accurately as possible the total amount of interest-bearing debt that the firm owes. Therefore, from the vantage point of the credit analyst concerned with measuring leverage accurately, *disclosure* precedes *accounting classification*. The analyst is at liberty to define debt in order to obtain a reliable measure for analytical purposes.

### What Happens When a Company Writes Off Goodwill?

Although the write-off, being a noncash transaction, does not affect cash flow and liquidity, it reduces shareholders' equity, which may trigger covenants in a Loan Agreement. In many companies' balance sheets, goodwill can be significant. **General Electric** wrote down $22.1 billion of it in the second half of 2018. Goodwill accounted for just over a quarter of the firm's balance sheet.

In contrast with debt, equity has no repayment schedule, no maturity, and no mandatory payments. Shareholders' equity is often confused with cash. Thus, the statement "Company ABC can draw cash from shareholders' equity to pay its bills" is incorrect. The first point to note is that shareholders' equity is on the liability side of the balance sheet, whereas cash is on the asset side. The second point is that shareholders' equity is the *owners' claim* against the assets of the company, which implies the money (to acquire the assets) has already been spent.

So, as a credit analyst, what do you look for in a balance sheet? Let us review some general principles. To begin with, lenders want to know if the borrower is safe to lend money to, the amount to lend, and the interest rates and terms to apply. Therefore, lenders evaluate the totality of the balance sheet. A useful way of thinking is to size up the borrower in two timeframes: short term and longer term. On the asset side, lenders look for strong liquid assets (cash, cash equivalents, and current assets) to support the borrower's ability to meet short-term obligations. For the longer term, lenders want to know about the firm's asset turnover and whether the company can effectively generate cash through its operations. On the liability side, lenders are interested in a borrower's *total* indebtedness and an accurate reading of its financial leverage. Therefore, obligations that are off-balance sheet must be added to the on-balance debt. The financial leverage is measured relative to a borrower's capital or equity. A lender is also interested in the shareholders' equity or the book value.

### The Statement of Cash Flows

The cash flow statement (CFS) is a mandatory part of a firm's financial reporting. The CFS reports the cash generated and used during the period of their occurrence in three categories:

1. Operating activities: Cash flow from operations (CFO) converts the items in the income statement from an accrual to a cash basis, which is another way of saying that not all transactions in the income statement are cash transactions. CFO makes adjustments for various non-cash items such as depreciation.
2. Investing activities: Cash flow from investing (CFI) reports the acquisition and disposal of long-term assets such as property, plant, and equipment.
3. Financing activities: Cash flow from financing (CFF) reports the issuance and purchase of the firm's own bonds and common stock, the repayment of long-term debt, and the payment of dividends.

The sum of the three balances is the net change in cash flow in a given period due to CFO, CFI, and CFF. In any given period, the total figure can be positive (net inflow) or negative (net outflow).

From the perspective of the credit analyst, the cash flow statement (CFS) serves four main purposes. First, it complements the P&L (profit and loss) and Balance Sheet statements especially where the other two are of limited value. Cash repays debt, so understanding the cash inflow and outflow is vital to assessing credit risk. Second, red flags go up when one observes that profit is consistently much higher than CFO, an indication that the firm is not effective in turning profit into cash. Finally, the CFS helps identify where a company fits in the Industry Life Cycle. Introductory or start-up companies are highly profitable but they require large external financing; mature companies tend to be net generators of cash flow (though less profitable) because their need for investment levels off as they become self-funding, whereas declining companies are net users due to deteriorating CFO and CFI. Fourth, the CFS is used to model the performance of a borrower to meet some given targets under plausible "what if" conditions. In Chap. 5, we present such a model.

## 2.3  Role of the Auditor

The auditor, a certified public accountant, is responsible for seeing that the company's financial statements conform to generally accepted accounting principles (GAAP) of the country or in accordance with International Accounting Financial Standards. Box 2.1 is an example of an Independent auditor's Report by *Arthur Anderson LLP*.[5] The auditor conducts the audit in accordance with standards generally accepted in the United States. Those standards require that the auditor perform certain procedures, depending on the auditor's judgement of the materiality of the risks, whether due to fraud or error. Significantly, it means that although management prepared the reports, the auditor performs an independent review. The auditor examines the firm's internal controls pertaining to the preparation of financial statements, and evaluates the appropriateness of accounting policies used, and the reasonableness of accounting estimates made by management. Audited financial statements are accompanied by the auditor's opinion.

The Report section of an annual report does not usually draw much public attention because it reads like a boilerplate (see Box 2.1). But, in fact, the text contains important declarations and assurances from the auditor. If you were a shareholder of Enron, Global Crossing, Tyco International, WorldCom, and Nortel Networks Corporation, all found guilty of defrauding shareholders over a long period, the auditor's statement should give you pause.[6] The fraudulent practices had been going on for years undetected. Enron had assets of $63.4 billion when it filed for bankruptcy on December 2, 2001. WorldCom's $107 billion in assets dwarfs Enron's when the company filed for bankruptcy in July 19, 2002. That the assets of these companies are many times larger than the combined GDPs of many countries gives you an idea of the unimaginable size of the losses that shareholders and lenders absorbed.

## 2.4  Ratio and Financial Analysis

**Some Preliminary Cautionary Notes**
Financial ratios are a useful standardisation; they enable comparative analysis of companies of different sizes in any given period or over many periods. In a common-size financial statement, line items can be expressed as percentages of a common base figure or scaling factor so that percentages add up to 100. For example, the balance sheet components are displayed as percentages of total assets; the income statement components are displayed as percentages of total sales (see Table 2.1); and the cash flow line items are expressed as a percentage

**Box 2.1: Excerpts from Arthur Anderson LLP Declaration**

- "To the Shareholders and Board of Directors of Enron Corporation"
- "We have examined management's assertion that the system of internal control of Enron Corp. (an Oregon Corporation) and subsidiaries as of December 31, 1999, 1998 and 1997 was adequate to provide reasonable assurance as to the reliability of financial statements and the protection of assets from unauthorised acquisition, use or disposition, included in the accompanying report on Management's Responsibility for Financial Reporting. Management is responsible for maintaining effective internal controls over the reliability of financial statements.......... Our responsibility is to express an opinion on management's assertion on our examination."
- "Our examinations were made in accordance with attestation standards established by the American Institute of Certified Public Accountants and, accordingly, included obtaining and understanding of the system on internal control, testing and evaluating the design and operating effectiveness of the system of internal control and such other procedures as we considered necessary in the circumstances. We believe that our examinations provide a reasonable basis for our opinion."
- "In our opinion, management's assertion that the system of internal control of Enron Corp. and its subsidiaries as of December 31, 1999, 1998 and 1997 was adequate to provide reasonable assurance as the reliability of financial statements and the protection of assets ......... in all material respects, based upon current standards of control criteria."
- "We have audited the accompanying consolidated balance sheet of Enron Corp. (an Oregon Corporation) and subsidiaries as of December 31, 1999, 1998 and 1997, and the related consolidated statement of income, comprehensive income, cash flows, and changes in shareholders' equity for each of the three years in the period ended December 31, 1999. The financial statements are the responsibility of Enron Corp.'s management. Our responsibility is to express an opinion on these financial statements based on our audits."
- "We conducted our audits in accordance with auditing standards generally accepted in the United States. Those standards require that we plan and perform the audit to obtain reasonable assurance about whether the financial statements are free of material misstatements. An audit includes examining, on a test basis, evidence supporting the amounts and disclosures in the financial statements. An audit also includes assessing the accounting principles used and significant estimates made by management, as well as evaluating the overall financial statement presentation. We believe that out audits provide a reasonable basis for our opinion."
- "In our opinion, the financial statements referred to above present fairly, in all material respects, the financial position of Enron Corp. and subsidiaries as of December 31, 1999 and 1998, and the results of their operations, cash flows and changes in shareholders' equity for each of the three years in the period ended December 31, 1999, in conformity with accounting principles generally accepted in the United States."

(Source: Enron Annual Report, 1999)

**Table 2.1** Income statement and common-sized income statement

Loblaw Companies Ltd.

Statement of earnings ($ mm)
(Fiscal year on the Saturday closest to December 31)

| | 2010 | 2011 | 2012 | 2013 | 2014 | 2015 |
|---|---|---|---|---|---|---|
| Revenue | 30,836 | 31,250 | 31,604 | 32,371 | 42,611 | 45,394 |
| Cost of merchandise inventories sold | 23,534 | 23,894 | 24,185 | 24,701 | 32,063 | 32,846 |
| Gross margin | 7302 | 7356 | 7419 | 7670 | 10,548 | 12,548 |
| Other operating expenses | | | | | | |
| SG & A expense | 5154 | 5088 | 5309 | 5369 | 8258 | 8741 |
| Rent expense[a] | 173 | 185 | 137 | 156 | 156 | 614 |
| Depreciation and amortisation (D&A)[b] | 628 | 699 | 777 | 824 | 1472 | 1592 |
| Operating income | 1347 | 1384 | 1196 | 1321 | 662 | 1601 |
| Interest expense[a] | 452 | 442 | 437 | 516 | 625 | 674 |
| Interest income[a] | −99 | −115 | −106 | −48 | −41 | −30 |
| Earnings before income taxes | 994 | 1057 | 865 | 853 | 78 | 957 |
| Income taxes | 319 | 288 | 215 | 226 | 25 | 334 |
| Net earnings | 675 | 769 | 650 | 627 | 53 | 623 |
| | **As % of revenue** | | | | | |
| Revenue | 100% | 100% | 100% | 100% | 100% | 100% |
| Cost of merchandise inventories sold | 76.3% | 76.5% | 76.5% | 76.3% | 75.2% | 72.4% |
| Gross margin | 23.7% | 23.5% | 23.5% | 23.7% | 24.8% | 27.6% |
| Other operating expenses | 0.0% | 0.0% | 0.0% | 0.0% | 0.0% | 0.0% |
| SG & A expense (excluding D&A) | 16.7% | 16.3% | 16.8% | 16.6% | 19.4% | 19.3% |
| Rent expense | 0.6% | 0.6% | 0.4% | 0.5% | 0.4% | 1.4% |
| Depreciation and amortisation (D&A) | 2.0% | 2.2% | 2.5% | 2.5% | 3.5% | 3.5% |
| Operating income | 4.4% | 4.4% | 3.8% | 4.1% | 1.6% | 3.5% |
| Interest expense | 1.5% | 1.4% | 1.4% | 1.6% | 1.5% | 1.5% |
| Interest income and other financing charges (net) | −0.3% | −0.4% | −0.3% | −0.1% | −0.1% | −0.1% |
| Earnings before income taxes | 3.2% | 3.4% | 2.7% | 2.6% | 0.2% | 2.1% |
| Income taxes | 1.0% | 0.9% | 0.7% | 0.7% | 0.1% | 0.7% |
| Net earnings | 2.2% | 2.5% | 2.1% | 1.9% | 0.1% | 1.4% |

[a]Figures are from the Notes to the Statement of Earnings; [b]Figures are from the Cash Flow Statement
Source: Loblaw Annual Reports

of total cash flow (or total operational cash flow for the components of cash flows from operations). In order to obtain meaningful comparisons, the credit analyst needs to be aware of a few important points on using common-size financial statements and other ratios for intercompany comparisons.

## Accounting Systems and Methods

The credit analyst should determine before spreading the financial statements which accounting system the firm uses, such as U.S. GAAP or IAS because of important differences. Within the given system, the choice of accounting methods allowed directly affects the values of line items of financial statements and thus the ratios derived from them. Ratios are not comparable between firms that use different accounting methods, or a firm over time when it adopts new accounting methods.

### Benchmarks and Comparative Ratio Analysis

A company's ratios by themselves provide limited insight unless one knows how well the firm is performing relative to its industry. The comparison works well when a firm's product line does not span a range of industries. Benchmarking is necessary to evaluate how well a company is performing; it *indicates* such information on whether a firm has accumulated too much debt, has insufficient cash to service its debt, or is not collecting receivables fast enough. Large deviations from the benchmarks might be a clue to unscrupulous financial reporting. For example, the financial statements of a company that is consciously not writing off past-due accounts aggressively would show a lower ratio of sales to accounts receivable than the industry average. But by keeping uncollectible accounts receivable off the books, rather than provisioning for losses and writing them off, the business appears profitable and the balance sheet looks healthy.

Although as a general practice benchmarking is recommended, it is of no value as a tool for comparative analysis if a particular industry is in decline or the big firms in the industry are doing poorly. There are other limitations to benchmarking. Finding suitable industry averages can be problematic for a firm whose product line spans many industries. Finally, benchmarking is industry-specific and, as such, using an industry average for comparisons between firms in different industries is useless.

Another tool of comparative analysis is peer-to-peer grouping, which enables closer analysis of companies of similar size and lines of business. For example, in terms of assessing profitability and efficiency, firms in the supermarket sector generate low profit margins and high turnover, compared to companies in the aircraft-manufacturing sector. As with the benchmarking, creating a homogeneous group of firms is a challenge because sample size decreases with increasing heterogeneity. A comparison with one or two companies would not be as informative as one with twenty or more.

### Negative Book Values: Signs Can Play Tricks

Particular attention is required to interpret negative ratios and absolute numbers derived from the line items.

- **Example 1: Negative Equity in an accounting sense is not synonymous with insolvency or bankruptcy.**

Share repurchase can reduce shareholders' equity. If Company ABC repurchases from the open market 100 of its stock at $10 each, it will credit the cash account with $1000 and debit Treasury Stock—a contra equity account—$1000. Thus, a share buyback reduces total shareholders' equity. For example, Domino's Pizza started to buy back its stock in 2011 and the book value of shareholders' equity and return on equity (ROE) turned negative in recent years. But the negative figures were not a sign of insolvency because the company was profitable and the share buyback was being financed by the cash generated from the operations.

- **Example 2: Negative net income and negative equity resulting in positive ROE**

In contrast with Example 1, Company XYZ reports negative net income and negative shareholders' equity. The positive value of the ratio will be misleading. Moreover, if ROE figures are computer-generated, the credit analyst would be misled by the positive values in such cases.

- **Example 3: Share buyback – Case of Improved Performance Metrics**

In a share buyback a company debits cash, which reduces the company's cash holdings, and consequently total assets, by the amount of the cash expended. The buyback will simultaneously reduce shareholders' equity on the liabilities side by the same amount. As a result, performance metrics such as return on assets (ROA) and return on equity typically improve subsequent to a share buyback.

## 2.5 Categories of Ratios

For credit analysis, we will be discussing four groups of ratios:

1. Profitability
2. Asset utilisation and efficiency
3. Liquidity
4. Debt and solvency

One point to bear in mind is that the grouping of ratios is somewhat arbitrary because financial ratios are interrelated and hence, are not standalone categories. A few examples will suffice. For example, asset utilisation and efficiency overlap with profitability. A firm that employs its assets efficiently is more likely to more profitable than one that does not make the best use of its resources. Productive efficiency means the firm is producing the maximum amount of goods and services with a given amount of inputs at the lowest possible average cost. Therefore, efficiency overlaps with profitability. Likewise, liquidity overlaps with efficiency. The ability of a company to turn inventory into sales, and sales into cash determines cash flow. Liquidity and solvency go hand in hand.

There are numerous financial ratios but the credit analyst need only look at a handful because many are redundant due to high correlation and high collinearity. Therefore, the informational value does not necessarily increase with the number of ratios employed.[7] This chapter focuses on a subset of ratios that have proven over time to be reasonably reliable indicators and predictors of creditworthiness.[8] Although a small set of ratios applies to most industries, the credit analyst usually replaces or supplements them with indicators that measure the characteristics of an industry better than the generic ones. Perfect examples are banking, farming, commercial real estate, and energy. We will see examples of this in Chaps. 6 and 7, which focus on the credit assessment of a counterparty in commercial real estate and banking.

A final note is that that the analyst must often adjust various metrics to improve their accuracy and to maintain consistency through time and across companies. For example, if you are measuring the profitability of a firm's core operations, you would exclude one-off income gains from discontinued business and gains from the sale of assets. When calculating total debt, it will often be necessary to add back off-balance sheet obligations for a more accurate picture of leverage and debt-servicing strength.

Purely for illustration purposes, we use the historical financial information from publicly available annual reports of Loblaw Companies Limited (Loblaw), a Canada-based public company listed on the TSE (Toronto Stock Exchange). The Company's subsidiaries include Loblaws Inc., Shoppers Drug Mart Inc., Choice Properties Limited Partnership, Choice Properties Real Estate Investment Trust, and President's Choice Bank. The Company, through its subsidiaries, sells products and services related to food, general merchandise, drugs, health and beauty, and apparel. The Company operates through three segments: Retail, Financial Services, and Choice Properties. The discount supermarket operation dominates the retail segment, which has accounted for almost 98% of consolidated revenue in recent years.

We begin the discussion using *only* the line items reported on the balance sheet and in the consolidated financial statements. We consider off-balance sheet (OBS) items, specifically OBS obligations in subsequent sections. We present methods to capitalise such liabilities in order to obtain an accurate picture of the total debt.

## 2.5.1 Profit and Profitability

Profit is measured in terms of absolute monetary units, whereas profitability is measured by ratios. Firms pursue many strategies or objectives such as maximising profits, increasing market share, industry leadership, or growing and diversifying in other lines of business through mergers and acquisitions. Profitability ratios measure the ability of management to use resources efficiently to maximise profits.[9] There are numerous ways to measure profitability. Differences in accounting systems and methods contribute to the proliferation of profitability ratios.

The reliability of the sales or revenue number is critical and the credit analyst needs to be aware of aggressive income recognition that results in fraudulent and unethical reporting. An example of the latter is window dressing to portray the firm in a more favourable light at the end of the accounting period (quarter or year). The income statement provides many opportunities for window dressing. Take, for example, accelerating sales from a future period to the current through early shipment discounts which save on shipping costs and entice buyers to make current purchases. The current period's sales will look strong, and so would the profitability ratios and the solvency ratios that also use an income measure as numerator.

With these qualifying comments, let us look at four commonly used profitability ratios:

1. Gross Profit Margin
2. Operating Profit Margin
3. Pre-tax Profit Margin
4. Net Income Margin

**Gross Profit Margin**
The gross margin is a key performance measure because all other costs must be recovered from gross profit, and any income earned is the balance remaining. The gross margin is measured as sales minus cost of goods sold, or costs or sales, divided by revenue or sales:

$$\text{Gross profit margin} = \frac{\text{Sales} - \text{Costs of Goods Sold}}{\text{Revenue}}$$

Applying this definition to Loblaws' Income Statement (Table 2.1), the gross profit margin in 2015 was 27.6%:

$$\text{Gross profit margin}_{2015} = \frac{45,394 - 32,846}{45,394} = 27.6\%$$

### Analysis

The gross margin represents the portion of each dollar of revenue that the company retains as gross profit. The 27.6% means that for every dollar of sales, there is almost 28 cents of gross income to cover operating and non-operating expenses.

### Operating Profit Margin

Operating profit margin is measured as:

$$\text{Operating profit margin} = \frac{\text{Operating income}}{\text{Revenue}}$$

This metric excludes the effects of interest expense (financing), income from affiliates and asset sales (investment) and taxes. Operating income is considered an official financial measure under GAAP. It is income from core business, excluding the effects of (a) income from affiliates and asset sales, (b) financing, and (c) tax position. A measure of operating income is EBIT (earnings before interest and taxes) derived from subtracting operating costs and expenses—which is the sum of cost of goods sold, operating expenses, and depreciation & amortisation—from top line sales or revenue. The figure for net sales may also be used.

$$\text{Operating income} = \text{Sales} - (\text{cost of goods sold} + \text{other operating expense})$$

Operating expenses include broadly, cost of sales, and SG&A (selling, general and administrative expense). SG&A expense includes rental expense, and depreciation (for tangible assets) and amortisation (for intangible assets). Items that are unrelated to the firm's core operations are not included.

Applying this definition to Loblaws' Income Statement (Table 2.1), the operating profit margin in 2015 was 3.5%:

$$\text{Operating profit margin}_{2015} = \frac{45,394 - 32,846 - 10,947}{45,394} = 3.5\%$$

## Analysis

Interpreting changes in operating profit margin requires looking into the underlying factors and understanding the causes for the changes in the factors. The operating profit margin ratio indicates how the firm is supporting its operations. A good indicator of financial strength is that the firm is earning enough money from its operations to support the business. The 3.5% in 2015 means that for every dollar of operating income, nearly 4 cents remain after the operating expenses have been paid to cover the non-operating expenses, such as interest. A higher operating margin is clearly more favourable than a lower ratio because it means that the firm is generating enough cash from its core business to pay for variable and fixed costs. We note that low profitability ratios are typical in the retail grocery and food industry.[10] In a global context, 3.5% appears to be average performance.

## Margin before Interest, Taxes, and Depreciation/Amortisation

EBITDA has its litany of weaknesses or, as some might add, abuses[11]; nonetheless, like many financial ratios, EBITDA provides useful information if used properly. It is widely used in credit analysis as a proxy for cash flow generated from operations since depreciation and amortisation are non-cash expenses charged against income. It is a useful measure for comparing companies with different depreciation policies. Other strengths would include the fact that it is a profit margin that is independent of interest expense and taxes, similar to EBIT (or operating margin), and therefore it is a useful measure of debt servicing capacity. EBITDA is based on operating income and necessary day-to-day operating expenses; hence, uncluttered by cash flows from capital investments and financing. It is simple to calculate. But the same strengths are also its weaknesses. For instance, EBITDA does not account for changes in capital expenditures, and it can overstate cash flow in periods when working capital needs (for inventory and accounts receivable) are increasing fast.

EBITDA is derived from adding depreciation and amortisation to EBIT; alternatively, it is the sum of net income before tax, interest expense, and depreciation and amortisation. The EBITDA margin is defined as:

$$\text{EBITDA Margin} = \frac{\text{EBITDA}}{\text{Revenue}}$$

$$\text{EBITDA} = \text{Net income} + \text{Interest expense} + \text{Taxes} + \text{Depn / Amort.}$$

Applying these definitions to Loblaw's Income Statement, EBITDA is measured as:

$$\text{EBITDA}_{2015} = 623 + 674 + 334 + 1592 = 3223$$

$$\text{Margin before interest and taxes} = \frac{3223}{45,394} = 7.1\%$$

**Analysis**

The EBITDA margin ratio shows that every dollar in sales earned results in nearly 7 cents of cash profits is available to cover taxes and interest. The interpretation of this ratio is thus similar to the operating profit margin.

**Net Profit/Income Margin**

The overall profit margin is net of all expenses and reported at the bottom of the income statement. The net profit margin shows how good a company is at converting sales into profits available for shareholders. The ratio is defined as follows:

$$\text{Net margin} = \frac{\text{Net income}}{\text{Revenue}}$$

Applying this definition to Loblaws' Income Statement, the operating profit margin in 2015 was 1.4%:

$$\text{Net margin}_{2015} = \frac{623}{45,394} = 1.4\%$$

**Analysis**

The 1.4% shows that for every dollar of sales, 1.4 cents are available for shareholders after all expenses are covered. We note that such a low figure is in line with the average performance of companies in the grocery and food retailing business.[12] Interpreting changes in net margin requires looking into the underlying factors and understanding the causes for the changes in the factors.

**Note**

Discretionary items can make a big difference in the way profit is measured. For family-owned or closely held businesses in which a small group of shareholders control the operating and managerial policies of the firm, the *net income* figure can be a misleading measure of profit because of various discretionary expenses. The biggest is management compensation to family members who hold senior positions in the company. To measure profit more accurately for this form of business organisation, the analyst would add back taxes, management compensation, and depreciation, which is a significant non-cash expense:

$$\textbf{Profit} = \textbf{Net income before tax} + \textbf{M'gt compensation} + \textbf{Depreciation}$$

## 2.5.2 Return on Investment

Return on investment (ROI) measures the relationship between return and the amount invested. The amount invested is called the finance base consisting of equity and debt. ROI evaluates profitability of a firm. ROI is measured before tax or after tax.

**Return on Assets (Before Tax)**

The before-tax definition is:

$$\text{ROA} = \frac{\text{EBIT}}{\dfrac{\text{Beginning total assets} + \text{Ending total assets}}{2}}$$

Where EBIT (a measure of operating income) is defined earlier. The calculated ratio for 2015 is:

$$\text{ROA}_{2015} = \frac{957 + 674}{\dfrac{33,759 + 33,939}{2}} = 4.8\%$$

## Analysis

For every dollar of assets, Loblaw made almost five cents in 2015. Return on assets is typically low in grocery and food retail, but Loblaw's 4.8% ROA is dwarfed by 13.8% for Metro Inc., a major Canadian competitor. The credit analyst looks for the underlying causes for changes in ROA, which is composite of the sales to asset ratio times the EBIT to sales ratio.

$$\text{ROA} = \frac{\text{Sales}}{\text{Assets}} \times \frac{\text{EBIT}}{\text{Sales}}$$

The analysis requires a deep inquiry into the causes of the changes in the two components. Changes in the sales to asset ratio (an efficiency or the activity ratio discussed in Sect. 2.5.3) result from poor asset management, whereas low profitability captured by the EBIT to sales ratio may be due to weaknesses in cost management and marketing, or just poor service and product quality. Notice that EBIT/Sales measure profitability independently of the firm's capital structure (because it excludes interest expense) and the tax position (because it excludes tax expense).

## Return on Equity

Return on Equity (ROE) measures the ability of a firm to earn income from its shareholders' investments in the company. ROE is an after-tax measure of return on investment and is defined as follows:

$$\text{ROE} = \frac{\text{Net income}}{\dfrac{\text{Beginning total equity} + \text{Ending total equity}}{2}}$$

Applying this definition to Loblaw's Income Statement and Balance Sheet, the ROE in 2015 was 4.8%.

$$\text{ROE}_{2015} = \frac{623}{\dfrac{12,787 + 13,164}{2}} = 4.8\%$$

**Analysis**

Return on equity measures how efficiently Loblaw uses the shareholders' money to make profits and grow the company. Each dollar of common stockholders' equity generates nearly 5 cents return. Companies like to report ROE because they know that investors are looking for profitable companies. ROE is also a composite ratio:

$$\text{ROE} = \frac{\text{Income}}{\text{Sales}} \times \frac{\text{Sales}}{\text{Assets}} \times \frac{\text{Assets}}{\text{Equity}}$$

Therefore, a clearer understanding of changes in ROE requires looking into changes in Loblaws' profitability (income to sales ratio), the activity (sales to assets ratio), and its solvency or leveraging (assets to equity ratio). A rising ROE can be a misleading indicator of sustainable performance if increasing leverage ratio contributes the most.

## 2.5.3 Asset Utilisation and Efficiency

We stated earlier that efficiency and profitability go together. To be clear we use the term *efficiency* in a very restricted sense rather than in its broadest meaning that captures the three types of efficiency of a business process: (a) technical efficiency, (b) allocative efficiency, and (c) scale efficiency. The measures that we present in this chapter do not capture the technical or *Pareto-type* efficiency introduced by Charles Koopmans (1951).[13] The efficiency ratios we will be using are known by other names, such as activity ratios, or turnover ratios because they indicate how best a company uses its assets to earn income. We can measure how best a firm employs its resources by calculating how long it takes a firm to convert accounts receivable and inventory into cash. A perfect example of the cash conversion cycle is retailing. Costco and Wal-Mart, for example, are extremely good at turning inventory, thus able to sell low-margin products at high volumes. If sales are profitable, the higher is the asset turnover ratio, the higher is the level of profit, and the higher is the ROE. With limited shelf or retail space, increasing asset turnover can be the best method to raise the ROE.

Two important efficiency ratios for manufacturing and merchandising firms are:

1. Accounts Receivable Turnover
2. Inventory Turnover

For enterprises that produce services rather than products, for example, passenger airline companies, the inventory turnover ratio is still relevant but must be defined differently to convey the same meaning. We discuss this point in Chap. 6 where we analyse a fictional airline.

**Accounts Receivable Turnover**

Accounts receivable turnover measures how many times a firm turns its accounts receivable into cash during a period. The measure shows the efficiency with which a company is collecting its credit sales from customers. If the period is a year (365 days), accounts receivable turnover is defined as:

$$\text{Accounts receivable turnover} = \frac{\text{Net credit sales}}{\dfrac{\text{Beginning AR} + \text{Ending AR}}{2}}$$

$$\text{Days of Accounts Receivable} = \frac{365}{\text{AR Turnover}}$$

We use credit sales because cash sales do not create receivables; however, not all companies report cash and credit sales separately and usually only total sales or net sales are reported in the income statement. In this case, the practice has been to use total sales or net sales, which implicitly assumes all the sales are made on credit. If the assumption is wrong and a significant portion of sales is cash, the ratio would be less useful for any given year. If the cash proportion tends to be stable over time, the ratio would still be useful for year-to-year comparison since the changes in the cash portion will be insignificant.

The accounts receivable turnover is defined alternatively as:

$$\text{Accounts Receivable Turnover} = \frac{\text{Average Accounts Receivable}}{\text{Revenues}} \times 365$$

The Loblaw income statement did not report credit sales, so we use total revenues instead. Applying the definition to the Income Statement and Balance Sheet, the accounts receivable turnover in 2015 was almost 36.

$$\text{Accounts receivable turnover}_{2015} = \frac{45,394}{\dfrac{1209 + 1325}{2}} = 35.8 \times$$

$$\text{Accounts receivable turnover}(\text{days})_{2015} = \frac{365\,\text{days}}{35.8} = 10.2\,\text{days}$$

**Analysis**

On average, Loblaw collected its receivables 36 times a year in 2015, which means the company collected its receivables once every 10 days. One may interpret the receivables turnover ratio as a liquidity ratio because the higher the turnover, the shorter the time to convert receivables into cash (recall what we said about the overlapping of ratio categories).

**Inventory Turnover (Using Cost of Sales)**

The inventory turnover is defined as:

$$\text{Inventory turnover} = \frac{\text{Cost of goods sold}}{\dfrac{\text{Beginning Inv} + \text{Ending Inv}}{2}}$$

Inventory turnover is a measure of the efficiency with which a firm controls its merchandise to avoid excessive holding of inventory. Companies realise a cost efficiency—a saving on the interest cost of inventory by employing just-in-time inventory methods. If the company does not fund its inventory through an operating line of credit, it still costs the company in terms of forgone interests income, an opportunity cost. Accountants use cost of sales for the numerator because inventory is at cost and not valued at selling or market prices, which is usually higher than unit COGS by a profit markup. The turnover metrics show how easily a company turns its inventory into cash. As we saw in accounts receivable turnover, inventory turnover is also a measure of liquidity. For big retailers like Costco and Wal-Mart, inventory is the biggest item of the current assets on the balance sheet. For example, in 2014 and 2015, Wal-Mart's inventory share in current assets was 73% and 71%, respectively. Holding unsellable inventory uses up working capital, which is costly.

Applying this definition to Loblaw's Income Statement and Balance Sheet (Tables 2.2 and 2.3), the inventory turnover in 2015 was almost 8.

$$\text{Inventory turnover}_{2015} = \frac{32{,}846}{\dfrac{4309 + 4322}{2}} = 7.6\times$$

**Table 2.2** Balance sheet ($ mm)

| Loblaw Companies Ltd. | | | | | |
|---|---|---|---|---|---|
| (Fiscal year on the Saturday closest to December 31) | | | | | |
| | 2011 | 2012 | 2013 | 2014 | 2015 |
| Assets | | | | | |
| Current assets | | | | | |
| Cash and cash equivalents | 966 | 1079 | 2260 | 999 | 1018 |
| Short-term investments | 754 | 716 | 290 | 21 | 64 |
| Accounts receivable | 467 | 456 | 618 | 1209 | 1325 |
| Inventories | 2025 | 2007 | 2084 | 4309 | 4322 |
| Credit card receivables | 2101 | 2305 | 2538 | 2630 | 2790 |
| Prepaid expenses and other assets | 117 | 74 | 75 | 214 | 265 |
| Assets held for sale | 32 | 30 | 22 | 23 | 71 |
| Total current assets | 6462 | 6667 | 7887 | 9405 | 9855 |
| Fixed assets | 8725 | 8973 | 9105 | 10,296 | 10,480 |
| Investment properties | 82 | 100 | 99 | 185 | 160 |
| Goodwill & intangible assets | 1029 | 1057 | 1054 | 12,993 | 12,526 |
| Deferred income tax assets | 232 | 260 | 253 | 193 | 132 |
| Security deposits | 266 | 252 | 1701 | 7 | 2 |
| Franchise loans receivable | 331 | 363 | 375 | 399 | 329 |
| Other assets | 301 | 289 | 285 | 281 | 455 |
| Total assets | 17,428 | 17,961 | 20,759 | 33,759 | 33,939 |
| Liabilities | | | | | |
| Current liabilities | | | | | |
| Bank indebtedness | 0 | 0 | 0 | 162 | 143 |
| Trade payables and other liabilities | 3677 | 3720 | 3797 | 4774 | 5106 |
| Provisions | 35 | 78 | 66 | 84 | 127 |
| Income taxes payable | 14 | 21 | 37 | 34 | 82 |
| Short-term debt | 905 | 905 | 1008 | 605 | 550 |
| Long-term debt due within one year | 87 | 672 | 605 | 420 | 998 |
| Associate interest | 0 | 0 | 0 | 193 | 216 |
| Capital securities | 0 | 0 | 0 | 225 | 0 |
| Total current liabilities | 4718 | 5396 | 5513 | 6497 | 7222 |
| Provisions | 50 | 59 | 56 | 76 | 131 |
| Long-term debt | 5493 | 4997 | 6672 | 11,042 | 10,013 |
| Trust unit liability | 21 | 18 | 688 | 722 | 821 |
| Deferred income tax liabilities | 222 | 223 | 34 | 1853 | 1834 |
| Other liabilities | 917 | 851 | 778 | 782 | 754 |
| Total liabilities | 11,421 | 11,544 | 13,741 | 20,972 | 20,775 |
| Equity | | | | | |
| Preferred share capital | 0 | 0 | 0 | 0 | 221 |
| Common share capital | 1540 | 1567 | 1642 | 7857 | 7851 |
| Retained earnings | 4414 | 4790 | 5289 | 4810 | 4954 |
| Contributed surplus | 48 | 55 | 87 | 104 | 102 |
| Accumulated other comprehensive income | 5 | 5 | 0 | 8 | 23 |
| Total equity attributable to shareholders of the company | 6007 | 6417 | 7018 | 12,779 | 13,151 |
| Non-controlling interests | 0 | 0 | 0 | 8 | 13 |
| Total equity | 6007 | 6417 | 7018 | 12,787 | 13,164 |
| Total liabilities and equity | 17,428 | 17,961 | 20,759 | 33,759 | 33,939 |

Source: Loblaw Annual Reports

**Table 2.3** Statement of cash flows ($ mm)

| Loblaw Companies Ltd. | | | | | |
|---|---|---|---|---|---|
| Statement of earnings ($ MM) | | | | | |
| | 2011 | 2012 | 2013 | 2014 | 2015 |
| Operating activities | | | | | |
| Net earnings | 769 | 650 | 627 | 53 | 623 |
| Adjustments for: | | | | | |
| Income taxes | 288 | 215 | 226 | 25 | 334 |
| Net interest expense and other financing charges | 327 | 331 | 468 | 584 | 644 |
| Depreciation and amortisation | 699 | 777 | 824 | 1472 | 1592 |
| Future income taxes | 0 | 0 | 0 | 0 | 0 |
| Income taxes paid | −216 | −232 | −272 | −293 | −296 |
| Income taxes received | 60 | 52 | 49 | 29 | 7 |
| Settlement of equity forward contracts | −7 | 0 | −16 | 0 | 0 |
| Settlement of cross currency swaps | 0 | 0 | 94 | 0 | 0 |
| Change in credit card receivables | −104 | −204 | 0 | −92 | −160 |
| Change in non-cash working capital | 8 | 55 | −224 | −321 | 235 |
| Net fixed asset and other related impairments | 5 | 19 | −32 | 16 | 73 |
| (Gain) loss on disposal of assets | −18 | −12 | −1 | 3 | −5 |
| Recognition of fair value increment on inventory sold | 0 | 0 | 0 | 798 | 0 |
| Charge related to inventory measurement and other conversion differences | 0 | 0 | 0 | 190 | 4 |
| Gain on defined benefit plan amendments | 0 | 0 | −51 | 0 | 0 |
| Other | 3 | −14 | 32 | 105 | 28 |
| Cash flows from operating activities | 1814 | 1637 | 1724 | 2569 | 3079 |
| Investing activities | | | | | |
| Fixed asset purchases | −987 | −1017 | −865 | −996 | −1008 |
| Intangible asset additions | 18 | 20 | −12 | −90 | −233 |
| Acquisition of Shoppers Drug Mart Corporation, net of cash acquired | 0 | 0 | 0 | −6619 | 0 |
| Cash assumed on initial consolidation of franchises | 0 | 0 | 0 | 0 | 33 |
| Change in short-term investments | 0 | 0 | 451 | 269 | −43 |
| Proceeds from disposal of assets | 57 | 62 | 26 | 129 | 36 |
| Change in franchise investments and other receivables | −18 | −22 | 5 | −25 | 0 |
| Goodwill and intangible asset additions | −14 | −43 | 0 | 0 | 0 |
| Change in security deposits | 92 | 11 | −1444 | 1694 | 5 |
| Investment in joint venture | 0 | 0 | 0 | −6 | 0 |
| Other | −4 | 0 | 0 | −40 | −28 |
| Cash flows used in investing activities | −856 | −989 | −1839 | −5684 | −1238 |
| Financing activities | | | | | |
| Change in bank indebtedness | −10 | 0 | 0 | −133 | −19 |
| Change in short-term debt | 370 | 0 | −300 | 19 | −55 |
| Long-term debt | | | | | |
| Issued | 287 | 111 | 2770 | 5865 | 1186 |
| Retired | −909 | −115 | −871 | −3336 | −1783 |

(continued)

**Table 2.3** (continued)

| Loblaw Companies Ltd. | | | | | |
|---|---|---|---|---|---|
| Redemption of capital securities | 0 | 0 | 0 | 0 | −225 |
| Deferred debt financing costs | 0 | 0 | −21 | −28 | 0 |
| Issuance of trust units (note 30) | 0 | 0 | 660 | 1 | 0 |
| Trust unit issuance costs | 0 | 0 | −44 | 0 | 0 |
| Interest paid | −380 | −356 | −370 | −506 | −491 |
| Dividends paid on common and preferred shares | −193 | −177 | −259 | −496 | −416 |
| Common share capital | | | | | |
|   Issued | 0 | 0 | 75 | 629 | 63 |
|   Purchased and held in trust | 21 | 22 | −46 | 0 | −63 |
|   Purchased and cancelled | −39 | −16 | −73 | −178 | −280 |
| Issuance of preferred share capital | 0 | 0 | 0 | 0 | 221 |
| Contribution from non-controlling interests | 0 | 0 | 0 | 8 | 0 |
| Other | 0 | 0 | 0 | 0 | 23 |
| Cash flows (used in) from financing activities | −853 | −531 | 1521 | 1845 | −1839 |
| Effect of foreign currency exchange rate changes on cash and cash equivalents | 4 | −4 | 8 | 9 | 17 |
| Change in cash and cash equivalents | 109 | 113 | 1414 | −1261 | 19 |
| Cash and cash equivalents, beginning of period | 857 | 966 | 1079 | 2260 | 999 |
| Cash and cash equivalents, end of period | 966 | 1079 | 2493 | 999 | 1018 |

Source: Loblaw Annual Reports

$$\text{Inventory turnover}\left(\text{days}\right)_{2015} = \frac{365\,\text{days}}{7.6} = 48\,\text{days}$$

**Analysis**

Loblaw's inventory turnover was close to 8× in 2015, which means the company took 48 days to sell the entire inventory. The higher is the turnover, the shorter is the time to convert inventory into cash. For retailers of low-margin products, the one big contributor to their profitability is moving inventory or products fast. For example, look no further than the US retailing giant, Wal-Mart. Its inventory turnover averaged 8.2 in the period 2012-2015, which means the company took 45 days to sell its entire inventory, or complete one turn. The sector average is 11× or 33 days.

**Inventory Turnover (Using Sales or Net Sales)**

We stated earlier that cost of sales is used for the numerator because inventory is at cost. Another measurement of inventory turnover uses sales for the numerator.

$$\text{Inventory turnover} = \frac{\text{Revenue}}{\dfrac{\text{Beginning Inv} + \text{Ending Inv}}{2}}$$

Applying this definition to Loblaw's Income Statement and Balance Sheet (Tables 2.2 and 2.3), the inventory turnover was 10.5× compared to 7.6× using COGS in 2015.

$$\text{Inventory turnover}_{2015} = \frac{45,394}{\dfrac{4309 + 4322}{2}} = 10.5\times$$

**Analysis**
By the sales approach, the inventory turned over 10.5 times in 2015. The cost-of-sales approach is preferred conceptually and for accuracy because sales includes a markup over cost, so it gives an upward bias to the turnover. Using the cost-of-sales method, the turnover was 10.5× in 2015. *Whichever approach you decide to use for trend or intercompany analysis, be consistent and only compare inventory turnover that uses the same approach.*

**Accounts Payable Turnover**
This turnover metric applies to the liabilities side of the balance sheet, and is defined as:

$$\text{Accounts Payables Turnover} = \frac{\text{Average Accounts Payable}}{\text{Purchases}} \times 365$$

$$\text{Purchases} = \text{Adjusted COGS} + \left(\text{Ending Inventory} - \text{Beginning Inventory}\right)$$

Purchases are not usually reported separately in financial statements, so for *merchandise* companies it is estimated by adjusting COGS for depreciation and other non-cash items and adding the resulting figure to the change in inventory. Depreciation expense is usually included in operating expenses and cost of goods sold. Whether depreciation is included in COGS or in operating expenses depends on the asset being depreciated. If asset is directly used in the production of inventory, it is included in COGS. If the depreciation is associated with fixed assets for SG&A (selling, general, and administrative) purposes, the cost is listed in operating expense.

Loblaw's financial statements did not separate depreciation between fixed assets for inventory production and for SG&A, whilst depreciation was listed in operating costs. Based on the reported figures, the payables turnover ratio in 2015 was nearly two months.

$$\text{Payables turnover}_{2015} = \frac{4940}{32,846} \times 365 = 54.9 \text{ days}$$

**Analysis**

The figure means that Loblaw paid its suppliers every 55 days on average. The higher is the turnover, the faster the company is paying off suppliers. The time interval between the payment to suppliers and payments received is critical for retail and wholesale companies because it represents an important source of financing for operating activities. A turnover figure should always be compared to the benchmark for the industry, in this case, supermarket and grocery stores, to determine whether it is high or low.

**LIFO Versus FIFO**

We stated earlier that the choice of accounting method influences the results of a calculation. In evaluating inventory turnover, the analyst must be aware of which accounting method the enterprise used for inventory evaluation. The U.S. GAAP (Generally Accepted Accounting Principles) allows *both* methods: Last-In-First-Out (LIFO) and the First-In-First-Out (FIFO), and changes in the accounting method will affect year-to-year comparisons. Under IFRS (International Financial Reporting Standards), LIFO is prohibited in preference for FIFO or weighted average is permitted. Under LIFO the balance sheet inventory figure is understated when prices are rising because it is based on the oldest costs. Because of the understatement of inventory, the calculated ratio overstates the turnover.

## 2.5.4 Liquidity

Liquidity and solvency mean different things. A firm is liquid if it is able to raise enough cash—either by borrowing or by selling assets—to pay current obligations or contractual payments. A firm is solvent if its revenues (in a discounted present value sense) exceed its expenditures. Liquidity is a short-term concept that refers to the ability of the firm to convert assets into cash or to obtain cash for current obligations. However, liquidity may also be related to solvency; a company that cannot meet its current or short-term obligations is not one that will survive and be profitable for much longer.

Let us look at three liquidity metrics:

1. Current ratio
2. Acid-Test (Quick) ratio
3. Funds from operations ratio

We stated that grouping financial ratios is, in a sense, artificial and, not surprisingly, one does find inventory turnover and accounts receivable turnover listed under liquidity as well as activity measures.

**Current Ratio**

The current ratio is calculated as:

$$\text{Current ratio} = \frac{\text{Current assets}}{\text{Current liabilities}}$$

A measure of liquidity is working capital in absolute monetary values (in yuan, yen, rupee), and it is the difference between a company's current assets and current liabilities. Negative working capital means current assets are less than current liabilities and a firm must borrow money or sell non-current assets, which is not the usual course of action, to pay off its bills. Monetary values are, however, not meaningful for comparative analysis of firms that vary in size and, instead, the ratio of current assets to current liabilities is used. A current ratio of 1:1 means the firm's current assets just matches the current liabilities, leaving no buffer. Thus, a ratio that is greater than 1:1 is desirable. It gives assurance that the latter will not only be repaid in the next 12 months, but also that the firm has additional liquidity. The greater is the buffer, the lower is the risk of the firm liquidating non-cash current assets and even long-term assets that generate revenue. A current ratio below 1:1 is a sign that the company may have problems meeting its short-term obligations. If there is no external source of emergency cash, such as bank loan or cash injections from the owners, the firm may be forced into bankruptcy.

High current ratios in and of themselves are, however, not always a positive indicator and the credit analyst needs to look at the composition of current assets. For example, a firm's current assets may have a high proportion of inventory and uncollectible accounts receivable. In this case, the credit analyst should assess the turnover ratios in order to evaluate better the real strength of the current ratios. One of the problems the analyst encounters, however, is that financial statements do not provide information on the quality of both assets and liabilities.

A high current ratio and low turnover may be signaling slow-moving inventory and uncollectible accounts receivable. High current ratios may be due to a high proportion of cash, which is a non-earning asset and an opportunity cost in terms of interest income. A firm that is managing working capital efficiently minimises its need to hold cash. The cash is held as a precautionary reserve against temporary cash shortfalls. In the normal course of business, the firm meets its working capital requirements by drawing from a revolving bank credit line. It allows the firm to draw up to a certain amount, and to borrow again once the outstanding amount is repaid.

Using the information in Table 2.3, the current ratio for 2015 is calculated as:

$$\text{Current ratio}_{2015} = \frac{9855}{7222} = 1.4 \times$$

Using the same definition, the five-year trend is 1.37, 1.24, 1.43, 1.45, and 1.36 for the years 2011–2015, respectively.

**Analysis**
The company has enough assets to cover all short-term liabilities in the next 12 months, and with a bit left over as a buffer. Notice that prepaid expenses is part of current assets and this item is usually small relative to other assets like cash, inventory, and receivables. A large prepaid amount is not necessarily a good sign because the figure can be inflated by adding deferred charges and other dubious forms of short-term liquidity. Due diligence is required to determine whether there is sufficient explanation in the footnotes to the financial statements.

Changes in the current ratios need careful interpretation in the presence of seasonal and cyclical patterns, and window dressing. In an economic recession, inventories and accounts receivables accumulate, whilst the firm is managing to pay its short-term debts. This results in an upward bias in the ratio in a downturn. Firms in the retailing business accumulate inventory over the summer in preparation for the increase in sales in the fall and winter seasons. Therefore, the current ratio will tend to rise in the summer. The other timing effect has to do with window dressing that makes the end-of-period current ratio look good. For example, a company uses cash to reduce payables. The current ratio improves even if current assets are unchanged.

The use of the current ratio assumes that the company will sell off its current assets in the event of a liquidity crunch. In fact, this rarely happens because firms need some minimum level of inventories and accounts receivable to maintain operations. Another consideration is that in such a sale, the firm might have to sell its inventory at a discount and, thus, the effective ratio at the market prices would be lower.

### Acid-Test (Quick) Ratio

A more conservative liquidity metric is the acid-test (quick) ratio:

$$\text{Quick ratio} = \frac{\text{Cash} + \text{Cash equivalents} + \text{Marketable securities} + \text{ARs}}{\text{Current liabilities}}$$

The numerator of this ratio uses quick assets that are convertible to cash within 90 days. Marketable securities are traded and priced in the open market. Such financial instruments can be easily sold on any trading day at known prices. Inventories take longer to convert to cash and the realisable market values could be lower than the book values. (The name "acid-test" harkens back to a time when gold miners used acid to distinguish pure gold from other metals or alloys. Pure gold does not corrode because it does not react with acid. If the metal corroded, it failed the test of pure gold.)

Using the information from the balance sheet, the current ratio for 2015 is calculated as selecting the appropriate line items:

$$\text{Quick ratio}_{2015} = \frac{1018 + 64 + 1325}{7222} = 0.33\times$$

### Analysis

Generally, the acid-test ratio should be 1:1 or higher; however, it varies widely by industry. As with the current ratio, the higher is the ratio, the greater the company's liquidity. But in food retailing, ratios of under 1:1 are normal. Loblaw's 0.33× is in the same range as those of Wal-Mart (USA) and Tesco PLC (UK). The business environment for the consumer-products industry is relatively stable because the demand for consumer goods is relatively unresponsive to changes in the prices and disposable incomes. Also, firms in the retail sector tend to expand slowly, and can maintain lower acid-test ratios without exposing themselves to liquidity shortages. The use of the quick ratio assumes that the company will sell off its accounts receivable. The point made earlier for the current ratio also applies in this case.

**Funds from Operations (FFO)**
The current and quick ratios are static in that they measure liquidity at one point in time. A less static metric uses operating cash flow in the numerator, which is measured for a period of time, thus incorporating the changes over the defined time period. FFO, a cash flow metric, essentially converts the operating section of the accrual income statement to a cash basis statement:

$$FFO = \text{Net Income} + / - \text{Change Working Capital} + \text{Non} - \text{cash Expenses}$$

The denominator of the ratio is total funded debt, which comprises *interest-bearing liabilities* such as bank loans, bonds, and financial/capital leases, and OBS (off-balance sheet) debt such an operating lease to which interest is imputed. It is called funded debt because it is funded by explicit and imputed interest payments. For credit risk assessment, a postponed debt is not a liability because no interest is charged on the amount, and is thus excluded from the definition of funded debt. The off-balance sheet (OBS) liabilities are reported in the footnotes, and in the case of Loblaw, in the section Off-Balance Sheet Arrangements. For now, to simplify the discussion and the calculations, we ignore OBS obligations, which we will return to later in this chapter.

Using the figures of Tables 2.3 and 2.4, the Funds From Operations (FFO)/Total Funded Debt ratio for 2015 is:

$$\frac{FFO}{\text{Total funded debt}_{2015}} = \frac{3079}{143 + 550 + 998 + 10,013} = 26.3\%$$

**Table 2.4** Symmetrical effects of using financial leveraging

| Investors | Equity | Borrowing | Cost of investment | Value of investment 1 year later | Return on equity |
|---|---|---|---|---|---|
| **Price increases by 50%** | | | | | |
| Donald | $1000 | $0 | $1000 | $1500 | 50% |
| Susan | $1000 | $2000 | $3000 | $4500 | 150% |
| **Price decreases by 50%** | | | | | |
| Donald | $1000 | $0 | $1000 | $500 | −50% |
| Susan | $1000 | $2000 | $3000 | $1500 | −150% |

Notes:
(1) Investment is 100 Christmas trees, (2) Cost/tree $10

**Analysis**

The ratio can vary between negative values (for a bankrupt firm not operating) to over 75% for firms with little debt. Thus, funds from operations could cover 26.3% of the total debt. A borrower with a high ratio can more easily repay its debt and incur more debt than one that has a lower ratio. Ratios below the 15–20% range may be considered weak.

**FOCF (Free Operating Cash Flow) Ratio**

The FOCF/Total debt ratio is another useful measure of liquidity that is commonly used to analyse companies with large and recurrent capex (capital expenditure) needs. We will be using this measure in Chap. 6 to analyse a company in the passenger airline industry, which is highly capital intensive. The FOCF ratio is defined as follows:

$$FOCF = \frac{\text{Operating cash flow} - \text{Capex} - \text{Dividends}}{\text{Total funded debt}}$$

$$FOCF_{2015} = \frac{3079 - 1008 - 416}{11,704} = 14.1\%$$

This is a more conservative measure than Funds from Operations and, as you would observe, it can be made more conservative if deductions for non-cancellable financial lease payments and rental payments are included in the definition.

## 2.5.5 Debt and Solvency

A firm finances its operations and long-term growth by equity financing and debt financing. Debt comes in the form of bank loans and bonds; equity comes in the form of common stock, preferred stock, and retained earnings. Financial leverage (or capital leverage) refers to the use of borrowed money (debt) rather than one's own accumulated savings (equity) to acquire assets (remember: assets generate income or a return). The leverage is the relationship between debt and equity. The higher the ratio of debt to equity, the more levered the investor. The notion of leverage comes from physics. A lever, as you know from everyday experience, is a tool that gives *mechanical leverage* for moving or lifting heavy stuff. Similarly, the use of debt gives *financial leverage* to reap excess returns with just a small amount of one's money. But leverage can also amplify loses, as we will see. This simple example illustrates these two observations. Donald buys 100 pine Christmas trees cultivated in a farm for $10 each with his own money with the expectation of selling the trees a year later at a higher price. Susan is in the same investment and uses $1000 of her own money but unlike Donald borrows $2000 to buy 300 trees at $10 each. A year later, in December, the trees have increased in value by 50% and they are sold in Christmas.

Donald's $1000 realises a 50% return, whereas Sue earns three times Donald's returns with the same investment. Borrowing or financial leverage magnifies success. That said, leverage works in both directions. What if there was an over-supply of live Christmas trees in December and prices fell by 50%? The question then becomes one of solvency. Susan cannot repay the loan because she will make a loss of 150% on her $1000 investment. She will lose the $1000 equity and she will need $500 more just to pay off the principal. This example shows that with the benefits of financial leverage also comes significant downside risk. Donald, in contrast, manages to hold on to half of his investment.

A firm is solvent if its revenues exceed its expenditures and thus, solvency is the ability of a company to pay interest and the principal as they come due and pay off the debt. A solvent enterprise is thus more likely to survive over long period of time than one that is struggling to keep up with repayments on its funded or interest bearing debts. We discuss the main ratios:

- Leverage: Total Funded Debt/Capital; and Total Funded Debt/EBITDA
- Debt-service coverage: EBITDA/Interest + Principal
- Interest coverage: EBIT or EBITDA/Interest

Clearly, the first requirement of analysing leverage is to get an accurate measure of the *total* amount of funded debt.

On the liability side of the balance sheet are listed various obligations. Debt terminology has two meanings. In the broad sense, debt means all liabilities. In the narrow sense, as applied here, debts are written financing agreements, which are legally enforceable contracts. The borrower has the obligation to pay interest and principal at certain fixed periods. The debt instruments may take the form of traditional bank loans (short- and long-term) and bonds. With a bank loan, the obligor repays the principal and a certain amount of interest with each instalment; with a bond, the borrower or issuer pays the holder fixed interest at regular periods and repays the principal amount on maturity of the bond. The Balance Sheet reports four line items that conform to the narrow definition:

1. Bank indebtedness
2. Short-term debt
3. Long-term debt due within one year
4. Long-term debt

**Leverage**

The leverage ratio is defined as:

$$\frac{\text{Total balance sheet debt} + \text{Total OBS debt}}{\text{Capital}}$$

The debt to capital ratio shows the percentage of debt in the company's total financing comprising total debt, equity (including minority interest), and postponed debt. Both the numerator and denominator are measured at book value. A higher debt to capital ratio indicates that more creditor financing (bank loans and bonds) is used than investor financing (common shares) to fund the firm's operations and growth.

Total OBS debt drops out because we assume for now that it is zero. Applying the formula to 2015, the calculated ratio is:

$$\frac{\text{Total debt}}{\text{Capital}_{2015}} = \frac{143 + 550 + 998 + 10{,}013}{11{,}704 + 13{,}164} = 0.47 \times$$

**Analysis**

The total debt/capital ratio varies between zero if the firm has no interest or imputed interest bearing debt, and more than 100% or even negative for a bankrupt company that owes the bank and other creditors. Moderately leveraged companies tend to have debt/capital ratio of around 50%. The ratio for Loblaw falls below 50%, which puts the company in a slightly better position and suggests it is not highly leveraged. A lower debt/capital ratio usually implies a more financially stable business, especially in a period of falling sales. Companies with a higher debt/capital ratio are considered more risky to creditors and investors than companies with a lower ratio. Creditors view a higher debt/capital ratio as risky, for it shows that the investors have not funded the operations as much as creditors have.

The leverage ratio is measured in two ways depending on whether the company has or does not have OBS (off-balance sheet) liabilities:

$$\frac{\text{Total debt}}{\text{EBITDA}} \quad \text{or} \quad \frac{\text{Total debt}}{\text{EBITDAR}}$$

If the company has no OBS debt, the calculation of the ratio is simple because all the inputs come straight from the income statement and the balance sheet. But if the borrower has OBS liabilities, such as operating leases, pension liabilities, and so forth, the credit analyst needs to estimate the debt equivalent of the OBS liabilities, and the second measure is used. The total debt includes debt reported on and off the balance sheet, so that the estimate of cash flow (EBITDAR) must now add back the rental payments for the operating leases. For the time being, for illustration purposes, we avoid this complication and use the first measure. But later in this chapter, we present various methods of approximating the debt equivalent of OBS liabilities. Applying the first of the two formulae, the calculated ratio for 2015 is:

$$\frac{\text{Total debt}}{\text{EBITDA}_{2015}} = \frac{143 + 550 + 998 + 10{,}013}{957 + 674 + 1592} = 3.63\times$$

**Analysis**
The higher is the debt-to-EBITDA ratio, the higher the debt payments as a percentage of cash earnings (approximated by EBITDA). All other things being equal, high and rising debt-to-income ratios indicate the company may not be able to service its debt. A high debt-to-income ratio constrains additional borrowing, because either creditors are unwilling to lend, or the interest rate is too high.

**Debt-Service Coverage (DSC)**
This ratio measures the extent to which cash flow (approximated by EBITDA) is available to cover debt service payment. The ratio is defined as:

$$\text{Total debt service ratio}\,(\text{TDSR}) = \frac{\text{EBITDA}}{\text{Interest expense} + \text{principal repayment}}$$

The interest expense is reported in the income statement and the principal on the long-term debt is reported as the current portion of long-term debt, which is the amount of principal coming due within one year of the date of the balance sheet. Using the information of the Income Statement and the Balance Sheet, the ratio is calculated as:

$$\text{TDSR}_{2015} = \frac{957 + 974 + 1592}{974 + 998} = \frac{3223}{1672} = 1.9\times$$

Interest coverage is the ratio of EBITDA or EBIT to interest expense and is calculated as:

$$\text{Interest coverage} = \frac{\text{EBITDA}}{\text{Interest}} = \frac{3223}{674} = 4.8 \times$$

$$\text{Interest coverage}_{2015} = \frac{\text{EBIT}}{\text{Interest}} = \frac{957 + 674}{674} = \frac{1631}{674} = 2.4 \times$$

Because the accrual accounting for income does not always give a good measure, the cash provided by the operations, EBITDA is preferred over EBIT as a proxy for cash flow.

## Analysis

Note that these ratios are stated as multiples or ratios rather than percentages. The higher are the ratios, the higher the capacity to carry more debt, and hence, the lower the risk of default. A total debt-service ratio of 2× means that Loblaws generated enough EBITDA, a proxy for cash, to pay for its interest expense and principal 2 times over. Similarly, an EBIT coverage ratio of 2.4× means the company's operating income pays for its interest expense 2.4 times over. Is 2.4× a good ratio? Regarding optimal interest coverage, there is not standard because it varies across industries and companies in the same industry. That said, a coverage ratio of at least 1 is considered the minimum. A coverage ratio below 1 means a company cannot meet its current interest payment obligations. As you can see as the ratio rises above 1, the buffer to absorb a decrease in EBIT increases. For example, coverage of 1.5× means EBIT can fall 33.3% (0.5/1.5) and the company will still be able to pay the interest. In the case of Loblaws, the EBIT has to fall by more 60% (1.5/2.5) before the company cannot cover the payments.

## Which Coverage Ratio to Use

We examine five coverage ratios:

1. $\dfrac{\text{EBIT}}{\text{Interest}}$

2. $\dfrac{\text{EBIT}}{\text{Interest} + \text{Principal}}$

3. $\dfrac{\text{EBITDA}}{\text{Interest}}$

4. $\dfrac{\text{EBITDA}}{\text{Interest} + \text{Principal}}$

5. $\dfrac{\text{EBITDAR}}{\text{Interest} + \text{Principal}}$

The question is which one is most meaningful, considering the fact that regardless of whether the borrower fails to pay only interest or only principal on time, the borrower has defaulted on the loan. The answer is all four are important and the context is important in deciding which one to use. The key is determining whether the company can always roll over its maturing debt or can borrow to cover the current portion of long-term debt that comes due. Thus, the *net* burden of the debt is just the interest expense. Some companies have little or no term debt but large operating lines of credit for their working capital needs. The credit line revolves and requires only interest payment on the amounts drawn from the facility.

Consider the numerator. As we noted earlier, EBITDA is preferred over EBIT because it is a measure of cash flow. Therefore, in the case where maturing debt is automatically rolled over, or nearly all of the debt is a revolving line of credit, EBITDA/Interest apply. However, if rollover of maturing debt is not automatic—a likely outcome when capital markets are unsettled—the principal payment becomes a significant fixed claim on a borrower's cash flow. In this case, the EBITDA/Interest + Principal applies. Where *operating leases* are significant, then EBITDAR/Interest + Principal applies.

## 2.6   Off-Balance Sheet Debt

> An accurate accounting of total funded debt consisting of balance sheet debt and off-balance sheet debt is necessary in order to assess creditworthiness.

In previous sections, we took the simplistic view that Loblaws had no off-balance sheet debt. But the company reported significant OBS debt, so the credit analyst cannot overlook this in the calculation of the coverage and solvency ratios. In this section, we take up the subject of adjusting OBS debt and its effects on the ratios. As an example, we will show how to capitalise an operating lease. You will see how the capitalisation of an operating lease makes a company's performance look worse because it increases the asset and liability of a company. Therefore, return on assets, leverage/indebtedness ratios, and coverage ratios are negatively affected. Businesses often structure leases in such a way so they can report them as operating leases.

OBS debt arises from a variety of financing transactions, some of which are normal for the industry, for example, operating equipment leases in the airline industry, and operating land leases in commercial real estate. Take a cross-section of company financial statements and you are likely to encounter one or more of the following types of OBS debt.[14]

- Operating leases
- Guarantees
- Pension liabilities
- Sale of receivables
- Take-or-Pay and throughput arrangements
- Finance subsidiaries
- Joint ventures and investment in affiliates

Each of the above shares the common characteristic of debt, in that non-payment by the borrower on time is an event of default and the lender can take legal proceedings to recover the loan, which could trigger bankruptcy in many cases. We focus on operating leases because companies commonly fund their capital expenditures through operating leases than capital leases reported on the balance sheet. Regardless of the structure, both involve fixed repayment—a vital piece of information a credit analyst must have to assess creditworthiness.

Conforming to IFRS 16 (Leases), Loblaw reports the amounts of minimum lease payments (MLP) at balance sheet date under non-cancellable operating leases for each of the next five years, the total after year 5, and the present value of the remaining minimum lease payments as of the current fiscal year-end. Table 2.5 shows the MLPs for the firm's capital and operating leases at the balance sheet date of January 2, 2016. The MLPs are a series of future cash flows. There are two approaches to *estimate* the debt equivalent in the current period.

1. Present value
2. Rent expense multiple

Table 2.5  Capital and operating leases ($ mm)

| Year | Capital lease | Operating lease |
|---|---|---|
| 2016 | 89 | 682 |
| 2017 | 82 | 658 |
| 2018 | 69 | 617 |
| 2019 | 62 | 571 |
| 2020 | 58 | 504 |
| 2021 and thereafter | 700 | 2606 |
| | 1060 | 5638 |
| Less future finance charges | 431 | |
| Present value of minimum lease payments | 629 | |

Source: Loblaw 2015 Annual Report

## 2.6.1 The Present Value Approach

The present value of a future stream of cash payments over discrete periods is the following summation notation:

$$PV_{Perpetuity} = \sum_{n=1}^{N} \frac{CF_n}{(1+r)^n}$$

where

CF = Cash flow
$N$ = Lease term (number of discounting periods)
$n$ = Time $n$, starting $n = 1$ and ending at $n = N$
$r$ = Discount rate.

Net present value (NPV) is:

$$NPV_{Perpetuity} = \sum_{n=1}^{N} \frac{CF_n}{(1+r)^n} - C_0$$

$C_0$ = initial investment

The inputs of this formula are the periodic cash flows, the discount rate, and the number of discounting periods.

### Step 1: Estimate the Minimum Lease Payments (MLPs) and the Lease Term

For the annual payments profile, we use two assumptions:

1. A constant rate of $504/year; or
2. Declining rate

Consider the operating lease payments of Table 2.6. Under the constant rate assumption, one uses the 5th year's MPL for the 6th year and thereafter. This means $504 in year 2020 and subsequent years, which suggests 5.1 years left in the lease term ($2606/$504) and $N$ is 10 years (initial 5 plus remaining 5, rounded to the nearest year). The final payment of $590 is the residual that reconciles the sum to the aggregate MLPs of $5638.

**Table 2.6** Estimating PV of operating lease payments

| Year | Constant rate | Declining rate (7.2%) |
|---|---|---|
| 2016 | 682 | 633 |
| 2017 | 658 | 587 |
| 2018 | 617 | 545 |
| 2019 | 571 | 506 |
| 2020 | 504 | 469 |
| 2021 | 504 | 436 |
| 2022 | 504 | 404 |
| 2023 | 504 | 375 |
| 2024 | 504 | 348 |
| 2025 | 590 | 323 |
| 2026 | – | 300 |
| 2027 | – | 278 |
| 2028 | – | 258 |
| 2029 | – | 175 |
| Total | 5638 | 5638 |
| Present value | 4406 | 4235 |

Source: Estimation based on company data (see Table 2.5)

Under a reducing rate assumption, we assumed a 7.2% decline rate, which is the average of the rates of decline over the period 2016–2020. The final MLP of $175 has the same meaning of the residual in the case of a constant rate. The estimated MLPs under both assumptions are shown in Table 2.6.

**Step 2: Estimate the Discount Rate**
The interest rate ($r$) is estimated by solving for the implicit rate that makes the Net Present Value of the *capital lease* payments zero. It is the internal rate of return that equates the MPLs to the initial cost, which is represented by the present value disclosed in the notes to the financial statement. This value is $629 (see Table 2.7). Dividing the remaining payment of $700 by the 2020 payment of $58, we get 12 years, implying a lease term of 17 years (5 + 12). Assuming a constant rate of payment and applying the procedures in Step 1, we derive the annual MPLs. The implicit rate of interest is 7%, which is the IRR (internal rate of return) that makes the net present value zero. Note: We could have assumed a declining rate of payment, as we show in Table 2.7, but the differences are not significant.

The WACC (weighted average cost of capital) comprising equity and debt is a broad measure of what the company is expected to pay to holders of all its security. It is a better proxy for the discount rate than the implicit rate.[15] The WACC, although simple to calculate, is not easy to obtain because the annual reports do not contain the basic information. The implicit rate is easy to calculate (see Table 2.8). The average of the five years is 5%.

**Table 2.7** Finding IRR from capital lease

| Year | MLP |
| --- | --- |
| PV | 629 |
| 2016 | 89 |
| 2017 | 82 |
| 2018 | 69 |
| 2019 | 62 |
| 2020 | 58 |
| 2021–2032 | 58 |
| 2033 | 4 |
| Total MPLs | 1060 |
| Implicit rate | 7% |

**Table 2.8** Implicit interest rate on L-T debt

|  | 2011 | 2012 | 2013 | 2014 | 2015 |
| --- | --- | --- | --- | --- | --- |
| Interest | 282 | 285 | 287 | 644 | 584 |
| L-T debt | 5580 | 5669 | 7277 | 11,462 | 11,011 |
| Implicit interest rate | 0.051 | 0.050 | 0.039 | 0.056 | 0.053 |

### Step 3: Calculate the Present Value of the MPLs

Because we do not have an estimate of the WACC, for an estimate of the discount rate we use 6%, found by averaging the implicit rate (5%) and the IRR (7%). Using 6% as the discount rate, the capitalised value of the operating leases under constant rate and declining rate assumptions are $4406 and $4235, respectively as of January 2, 2016 (end of 2015 fiscal year). See Table 2.6.

## 2.6.2 Rent Expense Multiple Approach

In contrast to the PV approach, an alternative is a rule of thumb based on rent multiples. Moody's applies a sector multiple to the annual rental payment. The longer is the economic life of the asset, the higher the multiple. For example, airlines, shipping and public utilities have the highest multiple. Moody's adopts a conservative present value-adjusting approach:

> Under the updated methodology, Moody's will continue adjusting debt by calculating a present value for each company. The rating agency will use this amount or the amount derived from the use of a sector multiple applied to annual rents. However, present value will be the basis for the capitalized debt amount for many more companies than before because the sector multiples will be lower than they were previously in almost all cases. Ranging from 3× to 6×, rather than 5× to 8×, the new multiples will serve as a minimum floor to the present value calculation because Moody's expects that companies with very short lease tenors will renew most leases.[16]

In its 2015 annual report, Loblaw reports $686 in the current year's (2015) rent expense. Assuming Moody's 5× multiple for retail, the debt equivalent of the operating leases is $3.430, lower than the present value of $4406 (see Table 2.6). Which of the two should the credit analyst use? Since both are approximations that are likely to underestimate the true value, we go for the higher PV estimate.

## 2.6.3  Financial Statement Effects

The adjustment involves the following:

- The estimated debt equivalent of the operating leases is added to debt on the balance sheet and recognised as an increase in assets in property, plant, and equipment.
- The rental expense is allocated to interest and principal repayment, which goes as depreciation expense.
- The interest amount is derived by multiplying the present value of the operating leases by the implicit interest rate of 6%. Since rental expense is an operating expense, a lower figure resulting from capitalising the lease has the effect of increasing operating income.

Table 2.9 reports the effects of the adjustments. A capitalised lease increases the total value of the assets on a balance sheet; however, total debt increases by the same amount, in this illustration by $4.5 billion and the debt/equity ratio increases from 0.9× to 1.2×, a significant increase, though the ratio stays below 2×. Note that we are still using book value terminology for equity and not some market or fair value of equity. Operating income increases by the allocation of the 2015 rent expense of $614 million: $267 million goes to interest (not an operating expense), and $347 million goes to depreciation expense (an operating expense). Thus, EBIT increases by the interest expense; EBITDA by the interest and lease depreciation expense. CFO (cash flow from operations) increases by the implicit depreciation, and fixed asset purchase in CFI (cash flow from investing) reduces by the same amount. Although operating income increases, net income is unchanged because the allocations do not entail any net increase or decrease. In short, the capitalisation of an operating lease makes the company's performance look worse, so businesses often structure leases in such a way so they can report them as operating leases.

**Table 2.9** The effects of operating lease adjustments, 2015 ($ mm)

| | As reported | After adjustment | Impact of adjustment |
|---|---|---|---|
| *Balance sheet* | | | |
| Debt equivalent of operating leases | – | 4456 | Increase |
| Total debt | 11,704 | 16,160 | Increase |
| Average assets | 33,849 | 38,255 | Increase |
| *Financial statement ($ mm)* | | | |
| Revenue | 45,394 | 45,394 | No effect |
| Net income | 623 | 623 | No effect |
| Operating income | 1601 | 1868 | Increase |
| Rent expense | 614 | – | – |
| Interest expense[a] | 674 | 941 | Increase |
| Depreciation & amortisation expense[b] | 1592 | 1939 | Increase |
| Principal payment[c] | 998 | 1345 | Increase |
| EBIT | 1631 | 1898 | Increase |
| EBITDA | 3223 | 3837 | Increase |
| *Cash flow statement* | | | |
| CFO (cash flow from operations) | 3079 | 3426 | Increase |
| CFI (cash flow from investing) | –1238 | –1585 | Decrease |
| *Ratios: Debt, solvency, & profitability* | | | |
| Debt/Equity (x) | 0.89 | 1.23 | Increase |
| EBIT/Interest expense (x) | 2.42 | 2.02 | Decrease |
| EBITDA/Interest expense (x) | 4.78 | 4.08 | Decrease |
| Cash flow from operations/Total debt | 26.31% | 21.20% | Decrease |
| Return on average assets (ROAA) | 1.84% | 1.63% | Decrease |
| Net income/Revenue | 1.37% | 1.37% | No effect |
| Operating income/Revenue | 3.53% | 4.12% | Increase |

[a]Interest portion = Rate × PV of Leases (0.06 × $4456) = $267
[b]Depreciation = Rent expense – interest = $614 – $267 = $347. This is the "principal" portion that goes as depreciation
[c]Includes the current portion of the capitalised lease = PV of Lease/Lease term = $4456/10 = $446

# 2.7    Uses and Limitations of Ratio Analysis

Financial statements analysis is reviewing and analysing a firm's income statement, balance sheet, statement of cash flows, and a statement of changes in equity, in order to gain insights into the company's performance and financial health. Although ratio analysis is the principal tool for a comprehensive analysis, it is not without limitations. For example, *financial manipulations*[17] are hard to detect. Below are some of the important ones to keep in mind.

**Window Dressing and Financial Statement Manipulation**

*Window dressing* are tricks to make operating results and the statement of assets and equity more favourable than they would otherwise show at reporting time. Whereas all fraudulent financial reporting are illegal, not all window dressing are, though they all are misleading (unethical). In some cases, window dressing can be illegal. Some well-known examples are *Enron Corporation*, *WorldCom*, and *Nortel*. There is political debate on what is technically accurate and materially misleading. For example, *Lehman* (no longer in business) moved $50 billion off its balance sheet on the last day of each quarter, an accounting manoeuvre known as Repo 105. The Securities Exchange Commission did not see it fit to take any action, implicitly admitting that "window dressing" is not fraud.

1. **Backward looking versus forward looking:** Critics of ratio analysis argue that it is a futile exercise to predict the future from historical data or past performance. Defenders of ratio analysis argue that one has to begin somewhere and even current and past data are a better starting point than no data. In addition, it is the credit analyst's job to assess the reliability of the historical data. And if they are not, then the analyst performs the ratio analysis on *pro forma* financials, which in any case starts with an understanding of the company's past and present performance. In Chap. 5, we provide an example of the use of a financial forecast.

2. **Industry benchmarks are not always the "norm":** A common practice in ratio analysis is to compare a firm's ratios with industry benchmarks to determine the strength of the performance. But this analysis implicitly assumes that the industry is healthy. If the industry is doing poorly, however, the benchmarks are useless information on how well a company compares. There are dozens of industries that are in decline or in transition.

3. **Financial manipulation is more frequent than one may believe:** Some of the relatively minor red flags include changes in accounting standards and methods that can distort period-to-period performance measures. Accountants use timing tricks to window dress or portray a firm in a more favourable light. For example, high accounts receivable (ARs) and inventory make financial position look good, but dig deeper and you may find the collectability of the ARs is doubtful as much of the inventory might be valueless due to impairment. This means that the net worth of the company is overstated and after the required write-off, the company may well be insolvent (negative net worth). In severe cases, what may appear as minor yellow and red flags may be signalling a "smoking gun" as in the case of Enron and WorldCom.

4. **Operational changes can distort trends:** Firms "reinvent" themselves and the way they operate changes over time. Thus, even the same ratio at two different points in time could have different interpretations of financial strength or weakness.

# Notes

1. See Bernstein, Leopold and Wild, John (1998), *Financial Statement Analysis, Theory, Application, and Interpretation*, 6th edition, Irwin McGraw-Hill. Also, White, Gerald, Sondhi, Ashwinpaul, and Fried, Dov (1997), *The Analysis and Use of Financial Statements*, 2nd edition, John Wiley and Sons; Kimmel, Weygandt, Kieso, and Trenholm (2009), *"Financial Accounting, Tools for Business and Decision Making"*, 4th Canadian ed., John Wiley and Sons.
2. Fridson, Martin, and Alvarez, Fernando (2011), *Financial Statement Analysis, A Practitioner's Guide*, 4th ed. John Wiley & Sons Inc. In Chap. 1, the authors discuss "the importance of being skeptical". This theme carries through the rest of this book, an indispensable resource for credit analysts and for first-time users of financial statements. This book looks at some of the biggest financial scandals in recent times, such as Enron, WorldCom, and Nortel Networks.
3. Chartered professional accountants provide three types of financial statements. (1) Audited Engagement: It provides the highest assurance that the financial statements are free of material misstatement and are fairly presented based upon the application of generally accepted accounting principles (GAAP). The assurance is supported by testing procedures performed in the compilation of the figures. (2) Review Engagement: It provides only limited or reasonable assurance on a company's financial statements. (3) Compilation Engagement: They provide no assurance on a company's financial statements. The accountants merely compile them in a financial statement format that complies with generally accepted accounting principles without any testing performed.
4. International Financial Reporting Standards (IFRS), the reporting rules for making company accounts understandable and comparable across international boundaries, are issued by the International Accounting Standards Board (IASB) of the International Accounting Standards Committee (IASC). The IASC has no authority to require international compliance, but many countries including Australia, Brazil, Canada, and the European Union have adopted the accounting standards. The financial statements of publicly traded companies in these jurisdictions are prepared in accordance with IAS. The Financial Accounting Standards Board (FASB) of the United States establishes and communicates standards of financial accounting and reporting, known as generally accepted accounting principles (GAAP). The United States has not adopted IFRS, but the FASB also requires the reporting of comprehensive income.
5. Arthur Andersen LLP was the public accounting firm that audited Enron Corp. The firm cofounded as Andersen, DeLany & Co. in 1913 by Arthur E. Andersen, no longer exists. On June 15, 2002, Arthur Andersen was found guilty of obstructing justice (shredding evidence) in the Enron scandal, and lost its licence to engage in public accounting.

6. Such data are available from various business services companies. Sources include Risk Management Association (RMA). Banks use RMA Annual Statement Studies as a standard source to evaluate businesses applying for financing. Another source is online web access to Dun & Bradstreet's Key Business Ratios to benchmarking data. A third source is Wolters Kluwer's Almanac of Business and Industrial Financial Ratios for 199 industries in all of North America (Canada, the United States, and Mexico).

7. The widely used variable reduction techniques are Principal Components Analysis and Factor Analysis. The procedures partition a smaller number of metrics from the larger multivariate data set. The result is a subset whose ratios have zero correlation with each other but are strongly correlated with the excluded ratios. The zero or low correlation ensures maximum information or explanatory power is achieved. The strong correlation ensures that the ratios of the subset capture information in the excluded ratios. Bernstein & Wild, op. cit. Lists 48 financial ratios in the front cover; and there are as many as 100 as stated in White, Sondhi, and Fried, op. cit. Page 192.

8. Sathye, M. V. James, and B. Raymond (2013), *Credit Analysis and Lending Management*, 3rd Edition, Tilde University Press. Refer to Chapter 2, page 81. The authors list ten ratios that loan officers consider important.

9. Herbert A. Simon coined the word satisficing by combining "satisfy" and "suffice" to explain the behaviour of decision-makers working with limited information. In such a situation, he argued that an optimal solution is indeterminate. He referred his satisficing theory of the firm as *bounded rationality* in contrast with *unbounded rationality* that underpins the classical theory, which assumes that the firm knows with *certainty* its demand and cost function and can therefore maximise profit. Herbert Simon received the Nobel Memorial Prize in Economics "for his pioneering research into the decision-making process within economic organizations" in 1978.

10. See online data prepared by Aswath Damodaran, NYU Stern School of Business, Operating and Net Margins by Industry Sector. Data of last update: January 5, 2017. http://people.stern.nyu.edu/adamodar/New_Home_Page/datacurrent.html. See also Grocery Stores Industry Profitability on CSI Market. Web site: http://csimarket.com

11. See Ganguin, B., J. Bilardello (2005), op. cit., page 99 where the authors examine the pros and cons of using EBITDA; and Martin Fridson & Fernando Alvarez (2011) op. cit., Chapter 8.

12. Refer to Aswath Damodaran, op. cit. The average for 163 global firms in the industry was 1.92% as of January 2017. Data from CSI Market show that average the Net Income margin for US firms was 2.35% in 2016 and 2.13% in 2015.

13. Koopmans, Tjalling C., ed. (1951), *Activity Analysis of Production and Allocation.* New York: Wiley. Koopmans' notion of technical efficiency is that

an input–output vector is technically efficient if, and only if, increasing any output or decreasing any input is possible only by decreasing some other output or increasing some other input.

14. White, Sondhi, and Fried, op. cit. on methods to adjust leverage ratios to include various off-balance sheet liabilities. In particular, this chapter shows how to capitalise operating leases. Also, Moody's, "Guideline Rent Expense Multiples for Use with Moody's Global Standard Adjustment to Capitalize Operating Leases", Revised March 2006. Refer to Chapter 11.

15. The general formula for WACC is: $\mathrm{WACC} = \dfrac{\sum_{j=1}^{N} r_j V_j}{\sum_{j=1}^{N} V_j}$ where $N$ is the number of sources of capital, $r$ is the required rate of return for security $j$, and $V$ is the market value of all outstanding securities $j$. Applying the formula to two securities, equity and debt, $\mathrm{WACC} = \dfrac{E}{E+D} r_e + \dfrac{D}{E+D}(1-t)r_d$ where $E$ is the market value of equity, $D$ is the market value of debt, and $t$ is the marginal tax rate.

16. Moody's Investors Services (2015), *Announcement: Moody's updates its global methodology for financial statement adjustments*. The methodology is provided in the publication June 2015 article, *Financial Statement Adjustments in the Analysis of Non-Financial Corporations*. Before the recent revision, the sector multiples ranged from 5× to 8×.

17. There are numerous readings on financial manipulation. The reader may wish to look up these sources: (1) Martin Fridson and Fernando Alvarez, ibid., Chapter 9, The Reliability of Disclosure and Audits; (2) Roman Weil and Michael Mahler, *Handbook of Cost Management,* 2nd Edition, John Wiley & Sons, 2005, Chapter 31, Section 41.4, Specific Methods to Manipulate Financial reports; (3) Al Rosen and Mark Rosen, *Financial Shenanigans: How to Detect Accounting Gimmicks & Fraud in Financial Reports*, Third Edition Hardcover, May 5, 2010.

# 3

# The Criteria-Based Approach to Credit Risk Assessment and Credit Risk Rating

**Chapter Objectives**

1. Introduce the key elements of a risk rating system
2. Introduce the criteria-based approach to credit risk assessment and credit risk rating
3. Explain the borrower risk rating (BRR) scorecard and its components
4. Understand the purpose of overrides
5. Discuss a method to deal with the effect of information asymmetry on risk rating

## 3.1 Introduction

In this chapter, we continue the discussion of how lenders assess creditworthiness and grade borrowers according to some predetermined rating scale. Commercial banks and rating agencies use letters and numbers, or alphanumeric grades, such as "AA" and "Baa2", and plus/minus modifiers such as "BBB–" and "BBB+". Risk ratings are critical in many of the day-to-day processes or decisions in a bank's operations. The following seven applications of BRRs (borrower risk ratings) cover the gamut of the lending business:

---

**Electronic Supplementary Material:** The online version of this chapter (https://doi.org/10.1007/978-3-030-32197-0_3) contains supplementary material, which is available to authorized users.

1. Approving or declining a loan application
2. Pricing or setting the interest rate on a loan
3. Estimating the profitability of a customer or a relationship
4. Setting exposure limits of a customer or a relationship
5. Transferring credit risk through financial guarantees
6. Determining RAROC (risk-adjusted rate of return on capital)
7. Estimating loan losses and provisioning for risk capital

It is clear from the applications that the development of an effective risk-rating system has as much to do with the profitability of a bank as with regulatory compliance such as capital provisioning and assigning counterparty risk.

There are various methodologies to assess and classify credit quality. One may view them as a spectrum of methodologies ranging from the lowest level of formalisation (high level of subjectivity) to the highest level of formalisation (low level of subjectivity). All these methods have their rightful place because there is no preferred method or methods to assess credit risk (recall from Chap. 1: credit risk assessment is both art and science). In fact, the level of formalisation in credit risk assessment varies. Arranged in ascending order of formalisation are the following three methodologies that are in common use:

1. Pure judgement (e.g., qualitative analysis based on expert knowledge)
2. Midway or hybrid approach (e.g., criteria-based approach) combining features of pure judgement and pure model
3. Pure model (e.g., linear and non-linear probability models)

The major deficiency of pure judgement is the fact that the analysis and the conclusions result almost exclusively from the risk assessor's expertise, derived from practical experience and observations. For this reason, the method is prone not only to inconsistency in risk ratings across industry segments of a portfolio, but also to rating inconsistency within a particular industry. Further, a pure judgement model lacks a link between the analysis and the probability of default.

At the other end of the spectrum are purely statistical and mathematical models, which we will present in Chaps. 8 and 9. Some of the essential tools include linear regression, discriminant analysis, and logit analyses. The big advantage of statistical models is that the selection and weighting assigned to the predictors is *objective*, in the restricted sense that the data rather than judgement determine the selection of predictors and their relative importance. We qualify objectivity because there is still some judgement that comes into play, for example, in deciding the final model. Since data are the deciding factor, the quality of the data is crucial in statistical models. In building such models, the selection of predictors and their weighting are geared towards estimating the best model that accurately classifies solvent and insolvent borrowers, or predicts the likelihood of defaults. Further, the output of a statistical model can be calibrated to default probabilities.

Lending institutions use a variety of methods to assess creditworthiness. A hybrid model that combines features of qualitative models and mathematical models is one of them. As the name implies, it is a midway approach and its strength derives from the shortcomings of a pure judgement model and a pure model. The criteria-based method[1] is heuristic (by definition) but has a number of advantages, which make it an essential methodology in the credit assessment structure of a lending institution.

1. It facilitates consistency in risk rating.
2. It accommodates expert knowledge in a formalised structure capable of processing qualitative information to produce BRRs. Therefore, it complements statistical models incapable of processing qualitative information directly or indirectly.
3. It can process a large number of quantitative and correlated variables, though, in practice, a limited number is used because of the redundancy due to the correlation.
4. The hybrid approach does not involve parameter estimation, so the high correlation between predictors is not a problem.

Figure 3.1 depicts the steps in credit risk analysis based on the criteria approach. As you can see for a hybrid model, the ultimate decision on a final credit rating rests with the risk assessor. The override functionality allows the credit analyst to override the criteria-based output. Conversely, in a purely statistical model, the override is only for exceptions. The last step in the chart is validation. As we stated earlier, a model must be validated at regular intervals as data become available to verify that it is performing as expected. Based on the validation results, users can then decide whether the model is no longer reliable in its predictions and, therefore, needs to be re-estimated or modified to include new predictors. In the rest of the chapter, we go through the steps reported in Fig. 3.1.

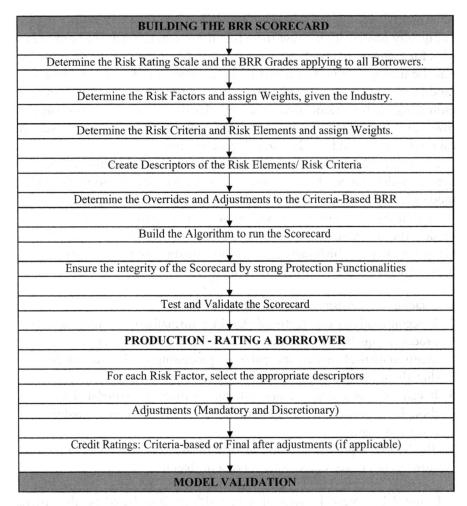

**Fig. 3.1** Methodology of building and deploying hybrid model

## 3.2 The Framework of CRA (Credit Risk Assessment)

Credit risk rating is part of the larger framework called a credit rating system[2] so we need to touch on this subject in order to fill in essential background. We may start by asking what minimal characteristics such a system must have to be effective. The list would include these key elements:

- Two-dimensionality: The obligor credit rating is independent of the facility or transaction ratings.
- A defined time horizon: The risk rating must be forward looking. This means rating through-the-cycle (TTC) rather than at a point-in-time (PIT).
- Rating consistency: The credit ratings of borrowers across segments, or within a segment across geographies, should be consistent.
- Rating replicability: Regardless of who is doing the rating, a scorecard should yield the same counterparty risk rating based on the same data.
- Rating granularity: An appropriate degree of granularity in the risk ratings is essential to differentiate the riskiness of obligors.
- Model validation: In *SR 11-7: Guidance on Model Risk Management*, the US Federal Reserve defines model validation as "the set of processes and activities intended to verify that models are performing as expected, in line with their design objectives and business uses (9)". Therefore, the people who do the testing cannot be the model developers but an independent team, which could be within the organisation or an external third party. Inconsistencies between a bank's actual loan loss experience and the BRR profiles indicate inaccurate calibration of the default probabilities.

Under the Basel II Accord, the design of the rating system of financial institutions must be based on two dimensions. One dealing exclusively with borrower characteristics indicating the propensity of the borrower to default; the other dealing exclusively with the transaction-specific characteristics, such as collateral, terms of repayment, and the nature of the facility or loan product. A two-dimensional rating system ensures that the default risk associated with the borrower is separate from the default risk associated with the credit exposure.

An effective risk rating system differentiates creditworthiness over a defined *time horizon*. With a relative rating system, one can order the ratings according to the implied likelihood of default. An important consideration is how far out into the future the ratings are to apply. The answer depends partly, but significantly, on the degree of cyclicality of the industry and the position of the industry on the cycle (see Table 4.2 of Chap. 4 where we discuss industry risk). If the industry is highly cyclical and the analysis employs current or point-in-time data, the counterparty risk rating will be pro-cyclical. This means that at annual reviews through the cycle, the BRR will fluctuate. The BRR will improve during the recovery and expansion phase as financial performance data improve, but weaken in the down phase as performance data worsen. Clearly, such frequent upgrades and downgrades are unsatisfactory.

Many financial institutions define the time horizon of their credit ratings anywhere between one and three years, some as many as five or seven in the case of a project loan. The rating agencies claim to rate through-the-cycle when assigning corporate credit ratings. To dampen or remove the cyclical effect on the risk rating, the credit analyst has two options. One is to construct *pro forma* financial statements. For most counterparty risk ratings, the time horizon is typically three years. For specialised lending such as project finance, a longer period is appropriate as noted earlier. The other procedure, called *through-the-cycle* method, is one whereby the scorecard adjusts for the counter-cyclical bias based on the position of the industry in the business cycle. We revisit these considerations in more detail in the theory in Chap. 4 and in the case study in Chap. 5.

We will be introducing an important functionality called overrides in the criteria-based model (see Fig. 3.1). The override is a necessary feature because no model can capture the full complexity or the extreme peculiarities of a system. For this reason, the credit analyst must have the option, albeit subject to strict criteria, to override the results with an alternative rating. One of the criteria is that an override must be based on credit risk factors and not, for example, client relationship matters. As you will see later, country risk and sovereign risk factors are some of the important overrides to the overall criteria-based rating, but there could be other overrides to the component ratings. That said, overrides must be kept to a minimum. First, the excessive use of overrides indicates the scorecard is inadequate on many levels. For example, it might call for more risk criteria, a review of the weights, better predictors, and more granularities. Banks review their rating models/scorecards periodically. We will comment on these deficiencies later under the section *Testing and Validation*. Second, the excessive or arbitrary use of overrides undermines rating consistency.

We use the term rating "model" broadly to include expert judgement, questionnaire, hybrid, neural network, and mathematical models. We also use "scoring" interchangeably with "rating". Therefore, "scorecard" is a part of the rating methodology and is not to be confused with *application scorecard* and *behavioural scorecard*, tools that lenders use to assess loan applications such as credit cards and consumer loans. What follows are the broad outlines of the criteria-based approach. We leave the details for Chap. 4.

## 3.2.1 The BRR Scorecard

### Criteria-Based Rating

The criteria-based approach that we present in this chapter is based on fundamental credit analysis of four types of risks to assess creditworthiness. The four building blocks or criteria of the BRR scorecard are the following risk criteria:

1. Industry risk
2. Business risk
3. Management risk
4. Financial risk

Risk criteria subdivide into *risk factors*, which are broken down further into *risk elements*. Each risk element is defined by *descriptors* that differentiate the 16 grades reported in Table 3.1. The Scorecard is the tool to process the quantitative and qualitative variables consistently into a composite rating, which we call the BRR. In Appendix 3.1, we review the types of variables you will be encountering throughout this book. Analytically, a scorecard divides into two parts. The first part processes information that is typical of the majority of borrowers, and covers what we may call normal situations or conditions. The second part constitutes mandatory overrides to the criteria-based rating, because of exceptional or abnormal situations. The adjustments are mandatory. *Remember: the whole purpose of the credit assessment is to obtain an accurate BRR.*

As an example of how these subdivisions relate to each other, take one of the risk criteria, financial risk. It can be defined by many risk factors like profitability, liquidity, asset quality, cash flow, and so forth. We can define each of these further by various risk elements. For example, we can describe profitability quantitatively by net income/sales, return on equity (ROE), return on assets (ROA), and so on. Then the question becomes: how do we assign a particular value of a ROA to a default risk? The answer is in the descriptors (see Appendix 3.2 for example). Since we have 16 risk grades, we need to come up with 16 sets of descriptors. In

**Table 3.1** Mapping between rating category, letter grade, and composite numeric score

| Rating category | Score | Letter grade | Composite numeric score |
|---|---|---|---|
| Very low | 16 | AA+ | $15.1 < x \leq 16.0$ |
| | 15 | AA | $14.1 < x \leq 15.0$ |
| | 14 | AA− | $13.1 < x \leq 14.0$ |
| Low | 13 | A+ | $12.1 < x \leq 13.0$ |
| | 12 | A | $11.1 < x \leq 12.0$ |
| | 11 | A− | $10.1 < x \leq 11.0$ |
| Moderate | 10 | BBB+ | $9.1 < x \leq 10.0$ |
| | 9 | BBB | $8.1 < x \leq 9.0$ |
| | 8 | BBB− | $7.1 < x \leq 8.0$ |
| High | 7 | BB+ | $6.1 < x \leq 7.0$ |
| | 6 | BB | $5.1 < x \leq 6.0$ |
| | 5 | BB− | $4.1 < x \leq 5.0$ |
| Very high | 4 | B+ | $3.1 < x \leq 4.0$ |
| | 3 | B | $2.1 < x \leq 3.0$ |
| | 2 | B− | $1.1 < x \leq 2.0$ |
| Default | 1 | D | $\leq 1.0$ |

practice, this is not possible due to the lack of historical data to validate the definitions. The more granular the rating system, the more difficult it is to find descriptors for every point of the scale.

A descriptor must meet two important conditions:

1. The predictors must have a *monotonic* relationship—always increasing or always decreasing but never both—with the BRR grades. In a non-monotonic function, the relationship between the predictors and the likelihood of default is ambiguous. For example, consider a total debt/earnings before interest, taxes, depreciation, and amortisation (EBITDA). If *on average* for a large sample of borrowers the BRR sometimes increases, sometimes decreases, or shows no change to increasing values of the ratio, the ratio cannot serve as a reliable predictor of default.
2. Both numerical and qualitative descriptors must be discrete, or specific to a particular risk grade. Put simply, segments cannot overlap.

**Adjustments: Mandatory Overrides Including Information Asymmetry**
The override functionality is an integral part of expert-based judgement models and it says that *notwithstanding*[3] the criteria-based BRR, material information that the first part of the scorecard cannot capture may call for a different rating. One of the common overrides that we mentioned before is sovereign risk, which serves to *limit* the criteria-based BRR, and the rationale being that the borrower cannot be stronger than the country in which it operates, or the government, which has the power of taxation and controls foreign reserves and hard currency leaving the country. Consider, for example, a situation where the criteria-based BRR of an Indonesian bank is *higher* than the risk ratings of the country and the government. Applying the override, the risk assessor selects the lower of the SSR/CRR (sovereign risk rating/country risk rating).

Another important adjustment is related to information asymmetry. It poses a major problem for BRR assessment. In this book, we propose a novel way to address the problem in regard to manipulated financial records. *Fraudulent financial reporting* is the wilful misrepresentation or omission of financial information, designed to improve the appearance of financial statement with the intent to deceive investors and lenders to obtain financing. Fraudulent financial reporting can result in civil litigation and costly settlements; hence, litigation risk can materially affect a risk rating. In recent months there have been a surge in opioid-related lawsuit filings in the United States against pharmaceutical companies—a situation that is reminiscent of the civil litigation against tobacco companies by 46 US states and the massive settlement in 2015 amounting to US$206 billion over 25 years.[4]

The question is: which section of the scorecard is the best place to incorporate information asymmetry risk? In the light of the numerous financial scandals within recent times, *information asymmetry* can be considered a risk factor in management risk. Alternatively, it can be housed in financial risk because the repercussions from not disclosing full information are financial. Whilst there is merit in both arguments, we prefer to have information asymmetry as an override to the composite BRR, operating like the SRR/CRR override in the scorecard, except that it is not mandatory. We label it "information asymmetry override" to address situations where the credit analyst can show that quantitative or qualitative information that is material to the BRR assessment is not transparent or is withheld. To support such a case, the analyst must be able to quantify the effects of the data omission on the profit and loss (P&L) statement and the balance sheet and run a second scorecard to show how the BRRs compare.

---

**Can a Lender Knowingly Worsen the Information Asymmetry Problem?**

There is always the risk that senior management might interfere with the independent assessment of credit analysts and internal auditors. Risk analysts might fail to do proper due diligence because they do not understand the risk or are afraid of pushback from senior management.

---

The risk assessor arrives at her/his decision to apply the override after a thorough decision process:

- First, gather the information. Are there yellow and red flags of fraudulent financial reporting (which includes withheld information)?
- If the answer is yes, document the findings: Activities that demand answers, but may not be bad in and of themselves are yellow flag. For example, a big part of Enron's business was high-exposure derivative positions marked to model, and the value of the contracts depended critically on assumptions. But Enron's management was not forthcoming with sufficient information.
- Make every effort to obtain the information, first from the borrower (if possible). If management does not attempt to provide information but reacts angrily to the suggestion that it should, make a note of this as a warning sign. Otherwise, look to external rating agencies and the media (print and digital) for information.
- Assess if the resulting misstatement or lack of sufficient information is *material* to the financial statements. To be material, the information gap must be large enough to affect the risk rating. We will not go into the area of *accounting irregularities* because they are numerous; however, see Chap. 2 for a list of books that deal with this very subject and the detection methods.

- Run the BRR scorecard using alternative information that would include plausible estimates; then compare the BRRs to check for material difference in credit rating.
- Two or more notches are material. Internal policy would specify the BRR for such cases.

The override will have the desired effect of increasing the lending rate to compensate for the higher perceived risk, or of declining the transaction because its RAROC fails the hurdle rate test. Note that in the presence of mandatory overrides, such as SRR and CRR, these still apply, but the final BRR would be the lowest.

## 3.2.2  Designing the Risk-Rating Scale and Rating Granularity

One can build the criteria-based model in a scorecard format in Excel, or Visual Basic, complete with an algorithm to perform the calculation automatically. The risk rating scale is the standard to which the credit worthiness of counterparties is assessed on a relative basis. A common standard ensures consistency in the BRRs within a particular industry or sector, and across diverse industries or sectors. Let us call this the *master scale* of the default probability attached to each rating or score. For illustration, we work with a manageable set of BRR grades with modifiers of "+" and "−" signs. Table 3.1 shows six categories, the mid-points of the scale, representing the least to the greatest credit risk: AA, A, BBB, BB, B, and D. With the modifier, the BRR rating scale consists of 16 grades. The default category (D) includes borrowers who are unlikely to repay the debt in full and at the original terms, delinquent for at least 90 days, and are under bankruptcy protection.

These alpha grades with the modifiers are mapped to numeric scores ranging from 0 (default) to 16 (least risk). As we showed in Table 1.1 back in Chap. 1, a commercial bank would have as many as 20 risk grades or notches, which allows it to cross-tabulate its BRR rating system with those of the rating agencies and ensure that internal ratings are consistent with external ratings. This practice by many banks is, however, not without serious consequences and requires heroic assumptions. First, it assumes that the default probabilities of the external ratings are monotonic but they are not always so in any given year. Second, it assumes that historical default frequencies of rated companies from external agencies are representative of the total portfolio of banks; however, a large swath of a bank's portfolio consists of unrated companies.

> **Commercial Banks Rely on the Ratings of External Credit Rating Agencies at Their Peril**
>
> Joseph Stiglitz (2009),[5] who won the Nobel Prize for his work on Information Asymmetry in economics, wrote: "Rating agencies played a central role (in the 2008 financial crisis). They believed in financial alchemy, and converted F-rated subprime mortgages into A-rated securities that were safe enough to be held by pension funds (2)."

There are no standards for the level of granularity, though it is obvious that if there are too few grades the rating system as a tool will be blunt (see Sect. 3.2); it will fail to differentiate risk effectively to support credit decisions. Conversely, too fine a rating scale is not an unqualified virtue because it increases the likelihood of the problem of non-monotonicity. The BRR represents the probability of default (PD). Commercial banks[6] estimate the probabilities from records of their internal default frequencies. For example, in our illustration, "AA+" the highest grade in our system would be some non-zero number like 0.04%, whereas "D" could be 100%.

Table 3.1 gives the risk-rating scale, which is a linear continuum of scores equally spaced from 1 to 16, with each numeric score attached to a letter grade. This mapping is what enables the scorecard to quantify the various risks through the placement of the descriptors in the BRR scorecard. The descriptors are the core of a scorecard. They define the predictors and differentiate the grades. In theory, each predictor can have as many *sets* of predictors or bins as the number of grades. For example, the historical values of earnings before interest and taxes (EBIT)/interest can be grouped into 16 disjunctive intervals. For qualitative predictors such as management quality, theoretically there can be 16 discrete sets of attributes, though unlikely in practice. If the data are available, every predictor will have discrete sets of descriptors for each grade, but, in practice, the validating data might not exist. Another reason is that qualitative predictors of creditworthiness are difficult to define at a granular level. All these result in a scorecard with undefined grades. This does not mean, however, that the scorecard will fail to assign the composite BRR, which we will show in later chapters.

Obviously, it is much easier to categorise numerical variables. Look again at the EBIT/interest expense ratio. It is a continuous variable so that it lends itself to distinct groupings. Regardless of whether the (independent) variables are qualitative or quantitative, however, for them to have any predictive and explanatory power, the relationship between them and the default frequency (the dependent variable) must be monotonic and based on accepted theory and evidence. Again, consider the EBIT/interest expense ratio that predicts solvency. The likelihood of default is expected to vary inversely with the ratio over the specified domain of values for this ratio.

For debt/equity, we would expect the opposite pattern over a defined range of values. Monotonicity rules out reversals in the relationship within the defined range of values (or the domain), which in the BRR scorecard includes both numerical and qualitative information. Let us turn to the risk rating scale shown in Table 3.1 to see how they fit in the model. Consider the letter grade column. In Sect. 3.2.1, we stated the risk analyst does not directly assign grades but indirectly does so through the placements of the descriptors. You could see from the mapping in Table 3.1 that selecting a descriptor for "A+" means also selecting a score of 13. After making all the selections on the scorecard, it will calculate the composite score and assign the risk grade. Let us say the composite score is 5.686. The scorecard rounds the number to 5.7 (assuming 1 decimal place is the chosen rule) and looks up the risk-rating scale. It locates the $[5.1 < x \leq 6.0]$ range which attaches to "BB". Recall that default probabilities are attached to each grade. In designing the scorecard, it is sufficient to display only the grade instead of both.

## 3.2.3 The Time Horizon: Trade-Off Between Timeliness and Stability of the BRRs

A risk rating must have a forecast horizon for it to have any meaningful policy application. In commercial banking, the typical time horizon is three years but it can extend to five years. At any given point-in-time (PIT), the assigned rating—called a PIT rating—indicates the credit default risk based on an assessment of the borrower's current and future condition and, thus, combines both cyclical and permanent factors. PIT ratings tend to ride the cycle, improving over the expansion but worsening over the downturn. A through-the-cycle (TTC) rating stays stable, but the stability comes at a cost: a TTC rating is slow to adjust, even as a borrower is heading to default.

### When to Adjust for Industry Cyclicality?

Let us start with the premise that the BRR is a forward looking or through-the-cycle assessment of the risk of default. For many banks, the time horizon is usually three years. At the same time, the industry is going through its regular ups and downs, so the question becomes: how does the credit analyst measure a

(continued)

> **(continued)**
>
> company's financial strength in such volatile conditions. If point-in-time *financial performance* is what mainly determines the BRR, the use of current financial information would be biased, favouring high BRRs in the very short term, but in twelve months' time the BRR would be downgraded if the industry is in recession. The opposite would occur a year later coinciding with the next annual BRR review, if the industry is in an upswing. But such rating actions are inconsistent with the fundamental premise. This warrants dampening the point-in-cycle effect on the rating to minimise downgrades and upgrades based *primarily* on current financial performance tied to the industry cycle.

The TTC downgrade comes too late, however, and a large steep adjustment, referred to as the cliff effect, results. Therefore, for timeliness, a PIT rating performs better because it is more sensitive to the business cycle. The disadvantage is that the frequent downgrades and upgrades are administratively cumbersome and the effects on the return on capital over a complete cycle—or over several, for that matter—may be neutral or marginally profitable at best. If the rating system is very sensitive then as business conditions improve over an economic upswing, upgrades in risk ratings would become common, more borrowers would qualify, and the loan book would expand, but as business conditions reverse, the opposite would occur: credit risk would deteriorate, downgrades would increase, and loan portfolios would contract.

Lenders want rating sensitivity for accuracy but they also want rating stability because frequent adjustments to BRRs across segments involve administrative and opportunity costs. Another argument in favour of a longer forecast horizon than just the current period is that the PDs, calibrated against the BRRs, reflect the lender's loan loss experience across an entire economic cycle. Thus, a PIT-based rating system would predict differently than TTC-based rating system. Graphically, the PIT and TTC curves, PD plotted on the vertical axis and time on the horizontal axis, would mimic the shape of a sine wave over an average business cycle, say 20 quarters, but the PIT would have the highest amplitude. The TTC would be more flattened out.

Credit practitioners accept the fact that there is no fully satisfactory solution to the trade-off. In Chap. 4, we deal with this theme in detail but, for now, we provide a flavour of what the adjustments entail. For highly cyclical industries, best practices involve a counter-cyclical adjustment for the behaviour of the BRR six to nine months away, or longer. A model based on the criteria-based approach largely achieves both desirable features of rating timeliness and stability.[7]

One method is to assess financial risk on *current period* financial statement and *pro forma* financial statements, derived from stress testing the borrower under various worst-case assumptions. The use of *pro forma* financial statements depends only on one criterion: whether recent and current history are reliable. In this case, the cyclicality makes the historical data (including current) unreliable. There could be other reasons. The other method is to incorporate the business cycle in business risk by adding a counter-cyclical adjustment. To achieve this effect on the BRR, we would add another risk factor that we label *Cyclical Adjustment Factor*. In the usual fashion, it will be assigned a weight and it will be defined by descriptors of the position of the industry in the cycle. We discuss the economics underlying the descriptors and illustrate the application of the procedure in Chap. 4.

Let us look at a complete business cycle illustrated in Fig. 3.2. One measures the length of a business cycle from peak to peak, or trough to trough. We see that the PIT adjustment dampens the cyclical effect on the overall risk rating. At or nearing time $t_1$ at the top of the cycle firms are reporting their strongest performance, but at the same time the risk of a downturn is also at its highest. As designed, the financial risk assessment of the scorecard captures the financial performance through current measurements of the financial metrics, but this positive effect on the risk grade is offset concurrently by the PIT adjustment in business risk assessment through the higher risk of default after time $t_1$. As you can see, the reverse applies as the industry approaches time $t_2$ at the bottom of the cycle. To anticipate what we intend to do, we want to be able to locate the position of the industry on the business cycle, but to do this we first need to understand the dynamics of each phase of the cycle, which will allow us to identify certain differentiating characteristics or patterns. This determination is key to creating the descriptors for the risk ratings. In Chap. 4, we will examine the use of current and leading economic indicators

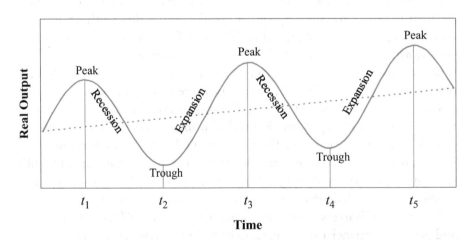

**Fig. 3.2** The four phases of the business cycle

to help locate the position and define the characteristics in the PIT adjustment in business risk. In Chap. 5, we extend the analysis of cyclical adjustment by applying the PIT adjustment in business risk and alternatively in financial risk in a case study, and compare the results.

## 3.2.4 The Structure of a BRR Scorecard: Risk Criteria, Risk Factors, Risk Elements, and Weights

We now turn to the theoretical part of designing a scorecard and the discussion comes down essentially to determining the risk criteria, the risk factors, the risk elements, and their relative importance. The main criterion for selecting variables is their explanatory and predictive power. For guidance, the risk analyst relies on all relevant finance and economic theories, statistical studies, observation, and expert knowledge. For example, the debt/total capital ratio is considered a reasonably good predictor of insolvency and default based on theory and observation. The template in Table 3.2 illustrates at an abstract level the arrangement of the *risk criteria*, the *risk factors*, and the *risk elements* described by *descriptors* denoted "d" in a typical BRR scorecard. The descriptors are usually both qualitative and quantitative. Later we will look at descriptors in detail but for now, you may think of a descriptor as a unique characteristic or set of characteristics of the predictor variable. For instance, the descriptors for the ratio of current assets to current liabilities, a predictor of liquidity strength in financial risk, would be the set of all positive values on the real number line, or, usually, discrete ranges on the number line. Obviously, qualitative descriptors that by definition are unquantifiable are more challenging to define. Table 3.5 in Appendix 3.2 gives the definitions of the financial ratios.

The weights are a critical component of a scorecard. For the most part, they are subjectively assigned, but regression and correlation analyses are used to provide information on the relative importance of the predictors. The *distribution* of the weights is, however, more important that the *absolute* values. For example, if we judge financial risk to be the most important factor in creditworthiness, we accord it biggest weight so that the composite BRR becomes sensitive to relatively small changes in the financial BRR. This makes the composite rating sensitive to changes in financial information. A reduction in the weight for financial risk from, say, 50% to 45% is just a 10% decrease and not enough to make financial risk less of a swing factor in the overall BRR. But a change from 50% to 20% is a 60% decrease, so the composite rating will be less sensitive to changes in financial risk.

**Table 3.2** BRR scorecard template

| BRR COMPONENTS | WEIGHT | AA+ 16 | AA 15 | AA- 14 | A+ 13 | A 12 | A- 11 | BBB+ 10 | BBB 9 | BBB- 8 | BB+ 7 | BB 6 | BB- 5 | B+ 4 | B 3 | B- 2 | D 1 | SCORE | BRR |
|---|---|---|---|---|---|---|---|---|---|---|---|---|---|---|---|---|---|---|---|
| | | | | | | | DESCRIPTORS | | | | | | | | | | | | |
| **1. INDUSTRY RISK** | 10.0% | | | | | | | | | | | | | | | | | | |
| **1-A Stability of Revenue and Profitability** | 50.0% | | | | | | | | | | | | | | | | | | |
| *profitability during an economic downturn* | 100.0% | d | d | d | d | d | d | d | d | d | d | d | d | d | d | d | d | 4 | B+ |
| **1-B Outlook for Growth and Profitability** | 50.0% | | | | | | | | | | | | | | | | | | |
| *1 Entry and Exit Barriers* | 100.0% | d | d | d | d | d | d | d | d | d | d | d | d | d | d | d | d | 11 | A- |
| **INDUSTRY RISK BRR BASED ON THE CRITERIA** | | d | d | d | d | d | d | d | d | d | d | d | d | d | d | d | d | 7.5 | BBB- |
| OVERRIDE | | | | | | | | | | | | | | | | | | | |
| **2. BUSINESS RISK\*** | 30.0% | | | | | | | | | | | | | | | | | | |
| **2-A Competitive Position** | 33.3% | d | d | d | d | d | d | d | | d | d | d | d | d | d | d | d | 12.0 | BBB+ |
| **2-B Market Position** | 33.3% | d | d | d | d | d | d | d | d | d | d | d | d | d | d | d | d | 11.0 | BBB+ |
| **2-C Cyclical Position (Cyclical Adjustment Factor)** | 33.3% | d | d | d | d | d | d | d | d | d | d | d | d | d | d | d | d | 4.0 | B+ |
| **BUSINESS RISK BRR BASED ON THE CRITERIA** | | | | | | | | | | | | | | | | | | 9.0 | BBB- |
| OVERRIDE | | | | | | | | | | | | | | | | | | | |
| **3. MANAGEMENT RISK** | 20.0% | | | | | | | | | | | | | | | | | | |
| **3-A Management Quality** | 33.3% | d | d | d | d | d | d | d | d | d | d | d | d | d | d | d | d | 10.0 | B+ |
| **3-B Business Strategy** | 33.3% | d | d | d | d | d | d | d | d | d | d | d | d | d | d | d | d | 10.0 | B+ |
| **3-C Financial Strategy** | 34.0% | d | d | d | d | d | d | d | d | d | d | d | d | d | d | d | d | 8.0 | B |
| **MANAGEMENT RISK BRR BASED ON THE CRITERIA** | | | | | | | | | d | | | | | | | | | 9.3 | BBB+ |
| OVERRIDE | | | | | | | | | | | | | | | | | | | |
| **4. FINANCIAL RISK** | 40.0% | | | | | | | | | | | | | | | | | | |
| **4-A Financial Performance** | 80.0% | | | | | | | | | | | | | | | | | | |
| **4-A-1 Profitability** | 25% | | | | | | | | | | | | | | | | | | |
| *1. EBITDA Margin* | 50% | d | d | d | d | d | d | d | d | d | d | d | d | d | d | d | d | 11.5 | |
| *2. ROA* | 50% | d | d | d | d | d | d | d | d | d | d | d | d | d | d | d | d | 12.0 | A |
| **4-A-2 Liquidity** | 25% | | | | | | | | | | | | | | | | | | |
| *1. Current Ratio* | 50% | d | d | d | d | d | d | d | d | d | d | d | d | d | d | d | d | 12.0 | A |
| *2. FCF/Adjusted Debt* | 50% | d | d | d | d | d | d | d | d | d | d | d | d | d | d | d | d | 14.0 | AA- |
| **4-A-3 Leverage** | 25% | | | | | | | | | | | | | | | | | | |
| *1. Funded Debt/EBITDA* | 50% | d | d | d | d | d | d | d | d | d | d | d | d | d | d | d | d | 10.0 | BBB+ |
| *2. Total Liabilities/TNW* | 50% | d | d | d | d | d | d | d | d | d | d | d | d | d | d | d | d | 13.0 | A+ |
| **4-A-4 Debt Coverage** | 25% | | | | | | | | | | | | | | | | | | 10.5 | |
| *1. Debt Service Coverage* | 50% | d | d | d | d | d | d | d | d | d | d | d | d | d | d | d | d | 10.0 | BBB+ |
| *2. Fixed Charge Coverage Ratio* | 50% | d | d | d | d | d | d | d | d | d | d | d | d | d | d | d | d | 11.0 | A- |
| **4-B Financial Flexibility** | 20% | | | | | | | | | | | | | | | | | | 11.0 | |
| *1. Ability to raise Debt and Equity Financing* | 100% | d | d | d | d | d | d | d | d | d | d | d | d | d | d | d | d | 11.0 | A- |
| **FINANCIAL RISK BRR BASED ON THE CRITERIA** | 100% | | | | | | | | | | | | | | | | | 11.5 | A |
| OVERRIDE | | | | | | | | | | | | | | | | | | | |

\* If the Cyclical Adjustment Factor is warranted then all Risk Factors are assigned the pre-determined weights; otherwise Cyclical Adjustment Factor is unweighted.

| | | | BRR |
|---|---|---|---|
| A. CRITERIA-BASED COMPOSITE BRR | | 9.9 | BBB+ |
| B. INFORMATION ASYMMETRY OVERRIDE (YES/NO) | | | NO |
| C. CRR RATING OVERRIDE (YES/NO) | | | A+ |
| D. SOVEREIGN RISK RATING OVERRIDE (YES/NO) | | | A+ |
| FINAL COMPOSITE BRR = LOWEST OF A, B, C, AND D | | | BBB+ |

## 3.2.5 The Functional Relationship Between Predictors and Default Frequency

In Sect. 3.2.2, we introduced the descriptors, their functional properties, and the central role they play in the workings of a BRR scorecard. In this section, we focus on how the credit analyst might go about creating the descriptors for the financial ratios. First, we need to get an idea for selecting financial variables and transforming them into a form suitable for the scorecard. Let us use the EBIT/interest ratio as example. From theory and observation, the higher is the ratio, the stronger the coverage and thus the lower the likelihood of default, *ceteris paribus*. The expected functional relationship is negative. The next step is to obtain a large sample of coverage ratios for firms across industries. We may want to use average values rather than a single year's value to iron out dips and spikes. The next step is cleaning the data of outliers and clerical inaccuracies, such as wrong codes in the downloading process. "Garbage in, garbage out" is a sound principle to guide the cleaning process without affecting the integrity of the data.

Once we have a clean sample of data, the next step is to reduce the large number of data points to a small, manageable subset but with minimal loss in information value. We apply a grouping procedure. As we mentioned before, the number of BRR grades sets the *maximum* number of intervals/bins for a given predictor in a scorecard. In our example, we have 16 grades from D to AA+. Table 3.1 gives the list of the 16 risk grades mapped to the 16 intervals or bins.

We use a grouping procedure of data analytics called coarse classifying. In general, the procedure is used to gain an understanding of the strength of the relation between the explanatory/independent variable and the dependent/explanatory variable. This is not surprising because we want the independent variable to be highly predictive of default. Let us consider in particular the relationship between EBIT/interest (the explanatory variable/predictor) and the frequency of default (the dependent variable). Our first step called *fine classing* is creating $X$ number of equal and distinct groups called *bins* for the values of EBIT/interest, and associating each bin with the frequency of default (the dependent variable). We would find that high ratios are associated with low probabilities. The next step called *coarse classing* is to create fewer categories by merging similar adjacent groups to remove redundancy.

Once we have a reduced number of groups to work with, the next step is to test the relationship between them and the default frequencies to ensure monotonicity. A positive relationship between default rates and EBIT/interest would be rejected, but let us assume we have the expected negative slope. If the relationship is not monotonic, even for one group of values, keep merging adjacent groups one by one until the monotonicity takes shape. The choice of which bins to merge first depends on the maximum likelihood principle: choose the one that maximises the (log) likelihood of the dependent variable (in this case, the default frequency) given the values of the explanatory variable (EBIT/interest). For robustness, Thomas (2009)[8] recommends that each bin should have a "reasonable percentage of the population in it – certainly at least 5 percent of the population".

Although coarse classing is a rigorous statistical procedure, it leaves open much room for judgement. In practice, the intervals do not always have to be equally spaced, though the monotonicity condition must always be present. Table 3.3 shows two gradations. Interval A is a linear gradation, with constant and equal widths. As we hinted, it is not unusual to have non-linear relationships. For example, the lender might want to make it increasingly hard for a borrower to reach the top ratings, or it might just be the case—based on industry data or the lender's own internal data—that no borrower in the industry has the attributes for, say, "AA+" signifying almost zero probability of default. In this case, the relationship will be geometric, such as Interval B, with the interval widths getting increasingly wider as the BRR increases by one notch towards the highest rating. As Thomas (2009) notes, "the binning process is an art as much as a science (72)."

**Table 3.3** EBITDAR margin descriptors

| Grade | Score | Interval (A) | Interval (B) |
|-------|-------|--------------|--------------|
| D     | 1     | ≤0           | ≤0           |
| B–    | 2     | 0.1–2.5      | 0.1–1.1      |
| B     | 3     | 2.6–4.4      | 1.2–2.2      |
| B+    | 4     | 4.5–6.4      | 2.3–3.3      |
| BB–   | 5     | 6.5–8.4      | 3.4–5.5      |
| BB    | 6     | 8.5–10.4     | 5.6–7.7      |
| BB+   | 7     | 10.5–12.4    | 7.8–9.9      |
| BBB–  | 8     | 13.5–14.4    | 10.0–13.0    |
| BBB   | 9     | 15.5–16.4    | 13.1–16.1    |
| BBB+  | 10    | 17.5–18.4    | 16.2–19.2    |
| A–    | 11    | 19.5–20.4    | 19.3–22.9    |
| A     | 12    | 21.5–22.4    | 23.0–28.0    |
| A+    | 13    | 23.5–24.4    | 28.1–34.2    |
| AA–   | 14    | 25.5–26.4    | 34.3–41.2    |
| AA    | 15    | 26.5–28.4    | 41.3–49.3    |
| AA+   | 16    | ≥28.5        | ≥49.4        |

## 3.3 Building the Risk Criteria in a Computer Spreadsheet

### 3.3.1 Assignment of Scores to the Risk Factors/Sub-Factors and Calculation of the Risk Scores

The calculation of the composite risk score is based on a weighted sum (also called weighted average) model. It is not a statistical model that is based on estimated parameters derived from the set of data, but it is a model nonetheless. It essentially combines expert judgement with statistical analysis. As the name implies, the tool involves summing a set of well-defined risk criteria, each assigned a subjective weight that reflects its relative importance in predicting default. The most serious criticism of the criteria-based approach is that it requires personal judgement on the weighting and the selection of the default predictors, both quantitative and qualitative. But as we argued in Chap. 1, expert judgement based on experience and observation is not guesswork and has a valid place in probability analysis. That said, the criteria-based approach has certain advantages over a purely econometric or mathematical model and it is widely used by banks and rating agencies for the following reasons:

1. It is unconstrained by the estimation problems ordinarily encountered in applying econometric tools.
2. It can process more information by evaluating numerous predictors. In principle, there is no limit to the number of material predictors.
3. It can quantify qualitative factors that are material to risk rating. Qualitative factors are as important as quantitative factors in the assessment of creditworthiness.
4. It is best suited to process exceptional situations, or outliers, through the proper use of the override functionality.

We begin with a quantitative presentation of the scorecard. Let us first write down the aggregate equation for 4 risk criteria and 100 borrowers in a loan portfolio. The equation for the composite score is expressed in the following summation notation:

$$\left(\text{Composite risk score}\right)_b = \sum_{k=1}^{4} \left(\text{Risk criteria score}\right)_{kb} \times \left(w_k\right) \quad (3.1)$$

where:

$b$ = 1, 2, 3, ...., 100 borrowers
$k$ = 1, ..., 4 risk criteria

From the equation, $w_k$ is the relative weight of risk criteria $k$, and (risk criteria score)$_{kb}$ is the value of a risk criterion when it is evaluated in terms of risk criteria $k$ for borrower $b$. The calculation is repeated for all 100 borrowers.

If you examine Eq. (3.2) carefully, you would notice it describes the aggregation of the four risk criteria, so a key question we will be considering is what determines the risk criteria scores. A risk criterion score is a weighted average of the risk factors, each of which is a weighted average of the risk elements:

$$\text{Risk factor score}_{jk} = \sum_{i=1}^{N}\left(\text{Risk element}_{ijk} . w_{ijk}\right) \tag{3.2}$$

where there are $j$ risk factors, and $i$ risk element. The equation says for the $j^{\text{th}}$ risk factor of the $k^{\text{th}}$ risk criterion, the risk factor score is a weighted average of the $i^{\text{th}}$ risk element score multiplied by its weight ($w_{ikj}$).

A risk criterion score is a weighted average of the risk factor scores. For any given borrower, the risk criterion score for the $k^{\text{th}}$ risk criterion is calculated according to the equation:

$$\text{Risk criterion score}_{k} = \sum_{j=1}^{M}\left(\text{Risk factor score}_{jk} . w_{jk}\right) \tag{3.3}$$

Equation (3.3) says the $k^{\text{th}}$ risk criterion score is the sum of the $j^{\text{th}}$ risk factor multiplied by its weight ($w_{jk}$). Thus, by adding up the risk criteria scores we arrive back at Eq. (3.1) that we introduced earlier.

$$\left(\text{Composite risk score}\right)_{b} = \sum_{k=1}^{4}\left(\text{Criteria risk score}_{k} . w_{k}\right)$$

Table 3.4 gives the building blocks and anticipates the use of the Cyclical Adjustment Factor in business risk that we will take up in Chap. 4. It is worth

Table 3.4 Summary of scorecard calculations

| Risk criteria | Weight (%) | Score | Risk grade |
|---|---|---|---|
| Industry risk | 10 | 7.5 | BBB− |
| Business risk | 30 | 9.0 | BBB+ |
| Management risk | 20 | 9.3 | BBB+ |
| Financial risk | 40 | 11.5 | A |
| **Composite** | **100** | **9.9** | **BBB+** |

noting that a scorecard is designed specifically for the given industry and the type of financing, such as commercial real estate and project financing. Although the aggregation rules are the same for all scorecards, the details in regard to the risk criteria and the weights will vary to capture the essential features of the industry or the asset being funded. Notice in the template that risk elements are not required for every risk factor, which often stands in place of the risk elements. In management risk, for example, we have three risk factors that are not broken down further, in contrast with financial performance. The shaded areas of the template represent the placements for the descriptors. For illustration purposes, we show no blank cells for descriptors but keep in mind that in practice many cells are usually blank due to the unavailability of validating data.

Imagine you are the credit analyst and you are rating a highly cyclical firm. All the leading economic indicators point to a recession within the next six to nine months and the next BRR refresh is 12 months away. You correctly anticipate that the current financial performance will not continue but will worsen. A point-in-the-cycle or a point-in-time BRR assessment will overstate the BRR, so you apply the Cyclical Adjustment Factor to capture the expected deterioration in the business environment during the down phase of the cycle. Accordingly, you assign a rating of "B+". Based on the strong point-in-cycle performance, you rate financial risk "A". We summarise Table 3.2 results in Table 3.4.

The effect of the BRR Cyclical Adjustment Factor is to temper the financial risk rating. For, without the cyclical adjustment, the composite score is 10.7 (BRR "A–") instead of 9.9 ("BBB+"), as shown in Table 3.4. The reason we get the "A" rating is that ***Business Risk***, without the Cyclical Adjustment Factor, is 11.5 ("A"), while holding the ratings of the other Risk Criteria unchanged. Recall that the descriptors of a scorecard are mapped to the predetermined rating system shown in Table 3.1. Therefore, once the analyst completes the placement of the descriptors (and other mandatory fields as applicable), the scorecard—programmed with the formulas and a look-up table for the score-BRR mappings—computes the composite score and attaches the corresponding BRR. Given the placements, the scorecard rates industry risk, business risk, management risk, and financial risk "BBB–", "BBB", "BBB+", and "A" respectively. The weighted average of the four risk grades is a composite score of 9.9, which maps to a BRR of "BBB+". The SRR/CRR override does not apply because the ratings are higher. *As a learning experience of how the scorecard adds up, the reader is encouraged to "do the maths" and derive the same results.*

### 3.3.2 Assignment of Counterparty Risk Rating after Overrides

A clear advantage of an expert knowledge-based model over statistical models is that the risk assessor can override BRRs derived from the criteria, although subject to internal credit policy. There are two types of overrides and they follow from the structure of the scorecard. First, in the criteria-based part of the scorecard, the risk assessor can notch up or notch down the BRR of one or more sections of the scorecard shown in Table 3.2. That said, the scorecard must be so designed to prevent deletion of the criteria-based BRRs. Moreover, the risk assessor must complete a mandatory field for the rationale, or the scorecard will not calculate. These are critical design features to protect the integrity of a BRR scorecard.

In the second type of BRR override, the risk assessor can and is often required to notch down the criteria-based BRR. Let us look at the mandatory overrides for rating a foreign borrower, which involves cross-border risk due to any number of factors. In this case, the CRR and the SRR serve as ceilings on the criteria-based BRR. The CRR and SRR are usually the same, but there are many recent cases of divergence.[9] In Table 3.2, the final BRR after SRR/CRR override remains "BBB+" because the override ratings exceed the criteria-based rating. Another mandatory override that also serves as a ceiling is the credit risk of the national or provincial/state government. A university, school board, hospital, or municipality cannot be rated higher than its province/state on which it relies for funding. Nor can the rating of a state/province exceed the rating of the national government where there is a similar dependency. Mandatory override includes borrowers who are classified as impaired. They are automatically assigned the default rating. In this second type are non-mandatory overrides, for example, information asymmetry override that directly addresses fraudulent financial reporting. The override is discretionary though subject to internal credit policy guidelines. The risk assessor is required to substantiate the claim and document the evidence.

## 3.4  Model Validation

All models, pure judgement, hybrids, and mathematical, must be tested and validated. Validation is an essential procedure of the credit assessment framework. In validation, we compare a model's predictions against the actual outcomes over a period of varying lengths and at regular intervals. The procedure involves testing a sample of scorecards of borrowers from a cross-section of industries for the following characteristics:

1. Discriminatory power: The ability of a rating model to differentiate between good and bad credits represented by the BRRs. This test for the criteria-based models equates to testing for systematic bias in a regression model. And it involves testing *ex post* data for samples of borrowers representing the industries of a portfolio. For this sample of "good" and "bad" cases, appropriately defined, a lender must maintain a databank of the *initial* ratings and of the status of "good" or "bad" 12 months after the assignment of the ratings.
2. Stability: To determine whether a model is stable, one tests the discriminatory power of a rating model over more than one forecasting horizon of varying length (see characteristic 1 above for the procedure). If the model is unstable, the *ex ante* assigned ratings will over-predict or under-predict, or drift over time.

The purpose of the validation is to improve the discriminatory and predictive power of the model, which may involve one or all of the following:

1. Replacing outdated predictors
2. Adding new predictors and therefore creating new descriptors subject to data availability
3. Redefining descriptors to improve their discriminatory power
4. Reviewing the ranges for grouped financial data
5. Adjusting the weights based on recent experience and statistical analysis

The process is iterative and the goal is to reach a sufficient level of comfort with the scorecard's performance. It is quite possible for a model to fail the validation tests. A main cause is a significant shift in the risk profile of the population. In the case of a hybrid model, there are many fixes as we listed above. Models based on regression analysis might have to be redeveloped because the estimated parameters might have changed. The model developer would first perform statistical tests on the model parameters such as its mean and variance to determine that a shift has occurred.

## 3.5 Summary

Chapter 4 covers a great deal of the groundwork, so it seems appropriate to highlight the main technical points. The basic principles and ideas are the same and these will come in handy for designing a BRR scorecard for any industry.

1. **What is the BRR scorecard**

   The Scorecard is the tool to process the quantitative and qualitative information consistently into a composite rating, which we call the BRR. Table 3.2 gives a template.

2. **What are the building blocks of a scorecard?**

   The scorecard consists of the risk criteria, which determine the criteria-based BRR, and overrides:

   i. Industry risk assessment
   ii. Business risk assessment
   iii. Management risk assessment
   iv. Financial risk assessment
   v. Overrides to the criteria-based BRR

   Overrides are integral to the scorecard. This is just a recognition that there are exceptions and abnormal conditions. Overrides can be discretionary or mandatory as with the SRR/CRR ratings. In this book, we propose the information asymmetry override for financial misrepresentation or fraudulent financial reporting that includes withheld information. The override is discretionary. In general, overrides are essential because a consideration of other qualitative and quantitative risk factors will result in a more accurate BRR than the criteria-based BRR.

3. **How are the weights determined?**

   The weights are subjective in that they are derived from expertise and observation. Nonetheless, statistical analysis is also used to determine the weights. For the situations where there are no strong reasons to assign different weights, the risk analyst defaults to equal weighting.

4. **What are descriptors?**

   The *descriptors* are verbal and numerical definitions. They relate a predictor/financial measure to the likelihood of default reflected in the BRR grades. Descriptors must satisfy two mathematical conditions to be predictive. First, the functional relationship between the values/definitions of a predictor and the BRR grades must be monotonic. Second, the subgroups or bins must be distinct.

5. **How does the scorecard adjust the BRR for business cycle effects?**

   The model includes a built-in functionality called *Cyclical Adjustment Factor* in the business risk assessment section of the scorecard. Alternatively, the analyst may use *pro forma* financials provided by the borrower, or construct his or her own, in order to complete the financial risk assessment of the scorecard.

6. **How does the scorecard adjust the BRR for information asymmetry effects?**

   The scorecard includes information asymmetry override. The functionality allows the risk assessor to override the criteria-based BRR if she/he can show and document fraudulent financial reporting by the borrower, or unwillingness to provide material information. The latter is more applicable to an existing borrower or a new customer applying for a loan.

7. **Can a risk assessor use his/her own judgement to override the overall BRR or a component BRR?**

   Yes, but supported by a risk-based rationale; moreover, the rationale must be documented in the scorecard to preserve its integrity. Considerations related to the credit structure and the collateral cannot serve as rationale because they are in direct opposition to the requirements of two-dimensional risk-rating system that separates borrower risk (PD) from transaction/facility risk rating (FRR). Likewise, reasons related to the profitability or unprofitability of the client relationship cannot be valid for a BRR override.

# Appendix 3.1: Function, Variables, and Grouped and Ungrouped Data

Throughout this book, we would often be using "function" and "variable" explicitly and implicitly. Therefore, a brief backgrounder would be useful. Simply put, a function is like a gizmo that takes an input at one end and gives out *only* one output at the other end, not unlike a meat grinder. Take the example of a simple function:

$$g(x) = 2x$$

or explicitly as:

$$y = 2x$$

where $x$ is the input. This particular function "$g$" takes any value of $x$, multiplies it by a constant number "2", and gives you a result "$y$". The "2" is called a parameter. It is clear from the example that the variable "$x$" can take any real number, and likewise "$y$". There are an infinite number of functions, but that does not change the fact that they perform the very same task.

This brings us to the words "variable" and "value". Whilst the two formulations above usually involve real numbers, it is not necessary that they always be that way. So let us define a variable as *anything* that has a *quantity* or *quality* that *varies*. The operative words are deliberately italicised. Figure 3.3 gives the type of variables we will be using in the models presented in this book.

**Numerical variable:** The values of a numerical variable are numbers. They include continuous and discrete variables. Another name for numerical variable is *quantitative variable*. Therefore, by definition, any variable that one can add is quantitative. ROE of 12.7% plus ROE of 14.3% sums to 27.0%.

**Qualitative variable:** It is a variable that is not numerical but consists of ordinal and nominal variables. Therefore, by definition one cannot add qualitative variables, such as BRR of "A" plus BRR of "B" (see ordinal variable).

**Random variable:** It is a quantity that can have a range of values. In statistics, a random variable is a numerical description of the outcome of a statistical experiment. For example, the number of firms that default on their debts in any given year is a discrete random variable. The next EBITDA/interest ratio is an example of a continuous random variable.

**Continuous variable:** It is a variable with infinite number of values, like profit and current assets to current liabilities.

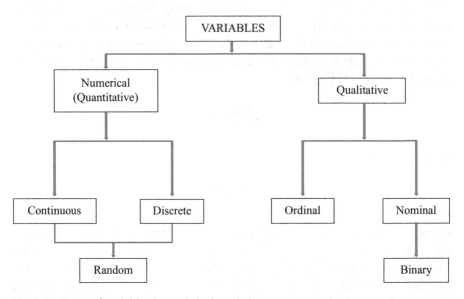

**Fig. 3.3** Types of variables in statistical analysis

**Discrete variable:** It is a variable that can only take on a certain number of values (i.e., integer values), for example, the population of a city.

**Ordinal variable:** It is a variable with a clear ranking, so that every data point can be put in order (1st, 2nd, 3rd, 4th, and so on), or (low, middle, high). Examples include BRR (borrower risk rating), management quality, and financial flexibility.

**Nominal variable:** It is another name for a *categorical variable*. It includes binary variables.

**Binary variable:** It is a variable that can only take on two values. For example, default or no default.

**Dichotomous variable:** It is the same as a binary variable.

**Dummy variables:** In this book, a dummy variable is a categorical variable used in regression analysis for assigning relationships to unconnected categorical variables. For example, if you have the categories "default" and "no default" you might assign a 1 to mean "default" and 0 to mean "no default". More generally, a dummy variable can also represent a variable for which a direct measurement is not available. For example, it is customary to represent "trend" or "technical change" by a dummy variable taking values $1, 2, 3 \ldots N$.

**Independent variable:** It is a variable that does not depend on another variable in the model; therefore, it is not affected by anything the modeller does.

**Explanatory variable:** In the context of a single equation, it is the same as *independent variable* or *predictor variable*.

**Dependent variable:** It is a variable that is affected by the independent variable or variables. It is what one measures from assuming certain value of the independent variable and the estimated parameters.

**Parameter:** In statistics, a parameter is a characteristic of a population such as its mean and variance, which we *estimate* by sampling a population. In maths, a parameter (or *estimated parameter*) is a special type of *variable* that is meant to stay fixed *but* for a certain application.

**Ungrouped data:** These are numerical data given as *individual* data points, for example, 2.3%, 2.4%, and 2.5%.

**Grouped data:** These are numerical data given in closed *intervals*, for example [2.51–4.51], [4.52–6.52], and [6.53–8.53]. They are *discrete* or *disjunctive* (meaning mutually exclusive). In the criteria-based approach, grouped data are commonly used.

# Appendix 3.2: Definition of Financial Variables Used as Predictors

**Table 3.5** Definitions of financial predictor variables

| Definitions |
| --- |
| **EBITDA margin:** (Earnings before interest, taxes, depreciation/amortisation) divided by revenue |
| **EBITDAR margin:** (Earnings before interest taxes, depreciation/amortisation, and rent) divided by revenue |
| **Operating ratio:** Total expenses minus interest expense divided by operating revenue |
| **Net profit margin:** Net profit divided by revenue |
| **ROA:** Return on average assets. EBIT divided by average assets |
| **Current ratio:** Current assets divided by current liabilities |
| **FCF/adjusted funded debt:** Free cash flow divided by the sum of funded debt and capitalised off-balance sheet debt. |
| **Funded debt:** On-balance sheet and off-balance sheet obligations for borrowed money that bears explicit interest or imputed interest, plus guarantees for third-party liabilities, but excludes postponed debt. |
| **TNW:** Tangible net worth is total equity plus postponed debt minus intangibles, deferred charges, and leasehold improvements |
| **Total liabilities/TNW:** All liabilities excluding deferred tax liabilities and postponed debt divided by TNW |
| **Postponed debt:** Debt fully postponed and subordinated to the debt owing to the lender. |
| **EBIT:** Earnings before interest and taxes (same as net operating income) |
| **Debt service coverage:** EBIT divided by interest expense; or EBITDA divided by interest expense and scheduled principal payments |
| **Fixed charge coverage ratio (FCCR):** EBIT plus FCBT (lease expense and other fixed charges before tax) divided by FCBT plus interest expense and scheduled principal payments. |
| A FCCR of less than one means that the company lacks enough money to cover its fixed charges. Note: There is no standard definition of FCCR, and thus the specific components depend on the loan agreement. |

# Notes

1. The criteria approach is the workhorse for credit risk assessment and is discussed extensively in the literature. For example, see Standard and Poor's, *Fundamentals of Corporate Credit Analysis*, op. cit.

2. See Paragraph 394 under Rating System Design of International *Convergence of Capital Measurement and Capital Standards*, op. cit: "The term *rating system* comprises all of the methods, processes, controls, and data collection and IT systems that support the assessment of credit risk, the assignment of internal risk ratings, and the quantification of default and loss estimates."

3. The override is the equivalent of the *notwithstanding clause* that gives power to a government to override certain protections in a country's charter.

4. Tobacco Control Legal Consortium (2015), *The Master Settlement Agreement: An Overview*. In addition to the 2015 settlement ($206 billion) with 46 states, there was the 1998 settlement ($40 billion) with Florida, Minnesota, Mississippi, and Texas.

5. Stiglitz, Joseph (2008), *The Anatomy of a Murder: Who Killed America's Economy?* Critical Review June 2009, Vol. 21, Issues 2 & 3.

6. For an actual example of a commercial bank's rating system, see Royal Bank of Canada Annual Report 2017, page 9, Table 46. There are 22 BRR grades, each with a PD calibrated against it.

7. John Kiff., Kisser M., and Schumacher L. (2013), *Rating Through-the-Cycle: What does the Concept Imply for Rating Stability and Accuracy?*, I.M.F Working Paper. Also Rebekka Topp and Robert Perl (2010), *Through the cycle ratings* versus *point in time ratings and implications of the mapping between both rating types*. Financial Markets, Institutions and Instruments, 19:47–61, 2010. Topp and Perl investigated Standard and Poor's corporate ratings and showed the ratings behave pro-cyclically, even though the credit rating agencies claim to focus only on the permanent risk factors.

8. Thomas, Lyn, C (2009), *Consumer Credit Models*, Oxford University Press. This book is about credit scoring. It provides the theory and the application of credit scoring methods.

9. See S&P Capital IQ, Marcel Heinrichs and Ivelina Stanoeva (2012), *Country risk and sovereign risk – building clearer borders*, The Euromoney Risk Management Handbook, 2nd Edition.

# 4

# The Building Blocks of Credit Analysis and Credit Risk Rating

**Chapter Objectives**

1. Understand why country and sovereign risk are material to credit rating
2. Understand the structure of each of the four building blocks: industry risk, business risk, management risk, and financial risk
3. Discuss industry analysis and understand why industry risk is material to credit rating
4. Learn to construct a criteria-based model
5. Develop a borrower risk rating (BRR) scorecard template (template is available online)
6. Apply the BRR scorecard template to calculate a composite score and assign a composite borrower risk rating

## 4.1   Introduction

Chapter 3 laid the foundations of the criteria-based approach and a risk rating system. In this chapter, we do the construction—block by block. Imagine your task as a credit analyst is to design and build a borrower risk rating (BRR) scorecard. As you will learn in this chapter, each block is designed to capture and process information that you determine is relevant

---

**Electronic Supplementary Material:** The online version of this chapter (https://doi.org/10.1007/978-3-030-32197-0_4) contains supplementary material, which is available to authorized users.

for a given risk criterion of the BRR; combined, the scorecard gives the overall risk rating. A common practice is that the commercial credit risk cannot be better than the country risk rating (CRR) for its country of domicile; it applies to domestic and foreign borrowers, but the practice is particularly relevant to evaluating the BRR of a foreign borrower, or one whose business is based in the country of domicile. Because the likelihood of repayment can be adversely affected by country and sovereign risks, country risk takes precedence. We start with a brief examination of country risk and sovereign risk because they are integral in evaluating the final BRR of a foreign obligor.

## 4.2   Country Risk and Sovereign Risk

To recall from Chap. 3, the BRR scorecard has an override functionality, which allows the risk assessor to notch down the BRR that the scorecard produces. We call this BBR, derived directly from the scorecard, the *criteria-based BRR*. If the country risk rating/sovereign risk rating (CRR/SRR) is lower than the criteria-based rating, the risk assessor must override the latter with the CRR/SRR (the lower of the two). CRRs establish a ceiling for commercial credit risk ratings, which mean a borrower's commercial risk rating cannot be better than the CRR of its country of domicile. As we noted earlier, the override is mandatory. Country risk is an additional layer of credit risk on the standalone counterparty risk. Country risk is the likelihood of economic and political forces in the country adversely affecting the borrower's willingness and ability to repay the debt to the foreign creditor. In regard to the debt, political risk captures the *willingness* of a country to repay, whereas the economic risk captures the *ability* to repay. The ability reflects many factors such as *transfer risk*, caused by foreign exchange shortage and exchange rate devaluation, and *sovereign risk* (SR), which is the risk of a government defaulting on its commercial loan obligations. Sovereign risk is a proxy for country risk and, most times, the political and economic conditions mirror each other. But as we noted in the previous chapter, the two risks are not necessarily identical. Governance is also an important factor in country risk and sovereign risk. The World Bank publishes Worldwide Governance Indicators for six dimensions of governance:

1. Political voice and accountability
2. Political stability and absence of violence

3. Government effectiveness
4. Regulatory quality
5. Rule of law
6. Control of corruption

A commonly used predictor variable in country risk analysis is the rate of growth in real income per capita over many years. One *quick* way to size up economic progress and the level development (but not the distribution of income) in a country is to look at panel data consisting of real gross domestic product (GDP) per capita income, or real GDP divided by the population. Table 4.1 gives the figures for a sample of 18 developed and developing countries. The data reveal some important facts:

1. Economic performance varies widely over time and across countries. Average growth rates in 1989–2017 period ranged between −0.3% and 8.0%.
2. Many developing countries experienced long periods of economic stagnation during the period.
3. Economic stagnation, which is a reliable barometer of social instability, directly affects a country's external debt-servicing capability. A prolonged period of economic weakness, interacting with political instability, is often a precursor of sovereign debt defaults.
4. Economic shocks, such as the 2008–2009 financial crisis, quickly spread globally and small open economies that are heavily dependent on trade are particularly vulnerable. We see negative growth rates for many developing countries during this period.

The CRR (country risk rating) and the SRR (sovereign risk rating) capture these considerations and many more using the same criteria-based method to rate a corporate borrower. There are statistical methods as well and we present these in Chaps. 8 and 9.

Whilst a general understanding of country risk analysis[1] is helpful in rating a foreign borrower, the risk assessor is not usually required to perform country risk analysis to come up with the appropriate CRR/SRR for the override. Banks find it cost-effective to outsource the work to specialised financial services vendors like the Economic Intelligence Unit (EIU) and the rating agencies instead of building their own models, although it was standard operation in the heyday of country risk lending during the 1970s and 1980s. Banks had invested huge sums to develop and maintain country-risk rating models. Country risk management is usually integrated with risk management

Table 4.1 GDP per capita growth (annual)

| Year | Bahamas | Botswana | Chile | Jamaica | Brazil | India | Australia | Greece | China | Singapore | Barbados | Malaysia | South Africa | Canada | Sweden | United States | Saudi Arabia | Germany |
|---|---|---|---|---|---|---|---|---|---|---|---|---|---|---|---|---|---|---|
| 1989 | 4.9 | 9.9 | 8.1 | 6.5 | 1.4 | 3.7 | 2.1 | 3.3 | 2.6 | 7.0 | 3.2 | 5.9 | 0.2 | 0.5 | 2.0 | 2.7 | -4.3 | 3.1 |
| 1990 | -3.3 | 3.8 | 1.6 | 3.5 | -4.8 | 3.4 | 2.0 | -1.1 | 2.4 | 5.8 | -3.6 | 6.0 | -2.5 | -1.3 | 0.0 | 0.8 | 11.2 | 4.4 |
| 1991 | -5.9 | 4.5 | 6.1 | 4.0 | -0.2 | -1.0 | -1.6 | 1.9 | 7.8 | 3.7 | -4.2 | 6.6 | -3.3 | -3.4 | -1.8 | -1.4 | 11.3 | 4.3 |
| 1992 | -5.6 | 0.2 | 9.4 | 1.1 | -2.1 | 3.4 | -0.8 | -0.1 | 12.8 | 3.9 | -7.3 | 6.1 | -4.4 | -0.3 | -1.7 | 2.1 | 0.9 | 1.2 |
| 1993 | -1.6 | -0.7 | 5.0 | 8.4 | 3.0 | 2.7 | 3.0 | -2.2 | 12.6 | 8.8 | 0.9 | 7.2 | -1.1 | 1.5 | -2.6 | 1.4 | -4.0 | -1.6 |
| 1994 | 1.4 | 1.1 | 3.5 | 0.4 | 3.6 | 4.6 | 2.9 | 1.5 | 11.8 | 7.5 | 3.4 | 6.5 | 0.9 | 3.5 | 3.4 | 2.8 | -1.9 | 2.1 |
| 1995 | 2.8 | 4.5 | 7.4 | 1.4 | 2.7 | 5.5 | 2.6 | 1.6 | 9.8 | 3.8 | 1.6 | 7.1 | 1.0 | 1.8 | 3.5 | 1.5 | -2.1 | 1.4 |
| 1996 | 2.9 | 3.5 | 5.3 | -1.1 | 0.6 | 5.5 | 2.5 | 2.4 | 8.8 | 3.2 | 3.6 | 7.2 | 2.3 | 0.5 | 1.4 | 2.6 | 0.5 | 0.5 |
| 1997 | 0.9 | 5.8 | 6.0 | -2.1 | 1.8 | 2.1 | 2.8 | 4.0 | 8.1 | 4.7 | 4.3 | 4.6 | 0.9 | 3.2 | 2.8 | 3.2 | -0.8 | 1.7 |
| 1998 | 3.6 | -1.2 | 3.0 | -3.3 | -1.2 | 4.2 | 3.5 | 3.3 | 6.8 | -5.5 | 3.3 | -9.7 | -1.1 | 3.0 | 4.2 | 3.2 | 0.9 | 2.0 |
| 1999 | 5.9 | 7.7 | -1.7 | 0.1 | -1.0 | 6.9 | 3.8 | 2.7 | 6.7 | 5.3 | 0.0 | 3.6 | 0.8 | 4.3 | 4.4 | 3.5 | -5.7 | 1.9 |
| 2000 | 2.6 | 0.3 | 4.0 | 0.0 | 2.6 | 2.0 | 2.7 | 3.5 | 7.6 | 7.0 | 1.9 | 6.4 | 2.6 | 4.3 | 4.6 | 2.9 | 3.2 | 2.8 |
| 2001 | 0.9 | -1.3 | 2.1 | 0.6 | 0.0 | 3.0 | 0.6 | 3.6 | 7.6 | -3.6 | -2.7 | -1.7 | 1.3 | 0.7 | 1.3 | 0.0 | -3.7 | 1.5 |
| 2002 | 0.7 | 4.6 | 1.9 | 1.3 | 1.7 | 2.1 | 2.7 | 3.5 | 8.4 | 3.3 | 0.5 | 3.2 | 2.3 | 2.1 | 1.7 | 0.8 | -5.5 | -0.2 |
| 2003 | -3.3 | 3.2 | 2.9 | 3.0 | -0.2 | 6.1 | 1.7 | 5.5 | 9.4 | 6.0 | 1.9 | 3.7 | 1.6 | 0.8 | 2.0 | 1.9 | 8.0 | -0.8 |
| 2004 | -1.2 | 1.3 | 6.0 | 0.7 | 4.5 | 6.2 | 2.8 | 4.8 | 9.5 | 8.2 | 1.1 | 4.7 | 3.3 | 2.1 | 3.9 | 2.8 | 4.8 | 1.2 |
| 2005 | 1.3 | 3.1 | 4.6 | 0.3 | 2.0 | 7.6 | 1.8 | 0.3 | 10.7 | 5.0 | 3.7 | 3.3 | 4.0 | 2.2 | 2.4 | 2.4 | 2.6 | 0.8 |
| 2006 | 0.5 | 6.7 | 5.2 | 2.3 | 2.8 | 7.6 | 1.3 | 5.3 | 12.1 | 5.5 | 5.3 | 3.6 | 4.4 | 1.8 | 4.1 | 1.7 | 0.0 | 3.8 |
| 2007 | -0.5 | 6.6 | 3.8 | 0.9 | 4.9 | 8.2 | 3.1 | 3.0 | 13.6 | 4.7 | 1.4 | 4.4 | 4.3 | 1.1 | 2.6 | 0.8 | -0.9 | 3.4 |
| 2008 | -4.1 | 4.5 | 2.5 | -1.3 | 4.0 | 2.4 | 1.6 | -0.6 | 9.1 | -3.5 | -0.3 | 3.0 | 2.1 | -0.1 | -1.3 | -1.2 | 3.4 | 1.3 |
| 2009 | -5.8 | -9.2 | -2.5 | -4.8 | -1.1 | 7.0 | -0.2 | -4.6 | 8.9 | -3.6 | -4.4 | -3.3 | -2.6 | -4.1 | -6.0 | -3.6 | -4.7 | -5.4 |
| 2010 | -0.1 | 6.7 | 4.8 | -1.9 | 6.5 | 8.8 | 0.5 | -5.6 | 10.1 | 13.2 | -0.1 | 5.5 | 1.8 | 1.9 | 5.1 | 1.7 | 2.1 | 4.2 |
| 2011 | -1.0 | 4.2 | 5.1 | 1.3 | 3.0 | 5.2 | 1.0 | -9.0 | 9.0 | 4.2 | 0.3 | 3.4 | 1.9 | 2.1 | 1.9 | 0.8 | 6.8 | 5.6 |
| 2012 | 1.6 | 2.6 | 4.4 | -1.0 | 1.0 | 4.1 | 2.1 | -6.8 | 7.3 | 1.6 | -0.1 | 3.5 | 0.8 | 0.6 | -1.0 | 1.5 | 2.3 | 0.3 |
| 2013 | -1.8 | 9.3 | 3.1 | 0.1 | 2.1 | 5.1 | 0.9 | -2.5 | 7.2 | 3.4 | -0.3 | 2.8 | 1.0 | 1.3 | 0.4 | 1.0 | -0.2 | 0.2 |
| 2014 | -1.4 | 2.2 | 0.9 | 0.3 | -0.4 | 6.1 | 1.0 | 1.4 | 6.8 | 2.5 | -0.3 | 4.2 | 0.4 | 1.7 | 1.6 | 1.8 | 0.8 | 1.5 |
| 2015 | -0.2 | -3.5 | 1.4 | 0.5 | -4.4 | 6.9 | 0.9 | 0.4 | 6.4 | 1.0 | 0.6 | 3.3 | -0.1 | 0.2 | 3.4 | 2.1 | 0.8 | 0.9 |
| 2016 | -2.8 | 2.4 | 0.4 | 1.0 | -4.3 | 5.9 | 1.3 | 0.2 | 6.1 | 1.1 | 1.7 | 2.7 | -0.7 | 0.2 | 1.9 | 0.7 | 1.5 | 1.1 |
| 2017 | 0.4 | 0.5 | 0.7 | 0.2 | 0.2 | 5.4 | 0.3 | 1.5 | 6.3 | 3.5 | 1.4 | 4.4 | 0.1 | 1.8 | 0.8 | 1.5 | -0.6 | 1.8 |
| Average | -0.3 | 2.9 | 3.6 | 0.8 | 1.0 | 4.9 | 1.7 | 0.7 | 8.5 | 3.7 | 0.6 | 3.7 | 0.8 | 1.2 | 1.5 | 1.5 | 0.8 | 1.6 |

Source: World Bank

responsible for risk rating. With the outsourcing arrangement, country risk ratings from external sources are scaled so that they dovetail with a bank's internal rating system.

## 4.3   Industry Risk Assessment

Industry risk is the likelihood of any firm losing sales or market share, or failing owing to disruptions and trends in the industry. Therefore, industry risk analysis sets the stage for the assessment of the company. And for good reason, the first risk criterion of a BRR scorecard is industry risk, and what follows after are the company-specific risks. As a backdrop, it might be useful to review the purposes of industry analysis and some of the analytical approaches that credit practitioners continue to use. In this practical business of credit analysis, the analyst does not have the ideological luxury of picking favourite models because none is perfect, so an eclectic approach is the one that is most likely to assure completeness of assessment. A traditional approach, called the Industry Life Cycle (ILC) model, borrows from the phenomenon of the *life cycle* in the biological sciences. Like the life cycle of an organism, an industry goes through distinct stages from birth to death. Another approach, the Five Forces model, was developed by Michael Porter in the late 1970s and popularised in Porter (1980).[2] Porter's framework may be seen as a critique of models that adapt the physical phenomenon of a life cycle to explain and predict the evolution of an industry, firm, or, at the more basic level, the product. A common criticism of the ILC model is the following observation that Porter (1980)[3] makes:

> The real problem with the product life cycle as a predictor of industry evolution is that it attempts to describe one pattern of evolution that will invariably occur. Moreover, except for the industry growth rate, there is little or no underlying rationale for why the competitive changes associated with the life cycle will happen. Since actual industry evolution takes so many different paths, the life cycle pattern does not always hold, even if it is a common or even the most common pattern of evolution. Nothing in the concept allows us to predict when it will hold and when it will not.

### The Importance of Industry Risk

In banking circles, there is some debate on whether industry risk analysis should be a part of the overall risk rating of a business because, so goes the argument, illiquidity triggers default. It is a false argument because the BRR is meant to capture cash flow strength in both the short- and longer-term. High IRRs do not assure a firm will never default, but a low IRRs increase the likelihood and thus tempers the potential BRR.

The Five Forces model is, however, not without its blind spots and much has been written on this subject, which will take us astray from credit analyses if we were to go down that path. From the perspective of the credit analyst, however, it is worth noting that the major criticism of Porter's model is its static property, which is to say that time as an independent factor is virtually ignored. Nonetheless, the global business environment has changed significantly since the 1980s due to technology and global supply chains (globalisation). These are essentially dynamic forces that affect competitiveness, and they have been changing so fast that a static model would always be lagging. That said, although neither of the two approaches to industry analysis is wholly satisfactory, they both are useful in trying to understand the competitive position of a firm, its profitability and growth outlook, and the behaviour of its cash flows (Fig. 4.1). We propose an eclectic approach that combines the following elements:

1. Porter's Five Forces model
2. The ILC model
3. The business Life Cycle model
4. Cost and cost structure
5. Country and political risk
6. Demographic and social trends
7. Global markets

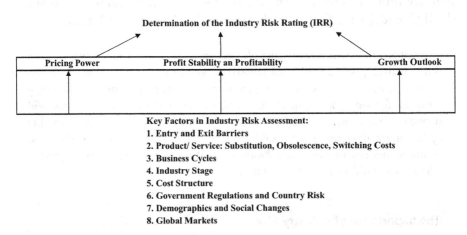

**Fig. 4.1** Map for industry analysis

## 4.3.1 Porter's Five Forces Framework Model of Industry Analysis

Let us first explore the Five Forces model. It is a popular management tool to analyse industry competition and the threats to a firm's profitability. A firm's competitive position is influenced by the threats and opportunities facing the industry. Porter's Five Forces model is a framework that models an industry as being influenced by five forces: (1) threat of new entrants, (2) supplier power, (3) buyer power, (4) threat of substitutes, and (5) degree of rivalry. As a widely used business tool for planning and strategy, managers use the model to develop a competitive edge over rival firms. From the vantage point of the credit analyst, however, it is more important to understand the threats and opportunities and how they affect competitive strength. The Porter model helps assess industry attractiveness and emerging trends that affect industry competition. Table 4.2 summarises the Porter model. It gives the five forces, the factors related to each of them, and the direction of the relationship between the factors and competition or the intensity of competition in the industry. From the vantage point of the credit analyst, the implications for growth, profitability, and the cash flow are what matters in reading the table. Any factor that diminishes competition or rivalry is a positive for the incumbent firms of the industry.

**Barriers to Entry and Exit**

A barrier to entry is something that stops a company from entering into an industry. High barriers to entry favour low production capacity, high prices, and high profitability of the subject industry. In many cases, the barriers are natural or structural to the industry, but they could also be created by the incumbent firms as part of their growth strategy to limit rivalry. Let us look at some of the important barriers to entry:

1. **Economies of large-scale production:** This is the need for large volume of production and sales to enable a firm to produce at the lowest possible unit cost.[4] New entrants are deterred from entering the industry when significant economies of scale have already been exploited by the incumbent firms.
2. **Capital requirements and technology:** This relates to the cost of capital investment per unit of output in production facilities. High capital costs impede entry. The capital investment includes plant and equipment, infrastructure, advertising, and research and development (R&D). The costs are also natural barriers. The costs are fixed because they are unrecoverable

**Table 4.2** Porter's five forces and their effects on competition in the industry

| Forces and their factors | The connections between the force factors and rivalry | Direction of the relationship between force factors and rivalry |
|---|---|---|
| **1. Threat of new entrants** | | |
| Economies of scale | Barrier to entry. Companies in markets with high entry barriers face less competition than those in markets with low entry barriers. | Inverse relationship |
| Access to inputs | Same as for economies of scale | Inverse relationship |
| Capital requirements | Same as for economies of scale | Inverse relationship |
| Brand identity/product differentiation | Same as for economies of scale | Inverse relationship |
| Switching cost | The one-time cost of a buyer switching from an existing seller to a new entrant is a disincentive to change product. Switching cost is an entry barrier. | Inverse relationship |
| Access to distribution channels | Same as for economies of scale | Inverse relationship |
| Absolute cost advantages | Same as for economies of scale | Inverse relationship |
| Government policy that limits or prevents entry to industries | Same as for economies of scale | Inverse relationship |
| **2. Supplier power** | | |
| Concentration of suppliers | Where the supply of inputs is concentrated in a few firms, sellers have higher negotiating leverage to charge high prices than firms in an industry with low supply concentration. Strengthens supplier bargaining power. | Inverse relationship |
| Importance of volume sales | Firms in an industry where volume purchasing of inputs is important face less competition than firms in an industry where volume purchases are not important. Strengthens supplier bargaining power. | Inverse relationship |
| Presence of substitute inputs | Firms in an industry where substitute inputs are readily available face more competition than firms in an industry where substitute inputs are unavailable or limited. Weakens supplier bargaining power. | Positive relationship |
| Switching costs of firms in the industry | Suppliers of inputs benefit from high switching cost because it promotes dependency, which helps to keep supplier prices high. High switching cost of moving from one supplier to another strengthens supplier bargaining power. | Inverse relationship |

## 3. Buyer power

| | | |
|---|---|---|
| Bargaining leverage | Firms in an industry where buyers have bargaining leverage compete more intensely than those in an industry where buyers have no bargaining power. | Positive relationship |
| Buying in large volume | Firms in an industry where buyers prefer bulk buying have to compete more for those customers than the firms in an industry where customers buy in any amounts. | Positive relationship |
| Price sensitivity | Firms in an industry where demand is sensitive to price compete more on price than firms in an industry where the demand for the good is price-insensitive. | Positive relationship |
| Brand identity | Strong brand identity is a form of product differentiation, which makes substitution more difficult. | Inverse relationship |
| Substitutes available | The availability of substitutes outside the industry lessens consumer dependency on a given product. The availability of substitutes lowers switching cost and strengthens the bargaining power of buyers. The existing firms have to compete more to retain customers. | Positive relationship |
| Product differentiation | In an industry where the good is standardised or undifferentiated, firms compete more intensely on price compared to an industry where the good differentiated. | Inverse relationship |

## 4. Threat of substitutes

| | | |
|---|---|---|
| Switching cost | High one-time switching cost is a disincentive to switching between products. | Inverse relationship |
| Tradeoff between price and product performance | The threat of a substitute from another industry is high when it offers an attractive price-performance trade-off compared to the industry's product. The threat discourages new entrants. | Inverse relationship |

## 5. Degree of rivalry

| | | |
|---|---|---|
| Exit barriers | High exit barriers keep firms from leaving an industry and leads to overcapacity. | Positive relationship |
| Industry concentration | High industry concentration amongst a handful of firms accounting for the bulk of industry sales reduces rivalry. | Inverse relationship |
| Industry growth | Slow growth in the industry causes more intense rivalry for market share. | Positive relationship |
| Operating leverage (fixed costs/ total costs) | The higher the operating leverage ratio, the higher the level of production required to achieve the lowest unit cost. This leads to oversupply or overcapacity. | Positive relationship |
| Product differentiation | Product differentiation reduces competition. | Inverse relationship |
| Brand loyalty | Brand loyalty is a form of product differentiation. | Inverse relationship |
| Switching cost | When a consumer can easily switch between goods, sellers struggle to retain or attract customers. The presence of high switching cost reduces competition amongst existing firms and discourages new entrants. | Inverse relationship |

should a firm decide to shut down. R&D expense is high in oligopolistic markets such as pharmaceuticals, and, in order to compete, new firms have to match, or exceed, the level of such spending by the incumbent firms. Because of the high cost of R&D in bringing new drugs to the market, the government grants a monopoly, usually lasting for a limited period of 20 years or so, to the drug company, thereby permitting it to recoup the investments made during the drug's development.

The industry's rate of technical innovation, or the rate of product obsolescence, is also a source of entry barrier. Innovation shortens the useful life and the adaptability of existing products, and the incumbents invest huge sums to ensure they stay ahead of the product curve. In the consumer electronics industry, which includes big companies like Apple, Samsung, and Huawei, the rate of product obsolescence is very high and consumers come to expect the development of new products. The retention of highly skilled employees and an effective R&D process are vital to such fast-changing pace of innovation.

3. **Access to supplier:** This refers to a firm's need for access to parts and raw material to enable production to occur without serious disruptions. For example, in the automotive industry, a major disruption to the complex global supply chain can cripple the industry. Scale and complexity of an operation make very effective barriers.

4. **Switching costs:** This refers to the one-time costs that a consumer incurs by switching from one provider to another. The costs can be monetary, such as the purchase and installation of new equipment, or non-monetary, such as the inconvenience from the loss of service during the switching process. Switching costs are common to suppliers of cable TV, telephone service, and energy. The barriers—the inconvenience, effort, and money— deter buyers from switching from one market to another, thereby creating a captive demand within the industry.

5. **Strong brand and brand loyalty:** The presence of strong brands and customer loyalty helps to deter new firms or latecomers from creating a new brand of product.

6. **Government regulations:** The barrier may include permits and licences to establish production, or rigid industry standards.

## Government Regulations

As we have discussed above government regulations can significantly influence the profitability and growth prospect of an industry. If they serve as entry barriers, the firms in the industry benefit. But government regulations are also intended to promote competition and reduce profit margins. There are four broad categories of government regulations:

1. **Public interest regulations:** These are regulations intended to promote health and safety in regard to the environment, labour, food, drugs, transportation, and health care. Governments use a variety of instruments, including licences, product standards, and foreign ownership restrictions.
2. **Special interest regulation:** In response to domestic political pressure, governments shield certain industries or consumer groups. The agricultural sector comprising dairy, poultry, pork, beef, grain, and fruit is a perfect example of supply management to support prices in order to stabilise farmers' incomes. Government's licensing is another form of supply management to keep out foreign competition and limit capacity.
3. **Deregulation:** These are regulations that prohibit or lower entry barriers to encourage competition. The rationale for such regulations is that competition lowers prices, improves living standards, and stimulates innovation.
4. **Red tape:** Government red tape, such as delays in approvals and licensing, is a common practice and a barrier to entry.

**Product Substitution and Obsolescence**

Industry profitability suffers as a result of product substitution when a new product or service meets the same needs in a different way. E-mail substitutes for express mail through the postal service. Steel, glass, and plastic can substitute for aluminium for making beverage containers. A major cause of product obsolescence is technological innovation. Obsolescence is either *natural or planned*. From the nineteenth century onward, iron and steel replaced wood in the building of ships. In the industrialised world, the motor vehicle has replaced horse-drawn carriages as the common mode of transportation. These are examples of natural obsolescence. Product upgrades are examples of planned obsolescence, which is a business strategy to keep consumers loyal to the product, and hence, it is a defence against substitution risk.

## 4.3.2 Industry Life Cycle Model

Figure 4.2 depicts the life cycle of an industry, tracked by total industry revenue or sales and over a long period. Industry life cycle is often presented as stylised facts or general tendencies.

The ILC model is useful for its classification and depiction of the stages according to certain characteristics. For example, if we know the stage that an industry is at, we have some *a priori* knowledge of the cash-flow needs and the relative profitability of the average firm in the industry. A young growth company is usually more profitable than a mature company is but it requires relatively larger cash from external sources. Think of Microsoft when it was

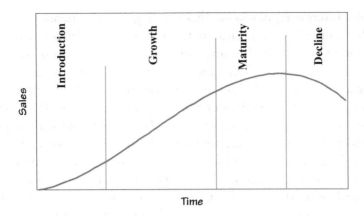

**Fig. 4.2** Industry life cycle curve

just a start-up company in the 1970s, then experiencing rapid growth in the 1980s and 1990s and has become a mature company in the 2000s. This is not to say that the next phase is necessarily "decline", though that could happen as we observe the declining performance of IBM and similar firms that used to be industry giants in the information technology industry.

Usually, however, instead of framing the analysis in terms of a predetermined progression from one stage to the next, we can get more analytical mileage from the model by trying to identify the stage of the industry through its dominant characteristic. That is to identify whether the company is representative of a growth industry, a mature industry, or a declining industry. All this is helpful information for the credit analyst to get a good sense of an industry's profitability, cash-flow needs, and future growth. From a correct identification of the industry in the first place, the credit analyst can then focus on sales, profitability, and growth outlook for the firm under review. Let us make use of the industry classifications of the life cycle model to define the type of industry:

- Pioneering
- Growth
- Mature (including niche)
- Declining

**Pioneer Industry**

A new or pioneer industry is formed when a few start-up firms launch a new product or service that often substitutes for products offered by another industry. A new industry has high risk of failure and low profits, the latter due to high input and promotion costs, and a strategy that favours growth over profit maximisation. Firms require large sources of external financing, but the upside is high profit margins as the product gains buyers' acceptance.

**Growth Industry**

A growth industry experiences consistently higher-than-average growth in size as measured by total industry revenue. Its cash needs are also relatively high as a pioneer industry. A key characteristic of the expansion phase is rising prices as growth in demand outpaces capacity. In such an environment, firms in the industry have market power to price products or services above marginal cost and realise high profit margins. Market power translates into *pricing power*. Pricing power depends on the sensitivity of demand for the good to changes in the price. In technical terms, this sensitivity is measured by the *price elasticity of demand*, elegantly captured by the following markup rule[5]:

$$P = MC\left(\frac{1}{\eta + 1.}\right)$$

where:

$P$ = price of the good or service
$MC$ = Marginal cost of production
$\eta = \dfrac{1}{\in_p}$ is the reciprocal of the price elasticity of demand ($\in_p$), measured by the percentage change in quantity demanded divided by the percentage change in the price.

This rule says that a firm can price its product well above the marginal cost of production if the term in the bracket is greater than 1. The condition obtains if $\in_p < -1$. Conversely, $\eta \approx 0$ as $\in_p$ becomes larger and larger in absolute value, which is the situation facing a firm with no ability to set prices above marginal cost pricing. This is the case of a purely competitive market for an undifferentiated product. A firm has no choice but to price its product at the extra cost of materials and the direct labour to produce an extra unit, that is, $P = MC$ in this limiting case.

In credit analysis the determinants of $\in_p$ rather than its precise value are the main concerns. The factors include (a) availability of substitute goods, (2) the type of good (inferior, necessary/normal, or luxury), and (3) brand loyalty. The availability of substitute goods increases the choice, thus enabling consumers to switch from one good to another due to changes in their prices. The less discretionary the demand for the good, the less sensitive it is to prices and income. For example, food and medicines are non-discretionary in a typical household's budget. Consumers who are loyal to a certain brand name of a given product (e.g., smart phones and toothpaste) are not likely to switch brand if its price were to increase. Maybe for a large price change or large price differentials, consumers might consider switching.

The health-care industry is a perfect example of pricing power stemming from market power of the incumbent firms. For example, just overnight, Turing Pharmaceuticals raised the price of a drug called *Daraprim* from $13.50/tablet to $750/tablet.[6] Pricing power in the pharmaceutical industry is the driving force behind the double-digit growth rates (see comparative growth rates in Table 4.3). The data are for the last five-year period ending January 2019; however, the growth pattern has been consistent going back a longer period.

Demographic factors such as longer life spans and a growing population of seniors push up demand for drugs. There are economic drivers as well. Health care and many life-saving drugs are a necessity, which makes the demand relatively price inelastic. In addition, patent protection allows drug companies to maintain high prices that are well over the marginal cost of production.

**Mature Industry**
A mature industry is one that has passed through the introduction and the growth phases of industry cycle, and is now encountering less growth potential and more rivalry amongst competitors for market share. Thus, the main characteristic of a mature industry is slower growth in sales and less pricing power due to the competition to maintain market shares. Although growth in revenues has moderated, firms of a mature industry tend to benefit from greater stability in sales. The cash requirements of existing firms from external sources are relatively low owing to relatively high cash inflow from operations but relatively low cash needs for investment like research and development that is crucial in the introductory and growth phases. This stability pattern is not assured, however, because technological and scientific progress leads to substitute goods. As we saw in the Porter model, if the price–performance trade-off is attractive, buyers would switch to the substitute; likewise, if the switching cost is low.

A special type of a mature industry is the *niche industry*, which is part of a supply chain and thus owes its survival and success to the bigger firms that buy their products. If these firms were to reorganise their production in another way or start making the parts, the niche industry will disappear. A good example is in the automotive industry where there are hundreds of Tier 3, Tier 2, and Tier 1 suppliers of diverse automotive products in the supply chain leading to the OEMs (original equipment manufacturer) like Ford,

**Table 4.3** Historical growth rate in earnings by industry (global)

| Industry name | Compound annual growth rate in revenues-last 5 years | Industry name | Compound annual growth rate in revenues-last 5 years |
|---|---|---|---|
| Advertising | 10.24% | Insurance (Prop/Cas.) | 6.65% |
| Aerospace/Defence | 7.37% | Investments & asset management | 13.28% |
| Air transport | 8.01% | Machinery | 6.01% |
| Apparel | 4.01% | Metals & mining | 10.93% |
| Auto & truck | 9.28% | Office equipment & services | 2.62% |
| Auto parts | 7.00% | Oil/Gas (Integrated) | −0.45% |
| Bank (Money centre) | 12.67% | Oil/Gas (Production and exploration) | 1.98% |
| Banks (Regional) | 8.66% | Oil/Gas distribution | 11.02% |
| Beverage (Alcoholic) | 5.97% | Oilfield Svcs/Equip. | −0.91% |
| Beverage (Soft) | 4.93% | Packaging & container | 7.68% |
| Broadcasting | 4.73% | Paper/forest products | 7.35% |
| Brokerage & investment banking | 19.48% | Power | 8.34% |
| Building materials | 6.23% | Precious metals | 4.65% |
| Business & consumer services | 9.54% | Publishing & newspapers | 0.68% |
| Cable TV | 7.54% | R.E.I.T. | 12.68% |
| Chemical (Basic) | 7.55% | Real estate (Development) | 12.63% |
| Chemical (Diversified) | 4.08% | Real estate (General/Diversified) | 11.24% |
| Chemical (Specialty) | 6.41% | Real estate (Operations & services) | 8.89% |
| Coal & related energy | 6.00% | Recreation | 3.55% |
| Computer services | 8.32% | Reinsurance | 6.00% |
| Computers/Peripherals | 4.05% | Restaurant/Dining | 6.41% |
| Construction supplies | 5.84% | Retail (Automotive) | 9.21% |
| Diversified | 8.72% | Retail (Building supply) | 5.21% |
| Drugs (Biotechnology) | 23.79% | Retail (Distributors) | 8.97% |
| Drugs (Pharmaceutical) | 16.79% | Retail (General) | 3.40% |
| Education | 6.56% | Retail (Grocery and food) | 5.67% |
| Electrical equipment | 7.23% | Retail (Online) | 12.23% |
| Electronics (Consumer & Office) | 0.50% | Retail (Special lines) | 3.04% |
| Electronics (General) | 5.99% | Rubber & tires | 0.37% |
| Engineering/Construction | 5.49% | Semiconductor | 6.44% |
| Entertainment | 12.25% | Semiconductor equip | 12.47% |
| Environmental & waste services | 10.49% | Shipbuilding & marine | 3.00% |
| Farming/Agriculture | 8.60% | Shoe | 0.54% |

(*continued*)

**Table 4.3** (continued)

| Industry name | Compound annual growth rate in revenues-last 5 years | Industry name | Compound annual growth rate in revenues-last 5 years |
|---|---|---|---|
| Financial Svcs. (Non-bank & insurance) | 14.37% | Software (Entertainment) | 15.07% |
| Food processing | 7.72% | Software (Internet) | 28.69% |
| Food wholesalers | 8.76% | Software (System & application) | 13.20% |
| Furn/Home furnishings | 7.83% | Steel | 2.89% |
| Green & renewable energy | 18.75% | Telecom (Wireless) | 2.24% |
| Healthcare products | 12.44% | Telecom. equipment | 8.84% |
| Healthcare support services | 13.52% | Telecom. services | 9.35% |
| Healthcare information and technology | 17.78% | Tobacco | 7.25% |
| Homebuilding | 10.31% | Transportation | 12.19% |
| Hospitals/Healthcare facilities | 7.84% | Transportation (Railroads) | 5.33% |
| Hotel/Gaming | 14.19% | Trucking | 6.14% |
| Household products | 8.82% | Utility (General) | 2.31% |
| Information services | 16.40% | Utility (Water) | 13.42% |
| Insurance (General) | 8.21% | Total market | 8.65% |
| Insurance (Life) | 7.12% | Total market (without financials) | 8.18% |

Source: http://people.stern.nyu.edu/adamodar/New_Home_Page/datacurrent.html.
Data of last update: January 5, 2019

Toyota, Mercedes-Benz, and Renault. Take, for example, the Tier 3 niche. Their main market are the Tier 2 s. Thus, they face *concentration risk* in sales, in addition to the risk from industry reorganisation. Furthermore, a niche industry faces substitution and obsolesce risks, as do most industries. All of these make niche industries high risk in industry analysis.

**Declining Industry**

The telltale signs of a declining industry are stagnant or decreasing sales due to declining demand, excess capacity that worsens the price decline caused by the fall in consumption, and consolidation of market shares amongst a handful of firms that survive. Notable examples of consolidation are the global cigarette industry that is dominated by five companies, and the US coal industry dominated by two companies that account for slightly over a third of total US production in 2017. Coal competes with nuclear power, oil, natural gas, and solar and wind power. Moreover, natural gas and renewable power are inexpensive and they are not going away. The last decade has seen many US coal companies go out of business, saddled with high debt and declining sales. A recovery in coal demand in the United States is unlikely. Another industry that is in rapid decline globally or is already dead in many countries is asbestos mining and production. Asbestos can cause lung cancer and the legal costs from the settlement of lawsuits have been high. Over the years, asbestos substitutes have replaced asbestos fibre in the manufacturing of construction materials.

Declining industries like coal and asbestos usually need massive government support like subsidies and tax breaks to show a profit.[7] The cigarette industry is, however, the most notable exception because it has been considered a declining industry for a very long time. The global industry has seen a steady drop in volumes since 2012. Yet it is one of the most profitable industries in the world. The profitability of the tobacco industry is due to the fact that nicotine is addictive, which makes the demand for cigarettes highly price and income inelastic. Note, however, that the cigarette industry faces high competition—no pun intended—from marijuana, the cultivation and use of which are becoming increasingly legal in the consuming countries.

From the vantage point of the credit analyst, it is always important to know whether the drop in sales is global or national in scope. The industry might be in decline nationally or locally, but growing globally. The credit analyst needs to consider both demand and supply factors. Let us examine some examples. Higher production costs account for the decline in clothing manufacturing and consumer electronics in developed countries; in response, production has shifted to developing countries. Social and demographic changes affecting demand also account for some of an industry's decline. Production of household sewing machines has disappeared in developed markets due to both relative costs and socio-demographic factors (e.g., more women are working outside the home). But in the developing part of the world, both supply and demand conditions favour a vibrant market for sewing machines. As a result, manufacturers have shifted production to the emerging markets. International cigarette companies target the emerging markets to make up for declining demand in domestic markets. Some 80% of the world's smokers live in low- to middle-income countries. Furthermore, in response to cost pressures, the production of the numerous parts of a product has spread globally. Many such products are integrated into the global supply chains of large multinationals. The entire competitive structure is built on the global supply chains. This spatial allocation of resources and production, the global equivalent of Adam Smith's concept of the division of labour, enables firms to minimise cost (or maximise efficiency) and raise the quality of their products.

## 4.3.3 The Business Cycle

A cyclical industry is one that is sensitive to fluctuation in the wider economy, measured by growth in real GDP (gross domestic product). Sales and profits of cyclical industries are higher during economic expansions, and lower during economic contractions. The business cycle is an enduring feature of all mature or developed economies. Take the largest economy in the world, the United States, for example. Between 1945 and 2019, there have been 11 business cycles averaging 69 months. The cycles differ in both their length (measured from peak to peak) and severity (measured by the cycle amplitude). The average expansion during this period lasted 58.4 months, and the average contraction lasted 11.1 months.[8]

Understanding the cyclicality of a business is crucial to assessing the financial stability of a company. Cyclicality is a negative factor in industry risk assessment because default frequency increases during an economic downturn. In credit analysis, determining whether the industries are or are not highly pro-cyclical is essential. To do this, the analyst compares the level of economic activity with industry revenue over time and quantifies the co-movements. Table 4.4 gives the correlation coefficients for final demand for diverse industries and the level of economic activity represented by real GDP.[9] The relative strength of the correlation could be classified as follows:

1. Perfect: correlation coefficient approaching ±1
2. High or strong correlation: value lies between ±0.50 and ±1
3. Moderate or medium correlation: value lies between ±0.30 and ±0.49
4. Low-degree or small correlation: value lies below ±0.29
5. No correlation: value is zero

*Cyclical industries* are positively correlated with the economic cycle. As you can see from the table, the highly cyclical industries include construction, retail trade, motor vehicles and equipment, and rail and air transportation. Sales volume in such industries tends to move in step with the cycle. Conversely, *counter-cyclical industries* are negatively correlated with the economic cycle, tending to do well during downturns and poorly during upturns. As shown in the table, the food, insurance, and health-care industries are negatively correlated with the economic cycle. In between these two are the industries that are weakly correlated with the business cycle. These are shielded from the business cycle and competition through the fact that demand for their products and services is relatively income and price inelastic

**Table 4.4** Industry correlation with GDP

| Industry | Correlation coefficient |
| --- | --- |
| Retail trade except eating and drinking places | 0.9175 |
| Construction | 0.8975 |
| Wholesale trade | 0.8412 |
| Miscellaneous fabricated textile products | 0.8101 |
| Sawmills and planing mills | 0.8036 |
| Household furniture | 0.7713 |
| Motor vehicles and equipment | 0.7575 |
| Household appliances. | 0.7248 |
| Real estate | 0.7142 |
| Air transportation | 0.6625 |
| Construction and related machinery | 0.6281 |
| Fabricated structural metal products | 0.5459 |
| Books | 0.5240 |
| Office and miscellaneous furniture and fixtures | 0.5227 |
| Engines and turbines | 0.4452 |
| Measuring and controlling devices | 0.3627 |
| Apparel. | 0.2993 |
| Computer and office equipment | 0.2862 |
| Electrical utilities | 0.2739 |
| Toys and sporting goods | 0.2014 |
| Health services | 0.1602 |
| Dairy products | 0.1599 |
| Bakery products | 0.1295 |
| Drugs | 0.0858 |
| Tobacco products | 0.0489 |
| Miscellaneous food and kindred product | −0.0639 |
| State and local government enterprises | −0.1599 |
| Insurance carriers | −0.1723 |
| Footwear, except rubber and plastic | −0.2338 |
| Hospitals, private | −0.4714 |

Source: Monthly Labour Review, February 1997

The rates of decline from peak to trough in industry revenue, profit (measured by earnings before interest and taxes [EBIT]) and cash flow (measured by earnings before interest, taxes, depreciation, and amortisation [EBITDA]), calculated for many cycles across many industries serve as indicators of the cyclicality and volatility. The more cyclical the industry, the more volatile the revenues, profits, and cash flow. Traders like volatility because they can make bets on the highs and lows and the directions. In contrast, the credit analyst looks for a strong monotonic relationship between the changes in these predictors (EBIT and EBITDA) and the likelihood of default represented by the risk grades. In credit analysis, the instability of these measures is a negative in the assessment of creditworthiness.

### 4.3.4 Costs and Cost Structure

The cost of raw material, energy, and labour is a big factor in profitability and some industries are more sensitive than others are to input-price changes. For example, rising cost of jet fuel and labour have a big impact on profits and profitability in the airline industry because these two items represent the biggest expense of running an airline. Similarly, the profitability of the paper industry is highly sensitive to changes in the price of energy because paper manufacturing is energy intensive, but paper producers lack bargaining power on the input side and also lack pricing power on the product side. In credit analysis, earnings volatility is a negative so it is necessary to analyse a firm's cost structure and its operating advantage. *Operating leverage* is something intrinsic to the operation of certain production activities that require a large proportion of fixed costs in total costs. A fixed cost or expense is an expenditure that does not vary with the level of production and related activities in the short run. Conversely, variable costs vary with the level of production, so strictly speaking variable cost is zero when activity level is zero. Low (high) operating leverage means most costs are variable (fixed).

High fixed to variable cost structures limit the ability of a firm to cut costs when the market is slack and sales are tumbling. Figure 4.3 illustrates the effect of operating leverage on operating profit margin, measured by the ratio of EBIT to sales. Consider the two industries with the cost structures depicted. EBIT varies with sales but operating leverage changes the shape of the curve. High operating leverage steepens the curve.

The implications are significant in terms of income volatility and profitability. When sales are $40 million, the profit margin is 10% for both industries. With higher sales, operating profit of ABC rises faster than XYZ's, but

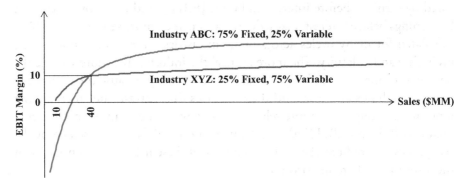

**Fig. 4.3** Operating leverage and operating profit

at lower levels of sales, such as $10 million, XYZ breaks even whereas ABC makes a loss. In a downturn, industry ABC is losing money and at a faster rate.

The higher the operating leverage for a given contribution margin (selling price minus average variable cost), the higher the sales volume to break even. We see this from the break-even relationship where total sales (selling price/ unit × sales volume) equal the sum of total variable costs and fixed costs so that operating profit (EBIT) is zero. By isolating sales volume to the left of the equation, we can express it as a function of fixed costs, selling price per unit, and variable cost per unit.

$$\text{Sales volume} = \frac{\text{Fixed costs}}{\text{Selling price per unit} - \text{Variable cost per unit}}$$

Furthermore, by rearranging this equation we see that the higher the fixed costs, the higher the sales volume required for the desired or the lowest average variable cost, given the price per unit.

$$\text{Variable cost per unit} = \text{Selling price per unit} - \frac{\text{Fixed costs}}{\text{Sales volume}}$$

High operating leverage interacting with high financial leverage makes for a volatile combination when sales are falling, and the result can lead to default or bankruptcy. Consider the expression for operating profit after tax for a borrower:

$$\textbf{Operating profit after tax} = \textbf{EBIT} - i * d (1 - t)$$

where $i$ = interest rates, $t$ = tax rate, and $d$ = stock of debt.

As we showed in Chap. 2, financial leverage increase returns on equity by borrowing rather than using one's own money; however, leverage works in reverse in bad times. As sales recede during a recession so does EBIT but the interest payments on the debt ($i$ times $d$) is a fixed expense. The firm makes a loss if the after-tax interest payment exceeds EBIT. At the same time, whilst sales are falling the firm realises it is unable to generate revenue to contribute to the high fixed costs so EBIT falls faster. If the loss is large enough or persistent, bankruptcy or insolvency is likely to happen. The firms with high fixed costs and high debt are considered more risky than firms with low operating leverage and low financial leverage when economic conditions are weakening.

Although high operating leverage works against profit margins in a downturn, the opposite occurs in an upturn. The reason is total costs do not rise as fast due to the high fixed component whilst sales rebound, so profit margins rise faster than sales do (see Fig. 4.3). You can say that the fixed costs, performing as a mechanical lever, gives the firm *operating leverage* to realise bigger profitability in good times. For example, drug and software companies invest large sums upfront for development and marketing. This fixed component of costs will not change much irrespective of sales. Table 4.5 gives a summary of the conclusions.

Companies characterised by high ratios of fixed assets to total assets are by nature capital intensive so there is a positive correlation between capital intensity and operating leverage. Table 4.6 shows that labour-intensive industries such as business and consumer services, agriculture, and retail tend to have low operating leverage.[10] It is, however, not always the case that low capital intensity means low fixed costs in total because some types of labour costs are fixed. For example, the property, plant, and equipment (PP&E)/total assets ratio is low for biotechnology and pharmaceutical but these industries cannot survive without their highly specialised workers. The same applies to the airline industry, which happens to be very capital intensive at the same time. Capital-intensive industries such as oil and gas, telecommunications, coal, and utilities have high operating leverage. The US coal mining industry stands out as a good example of the volatile mixture of high operating leverage and high financial leverage in a market where demand is dropping.

To sum up:

- In a period of rising sales, industries with high operating leverage experience a rapid rise in operating profit.
- In a period of falling sales, low operating leverage supports cost reduction.
- In a period of falling sales, high financial leverage amplifies the contractionary effect of high operating leverage on operating profit.
- In a period of lower levels of sales, industries with low operating leverage are more likely to be profitable than industries with high operating leverage.

**Table 4.5** Comparison between low and high operating leverage

|  | Low operating leverage | High operating leverage |
|---|---|---|
| Fixed costs | Low | High |
| Variable costs | High | Low |
| Profit margin stability | Higher | Lower |
| Economic expansion | Lower profits | Greater profits |
| Economic contraction | Lower losses | Greater losses |
| Break-even point | Lower | Higher |

**Table 4.6** Net property, plant, and equipment to total assets (global)

| | PP&E/ Total assets | | PP&E/ Total assets |
|---|---|---|---|
| Advertising | 6.6% | Insurance (Life) | 0.6% |
| Aerospace/Defence | 12.8% | Insurance (Prop/Cas.) | 1.2% |
| **Air transport** | **59.6%** | Investments & asset management | 5.7% |
| Apparel | 19.1% | Machinery | 18.8% |
| Auto & truck | 19.3% | Metals & mining | 51.8% |
| Auto parts | 29.4% | Office equipment & services | 19.3% |
| Bank (Money centre) | 0.7% | **Oil/Gas (Integrated)** | **57.3%** |
| Banks (Regional) | 1.1% | **Oil/Gas (Production and exploration)** | **74.0%** |
| Beverage (Alcoholic) | 21.2% | **Oil/Gas distribution** | **62.3%** |
| Beverage (Soft) | 17.9% | Oilfield Svcs/Equip. | 38.6% |
| Broadcasting | 13.8% | Packaging & container | 35.7% |
| Brokerage & investment banking | 1.1% | Paper/Forest products | 49.1% |
| Building materials | 25.5% | Power | 62.6% |
| Business & consumer services | 10.9% | Precious metals | 62.8% |
| Cable TV | 20.9% | Publishing & newspapers | 16.3% |
| Chemical (Basic) | 37.5% | R.E.I.T. | 63.0% |
| Chemical (Diversified) | 28.4% | Real estate (Development) | 3.8% |
| Chemical (Specialty) | 34.8% | Real estate (General/Diversified) | 23.5% |
| Coal & related energy | 45.7% | Real estate (Operations & Services) | 53.0% |
| Computer services | 8.1% | Recreation | 28.7% |
| Computers/Peripherals | 16.4% | Reinsurance | 0.1% |
| Construction supplies | 27.5% | Restaurant/Dining | 35.3% |
| Diversified | 14.7% | Retail (Automotive) | 24.1% |
| **Drugs (Biotechnology)** | **9.5%** | Retail (Building Supply) | 43.1% |
| **Drugs (Pharmaceutical)** | **13.6%** | Retail (Distributors) | 13.3% |
| Education | 21.8% | Retail (General) | 37.9% |
| Electrical equipment | 17.6% | Retail (Grocery and food) | 35.9% |
| Electronics (Consumer & office) | 14.0% | Retail (Online) | 14.6% |
| Electronics (General) | 23.2% | Retail (Special lines) | 20.4% |
| Engineering/Construction | 9.1% | Rubber & tires | 39.9% |
| Entertainment | 13.2% | Semiconductor | 31.0% |
| Environmental & waste services | 27.9% | Semiconductor equip | 22.1% |
| Farming/Agriculture | 27.6% | Shipbuilding & marine | 49.3% |
| Financial Svcs. (Non-bank & insurance) | 0.8% | Shoe | 18.5% |
| Food processing | 26.4% | Software (Entertainment) | 16.8% |
| Food wholesalers | 19.6% | Software (Internet) | 15.8% |
| Furn/Home furnishings | 16.6% | Software (System & application) | 8.4% |
| Green & renewable energy | 68.5% | Steel | 43.4% |
| Healthcare products | 11.8% | Telecom (Wireless) | 29.0% |
| Healthcare support services | 7.7% | Telecom. equipment | 8.5% |
| Healthcare information and technology | 9.8% | Telecom. services | 33.8% |
| Homebuilding | 6.6% | Tobacco | 7.8% |
| Hospitals/Healthcare facilities | 42.1% | Transportation | 23.3% |
| Hotel/Gaming | 46.1% | **Transportation (Railroads)** | **72.8%** |
| Household products | 17.8% | Trucking | 31.1% |
| Information services | 3.8% | Utility (General) | 50.6% |
| Insurance (General) | 0.7% | Utility (Water) | 47.3% |

Source: http://people.stern.nyu.edu/adamodar/New_Home_Page/datacurrent.html.
Data of last update: January 5, 2019

### 4.3.5 Country Risk and Political Risk

Certain industries, such as the extractive industries like mining, are often highly exposed to country risk, involving tax regime, royalty frameworks, and licensing processes. There is also political risk of expropriation or nationalisation. For example, ExxonMobil had been a target of expropriation long before Venezuela, under a leftist government, nationalised the company in 2007.

### 4.3.6 Demographics and Social Trends

We have examined many examples in previous sections where demographic changes and social trends influence the demand for a product. To recall, demographic changes include the ageing of the population and longer life spans for the aged. Rising incomes, a growing middle class, and increasing urbanisation are additional social factors to consider.

### 4.3.7 Global Markets

Foreign markets are the natural outlet for domestic industries that have excess capacity and depend on volume sales to drive profit margins. Examples include steel, chemicals, and motor vehicles. In this age of globalisation, companies compete by reallocating resources globally through supply chains to keep their costs low in order to compete globally. We see this production arrangement not only with the automotive industry, but also across many industries.

> As the book goes to press, multilateral trade and globalisation are facing many challenges.

## 4.4   Scoring Industry Risk

We covered a lot of ground identifying and analysing the important information needed in industry risk analysis. With this knowledge and the methodology presented in Chap. 3, we are now in a position to build an industry scorecard using two factors: (1) stability of revenue and profitability (during a cyclical downturn), and (2) outlook for growth and profitability. For illustrative purposes, we work with a few rating categories for the passenger airline industry. We will assign a weight of 40% to the first criterion and a higher weight (60%) to the second because it is forward looking, in contrast with historical cash-flow stability. We will default to equal weights for the growth and profitability sub-factors.

Before we get to the scorecard, the cyclicality of an industry deserves some comment. It is relatively easy for the analyst to determine which industry is cyclical or not and which financial indicators to use to describe the cycle; however, the practical problem is measuring the cyclicality in a format suited to the criteria-based approach. The method that we use is an application of Standard and Poor's—S&P (2013).[11] The S&P methodology involves extensive data analytics on "big data", which is outside the scope and requirements of this book. Still, it is instructive to present the following summary to give you the general idea of the methodology:

- S&P looked at two components of the economic cycle, *industry revenue* and *industry cash flow*, from peak to trough for 38 industries. They used EBITDA as a proxy for cash flow because they lacked globally consistent and comparable data. They calculated peak-to-trough declines in the two components for all industries in the recessions from 1950 to 2010 in the United States, and in other major economies from 1987 to 2010.
- S&P calibrated the cyclicality assessments—changes in industry revenue and changes in EBITDA—against "BBB" and "BB" stresses/recessions[12] in the 1950–2010 period to enhance ratings comparability across industries and time.
- They set about creating criteria for the two components for six discrete segments. They used a statistical clustering technique to categorise the data.
- The pairing of descriptors for revenue decline and cash-flow decline is what ultimately defines the risk category/grade.

Table 4.7 summarises the S&P method. For example, "Industry revenues decline by up to 4% during a cyclical downturn" combines with "Profitability ratio declines between 3% and up to 7% during a cyclical downturn" to define a risk grade of 2. The worst case is defined by cash flow declining many times faster (more than 72%) than the rates of decline in revenue. For our purposes, we use the same predictors, industry revenue and EBITDA (proxy for cash flow), and we also use EBIT (for operating profit) and seasonality; however, since we do not have the data to construct the numerical groupings for industry revenue, EBITDA, and EBIT, we use qualitative descriptors. This allows us to capture a similar cyclical effect and serves to illustrate how the descriptors work. We combine all to define the five risk grades in Table 4.7. As we saw in the previous chapter, once the scorecard is set up, the risk analyst may only *select* the appropriate descriptor, and computation and the BRR rating are purely a scorecard function.

**Table 4.7** Summary of S&P industry risk assessment

| | | Profitability declines during a cyclical downturn | | | | | |
|---|---|---|---|---|---|---|---|
| | | ≤3%* | 3.0 to ≤7.0 | 7.0 to ≤12.0 | 12.0 to ≤24.0 | 24.0 to ≤72.0 | >72.0 |
| | ≤4%* | 1 | 2 | 3 | 4 | 5 | 6 |
| | 4.0 to ≤8.0 | 1 | 2 | 3 | 4 | 5 | 6 |
| Industry revenue declines during a cyclical downturn | 8.0 to ≤13.0 | 1 | 2 | 3 | 4 | 5 | 6 |
| | 13.0 to ≤20.0 | 2 | 3 | 4 | 4 | 5 | 6 |
| | 20.0 to ≤32.0 | 2 | 3 | 4 | 4 | 5 | 6 |
| | >32.0 | 3 | 3 | 4 | 5 | 5 | 6 |

The risk categories are: very low risk (1), low risk (2), intermediate risk (3), moderately high risk (4), high risk (5), and very high risk (6).

Source: Standard & Poor's, *increase/decrease

## 4.4.1 Industry Risk Scorecard

In this section, our aim is not to suggest a formulaic approach or something resembling a tick-sheet of predictors. Rather, our aim is to show that whatever the combination of explanatory variables one selects for a given industry, they should be *robust*, which is to say they should at least be *stable predictors* of industry revenue and the future growth of the industry. We use two risk criteria to determine the industry risk rating (IRR):

1. Stability of revenue and profitability
2. Outlook for growth and profitability

The previous discussion gives us a vast amount of information. To make the analysis manageable, we group the information. An inexhaustive list of risk factors includes the following (listed also in Fig. 4.1):

1. Entry and exit barriers
2. Product/service: substitution, obsolescence, switching costs
3. Business cycles
4. Industry stage
5. Cost structure
6. Government regulations and sovereign debt crisis
7. Demographics and social changes
8. Global markets

The first criterion is essentially historical, and to measure it one analyses the actual volatility of revenue and profit margins over many business cycles. The second criterion is essentially forward looking, so we give it more weight than the first in the computation of the IRR.

Table 4.8 presents the scorecard with the risk factors in the first column and the descriptors that define and differentiate the ratings in the top row. With the benefit of the foregoing discussion on industry analysis combined with knowledge of the airline industry, a credit analyst would make the best judgement in selecting the descriptors for the eight risk factors. The shaded areas represent the placements. We leave it to the reader to confirm that the weighted score for industry risk is 6.9, which maps to "BB+" according to the rating scale. In other words, according to the rating system, industry risk for an airline company falls in the high-risk range of $6.1 < \times \leq 7.0$.

Although the template we have provided is a simplified version of a detailed industry risk analysis, the "high-risk" rating aligns with the ratings of more comprehensive industry analysis. For example, Standard & Poor's (2010, 3)[13] notes "In our opinion, the airline industry usually involves greater credit risk than most other industries and sectors, as reflected in the fact that we characterize the business risk profiles of more than two-thirds of rated airlines as either weak or vulnerable."

We encourage the reader to apply the template, with appropriate modifications, to evaluate the IRR (industry risk rating) for the pharmaceutical industry and the coal industry. If the results obtained are low risk for pharmaceuticals and high risk for coal, they align with the consensus. *The exercise will test both your understanding of the fundamental concepts of the criteria-based methodology and your ability to apply the knowledge.*

## 4.5   Business Risk Assessment

The business risk facing a firm is the likelihood of its profits falling below expectations or making a loss. The risk is determined by a host of factors, many of which not surprisingly are related to the same set of factors that affect industry risk. They include:

- Brand name, quality, reliability, and so on
- Operating cost: cost level and cost structure (ratio of fixed to variable costs)
- Internal economies of scale: effect on pricing, purchasing, administrative savings, financial saving, risk bearing
- Barriers to entry

**Table 4.8** Industry risk assessment – passenger airline industry

| Risk criteria and factors | W (%) | AA | A | BBB | BB | B |
|---|---|---|---|---|---|---|
| | | 15 | 12 | 9 | 6 | 3 |
| I: Stability of revenue and profitability | 40.0% | | | | | |
| Cyclical and seasonal volatility of revenue and profitability during an economic downturn | 100.0% | The historical data support one or a combination of the following: Industry operating revenue stagnates or grows even as the economy (GDP) is contracting. Operating profit margin declines roughly in sync with industry revenue, but stays positive. Revenue and profits margins exhibit relatively low seasonal fluctuations. | The historical data support one or a combination of the following: Industry operating revenue declines faster than the economy (GDP). Operating profit margin declines, but at a slower pace vis-à-vis industry revenue. Operating cash flow (represented by EBITDA) worsens, but stays positive. Revenue and profits margins exhibit low seasonal fluctuations. | The historical data support one or a combination of the following: Industry operating revenue declines at a much faster pace than the economy (GDP). Operating profit (EBIT) declines, but at a moderately faster pace vis-à-vis industry revenue. Operating cash flow (represented by EBITDA) worsens, but stays positive. Revenue and profits margins exhibit moderate seasonal fluctuations. | The historical data support one or a combination of the following: Operating revenue declines many times faster than the economy (GDP). Operating profit (EBIT) approaches zero or may dip below. Operating profit (EBIT) declines at a faster pace vis-à-vis industry revenue. Operating cash flow (represented by EBITDA) approaches zero, or may dip below. Revenue and profits margins exhibit high seasonal fluctuations. | The historical data support one or a combination of the following: Industry operating revenue declines many times faster than the economy (GDP). Operating profit (EBIT) turns sharply negative. Operating profit (EBIT) declines many times faster vis-à-vis industry revenue. Revenue and profits margins exhibit very high seasonal fluctuations. |
| II: Outlook for growth & profitability | 60.0% | | | | | |
| 1. Entry and exit barriers | 12.5% | High barriers to entry (e.g., legal monopoly, high financing requirements to fund capital investments and R&D, rapid technological change). Very limited options available to overcome entry barriers, for example leasing rather than owning equipment. High cost advantages. Significant switching costs | | Low to moderate barriers to entry; barriers to exit substantial. Options available to overcome entry barriers, e.g., leasing rather than owning equipment. Low cost advantages. Low switching costs | Few barriers to entry; barriers to exit relatively high. However, many options available to overcome entry barriers. Limited cost advantages. New entrants face low costs. Virtually no switching costs | |
| 2. Product/ service: substitution, obsolescence, switching costs | 12.5% | Substantially all of the following: No substitute product/ service currently available outside the industry. Usability of the product/ service not threatened by new technology | | Substantially all of the following: Some substitute products/ services already available outside the industry. Usability of the product/ service threatened by new technology | Substantially all of the following: Many substitute products/ services available outside the industry. Usability of the product/ service significantly threatened by new technology | Substantially all of the following: Many substitute products/ services available outside the industry in decline globally. Usability of the product in decline. Product banned by most countries |
| 3. Industry stage | 12.5% | One or a combination of the following: Growth stage. Demand increasing faster than supply. Sales and earnings expanding at a faster rate than in other industries | | One or a combination of the following: Mature stage and profits are relatively stable. High competitive pressures. Industry growth closely matches GDP growth | One or a combination of the following: Mature stage but profits are volatile. High competitive pressures. Industry growth unevenly matches GDP growth | One of the following: Decline stage (declining revenue and profit). Introductory stage (too rapid growth at the expense of profitability, new technology, and new business model) |
| 4. Cost and cost structure | 12.5% | One or a combination of the following: Vertically integrated operation is the norm. Easy access to supplies. Ability to recover or hedge costs (e.g. regulated industry structure). Low fixed to variable costs by industry comparisons. Low financial leverage by industry comparisons. Low financial leverage by industry comparisons. Firms face low switching costs in changing suppliers. Numerous suppliers | | One or a combination of the following: Mostly vertically integrated operation. Ability to recover or hedge costs (e.g. regulated industry structure). Long-term contracts provide some predictability to pricing and material availability. Fixed to variable costs average by industry comparisons. Financial leverage average by industry comparisons. Firms face moderate switching costs in changing suppliers. Significant industry concentration amongst suppliers | One or a combination of the following: Limited access to supplies. Limited ability to pass on cost increases; hedging is costly. Long-term contracts provide limited predictability to pricing and material availability. Fixed to variable costs high by industry comparisons. Financial leverage high by industry comparisons. Firms face relatively high switching costs in changing suppliers. Relatively high industry concentration amongst suppliers | One or a combination of the following: No access to supplies; hedging is costly. Mostly spot purchases with suppliers. Fixed to variable costs high by industry comparisons. Financial leverage high by industry comparisons. Firms face high switching costs in changing suppliers. Few suppliers |

| | Weight | | | | |
|---|---|---|---|---|---|
| 5. Degree of unionisation | 12.5% | Unionisation not permitted or, no effective collective bargaining occurs | Industry is unionised but labour relations have been relatively peaceful<br>Susceptible to strikes and work stoppages | Highly unionised industry; labour relations contentious<br>Frequent strikes and work stoppages | Unions highly organised and militant<br>Labour relations highly contentious<br>Frequent strikes and work stoppages |
| 6. Government regulation and country risk | 12.5% | One or a combination of the following:<br>Very weak safety and environmental requirements in place<br>Firms have the ability to recover the associated costs (e.g. from taxpayers)<br>Very high protectionist regulations | One or a combination of the following:<br>Weak safety and environmental requirements in place<br>Firms have some leeway to recover the associated costs (e.g. from taxpayers)<br>Relatively high protectionist regulations | One or a combination of the following:<br>Strict safety and environmental requirements in place<br>Firms have limited ability to recover the associated costs (e.g. from taxpayers)<br>Limited protection from foreign competition<br>Foreign operation at some risk of nationalisation<br>Profit repatriation at some risk | One or a combination of the following:<br>Tough safety and environmental requirements in place<br>Firms have no ability to recover the associated costs (e.g. from taxpayers)<br>Weak or no protection from foreign completion<br>Foreign operation at risk of nationalisation<br>Profit repatriation at significant risk |
| 7. Demographics and social trends | 12.5% | Global demographic and social changes highly favouring strong long-term growth in demand | Global demographic and social changes favouring long-term growth in demand | Global demographic and social changes weakly favouring long-term growth in demand | local demographic and social changes do not or hardly favour long-term growth in demand |
| 8. Global markets | 12.5% | One or a combination of the following:<br>Low capacity worldwide<br>Highly concentrated with a few companies controlling the global market<br>High demand worldwide<br>Product/ service highly differentiated | One or a combination of the following:<br>Relatively high overcapacity worldwide<br>Fierce global competition<br>Product/ service somewhat commoditised | One or a combination of the following:<br>Very high overcapacity worldwide<br>Fierce global competition<br>Fragmented market<br>Product/ service highly commoditized | One or a combination of the following:<br>Very high overcapacity worldwide<br>Fierce global competition<br>Low or declining demand for product/ service<br>Product/ service undifferentiated |

- Market share
- Diversification (by product, geography, and customer)
- Government regulations
- Input costs

All these influence the business risk through these channels:

- Market position
- Pricing
- Competitiveness
- Business consistency and stability

## 4.5.1  Market Position, Pricing, and Competitiveness

Market position is the competitive standing of a firm or of its products consumed in a defined market. Measures of market size include volume sales, number of customers, revenue, distribution coverage, and product usage. A related concept is market dominance, and in many countries governments have regulations to prevent the abuse of market power. The question is this: how does one measure market power? The Canadian Competition Bureau notes:

> The Bureau considers market dominance to be synonymous with market power. Although it can be difficult to measure market power directly, the Bureau places greatest emphasis on key factors such as market share and barriers to entry. In defining market dominance, the Competition Bureau looks at whether a firm, or a group of firms, substantially, or completely, controls a product or service in a given geographic area.[14]

A firm's market position is usually measured by the firm's market share, measured directly in various ways such as dollar sales (revenues), unit sales (volume), or reserves in certain resource industries. There is no correct way to measure market share, defined as the percentage of the total market served by the firm or brand. Firms probably track both because they have access to market data to calculate the metrics. If the products are very similar and firms are operating at capacity, relative market shares should be similar regardless of measurement unit. This result is reported in Table 4.9A for homogenous products and similar prices. The relative market shares are also similar regardless of unit measurement.

**Table 4.9A** Unit market share with homogenous products

| Brand | Average price | Unit sales | Unit market share | Sales | Revenue market share |
|---|---|---|---|---|---|
| A | $2.50 | 15,000 | 50% | $37,500 | 46% |
| B | $3.00 | 9000 | 30% | $27,000 | 33% |
| C | $2.75 | 6000 | 20% | $16,500 | 20% |
| Total | $2.70 | 30,000 | 100% | $81,000 | 100% |

**Table 4.9B** Unit market share with differentiated products

| Brand | Average price | Unit sales | Unit market share | Sales | Revenue market share |
|---|---|---|---|---|---|
| D | $2.00 | 15,000 | 54% | $30,000 | 25% |
| E | $8.00 | 9000 | 32% | $72,000 | 59% |
| F | $5.00 | 4000 | 14% | $20,000 | 16% |
| Total | $4.36 | 28,000 | 100% | $122,000 | 100% |

In contrast, where product differentiation and price differences are significant, as in Table 4.9B, the choice of the measurement unit for market share will make a marked difference in the calculation measurements. The unit method yields a market share of 54% for brand D, but brand E generates the bulk of the industry's total revenue due to the higher price of $8.00, which is more than the industry average. The revenue market share for brand E is 59%. This example shows that in the presence of product differentiation and substantial price differences, the choice of the measurement unit is key to the determination of market dominance. There could be many dominant firms in an industry depending on method of calculation. Credit analysts need to be wary of company annual reports that make vaunted claims of market dominance or market leadership.

The following statements from regulatory body, Canada's Competition Bureau, may serve as a useful guide for determining market dominance from relative market shares.

*Though there are no hard and fast rules governing the relationship between market share and market dominance, the Bureau is guided in its approach by the following general criteria when examining market conditions:*

- *A market share of less than 35%, held by one firm, does not generally raise concerns with the Bureau.*
- *A market share of 35% and over, held by one firm, generally raises some concern and prompts further examination by the Bureau.*
- *In the case of a group of firms, a combined market share exceeding 60% generally raises concerns and prompts further examination by the Bureau.*[15]

Companies can improve their market position through price competition, quality improvements, product innovation, increased or targeted distribution, or by influencing consumer perceptions through advertising and marketing. Clearly, market share, pricing, and competitiveness are related. Firms attempt to expand their market shares through various means such as advertising, branding, and competitive pricing. Market shares fluctuate so it is better to gauge market dominance over a long period rather than for any one period, where increases and decreases may only be signalling the relative competitiveness of the company's products or service.

## 4.5.2  Business Consistency and Stability

Business consistency and stability relate to operating performance measures such as revenue, unit sales, profit, and cash flow through time. In credit analysis, performance that is dependable or consistent is a positive, whereas performance that fluctuates is a negative. Business stability is reflected in steady growth rates (e.g., sales) or stable performance ratios. Maintaining or increasing market share depends on the growth dynamics. To maintain market share, a firm's performance must be consistent and stable, enabling revenues to grow at the same rate as the total market. Moreover, to increase market share, a firm must be increasing sales faster than the total market by being super-competitive.

# 4.6   Scoring Business Risk

An airline company (which will be the focus of Chap. 5) is a good example to illustrate how the credit analyst goes about thinking of the relevant risk criteria, the risk factors, and the risk elements (as required) to build the scorecard for business risk. The analyst begins by asking what the critical areas are that an airline *must* prove effective, otherwise it will fail. The KSFs (key success factors) would include at least these four: (1) managing its finances, (2) managing its fleet, (3) attracting customers, and (4) managing its people. These KSFs may be grouped under two broad risk criteria and the risk factors: competitive position and market position. You would notice a third risk criterion, cyclical position. Although it is not a KSF, it plays a key role in adjusting the business risk score for the industry's position in the business cycle; hence the name point-in-time (PIT) adjustment. We will explain why the PIT adjustment factor is built into the model:

1. Competitive position (weight 1/2 or 1/3):

   a. Operating cost
   b. Operating revenue
   c. Fleet
   d. Customer service and safety record

2. The market position (weight 1/2 or 1/3):

   a. Diversification by geography and service
   b. Market share
   c. Route network

3. Cyclical position (weight 1/3):

   a. Cyclical Adjustment Factor

## 4.6.1 Designing the Scorecard to Accommodate Cyclical Correction

Let us first discuss the weighting of the risk factors in Table 4.10, to be discussed later, to take account of business cycle effects on the BRR. The scorecard is designed to handle cases where the industry is highly cyclical and the cyclicality primarily drives current performance that is reflected in the financial statements. The question that the assessor faces is what financial information to use given the phase of the economic cycle. Take, for example, the case where all or most economic indicators *point* to a recession in the next 12 months (NTM) or so (Note: no economic model can accurately forecast turning points). Using the LTM (last twelve months) financials of the current year and the previous two to three years would likely result in a BRR upgrade because the data driving financial risk and, hence, the model, improve during the boom phase. But at the next BRR review, say within a year or so, a rating downgrade seems more likely because data tend to worsen when the industry is in the down phase. The volatility of the BRR is unsatisfactory, as we discussed in Chap. 3.

In order to make the BRR sensitive to the economic cycle for highly cyclical industries, and particularly where the risk analyst has determined that the cycle is driving financial performance, the business risk includes a third risk criterion called Cyclical Adjustment Factor. It gives the assessor the choice of (a) applying PIT (point-in-time) adjustment to business risk, or (b) using the LTM data of the current year and financial forecast to assess financial risk. If the analyst chooses the PIT adjustment, the weights are equally distributed across three risk factors if there are no compelling theoretical or empirical reasons for unequal weighting. The effect of the Cyclical Adjustment Factor on the BRR is counter-cyclical. Alternatively, if the analyst chooses *pro forma* financials, the PIT adjustment becomes unnecessary, and the only risk factors for business risk are the first two, again equally weighted.

## 4.6.2 Competitive Position

### Operating Costs

- Non-fuel cost (in an appropriate currency) per available seat kilometre
- Load factor or seat-capacity rate (indicator of efficiency)[16]
- Ability to impose fuel surcharge without adversely affecting demand
- Financial resources to hedge or mitigate exchange rate risks and fuel price risks
- Relations between the airline and its employees and unions
- Legacy cost burdens, such as pension liabilities
- Flexibility to manage the fleet: redeploy planes or manage capacity to manage changes in demand

### Operating Revenue

- Relative growth in total revenue
- Relative stability of the load factor
- Ability to leverage market/demand segments for price discrimination to increase passenger yields
- Membership in global alliances (e.g., the Star Alliance) and with code-sharing partnerships
- Participation in joint ventures with many major international airlines

### Fleet

- Proportion of the fleet fully owned or leased by the airline
- Average age of the fleet relative to the industry
- Suitability between fleet mix and the routes served
- Ongoing fleet renewal programme with a good mix of firm and optional orders

### Customer Service and Safety Record

- Brand recognition
- Brand loyalty

- Safety record
- Reputation for quality service
- Ability to charge higher prices and fees for services without adversely affecting flight

### 4.6.3 Market Position

*Revenue Diversification by Geography and Services*

- Diversification across regions and continents
- Diversification across country regional and continental flights
- Alliances and network integration, with code-sharing deals
- Revenue share of non-passenger services

*Market Share*

- Market leadership and the number of important markets in which the airline leads

*Route Network*

- The profitability of the routes and the proportion of business travel
- Access to the key cities of markets served
- Flight frequency and the favourability of the time slots

### 4.6.4 Cyclical Position: Phase of the Economic Cycle

In designing the BRR scorecard, we need to decide how forward looking we want the model to be, and consider the pros and cons of PIT (point-in-time) and TTC (through-the-cycle). Obviously, the "fixes" are not perfect solutions but they are better than ignoring the issue because the risk and return implications from using unreliable BRRs are significant. The influence of the business cycle on the BRR depends on the correlation between the performance of an industry *as a whole*, and the performance of a particular firm belonging to that industry. We will be looking at a practical application in Chap. 5.

In order to develop the ideas for a cyclical adjustment, let us first understand the macroeconomic concept of an economic cycle and for this purpose, we use US data. The first thing to know is that the business cycle is a permanent feature of a market economy although economic science does not have a theory to explain and predict it. For this reason, we need to put together many pieces of information in a coherent story, not unlike completing a jigsaw puzzle. Quite often, some important pieces are missing from the picture. The second thing to know is that every cycle is different in terms of its duration (periodicity) and severity (amplitude). As Fig. 4.4 for the United States shows, an economy (represented by real gross domestic product) fluctuates in a sort of sinusoidal pattern. Thirty-three cycles preceded the current one in the 1854–2009 period. Figure 4.5 shows 11 cycles, each of a different length measured in months. The left side of the graph shows the lengths of the recessions, and the bars indicate the lengths of the expansion. The average life span of the last three cycles is 9.1 years. As the book goes to press, the expansion is already 124 months old, the longest run since records began in 1854.

We learn from history (using the United States as example) that all expansions eventually die.[17] From the vantage point of the credit analyst, the question is how to situate the industry in the correct phase of the cycle. We saw in Fig. 3.2 that the turning points are the top of the cycle (peak) and the bottom of the cycle (trough). Following these points are recession and expansion respectively. The credit analyst looks for guidance in economic indicators (remember we said earlier that there is no model that can predict turning points). High-frequency data are the best information and they go by the labels coincident economic indicators (CEI) and leading economic indicators (LEI).

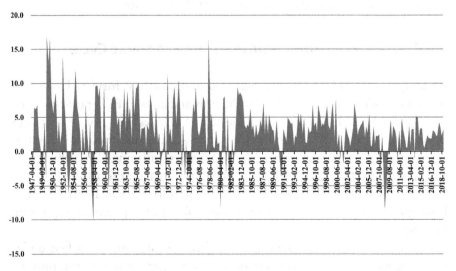

**Fig. 4.4** US real GDP growth during 1947–2019. (Source: FRED, Federal Reserve of St. Louis)

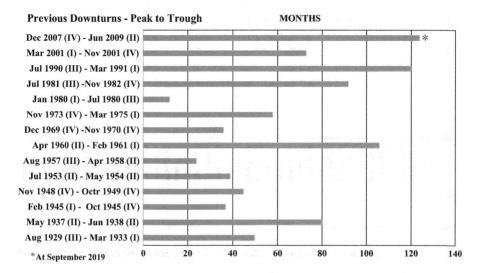

**Fig. 4.5**  Length of economic expansion. (Source: National Bureau of Economic Research)

The coincident indicators show the current state of the economy, whereas the leading indicators predict changes in the economy six to nine months away. A familiar example of a coincident economic indicator is retail sales. Examples of leading indicators that by definition are forward looking include building permits for new private housing units and consumer expectations. A drop in building permits signals lower housing construction in the months ahead, and negative readings of consumer sentiment point to lower spending on durable and non-durable goods in the months ahead. All these will have ripple effects on manufacturing and services and employment in these sectors.

Whilst it is worth noting that indices of leading economic indicators are far from being accurate predictors, they are overall successful. Again, as an example, let us look at US data and Fig. 4.6, which shows the monthly changes in the composite index. The index includes as many as ten leading indicators, as does the Conference Board's LEI. Leading indicators usually include the yield curve, or the interest rate difference/spread between a long-term government bond (e.g., a ten-year US Treasury bond) and an administered rate (e.g., US Federal Funds). In Chap. 6, we discuss briefly the yield curve and why the bond market is a relatively reliable indicator of a recession—the phenomena known as an inversion of the yield curve. A yield curve inversion occurs when long-term bond yields fall below yields on shorter-term government debt. Suppose the market becomes pessimistic about future growth—nine months away or even longer. It will expect the Fed to respond by cutting short-term

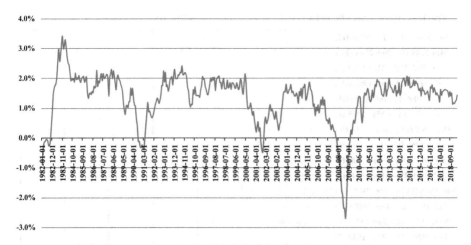

**Fig. 4.6** Leading index for the United States. (Source: Federal Reserve Bank of St Louis)

interest rates, and these expectations will be reflected in falling long-term rates. The normal shape of the curve is upward sloping indicating that the market is optimistic about economic growth and expects future short-term rates to rise, reflected in rising longer-term rates.

The first pattern to notice is the parabolic shapes through the jagged lines above the zero line. This is a graphical depiction of the economy losing momentum as the cycle progresses, eventually reaching a maximum point before starting its descent. The second pattern to notice is that changes in the LEI warn of economic slowdown before the turning point. Three or more consecutive changes in the LEI in the same direction suggest a turning point in the economy; in particular, three consecutive *negative* readings suggest a possible recession. This LEI (Federal Bank of St. Louis) shown in the figure was late in predicting the turning point, so the changes from month to month were still in positive territory prior to the recession that started in December 2007. Still, the changes in the index were signalling a downbeat tone many months before the turning point.

In contrast, the Conference Board's LEI successfully anticipated the turning point with negative changes many months prior to the recession and previous ones. Similarly, the Organisation for Economic Co-operation and Development's (OECD) composite leading indicators (CLI) gave the first warning in September 2007 and was able to anticipate the downturn five months ahead.[18] The EU entered recession in Q2:2008. The leading economic indicators for both the OECD and the Conference Board are, however, not an unqualified success because they sounded false alarms in previous cycles.

The mixed results reflect the fundamental problem that the precursors to a recession are different in each episode.[19]

In addition to the leading economic indicators, the credit analyst may find monetary indicators useful. They include central bank policy announcements that may convey information on the current state of the economy and its future path. The statutory mandate of many central banks is maximum price stability and maximum employment. Therefore, they compare their expectations of economic growth, inflation, and employment with realised performance. They also monitor labour-market conditions, and consider financial and international developments to determine the stance of monetary policy. The goals of price stability and full employment involve the question of economic slack.[20] Underlying this notion are three critical economic "speed limits":

1. The *potential rate* of growth or the sustainable growth rate when capital and labour are fully employed. In the United States, the Congressional Budget Office estimated the rate is 2% a year from 2018 to 2022.
2. The *full employment rate* of civilian unemployment. In the United States, the estimated rate is around 5%.[21]
3. The central bank's *target rate* of inflation—measured by the year-over-year rate of increase in the CPI (consumer price index). In the United States, the target is 2%, and as Fig. 4.7 shows the rate of inflation is in the 2% range.

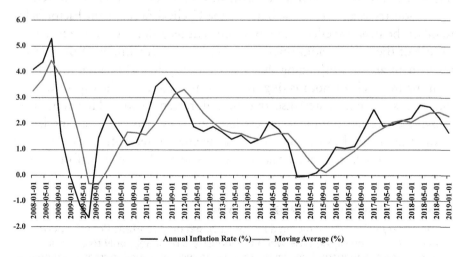

**Fig. 4.7**   US annual inflation rate (Y/Y). (Source: Federal Reserve Economic Data)

The current thinking in academic and professional circles is that the US economy does not have much slack remaining. This view is largely based on the fact that the economy is growing faster than its potential (see actual growth rates, Fig. 4.4) of 2% yearly, whereas the unemployment rate is running well below 5%, suggesting diminishing capacity. The less slack there is in economy, the more the pressure for prices to rise. Therefore, it is hardly a coincidence that the Federal Reserve started in December 2015 to step up the Fed Funds target rate from 0.25–0.50% to 2.25–2.50% in November 2018 and has held it at that range since then. At the November 2018 Federal Open Market Committee (FOMC) meeting when the Committee agreed to raise the range to 2.25–2.50%, the press release mentioned "a strong labor market and inflation near its symmetric 2 percent objective". Putting all the information, including the very puzzling fact that inflation is tame, a *reasonable* interpretation of the data would suggest that the industry is in the late stage of the cycle, though to emphasise, the turning point is unpredictable.

### Cyclical Adjustment Factor

Our aim is to find a way to reduce the sensitivity of the BRR to the effects of the cycle on current financial performance. One approach is to build a counter-cyclical bias in business risk through a risk factor that we label as Cyclical Adjustment Factor. The way it works is as follows. If the credit analyst determines that the industry is at or near the peak of the cycle, this calls for tempering the BRR with the Cyclical Adjustment Factor in business risk; conversely, if the industry is at or near the bottom, the Cyclical Adjustment Factor helps to offset the negative effects due to the current recession. Avoid the mechanical use of the cyclical adjustment. The obvious shortcomings of the cyclical adjustment are (a) misjudging the phase of the cycle and making the adjustment prematurely or not making the adjustment, and (b) the expected turning points do not materialise due to unforeseen factors. However, these weaknesses are not unique to expert-judgement models but to all models of credit default risk. In such situations, management intervention is required. If the key success factors are weak (strong), whereas financial performance is

---

**Point-in-Time Versus Through-the-Cycle**

Lenders try to avoid upgrading a borrower based on its current financial performance at the top of the cycle when the industry is booming, only to downgrade later when the industry is at the bottom of the cycle and the industry as a whole is struggling. This could lead to three significant distortions: (1) bad lending decisions, (2) incorrectly placing a borrower on the watch list, and (3) unstable risk concentrations in the loan portfolio.

strong (weak), this is a sign that the cycle is driving the results. An alternative approach to the Cyclical Adjustment Factor is the use of current and *pro forma* financial statements for the assessment of financial risk, which we will examine in a later section.

> **When to Apply Cyclical Adjustment?**
>
> The cyclical adjustment should be used only after a careful determination that the firm's PIT performance is due mainly to the business cycle rather than to key success factors in business strategy, competitiveness, and management. Furthermore, the cyclical adjustment is best applied when the odds of a recession or recovery are judged to be relatively high.

The descriptors for business risk, including those for the Cyclical Adjustment Factor, are shown in Table 4.10 for an airline company. Here is how we (or you the credit analyst) go about applying them. To differentiate the phases of the cycle, we look for clues in leading economic indicators, the stance on monetary policy, monetary policy announcements, and the actual trends in official interest rates. We then apply the scoring of business risk using the Cyclical Adjustment Factor and the other risk factors for a highly cyclical industry and we choose an airline company for this purpose. The credit analyst selects the appropriate descriptors in the usual fashion, and they are the ones highlighted. With these selections and the built-in formulas in the model, the scorecard does the calculation. The weighted score for business risk assessment is 5.0, which is a rating of "BB–". The overall score is sensitive to the cyclical adjustment, *ceteris paribus*. For example, if it were "BBB" instead of "BB", the overall score jumps to 7.5, which maps to "BBB–".

## 4.7  Management Risk Assessment

The management of any organisation requires developing a business plan consisting of broad goals, developing the strategies and the tactics to achieve the objectives, and executing the plan, given the resources of physical capital, human capital, financial capital, material inputs, and technology. Management necessarily includes the people who manage an organisation, so corporate governance plays a pivotal role in the success of the plan, the performance of the company, and, therefore, its creditworthiness. Management risk assessment, like business risk assessment, is qualitative and subjective for the most part. Because of this, it would be an understatement to say that getting an accurate assessment of management risk is more difficult than the financial

**Table 4.10** Business risk assessment (airline)

| Risk criteria | W (%) | A — 12 | BBB — 9 | BB — 6 | B AND BELOW — 5 |
|---|---|---|---|---|---|
| 1. Compositive position | 0.5 | | | | |
| Operating cost | 0.2 | A combination of the following: Effectively controls non-fuel cost. CASM (cost per available seat mile/kilometre) below the average of the peer group. Achieves consistently a high and relatively stable load factor. Able to pass on cost increase (e.g., fuel surcharges) with moderate impact on passenger loads. Has the required scale to negotiate lower prices with suppliers. Has sufficient financial resources to hedge effectively against exchange-rate and fuel-price risks. Not heavy burdened by legacy costs. Able to manage capacity in response to unforeseen changes in demand. Enjoys stable relations with unions. | A combination of the following: Reasonably effective in controlling costs. CASM in line with the average of the peer group. Achieves high load factors with fluctuations. Some leeway to pass on cost increases but passenger loads are adversely affected. Limited ability to negotiate lower prices with suppliers. Has adequate financial resources to hedge reasonably well against exchange-rate and fuel-price risks. Burdened by significant legacy cost. Has some ability to manage capacity in response to unforeseen changes in demand. Enjoys fairly stable relations unions. Minor disruptions occur. | A combination of the following: Limited ability to control non-fuel cost. CASM exceeds average of the peer group. Limited ability to pass on cost increases without adversely affecting passenger loads. Some ability to negotiate lower prices with suppliers. Achieves below-average load factor. Limited ability to pass on cost increases without adversely affecting demand. Has limited resources to hedge against a substantial portion of exchange-rate and fuel-price risks. Burdened by high legacy cost. Has limited flexibility to manage capacity in response to changes in demand. Experiences disruptions from labour disputes. | A combination of the following: Limited ability to control non-fuel cost. CASM well exceeds average of the peer group. Achieves a load factor that is often at or below the airline's breakeven. Unable to pass on cost increases. No ability to negotiate lower prices with suppliers. Very limited in its ability to hedge against exchange-rate and fuel-price risks. Burdened by material legacy costs. Limited flexibility to manage capacity in response to changes in demand. Adversarial relations between the airline and unions. |
| Operating revenue | 0.2 | A combination of the following: Above-average growth in total revenue exceeding 10.1 per cent over 1 year. Achieves consistently a high and relatively stable load factor well in excess of the airline's breakeven. Leverages its varied market/demand segments effectively for price discrimination to increase passenger yields. Participation in global alliances (e.g., the Star Alliance, Sky Team, Oneworld) and many code-sharing partnerships. Involved in joint ventures with many major international airlines. | A combination of the following: Average but stable growth in total revenue of between 5.1 per cent and 10 per cent over 1 year. Achieves a load factor that exceeds the airline's breakeven, although inconsistently. Has market/demand segments that allow for effective price discrimination to increase passenger yields. Participation in global alliances (e.g., the Star Alliance, Sky Team, Oneworld) and limited code-sharing partnerships. Involved in joint ventures with a few major international airlines. | Below-average growth in total revenue of between 0% and 5% over 1 year. Achieves a load factor that exceeds the airline's breakeven, but passenger loads fluctuate significantly. Has a relatively narrow market/demand segments for price discrimination to increase passenger yield significantly. Participation in global alliances (e.g., the Star Alliance, Sky Team, Oneworld) and limited code-sharing partnerships. | No growth or negative growth in total revenue over 1 year. Achieves a load factor that is often at or below the airline's breakeven. Has no leeway for price discrimination for passenger-yield increases. Not a member of a global alliances (e.g., the Star Alliance, Sky Team, Oneworld). Limited code-sharing opportunities |
| Fleet | **0.2** | A combination of the following: Airline owns a large proportion of its fleet. Leased planes are on long-term leases with staggered expiry dates. Modern fleet and equipment; fuel and maintenance efficient. Ongoing fleet renewal programme with a good mix of firm and optional orders. The fleet mix is compatible with the routes. | A combination of the following: Airline leases most of its planes on a combination of long- and short-term leases. Some bunching of the expiry dates exist. Good fleet and equipment. Ongoing fleet renewal programme with a fair mix of firm and optional orders. The fleet mix is compatible with the routes. | A combination of the following: Airline leases almost all of its planes on medium-term leases with some flexibility. The fleet mix is inadequate for the routes. Some fleet renewal planning occurs, but disrupted by late aircraft deliveries at times | A combination of the following: Airline leases almost all of its planes on medium-term leases with some flexibility. Age of the fleet well above average. Fuel and maintenance inefficient. The fleet mix is poorly matched with the routes. Limited fleet renewal planning occurs, and aircraft purchases tend to be opportunistic |

| Criteria | Weight | | | | |
|---|---|---|---|---|---|
| Revenue base | 0.2 | Above-average growth in total revenue exceeding 10.1 per cent over 1 year. Leverages its varied market/demand segments effectively for price discrimination to increase passenger yields. Participation in global alliances (e.g., the Star Alliance, Sky Team, One world) and many code-sharing partnerships. Involved in joint ventures with many major international airlines | Average but stable growth in total revenue of between 5.1 per cent and 10 per cent over 1 year. Has market/demand segments that allow for effective price discrimination to increase passenger yields. Participation in global alliances (e.g., the Star Alliance, Sky Team, One world) and limited code-sharing partnerships. Involved in joint ventures with a few major international airlines | Below-average growth in total revenue of between 0% and 5% over 1 year. Has too narrow market/demand segments to apply price discrimination for passenger-yield increases. Participation in global alliances (e.g., the Star Alliance, Sky Team, One world) and limited code-sharing partnerships. | No growth or negative growth in total revenue over 1 year. Has no leeway for price discrimination for passenger-yield increases. Not a member of a global alliances (e.g., the Star Alliance, Sky Team, One world). Limited code-sharing opportunities |
| Customer service and safety | 0.2 | A combination of the following: Well established and highly regarded name regionally or globally. Has a successful loyalty programme (confirmed by large and growing number of participants). Gets consistently high ratings from global systems that classify airlines and airports. Consistently high reputation for service quality. | A combination of the following: Established and recognised name regionally or globally. Moderately successful loyalty programme. Gets good ratings from global systems that classify airlines and airports. Solid reputation for service quality; mostly positive comments. | A combination of the following: Low name recognition globally but well recognised regionally. Has a loyalty programme or may be planning to introduce one. Gets satisfactory ratings from global systems that classify airlines and airports. Satisfactory reputation for quality service; no major unfavourable comments. | A combination of the following: Name recognition more confined to price-sensitive travellers. Does not have a loyalty programme. Unrated or gets poor ratings from global systems that classify airlines and airport. Mostly poor service quality. Offers the lowest prices among competitors flying the same routes. |
| 2. Market position | 0.5 / 0.33 | | | | |
| Revenue diversification by geography and services | 0.334 | A combination of the following: Highly diversified across regions and continents. Highly diversified across regional and intercontinental flights. Non-passenger services (cargo/ other) represent an important source of revenue (more than 10%) | A combination of the following: Well diversified across regions and continents. Well diversified across regional and intercontinental flights. Non-passenger services (cargo/ other) a meaningful source of revenue (between 5% and 10%) | A combination of the following: Limited diversification across regions and continents. Non-passenger services (cargo/ other) are an important source of revenue (less than 5%). | A combination of the following: The markets are mostly regional. Passengers are the only source of revenue. |
| Market share | 0.33333 | A leader in many key markets | Ranks in the middle in terms of market shares in some key markets | Ranks low in terms of market shares in some key markets | Not amongst the market-share leaders in terms of key markets. Amongst leaders of only small, or mostly niche markets |
| Route network | 0.33333 | A combination of the following: Very profitable routes with very high ratio of business/leisure travel. Accessibility to all key cities of markets served. High flight frequency with favourable time slots. Wide portfolio of international route and slot rights to support growth. Traffic routes have strong growth potential. | A combination of the following: Profitable routes with high ratio of business/leisure travel. Accessibility to most key cities of markets served. High flight frequency, most with favourable time slots. A decent portfolio of route and slot rights to support growth. Traffic routes have reasonable growth potential. | A combination of the following: Somewhat profitable routes with low ratio of business/leisure travel. Accessibility to some key cities of markets served. Fairly frequent flights, some with unfavourable time slots. Has a narrow portfolio of route and slot rights; inadequate for further growth. Traffic routes have reasonable growth potential. | A combination of the following: Primarily or only regional routes that serve as feeder to other airlines. Infrequent flights to key cities with usually unfavourable time slots. Lacks sufficient route and slot rights to support growth. Traffic routes have low growth potential. Low-margin chartered flights to vacation destinations. |

(continued)

**Table 4.10** (continued)

| 3. Cyclic position | 0 | | |
| | 0.33 | | |
| Cyclical adjustment factor | 1 | Changes in the monthly LEI (index of the leading economic indicators) suggest the business cycle may be at or approaching the trough.<br><br>Monetary policy remains expansionary<br>Official interest rates are not falling as fast as before or show signs of bottoming out. | Changes in the LEI suggest the business cycle is in the mid to late stages.<br><br>Monetary policy announcements suggest interest rates will rise in the future, a signal that the central bank expects growth to continue.<br>Official interest rates are rising in response to strong economic growth. | Changes in the monthly LEI point to economic slowdown but no clear warning of recession.<br><br>Monetary policy announcements suggest interest rates will fall in the future, consistent with the warning indicated by the changes in the LEI.<br>Central bank has stopped raising official interest rates or is holding them steady within the announced range. | Changes in the monthly LEI signal recession in the next 6-9 months.<br><br>Monetary policy announcements suggest interest rates will fall in the future, confirming the LEI warning.<br>Official interest rates are falling faster than usual as the target range expands. |

analysis. If there is any doubt about this observation, think of all the analyses performed over the years on these industry giants—Enron, WorldCom, Nortel, and Parmalat—but just a few might have yellow-flagged or red-flagged the serious management risks that ultimately brought down these industry giants.

A careful choice of evidence-based risk factors can reduce the subjectivity. We focus on three attributes of management risk and we give them equal weights shown in the brackets.

1. Management quality (weight 1/3)
2. Business strategy (weight 1/3)
3. Financial policy and strategy (weight 1/3)

## 4.7.1 Management Quality and Addressing Information Asymmetry in BRR Determination

From the perspective of the credit analyst, the assessment of management quality should at least cover four broad attributes:

1. Qualification
2. Experience
3. Competence
4. Character

The best management requires all four. Management quality brings into sharp focus corporate governance[22] and character that we examined in the "Five Cs" in Chap. 1. Character assessment focuses on the integrity or the ethical conduct of management and the quality of leadership, but obtaining information is very difficult. When the analyst eventually gets his/her hands on the information, it is often too late as we saw with the financial scandals such as Enron Corporation, WorldCom, Nortel Corporation, and many more. The management factor is the most difficult due to the principal–agency problems of information asymmetry that we examined in Chap. 1. To recall, information asymmetry in the loans market occurs when the borrower possesses better information than the lender in a credit relationship. Hidden information and actions prevent a lender from assessing creditworthiness and accurately determining a BRR. Given that information asymmetry poses a serious impediment, how might a lender attempt to reduce the problem in its risk rating process? The method that we propose is the use of the override functionality that we discussed in Chap. 3.

## 4.7.2 Business Strategy

A company is expected to have a business plan with clearly articulated goals and strategies that include an assessment of the risks to the plan and the mitigating actions. The goals typically include profitability, growth, and market share. The credit analyst starts at the macro level to determine whether the plan is realistic to begin with, and then assesses at the more micro level whether the plan is attainable with the resources at hand. Evaluating the aggressiveness of the plan is thus critical to determining whether the goals are feasible and sustainable without weakening the company's capital structure by taking on more debt. Complementing this forward assessment is an investigation into the company's past performance in plan execution; a history of failures is usually a good predictor of poor future performance.

Companies do not typically share their business plans, the actual document, with credit analysts; however, credit analysts who work for banks usually have access to the plans of private and closely held businesses that are the banks' customers (business borrowers). Companies are often willing to submit their business plans to a lender when they are in the market for a sizeable loan. Credit analysts learn about a public company's business plan through interviews with senior management, information in annual reports, and the call reports of account managers.

## 4.7.3 Financial Plan

The other important document is the financial plan, which translates the business plan in numbers—the language of accounting. The plan is communicated in *pro forma* or projected income statement, balance sheet, and cash-flow statement, and the performance measurements or targets. The credit analyst reviews the financial plan for consistency with the business plan and the *external* financing requirements. An understanding of industry risks helps in assessing the objectives. The previous comment on access to the business plan also applies to financial plan.

# 4.8   Scoring Management Risk

As we did for financial risk, industry risk, and business risk, we apply the same scoring methodology for management risk assessment. As shown in Table 4.11, the three factors discussed above—the weights, the grades, and the descriptors of the grades—make up the management risk section of the scorecard. For

**Table 4.11** Management risk assessment

| | | 12 | 9 | 6 |
|---|---|---|---|---|
| Management quality | 33.33% | Written or verbal financial policy and strategy for which some or all of the following apply:<br>Highly qualified and competent people in senior management<br>Highly qualified and competent people in lower levels of management<br>At least 20 years of exceptional performance relative to business plans and strategies through many business cycles<br>Ranks consistently in the second quartile of industry peers | Written or verbal financial policy and strategy for which some or all of the following apply:<br>Qualified and competent people in senior management<br>Qualified and competent people in lower levels of management<br>At least 10 years of solid performance relative to business plans and strategies and through one business cycle<br>Ranks consistently in the third quartile of industry peers | Professionally managed company for which one or more of the following apply:<br>A few qualified and competent people in senior management<br>A few qualified and competent people in lower levels of management<br>A choppy record of successful performance relative to business plans and strategies over a period of at least 5 years<br>May have had severe challenges in one economic downturn<br>Ranks consistently in the fourth quartile of industry peers |
| Business strategy | 33.33% | Written or verbal financial policy and strategy for which some or all of the following apply:<br>3-5 year time horizon<br>Goals, operating strategy, and financial strategy clearly defined<br>Plan is consistent with industry and economic environment<br>Goals are achievable within the current financial policy and strategy<br>Key performance indicators maintained and often exceeded in the past<br>Strong expectation the company would maintain its high competitive performance over the plan horizon | Written or verbal financial policy and strategy for which some or all of the following apply:<br>1-3 year time horizon<br>Goals, operating strategy, and financial strategy clearly defined<br>Plan is consistent with industry and economic environment<br>Goals are achievable within the current financial policy and strategy<br>Average performance in the recent past<br>Company is expected to maintain or slightly improve its competitive advantages over the plan horizon | Written or verbal business plan with one or more of the following:<br>1-2 year time horizon<br>Goals, operating strategy, and financial strategy not clearly defined<br>Plan is unrealistic in its assessment of the business and economic environment<br>Plan is more backward than forward looking with more effort directed to correcting past errors<br>Not likely to achieve all goals within the current financial policy and strategy<br>Low expectation the company would maintain its competitive position over the plan horizon |
| Financial strategy | 33.33% | Written or verbal financial policy and strategy for which some or all of the following apply:<br>Policy on spending, borrowing, and accounting practices consistent with business plan<br>Financial strategy translated into a financial plan, that is the *pro forma* financial statements with the key performance measurements<br>Projected debt levels and cash flow sustainable<br>Highly likely to maintain financial flexibility or accessibility to external funding | Written or verbal financial policy and strategy for which some or all of the following apply:<br>Policy on spending, borrowing, and accounting practices mostly consistent with business<br>Financial strategy translated into a financial plan, i.e., the *pro forma* financial statements with the key performance measurements<br>Projected leverage and cash flow ratios are average by industry comparisons<br>Likely to maintain some degree of financial flexibility or accessibility to external funding | Written or verbal financial policy and strategy vague with one or more the following:<br>Policy on spending, borrowing, and accounting practices unclear<br>Financial strategy and goals not measurable in some cases and not translated into a *pro forma* financial statements<br>Financial strategies of the past have failed to meet plan goals<br>Aggressive leverage policy<br>Limited financial flexibility |

illustration, we show a scorecard with grades A, BBB, BB, and their descriptors. In this illustration, a placement of "BBB" for each of the three risk factors and no override produce a weighted average score of 9, which is expected according to the mapping.

## 4.9    Financial Risk Assessment

In Chap. 2, we looked at financial ratios: how they are defined, how they are measured, what they are used for, and how they are to be interpreted for effective use. In this chapter, the focus is on the actual application of the ratios for the section, "Financial Risk Assessment". There are four quantifiable categories that cover the income statement, balance sheet, and the cash-flow statement and one qualitative category, financial flexibility.

1. Profitability
2. Asset utilisation and efficiency
3. Debt and solvency
4. Liquidity
5. Financial flexibility

We stated in the previous chapter that there are numerous financial ratios but, in practice, the credit analyst needs no more than 10–12 of them. Quantity does not necessarily mean quality when it comes to financial ratio analysis. The use of many ratios does not yield significantly more information because they are strongly correlated or collinear with other ratios being considered. Furthermore, even amongst the commonly used metrics some are unsuitable for certain industries and, in their places, the credit analyst must be selective. For example, it makes no sense assessing the efficiency of firms that provide services, such as banks and airlines, by looking at inventory turnover ratios. But for manufacturing and merchandising, such ratios are useful. For non-financial entities, the following metrics are commonly used to assess a firm's debt-servicing ability:

- Total debt/capital (%)
- FFO (funds from operations)/total debt (%)
- Free (operating) cash flow/total debt (%)
- EBITDA or earnings before interest, taxes, depreciation, amortisation, and rent (EBITDAR)/interest (×)
- EBIT/interest (×)

The fifth category, financial flexibility—a qualitative measure—is as much a significant determinant of creditworthiness as are the quantitative measures. Borrowers that have wide access to diverse sources of external financing are less likely to experience a liquidity crunch and, therefore, less likely to default. Think of an airline company, which typically faces very volatile cash flow due to cyclical and seasonal factors, and unpredictable factors such as fuel price, strikes, and terrorist attack. At the same time, airline companies are highly leveraged and access to financing is a vital input in an airline's "production function". The sources of external financing include the following:

### A. Equity Instruments:

    a. Cash from individuals with "deep pockets"
    b. Common and preferred shares sold to the public
    c. Private placement (stocks sold to a small number of investors rather than part of a public offering)

### B. Debt Instruments[23]:

    a. Committed and uncommitted loan facilities offered by banks and non-bank financial institutions (FIs). The loans are provided by individual banks or a syndicate of banks (such loans are called syndicated loans). Loans include term loans, revolving line of credit, commercial paper (CP)-back up line, bridge loan, and lease financing.
    b. Secured and highly monitored financing by banks and non-bank FIs (e.g., asset-based lending, and factoring)
    c. Secured and unsecured bonds (a long-maturity loan—up to 30 years for the US Treasury bond)
    d. Notes (a short-maturity bond)
    e. Debentures (unsecured bonds)
    f. Private placement (bonds sold to a small number of investors rather than part of a public offering)
    g. Commercial paper (CP), bankers acceptances (BA), and other short-term debt instruments
    h. Structured finance (non-conventional, complex, and high-risk financial transactions)[24]

### C. Sale of Assets

    • Sale of fixed assets, equipment, and rights.

Financial flexibility is a qualitative factor that is more difficult to define than financial ratios; however, asking the right questions enables a credit analyst to assess the risk:

1. Are all or many sources of financing available to the borrower?
2. Relative to the current portion of its total liabilities, is the borrower able to raise all or just a fraction of its funding requirements?
3. If the borrower is a public (externally rated) company, what are the ratings that will ease access to external funding?
4. If the borrower is a private (externally unrated) company, how does it compare to a public company in terms of financial strength?

Clearly, public companies that are investment grade or better are in a stronger position to obtain financing from many sources and in the amounts needed. In fact, external ratings are necessary for certain types of borrowing such as corporate bonds and commercial paper. Usually, the users are multinational corporations (listed on one or more stock exchanges) and very large private companies. The private companies that are as financially strong as the public companies would be expected to have similar access in terms of potential sources and the amounts that can be raised. In contrast, those that are below investment grade are at a relative disadvantage. Based on these questions, we define the three grades for financial flexibility (see Table 4.12).

## 4.9.1 Data Sources and the Scope of the Financial Risk Assessment

There are generally three levels of financial reporting in terms of the degree of assurance and due diligence performed by a chartered professional accountant (CPA). Audited financial statements are the standard for the primary source because this form of engagement with the CPA provides the highest level of assurance. It is often the case, however, that audited financial statements are unavailable, as with start-up businesses, and, in this situation, the risk analysts must use unaudited reports. The Review Engagement report is one of them. In this report, although an audit is not required, the accountant who prepares the financial statements expresses limited assurance.

A third source of financial information that requires neither an audit nor any opinion is the Compilation Engagement or Notice to Reader (NTR). Therefore, an uncertified accountant or professional bookkeeper can prepare a Compilation Engagement although CPAs perform this accounting service. Another type of unaudited financial report that should be used when formal financial statements are unavailable is the *pro forma* financial statement, which is based on estimates and assumptions of the firm's management.

Consider a borrower who already has a credit exposure with a lender, or is applying for a loan for the first time. The borrower either is obligated to provide financial statements under the loan agreement, or is required to provide all necessary financial information with the loan application. In order to determine the obligor's current and future financial strength, the credit analyst must first have a good idea as to whether current and recent historical information is reliable; hence, the type of financial information that the credit analyst has to work with is important. Let us examine the following three cases:

1. The firm is stable and is operating in an industry that is relatively non-cyclical (indicated by low correlation with the *overall economy* or its gross domestic product).
2. The firm's performance over the last three years is not indicative of future results.
3. The firm has acquired another company from a different industry.

Given these conditions, the credit analyst needs to decide whether historical (including current) data are sufficient, or should be supplemented with *pro forma* financial forecast.

In the first case where a borrower's performance has been stable in many years, once the credit analyst determines there will be no abrupt changes in the company's performance a year or two away, then the audited and interim financial reports are adequate. Stability does not mean no changes, for a company can be growing and gaining market share at a sustainable rate. Financial indicators for the last twelve months (LTM) of the current year and the previous two years would suffice for the financial risk assessment.

In the second case, for example a company in the very late phase of a highly cyclical industry, the predictive value of historical financial performance decays exponentially going back in the recent past. A more accurate assessment of future performance requires the LTM of the current year and the next twelve months (NTM) financial indicators derived from the *pro forma* financials.[25]

The third case is one where the particular change, such as an acquisition or sizeable increase in debt, materially affects the balance sheet (the capital structure), income statement (profit and profitability), and the cash-flow statement (the future cash flow). The financial information would consist of LTM financial performance adjusted for the changes that will affect all four ratio categories listed earlier: profitability, asset utilisation and efficiency, debt and solvency, and liquidity.

# 4.10 Scoring Financial Risk

Let us consider a straightforward case requiring no NTM financials; recent and current financials are just good enough. The firm's operating performance has been stable, the industry is weakly cyclical, and, furthermore, judging from all the coincident and leading economic indicators, the credit analyst determines the business cycle still has plenty of momentum. We also assume the firm has no off-balance sheet debt. With these complications assumed away, the performance measures are for the LTM and the previous two years. The next step is to spread the financial statements, calculate the financial measurements, and select the appropriate descriptors in the scorecard to calculate a financial risk score.

Let us examine the weighting applied (see Table 4.12) and the rationale. The financial risk assessment carries the largest weight of 40% in the composite risk rating. The first four risk criteria are quantitative and thus measurable: (1) profitability, (2) asset utilisation and efficiency, (3) debt and solvency, and (4) liquidity. We attach more weight to debt and solvency and liquidity because these are the key drivers in the ability to repay. Debt and solvency, and liquidity are each rated 25%. The fifth criterion, financial flexibility, is qualitative but, as you can see, it has a relatively large weight of 20% reflecting the fact that a liquidity crisis is what often triggers bankruptcy rather than unprofitability or even high indebtedness. Thus, lower weights are allotted to profitability and to asset utilisation and efficiency.

In this simplified example, we use 6 of the 16 risk grades shown in Table 3.1 of Chap. 3 and illustrative financial ratios (see below), which all increase or decrease monotonically with the risk grades for the defined ranges of the ratios. For example, the risk grade always increases as the EBITDA Margin rises; similarly, the risk grade always declines as the Debt/EBITDA ratio increases. To score financial risk assessment, we work with following hypothetical information:

- EBITDA margin: 10.2%
- EBIT/average assets: 12%
- A/R turnover: 40 days
- Inventory turnover: 39 days
- Debt/EBITDA: 3.6×
- Debt/capital: 50%
- Funds from operations (FFO)/total debt: 22%
- Current ratio: 2.0×
- Financial flexibility: company can draw from committed and uncommitted bank facilities, and so on.

**Table 4.12** Financial risk assessment

| RISK CRITERIA AND MEASURES | W (%) | AA | A | BBB+ | BBB | BBB– | BB |
|---|---|---|---|---|---|---|---|
| | | 15 | 12 | 10 | 9 | 8 | 6 |
| **1. PROFITABILITY** | **15%** | | | | | | |
| *EBITDA Margin (50%)* | *50%* | | 23.1–28.0 | 18.1–23.0 | 13.1–18.0 | 8.0–13.0 | |
| *EBIT/Avg Assets (50%)* | *50%* | | 20.3–25.8 | 15.2–20.2 | 10.1–15.1 | 5.0–10.0 | |
| **2. ASSET UTILISATION AND EFFICIENCY** | **15%** | | | | | | |
| *Accounts Receivable Turnover Days (50%)* | *50%* | | 19.0–29.0 | 30.0–35.0 | 36–45.0 | 46–55.0 | |
| *Inventory Turnover Days (50%)* | *50%* | | 14.0–24.0 | 25.0–30.0 | 30.1–40.0 | 40.1–50.0 | |
| **3. DEBT AND SOLVENCY** | **25%** | | | | | | |
| *Debt/EBITDA (50%)* | *50%* | | 0.6–1.5 | 1.6–2.5 | 2.6–3.5 | 3.6–4.5 | |
| *Debt/Capital (50%)* | *50%* | | 35.0–40.1 | 40.0–45.0 | 45.1–55.0 | 55.1–65.0 | |
| **4. LIQUIDITY** | **25%** | | | | | | |
| *FFO/Total Debt (50%)* | *50%* | | 60.1–70.0 | 50.1–60.0 | 35.1–50.0 | 20.0–35.0 | |
| *Current ratio (50%)* | *50%* | | 2.6–3.0 | 2.1–2.5 | 1.6–2.0 | 1.0–1.5 | |
| **5. FINANCIAL FLEXIBILITY** | **20%** | | | | | | |
| **Ability to raise equity and debt financing** | *100%* | A multinational company (public or private). Able to raise debt, equity, and mezzanine financing. If public company, it is rated high investment grade. If unrated company, financially strong as a medium-grade public company. | | NO DESCRIPTORS | Company can draw from committed and uncommitted bank facilities. Company listed on a major stock exchange and can raise equity. If public company, it is rated medium investment grade. If unrated company, financially strong as a high-grade public company. | NO DESCRIPTORS | Limited access to conventional bank loans, the bond, and equity markets. Access to asset based financing such as ABL and factoring. If public company, it is rated non-investment grade. If unrated company, financially weak a high-grade public company. |

The scorecard for financial analysis assessment is complete once the factors are grouped (bucketed) and assigned weights. As we saw for the other sections, the application of the financial risk scorecard is straightforward: the credit analyst makes a placement within the appropriate scorecard range. The algorithm in the background produces the composite score and the associated risk grade. We highlight the placements in Table 4.12. In this example, the scorecard uses the weighted sum formula, and the result is a score of 8.6 (rounded to 1 decimal place), representing "BBB" (medium risk) from Table 3.1.

## 4.11 Calculating the Composite BRR

The overall BRR is simply the weighted average of the four risk criteria: industry risk (6.9), business risk (7.5), management risk (9.0), and financial risk (8.6) from corresponding score cards discussed above. Assume risk criteria weights of 10%, 20%, 20%, and 50% respectively. Then the weighted average is as follows:

$$BRR = \sum_{i=1}^{4} w_i * \text{Risk Criteria Score}_i$$

$$BRR = (0.1)(6.9) + (0.2)(7.5) + (0.2)(9.0) + (0.5)(8.6) = 8.3$$

A composite score of 8.3 maps to "BBB".

## Notes

1. For a primer on this subject, see Nagy, Pancras J. (1984), *Country Risk: How to Assess, Quantify, and Monitor It*, London: Euromoney Publications, 1984; Mina Toksoz and The Economist, *Guide to Country Risk: How to Identify, Manage and Mitigate the Risks of Doing Business Across Borders*, December 2014. Country risk ratings are provided by credit risk rating agencies such as Fitch and Moody's, and political risk analysis organisations such as EIU (Economist Intelligence Unit). See EIU, *Country Risk Model: An Interactive Tool for Analysing Country and Sovereign Risk*.
2. Porter, M. (1980), *Competitive Strategy: Techniques for Analyzing Industries and Competitors*, The Free Press.
3. See Porter, op. cit. page 158. The author acknowledges certain "legitimate criticisms" of the life cycle approach and the S-curve depiction.
4. In a competitive market, a firm minimises costs at the lowest point on its short run average cost curve where $ATC$ (average total cost) = $MC$ (marginal cost) because $MC$ always cuts $ATC$ at the lowest point on the $ATC$ curve.

5. The markup rule says $P = MC\left(\dfrac{\epsilon_p}{1+\epsilon_p}\right)$. Divide the numerator and denominator of the term in bracket by $\epsilon_p$, and the result is $P = MC\left(\dfrac{1}{\eta+1}\right)$, where $\eta = 1/\epsilon_p$.

6. Reported in the New York Post. Andrew Pollack, *Drug Goes from $13.50 a Tablet to $750, Overnight*, September 20, 2015. The article states: "Specialists in infectious disease are protesting a gigantic overnight increase in the price of a 62-year-old drug that is the standard of care for treating a life-threatening parasitic infection. The drug, called Daraprim, was acquired in August by Turing Pharmaceuticals, a start-up run by a former hedge fund manager. Turing immediately raised the price to $750 a tablet from $13.50, bringing the annual cost of treatment for some patients to hundreds of thousands of dollars."

7. In the US coal industry, companies mine in Federal lands that the government leases at preferential rates to keep the mines in Appalachia open. In Canada, asbestos—declared by the international community the cause of *mesothelioma*, a form of cancer that develops in the lining of the lungs, abdomen, or heart, and banned outright by the European Union (EU) but not totally by the United States—had been a major industry (concentrated in Quebec) until 1973 when production peaked at around 1.7 million tonnes. In 2011 the last two remaining asbestos mines in Canada, which were both located in the province of Quebec (Jeffrey Mine and Thetford Mines), halted production. Previously, the firms survived with the help of government loans and guarantees and, significantly, Canadian government support for asbestos mining and exports, despite the total EU ban and the partial US ban on asbestos use. Most of the asbestos that Canada continued to produce went to developing countries, mostly India, as exports.

8. NBER (The National Bureau of Economic Research). NBER website: http://www.nber.org

9. Berman J., and Pfleeger J., (1997), Which industries are sensitive to business cycles? *Monthly Labor Review*, February.

10. Not all labour is variable cost. In the software and pharmaceutical industries, companies do not lay off R&D workers in response to lower sales. Typically, the jobs in sales positions are amongst the first to feel the cutbacks.

11. Standard and Poor's (2013), *General Criteria, Methodology: Industry Risk, S&P*, November, Ratings Direct, November 19, 2013.

12. See S&P (2008), *Understanding Standard & Poor's Rating Definitions*. "BBB" stress scenario: An issuer or obligation rated "BBB" should be able to withstand a moderate level of stress and still meet its financial obligations. A GDP decline of as much as 3% and unemployment at 10% would be reflective of a moderate stress scenario. A drop in the stock market by up to 50% would similarly indicate moderate stress.

"BB" stress scenario: An issuer or obligation rated "BB" should be able to withstand a modest level of stress and still meet its financial obligations. For example, GDP might decline by as much as 1% and unemployment might reach 8%. The stock market could drop by up to 25%.

13. Standard & Poor's (2010), *Key Credit Factors: Criteria for Rating the Airline Industry*.

14. Government of Canada, Competition Bureau (2015), *Abuse of Dominance: A Serious Anti-Competitive Offense*.

15. Government of Canada, Competition Bureau, op. cit.

16. Load Factor: The number of revenue passenger miles (RPMs) expressed as a percentage of available seat miles (ASMs), either on a particular flight or for the entire system. Load factor represents the proportion of airline output that is actually consumed. To calculate this figure, divide RPMs by ASMs. Load factor for a single flight can also be calculated by dividing the number of passengers by the number of seats. The increases in load factor as well as passenger revenue per available seat mile (PRASM) are positive indicators of efficiency, and reflect the company's strong operational capabilities. The increased load factor will result in higher margins as the company is able to generate more passenger revenue for the same fixed cost.

17. It is incumbent on those who dismiss history as guide to the future to explain why the expansion will go on expanding forever, just as in the reverse, when the economy is in recession, that it will go on declining forever.

18. Astolfi, R. (2016), *Did the OECD Composite Leading Indicator See It Coming?* OECD Statistics Directorate, OECD Insights.

19. The precursor to the 1980s economic recession—including the double dip—was the spiralling inflation that slightly topped 14% in the first half of 1980. The Federal Reserve tightened monetary policy and the Fed Funds rate climbed to as high as 20% in 1981 before the inflation rate fell back, to 2.4% by July 1982. In the early 1990s, the economy was already weak when business and consumer confidence had already taken a beating due to the spike in oil prices after Iraq invaded Kuwait on August 2, 1990. In the 2008–2009 recession, the underlying cause was the financial crisis, the worst since the Great Depression. Inflation had been rather tame and interest rates had been low and stable since the mid-1980s. A real estate bubble got underway in the mid-1990s, inflated by subprime mortgages, which in turn led to the proliferation of mortgage-backed securities known as CDOs (collateralised debt obligation). The collapse of the real estate market triggered a deep financial crisis, all of which contributed to the recession.

20. Congressional Budget Office (2016), *An Update to the Budget and Economic Outlook 2016–2026*, Congress of the US CBO. See projections for the unemployment rate and potential GDP growth in Tables 2.1 and 2.3 respectively. *The natural rate of unemployment (NAIRU) is the non-accelerating inflation rate of unemployment, or U\**. It is the lowest level that unemployment can reach

without generating excess inflation. Below this long-run rate, wage and price inflation spirals upward. NAIRU, like the natural rate of interest—the rate of interest at which the central bank is neither stimulating nor restraining the economy—is often called "starred" variables. The asterisk is used to indicate that the variables must be estimated as there is uncertainty around them depending on the measurement approach. It does not mean, however, that because NAIRU is unobservable it does not exist. Still, the Federal Reserve uses an estimate of the NAIRU to help guide monetary policy, In the FAQs, *What is the lowest level of unemployment that the U.S. economy can sustain?* The Board of Governors of the Federal Reserve System responded: "Many estimates suggest that the long-run normal level of the unemployment rate – the level that the unemployment rate would be expected to converge to in the next 5 to 6 years in the absence of shocks to the economy – is in a range between 4.5 and 6 percent. Policymakers' judgements about the long-run normal rate of unemployment in the Summary of Economic Projections are generally in this range as well. For example, in the September 2017 projections, FOMC participants' estimates of the longer-run normal rate of unemployment ranged from 4.4 to 5.0 percent." Economists have consistently underestimated $U^*$. The US unemployment rate has been steadily declining from 4.4% in March 2017 and has dipped below 4% since March 2019. Whilst wage inflation has been remarkably tame, around 3%, it has been approaching the 3.5% peak of Q1:2007. The economy went into recession three-quarters later in December 2008.

21. The *pre-emption* of inflation rests on (a) the fact that monetary (and fiscal) policy act slowly and with varying lags, and (b) the *Phillips Curve* model, or more accurately the *modified Phillips Curve* model. The modified version states that this year's inflation rate ($\pi_t$) is the result of this year's expectation of the inflation rate ($\pi_t^e$), the markup on prices ($m$), the various factors in wage determination ($z$), and the current unemployment rate ($U_t$). In symbols:

$$\pi_t^e = \theta \pi_{t-1}$$

$$\pi_t = \pi_t^e + (m+z) - U_t$$

$$\pi_t - \pi_{t-1} = (m+z) - \alpha U_t$$

The first equation of the model describes how people form their expectations of inflation; the higher the value of $\theta$, the more of last year's inflation leads workers and employers to revise their expectations of this year's inflation rate. The second equation says that this years' inflation rate is influenced by the expected inflation, the markup and the factors that influence wage determination ($z$), and the unemployment rate. This last one captures capacity utilisation. The third equation says that when $\theta = 1$, the change in the inflation rate $(\pi_t - \pi_{t-1})$, not the level $(\pi_t)$, is positively related to $(m + z)$ and negatively related to $U_t$. As a first cut, we looked at US data (1996–2018) and the correlations. The (negative) correlation coefficient between the unemployment rate and the capacity utilisation rate is relatively high ($-0.7$). The coefficient for the *change in the inflation rate* and the unemployment is, however, virtually zero, implying that the level of the unemployment rate and hence domestic capacity utilisation rate have been contributing very little to the change (acceleration or deceleration) in the level of inflation. Globalisation and hence *international* capacity utilisation appears to be a more important factor than *domestic* capacity utilisation in explaining domestic inflation. For a related article, see Federal Reserve Bank of San Francisco, *Inflation – Stress-Testing the Phillips Curve*, Òscar Jordà, Chitra Marti, Fernanda Nechio, and Eric Tallman, February 11, 2019.

22. For coverage of corporate governance, see B. Ganguin and J., Bilardello, *Fundamentals of Corporate Credit Analysis*, Chapter 4, ibid.

23. There are many textbooks on money market and fixed-income securities. Some of the better known ones include Marcia Stigum, *The Money Market*, McGraw-Hill, 3rd edition, December 1, 1989; and Frank J. Fabozzi, *The Handbook of Fixed-Income Securities*, McGraw-Hill Education, 8th edition, January 6, 2012.

24. Fabozzi, F.J., Davis, H.A, and Choudhry, M. (2006), *Introduction to Structured Finance*, John Wiley and Sons. The authors explain there is no single and all-encompassing definition of *structured finance*, although you know it by numerous characteristics. Some structured finance products include ABS (asset-backed securities). These are bonds or notes backed by financial assets such as receivables, auto loans, and home-equity loans. Structured finance also includes riskier CDOs (collateralised debt obligations) that were "backed" by pooled assets such as bonds, loans, and mortgages—including the notorious subprime mortgages that went sour in 2007 and caused a global financial crisis in 2008.

25. On financial forecasting methods, see Chapter 3 of Robert C. Higgins, *Analysis for Financial Management*, 5th edition, Irwin-McGraw Hill; Ganguin & John Bilardello, ibid., Chapter 6.

# 5

# How It All Fits

## Chapter Objectives

1. Demonstrate the application of the criteria-based approach to the passenger airline industry and a *fictional* airline company
2. Learn to prepare a *pro forma* financial statement and a cash-flow forecast
3. Apply stress tests to determine financing gap and credit quality
4. Build a borrower risk rating (BRR) scorecard for the commercial airline industry
5. Apply the scorecard to determine the credit rating of an airline company

## 5.1 Introduction

In Chap. 4, we focused on methods and methodology. We learned to design a scorecard from the bottom up, adding building block upon building block. The result was a borrower risk rating (BRR) scorecard. In this chapter, we customise the BRR template for the passenger airline industry and, through the exercise, the reader sees how the pieces fit together in a study of a fictional passenger airline company, *AY Intercontinental Airways* based in Texas, United States. Although the financial statements are made up, they are for all practical purposes the sort of information reported in the annual reports and financial releases of a medium-size airline company.

---

**Electronic Supplementary Material:** The online version of this chapter (https://doi.org/10.1007/978-3-030-32197-0_5) contains supplementary material, which is available to authorized users.

There are two ways to approach this chapter in order to get the most out of it. One way is to imagine you are the model developer of a commercial bank and you are building a BRR scorecard of the passenger airline industry. So you are more focused on model design and development. If that is your goal, this chapter will equip you with the necessary tools and ideas. Alternatively, pretend you are an employee of a major lending institution that is considering a loan application from AY Intercontinental, and you are doing the credit risk analysis to determine the BRR. So you are more focused on credit risk assessment. It is January 2018 and the analyst has all necessary financial information including the annual reports for 2017 and previous years and a December 2017 call report by the investment firm's relationship manager. This chapter explores the thinking or theorising that goes into the analysis and presents the methodology. This takes us to the case study.

## 5.2   A Case Study of AY Intercontinental Airways

### 5.2.1  Company Background and Profile

**AY Intercontinental Airways (AYIA)**
**Credit Risk Assessment: BBB− (Low Medium Risk)**
**Company Profile**

AY Intercontinental Airways (AYIA) is a full service airline based in Texas. AY Intercontinental began as a private company in Houston in 1938 as Houston Airways. The airline prospered in the 1970s, but after the early 1980s started to perform poorly because of management problems. The carrier started to report losses in 1984. In March 1987, Sky's The Limit, a venture capitalist firm based in Dallas, Texas, bought over the company and, shortly after, the airline went public. The stock is actively traded (listed AYIA). AY Intercontinental provides scheduled passenger service directly to over 90 million customers to more than 150 airports across Africa, North America, South America and the Caribbean, Asia, the Middle East, New Zealand, and Australia. AY Intercontinental operates a fleet of more than 195 mainline aircraft including 55 small-sized, 60 medium-sized, 35 wide-body, and 45 regional aircrafts. In addition to passenger service, AY Intercontinental generates revenue from its cargo division, operating as AY Cargo that provides direct services to over 100 international destinations and has sales offices in over 40 countries. The Company's route network includes alliances with other foreign airlines and membership in Sky Team, a passenger airline alliance.

## 5.2.2  Industry Risk Assessment (15%)

**Industry Risk Rating: BB+ (High Risk)**

A good understanding of the economics of the passenger airline industry is necessary to assess the creditworthiness of an airline company. It is a highly cyclical and seasonal industry in which the major factors driving the demand for air transportation and travel are consumer confidence, climate change, personal disposable income, and corporate profitability. The two biggest costs of operating an airline are jet fuel and labour, both of which are largely outside the control of an airline. Fixed to variable costs are particularly high in the industry due to the labour and capital-intensive nature of the business, limiting scope for adjustment when business is slow or contracting. At the same time, it is normal for passenger loads to fluctuate widely in both good and bad times. The competition, the cost structure, and the volatility in passenger loads, all combined, lead to low profit margins and unstable cash flow. Table 5.1 gives comparative expense ratios and fixed assets to total assets of six international airlines and they tell the same story about airline companies in general.

The table shows that the two biggest expenses of running an airline are jet fuel and labour. The two together account for between a third and a half of total operating costs. Airline operation is labour intensive and more than a fifth of total operating expense is salaries and benefits. Additionally, the industry is very capital intensive, with fixed assets of aircraft and equipment accounting for well over half of total assets.[1] Company size plays a key role in cost minimisation. The big carriers enjoy huge bargaining power to negotiate discounts on the prices of jet fuel and other supplies. Small airlines have no such bargaining power.

On the revenue side, the main drivers are the state of capacity and competition relative to demand for travel. Since 2000, the number of carriers has grown faster than the demand, resulting in chronic overcapacity. In Europe, in particu-

Table 5.1  Selected operating measures of major World Airlines (2014–2016 average)

| Airline | Air-line fuel and related charges/total operating expense | Employee costs/total operating expense | Fixed assets/ total assets |
|---|---|---|---|
| Air Canada | 21.0% | 18.8% | 55.4% |
| American Airlines | 20.0% | 26.9% | 56.7% |
| British Airways | 16.6% | 14.6% | 53.9% |
| Cathay Pacific | 34.6% | 19.6% | 47.9% |
| Qantas | 23.1% | 24.1% | 66.2% |
| United Continental | 25.9% | 29.9% | 56.1% |

Source: Annual reports/SEC filings of the listed airlines for years 2016 and 2015

lar, numerous airlines have gone bankrupt. The capital-intensive nature of the industry makes it difficult for marginal participants to exit from the industry, thus worsening the overcapacity and creating pressure for consolidation.[2]

To say that airlines compete aggressively would be an understatement. The history of the industry shows that since the deregulation of the airline industry in late 1970s—a global development that started in the United States and Canada—there has been no hiatus in the intensity of the competition; in fact, it has intensified. There are now many types of carriers, which are in a tight race to fill seats. They include the FSNCs (full service network carriers)—many of which used to be monopoly national airlines—regional airlines, holiday carriers (including charter operators), no frills or budget LCCs (low-cost carriers), and hybrid carriers that operate on more than one business model. The "no frills" LCCs focus on achieving lower cost than the more established international carriers because they compete on price. To stem the revenue loss, the FSNCs have embraced the LCC model by incorporating budget carriers into their regular fleet.

With this background information, we are in a position to flesh out the industry risk framework with details that are specific to the commercial airline industry. We illustrate the scorecard with five grades. Below are the risk criteria and their risk factors:

1. **Stability of revenue and profitability:**

   - Cyclical and seasonal volatility of revenue and profitability during an economic downturn

2. **Outlook for growth and profitability:**

   - Entry and exit barriers
   - Product/service substitution and obsolescence
   - Industry stage
   - Cost and cost structure
   - Degree of unionisation
   - Demographics and social trends
   - Global market and competition

The foregoing covers the important factors in industry risk analysis.

The passenger airline business is highly cyclical and seasonal and history shows that the industry takes more than a year to recover from a severe downturn. Figure 5.1 depicts the performance of the US airline industry during the period 2000–2016, which covers two economic downturns in

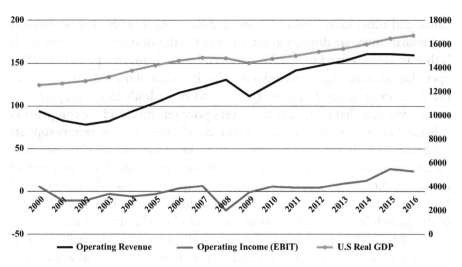

**Fig. 5.1** Performance of major US Airlines (2000–2016)

2000–2001 and in 2008–2009. In both recessions, we see very steep declines in operating income (EBIT). Operating cash flow tends to be volatile and in a recession, it can swing from positive to negative, increasing the risk of bankruptcy. Another characteristic of the airline industry is the wide gap between operating revenue and operating income, a reflection of the high costs of running an airline company.

Compared to the first criterion (stability of revenue and profitability) the second criterion, outlook for growth and profitability), is forward looking and, thus, more heavily weighted. From our understanding of the economics of the airline business, given what we know about the economics of the industry, our intuition tells us that industry risk should be relatively high, even before attempting to complete the scorecard. First, let us review the "negatives", starting with entry and exit barriers. The cost of acquiring a fleet is prohibitive and whilst the availability of leasing options and bank loans helps to lower the barrier for new entrants, capital remains the major obstacle. The exit barrier is also high due to the capital-intensive nature of the operation and the contractual arrangements between airlines and suppliers.

Passenger airline is a mature industry and, based on the industry life cycle model that depicts the various stages where businesses operate, we would expect profitability and cash flow to be relatively stable. On the contrary, volatility in revenue and cash flow is normal for the industry for a couple of reasons. An airline's biggest operating expenditures are jet fuel and labour, "bills" that an airline cannot control. Hedging to protect an airline against volatile fuel prices is costly, as are long-term labour agreements with pilots, flight attendants, and other crew workers to avoid strikes. The salaries of these workers and management are disproportionately fixed in the airline industry. The result is that an airline's fixed to variable costs tend to be high. In a period of falling operating revenue, high indebtedness—that is typical of the industry—magnifies the impact of fixed operating costs, and often leads to bankruptcy. The second reason is that travel demand is very price sensitive, and the competition is fierce due to overcapacity. On the "positives", however, two factors support long-term growth and profitability. First, substitution and obsolescence risks are low for air travel. Second, as personal incomes rise in the developing part of the world, demand for leisure air travel is also expected to rise. The International Monetary Fund (IMF; World Economic Outlook, April 2019) says that most of the growth in the world's gross domestic product (GDP) over the next five years will be in the emerging and developing economies and they will be growing more than twice as fast, whereas the advanced economies would expand by under 2%.

### Scoring Industry Risk

The risk assessor makes the appropriate placements in the scorecard, shown by the highlighted descriptors in Table 5.2. The assigned ratings are in brackets:

I. Stability of revenue and profitability:

- Cyclical and seasonal volatility of revenue and profitability during an economic downturn ("BB")

II. Outlook for growth and profitability:

- Entry and exit barriers ("BBB")
- Product/service substitution and obsolescence ("A")
- Industry stage ("BB")
- Cost and cost structure ("BB")
- Degree of unionisation ("BB")
- Government regulations and country risk ("BB")
- Demographics and social trends ("BBB")
- Global market and competition ("BB")

The weighted average for the scores of these grades is 6.9, which maps to a "BB+". According to the rating system, "BB+" represents high risk, which is a reasonable rating for the commercial airline industry. The value of the industry risk in the overall BRR should be obvious: given that the industry risk is high, a credit analyst should expect few airline companies with consistently high ratings.

**Table 5.2** Industry risk assessment—AY Intercontinental Airways

| Risk criteria and factors | W (%) | AA | A | BBB | BB | B |
|---|---|---|---|---|---|---|
| | | 15 | 12 | 9 | 6 | 3 |
| **I: Stability of revenue and profitability** | 0.4 | | | | | |
| Cyclical and seasonal volatility of revenue and profitability during an economic downturn | 1 | The historical data support one or a combination of the following: Industry operating revenue stagnates or grows even as the economy (GDP) is contracting. Operating profit margin declines roughly in sync with industry revenue, but stays positive. Revenue and profits margins exhibit relatively low seasonal fluctuations. | The historical data support one or a combination of the following: Industry operating revenue declines faster than the economy (GDP). Operating profit margin declines, but at a slower pace vis-à-vis industry revenue. Operating cash flow (represented by EBITDA) worsens, but stays positive. Revenue and profits margins exhibit low seasonal fluctuations. | The historical data support one or a combination of the following: Industry operating revenue declines at a much faster pace than the economy (GDP). Operating profit (EBIT) declines, but at a moderately faster pace vis-à-vis industry revenue. Operating cash flow (represented by EBITDA) worsens, but stays positive. Revenue and profits margins exhibit moderate seasonal fluctuations. | The historical data support one or a combination of the following: Operating revenue declines many times faster than the economy (GDP). Operating profit (EBIT) approaches zero or may dip below. Operating profit (EBIT) declines at a faster pace vis-à-vis industry revenue. Operating cash flow (represented by EBITDA) approaches zero, or may dip below. Revenue and profits margins exhibit high seasonal fluctuations. | The historical data support one or a combination of the following: Industry operating revenue declines many times faster than the economy (GDP). Operating profit (EBIT) turns sharply negative. Operating profit (EBIT) declines many times faster vis-à-vis industry revenue. Revenue and profits margins exhibit very high seasonal fluctuations. |
| **II: Outlook for growth & profitability** | 0.6 | | | | | |
| Entry and exit barriers | 0.125 | High barriers to entry (e.g., legal monopoly, high financing requirements to fund capital investments and R&D, rapid technological change) Very limited options available to overcome entry barriers, for example, leasing rather than owning equipment | High barriers to entry; barriers to exit substantial Limited options available to overcome entry barriers, for example, leasing rather than owning equipment | High barriers to entry; barriers to exit substantial Limited options available to overcome entry barriers, for example, leasing rather than owning equipment | High barriers to entry; barriers to exit relatively high However, many options available to overcome entry barriers | Very low or non-existent barriers to entry; barriers to exit high |
| Product/ service substitution and Obsolescence | 0.125 | Substantially all of the following: No substitute product/ service currently available outside the industry Usability of the product/ service not threatened by new technology | Substantially all of the following: Some substitute products/ services already available outside the industry Usability of the product/ service threatened by new technology | Substantially all of the following: Some substitute products/ services already available outside the industry Usability of the product/ service threatened by new technology | Substantially all of the following: Many substitute products/ services available outside the industry Usability of the product/ service significantly threatened by new technology | Substantially all of the following: Many substitute products/ services available outside the industry Usability of the product in decline globally Product banned by most countries |
| Industry stage | 0.125 | One or a combination of the following: Growth stage Demand increasing faster than supply Sales and earnings expanding at a faster rate than in other industries | One or a combination of the following: Growth stage Demand increasing faster than supply Sales and earnings expanding at a faster rate than in other industries | One or a combination of the following: Mature stage and profits are relatively stable High competitive pressures Industry growth closely matches GDP growth | One or a combination of the following: Mature stage but profits are volatile High competitive pressures Industry growth unevenly matches GDP growth | One or a combination of the following: Decline stage (declining revenue and profit) Introductory stage (too rapid growth at the expense of profitability, new technology, and new business model) |
| Cost and cost structure | 0.125 | One or a combination of the following: Vertically integrated operation is the norm. Easy access to supplies Ability to recover or hedge costs (e.g., regulated industry structure) Low fixed to variable costs by industry comparisons Low financial leverage by industry comparisons | One or a combination of the following: Mostly vertically integrated operation Ability to recover or hedge costs (e.g., regulated industry structure) Long-term contracts provide some predictability to pricing and material availability Fixed to variable costs average by industry comparisons Financial leverage average by industry comparisons | One or a combination of the following: Mostly vertically integrated operation Ability to recover or hedge costs (e.g., regulated industry structure) Long-term contracts provide some predictability to pricing and material availability Fixed to variable costs average by industry comparisons Financial leverage average by industry comparisons | One or a combination of the following: Limited access to supplies Limited ability to pass on cost increases; hedging is costly Long-term contracts provide limited predictability to pricing and material availability Fixed to variable costs high by industry comparisons Financial leverage high by industry comparisons | One or a combination of the following: No access to supplies; hedging is costly Mostly spot purchases with suppliers Fixed to variable costs high by industry comparisons Financial leverage high by industry comparisons |

(continued)

**Table 5.2** (continued)

| | | | | | | |
|---|---|---|---|---|---|---|
| Degree of unionisation | 0.125 | Unionisation not permitted or, no effective collective bargaining occurs | Industry is unionised but labour relations have been relatively peaceful. Susceptible to strikes and work stoppages | | Highly unionised industry; labour relations contentious. Frequent strikes and work stoppages | Unions highly organised and militant. Labour relations highly contentious. Frequent strikes and work stoppages |
| Government regulation and country risk | 0.125 | One or a combination of the following: Very weak safety and environmental requirements in place. Firms have the ability to recover the associated costs (e.g., from taxpayers). Very high protectionist regulations | One or a combination of the following: Weak safety and environmental requirements in place. Firms have some leeway to recover the associated costs (e.g., from taxpayers). Relatively high protectionist regulations | | One or a combination of the following: Strict safety and environmental requirements in place. Firms have limited ability to recover the associated costs (e.g., from taxpayers). Limited protection from foreign competition. Foreign operation at some risk of nationalisation. Profit repatriation at some risk | One or a combination of the following: Tough safety and environmental requirements in place. Firms have no ability to recover the associated costs (e.g., from taxpayers). Weak or no protection from foreign competition. Foreign operation at risk of nationalisation. Profit repatriation at significant risk |
| Demographics and social trends | 0.125 | Global demographic and social changes highly favouring strong long-term growth in demand | Global demographic and social changes favouring long-term growth in demand | | Global demographic and social changes weakly favouring long-term growth in demand | Local demographic and social changes do not or hardly favour long-term growth in demand |
| Global market & competition | 0.125 | One or a combination of the following: Low capacity worldwide. Highly concentrated with a few companies controlling the global market. High demand worldwide. Product/service highly differentiated | One or a combination of the following: Relatively high overcapacity worldwide. Fierce global competition. Product/service somewhat commoditised | | One or a combination of the following: Very high overcapacity worldwide. Fierce global competition. Fragmented market. Product/service highly commoditized | One or a combination of the following: Very high overcapacity worldwide. Fierce global competition. Low or declining demand for product/service. Product/service undifferentiated |

### 5.2.3 Business Risk Assessment (25%)

**Rating: BBB− (Medium Risk)**
The scorecard for business risk consists of the following three risk criteria and risk factors that are *specific* to passenger airlines:

1. **Competitive position**

    A. Operating cost
    B. Operating revenue
    C. Fleet
    D. Revenue base
    E. Customer service and safety record

2. **The market position**

    A. Revenue diversification by geography and services
    B. Market share
    C. Route network

3. **Cyclical position**

    A. Cyclical Adjustment Factor

Table 5.3 shows the scorecard with descriptors for a subset of ratings of the 16-point rating scale.

In this section, we examine the placements of the descriptors and discuss the criteria supporting the selections.

**Competitive Position**

A. Operating cost

**Rating: BBB**

CASM (Cost per Available Seat Mile) has been on a steady decline from almost 13 US cents in the mid-2000s to nearly 8 US cents in the last few years (2015–2017). The load factor—a commonly used metric in the industry for operating efficiency—has risen to over 80%, and the BELF (breakeven load factor) has been fluctuating in the range of 68–75% in the last ten years of the carrier's operation (2008–2017). The higher is the load factor, given the BELF, the higher the airline's efficiency and, thus, the lower the *unit operating cost*. The airline's breakeven was 75% in 2017, exceeding the industry average of 69%. Cost management is vital to survival in the business because of the high

**Table 5.3** Business risk assessment—AY Inter-Continental Airlines, Cont'd

| Business factor | W (%) | A | BBB | BB | B AND BELOW |
|---|---|---|---|---|---|
| | | 12 | 9 | 6 | 5 |
| 1. Competitive position | 50.0% | | | | |
| | 34.0% | | | | |
| Operating cost | 20.0% | A combination of the following: Effectively controls non-fuel cost. CASM (cost per available seat mile/kilometre) below the average of the peer group. Achieves consistently a high and relatively stable load factor. Able to pass on cost increase (e.g., fuel surcharges) with moderate impact on passenger loads Has the required scale to negotiate lower prices with suppliers. Has sufficient financial resources to hedge effectively against exchange-rate and fuel-price risks. Not heavy burdened by legacy costs. Able to manage capacity in response to unforeseen changes in demand Enjoys stable relations with unions. | A combination of the following: Reasonably effective in controlling costs. CASM in line with the average of the peer group. Achieves high load factors with fluctuations. Some leeway to pass on cost increases but passenger loads are adversely affected Limited ability to negotiate lower prices with suppliers. Has adequate financial resources to hedge reasonably well against exchange-rate and fuel-price risks. Burdened by significant legacy cost. Has some ability to manage capacity in response to unforeseen changes in demand. Enjoys fairly stable relations unions. Minor disruptions occur. | A combination of the following: Limited ability to control non-fuel cost. CASM exceeds average of the peer group. Limited ability to pass on cost increases without adversely affecting passenger loads Achieves below-average load factor. Limited ability to pass on cost increases without adversely affecting demand. Has limited resources to hedge against a substantial portion of exchange-rate and fuel-price risks Has limited flexibility to manage capacity in response to changes in demand Experiences disruptions from labour disputes. | A combination of the following: Limited ability to control non-fuel cost. CASM well exceeds average of the peer group. Achieves a load factor that is often at or below the airline's breakeven. No ability to negotiate lower prices with suppliers. Very limited in its ability to hedge against exchange-rate and fuel-price risks. Burdened by material legacy costs. Limited flexibility to manage capacity in response to changes in demand. Adversarial relations between the airline and unions. |
| Operating revenue | 20.0% | Above-average growth in total revenue exceeding 10.1 per cent over 1 year Achieves consistently a high and relatively stable load factor well in excess of the airline's breakeven. Leverages its varied market/demand segments effectively for price discrimination to increase passenger yields Participation in global alliances (e.g., the Star Alliance, Sky Team, Oneworld) and limited code-sharing partnerships Involved in joint ventures with many major international airlines | Average but stable growth in total revenue of between 5.1 per cent and 10 per cent over 1 year Achieves a load factor that exceeds the airline's breakeven, although inconsistently. Has market/demand segments that allow for effective price discrimination to increase passenger yields Participation in global alliances (e.g., the Star Alliance, Sky Team, Oneworld) and limited code-sharing partnerships Involved in joint ventures with many major international airlines | Below-average growth in total revenue of between 0% and 5% over 1 year Achieves a load factor that exceeds the airline's breakeven, but passenger loads fluctuate significantly. Has a relatively narrow market/demand segments for price discrimination to increase passenger yield significantly Participation in global alliances (e.g., the Star Alliance, Sky Team, Oneworld) and limited code-sharing partnerships. | No growth or negative growth in total revenue over 1 year Achieves a load factor that is often at or below the airline's breakeven. Has no leeway for price discrimination for passenger-yield increases Not a member of a global alliances (e.g., the Star Alliance, Sky Team, Oneworld) Limited code-sharing opportunities |
| fleet | 20.0% | A combination of the following: Airline owns a large proportion of its fleet. Leased planes are on long-term leases with staggered expiry dates Modern fleet and equipment; fuel and maintenance efficient Ongoing fleet renewal programme with a good mix of firm and optional orders The fleet mix is compatible with the routes. | A combination of the following: Airline leases most of its planes on a combination of long- and short-term leases. Some bunching of the expiry dates exist. Good fleet and equipment Ongoing fleet renewal programme with a fair mix of firm and optional orders The fleet mix is compatible with the routes. | A combination of the following: Airline leases almost all of its planes on medium-term leases with some flexibility Age of the fleet is higher than average. The fleet mix is inadequate for the routes. Some fleet renewal planning occurs, but disrupted by late aircraft deliveries at times | A combination of the following: Airline leases almost all of its planes on medium-term leases with some flexibility Age of the fleet well above average. Fuel and maintenance inefficient The fleet mix is poorly matched with the routes Limited fleet renewal planning occurs, and aircraft purchases tend to be opportunistic |
| Revenue base | 20.0% | Above-average growth in total revenue exceeding 10.1 per cent over 1 year Leverages its varied market/demand segments effectively for price discrimination to increase passenger yields Participation in global alliances (e.g., the Star Alliance, Sky Team, One world) and many code-sharing partnerships Involved in joint ventures with many major international airlines | Average but stable growth in total revenue of between 5.1 per cent and 10 per cent over 1 year Leverages its varied market/demand segments that allow for effective price discrimination to increase passenger yields Participation in global alliances (e.g., the Star Alliance, Sky Team, One world) and limited code-sharing partnerships Involved in joint ventures with a few major international airlines | Below-average growth in total revenue of between 0% and 5% over 1 year Has too narrow market/demand segments that allow for effective price discrimination for passenger-yield increases Participation in global alliances (e.g., the Star Alliance, Sky Team, One world) and limited code-sharing partnerships. | No growth or negative growth in total revenue over 1 year Has no leeway for price discrimination for passenger-yield increases Not a member of a global alliances (e.g., the Star Alliance, Sky Team, One world) Limited code-sharing opportunities |

| Criterion | Weight | | | | |
|---|---|---|---|---|---|
| Customer service and safety | 20.0% | A combination of the following: Well established and highly regarded name regionally or globally. Has a successful loyalty programme (confirmed by large and growing number of participants) Gets consistently high ratings from global systems that classify airlines and airports. Consistently high reputation for service quality. | A combination of the following: Established and recognised name regionally or globally. Moderately successful loyalty programme. Gets good ratings from global systems that classify airlines and airports. Solid reputation for service quality; mostly positive comments. | A combination of the following: Low name recognition globally but well recognised regionally. Has a loyalty programme or may be planning to introduce one. Gets satisfactory ratings from global systems that classify airlines and airports. Satisfactory reputation for quality service; no major unfavourable comments. | A combination of the following: Name recognition more confined to price sensitive travellers. Does not have a loyalty programme. Unrated or gets poor ratings from global systems that classify airlines and airport. Mostly poor service quality. Offers the lowest prices among competitors flying the same routes. |
| Market position | 50.0% | | | | |
| Revenue diversification by geography and services | 33.4% | A combination of the following: Highly diversified across regions and continents Highly diversified across regional and intercontinental flights Non-passenger services (cargo/other) represent an important source of revenue (more than 10%) | A combination of the following: Well diversified across regions and continents Well diversified across regional and intercontinental flights Non-passenger services (cargo/other) a meaningful source of revenue (between 5% and 10%) | A combination of the following: Limited diversification across regions and continents Non-passenger services (cargo/ other) are an important source of revenue (less than 5%). | A combination of the following: The markets are mostly regional Passengers are the only source of revenue. |
| Market share | 33.3% | A leader in many key markets | Ranks in the middle in terms of market shares in some key markets | Ranks low in terms of market shares in some key markets | Not amongst the market-share leaders in terms of key markets Amongst leaders of only small, or mostly niche markets |
| Route network | 33.3% | A combination of the following: Very profitable routes with very high ratio of business/leisure travel. Accessibility to all key cities of markets served. High flight frequency with favourable time slots. Wide portfolio of international route and slot rights to support growth. Traffic routes have strong growth potential. | A combination of the following: Profitable routes with high ratio of business/leisure travel. Accessibility to most key cities of markets served. High flight frequency, most with favourable time slots. A decent portfolio of route and slot rights to support growth. Traffic routes have reasonable growth potential. | A combination of the following: Somewhat profitable routes with low ratio of business/leisure travel. Accessibility to some key cities of markets served. Fairly frequent flights, some with unfavourable time slots. Has a narrow portfolio of route and slot rights; inadequate for further growth. Traffic routes have reasonable growth potential. Traffic routes have limited growth potential. | A combination of the following: Primarily or only regional routes that serve as feeder to other airlines Infrequent flights to key cities with usually unfavourable time slots Lacks sufficient route and slot rights to support growth Traffic routes have low growth potential Low-margin chartered flights to vacation destinations. |
| Cyclical position | 0.0% | | | | |
| Cyclical adjustment factor | 100.0% | Changes in the monthly LEI (index of the leading economic indicators) suggest the economy may be at or approaching the bottom of the cycle. Monetary policy remains expansionary Official interest rates are not falling as fast as before or show signs of bottoming out. | Changes in the LEI suggest the economy will continue to grow. Monetary policy announcements suggest interest rates will rise in the future, a signal that the central bank expects growth to continue. Official interest rates are rising in response to strong economic growth. | Changes in the monthly LEI point to economic slowdown. Monetary policy announcements suggest interest rates will fall in the future, which implies that the economy will enter a period of slower growth. Central bank has stopped raising official interest rates or is holding them steady within the announced range. | Changes in the monthly LEI signal recession in the next 6–9 months. Monetary policy announcements suggest interest rates will fall in the future, confirming the LEI warning. Official interest rates are falling faster than usual as the target range expands. |

ratio of fixed to variable costs. The management of AY Intercontinental seems determined to lower costs to overcome two limiting constraints. First, AY Intercontinental lacks the scale to negotiate lower prices for fuel. Second, the company has material legacy costs, comprising mainly pension obligations and long-term debt incurred prior to its going public.

B.  Operating revenue: diversification by geography and services

### Rating: BBB

Growth in total revenue has been hovering around 7%. Passenger load factor remains on an upward trend, averaging 81.40% in the 2013–2017 period, and exceeding the break even of 72.2% for the same period. The carrier participates in global alliances such as Star Alliance, and has code-sharing partnerships. AY Intercontinental has recently finalised a joint venture with Canada Goose, Canada's second largest passenger-cargo airline based in Montreal. The agreement will expand AY InterContinental's existing code-sharing partnership, as well as provide increased access to connecting domestic flights in both countries.

C.  Fleet

### Rating: A

AY Intercontinental has a fleet of over 195 planes of different sizes, with a mix of old and modern fuel-efficient planes. The fleet mix is compatible with the routes. More than half of the fleet is relatively new. It has a renewal programme with a fair mix of firm and optional orders. The airline owns most of its planes. Leased planes are on long-term leases with staggered expiry dates.

D.  Revenue base

### Rating: BBB

AY Intercontinental rebounded from the 2008–2009 global economic recession, reporting a 10.8% increase in operating revenue. Operating revenue growth slowed to 7.4% in 2010, hovering around the 5% mark since then. The airline appears to be making the right decisions to support growth. It joined Sky Team, and has code-sharing partnership with several international airlines. In 2016, the airline announced its first joint venture with a major Canadian carrier. The joint venture includes code-sharing, joint sales and marketing initiatives, colocation at key hubs to provide seamless passenger and baggage transit, and increased cargo cooperation across the Americas.

E.  Customer service and safety reputation

### Rating: BB

AY Intercontinental is well-known regionally. Outside the Americas, however, it lacks high name recognition. In all the years of operation since privatisation in 1987, AY Intercontinental has experienced minor accidents. Significantly, in the history of its operations, transportation authorities have never grounded the carrier for safety concerns or breaches. The airline gets a satisfactory rating from the global systems that classify airlines and airports.

## Market Position

A.  Revenue diversification by geography and services

### Rating: BBB

AY Intercontinental is fairly diversified across regions and flights. Non-passenger services (cargo and other) contributed 10% to operating revenue over the last years with cargo contributing roughly half of non-passenger revenue. Through its subsidiary, AY Cargo, with sales offices in over 40 countries, the company provides direct services to over 100 international destinations.

B.  Market share

### Rating: BBB

AY Intercontinental is a mid-size airline company by international standards. It ranks in the middle in terms of market share in its main market, concentrated in southeastern United States.

C.  Route network

### Rating: BBB

AY Intercontinental operates profitable routes for business passengers year round and for northern hemisphere leisure travellers to the Caribbean. Additionally, the company's routes give it access to some of the major cities including Rio de Janeiro, Miami, Boston, New York, Montreal, and Toronto.

However, the airline's growth potential is significantly limited by new low-cost entrants, its small portfolio of routes, and slot rights.[3] For these reasons the BBB ratings seems justified.

**Cyclical Position**

A. Cyclical Adjustment Factor

**Rating: BB**

The US expansion is now into its tenth year and is the longest on record. The coincident and leading economic indicators for the US economy suggest the passenger airline industry may be nearing the top of the cycle and economic slowdown or recession may be in the offing. Therefore, Cyclical Adjustment Factor and a rating of "BB" seem justified for the forecast horizon.

**Scoring Business Risk**

The assigned ratings are in brackets:

I. **Competitive position**

- Operating cost ("BBB")
- Operating revenue ("BBB")
- Fleet ("A")
- Revenue base ("BBB")
- Customer service and safety ("BB")

II. **Market position**

- Revenue diversification by geography and services ("BBB")
- Market share ("BBB")
- Route network ("BBB")

III. **Cyclical position**

- Cyclical Adjustment Factor ("BB")

The weighted average of these scores is 8.0, which maps to a "BBB–", representing medium risk.

## 5.2.4  Management Risk Assessment (20%)

**Management Risk Rating: BBB– (Medium Risk)**

We assess management risk of AY Intercontinental Airways by examining the four risk criteria that we introduced in Chap. 3:

- Management quality
- Business strategy
- Financial strategy

## Management Quality
### Rating: BB
Most of the employees in senior management roles are professionals with many years of industry experience in the areas they control. The majority have come up through the ranks with 10–20 years of service and, thus, they are thoroughly familiar with the operations of the company. As part of HR's (Human Resources) strategy to deepen the skills pool, the airline fills vacancies, particularly for the divisional heads, with fresh talent brought from outside the organisation. Middle- and low-layer management is, however, not as strong in terms of skills and experience. The company ranks in the fourth quartile of industry benchmarks. The weakness is partly reflected in surveys that show the quality of service is just satisfactory.

## Business Strategy
### Rating: BBB
The airline follows a three-year business plan. The strategy of the last five years has been to expand regionally to service more "regional corridors" and to expand internationally by growing its fleet, membership in global alliances, and code-sharing partnerships. The strategy has indeed strengthened the carrier's regional presence, but the airline is still far away from achieving its global reach. The passenger load factor improved noticeably to the high seventies. As for profitability, measured by net income, the airline's performance has not been as strong, partly because of the global recession in 2008–2009 and higher jet fuel prices. But despite the improvement in net income, the airline has been struggling to achieve the target of 3.0 US cents for unit profits, measured by operating profit in US cents per available seat mile. Unit profits, defined by the difference between RASM (revenue per available seat mile) and CASM (cost per available seat mile),[4] came in below the target in 2017 due mainly to jet fuel prices (Fig. 5.2).

## Financial Strategy
### Rating: BBB
Overall, replacing older fuel-inefficient planes has improved the financial performance of the airline, but reducing expenses remains a significant challenge due to fuel, labour, and debt servicing. The debt has grown to $23.1 billion at end-2017 owing to capex (capital expenditures) needs. We analyse financial risk in the next section, Financial Risk Assessment.

## Scoring Management Risk
As shown in Table 5.4, the selected descriptors are highlighted. Below are the associated ratings in brackets:

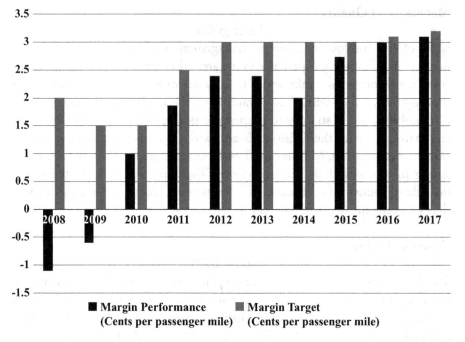

**Fig. 5.2** Unit profit of AY-Intercontinental Airways

I. Management quality ("BB")
II. Business strategy ("BBB")
III. Financial strategy ("BBB")

The weighted average of these scores is 8.0, which maps to a "BBB−", representing medium risk.

## 5.2.5 Financial Risk Assessment (40%)

**Risk Rating: BBB (Moderate Risk)**
We rated financial risk "BBB" based on financial performance defined by risk factors 1 through 5, and by financial flexibility defined by the risk factor 6.
**Financial Performance:**

1. Profitability (10%)

    i. Earnings before interest, taxes, depreciation, amortisation, and rent (EBITDAR) margin

2. Efficiency (10%)

    i. Load factor for consolidated operation

**Table 5.4** Management risk assessment—AY Intercontinental Airways

| Management Factor | W | AA 15 | A 12 | BBB 9 | BB 6 | B AND LESS 3 |
|---|---|---|---|---|---|---|
| Management quality | 33.4% | Substantially all of the following: Top professionals with deep experience, and highly competent throughout management. Well below-average employee turnover rates. Management has been "battle tested" though many business cycles; almost always on target according to the business plans. Ranks in the top quartile of industry benchmarks. | Substantially all of the following: Highly competent and experienced management at all layers. Below-average employee turnover rates. Management has been "battle tested" though many business cycles; strong performance recorded. Ranks in the top quartile of industry benchmarks. | Substantially all of the following: On balance, qualified and competent management at all layers. Average employee turnover rates. Management has been "battle tested" though a few business cycles; satisfactory performance recorded overall. Ranks in the third quartile of industry benchmarks. | Substantially all of the following: Many in the senior management ranks are competent and experienced; however, critical management skills are limited in the middle- and low-level layers. Above-average employee turnover rates. Management may have been "battle tested" though one complete business cycle. Ranks in the fourth quartile of industry benchmarks. | Substantially all of the following: Management lacks deep experience, sufficient knowledge, or critical skills. Well above-average employee turnover rates. Management may not have been "battle tested" though a complete business cycle; poor performance recorded. Ranks in the fourth quartile of industry benchmarks. |
| Business strategy | 33.4% | Substantially all of the following: A well-formulated and well-communicated strategy. The time horizon is right for any or a combination of the following: the current state of the company, the growth stage of the industry, and technological and demographic factors. Company consistently on target according to the business plans and often exceeds. Company would highly likely achieve the goals of the current strategy. | Substantially all of the following: A well-formulated and well-communicated strategy. The time horizon is right for any or a combination of the following: the current state of the company, the growth stage of the industry, and technological and demographic factors. Company mostly on target according to the business plans and often exceeds. Company would likely achieve the goals of the current strategy. | Substantially all of the following: A written and satisfactory formulation of the business goals and strategy. The time horizon is on balance right for any or a combination of the following: the current state of the company, the growth stage of the industry, and technological and demographic factors. Company mostly on target according to the business plans but seldom exceeds. Company would likely achieve most of the goals of the current strategy. | Substantially all of the following: A written or verbal business strategy. Strategy not clearly outlined and contains gaps. The time horizon is not right for any or a combination of the following: the current state of the company, the growth stage of the industry, and technological and demographic factors. Company inconsistently on target according to the business plans. Company would likely fall short of the goals of the current strategy. | Substantially all of the following: There is no clear written or verbal strategy. If a clear strategy exists, it is short-term and ad hoc (e.g., specific measures to restructure company debt and turn the company around). High likelihood the goals of the current strategy would not be achieved. |
| Financial strategy | 33.3% | Substantially all of the following: A flexible, sustainable, and well-communicated financial strategy to take the company from A to B. Financial strategy translated into a pro forma financial statement with well-defined performance targets. Planned spending and borrowing consistent with risk appetite and accessibility to external funding. | Substantially all of the following: On the whole, a fairly flexible, sustainable, and well-communicated financial strategy. Financial strategy translated into a pro forma financial statement with well-defined performance targets. Planned spending and borrowing consistent with risk appetite and accessibility to external funding. | Substantially all of the following: Sustainable financial strategy but with limited flexibility. Financial strategy translated into a pro forma financial statement with well-defined performance targets. Planned spending and borrowing may be aggressive relative to total cash resources available to fund expansion. | Substantially all of the following: An inflexible and unsustainable financial strategy. Financial strategy may not be translated into a pro forma financial statement with well-defined performance targets. Aggressive leverage policy. Financial strategies of the past have had limited success. | Substantially all of the following: An inflexible and unsustainable financial strategy. Financial strategy may not be translated into a pro forma financial statement with well-defined performance targets. Aggressive leverage policy. Financial strategies of the past have failed to meet plan goals. |

3. Leverage (20%)

   i. Adjusted debt/EBITDAR
   ii. Adjusted debt/adjusted capital

4. Coverage (20%)

   i. EBITDAR/(interest + rent)

5. Liquidity (10%)

   i. Free cash flow (FCF)/adjusted debt
   ii. Current assets/current liabilities

   **Financial Flexibility:**

6. Ability to raise equity and debt financing (30%)

## 5.2.6 Spreading Financial Statements for Risk Performance Variables

The first step in financial risk assessment is to spread the financial statements (see Tables 5.5–5.7) and calculate the financial ratios (see Table 5.8). This exercise calls for close attention to the footnotes in the annual reports. Because the airline business is highly cyclical, a three-year forecast rather than the current financial statements (quarterly) and the last three years' financial statements (annual) are more suitable but, for now, we use the historical data from 2014 through to 2017. In order to account for the business cycle effect on the risk rating, we incorporated the Cyclical Adjustment Factor in business risk assessment in Sect. 5.2.3. Later, we show how to apply the cyclical adjustment directly in the financial risk section of the scorecard with current and projected financial statements.

Table 5.8 gives the indicators of financial performance for the 2015–2017 period.

**Financial Performance**
AY InterContinental's financial performance improved during recent years. Some of the key ratios for profitability, solvency, liquidity, and debt coverage for the last three years are shown in Table 5.8. Profitability, measured by EBITDAR margin, improved. The factors that account for this are partly cyclical, partly external to the airline (e.g., oil prices fell sharply after 2014), and partly internal to the airline, positively reflecting management quality. Global economic expansion continues to support passenger traffic. Also, passenger efficiency in terms of load factor improved from the mid-70% mark to over 80% recently.

**Table 5.5** Consolidated statement of earnings for the years ended December 31

| AY Intercontinental Airways | | | |
| --- | --- | --- | --- |
| ($ millions) | 2015 | 2016 | 2017 |
| **Operating revenue:** | | | |
| Passenger | 22,738 | 24,707 | 26,510 |
| Cargo | 2301 | 2442 | 2516 |
| Other | 1712 | 1580 | 1657 |
| Operating revenue | 26,750 | 28,730 | 30,683 |
| **Operating expenses:** | | | |
| Aircraft fuel | 7383 | 6030 | 5448 |
| Regional airlines expense | 492 | 644 | 988 |
| Employee costs | 6891 | 8058 | 8969 |
| Airport and landing fees | 1846 | 1804 | 1869 |
| Aircraft maintenance | 1477 | 1520 | 1548 |
| Depreciation and amortization | 1624 | 1727 | 2109 |
| Selling costs | 1231 | 1314 | 1415 |
| Contractual services | 812 | 1263 | 801 |
| Aircraft leasing (rent) | 615 | 652 | 673 |
| Food and beverage service | 541 | 670 | 739 |
| Other (net) | 1698 | 2087 | 2136 |
| Operating expenses | 24,610 | 25,770 | 26,694 |
| **Operating income:** | **2140** | **2959** | **3989** |
| Non-operating expense (+) or income (−) | | | |
| Foreign exchange loss (+) of gain (+) | 390 | 495 | 578 |
| Interest income (−) | −85 | −88 | −94 |
| Interest expense (+) | 900 | 1049 | 1205 |
| Net financing expense relating to employee benefits | 564 | 641 | 643 |
| Loss (+) or gain (−) on disposal of property and equipment | −34 | 52 | −15 |
| Other (net) | 234 | 170 | 351 |
| Non-operating expense | 1969 | 2319 | 2669 |
| Income before taxes | 171 | 640 | 1319 |
| Income taxes | 60 | 224 | 462 |
| **Net income** | **111** | **416** | **858** |

We observe, however, that the ratio of total adjusted funded debt to EBITDAR climbed to 4.4:1 in 2015, and, although the debt burden has been easing, the level of adjusted funded debt has risen sharply, $23.1 billion at end-2017, almost 90% of total adjusted capital. The high level of funded debt directly translates into a low coverage ratio of 3.6 in 2017. The inverse of this figure means that nearly a third of EBITDAR went to interest and rental expense. More telling is the fact that nearly two-thirds of operating income, measured by earnings before interest, and taxes (EBIT)—not reported in the table—went to interest and rent in 2017. High indebtedness is a negative due to the carrier's high operating leverage and volatile cash flows.

Let's look closer at the calculation of funded debt, keeping in mind that nearly all airlines have excessive debt.[5] AY Intercontinental owns more than half its aircraft under capital leases and leases the rest. It leases airport and terminal

**Table 5.6** Consolidated statement of financial position at December 31

| AY Intercontinental Airways | | | |
| --- | --- | --- | --- |
| ($ millions) | 2015 | 2016 | 2017 |
| **Assets** | | | |
| Current assets: | | | |
| Cash and cash equivalents | 2058 | 2383 | 2485 |
| Short-term investments | 4109 | 4923 | 5923 |
| Total cash, cash equivalents and short-term investments | 6167 | 7306 | 8409 |
| Restricted cash | 286 | 387 | 350 |
| Accounts receivable | 2123 | 1993 | 2278 |
| Aircraft fuel inventory | 240 | 195 | 224 |
| Spare parts and supplies inventory | 305 | 336 | 317 |
| Prepaid expenses, deposits, and other | 1746 | 1954 | 1326 |
| Total current assets | 10,866 | 12,171 | 12,903 |
| Non-current assets: | | | |
| Property and equipment | 19,204 | 21,908 | 23,660 |
| Pension assets | 2191 | 2532 | 3148 |
| Intangible assets | 959 | 1289 | 862 |
| Goodwill | 1020 | 1172 | 849 |
| **Total assets** | **34,240** | **39,072** | **41,422** |
| **Liabilities and shareholders' equity** | | | |
| Current: | | | |
| Accounts payable and accrued liabilities | 3629 | 4298 | 4142 |
| Advance ticket sales | 4040 | 5079 | 5799 |
| Current portion of long-term debt and finance leases | 1293 | 1489 | 1583 |
| Total current liabilities | 8962 | 10,866 | 11,525 |
| Non-current liabilities: | | | |
| Long-term debt and finance leases | 14,218 | 16,380 | 17,418 |
| Pension and other benefit liabilities | 5102 | 5861 | 6153 |
| Maintenance provisions | 2300 | 2631 | 2678 |
| Other long-term liabilities | 921 | 746 | 731 |
| Total liabilities | 22,541 | 25,618 | 26,979 |
| Shareholders' equity: | | | |
| Share capital | 1045 | 1035 | 1007 |
| Contributed surplus | 79 | 77 | 76 |
| Hedge reserves | 0 | −11 | 3 |
| Retained earnings | 1613 | 1487 | 1832 |
| Total shareholders' equity | 2737 | 2587 | 2918 |
| **Total liabilities and shareholders' equity** | **34,240** | **39,072** | **41,422** |

facilities, office space, and other equipment. These lease items, reported in the footnotes of the company's annual reports, count as funded debt. The airline has no postponed debts in favour of any third party. Under the footnote section, *Contingencies, Guarantees and Indemnities*, the airline reports the aggregate amount of the loans that it has guaranteed for certain third parties that provide de-icing and other services for the airline. Whilst management views the loss potential of the guaranteed debt as "remote", a risk analyst must treat any guaranteed debt as part of total funded debt of the company. Table 5.9 gives

**Table 5.7** Consolidated statement of cash flows for the years ended December 31

AY Intercontinental Airways

| ($ millions) | 2015 | 2016 | 2017 |
|---|---|---|---|
| Cash flows from (used for) | | | |
| **Operating activities:** | | | |
| Net income | 111 | 416 | 858 |
| Items not involving cash: | | | |
| Depreciation and amortisation | 1624 | 1727 | 2109 |
| Unrealised foreign exchange loss (gain) | 68 | 134 | 104 |
| Change in maintenance provisions | 46 | 48 | 57 |
| Loss (gain) on disposal of property and equipment | −34 | 52 | −15 |
| Changes in non-cash working capital balances (net) | 8 | 1840 | 992 |
| **Net cash flows from operating activities** | **1824** | **4217** | **4105** |
| **Financing activities:** | | | |
| Proceeds from borrowings | 1223 | 2359 | 1132 |
| Reduction of long-term debt and finance lease obligations | −1191 | −1293 | −1489 |
| Issue of shares | 6 | 3 | 0 |
| Purchase of shares | −18 | −72 | −63 |
| Dividends paid | 0 | −25 | −60 |
| **Net cash flows from financing activities** | **20** | **972** | **−480** |
| **Investing activities:** | | | |
| Additions to property and equipment (capex) | −1391 | −2704 | −1753 |
| Short-term investments | −109 | −814 | −1000 |
| Other (net) | −149 | −1363 | −753 |
| **Net cash flows used in investing activities** | **−1649** | **−4881** | **−3506** |
| Cash flow from/(used in) operating, investing and financing activities | 196 | 308 | 119 |
| Effect of exchange rate changes on cash and cash equivalents | −13 | 18 | −17 |
| Net change in cash and cash equivalents | 183 | 326 | 102 |
| Cash and cash equivalents, beginning of year | 1875 | 2058 | 2383 |
| **Cash and cash equivalents, end of year** | **2058** | **2383** | **2485** |

**Table 5.8** Performance indicators of AY Intercontinental Airways

| Risk elements | 2015 | 2016 | 2017 | Average |
|---|---|---|---|---|
| EBITDAR margin (%) | 16.4 | 18.6 | 22.1 | 19.0 |
| Load factor for consolidated operation (%) | 81.1 | 82.0 | 83.1 | 82.1 |
| Adjusted funded debt/EBITDAR (X) | 4.4 | 4.1 | 3.4 | 3.9 |
| Adjusted funded debt/adjusted capital (%) | 87.5 | 89.4 | 88.7 | 88.5 |
| EBITDAR/(interest + rent) (X) | 2.9 | 3.1 | 3.6 | 3.2 |
| FCF/adjusted funded debt (%) | 2.3 | 6.8 | 10.0 | 6.4 |
| Current assets/current liabilities (X) | 1.2 | 1.1 | 1.1 | 1.2 |

operating lease payments in the annual reports for the periods 2016–2020 and beyond, 2017–2021 and beyond, and 2018–2022 and beyond.

The last two columns of the table show the debt equivalents of the rental payments using the two approaches explained in Chap. 2. For the present value (PV), the "apparent" or implied borrowing rate is calculated as follows:

**Table 5.9** Estimated debt equivalent of operating leases ($millions)

| | | | | | | | | | Total | Present value (b) | Five times (c) |
|---|---|---|---|---|---|---|---|---|---|---|---|
| 2016–2020 and beyond | 2016 | 2017 | 2018 | 2019 | 2020 | Beyond 2020 | | | | | |
| Operating lease commitments (a) | $615 | $578 | $540 | $497 | $454 | $1621 | | | $4305 | $3214 | $3076 |
| 2017–2021 and beyond | – | 2016 | 2017 | 2018 | 2019 | 2020 | Beyond 2021 | | | | |
| Operating lease commitments | – | $636 | $603 | $565 | $523 | $496 | $1910 | | $4733 | $3493 | $3260 |
| 2018–2022 and beyond | – | – | 2017 | 2018 | 2019 | 2020 | 2021 | Beyond 2022 | | | |
| Operating lease commitments | – | – | $643 | $603 | $552 | $534 | $512 | $1730 | $4574 | $3414 | $3363 |

[a]Aircraft operating lease, other equipment, airport property and hangers, and office space
[b]The higher of the PVs from discounting the stream of payments under a constant and a declining rate assumption. Discount rate of 7%
[c]Apply a 5x multiple to the most recent (current year's) rental expense

**Table 5.10** Comparison between adjusted funded debt and unadjusted funded debt ($ Millions)

| Year | Total funded debt on balance sheet[a] Current portion + long-term portion | OBS obligations Operating lease commitments[b] | Loan guarantees[c] | Total adjusted funded debt | Difference between adjusted and unadjusted funded debt |
|---|---|---|---|---|---|
| 2014 | 14,288 | 3106 | 405 | 17,799 | 3511 |
| 2015 | 15,511 | 3214 | 400 | 19,125 | 3614 |
| 2016 | 17,869 | 3493 | 415 | 21,777 | 3908 |
| 2017 | 19,001 | 3414 | 425 | 22,841 | 3839 |

[a]Consists of debt and finance leases
[b]Higher of the PV of annual lease payments
[c]Guarantees include various indemnification agreements with counterparties

$$\text{Borrowing rate} = \frac{\text{Interest expenses}}{\left(\text{Beginning of year debt} + \text{End of year debt}\right)/2}$$

The three rates for the 2015–2017 period averaged 7.24%. For the PV calculation, we use a round figure of 7% for the discount rate. We chose the higher of the two present value estimates of total adjusted funded debt (shown in Table 5.9). As you may expect, the difference between the adjusted and unadjusted funded debt is significant, accounting for nearly a fifth of the total adjusted debt in each of the three years as reported in Table 5.10.

Pensions are another type of off-balance sheet (OBS) financing that the risk analyst needs to watch carefully because underfunded pension liabilities are increasingly a significant OBS debt in many corporations. The difference between the PBO (projected benefit obligations) and the fair value of the plan assets is the funded or unfunded status of the plan. The PBO is an estimate of the future stream of benefit obligations discounted to the present. The funded/unfunded status is a number that is usually buried somewhere in the footnotes, but it must be disclosed. In the case of AY Intercontinental, the footnotes of audited financial statement (pensions and other benefit liabilities) for the 2014–2017 period showed that projected benefit obligations (PBO) were about the same as the fair value of plan assets and the differences were not material.

If there were material underfunding, the analyst would use the difference between the two values, reduced by the corporate tax rate, as an *approximation* of the debt equivalent, and include this figure in total debt. Company cash contributions are tax deductible. For example, a $1 billion unfunded pension plan with a corporate tax rate of 30% means the company owes $700 million to its employees. We emphasise approximation because, as you can see from the derivation of unfunded pension liability, the fair market value is less prone to subjectivity than the PBO whose value depends on many assumptions. A company can reduce the PBO (and thereby increase the funded status) by increasing the discount rate, and by lowering the projected rate of salary increases. Another reason to pay close attention to unfunded pension plan is that a large underfunded plan inevitably means larger cash contributions and thus increases in company expense in the future. Pension accounting[6] is outside the scope of this book, but this brief presentation suffices to show the importance of including pension liabilities in the estimation of total debt.

**Financial Flexibility**

The ability of a company to obtain funding in the capital and credit markets is an important factor in its risk rating. A company with easy access to external funding is more likely to avoid a liquidity shortage than one with limited access. The ability of a borrower to raise equity and debt financing is a qualitative variable, which differentiates the degree of access, ranging from low to high. Table 5.11 gives the descriptors. In order to judge the borrower's ability to access credit markets, the credit analyst looks at the company funding record, which includes its debt and equity issues, the credit ratings of the company's short- and long-term debt, the amounts raised, and the spreads. Additionally, the credit analyst looks at the company financial strength.

For AY Intercontinental, the record of the last five years shows the airline has relied mainly on bank credit and to a limited extent on equity for its external funding. The ability of the airline to take on more debt is, however, lim-

**Table 5.11** Financial risk assessment—AY Intercontinental Airways

| Risk criteria | W (%) | Score | AA | Score | A | Score | BBB | Score | BB | Score | B |
|---|---|---|---|---|---|---|---|---|---|---|---|
| A. Financial performance | | | | | | | | | | | |
| Profitability | 10% | | | | | | | | | | |
| | | 16 | ≥ 28.5 | 13 | 22.5–24.4 | 10 | 16.5–18.4 | 7 | 10.5 – 12.4 | 4 | 4.5 – 6.4 |
| EBITDAR margin (%) | 100% | 15 | 26.5 – 28.4 | 12 | 20.5–22.4 | 9 | 14.5–16.4 | 6 | 8.5 – 10.4 | 3 | 2.6 – 4.4 |
| | | 14 | 24.5 – 26.4 | 11 | 18.5–20.4 | 8 | 12.5–14.4 | 5 | 6.5–8.4 | 2 | 0.1 – 2.5 |
| Efficiency | 10% | | | | | | | | | | |
| | | 16 | 97.9–100 | 13 | 89.8–93.3 | 10 | 79.1–82.5 | 7 | 68.4–71.9 | 4 | 57.6–61.1 |
| Load factor for consolidated operation (%) | 100% | 15 | 95.5–97.8 | 12 | 86.2–89.7 | 9 | 75.5–79.0 | 6 | 64.8–68.3 | 3 | 54.0–57.5 |
| | | 14 | 93.4–95.4 | 11 | 82.6–86.1 | 8 | 72.0–75.4 | 5 | 61.2–64.7 | 2 | ≤ 53.9 |
| Leverage | 20% | | | | | | | | | | |
| | | 16 | ≤ 0.8 – 0.0 | 13 | 1.3–1.5 | 10 | 2.2–2.4 | 7 | 3.1–3.3 | 4 | 4.0–4.3 |
| Adjusted funded debt/EBITDAR (X) | 50% | 15 | 0.9–1.0 | 12 | 1.6–1.8 | 9 | 2.5–2.7 | 6 | 3.4–3.6 | 3 | 4.4–4.7 |
| | | 14 | 1.1–1.2 | 11 | 1.9–2.1 | 8 | 2.8–3.0 | 5 | 3.7– 3.9 | 2 | ≥ 4.8 |
| | | 16 | 0.0–27.8 | 13 | 39.1–44.6 | 10 | 55.9–60.4 | 7 | 69.7–74.2 | 4 | 83.5– 88.5 |
| Adjusted funded debt/adjusted capital (%) | 50% | 15 | 27.9–33.4 | 12 | 44.7–50.2 | 9 | 60.5–65.0 | 6 | 74.3–78.8 | 3 | 88.6–94.6 |
| | | 14 | 33.5–39.0 | 11 | 50.3–55.8 | 8 | 65.1–69.6 | 5 | 78.9–83.4 | 2 | 94.7–100 |
| Coverage | 20% | | | | | | | | | | |
| | | 16 | > 20 | 13 | 10.8–13.0 | 10 | 5.0–6.0 | 7 | 2.1–2.5 | 4 | 0.6–0.9 |
| EBITDAR/(interest + rent) (X) | 100% | 15 | 15.5–17.7 | 12 | 8.4–10.7 | 9 | 3.8–4.9 | 6 | 1.5–2.0 | 3 | 0.0–0.5 |
| | | 14 | 13.1–15.4 | 11 | 6.1–8.3 | 8 | 2.6–3.7 | 5 | 1.0–1.4 | 2 | < 0 |
| Liquidity | 10% | | | | | | | | | | |
| | | 16 | > 25 | 13 | 15.1–18.0 | 10 | 6.7–9.0 | 7 | –3.1 to –6.0 | 4 | –12.1 to –15.0 |
| FCF/adjusted debt (%) | 50% | 15 | 21.1–24.0 | 12 | 12.1–15.0 | 9 | 3.3–6.6 | 6 | –6.1 to–9.0 | 3 | –15.1 to –19.0 |
| | | 14 | 18.1–21.0 | 11 | 9.1-12.0 | 8 | 0.0 –3.0 | 5 | –9.1 to–12.0 | 2 | < –20 |
| | | 16 | > 3.1 | 13 | 2.6–2.7 | 10 | 2.0–2.1 | 7 | 1.4–1.5 | 4 | 0.8–0.9 |
| Current assets/current liabilities (X) | 50% | 15 | 3.0-3.1 | 12 | 2.4–2.5 | 9 | 1.8–1.9 | 6 | 1.2–1.3 | 3 | 0.6–0.7 |
| | | 14 | 2.8-2.9 | 11 | 2.2–2.3 | 8 | 1.6–1.7 | 5 | 1.0–1.1 | 2 | < 0.5 |

| Risk criteria and measures | W (%) | AA | A | BBB | BB | B AND WORSE |
|---|---|---|---|---|---|---|
| B. Financial flexibility | | 15 | 12 | 9 | 6 | 3 |
| Ability to raise Equity and Debt Financing | 30% | A multinational company (public or private). Able to raise debt, equity, and mezzanine financing. If public company, rated rating is AA– (high-investment grade) or better; if unrated, financially strong as a high-grade public company. | A multinational company (public or private). Able to raise debt, equity, and mezzanine financing. If public company, rated A– (medium-investment grade) or better; if unrated, financially strong as a medium-grade public company. | Company can draw from committed and uncommitted bank facilities. Company listed on a major stock exchange and can raise equity. If public company, rated BBB– (low-investment grade) or better; if company, the equivalent of a low-investment grade public company. | Limited access to conventional bank loans, the bond, and equity markets. Limited access to secured debt – asset Based Lending) and Factoring. If public company, rated B– (non-investment grade. highly speculative) or better; If unrated, the equivalent of a highly speculative public company. | Severely limited access to conventional bank loans, the bond, and equity markets. Severely limited access to secured debt – asset Based Lending) and Factoring. If public company, publicly CCC– (extremely speculative) or worse; if unrated, the equivalent of an extremely speculative public company for which default imminent with poor recovery prospects. |

ited by the fact that the airline's leverage ratios are relatively weak. For example, gearing ratio of equity to adjusted capital, is low, averaging 1.4% in recent years (2015–2017). The airline has committed bank lines. Overall, a rating of "BBB–" seems appropriate for AY Intercontinental.

## Financial Risk Scorecard

Table 5.11 shows the placements of the descriptors for financial performance, followed by the BRR of AY Intercontinental in Table 5.12a.

**Table 5.12a** Base case; BRR of AY Intercontinental Airways

| Risk criteria | Weight | Score | Grade |
|---|---|---|---|
| Industry risk assessment | 15% | 6.68 | BB+ |
| Business risk assessment | 25% | 8.01 | BBB− |
| Management risk assessment | 20% | 8.00 | BBB− |
| Financial risk assessment | 40% | 8.60 | BBB |
| **Borrower risk rating** | | 8.04 | BBB− |

# 5.3  The Composite Score and Sensitivity Tests

Let us compare this scorecard with two other cases shown in Table 5.12b. The aim of the comparison is to validate the following claims:

- The Cyclical Adjustment Factor in business risk criterion tempers the business cycle effect on the composite BRR.
- The alternative of assessing financial risk based on *pro forma* financial statements has the same effect of dampening the business cycle effect on the composite BRR.

**Point-in-Cycle (PIC):** With the 40% weighting for financial risk, the credit score is very sensitive to current data. We run two simulations: (a) No Cyclical Adjustment Factor + use of PIC financials, and (b) PIC adjustment to financial risk section using *pro forma* financials. Here are the comparative results under three scenarios:

- **Base case:** *Cyclical adjustment captured in business risk using cyclical adjustment factors.* The score is 8.0 ("BBB−").
- **Alternative 1:** *No cyclical adjustment.* The score is 8.3 ("BBB+"), higher than the base case as expected.
- **Alternative 2:** *Cyclical adjustment captured in financial risk using* pro forma *financial statements.* The score is 7.8 ("BBB−"), lower than the BRR of Alternative 1, as expected.

Some important conclusions follow from these sensitivity tests:

- If the current and recent financial performance is volatile or unstable, projected financial ratios are more reliable than point-in-time financial data, which will underestimate the default risk.
- If significant changes to the borrower's balance sheet are expected, *pro forma* financial statements are more predictive than last twelve months (LTM) and current financial statements. The credit analyst should use *pro forma financial statements* to give a more reliable picture of future business conditions.

**Table 5.12b** Comparison of BRRs with and without cyclical adjustments

Company name: TY Intercontinental Airways

| Risk Criteria | W | Base case | | Alternative case 1 | | Alterative case 2 | |
|---|---|---|---|---|---|---|---|
| | | Score | Rating | Score | Rating | Score | Rating |
| Industry risk | 15% | 6.7 | BB+ | 6.7 | BB+ | 6.7 | BB+ |
| Business risk | 25% | 8.0 | BBB– | 9.0 | BBB | 9.0 | BBB |
| Management risk | 20% | 8.0 | BBB– | 8.0 | BBB– | 8.0 | BBB– |
| Financial risk | 40% | 8.6 | BBB | 8.6 | BBB | 7.4 | BBB– |
| Total weight | 100% | | | | | | |
| **Criteria-based BRR** | | **8.0** | **BBB–** | **8.3** | **BBB+** | **7.8** | **BBB–** |
| CRR/SRR Override (yes/no) | | No | AA+ | No | AA+ | No | AA+ |
| IA Override (yes/no) | | No | AA+ | No | AA+ | No | AA+ |
| **Final BRR** | | **8.0** | **BBB–** | **8.3** | **BBB+** | **7.8** | **BBB–** |

IA = Information Asymmetry
Base case: Cyclical adjustment captured in business risk using cyclical adjustment factor
Alternative 1: No cyclical adjustment
Alternative 2: Cyclical adjustment captured in financial risk using *pro forma* financial statements

- The point-of-interest (POI) adjustment provides a more reliable BRR for borrowers of highly cyclical industries and therefore a more reliable indicator of loan pricing.
- The industry risk serves to constrain the BRR. Although we did not perform the test, it is obvious that with a lower industry risk rating (IRR), *ceteris paribus*, the BRR will also be lower.

For illustration, we present the complete scorecard for Alternative 2 in Table 5.13.

# 5.4    Cash-Flow Projections for AY Intercontinental Airways

In this section, we illustrate the practical applications of financial forecasts in credit analysis and provide the techniques to prepare them. We look at two generic types:

1. *Pro forma* financial statements: A one- or multi-period forecast of an entity's financial statements consisting of the income statement, balance sheet, and cash-flow statement.
2. Cash-flow forecasting or cash budgeting: A one- or multi-period forecast of an entity's anticipated cash receipts and cash disbursements. It is an indispensable tool to assess whether the entity has sufficient cash or liquidity to operate effectively.

**Table 5.13** Credit risk scorecard

Company name: TY Intercontinental Airways

| Risk criteria | W | Risk factors | W | Risk elements | W | AA | ... | ... | B– | Score | Rating |
|---|---|---|---|---|---|---|---|---|---|---|---|
| **Industry risk** | **15%** | **Stability of revenue and profitability** | 40.0% | | | | | | | 6.7 | BB+ |
| | | | | Cyclical and seasonal volatility of revenue and profitability | 100.0% | | | | | 6.0 | BB |
| | | | | | | | | | | 6.0 | BB |
| | | **Outlook for growth and stability** | 60.0% | | | | | | | 7.1 | |
| | | | | Entry and exit barriers | 12.5% | | | | | 6.0 | BB |
| | | | | Product/service substitution and obsolescence | 12.5% | | | | | 12.0 | A |
| | | | | Industry stage | 12.5% | | | | | 6.0 | BB |
| | | | | Cost and cost structure | 12.5% | | | | | 6.0 | BB |
| | | | | Degree of unionisation | 12.5% | | | | | 6.0 | BB |
| | | | | Government regulation and country risk | 12.5% | | | | | 6.0 | BB |
| | | | | Demographics and social trends | 12.5% | | | | | 9.0 | BBB |
| | | | | Global market & competition | 12.5% | | | | | 6.0 | BB |
| **Business risk** | **25%** | **Competitive position** | 33.4% | | | | | | | 8.01 | BBB– |
| | | | | | | | | | | 9.0 | |
| | | | | Operating cost | 20.0% | | | | | 9.0 | BBB |
| | | | | Operating revenue | 20.0% | | | | | 9.0 | BBB |
| | | | | Fleet | 20.0% | | | | | 12.0 | A |
| | | | | Revenue Base | 20.0% | | | | | 9.0 | BBB |
| | | | | Customer service and safety | 20.0% | | | | | 6.0 | BB |
| | | **Market position** | 33.3% | | | | | | | 9.0 | |
| | | | | Revenue diversification by geography and services | 33.4% | | | | | 9.0 | BBB |
| | | | | Market share | 33.3% | | | | | 9.0 | BBB |
| | | | | Route network | 33.3% | | | | | 9.0 | BBB |

| Risk category | Wt | Component | Wt | Factor | Wt | Score | Rating |
|---|---|---|---|---|---|---|---|
| Management risk | 20% | | | | | 6.0 | BB |
| | | Cyclical position | 33.3% | Point-in-time adjustment | 100.0% | 6.0 | BBB− |
| | | Management quality | 20.0% | Management quality | 33.4% | 8.00 | BB |
| | | | | Business strategy | 33.3% | 6.0 | BBB |
| | | | | Financial strategy | 33.3% | 9.0 | BBB |
| | | | | Financial strategy | 33.3% | 9.0 | BBB |
| Financial risk | 40% | | | | | 8.60 | BBB |
| | | Financial performance | | | | 4.7 | |
| | | Profitability | 10.0% | EBITDAR margin (%) | 10.0% | 9.0 | BBB |
| | | Efficiency | 10.0% | Load factor for consolidated operation (%) | 10.0% | 11.0 | A− |
| | | Leverage | 10.0% | Adjusted Funded debt/EBITDAR (X) | 10.0% | 5.0 | BB− |
| | | Leverage | 10.0% | Adjusted Funded debt/adjusted capital (%) | 10.0% | 2.0 | B− |
| | | Coverage | 20.0% | EBITDAR/(interest + rent) (X) | 20.0% | 7.0 | BB+ |
| | | Liquidity | 5.0% | FCF/adjusted debt (%) | 5.0% | 8.0 | BBB− |
| | | Liquidity | 5.0% | Current assets/current liabilities (X) | 5.0% | 4.0 | B+ |
| | | Financial flexibility | | | | 2.7 | B+ |
| | | Ability to raise equity and debt financing | 30.0% | Ability to raise equity and debt financing | 100.0% | 9.0 | BBB |
| Total weight | 100% | | 100% | | 100% | | |
| Criteria Based BRR | | | | | | 7.8 | BBB− |
| CRR/SRR override (YES/NO) | | | | | | | AA+ |
| IA override (YES/NO) | | | | | | | NO |
| Final BRR | | | | | | | BBB− |

IA: Information Symmetry
Base case: No PIT adjustment in business risk with use of current financial statements
Alternative 1: PIT adjustment in business risk with use of current financial statements
Alternative 2: No PIT adjustment with use of projected financial statements

In general, the decision to use forecast data hinges essentially on whether the historical information on a company's recent performance is a good indicator of the future. In the particular case of AY Intercontinental Airways, we begin with the premise that the passenger airline industry is nearing the peak of the cycle. We combine elements of both *pro forma* financials and cash budgeting to measure the airline's capacity to repay its debt. As you will see, a financial forecast requires rebuilding much of the income statement and the balance sheet. One main use of the forecast is to determine whether a business is generating a cash surplus or deficit, vital clues on whether the company is likely to default on its debts.

Financial forecast modelling uses the language of finance and accounting in order to define the relevant inputs, the linkages, and the output, all in a consistent way. A *pro forma* financial statement is an example of deterministic modelling[7] in which the assumptions and the initial conditions fully determine the projections, which are the output of the model. There are various ways of setting up a cash-flow model and the level of sophistication depends on the application. We illustrate the modelling process with one of the simpler methods. They involve essentially projecting the financial statements based on the assumptions and the initial conditions. In our example, our "jump off" point is 2016. We present the model in two tables, one showing the assumptions (mainly ratios expressed in percentages) in Table 5.14, and the other for the forecast (output) in Table 5.15. The best place to begin is the profit and loss statement because total revenue, total operating expenses, and total non-operating expenses serve as the bases or the scaling factors.

First, we outline the steps and follow up with the actual calculations to generate the forecast.

### Step 1: Forecast Revenue, Expenses, and Net Income

- Total revenue by forecasting each component: passenger revenue, cargo revenue, and other revenue.
- Total operating expense. Use total revenue as the base to drive the individual operating expense items by applying the percentages (the percentage of each expense in total revenue) except for rental payment on the operating lease. The scheduled figures for rental payments on operating leases are usually reported in the footnotes of the annual report.
- Non-operating expenses, using total operating expense as a base and applying the percentages (the ratio of non-operating expense [NOE] to operating expense)
- Net income before taxes (NIBT) from the above projections: NIBT = operating revenue—operating expense—non-operating expense
- Taxes from NIBT by applying the tax rate assumption
- Net income = NIBT—taxes

**Table 5.14** Assumptions of financial forecast for AY Intercontinental Airways

| | History | | | Forecast assumptions | | |
|---|---|---|---|---|---|---|
| | 2015 | 2016 | 2017 | 2018(F) | 2019(F) | 2020(F) |
| **Income and expense drivers** | | | | | | |
| Revenue ($ MM) | 26,750 | 28,730 | 30,683 | 28,568 | 30,697 | 32,691 |
| Passenger revenue ($ MM) | 22,738 | 24,707 | 26,510 | 24,503 | 26,595 | 28,589 |
| ASM (available seat mile) - (000,000) | 1558 | 1674 | 1688 | 1650 | 1732 | 1819 |
| LF (load factor) | 81.1% | 82.0% | 83.1% | 82.5% | 83.0% | 83.6% |
| RRPM (yield) - Revenue (¢) per RPM | 18.0 | 18.0 | 18.9 | 18.0 | 18.5 | 18.8 |
| Cargo revenue ($ MM) | 2301 | 2442 | 2516 | 2416 | 2452 | 2452 |
| ATM (available ton mile) - (000,000) | 323 | 335 | 332 | 330 | 335 | 335 |
| Cargo load factor (based on ATMs) | 58.8% | 60.7% | 61.1% | 61.0% | 61.0% | 61.0% |
| RRCM (yield) - revenue (¢) per RCM | 12.1 | 12.0 | 12.4 | 12.0 | 12.0 | 12.0 |
| Other revenue ($ MM) | 1712 | 1580 | 1657 | 1650 | 1650 | 1650 |
| Operating expenses/revenue: | | | | | | |
| Aircraft fuel | 27.6% | 21.0% | 17.8% | 25.0% | 24.0% | 25.0% |
| Regional airlines expense | 1.8% | 2.2% | 3.2% | 3.3% | 3.4% | 3.3% |
| Employee costs | 25.8% | 28.0% | 29.2% | 32.0% | 30.0% | 30.0% |
| Airport and landing fees | 6.9% | 6.3% | 6.1% | 6.5% | 6.3% | 6.1% |
| Aircraft maintenance | 5.5% | 5.3% | 5.0% | 6.0% | 5.5% | 5.0% |
| Depreciation and amortisation | 6.1% | 6.0% | 6.9% | 7.1% | 6.8% | 6.8% |
| Selling costs | 4.6% | 4.6% | 4.6% | 5.0% | 4.6% | 4.6% |
| Contractual services | 3.0% | 4.4% | 2.6% | 2.7% | 2.6% | 2.6% |
| Aircraft leasing (rent) | 2.3% | 2.3% | 2.2% | 2.3% | 2.0% | 1.7% |
| Food and beverage service | 2.0% | 2.3% | 2.4% | 2.4% | 2.5% | 2.5% |
| Other (net) | 6.3% | 7.3% | 7.0% | 0.0% | 0.0% | 0.0% |
| Operating expense/revenue: | 92.0% | 89.7% | 87.0% | 92.3% | 87.7% | 87.6% |
| Non-operating expense/operating expense | 8.0% | 9.0% | 10.0% | 14.0% | 12.0% | 11.0% |
| Average term of L/T debt (yrs) | 12 | 12 | 12 | 12 | 12 | 12 |
| Average borrowing rate | 6.0% | 7.2% | 8.5% | 8.0% | 7.5% | 7.5% |
| Average tax rate | 35.0% | 35.0% | 35.0% | 35.0% | 25.0% | 25.0% |
| **Liquidity and working capital drivers** | | | | | | |
| Unrestricted cash | 286 | 387 | 350 | 350 | 350 | 350 |
| Minimum cash desired/revenue | – | – | – | 0.0% | 0.0% | 0.0% |
| Short-term investments/Total expense | 15.5% | 17.5% | 20.2% | 15.0% | 15.0% | 15.0% |
| Receivables turnover (days) | 26.0 | 26.1 | 25.4 | 25.0 | 25.0 | 25.0 |
| Inventory turnover (days) | 6.7 | 6.8 | 6.4 | 6.4 | 6.4 | 6.4 |
| Payables turnover (days) | 56.9 | 60.2 | 62.7 | 62.0 | 62.0 | 62.0 |
| Capex/revenue | 5.2% | 9.4% | 5.7% | 4.0% | 5.0% | 6.0% |
| Depreciation/operating expense | 6.1% | 6.0% | 6.9% | 7.1% | 6.8% | 6.8% |

Table 5.15 The financial forecast for AY Intercontinental Airways

| ($ millions) | History | | | Forecast | | |
|---|---|---|---|---|---|---|
| | 2015 | 2016 | 2017 | 2018 | 2019 | 2020 |
| **Income and expense** | | | | | | |
| Revenue | 26,750 | 28,730 | 30,683 | 28,568 | 30,697 | 32,691 |
| Revenue growth | 7.0% | 7.4% | 6.8% | −6.9% | 7.5% | 6.5% |
| Operating expenses: | | | | | | |
|   Aircraft fuel | 7383 | 6030 | 5448 | 7142 | 7674 | 8173 |
|   Regional airlines expense | 492 | 644 | 988 | 943 | 1013 | 1079 |
|   Employee costs | 6891 | 8058 | 8969 | 9142 | 9209 | 9807 |
|   Airport and landing fees | 1846 | 1804 | 1869 | 1857 | 1873 | 1994 |
|   Aircraft maintenance | 1477 | 1520 | 1548 | 1714 | 1535 | 1635 |
|   Depreciation and amortisation | 1624 | 1727 | 2109 | 2028 | 2087 | 2223 |
|   Selling costs | 1231 | 1314 | 1415 | 1428 | 1412 | 1504 |
|   Contractual services | 812 | 1263 | 801 | 771 | 798 | 850 |
|   Aircraft leasing (rent) | 615 | 652 | 673 | 643 | 603 | 552 |
|   Food and beverage service | 541 | 670 | 739 | 686 | 767 | 817 |
|   Other (net) | 1698 | 2087 | 2136 | – | – | – |
| Total operating expense | 24,610 | 25,770 | 26,694 | 26,354 | 26,972 | 28,634 |
| EBIT (operating income) | 2140 | 2959 | 3989 | 2214 | 3725 | 4057 |
| Non-operating expense | 1969 | 2319 | 2669 | 3690 | 3237 | 3150 |
| o.w: Interest expense | 900 | 1049 | 1205 | 1457 | 1252 | 1148 |
| Operating expense - depreciation[a] | 22,986 | 24,044 | 24,585 | 24,326 | 24,884 | 26,411 |
| EBITDAR | 4380 | 5338 | 6770 | 4885 | 6416 | 6832 |
| NIBT (net income before taxes) | 171 | 640 | 1319 | −1476 | 489 | 908 |
| Taxes | 60 | 224 | 462 | −517 | 122 | 227 |
| Net income | 111 | 416 | 858 | −959 | 367 | 681 |
| **Determination of cash inflows & outflows** | | | | | | |
| Net income | 111 | 416 | 858 | −959 | 367 | 681 |
| Items not involving cash: | | | | | | |
|   Depreciation and amortisation | 1624 | 1727 | 2109 | 2028 | 2087 | 2223 |
|   Unrealised foreign exchange loss (gain) | 68 | 134 | 104 | – | – | – |
|   Change in maintenance provisions | 46 | 48 | 57 | – | – | – |
|   Loss (gain) on disposal of prop'ty. & equipment | −34 | 52 | −15 | – | – | – |
| Changes in non-cash working capital balances (net) | 8 | 1840 | 992 | 252 | −88 | 88 |
|   Receivables | 2123 | 1993 | 2278 | 1957 | 2103 | 2239 |
|   Inventory | 544 | 531 | 541 | 501 | 538 | 573 |
|   Advance ticket sales | 4040 | 5079 | 5799 | 5700 | 5700 | 5700 |
|   Payables | 3629 | 4298 | 4142 | 4132 | 4227 | 4486 |
| Operating cash flow | 1824 | 4217 | 4105 | 1321 | 2366 | 2992 |
| Proceeds from borrowings | 1223 | 2359 | 1132 | | | |
| Principal payments | −1191 | −1293 | −1489 | −1583 | −1451 | −1331 |
| Issue of shares | 6 | 3 | 0 | – | – | – |
| Purchase of shares | −18 | −72 | −63 | – | – | – |
| Dividends paid | 0 | −25 | −60 | – | – | – |

(continued)

**Table 5.15** (continued)

|  | History | | | Forecast | | |
|---|---|---|---|---|---|---|
| ($ millions) | 2015 | 2016 | 2017 | 2018 | 2019 | 2020 |
| Financing cash flow | 20 | 972 | −480 | −1583 | −1451 | −1331 |
| Restricted cash | 286 | 387 | 350 | 350 | 350 | 350 |
| Short-term investments | 4109 | 4923 | 5923 | 4285 | 4605 | 4904 |
| Property & Equipment | 19,204 | 21,908 | 23,660 | 24,803 | 26,338 | 28,299 |
| Restricted cash | −5 | −101 | 37 | 0.0 | 0.0 | 0.0 |
| Sale (+)/purchase (−) of short-term investments | −109 | −814 | −1000 | 1638 | −319 | −299 |
| Capex | −1391 | −2704 | −1753 | −1143 | −1535 | −1961 |
| Other (net) | −144 | −1262 | −789 | – | – | – |
| Investing cash flow | −1649 | −4881 | −3506 | 495 | −1854 | −2261 |
| Free cash flow (FCF) | 433 | 1513 | 2352 | 178 | 831 | 1030 |
| Net cash from oper., invest., and financing activities | 196 | 308 | 119 | 233 | −940 | −600 |
| Effect of exchange rate changes on cash/equivalents | −13 | 18 | −17 | – | – | – |
| **Determination of cash needs** | | | | | | |
| Cash and cash equivalents, beginning of year | 1875 | 2058 | 2383 | 2485 | 2718 | 1778 |
| Cash and cash equivalents, end of year | 2058 | 2383 | 2485 | 2718 | 1778 | 1179 |
| Minimum cash desired (assumed) | – | – | – | 0 | 0 | 0 |
| Cash surplus (deficit) | | | | 2718 | 1778 | 1179 |
| **Projected credit measures** | | | | | | |
|  | 2015 | 2016 | 2017 | 2018(F) | 2019(F) | 2020(F) |
| EBITDAR margin (%) | 16.4 | 18.6 | 22.1 | 17.1 | 20.9 | 20.9 |
| Adjusted Funded debt/EBITDAR (X) | 4.4 | 4.4 | 4.4 | 4.2 | 2.9 | 2.4 |
| Adjusted Funded debt/adjusted capital (%) | 87.5 | 89.4 | 88.7 | 91.3 | 88.9 | 84.7 |
| EBITDAR/(interest + rent) (X) | 2.9 | 3.1 | 3.6 | 2.3 | 3.5 | 4.0 |
| FCF/adjusted Funded debt (%) | 2.3 | 6.8 | 10.0 | 0.9 | 4.5 | 6.2 |
| Current assets/current liabilities (X) | 1.2 | 1.1 | 1.1 | 0.8 | 0.8 | 0.8 |
| **Determination of cash needs** | 2015 | 2016 | 2017 | 2018(F) | 2019(F) | 2020(F) |
| Cash and cash equivalents, beginning of year | 1875 | 2058 | 2383 | 2485 | 2718 | 1778 |
| Cash and cash equivalents, end of year | 2058 | 2383 | 2485 | 2718 | 1778 | 1179 |
| Minimum cash desired (assumed) | 0 | 0 | 0 | 2857 | 3070 | 3269 |
| Cash surplus (deficit) | | | | −139 | −1291 | −2090 |
| Assume 10% minimum cash desired/revenue | | | | | | |

[a]Proxy for purchases on credit

**Step 2: Forecast Net Cash Flow from Operating Activities**

- Project liquidity and working capital from its components:
  - Short-term investments
  - Receivables
  - Inventory
  - Advance ticket sales
  - Payables

- Project net cash flow from operating activities = net income + net changes in non-cash working capital balances (from the above).

**Step 3: Forecast Net Cash Flow from Financing Activities**

- Project total debt from its components:
  - Current portion of long-term debt and finance leases
  - Long-term debt and finance/capital leases
  - PV operating leases
  - Guarantees

- Project principal payments (based on assumptions about average maturity of the outstanding debts).

**Step 4: Forecast Net Cash Flow from Investing and Financing Activities**

- Project capex
- Project short-term investments from which the changes are derived

**Step 5: Forecast Net Cash Flow from Operation, Financing, and Investing**

- Combine the results from the previous steps to forecast the total (net) change in cash flow

## 5.4.1 Performing the Calculations

**Forecasting Passenger Revenue**

In this section, we explain the formulas that drive the forecast. We begin with revenue. For a passenger airline, revenue is the product of three components at an aggregate level.

1. ASM (available seat miles): It is a measure of production. ASM represents one seat flown one mile.
2. PLF (passenger load factor): It is the proportion of an airline's seats that are filled by revenue passengers, derived by dividing RPM (revenue passenger miles) by ASM.
3. Revenue per revenue passenger miles (RRPM [yield]): It is the average fare per passenger per mile, derived by dividing total passenger revenue by total RPM.

We use the following formula:

$$\text{Passenger revenue} = \text{ASM} \times \text{PLF} \times \text{RRPM} \qquad (5.1)$$

Given the values for the variables on the right side of the equation, the spreadsheet calculates passenger revenue. Below is an illustration for 2018 and the same procedure is repeated for the rest of the forecast period. Table 5.14 gives these and other assumptions, where the ASM figure is in millions (MM).

$$\text{Passenger revenue}_{2018} = 1650 \times 82.5\% \times 18 = \$24,503 \text{ MM}$$

**Projecting Cargo Revenue**

Similarly, for cargo revenue, the three metrics are:

1. ATM (available ton miles): Represents one ton flown one mile.
2. CLF (cargo load factor): It is the proportion of an airline's cargo space filled by revenue cargo, derived by dividing revenue cargo miles (RCM) by ATM.
3. Revenue per revenue cargo mile (RRCM [yield]): RRCM is the average fee per cargo per mile, derived by dividing total cargo revenue by total RCM.

In the formula below, we use 2018 for illustration. The values of the three factors on the right side of the equation are given in the same table, where ATM is in millions.

$$\text{Cargo revenue}_{2018} = \text{ATM} \times \text{CLF} \times \text{RRCM} = \$2416 \text{ MM} \qquad (5.2)$$

**Forecasting Expenses**

(A) Operating expense

The expenditure items are grouped into two segments, operating and non-operating, because we need to forecast EBIT, a measure of operating income.

In order to forecast the line items of operating expenditures, we apply the ratio of operating expense to total revenue (expressed in percent) for each type of operating expenditure. The general formula to calculate the $i^{th}$ operating expenditure in period $t$ is the following:

$$\text{Operating expenditure}_t^i \, (\text{OE}) = \text{OE ratio}_t^i \times \text{Total revenue}_t \qquad (5.3)$$

For example, airline fuel is one of the largest expenditures of an airline. Our forecast assumes a ratio of 25% and with total revenue of $28,568 MM in 2018, airline fuel is projected at $7142 MM in 2018.

$$\text{Airline fuel}_{2018} = 0.25 \times (\$28,568 \, \text{MM}) = \$7142 \, \text{MM}$$

This formula does not apply to rental payments, which is an operating expenditure. This line item is the minimum rental payment scheduled for 2017–2020 based on the capitalised operating leases at the end of 2016. Chapter 2 explains the capitalisation procedure.

(B)  Non-operating expense

For non-operating expense (NOE, we apply the non-operating expense ratio to total operating expense.

$$\text{NOE}_{ti} = \text{NOE ratio}_{ti} \times \text{Operating expense}_{ti} \qquad (5.4)$$

Let us illustrate how the formula works with 2018 assumptions shown on the right side of the equation:

$$\text{Non-operating expense}_{2018} = 0.14 \times \$26,354 = \$3690 \, \text{MM}$$

The formula does not apply to interest payments, which are non-operating expenses. A separate formula is used to calculate the payments based on the total outstanding debt and the interest rate, which is an average rate.

$$\text{Interest expense} = i \times \text{debt} \qquad (5.5)$$

where $i$ is the average borrowing rate and debt is the average of the previous and current period's funded debt and finance leases. In any year, the total debt consists of four components: (1) the current portion of the funded debt and finance leases, (2) the long-term portion of funded debt and finance leases, (3) the capi-

**Table 5.16** Projected debt of AY International Airways

| Total debt | 2015 | 2016 | 2017 | 2018F | 2019F | 2020F |
|---|---|---|---|---|---|---|
| Total adjusted debt | 19,130 | 21,777 | 22,841 | 20,589 | 18,535 | 16,652 |
| Current portion of long-term debt and finance leases | 1293 | 1489 | 1583 | 1451 | 1331 | 1220 |
| Long-term debt & finance leases | 14,218 | 16,380 | 17,418 | 15,966 | 14,636 | 13,416 |
| PV operating lease | 3214 | 3493 | 3414 | 2771 | 2168 | 1616 |
| Guarantees | 405 | 415 | 425 | 400 | 400 | 400 |

talised operating lease, and (4) guarantees. To simplify the forecast, we assume no long-term funded borrowing. This means the outstanding debts decline each year by the scheduled debt repayments including the scheduled minimum rental payment on the off-balance sheet operating leases. For guarantees, the balance was $425 MM at end-2016 and it is not a material amount. The forecast assumes a fixed amount of $400 MM throughout the forecast horizon (Table 5.16).

Let us apply the formula 5.5 assuming the average interest rates of 8% for 2018, where figures in parenthesis are in millions:

$$\text{Interest expense}_{2018} = 0.08 \times \frac{(1583 + 17,418 + 1451 + 15,966)}{2} = \$1457 \, \text{MM}$$

**Forecasting Working Capital**

We focus on the three main drivers of working capital (current assets minus current liabilities):

1. Accounts receivable
2. Inventory
3. Accounts payable

In order to forecast these items, we need to make assumption about the turnover ratios that we discussed in Chap. 2. To recap, these metrics are defined as follows:

$$\text{Receivables turnover} = \frac{\text{Average accounts receivable}}{\text{Revenue}} * 365 \, \text{days} \quad (5.6)$$

$$\text{Inventory turnover} = \frac{\text{Average inventory}}{\text{COGS}} * 365 \, \text{days} \quad (5.7)$$

$$\text{Payables turnover} = \frac{\text{Average accounts payable}}{\text{Purchases on credit}} * 365 \, \text{days} \quad (5.8)$$

Reviewing the recent history, we see that the airline's turnover rate for *accounts receivable* is close to 30 days, which means that on average the company collects revenue from its credit transactions a few days short of a month. Based on the recent pattern, we assume a turnover rate of 25 days throughout the forecast period. For a predominantly service business, such as an airline, the generic concept of an operating cycle and the measurement of *inventory turnover* ratio based on COGS (cost of goods sold) seem less important compared to a manufacturing and retailing business. The reason is that although available airline seats are inventory and seats are sold, *they cannot be inventoried at value but only in quantity.* Furthermore, the number of available seats is fixed.

However, airlines still carry other types of inventory that consist mainly of spare parts, the food and beverages served during a flight, and disposable utensils. These supplies are recorded at cost in the balance sheet. The calculation of an inventory turnover ratio requires COGS, which by definition, applies only to businesses that sell or make products. For a service-based entity, the alternative metric is cost of revenue[8]; hence the following formula:

$$\text{Inventory turnover} = \frac{\text{Average inventory}}{\text{Revenue}} * 365\,\text{days} \qquad (5.9)$$

Using Eq. (5.9), we obtain an average turnover rate of 6.4 days for the 2014–2017 period. We project the same turnover rate for the forecast.

For the calculation of *accounts payable* turnover using Eq. (5.8), you need data for *cash payments*, but you would not find the information in the income statement, nor in the footnotes. The best proxy for cash payments is obtained by subtracting depreciation expense, a non-cash item, from total operating expense.[9] Based on the carrier's recent history, the turnover rate averaged 62 days, roughly two months. We project the same turnover rate for the forecast.

In order to generate the volume of accounts receivable, inventory, and accounts payable, we rearrange the formulae, shown below with examples of the projections for 2018, where revenue and cost figures are in millions of dollars.

$$\text{Accounts receivable}\,(\$) = \frac{\text{Total revenue} \times \text{Turnover ratio}}{365} \qquad (5.10)$$

$$\text{Accounts receivable}_{2018} = \frac{28{,}568 \times 25}{365} = \$1957\,\text{MM}$$

$$\text{Inventory} (\$) = \frac{\text{Total revenue} \times \text{Turnover ratio}}{365} \qquad (5.11)$$

$$\text{Inventory}_{2018} = \frac{28,568 \times 6.4}{365} = \$501\text{MM}$$

$$\text{Accounts payable} (\$) = \frac{(\text{Operating expense} - \text{Dep'n}) \times \text{Turnover ratio}}{365}$$

$$(5.12)$$

$$\text{Accounts payable}_{2018} = \frac{24,326 \times 62}{365} = \$4132 \text{ MM}$$

**Forecasting Investments**

The investment activities of AY Intercontinental revolve around restricted cash, short-term investments, and capex (capital expenditures). In the footnotes of the annual reports, the airline explains that it holds restricted cash to comply with regulations applying to advance ticket sales and escrow accounts. The opening balance of $350 million included undrawn lines of credit of $200 million. We also observe that a portion of the restricted cash seems largely independent of changes in the cash-flow drivers, such as revenue and expenses. Airlines manage *liquidity risk* and *credit risk* by holding liquid assets. These are short-term financial instruments with a maximum term of 12 months. Using all this information, we project that the amount stays the same at $350 million during the forecast period.

Keynes (1936)[10] famously wrote about "the three divisions of liquidity preference" in his *General Theory of Employment, Interest and Money*. Keynes proposed the theory to explain an individual's demand for money but the theory applies with equal relevance to a business because the reasons or the motives for holding cash are the same for both:

1. **Transaction motive:** Governs cash an airline holds to pay for everyday operating expenses. The amount held is positively related to scale, or the level of economic activity.
2. **Precautionary motive:** Governs cash held to deal with unforeseen circumstances, which include unanticipated seasonal and cyclical trends, an unexpected rise in jet fuel price, pilot strike, and so on.

3. **Speculative motive:** Governs cash held to take advantage of investment opportunities. In the airline business, expanding carriers are always looking for opportunities to buy over other airlines that have profitable routes.

At any given time, the transactions motive would dominate. A passenger airline spends huge sums for supplies and labour. The industry is, however, characterised by substantial volatility in cash flows, a factor in the demand function for precautionary cash balances. Similar to individuals, transaction and precautionary demands by businesses are more important than the speculative demand. We assume AY Intercontinental desires to hold 15% of total expense in short-term securities to help manage liquidity and credit risks, a figure that compares roughly to the average of the last three years, 2015–2017. To forecast the volume of short-term investments, we use the ratio of short-term investment to revenue as the driver and, for lack of a better label, we call this metric, FIR (financial investment ratio):

$$\text{Short-term investments} = \text{Total revenue} \times \text{FIR} \qquad (5.13)$$

$$\text{Short-term investment}_{2018} = 28,568 \times 0.15 = \$4285\text{MM}$$

Although we capture the precautionary motive by including in the forecast "minimum cash desired", the base case forecast sets the minimum cash desired at zero.

**Forecasting Capital Expenditure (Capex)**
The forecast makes provision for capital expenditure, which is vital to the ability of an airline to operate successfully. In the case of AY Intercontinental, the need for major fleet overhaul is minimal; however, it has commitments to take delivery of planes. The forecast assumes the capex/revenue ratio moderates in 2018, but ramps up in 2019 and 2020. Since we assumed no further borrowings during period 2017–2020, the capex is unfunded. The following formula drives the capex forecast:

$$\text{Capex} = \text{Capex ratio} \times \text{Revenue} \qquad (5.14)$$

$$\text{Capex}_{2018} = 0.04 \times 28,568 = \$1143\,\text{MM}$$

## 5.5   Summary of the Financial Forecast

### 5.5.1   Forecast Results from Stress Testing

To stress test revenues and expenses, we frontload the scenario by letting the economic downturn occur in the first year of the forecast period rather than delaying it towards the end of the period. Table 5.17 gives a summary of the forecast in terms of financial ratios that predict default. The main results of the projections are as follows:

- Top line revenue contract by 7% in 2018 from the previous year, erasing the gain of the previous year.
- Operating expenses also fall but not nearly as fast as revenue.
- EBIT contracts from almost $4 billion in 2017 to slightly over $2.2 billion in 2018.
- The airline records a bottom-line loss of $959 million in 2018.
- Performance recovers in 2019 and 2020 based on conservative assumptions on business conditions.
- Liquidity weakens significantly in 2018, indicated by the drop in the free cash-flow ratio and the current ratio.
- Despite the projected net loss in 2018 and the deterioration in liquidity, the airline meets payments on the total debt, including the off-balance sheet liabilities, from operating income.
- Incorporating the financial deterioration in anticipation of an economic slowdown, the scorecard gives a lower BRR compared to using current and recent financial data.

### 5.5.2   Forecasting the Financing Gap

Treasurers use a financial forecast to determine the company financing needs and the extent of external funding. In credit analysis, the cash budget is a useful tool not only to quantify the gap, but also to assess the risk of default. One of

**Table 5.17** Summary of the financial forecast

|  | 2015 | 2016 | 2017 | 2018(F) | 2019(F) | 2020(F) |
|---|---|---|---|---|---|---|
| EBITDAR margin (%) | 16.4 | 18.6 | 22.1 | 17.1 | 20.9 | 20.9 |
| Adjusted Funded debt/EBITDAR (X) | 4.4 | 4.4 | 4.4 | 4.2 | 2.9 | 2.4 |
| Adjusted Funded debt/adjusted capital (%) | 87.5 | 89.4 | 88.7 | 91.3 | 88.9 | 84.7 |
| EBITDAR/(interest + rent) (X) | 2.9 | 3.1 | 3.6 | 2.3 | 3.5 | 4.0 |
| FCF/adjusted Funded debt (%) | 2.3 | 6.8 | 10.0 | 0.9 | 4.5 | 6.2 |
| Current assets/current liabilities (X) | 1.2 | 1.1 | 1.1 | 0.8 | 0.8 | 0.8 |

**Table 5.18** Projecting external financing gap due to minimum cash requirement ($MM)

| Determination of cash needs | 2015 | 2016 | 2017 | 2018(F) | 2019(F) | 2020(F) |
|---|---|---|---|---|---|---|
| Cash and cash equivalents, beginning of year | 1875 | 2058 | 2383 | 2485 | 1429 | 1026 |
| Cash and cash equivalents, end of year | 2058 | 2383 | 2485 | 1429 | 1026 | 1183 |
| Minimum cash desired[a] | – | – | – | 2857 | 3076 | 3284 |
| Cash surplus (deficit) | | | | −1428 | −2050 | −2102 |

[a]Assume desired 10% of total revenue

the things we learned in previous chapters is that defaults are often the result of illiquidity rather than insolvency. The determination of external funding is:

$$\text{External funding required} = \text{Total sources} - \text{Total uses}$$

We asked the "what if" question: Suppose the airline wants to hold 10% of revenue in cash for precautionary reasons; what would be the effect on the financing gap? We test the scenario by assuming a minimum cash ratio of 10%. The results are shown in Table 5.18.

The result is a financing gap of $1.4 BN in 2018 and rising through the rest of the period. This is useful information for the credit analyst, for it shows that the airline would have to borrow significant sums in the next three years. A cash-flow model is obviously indispensable for scenario analysis to quantify high, medium, and low financial outcomes.

# Notes

1. See Damodaran, Aswath (Stern School of Business at New York University), *Debt Ratio Trade Off Variables by Industry*, Data of last *update: January 5, 2017*. For the global air transport industry, the ratio of fixed assets/total assets was 59.25, which is in the top decile. The highest (77.64%) was in railroads. In general, the transportation sector is highly capital intensive.

2. A long string of airlines across the United States and in Europe have gone bankrupt. In October 2017, Monarch Airlines joined the list. In March 2018, Alitalia Airlines went bankrupt.

3. A route "right" is the right granted to a country's airline with the privilege to enter and land in another country's airspace. Airport slots are specific time periods in which an aircraft may land or take off at an airport. A slot right is therefore the right granted to an airline to land and take off at specific times.

4. Cost per available seat mile (CASM) is a measure of unit cost in the airline industry. CASM is calculated by dividing all operating expenses by the total number of available seat miles produced. Sometimes, fuel or transport-related

expenses are excluded from CASM calculations to better isolate and directly compare operating expenses. Revenue per available seat mile (RASM), called "unit revenue", is calculated by dividing the airline's total revenue by total available seat miles.

5. This definition of funded debt excludes underfunded pension obligations, measured by the excess of pension and benefit liabilities over pension and benefit assets. A broad definition of debt must include the unfunded pension and benefits since they represent a claim on future earnings.

6. See Bernstein, Leopold and Wild (1998) and White, Sondhi and Fried (1997), ibid. Chap. 12, "Pensions and other employee benefits".

7. The opposite of a *deterministic* model is the *stochastic* model in which the output is not fully determined but random. For example, the deterministic model, $N_t = N_0 \lambda^t$ describes geometric growth where, at any time, $N$ (stands for population at any time) is fully determined by the initial value $N_0$, and the constant or known value of $\lambda$, which is the geometric rate of increase. Still, a deterministic model can handle uncertainty. The growth model shown earlier can be made stochastic by allowing $\lambda$ to vary according to a probability distribution, and this makes the output stochastic. In financial forecasting, the uncertainties in the input can be handled through the technique of a *Monte Carlo* simulation that uses a range of probable values of the inputs or assumptions in order to drive a range of potential outcomes. Notice that in a deterministic model, the uncertainty is external or exogenous, whereas in stochastic model, the uncertainty in the inputs or parameters is built-in or endogenous.

8. The turnover rates based on COGS and revenue are obviously not the same, and trying to reconcile the two can be tricky. This is because unit COGS is measured at cost, whereas unit revenue—equivalently the selling price—combines unit cost of production and a profit margin. The selling price is market determined and it covers not only production cost but also a profit margin. Thus, in a normal situation, unit revenue is greater than unit COGS, so unit revenue gives a lower turnover rate compared to the COGS measure. That said, goods and services do sell below unit cost of production, but such a situation cannot be sustainable because it means that the companies involved will eventually go out pf business.

9. Vasigh, Bijan., Fleming, Basil., Humphreys, J., (2014), *Foundations of Airline Finance*, Routledge, 2nd edition. See Chapter 7, Assessment of financial statements.

10. Keynes, J. M (1936), op. cit. Page 170, Ch. 13.

# 6

# Credit Risk Analysis and Credit Risk Rating of Commercial Real Estate

**Chapter Objectives**

1. Differentiate between residential mortgage loans and commercial mortgage loans
2. Assess the risks associated with commercial real estate lending
3. Develop a financial forecast for a commercial property (template is available online)
4. Learn to design a borrower risk rating (BRR) scorecard for income-producing real estate (IPRE)

## 6.1  Introduction

In this chapter, we extend the criteria-based approach to commercial real estate (CRE), which is business and commercial property that is not owner-occupied and earns rental income for profit. Commercial real estate (CRE) property includes office, industrial property, retail, hospitality, multifamily housing, industrial buildings, medical or care facilities, warehouses, garages, parking structures, and so on. There are numerous factors in the supply and demand in the CRE market and some of these are reported in Table 6.1. As you can see from this list of variables, those that drive up the demand for

**Electronic Supplementary Material:** The online version of this chapter (https://doi.org/10.1007/978-3-030-32197-0_6) contains supplementary material, which is available to authorized users.

**Table 6.1** Factors that influence the CRE market and valuations

| Factors | Expected Influence on Supply | Expected Influence on Demand |
|---|---|---|
| Broad economic trends (real income, growth in real income, employment, growth in employment) | +ve | +ve |
| Land availability | +ve | |
| Government policies and regulations | +ve or −ve | +ve or −ve |
| Demographic (population and population growth) | +ve | +ve |
| Relative prices (domestic/foreign) for the sane asset type | +ve | −ve |
| Inventory/sales ratio | −ve | |
| Occupancy rates | +ve | |
| Vacancy rates | −ve | |
| Absorption rate (rate at which homes are selling) | +ve | +ve |
| Rent/square foot | +ve | −ve |
| Cap rate | +ve | |
| Availability of financing | +ve | |
| Availability of supplies and workers | +ve | |
| Cost of capital (mortgage interest rates) | −ve | |
| Cost of production (land, wages, building supplies, transaction fees) | −ve | |

rental property drive supply in the same direction, but not always. For example, the higher the rents for an apartment, the lower the *amount* of space demanded; however, rising rents attract developers, *ceteris paribus*. Therefore, the supply *curve* at the given rent shifts upwards.

An important point to bear in mind is that unlike many goods whose prices are determined by active trading, there are no such equivalents in real estate. This means that the value of a real estate asset is an estimate of the true, unknown market price. Contrast this with the valuation of a *public company* whose stock trades actively in the exchanges. The market value of the company is simply the number of outstanding shares times the market price/share. Obviously, the value will change constantly during the day as the stock price changes, but market-clearing prices are observable.

Two things about CRE credit analysis are worth noting at the outset. First, whereas national trends come into play in assessing a CRE loan, real estate is *essentially* local so that regional conditions are often more important. Second, *time* is an important factor in CRE price dynamics. Prices are higher in the short run because the construction takes time and supply is fixed—some buildings take longer to build than others even within the same property type. We say supply is inelastic in the short run, but with the passage of time, it becomes more elastic as the rise in rents encourages building. As more floor space becomes available whilst the demand for floor space stays unchanged or rises at a slower pace, rents would start to stabilise.

**The Difference Between CRE Lending and Other Business Lending**

The credit risk of a commercial mortgage fundamentally depends on the financial performance of the underlying collateral/property and the market environment. So the BRR is based on an understanding of the uncertainties surrounding the CRE asset and attempting to quantify them. In other types of business credit, the BRR assessment is on the operation of the company. Often, a business loan is unsecured.

This basic background information gives us a feel for the economics of commercial real estate. We can use the information to help us start thinking of the factors we might want to include in the scorecard based on the criteria-based approach to determine the BRR. In commercial real estate lending, a lender does not rate the creditworthiness of the real estate company that is applying for a mortgage loan. Instead, the lender assigns the BRR to the asset being acquired because it generates the income to repay the mortgage. The following diagram (Fig. 6.1) is a general depiction of the credit risk analysis of an income-producing real estate (IPRE) property that is being financed by a mortgage.

As shown in Fig. 6.1, a property has the four basic attributes related to the tenant, the lease, and the location and condition of the property. These factors determine the income from renting the property and they determine the operating expenses. The difference between the two is net operating income (NOI) that goes to repay the principal and cover interest on the loan. When a bank underwrites a commercial real estate mortgage, it looks to the cash flow of the *property* as the primary source of repayment and not to the bor-

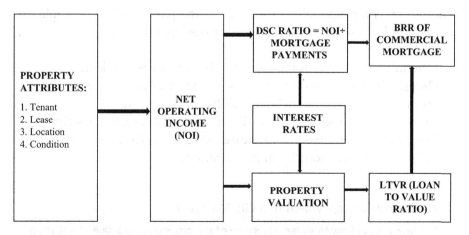

**Fig. 6.1** Factors determining commercial real estate lending

rower's collateral or other sources of repayment. In this sense, a lender determines first whether the property qualifies for the loan and secondarily the borrower.

Commercial mortgage lenders set minimum thresholds for the DSC ratio (debt service coverage ratio) and maximum thresholds for the LTV ratio (loan-to-value ratio), both of which vary by property type to reflect the relative risks. A riskier property will typically have higher DSC ratio requirements than other properties with more stable cash flows, such as apartments. The ratio of NOI to mortgage payments of interest and principal payments is the DSC ratio. The DSC ratio gives a lender a margin of safety. For example, by requiring a $1.50 \times$ DSC ratio, the lender is building in a cushion in the property's cash flow above the annual debt service. At this ratio, NOI could decline by 33.3% [Breakeven (%) = [(1.50 − 1.00)/1.50] and the loan payments would still be fully covered. In addition, the lender must know the value of the property and the down payment to determine the LTV ratio. A quick method to estimate the value of a property is the current NOI divided by the capitalisation rate (called the cap rate) observed in a particular market. The cap rate is the one-year rate of return from buying a property with cash and not a loan. Readers will recognise this formula as nearly identical to the *perpetuity formula*, which discounts a perpetual stream of annual income by the expected rate of return. In practice, lenders rely on more detailed valuation methods, which we will examine later.

## 6.2   Application of the Criteria-Based Methodology to CRE

The risk criteria methodology presented in the previous chapters applies to any type of loan, so let us recap the steps to design a scorecard:

- Determine the source of the cash flow that will repay the debt.
- Decide which set of Risk Criteria—industry, business, management, and financial—will form the building block of the scorecard.
- Specify the Risk Factors and the Risk Elements, and create Descriptors.
- Weight the Risk Criteria, the Risk Factors, and the Risk Elements.
- Build override functionality in the scorecard.

### The Sources of Repayment of a CRE Mortgage

1. Primary: Cash flow from rental income of the property or the sale of units/lots
2. Secondary: Liquidation of collateral
3. Tertiary: Personal guarantees offering an extra layer of protection

For illustration, we will be discussing these property types:

- Multifamily (apartment buildings)
- Hospitality (hotel, motel)
- Office
- Care facilities (medical, nursing homes, etc.)
- Retail stores

## 6.3 Risk Assessment Factors

We stated earlier that for CRE loans, lenders look primarily at the cash flow of the property for repayment. The demand for commercial premises has an overwhelming influence on cash. The demand for commercial real estate is a *derived demand*—a market demand for a particular product or service arising from another market demand for a different product or service. The demand for many goods we consume is a derived demand. For example, demand for *commuting* drives demand for *buses and trains*, two different goods. The demand for such modes of transportation is derived from the need to get to work. Using this economic principle, demand for apartments for example is a derived demand for dwelling space; demand for malls is a derived demand for consumer goods, and so on. Thus, the credit analyst needs to look at the risk factors that drive the profitability of the primary economic activity to assess the cash flow of the IPRE asset.

In designing the scorecard, the credit analyst needs to determine whether the IPRE is stabilised or un-stabilised because it has important implications for cash flow. A stabilised property is one that meets these characteristics:

- It is fully leased or leased at market occupancy
- Property rents are at market rates
- Tenant turnover is low and staggered
- It requires minimal capital improvements to maintain current standards

In contrast, an un-stabilised property typically is one that is being renovated or redeveloped and they tend to incur high maintenance expense.

A key characteristic of an un-stabilised property is that it charges below market rents and is struggling to raise occupancy rates to market levels. Because the cash flow is more uncertain than a stabilised property, the credit risk is higher. Thus, the prices of un-stabilised properties are listed below market in order to attract investors, which means that their cap rates are higher to compensate for the higher risk. The aim of a property owner in the un-stabilised property market is to make a profit by fixing deficiencies in the property and transforming it into a higher-valued stabilised property. It follows that a scorecard for un-stabilised IPRE will have different predictors and weights. In particular, for obvious reasons, lease maturity plays no role in the scorecard, tenant quality would be assigned the lowest weight, whereas the DSC ratio would have about a third of the total weight. This chapter does not cover un-stabilised properties.

The Risk Assessment Factors that really matter the most for an IPRE score-card are (a) Business Risk and (b) Financial Risk. The Business Risk Assessment is the qualitative part of the credit analysis, whereas the Financial Risk Assessment is the quantitative part. Industry Risk and Management Risk are not separate components, but they are not entirely ignored. The business risk reflects the physical and leasing characteristics of the property that make it desirable or undesirable for occupancy, whereas the financial risk reflects the debt-servicing strengths or weaknesses of the property once the property is leased up.

As for the weighting, it seems reasonable to default to equal weighting. A property will be unprofitable if the Business Risk is high. Business Risk rises with a deterioration in tenant quality, the location, the condition of the property, and the shorting of tenant lease terms. All are critical to the cash flow, so that it is hard to argue which is more important. First, let us look at Business Risk and its drivers (weights are in brackets):

1. Tenant quality (30–35% weighting)
2. Lease maturity (30–35% weighting)
3. Location (15–20% weighting)
4. Condition (15–20% weighting)

In order to come up with reasonable weights, the credit analyst must understand how the four attributes influence the cash flow. Tenant quality determines mainly the sustainability of the rental revenue, and determines significantly the cost of operating the property. Some of these costs or expenses are often not recoverable from the lease agreements, which means that either the property owner absorbs the costs or defers expenditures for maintenance and upgrades. Whereas tenant quality affects the level of revenue, the lease maturity determines its variability. A long-term lease, for example, provides more income stability than a lease that will expire after short periods without the certainty of renewal—called tenant rollover risk—or without the certainty of a new tenant. The location influences the marketability and the desirability of the property. The condition of the property also influences its marketability and desirability. At the same time, location affects the cost of operation. These are the various expenditures to maintain the property in a desirable state.

This background knowledge enables the credit analyst to rank the four attributes in order of importance. We give more weight to tenant quality than to location. A property in a good location may be fully rented up and still earn low NOI, or may even be losing money, if maintenance costs are too high. For this reason, property owners require tenants to show evidence of employment and income to screen out applicants who are likely to fall behind in their rent payments. Property owners do routine background checks such as credit reports and may ask for character references. Another desirable feature includes long-term tenants in the rent roll because the longer the lease term, the more stable the cash flow. We justify the equal ranking for location and condition for the reason that choosing between a poorly maintained apartment in a good location and a well-maintained apartment in a bad location, a tenant would likely be indifferent to the two.

## 6.4   Business Risk Assessment

### 6.4.1 Multifamily Property

The scorecard for Business Risk would consist of the property type and the descriptors (indicated by "d"), as shown in Table 6.2. We simplify it by listing a subset of the BRR grades. You would notice right away that the layout of the scorecard is relatively simple in that the attributes are just the Risk Criteria and there is no need to define Risk Factors and Risk Elements. The only important features you need to know are the descriptors. Let us examine each for a multifamily property and a retail property. The purpose is to illustrate how you go about defining the descriptors.

**Tenant Quality**
Tenant quality generally refers to the following:

1. The honesty and integrity of the tenant
2. The ability of the tenant to pay the rent on time for the remaining length of the lease
3. The ability of the tenant to meet the requirements of their lease

A lender cannot *quantify* quality directly but indirectly. One important source of information is the rent roll, which shows directly whether the tenants have the ability to pay their rents. Another measurable predictor of ten-

**Table 6.2** Business risk assessment of commercial real estate

| BUILDING TYPE | W | AA | A | BBB | BB | B | D |
|---|---|---|---|---|---|---|---|
| **MULTIFAMILY** | | | | | | | |
| Tenant Quality | 30% | | d | d | d | d | |
| Lease Maturity | 30% | | d | d | d | | |
| Location | 20% | d | d | d | d | d | |
| Condition | 20% | d | d | d | d | d | |
| **HOTEL** | | | | | | | |
| Tenant Quality | 30% | | d | d | d | d | |
| Lease Maturity | 30% | | d | d | d | d | |
| Location | 20% | | d | d | d | d | |
| Condition | 20% | d | d | d | d | | |
| **OFFICE** | | | | | | | |
| Tenant Quality | 30% | d | d | d | d | d | |
| Lease Maturity | 30% | d | d | d | d | d | |
| Location | 20% | d | d | d | d | d | |
| Condition | 20% | d | d | d | d | d | |
| **CARE** | | | | | | | |
| Tenant Quality | 30% | d | d | d | | | |
| Lease Maturity | 30% | d | d | d | | | |
| Location | 20% | d | d | d | d | d | |
| Condition | 20% | d | d | d | d | d | |
| **RETAIL** | | | | | | | |
| Tenant Quality | 30% | d | d | d | d | d | |
| Lease Maturity | 30% | d | d | d | d | d | |
| Location | 20% | d | d | d | d | d | |
| Condition | 20% | d | d | d | d | d | |
| **d: Descriptor** | | | | | | | |

ant quality is the vacancy rates. A borrower must provide the information to a lender in order to be considered for a loan. The aim of the following examples is to show that once you have the risk rating scale and the BRR categories established, your task as model builder or the credit analyst is to create the *sets of attributes* of the predictors that differentiate the default risks or the BRRs. To drive home the point, let us start with tenant quality for a few BRRs.

- A: It implies high tenant quality, with high occupancy (low vacancy) rates, and low turnover. The A-rated high-rise apartments would likely have more than 100 units and are professionally managed.
- BBB: It implies average tenant quality and relatively low vacancy rates. A BBB-rated apartment applies to a mid-rise apartment of 5–10 stories, with between 30 and 100 units, and elevator service.
- BB: It implies low tenant quality; high turnover with low occupancy (high vacancy) rates. The tenants would likely be receiving government assistance to help pay for the monthly rent.
- B: It implies very low tenant quality and high turnover. It is an undesirable place to rent. The tenants receive government assistance to help pay for the monthly rent.

**Lease Maturity**

For the average apartment building—rated "BBB"—the lease term is usually 12 months or less. Higher rated apartments—rated "A"—have a minimum lease term of 1 year and renewable. The lower-rated multifamily buildings—rated "BB" or lower—tend to see high turnover rates that reflect the location and condition, as well as the type of tenants, for example, out-of-town students who need accommodation for a school year, which is less than 12 months. Note, however, there are buildings that are designated student housing and they could be rated higher than "BB", but the question is how high? Given that the ability to pay is lower for students, even with government financial assistance, a rating of "BBB" seems a reasonable maximum. Apartments with monthly turnover or leased many times in a year are more likely to incur damage faster than an apartment rented at most once or twice a year, and they tend to be poorly and inadequately maintained.

**Location**

Location descriptors are rather easy to specify but because tastes are not homogenous, it is difficult to determine preferences from one individual to another. We can think of the "average tenant", however. He or she would likely consider the following in choosing a particular apartment building:

- Time travelling: uptown, midtown, or downtown
- Convenience: access to work place, public transportation, shops, restaurants, theatres, and so on
- Scenery, colour, and noise level: waterfront, beachfront, the landscape, a park, and so on

We can create descriptors for the five ratings, using this background information.

- AA: The location has many of the highly desirable locational features (see details listed earlier).
- A: The location is close to public transit, shops, grocery stores, and in walking distance to work. The property is typically in a major urban centre. Note: The population size would depend on a particular country's definition.
- BBB: The property is in the right location for the target market. Public transportation is of average quality and reliability.

- BB: The location is usually in small urban centres. The presence of negative externalities such as noise (from traffic, highway, and airport) and crime rate depress property values.
- B: The location is an economically depressed area. The apartment's vacancy rates are high.

**Condition**

The conditions of a mulita-unit residence would include all the following:

- The age of the building
- The level and quality of maintenance
- Internal appeal of the building: includes underground parking, fire alarm system and sprinklers, fire exits, and the amenities (fitness centre, swimming pool, communal space, etc.)
- Security, attendants, and janitorial services
- The external appeal of the building: includes landscaping, the front entrance, walkways, the parking entrance and exit, and so on

These are essentially all the details we need to create the descriptors:

- AA: The building is less than ten years old, was built to high standard, is well maintained, and has all the important external and internal attractive features. It is a well-managed property with full services provided.
- A: The building is well maintained, meets all the safety codes, and provides amenities that compare favourably with competing apartment buildings. Full services (security, attendant, and janitorial) are provided.
- BBB: The building is adequately maintained, meets all the safety codes, but provides limited amenities and other services required by the lease agreement.
- BB: Security, attendants, and janitorial services are poor. The property is inadequately maintained. Amenities are lacking.
- B: Lack of upkeep, with major repairs being deferred. The property is in a distressed location, evidenced by plight and poverty.

## 6.4.2 Retail Property

Retail properties include strip malls, community centres, and shopping malls. With the rapid growth in online shopping or e-commerce, the traditional bricks-and-mortar retailing, particularly the sprawling shopping malls, are struggling. Casualties of this trend include national and multinational household names, like Macy's, JC Penny, Sears, and Kmart—stores that have served as anchor stores, which are intended to draw shoppers for all other tenants. Sears (Canada) closed all of its stores in October 2017 after 65 years of operation in the country. Macy's, JCPenny, Sears Holdings Corp, Target, Kmart, and many more have been closing stores all across the United States. Meanwhile online retail giants like Amazon, Wal-Mart, E-bay, and Alibaba have been growing in leaps and bounds. The result has been a surge in demand for industrial property space for warehousing and shipping merchandise. As bricks-and-mortar retail continues to decline, the question becomes how fast owners can redevelop retail-shopping buildings or malls for alternative uses to support property values. These market trends will serve as background information to create the descriptors for the BRR grades.

## Tenant Quality

- AA: More than three-quarters of the GLA (gross leasable area) is rented to publicly rated retailers with credit ratings of AA−/ Aa3 and better, and whose products are not threatened by e-commerce. The complex houses at least one upscale department store.
- A: Rented by a few anchor stores that are national and multinational names that occupy at least a quarter of the GLA. They are publicly rated at least A−/A3. Most of the retail stores are not severely threatened by e-commerce.
- BBB: The tenants are mostly national names, occupying at least a third of the GLA. Other tenants are regional and local names. The national names are publicly rated at least BBB−/Baa3. The complex houses a mix of retail stores, but many are threatened by e-commerce.
- BB: The tenants are mostly unrated local names, usually cheap jewellery stores, hardware stores selling inferior kitchen utensils, nail salons, cheap imported curios, dry cleaners, cell phone repair, and shoe repair. The retail complex may have a grocery store.
- B: The tenants are local, unknown, and of questionable background. Their ability to pay is weak.

## Lease Maturity

All other things being equal, property owners prefer long-term leases for the stability of the monthly income. There is also tenant rollover risk that the credit analyst must think about. The risk arising from the possibility of the property owner being unable to release the space should a tenant vacate or, alternatively, sign a lease at less favourable terms than the previous one.

The terms of the lease have a bearing on the type of commercial leases[1] that a landlord may be willing to offer the tenant.

For long-term leases, escalating operating expenses—caused by inflation and inflating costs—are a big risk, and the property owner would prefer a lease that requires the lessee to pay for all increases in operating expenses. In such a situation, the Triple-Net (NNN) Lease or a Full Service Lease would be appropriate. Per Investopedia, "a **triple net lease** is a lease agreement that designates the lessee, which is the tenant, as being solely responsible for all the costs relating to the asset being leased, in addition to the rent fee applied under the lease." In contrast, a **full service lease** makes the landlord responsible for paying all of the property's operating expenses including maintenance, taxes, and insurance.

For shorter-term leases of between 1 and 36 months, rising inflation and costs are less of a factor, and the landlord would be more willing to offer a gross lease with the expectation that the flat rental or all-in fee will be adequate. A **gross lease** is one that has a flat rental fee that includes rent and all costs associated with ownership, such as taxes, insurance, and utilities. Gross leases are often found in lower priced properties. All other things being equal, the higher the volume of store traffic, the greater the amount of consumer spending. Hence, a highly rated property will have, as one of its key attributes, an anchor store with a lease term that exceeds the average lease term of the other stores.

We define the grades as follows:

- AA: The average of the remaining terms of the leases exceeds $X$ years, and the tenant rollover risk is less than or equal to $Y$ percent. The lease term of the anchor store exceeds the average for all tenants. (There are no standard values across countries or regions, so we use these notations and ordering: $X > X^1 > X^2 > X^3; Y < Y^1 < Y^2$.)
- A: The average of the remaining terms of the leases is between $X^1$ and $X$ years, and the tenant rollover risk is between $Y$ and $Y^1$ percent. The average lease term exceeds the average term of all loans secured by the property.
- BBB: The average of the remaining terms of the leases is between $X^2$ and $X^1$ years, and the tenant rollover risk is between $Y^1$ and $Y^2$ percent. The average lease term exceeds the average term of all loans secured by the property.
- BB: The average of the remaining terms of the leases is between $X^3$ and $X^2$ years, and the tenant rollover risk exceeds $Y^2$ percent. The building suffers from low occupancy rates. For short period lease terms, the simpler gross

lease may be commonly used rather than the Triple-Net (NNN) Lease, which may be the market's norm.

- B: Very short lease terms of between 1 month and 12 months. The building suffers from low occupancy rates. The leases may be gross lease type rather than the standard Triple-Net (NNN) Lease.

## Location

As we saw for a multi-unit residential property, location and access to transportation, including roads and highways, go hand in hand. That said, even with the convenience of transportation and the road and railway network, an undesirable area—rough, unsafe, and dirty—is a blight to a shopping mall in the area. We define the grades as follows:

- AA: The property has strong, general customer appeal, and is accessible through efficient and dependable public transportation and private taxis. The property is highly visible in a densely populated area, which has a strong and diversified economic base.
- A: The property commands above-average customer appeal. The transportation network is adequate. The property is easily recognisable and is located in a stable and growing urban area.
- BBB: The property is in the right location for the target market. The public transportation infrastructure is of average quality and reliability. There are no major locational concerns that detract from the attraction of the property.
- BB: The property value is somewhat affected by negative externalities from crime and social degradation. There is higher than average policing.
- B: The location is undesirable due to high poverty and crime rates or is in decline. There is high police presence.

## Condition

The considerations that we examined for a multi-unit residential property are similar for a retail property.

- AA: The building is less than ten years old, was built to high standard, is well maintained, and has all the important external and internal attractive features. Ample and free parking is available outside the property.
- A: The building is well maintained and the condition exceeds that of competing apartment buildings. There are onsite parking lots and they provide ample space.
- BBB: The building is adequately maintained. Limited parking is available outside the building.

- BB: It implies inadequately maintained (e.g., public washrooms, poor garbage disposal facilities). Onsite parking is inadequate. Deferred maintenance expense is higher than that for similar structures in the area.
- B: The property totally lacks upkeep and deferred maintenance expense are very high.

---

**Deferred Maintenance Expense Detracts from the BRR**

The real estate value using the income capitalisation approach must be reduced by the deferred maintenance estimates and by closing costs in order to derive a reliable loan-to-value ratio. Deferred maintenance represents deferred spending for necessary repairs to facilities and equipment. A company decides to put off maintenance for various reasons: (a) to report higher earnings in the short term, (b) when cash flow is inadequate, and (c) when the asset is approaching the end of its useful lives so the costs outweigh the benefits of maintenance and repairs.

---

We introduce a checklist of questions in Table 6.3 to help you develop a feel for the definitions of the four Risk Factors for Business Risk. As you can see from the questions, the descriptors are mostly qualitative; however, as we mentioned earlier, they must be clearly defined so that each set of descriptors or attributes effectively differentiates the BRR grades.

## 6.5    Financial Risk Assessment

For IPRE property, the two most important loan underwriting criteria are the LTV ratio and the DSC ratio. The ratios are defined as follows:

$$\text{Debt Service Coverage} = \frac{\text{Net Operating Income}}{\text{Annual Debt Service}}$$

$$\text{Loan to Value} = \frac{\text{Loan Amount}}{\text{Property Value}}$$

The DSC ratio is used to determine the extent of debt service coverage from the cash flow generated by a property; therefore, it serves as the primary measure of a property's debt-servicing capacity. The calculation of this ratio requires *pro forma* financial statements and the rent roll. The level of debt service is sensitive to the lending rate and the term of the loan. In assessing creditworthiness, the credit analyst must also consider the rollover or refi-

**Table 6.3** Selected qualitative characteristics of CRE properties

| Building type | Tenant quality | Lease maturity | Location | Condition |
|---|---|---|---|---|
| Multifamily | Tenant quality based on ability to pay rent and social behaviour? Occupancy rates? | Lease terms (long lease terms are a positive)? Percentage of lease term >1 year? Percentage of lease term ≤1 year? High turnover of tenants? | Checklist of desirability features (e.g., downtown, midtown, uptown, surrounding view, proximity to shopping, public transportation, parks, entertainment) Is the property in an undesirable, unsafe, or suffering area? | Property age? Quality and range of facilities? Well maintained? Curb appeal? |
| Office | Well know tenants or unknown/national and international names/undesirable/shady? Publicly rated? Class of tenants (high quality is a positive) who occupy the GLS (gross leasable area) Percentage of GLS (gross leasable area) rented by high quality tenants? | Lease terms (long lease terms are a positive)? Percentage of lease term >1 year? Percentage of lease term ≤1 year? High turnover of tenants? | Proximity to an urban market? Checklist of desirability features (e.g., downtown, midtown, uptown, view, proximity to public transportation). | Property age? Construction standards? Well maintained? Desirable area of location? Management quality? Classify the building (A is the best, C is the worst, and B is in the middle)? |
| Retail stores | Well know tenants or unknown/national and international names/undesirable/shady? Publicly rated? Class of tenants (high quality is a positive) who occupy the GLS (gross leasable area) Percentage of GLS (gross leasable area) rented by high quality tenants? | Lease terms (long lease terms are a positive)? Percentage of lease term >1 year? Percentage of lease term ≤1 year? High turnover of tenants? | Access to public transportation? Visibility of property? Property is close to or within the intended market? Is the property in an undesirable, unsafe, or suffering area? | Property age? Construction standards? Well maintained? Desirable area of location? Does the complex include value-added elements to entice visitors? Parking space adequate? |

(continued)

**Table 6.3** (continued)

| Building type | Tenant quality | Lease maturity | Location | Condition |
|---|---|---|---|---|
| Care facilities (hospitals, nursing homes, etc.) | Financial strength of tenants? Percentage of beds paid for through take-or-pay contract with a government body (contract with a government body is a positive)? | Lease terms (long lease terms are a positive)? Percentage of lease term >1 year contracted with a government body? | Property is close to or within the intended market? Demographic factors favour high demand for personal care? Property is located in a large population Centre (urban Centre is a positive)? Is the property in an undesirable, unsafe, or suffering area? | Property age? Construction standards? Well maintained? Desirable area of location? Management quality? Classify the building (A is the best, C is the worst, and B is in the middle)? |
| Hospitality | Quality of guests? Mix of business and leisure guests? | Seasonal occupancy rates (peak minus trough)? Hotel rooms rented out (a negative)? | Proximity to shopping, dining, entertainment? Tourist resort? Is the property in an undesirable, unsafe, or suffering area? | Property age? Construction standards? Well maintained? Curb appeal? Desirable area of location? Management quality? Classify the building (A is the highest, C is the lowest, and B is in the middle)? |

Many hoteliers are striving for a high occupancy rate for their properties without realising that selling rooms at low rates to increase occupancy does not mean profitability for the hotel

Hotels need to understand that it is not high occupancy but a high RevPar that they should be targeting. 100% occupancy with a low room rate is not a great achievement

It is important that a hotel has a strong occupancy without compromising on their Average Daily Room Rate (ADR). This is the main indicator on whether the hotel is doing well or not

RevPAR is a better indicator of hotels profitability because it is also an accurate indicator of optimum occupancy

That is, gross leasable area is the area for which tenants pay rent, and thus the area that produces income for the property owner

Gross leasable area. Gross leasable area (GLA) is the amount of floor space available to be rented in a commercial property

nancing risk that a borrower may not be able to take out a new loan at a higher interest rate to repay an existing debt at the final maturity date.[2] Thus, for analytical purposes, the credit analyst should use a rate that is higher than the current market rate or the point-in-cycle rate. The higher test rate may be viewed as a through-the-cycle rate. The test rate functions like a stress test rate and for this reason is set higher than the current interest rates.

Different banks have different policies and underwriting standards with regard to property valuation and the maximum LTV ratios. Banks follow internal guidelines for the LTV limits that vary with property type. For example, banks view industrial property loans to be riskier than multifamily loans because of higher vacancy and obsolescence risks. Consequently, the maximum LTV ratio for a warehouse (industrial property) is lower than that of a mid- or high-rise apartment, and the cost of borrowing is higher for industrial property than for a multifamily property. You could say that the LTV ratio, along with the DSC ratio, is the quantitative expression of a bank's strategic growth goals, its assessment of the relative risks of the property type, and existing portfolio concentrations. The LTV ratio measures the severity of loss in the event of a default. Therefore, lenders look for material down payment because it evidences *skin in the game*—a phrase that means the borrower is committed to the success of the project because the individual has invested much of his or her own money. A borrower with skin in the game would be more likely to inject cash to preserve the value of his or her equity if the DSC ratio were to fall below $1.0 \times$.

## 6.5.1  The Calculation of NOI

Without loss of generality, let us consider the retail property ABC Shopping Plaza with parking space and located in a middle-class area of a city. Table 6.4 provides information about the property and the transaction. We assume that the owner will buy the asset with a first mortgage with no prior liens and subsequent charges. The assumption allows us to focus on just one debt, the mortgage loan. The borrower will typically submit past income statements showing the operating expenses, a rent roll and the *pro forma* financial statements; however, banks prefer to prepare their own projections of the income statement.

> **Refinancing Risk**
>
> Refinancing risk in banking and finance is the possibility that a borrower cannot obtain a new loan to repay an existing debt. Rising NOI or stable NOI reduces refinancing risk. Unstable or declining NOI, indicators of a distressed property, increases refinancing risk. The higher the interest rate and the higher the vacancy rate, the higher the refinancing risk. *Therefore, a reliable estimate of the NOI is crucial to determining the risk rating of the property.*

**Table 6.4** Information sheet of ABC shopping plaza

| Address | 100 Bloor Street, Toronto |
| --- | --- |
| Purchase price | $30,000,000 |
| Closing cost | $600,000 |
| Income tax rate | 20.0% |
| Downpayment | $9,000,000 |
| Land value estimate | $500,000 |
| Land improvements estimate | $29,500,000 |
| Depreciation (years)—land improvements | 27 |
| Loan amount | $21,600,000 |
| Amortisation term (years) | 30 |
| Term of the loan (years) | 5 |
| Mortgage rate (rate of interest charged by a mortgage lender) | 5.0% |
| Cap rate (expected rate of return on a CRE property) | 8.1% |
| Monthly PMT | $2081 |
| Monthly rent per square foot | $60 |

In this example, we assume that this is a stabilised property. Thus, the income and expenses are the *stabilised* values using average growth rates over the five years of *normal* operation; this way, no one year is overstated or understated relative to the others. In this example, the term is five years and, at the maturity date, the expectation is that the loan will be refinanced by a new loan. To rate any commercial property, a lender would tend to use conservative assumptions, a practice akin to stress testing. A commercial mortgage lender would use a higher average vacancy rate and a higher test rate than the current rates observed in the market. The higher interest rate and the higher vacancy rate used to test whether the property can maintain the NOI to sustain debt repayment during the holding period. As we stated before, the higher vacancy and interest rates may be thought of as *through-the-cycle* measures. In Tables 6.4 and 6.5, we assume through-the-cycle interest rates and vacancy rates.

In order to create a *pro forma* profit-and-loss statement such as the one shown in Table 6.5, the credit analyst needs the following information:

1. The rent roll to derive normalised earnings
2. Tenant list and lease terms
3. Detailed history of operating expenses to derive normalised expense items

Normalisation removes the effects of seasonality, and unusual or one-time transactions, which distort the amount and behaviour of "bottom line" income and operating expense. The use of a computer spreadsheet greatly simplifies the calculation and the sensitivity testing. It suffices to look at Year 1 in Table 6.5 because the rest of the period involves repetitive projections. Pay attention to the individual line items under operating expenses and make

**Table 6.5**  Projected profit and loss statement of ABC property

|  | Year 1 | Year 2 | Year | Year 4 | Year 5 |
|---|---|---|---|---|---|
| Rental space (square feet) | 75,000 | 75,000 | 75,000 | 75,000 | 75,000 |
| Vacancy rate | 10% | 10% | 10% | 10% | 10% |
| Rented space (square feet) | 67,500 | 67,500 | 67,500 | 67,500 | 67,500 |
| Rent per square foot[a] | $60.00 | $62.10 | $64.27 | $66.52 | $68.85 |
| Rent income[a] | $4,050,000 | $4,191,750 | $4,338,461 | $4,490,307 | $4,647,468 |
| Effective gross income | $4,050,000 | $4,191,750 | $4,338,461 | $4,490,307 | $4,647,468 |
| Operating expenses:[a] | | | | | |
| Administration | $82,000 | $84,460 | $86,994 | $89,604 | $92,292 |
| Management fees | $114,100 | $117,523 | $121,049 | $124,680 | $128,421 |
| Personnel—wages and salaries | $410,000 | $422,300 | $434,969 | $448,018 | $461,459 |
| Insurance | $130,000 | $133,900 | $137,917 | $142,055 | $146,316 |
| Utilities | $110,000 | $113,300 | $116,699 | $120,200 | $123,806 |
| Contract services | $115,000 | $118,450 | $122,004 | $125,664 | $129,434 |
| Property taxes | $504,000 | $519,120 | $534,694 | $550,734 | $567,256 |
| Maintenance and repairs | $163,000 | $167,890 | $172,927 | $178,115 | $183,458 |
| Total operating expense | $1,628,100 | $1,676,943 | $1,727,251 | $1,779,069 | $1,832,441 |
| **Net operating income** | **$2,421,900** | **$2,514,807** | **$2,611,210** | **$2,711,239** | **$2,815,027** |
| Interest expense | $1,080,000 | $1,063,744 | $1,046,676 | $1,028,754 | $1,009,937 |
| Depreciation expense (land improvements) | $1,114,815 | $1,114,815 | $1,114,815 | $1,114,815 | $1,114,815 |
| Income before income taxes | $227,085 | $336,248 | $449,719 | $567,669 | $690,276 |
| Income tax expense[b] | $45,417 | $67,250 | $89,944 | $113,534 | $138,055 |
| **Net income** | **$181,668** | **$268,998** | **$359,775** | **$454,135** | **$552,221** |

[a]Growth rate assumptions: rent income 3.5%; operating expenses by 3%
[b]Tax rate of 20%

provision for the fact that occupancy will be significantly less than 100% on average through the year; hence, a realistic assumption for the vacancy rate is necessary for the projections. NOI for Year 1 is forecast at $2.4 million. The interest expense and the depreciation are *non-operating expenses*. Depreciation expense of $1.1 million arises from land improvement cost of $29.5 million (see Table 6.4) plus closing cost of $0.6 million.

The scheduled annual interest payments are derived from the $21.6 million loan at 5% interest, amortised over 30 years, and repaid in monthly instalments of principal and interest.[3] The loan amount is the sum of the purchase price of $30.0 million and closing cost of $0.6 million less the down payment of $9.0 million. The annual depreciation is this sum of land improvements and closing cost divided by the depreciation period (27 years). Rent income in Year 1 is $4,050,000 and is projected to rise by an average rate of 3.5% a year until Year 5. After subtracting non-operating expenses from NOI, the

**Table 6.6** Projected balance sheet of ABC property

|  | Year 1 | Year 2 | Year 3 | Year 4 | Year 5 |
|---|---|---|---|---|---|
| Current assets |  |  |  |  |  |
| Cash | $971,372 | $2,013,818 | $3,129,974 | $4,322,567 | $5,594,428 |
| Fixed assets |  |  |  |  |  |
| Property | $30,263,000 | $30,430,890 | $30,603,817 | $30,781,931 | $30,965,389 |
| Land | $500,000 | $500,000 | $500,000 | $500,000 | $500,000 |
| Accumulated depreciation | $1,114,815 | $2,229,630 | $3,344,444 | $4,459,259 | $5,574,074 |
| Total | $29,648,185 | $28,701,260 | $27,759,372 | $26,822,672 | $25,891,315 |
| **Total assets** | **$30,619,557** | **$30,715,079** | **$30,889,346** | **$31,145,239** | **$31,485,743** |
| Long-term liability |  |  |  |  |  |
| Mortgage payable | $21,274,889 | $20,933,522 | $20,575,088 | $20,198,731 | $19,803,557 |
| Owner equity |  |  |  |  |  |
| Owner capital | $9,163,000 | $9,512,558 | $9,954,483 | $10,492,373 | $11,129,966 |
| Net income | $181,668 | $268,998 | $359,775 | $454,135 | $552,221 |
| Total equity | $9,344,668 | $9,781,556 | $10,314,258 | $10,946,508 | $11,682,187 |
| **Total liabilities and owners equity** | **$30,619,557** | **$30,715,079** | **$30,889,346** | **$31,145,239** | **$31,485,743** |

result is net income before tax of $227,085 in Year 1. Income tax expense is $45,417, leaving a net income of $181,668.

The *pro forma* balance sheet and cash flow are shown in Tables 6.6 and 6.7. The cash flow is derived by adding back depreciation expense (because it is non-cash) and subtracting the principal payment on the balance of the loan. In Year 1, ABC Shopping Plaza generates a cash flow of $971,372. We now have all the information to calculate DSC ratio in Year 1:

$$\text{DSC ratio} = \frac{2,421,900}{(325,111+1,080,000)} = 1.72\text{x}$$

We now turn to the LTV ratio and property valuation. There are various valuation methods. Regardless of the method chosen, all valuation models are sensitive to the assumptions.[4] Appraisers usually employ more than one method for cross-referencing as none is perfect:

1. Comparison method
2. Replacement cost method
3. Income method

**Table 6.7** Projected statement of cash flows

|  | Year 1 | Year 2 | Year | Year 4 | Year 5 |
|---|---|---|---|---|---|
| Cash at beginning of year | $0 | $971,372 | $2,013,818 | $3,129,974 | $4,322,567 |
| Net income | $181,668 | $268,998 | $359,775 | $454,135 | $552,221 |
| Increase from P&L | $181,668 | $268,998 | $359,775 | $454,135 | $552,221 |
| Add: Depreciation expense | $1,114,815 | $1,114,815 | $1,114,815 | $1,114,815 | $1,114,815 |
| Minus: Principal paid | $325,111 | $341,367 | $358,435 | $376,357 | $395,174 |
| Cash increase/(decrease) | $971,372 | $1,042,446 | $1,116,155 | $1,192,594 | $1,271,861 |
| Cash at end of year | $971,372 | $2,013,818 | $3,129,974 | $4,322,567 | $5,594,428 |

**Table 6.8** Valuation based on comparable properties in locale A

| Item | Property 1 | Property 2 | Property 3 | Average |
|---|---|---|---|---|
| Sale date | 06-Jan-07 | 26-Jun-17 | 07-Aug-17 | – |
| Price | $20,000,000 | $19,200,000 | $27,125,000 | – |
| Gross annual rent | $5,000,000 | $4,800,000 | $7,000,000 | – |
| Gross square feet | 1,000,000 | 800,000 | 875,000 | – |
| Price per square foot | $20.00 | $24.00 | $31.00 | $25.00 |
| Rent per square foot | $5.00 | $6.00 | $8.00 | – |
| Price/gross rent (X) | 4.00 | 4.00 | 3.88 | 3.96 |
| Characteristic n | Age | Age | Age | – |
| Characteristic n + 1 | Parking space | Parking space | Parking space | – |
| Characteristic n + 2 | Exterior | Exterior | Exterior | – |
| Characteristic n+...... | No. elevators | No. elevators | No. elevators | – |

Price based on price/sq. foot: 1500 × $25.00 = $37,500,000
Price based on price/gross rent multiple: $10,000,000 × 3.96 = 39,600,000

A lender may look at two or three methods to corroborate the appraiser's *opinion of value*. A prudent lender[5] reviews each of the methods and the reliability of the information before deciding on the final value of the property for credit risk assessment. The strengths and weaknesses of each of the three methodologies are illustrated in Table 6.8.

## 6.5.2   Comparison Method

This method is also known as the market approach because it uses market data to approximate the true value of a property. On the comparison method, Brueggeman and Stone (1981)[6] note:

> The rationale for the market comparison approach lies in the principle that an informed investor would never pay more for a property that what other investors have recently paid for comparable properties.

For the market approach to work well, these conditions for properties within a given class must be met:

- The properties that are being compared (the comparables) were recently sold.
- The prices of the comparables are the outcome of normal, arm's length transactions. Properties involving power of sales, foreclosure, and government intervention will not be suitable comparables because the transactions between the buyer and the seller are not independent.
- The comparables are in the same locale.
- The comparables, by definition, have similar physical and aesthetic *characteristics* that are to be compared. The more the similarities the more accurate the method, but they do not have to be the same across properties.

Table 6.8 illustrates the sort of information an appraiser would use for the market approach. In this example, the property is a 1500 thousand square feet commercial building in Locale A. We assume the characteristics are very similar, otherwise the appraiser needs to adjust the price/square foot for each of the comparable properties (based on their characteristic) or alternatively, adjust the price/gross income multiple for each of the comparables. The more adjustments are required, the less desirable is the market method because they detract from the market appeal. Based on the average price per square foot of $25.00, the building is valued at $37,500,000, whereas based on the price/gross rent multiple of 3.96, the building is worth $39,600,000.

## 6.5.3 Replacement Cost Method

When there is no active market for the comparison method to apply, the next preferred method is the replacement cost approach that applies the substitution principle of economics. This concise and complete statement of the cost method comes from Brueggeman and Stone (1981)[7]:

> The rationale for using the cost approach to valuing (appraising) properties is that an informed buyer of real estate would not pay more for a property than what it would cost to buy the land and reproduce the structure.

Clearly, the condition of rational choice based on available information is fundamental to any method that attempts to approximate a market-determined price. The cost approach can be expressed by two simple relations:

Value of property $\approx$ Value of the Land + Value of the structure

$$\text{Value of the structure} = \text{Replacement cost} - \text{Depreciation}$$

The mechanical simplicity of the cost method (see the example in Brueggeman and Stone) is deceiving because its accuracy depends entirely on accurate data. The appraiser needs to identify all hard construction costs (e.g., cost of renting earth-moving equipment), all soft costs for legal and accounting work, fees for construction and civil engineers, builder's profit, and so forth. The method provides a reasonably accurate measure if the structure is relatively new so that few adjustments are required, particularly for depreciation. Older structures are harder to value because adjustment must be made for depreciation due to various types of obsolescence—functional, economic, and locational. For example, certain design features might be outdated, construction material might not be available, comparable land might not be available, and so on. The more adjustments that are warranted, the more room exists for personal bias, and hence the less accurate the final estimate.

## 6.5.4 The Income Method

This method is also known as the DCF (discounted cash flow) method for which the concept of the time value of money, or present value (PV), is applied. Brueggeman and Stone (1981)[7] state:

> The rationale for the income capitalisation approach to value is based on the premise that because improved real estate is capable of producing a flow of income over its economic life, investors will pay a present value for that flow of income that will provide them with a competitive return on capital invested in the property.

Under the rubric of the income approach are three commonly used methods: gross income multiplier (GIM), direct capitalisation, and the more detailed discounted cash flow (DCF).

### *Gross Income Multiplier (GIM)*
A gross income multiplier is a quick method to "size up" the value of a prospective sale. Thus, GIM is useful for rental houses, duplexes, and simple commercial properties when used in addition to more well-developed methods. The appraiser locates a number of comparable properties recently sold in the same neighbourhood, calculates for each the selling price/gross rental income, and from the results, establishes a multiple to apply to the gross rental income of the property. For example, if the rental income of the prop-

erty is $50,000 and the multiple is 8 (based on the comparable), the rough value of the property is 8 × $50,000, or $400,000.

### Valuation Based on the Concept of Present Value

Consider a property earning rental income that we can accurately forecast *over its economic life*. The value of the property today will be the present value (PV) of the NOIs and the *terminal or exit value* of the asset (TVA), which is the market value of a property at the end of an assumed holding period.

$$V = \frac{NOI_1}{(1+i)^1} + \frac{NOI_2}{(1+i)^2} + \ldots + \frac{NOI_n}{(1+i)^n} + \frac{TV_n}{(1+i)^n} \qquad (6.1)$$

where

$V$     value of the property

$i$     compound rate of return on total investment, or the IRR (internal rate of return) on the total investment that includes both the income flow *and* the terminal value

TV    terminal value of the property at the end of the investment holding period

$n$     service life of the building.

You could see from the PV calculation that the life expectancy of the structure is an important factor. Most well-constructed concrete and steel building last up to half a century or a bit more. All long-range forecasts are highly inaccurate, least of all a 50-year projection; hence, appraisers seldom attempt. Furthermore, buildings are bought and sold many times before they reach the end of their economic lives. Various techniques use a much-shortened investment horizon or holding period, five to ten years, for cash flow discounting.

### A Key Point in Investment Decisions

There are many competing investment vehicles in the capital market. Investors constantly compare the returns on their current investments to what they could earn elsewhere in the market, and the concept of *opportunity cost* plays a central role in the portfolio-rebalancing process. Furthermore, each return is the sum of a risk-free rate such as that for a government bond, and a risk premium that depends on risk profile of a particular asset class.

### Direct Capitalisation

The easiest approach is the back-of-the-envelope method called *direct capitalisation*. As Brueggeman and Stone (1981)[7] note:

> "It is based on the idea that at any given point in time the current net operating income (NOI) produced by a property is related to its current market value." Symbolically:

$$\frac{NOI_1}{V} = r \tag{6.2}$$

where

NOI    net operating income in the first year of normal operation, or stabilised annual operating income

$V$      property value

$r$      *current* return on total investment $V$ (also called cap rate).

An investor who purchased a property for the price of $V$ would realise a current return before any financing or income tax consideration of $r$:

$$r = \frac{NOI_1}{V} \tag{6.3}$$

Whilst the formula is deceptively simple to work with, there are a few subtleties about the cap rate to keep in mind so that you understand not only why it is so commonly used but also how it could be misused.

First, it is based on the NOI of a *stabilised* property, which is one that is operating in a *normal* fashion. Obviously, factors such as speculation and government rent controls can distort NOI and the cap rate. The "$r$" in Eq. (6.3) is not the same as the "$i$", the internal rate of return (IRR), *over the entire life of the property*, given by Eq. (6.1). So on what basis are we allowed to use a current return as a *reasonable* approach to determine value? Three conditions must hold, according to Brueggeman and Stone (1981)[7]:

1. There are many comparable properties bought and sold. If investors value properties to earn a *competitive* return $i$ over the life of an investment, then they must also value properties so that $r$ represents a competitive current return.
2. The buyers of those properties are also earning the same current return $r$ based on *1 year's NOI*.

3. There is a stable relationship between current returns and long-term investment returns. This requirement rules out market distortions and their effects on NOI.

Second, one way to think about the cap rate is that it consists of two components, a *risk-free return* and a *risk premium*. In developed markets, the yield on a ten-year government bond serves as a proxy. So the riskier the CRE asset, the higher the cap rate. Third, as we saw in the calculation of NOI, mortgage or interest payments are not included. Excluding debt is part of the reason the cap rate is so useful because it focuses on the property alone and not the financing of the purchase and tax considerations. An investor usually takes out a mortgage to finance the purchase. A cap rate assumes that the investor buys the property in cash, so this lets the investor compare the risk of one property with another. Finally, a cap rate can be generalised for an entire market for some given type of property. The cap rate is thus an average for a large group of properties of a specific market. In this sense, investors use the cap rate as an independent variable to value a property or to compare the risk of a market to another and to compare different locations for a given market.

From the previous discussions we can identify three major factors that influence cap rates and, hence, property valuation or prices.

1. Macro-variables: economy, demographics, land availability, government policy, and so on (see Table 6.1)
2. Micro-variables: the classification of the CRE property
3. The type of CRE property

Let us look briefly at each. First, macro-variables such as a strong and diversified economy, low unemployment rates, high population growth, land shortage, and regulatory restrictions for CRE development, all favour rising and stable rental income. Income stability means lower risk, all things being equal. The real estate market in a region enjoying these favourable conditions would have a lower perceived risk than one with undesirable features. Therefore, investors and property owners there would be willing to accept lower-income *returns* because of the lower risk.

Credit conditions influence the cap rate *directly* through the risk-free rate we mentioned before. As a central bank takes measures to tighten or loosen the money supply in order to move the entire maturity spectrum of interest rates up or down to affect aggregate demand, the risk-free rate moves accordingly.[8] Indirectly, monetary conditions influence cap rates because CRE assets compete with bonds, stocks, and other investment vehicles. For example, a tightening of monetary policy causes longer-term market interest rates to go up because the whole spectrum of financial assets ranging from overnight loans to 30-year bonds move in sync. New bond issues typically carry coupon rates at or close to the prevailing interest rate. Now that they are higher (or expected to rise further), investors will bid down the prices of the older bonds in order to realise the higher coupon rates. But this behaviour is not confined to the fixed income market because investors will opt to pay less for property in order to earn similar, risk-adjusted returns (recall profit maximising investors look at a portfolio of assets and the concept of opportunity cost driving asset allocation). The result, at least *in theory,* is higher cap rate.[9] Conversely, when interest rates are falling, lower cap rates result, *ceteris paribus.* In an environment of falling interest rates and portfolio rebalancing, stocks become attractive but so do real estate assets. As investors bid up the prices of real estate, risk-adjusted rates of return across markets would tend to converge.

Second, at the micro level, we observe that CRE property is graded according to both location- and property-specific features. A classification system might relate "Class A" to "best", whilst B, C, and D get progressively less desirable or attractive. North American data show that cap rates vary inversely with property class, confirmation of the principle of higher return in exchange for higher risk. The classification allows an investor or a homeowner to compare properties in similar locations and to adjust cap rates accordingly. In general, the higher (lower) the risk the higher (lower) the cap rate.

Finally, the type of property affects cap rates. For example, multifamily property is less risky than retail property (look at Table 6.10) because rental income is more stable for apartments owing to the relative insensitivity of the demand to income and rent. Consequently, the lower cap rate observed for multifamily real estate reflects the lower risk.

Capitalisation rates are estimated or obtained in three ways.

1. Finding properties in the same neighbourhood or locale that are similar to the prospective sale and establishing a representative rate based on the sample data.
2. Using cap rates based on the *survey responses* by commercial real estate services firms[10] of real estate investors regarding their expected returns.
3. Applying an appropriate DCF model.

$$\text{Value}\,(V) = \frac{\text{Cash Flow}\,(\text{CF})}{\text{discount rate}\,(r) - \text{perpetual growth rate}\,(g)}$$

Rearranging terms and isolating $\dfrac{\text{CF}}{V}$ on the left gives:

$$\frac{CF}{V} = r - g$$

By definition, $\frac{CF}{V}$ is the **cap rate**, which is the result we want. Example: Given a discount rate of 15% and a growth rate for net operating income of 5%, the cap rate is 10%.

### Discounted Cash Flow

The DCF methodology proves useful in situations where the capitalisation rate cannot be easily calculated because comparable properties (such as special purpose structures) in the same neighbourhood do not exist, or where a property's cash flow is so complex and volatile that more sophisticated versions of the DCF model are required. Regardless of the approach, the mathematics of DCF models follows familiar methods for stock valuation and bond pricing, with some modifications that accommodate the peculiarities of the real estate assets.

Let us write down one commonly used version of the model:

$$V = \sum_{t=1}^{t=N} \frac{FCF_t}{(1+r)^t} + \frac{TV}{(1+r)^N} \tag{6.4}$$

To apply this model, the appraiser needs to estimate:

1. The FCF (future cash flow) for every period of the investment horizon
2. The appropriate discount rate $r$, which is the *weighted average cost of capital* (WACC) because financing comprises debt (mortgage loan) and equity of the owner
3. The terminal value of the structure

The terminal value is the present value of the FCF expected after the investment horizon ending in year $N$. It is assumed that FCF in the terminal year $N$ will continue to grow at a constant rate $g$ in perpetuity. This is modelled as an infinite geometric series:

$$TV = \frac{FCF_N(1+g)}{(1+r)} + \frac{FCF_N(1+g)^2}{(1+r)^2} + \frac{FCF_N(1+g)^3}{(1+r)^3} + \dots \tag{6.5}$$

or written compactly:

$$TV = \sum_{t=1}^{\infty} \frac{FCF_N (1+g)^{t-1}}{(1+r)^t} \tag{6.6}$$

where
$g$ constant growth rate of FCF in perpetuity
$r$ WACC.

The constant growth rate is usually set at or below the rate of nominal GDP growth. With the further assumption that $g <$ WACC, then $0 < \frac{1+g}{1+r} < 1$ and the infinite series described by (6.6) converges to:

$$TVA = \frac{FCF_{N+1}}{(r-g)} \tag{6.7}$$

The WACC is derived from the Capital Asset Pricing Model (CAPM). As the name suggests, the rate is the result of averaging the cost of equity and the cost of debt according to the weight—the contributions of equity and debt in total capital—attached to each item:

$$WACC = COE. \frac{E}{D+E} + COD.(1-t_c) \frac{D}{D+E} \tag{6.8}$$

where
$E$          market value of equity
$D$          market value of debt
COE       cost of equity or return on equity
COD       cost of debt or the return on debt
$t_c$          corporate tax rate
$(D + E)$   total capital

The WACC is the expected return on capital (equity owners and debt holders) as it represents the investor's opportunity cost of putting money in CRE asset.

In this formulation, it is assumed that the debt is not repaid until the end of the holding period, for example, for a balloon loan, and thus the ratio of debt to total capital remains fixed over the investment period. The *simplification* avoids the effects of changing capital structure in the weighting procedure. For example, for a mortgage loan that is amortising over time, the equity weighting (debt weighting) will be increasing (decreasing) over the investment horizon.[11] The cost of equity (COE) (or the return on equity) is estimated by the following equation[12]:

$$COE = r_f + \beta\left(r_m - r_f\right) \tag{6.9}$$

where

$r_f$      risk-free rate
$\beta$      estimated coefficient (represents the volatility of the property-type relative to the market portfolio that includes *all assets in the economy*)
$r_m$      market rate
$(r_m - r_f)$    measures the risk premium.

The following is an example of the DCF (discount cash flow) method of valuation that applies a discount rate, derived from the CAPM, to a property's cash flow:

COD = 8%
$r_f = 11\%$
Risk premium = 5%.
$\beta = 0.8$

$$\frac{E}{D+E} = 30\%$$

$t_c$ = 25%. Plug these numbers in the set of equations of the DCF method and we get a WACC of 8.7%, which serves as the discount rate in the expression (6.4). The procedure is shown below:

$$COE = 11\% + 0.8\left(5\%\right) = 15\%$$

WACC = 15(0.3) + 8(.75) (0.7) = 8.7%

### The Growth Rate of NOI or FCF

Growth in NOI or FCF is an important variable to consider when comparing real estate because valuation is very sensitive to changes in growth assumptions. All things being equal, the higher the growth rate of NOI or FCF, the higher the valuation.

$$TVA = \frac{FCF_{N+1}}{(r-g)}$$

$$\text{Valuation}(V) = \sum_{t=1}^{t=N} \frac{FCF_t}{(1+r)^t} + \frac{FCF_{N+1}}{(r-g)(1+r)^N} \tag{6.10}$$

Note that the equation is not defined at $r = g$ (denominator becomes zero), and for $g > r$ (negative discount rate is nonsensical). A negative discount rate means that it is not worth investing in the asset knowing that its future value is certain to dwindle during the holding period. The present discounted value of the asset will be greater than the future value just by the maths.

It is clear from (6.10) that the discount rate compresses the stream of future cash flow into a single present value ($V$), which is the valuation of the asset today. As an example, consider the sale of a commercial property that the buyer intends to keep for five years and the estimated cash flow during the holding period in millions: $1.5, $1.7, $1.6, $1.4, and $1.8 in years 1–5, respectively. Also, assume FCF is expected to grow by 3% forever after Year 5. With this information fed into Eq. (6.10), the valuation is $27.7 million:

$$V = \frac{\$1.5}{(1.087)} + \frac{\$1.7}{(1.087)^2} + \frac{\$1.6}{(1.087)^3} + \frac{\$1.4}{(1.087)^4}$$
$$+ \frac{\$1.8}{(1.087)^5} + \frac{\$1.8(1.03)}{(0.087-0.030)(1.087)^5} = \$27.7\text{MM}$$

*The Sensitivity of Valuation and the Maximum Mortgage to the Interest Rate*
To see how valuation and the maximum mortgage are very sensitive to the interest rate, let us assume that the WACC was 7.7% rather than 8.7% in the PV equation, which gives:

$$V = \frac{\$1.5}{(1.077)} + \frac{\$1.7}{(1.077)^2} + \frac{\$1.6}{(1.077)^3} + \frac{\$1.4}{(1.077)^4} + \frac{\$1.8}{(1.077)^5}$$
$$+ \frac{\$1.8(1.03)}{(0.077-0.030)(1.077)^5} = \$33.6\text{MM}$$

We see that a 1-percentage point drop in the interest rate raises the valuation by almost $6 million to $33.6 million, *ceteris paribus*. Furthermore, let us

**Table 6.9** Relationship between valuation and interest rates

| Interest rate (%) | Valuation (mm) ($) | Max loan (mm)[a] ($) |
|---|---|---|
| 4.70 | 93.70 | 70.20 |
| 5.70 | 58.80 | 44.10 |
| 6.70 | 42.80 | 32.10 |
| 7.70 | 33.60 | 25.20 |
| 8.70 | 27.70 | 20.80 |

[a]Assume a maximum loan to value ratio of 80%

reduce successively the interest rate by 1 percentage point and calculate the valuation and the maximum loan a mortgage lender is willing to approve. The table gives the results for five successive decreases. By inspection, you can see that the relationship between valuation and interest rate is not linear but geometric: As the interest rate declines by 1 percentage point, the valuations increase at an increasing rate, or vice versa, as shown in Table 6.9.

We may now review the main points of this section:

1. Numerous calculations are required for future NOI. The inputs, such as the discount rate, leave plenty of room for assumption bias or subjectivity.
2. Valuation results are very sensitive to slight changes in the assumptions, such as the expected growth rate in NOI and WACC (expected return on capital).
3. The parameters in the DCF method, such as debt-to-equity ratio and the corporate tax rate, are static. A fixed debt/equity ratio is a hidden assumption of some "optimal" or "target" capital structure. Corporate tax rates are not fixed. These financing parameters influence the WACC and hence the valuation.
4. There is no one best valuation methodology.
5. It is impossible to reconcile the valuations based on the three methodologies to a single value.
6. The results of the methods used should corroborate. Big differences in the valuations should prompt the credit analyst to review the methodologies, the information, and the assumptions.
7. Effective collateral valuation is a critical part of credit risk analysis. The estimates derived from applying proper valuation techniques are better than guesswork and back-of-the-envelope calculations.
8. The benefit of a professional appraisal is that the lender can assess the quality of the information and the model's assumptions. The reliability of the data determines which valuation methodology is acceptable (remember: garbage in, garbage out, regardless of the sophistication of the model).

The pros and cons of the three evaluation methods are presented in Table 6.10.

**Table 6.10** Pros and cons of three commonly used valuation methods

| Valuation method | Methodology | Pros | Cons |
|---|---|---|---|
| **Comparison method** | Comparing the building being appraised with other properties in the same location, with roughly the same characteristics and quality, that had sold recently | Closest approximation to the true/fair value of the appraised property<br>Information on the selling prices is easily available; hence, no need to (explicitly) estimate discount rates and cash flows<br>The prices reflect current economic trends, such as inflation, interest rates, housing regulations<br>Easy to value non-cash flow producing property such as a primary residence whose price can be estimated by looking at similar properties in the same area | In practice, it is difficult to find buildings built in different periods that are exactly alike in terms of all possible physical features, including condition<br>Prices may reflect unquantifiable sentimental or aesthetic value, in addition to the quantifiable characteristics such as occupancy rates and size |
| **Income method** | Discounting pre-tax cash flow (NOI—debt service) for a (shortened) holding period and the terminal value of the property at the end of the holding period<br>Directly capitalising the current or first year's NOI with current return on total investment ($r$). The method is based on the idea that at ant time the *current* NOI to its *current* market value:<br>$NOI \div V = r$, where NOI is normal income in the first year of operation | It is easier to calculate current NOI than attempt to estimate the cash flows for the entire economic life of the property and the terminal value (or the reversion value of land at the end of the economic life)<br>The economic life of a property can be as long as 50–60 years and cash-flow projections for such long periods are inaccurate. Capitalising current income by a normalised cap rate is easier and produces a more reliable estimate<br>The DCF method proves useful when comparable properties do not exist and where the cash flow is complex and volatile | Capitalising the current year's NOI with the cap rate rests on assumptions that may not hold: (1) there is an active market for comparable properties, (2) buyers of the properties are also earning the same rate of return as the cap rate, and (3) there is no speculation persisting over a long period of time to distort the stable relationship between current returns (proxies by the cap rate) and long-term investment returns)<br>Estimates of value are extremely sensitive to the rate chosen for capitalisation in any present value calculation<br>Discount rates are difficult to estimate and WACC bundles financing side effects in the discount rate<br>Cash flows and the terminal value difficult to estimate |

(continued)

**Table 6.10** (continued)

| Valuation method | Methodology | Pros | Cons |
|---|---|---|---|
| **Replacement cost method** | Finding recently sold sites. To the cost of the raw land, add all the (hard) construction costs of the improvements (e.g., the building, landscape, etc.) and all soft costs (professional fees, licenses, builder's profit, etc.) | Ationale based on the economic principle of substitution whereby a rational and informed buyer of a real estate would not pay more for what it costs to buy the land and build a similar structure<br><br>Provides a fairly accurate estimate of value if the property value is new and requires few changes | Difficult to apply for old property with variations in structural design and locational features<br><br>For an existing improvement, the cost has to be refined downward for wear and tear, and for functional or structural obsolescence. These are difficult items to estimate |

## 6.6    Creating Descriptors for DSC and LTV

### 6.6.1 Preliminary Considerations

Credit risk varies significantly within and across property types. Let us start with the *within* variation. The reason for the differences is that the demand for rental space is affected by the demographics of the location, in particular, the population size and population growth, which reflect market size and market growth. Demand for CRE properties is a *derived demand*, as we noted earlier. For example, demand for apartments is a derived demand for housing and shelter. Population size determines demand for floor space and the going rents. Therefore, all other things being equal, occupancy rates are likely to be higher and more stable for a property that is located in a large population centre than the one in a small population centre. The bigger (smaller) the population centre, the lower (higher) the vacancy risk, and thus the lower (higher) the minimum required DSC ratio, or the smaller the required buffer for underwriting a property. Rents are more likely to be higher in populated centres compared to the less populated.

Credit risk also varies *across* property types, reflecting different risk profiles. For example, a hotel with high turnover is more risky than an apartment building with higher occupancy rates and hence, a more stable cash flow. This observation means that rates of return among property types vary according to the risk premium associated with a particular property type. The risk premium is a big component of the rate of return. If we add a risk premium to the Fisher equation,[13] we get the familiar *ex post* expression of the nominal rate of return:

$$r = i + \pi + p \qquad (6.10)$$

where
$r$  nominal return
$i$  prevailing interest rate
$\pi$  inflation rate
$p$  risk premium (in percent).

Equation (6.10) applies to commercial properties where the risk premium ($p$) captures property-specific risks. The *ex ante* form of the Fisher Eq. (6.10) uses the expected (denoted by the $e$ superscript) rate of inflation:

$$r^e = i + \pi^e + p \qquad (6.11)$$

The expected or target rate of return ($r^e$) is the discount rate used to derive the present value of a future income stream. An *approximation* of the risk premium by property type is derived by comparing the rate on a medium-term government bond to published capitalisation rates, which are provided by firms that specialise in real estate services. The firms get the rates from periodic surveys of real estate brokers. The difference or spread is thus an estimate of the risk premium that captures unique risk features of a property type. The rate of return an investor expects to earn from a risk-free ten-year government bond is used to measure the ($i+\pi^e$) term, which represents the investment's opportunity cost.

Let us look at the US data in Table 6.11 for stabilised property acquisitions. The data show a consistent pattern in the yield spreads—a measure of risk—in each of the half-year periods across property types in the period 2015–2017:

1. Multifamily (lowest risk) < office < industrial < retail < hospitality/hotel (highest risk).
2. Multifamily has the lowest spread over the risk-free ten-year treasury yield.
3. Hotel exhibits the highest yield spread.
4. The spread between multifamily and hotel is consistently well over 2 percentage points.

The differences in yield reflect differences in the derived demand functions with respect to price and income. The more insensitive or inelastic the demand to these variables, the more stable the cash flow, hence the lower the repayment risk. For example, housing and accommodation are a necessity and are relatively insensitive to changes in personal income and rentals. Therefore, *a priori*, we expect the cash flow from apartments to be more steady and predictable compared to hotels, because the demand for hotel accommodation is more discretionary. The demand for the other types of commercial property is also relatively income elastic. For example, in a recession, stores that are struggling do not stay open and absorb losses, so they leave and the result is higher vacancy rates.

LTV ratios across property types reflect differences in default risk due to the effects of population size and income. Consider, for example, two similar apartment buildings located in two different population centres. We start with the premise that mortgage lenders attempt to minimise risk of loss by limiting exposure. They achieve this through their lending policy on the maximum LTV ratios of property types.[14] The higher the perceived risk the lower

Table 6.11 US national-level capitalisation rates by property type

| Property type | H2 2015 (%) | Spread over 10-year treasury rate (2.27%, e.o.p) | H1 2016 (%) | Spread over 10-year treasury rate (1.49%, e.o.p) | H2 2016 (%) | Spread over 10-year treasury rate (2.45%, e.o.p) | H1 2017(%) | Spread over 10-year treasury rate (2.31%, e.o.p) | H2 2017 (%) | Spread over 10-year treasury rate (2.45%, e.o.p) |
|---|---|---|---|---|---|---|---|---|---|---|
| Multifamily | 5.26 | 299 | 5.26 | 377 | 5.32 | 287 | 5.27 | 296 | 5.59 | 319 |
| Office | 6.54 | 427 | 6.61 | 512 | 6.63 | 418 | 6.66 | 435 | 6.64 | 424 |
| Industrial | 6.71 | 444 | 6.72 | 523 | 6.73 | 428 | 6.66 | 435 | 6.51 | 411 |
| Retail | 6.88 | 461 | 7.36 | 587 | 7.12 | 467 | 7.23 | 492 | 9.02 | 557 |
| Hotel | 8.23 | 596 | 7.72 | 623 | 7.91 | 546 | 7.98 | 567 | 8.53 | 613 |

Source: CBRE (Coldwell Banker Richard Ellis (Boston, MA), North America Cap Rate Survey

the maximum LTV ratio. Large population centres have size advantages over small centres; hence, rents and occupancy rates are likely to be higher and more stable for a property in an urban area. Land—an input in the supply of property—is a big factor influencing property prices. Large population clusters are usually larger cities where land scarcity drives up property prices and ultimately rents. As we learned from the valuation methodologies, the level of the rental income and its stability are the two main inputs into the valuation of a property.

In creating the descriptors for the DSC ratio and the LTV ratio, monotonicity between the predictors and the rating grades within and across property types is crucial. Let us begin with the DSC ratio. Within a given property type, DSC is inversely related to the likelihood of default. We saw before that refinancing risk decreases with higher DSC. Across property types, identical DSC ratios are expected to be associated with different levels of credit risks, or stated another way, identical BRR grades across property types are expected to be associated with different levels of debt service coverage. For example, the DSC ratio for an apartment building (multifamily) would be lower than the DSC ratio for the riskier trailer park (manufactured home park). An office building falls in between the two properties in terms of the credit risk, and the DSC ratio would be an intermediate value. Maintaining this consistency is necessary for the predictive power of the scorecard. Across property types, the LTV ratio would vary inversely with the default risk of the property type. We expect that lending policy will be less restrictive for an apartment building than that for the trailer park, and therefore the maximum LTV ratio would be higher. For an office building that is less risky than a trailer park but more risky than an apartment, the LTV ratio would be somewhere between these two.

## 6.6.2 Creating the Descriptors

The focus of this section is creating the descriptors, applying the principles outlined in the previous section. For the illustration, we work with three population segments using as our standard the UN classifications[15] for defining population clusters or localities. Population is a discrete variable.

1. >500,000 inhabitants
2. 100,000–500,000 inhabitants
3. <100,000 inhabitants.

Population density, *ceteris paribus*, has a positive effect on the level of demand for rental property. Property prices and rents are more likely to rise in areas that are growing fast. This is a universal phenomenon. Numerous econometric studies using regression analysis on longitudinal data of many countries confirm this tendency.

Before going into the specifics, let us interpret the ratios regardless of property type. The DSC ratio of 1.0 serves as a reference mark. A value of less than 1.0 means that the NOI of the property cannot cover the current debt obligations of principal and interest (or interest alone for a balloon loan). It follows that DSC ratio of 1.0 provides no cushion against default. Lenders consider 1.0 high default risk. Conversely, a ratio greater than 1.0 means that the property is generating NOI for the current obligations and for a buffer. A DSC ratio like 1.1, which barely exceeds 1.0, also represents a high default risk. This is because even a minor decline in cash flow could quickly drive the ratio below 1.0. The lending policy of mortgage providers specifies minimum DSC ratios, which vary across CRE assets because the risks are not equal. For example, we saw that apartments are the least risky of all CRE assets, whereas hospitality is one of the most risky. Therefore, the minimum DSC ratio for multifamily may be 1.25:1, whereas the ratio for a hotel would be 1.45:1. What all this means is a property must earn additional income to raise the ratio well above 1.0 before it qualifies for a loan. The higher is the DSC ratio, the bigger the cushion, and the higher the BRR.

In the case of the LTV ratio, defining a reference point or even a reference range is not as obvious as the DSC ratio. For one thing, lenders look for a substantial down payment—from as low as 25% for relatively low-risk multifamily properties to as high as 50% for high-risk properties with unstable cash flows and valuations. For another, a mortgage loan with a LTV ratio $\geq 1.0$— the case where the borrower owes more than the property is worth—is one that is likely non-performing or is in foreclosure; hence, the DSC ratio is well below 1.0.

For the illustration, using six BRR grades for the scorecard construction, let us consider three property types (Multifamily, Retail, and Hotel) in the three population centres. The grid displays the BRR grades and the DSC descriptors. The H, M, L modifiers are the counterparts to the "+", "Mid", and "−" respectively of Table 3.1 that give the rating scale. Moving across the grid, for a given property type and population centre, we see that the BRRs are always *positively* related to the DSC ratios, which meet the necessary monotonicity condition. The functional relationship makes sense: the *higher* the DSC ratio, the lower the risk of default and, hence, the *higher* the

BRR, ceteris paribus. For example, consider a multifamily property in a population centre of <100,000. A DSC ratio $\geq 1.63$ defines a rating of "A–High", whereas a lower DSC ratio of 1.10 defines a rating of "B–Mid". For a given property type, the High, Mid, and Low grades are *positively* related to ratio size.

Another important property of the grid is that for a given population centre, the risk grades vary inversely with the riskiness of the property type. Multifamily is less risky than retail, which in turn is less risky than hotel. Accordingly, for the same ratio and population centre, the rating for multifamily must be higher than retail, which in turn must be higher than hotel. For example, consider a DSC ratio of 1.45 and a population centre 100,000–500,000. From Table 6.12, the ratings for multifamily, retail, and hotel are A–Low, BBB–Mid, and BBB–Low, respectively.

Let us examine the LTV ratio reported in Table 6.13. Here again, consistency and monotonicity conditions must obtain:

- For a given property type, population centre, and modifier (H-M-L), the BRRs are always *inversely* related to the LTV ratios. The functional relationship makes sense: The *higher* the LTV ratio (meaning higher risk exposure to the lender), the *higher* the risk of default and, hence, the *lower* the BRR, other things being constant. For example, look at Multifamily in a population centre of >500,000 in Table 6.12. The LTV ratio (54.99–57.09) defines A-high, whereas the higher risk exposure represented by the LTV ratio (74.02–76.12) defines B-high.

- For a given property type and population centre, the low, mid, and high grades are always *inversely* related to the LTV ratios. The functional relationship makes sense: the *higher* the LTV ratio, the *lower* the risk of default and, hence, the *lower* the BRR. Consider, for example, a retail property in a population centre <100,000 in Table 6.12. The LTV ratio of (40.05–42.57) defines A-low, whereas a lower risk exposure of (34.99–37.51) defines the higher rating of A-high.

- For a given population centre, the ratios follow a consistent pattern in relative risk across property type. For example, consider a population centre >500,000 and an LTV ratio of 65%. The ratings for multifamily, retail, and hotel are BBB–Mid, BB–Mid, and D–Default, respectively. The ranking makes sense: all things being equal, for the *same risk exposure*, the risk of default is lowest for multifamily and highest for hotel. Accordingly, the BRR grades must reflect the risk profile across property types.

**Table 6.12** Debt service coverage ratio

| Property type | Population | Low mid high | AA | A | BBB | BB | B | D |
|---|---|---|---|---|---|---|---|---|
| Multifamily | >500,000 | L | | 1.416–1.460 | 1.282–1.325 | 1.147–1.191 | 1.000–1.057 | |
| | | M | ≥1.550 | 1.461–1.504 | 1.326–1.370 | 1.192–1.236 | 1.058–1.102 | <1.00 |
| | | H | | 1.505–1.549 | 1.371–1.415 | 1.237–1.281 | 1.103–1.146 | |
| | 100,000–500,000 | L | | 1.447–1.494 | 1.302–1.349 | 1.158–1.205 | 1.000–1.060 | |
| | | M | ≥1.600 | 1.495–1.542 | 1.350–1.387 | 1.206–1.253 | 1.061–1.108 | <1.00 |
| | | H | | 1.543–1.590 | 1.388–1.446 | 1.254–1.301 | 1.109–1.157 | |
| | <100,000 | L | | 1.491–1.543 | 1.332–1.364 | 1.172–1.224 | 1.000–1.065 | |
| | | M | ≥1.650 | 1.544–1.596 | 1.365–1.437 | 1.225–1.277 | 1.066–1.118 | <1.00 |
| | | H | | 1.597–1.649 | 1.438–1.490 | 1.278–1.331 | 1.119–1.171 | |
| Retail | >500,000 | L | | 1.491–1.543 | 1.332–1.364 | 1.172–1.224 | 1.000–1.065 | |
| | | M | ≥1.650 | 1.544–1.596 | 1.385–1.437 | 1.225–1.277 | 1.066–1.118 | <1.00 |
| | | H | | 1.597–1.649 | 1.438–1.490 | 1.278–1.331 | 1.119–1.171 | |
| | 100,000–500,000 | L | | 1.528–1.585 | 1.357–1.413 | 1.185–1.241 | 1.000–1.069 | |
| | | M | ≥1.700 | 1.586–1.642 | 1.414–1.470 | 1.242–1.298 | 1.070–1.127 | <1.00 |
| | | H | | 1.643–1.699 | 1.471–1.527 | 1.299–1.356 | 1.128–1.184 | |
| | <100,000 | L | | 1.566–1.726 | 1.382–1.442 | 1.197–1.258 | 1.000–1.073 | |
| | | M | ≥1.750 | 1.627–1.788 | 1.443–1.503 | 1.259–1.319 | 1.074–1.135 | <1.00 |
| | | H | | 1.689–1.749 | 1.504–1565 | 1.320–1.381 | 1.136–1.196 | |
| Hotel | >500,000 | L | | 1.603–1.668 | 1.407–1.471 | 1.210–1.274 | 1.000–1.078 | |
| | | M | ≥1.800 | 1.669–1.733 | 1.472–1.537 | 1.275–1.340 | 1.079–1.143 | <1.00 |
| | | H | | 1.734–1.799 | 1.538–1.602 | 1.341–1.406 | 1.144–1.209 | |
| | 100,000–500,000 | L | | 1.641–1.710 | 1.432–1.500 | 1.222–1.291 | 1.000–1.082 | |
| | | M | ≥1.850 | 1.711–1.779 | 1.501–1.570 | 1.292–1.361 | 1.083–1.152 | <1.00 |
| | | H | | 1.780–1.849 | 1.571–1.640 | 1.362–1.431 | 1.153–1.221 | |
| | <100,000 | L | | 1.678–1.751 | 1.457–1.529 | 1.235–1.308 | 1.00–1.086 | |
| | | M | ≥1.900 | 1.752–1.725 | 1.530–1.603 | 1.309–1.382 | 1.087–1.160 | <1.00 |
| | | H | | 1.826–1.899 | 1.604–1.677 | 1.383–1.456 | 1.161–1.234 | |

**Table 6.13** Loan to value ratio (%)

| Property type | Population | High mid low | AA | A | BBB | BB | B | D |
|---|---|---|---|---|---|---|---|---|
| | >500,000 | H | | 54.99–57.09 | 61.33–63.44 | 67.68–69.78 | 74.02–76.12 | |
| | | M | 0–55 | 57.10–59.21 | 63.45–65.55 | 69.79–71.89 | 76.13–78.24 | [80.36, 100] |
| | | L | | 59.22–61.32 | 65.56–66.67 | 71.90–74.01 | 78.25–80.35 | |
| Multifamily | 100,000–500,000 | H | | 49.99–52.09 | 56.33–58.44 | 62.68–64.78 | 69.02–71.12 | |
| | | M | 0–50 | 52.10–54.21 | 58.45–60.55 | 64.79–66.89 | 71.13–73.24 | [75.36, 100] |
| | | L | | 54.22–56.32 | 60.56–62.67 | 66.90–69.01 | 73.25–75.35 | |
| | <100,000 | H | | 44.99–47.09 | 51.32–53.43 | 57.67–59.77 | 64.01–66.11 | |
| | | M | 0–45 | 47.10–49.21 | 53.44–55.54 | 59.78–61.88 | 66.12–68.23 | [70.35, 100] |
| | | L | | 49.22–51.32 | 55.55–57.66 | 61.89–64.00 | 68.24–70.34 | |
| | >500,000 | H | | 44.99–47.51 | 52.58–55.10 | 60.18–72.70 | 67.77–70.29 | |
| | | M | 0–45 | 47.52–50.04 | 55.11–57.63 | 62.71–65.23 | 70.30–72.82 | [75.24, 100] |
| | | L | | 50.05–52.57 | 57.64–60.17 | 65.24–67.76 | 72.83–75.23 | |
| Retail | 100,000–500,000 | H | | 39.99–42.51 | 47.58–50.10 | 55.18–57.70 | 62.77–65.29 | |
| | | M | 0–40 | 42.52–45.04 | 50.11–52.63 | 57.71–60.23 | 65.30–67.82 | [70.36, 100] |
| | | L | | 45.05–47.57 | 52.64–55.17 | 60.24–62.76 | 67.83–70.35 | |
| | <100,000 | H | | 34.99–37.51 | 42.58–45.10 | 50.18–52.70 | 57.77–60.29 | |
| | | M | 0–35 | 37.52–40.04 | 45.11–47.63 | 52.71–55.23 | 60.30–62.82 | [65.36, 100] |
| | | L | | 40.05–42.57 | 47.64–50.17 | 55.23–57.76 | 62.83–65.35 | |
| | >500,000 | H | | 29.99–32.93 | 38.83–41.77 | 47.68–50.61 | 56.52–59.46 | |
| | | M | 0–30 | 32.94–35.88 | 41.78–44.72 | 50.62–53.56 | 59.47–62.40 | [65.36, 100] |
| | | L | | 35.89–38.82 | 44.73–47.67 | 53.57–56.51 | 62.41–65.35 | |
| Hotel | 100,000–500,000 | H | | 24.99–27.93 | 33.83–36.77 | 42.68–45.61 | 51.10–54.04 | |
| | | M | 0–25 | 27.94–30.88 | 36.78–39.72 | 45.62–48.56 | 54.05–56.99 | [59.36, 100] |
| | | L | | 30.89–33.82 | 39.73–42.67 | 48.57–51.09 | 57.00–59.93 | |
| | <100,000 | H | | 19.99–22.93 | 28.83–31.77 | 37.68–40.61 | 46.52–49.46 | |
| | | M | 0–20 | 22.94–25.88 | 31.78–34.72 | 40.62–43.56 | 49.47–52.40 | [55.36, 100] |
| | | L | | 25.89–28.82 | 34.73–37.67 | 43.57–46.51 | 52.41–55.35 | |

## 6.7   Calculating the Composite BRR of ABC Shopping Plaza

As we saw in previous chapters, the calculation of the overall credit score is a straightforward procedure of selecting the appropriate descriptors in the scorecard. Let us illustrate the procedure for ABC Shopping Plaza. We would select the scorecard for Retail Property to derive the BRR (Table 6.14).

ABC Shopping Plaza is located in a population centre of more than 500,000 inhabitants. The descriptors that are highlighted generate the BRR for Business Risk. The DSC ratio is 1.72 × (calculated earlier) and the LTV ratio is 64.66. These two ratios generate the BRR for financial risk. The LTV ratio is derived by using the direct capitalisation method and a cap rate of 7.25%. Banks prefer an appraised value but for illustration of how the scorecard

**Table 6.14**   BRR scorecard—ABC shopping plaza

| RISK CRITERIA/ RISK FACTOR | W | | AA | A | BBB | S | R |
|---|---|---|---|---|---|---|---|
| **BUSINESS RISK** | 50% | | | | | 5.0 | BB- |
| Tenant Quality | 35% | | -More than 75 percent of the GLA is rented to publicly rated retailers. -Publicly rated AA-/Aa3 and better. -Online shopping is not a major threat to store traffic. -Stores Include at least one upscale department store. | -More than 75 percent of the GLA (gross leasable area) is rented to national and multinational names. -Publicly rated at least A-/A3. -Online shopping a limited threat to store traffic. | -The tenants are mostly national names, occupying at least a third of the GLA. Other tenants are regional and local names. -The national names are publicly rated at least BBB-/Baa3. -A mix of retail stores; some vulnerable to online shopping. | 12.0 | A |
| Lease Maturity | 35% | | -The average of the remaining terms of the leases exceeds 6 years. -The lease term of the anchor store exceeds the average. -Tenant rollover risk ≤10 percent -High and stable occupancy rates. | -The average of the remaining terms of the leases is between 4 and 5 years. -The term of the loan for the property is less than the average lease terms. -Tenant rollover risk between 10 and 15 percent. -Occupancy rates very good and very stable. | -The average of the remaining terms of the leases is between 1and 3 years. -The term of the loan for the property is less than the average lease terms of the tenants. -Tenant rollover risk is between 15 and 20 percent Occupancy rates good and stable. | 9.0 | BBB |
| Location | 15% | | -The property has strong, general customer appeal. -Accessible through efficient and dependable public transportation and private taxis. -The property is highly visible in a densely populated area with a strong and diversified economic base. | -The property commands above-average customer appeal. -The transportation network is adequate. -The property is easily recognisable and is located in a stable and growing urban area. | -The property is in the right location for the target market. -The public transportation infrastructure is of average quality and reliability. -There are no major locational concerns to doubt the ability of the property to draw visitors. | 9.0 | BBB |
| Condition | 15% | | -Modern complex built to high construction standards and well maintained. -Complex incorporates a full range of value-added elements for shoppable entertainment (concerts, arts centres, spas, fitness clubs, and farmer's markets, etc) to attract traffic. -Ample and free parking is available outside the property. | -Modern complex exceeding the condition of competing structures. -Complex incorporates value-added elements for shoppable entertainment to attract traffic. -Available onsite parking lots provide ample space. | -The complex is fairly modern and adequately maintained. -Complex incorporates limited value-added elements for shoppable entertainment to attract traffic. -Limited parking outside the building is available. | 9.0 | BBB |
| **FINANCIAL RISK** | 50% | | | | | 6.8 | BB+ |
| DSC (Pop > 500,000) | 75% | L | | 1.491–1.543 | 1.332–1.364 | | |
| | | M | ≥ 1.650 | 1.544–1.596 | 1.385–1.437 | 15.0 | AA |
| | | H | | 1.597–1.649 | 1.438–1.490 | | |
| LTV (Pop > 500,000) | 25% | H | | 52.58–55.10 | 60.18–72.70 | | |
| | | M | 0–45 | 55.11–57.63 | 62.71–65.23 | 9.0 | BB |
| | | L | | 57.64–60.17 | 65.24–67.76 | | |
| CRITERIA-BASED BRR | | | | | | 11.8 | A |
| CRR/SRR OVERRIDE (YES/NO) | | | | | | | NO |
| INFORMATION ASYMMETRY OVERRIDE (YES/NO) | | | | | | | NO |
| FINAL BRR | | | | | | | A |

GLA = Gross leasable area, W = Weight, S = Score, R = Rating, L = Low M = Mid  H = High

works, the direct method would suffice. The current NOI is $2,421,900 (see Table 6.5). Plug these numbers into Eq. (6.2), and we derive the LTV ratio:

$$\text{PROPERTY VALUE}(\$) = \frac{2{,}421{,}900}{0.0725} = \$33{,}405{,}517$$

$$\text{LTV}(\%) = \frac{21{,}600{,}000}{33{,}405{,}517} = 64.66\%$$

The weighted average is a score of 11.8, which maps to a composite BRR of "A" according to the Risk Rating Scale (see Table 3.1). As you can see from the scorecard, the BRR reflects the attributes of the property. Therefore, the factors that directly influence the BRR are market conditions that affect property valuations and DSC ratios. Qualitative factors related to tenant quality, lease maturity, location, and condition also influence the BRR. The amount that a lender is willing to provide will depend on the internal credit policy. The LTV ratio sets the maximum the lender would be willing to provide. In this example, 75% of the property value is $25.1 million, and since the loan application is for $21.6 million, the borrower is well inside the limit to qualify.

## 6.8   Summary of Key Points

- Real estate is the land plus any structure and resources on that land. Real estate can be differentiated into two types: residential/dwelling and non-residential:

  1. Residential (undeveloped land, single-family and multifamily dwellings, care facilities, etc.)
  2. Commercial (office buildings, retail stores that are free standing or in shopping malls)
  3. Industrial (manufacturing, production, research and development, storage and distribution facilities)
  4. Lodging and meals (hotels and motels)
  5. Other (gas stations, restaurants, etc.)

- Defined according to use—for income production or not for income production—real estate is either commercial or residential. Commercial real estate is property used solely for business, whereas residential is solely for private household, owner-occupied living space. By definition, commercial real estate therefore includes dwellings (e.g., apartment buildings and town houses) that are used for income production. Also by definition, *all* income-producing real estate comes under the rubric of commercial real estate (CRE), except residential real estate that is used solely for living space. CRE properties are usually non-owner-occupied.

- For entities whose principal business is holding or developing IPRE that are not owner-occupied, the BRR is determined by two Risk Criteria: Business Risk and Financial Risk. The Business Risk reflects four attributes of the property: Tenant quality, lease maturity, condition of the property, and the location of the property. The Financial Risk reflects the debt-servicing capacity of the property (measured by the DSC ratio) and the severity of the loss along with the equity participation by the borrower (measured by the LTV ratio). The DSC ratio is the ratio of normalised net operating income to mortgage payments. LTV ratio is the ratio of the loan amount to the appraised value of the property. Lenders prefer significant down payment, which gives them comfort that the borrower will inject capital if the DSC ratio were to fall below 1 × the NOI.

- The BRR assessment factors and the weights for a stabilised IPRE property are different from an un-stabilised property.

- Population density is an important factor in the behaviour of prices and rents of CRE assets. The BRR scorecard controls for the population effect by explicitly including population centres in Financial Analysis.

- Collateral valuation is the bedrock of all underwriting processes and, in CRE lending, an inaccurate estimate (such as an over-appraisal) increases risk exposure. Markets for IPRE assets are illiquid so that price discovery is problematic. Therefore, "out of an abundance of caution", lenders require more than one method of evaluation. The valuations are very sensitive to the assumptions, especially the discount rate. Professional appraisers provide three estimates to corroborate their *opinion of market value* based on three estimates: (a) prices of comparable properties, (b) the cost of replacing the property, and (c) present value of the discounted cash flow.

- REITs (real estate investment trusts) and REOCs (real estate operating companies) also hold and develop income-producing real estate. Their shares trade on a public exchange. The vast majority of these companies invest in large portfolios of stabilised IPRE properties. REITs focus their investment and portfolio strategy on generating cash flow through the rent or leases from the properties. The net income is distributed to investors. In contrast, REOCs focus their investment and portfolio strategy in reinvesting the earnings in the business rather than distributing them to unit holders. *Thus, company strategy and management are critical risk factors in assessing both REITs and REOCs.* In addition to the usual characteristics such as tenant quality and lease maturity to assess an IPRE asset financed by a mortgage, credit analysts include in their credit evaluation of REITs and REOCs specific features of the portfolio, such as the quality of the assets and the geographic diversification because they determine the stability and growth in the income generated. Therefore, in designing the BRR scorecards, one would capture three building blocks: Business Risk (including Business Strategy), Management Risk, and Financial Risk (including access to financing).

## Notes

1. A *Gross Lease* is a type of commercial lease where the property owner pays for the operating expenses that include property taxes, insurance, and maintenance. A *Gross Lease* allows the tenant to pay one flat or all-in fee in exchange for use of the space or property. The property owner absorbs any increase in the operating cost. The direct opposite of the Gross Lease is the Net Lease, meaning that the tenant pays for costs that would normally be paid by the owner. Specifically, a *Triple Net Lease* or a Net-Net-Net (NNN) lease designates the tenant as being solely responsible for all the operating costs of maintenance and repair, utilities, taxes, and insurance. A *Full-Service Lease* is another type of commercial lease, similar to the Gross Lease, except that it contains provisions to pass on escalating operating costs to the tenant.

2. The mortgage term or the term of a loan (in general) is the length of time the borrower is committed to a mortgage rate and the other terms set by the lender. The term can run for several months up to 30 years. After the term period expires, the expectation is that the outstanding balance will be rolled over or repaid by a new loan. The interest rate is not likely to be the same as that of the current loan. The **term of a loan** must be distinguished from another time span, the **mortgage period**, which is the length of time it takes for the borrower to pay off or amortise the entire mortgage, for example, over 30 years. The longer the mortgage period, the smaller the periodic principal payments. Assuming no balloon payment at the final maturity date, each payment includes principal and interest. The term of a mortgage loan that is fully paid off at maturity will be the same as the amortisation period. Usually, however, the amortisation period will be longer than the term. For example, a loan that is amortised after 30 years matures after 5 years.

3. There are two ways to derive the amortisation and interest schedule. First, the easiest is to use Excel and its built-in PMT function: = PMT(r,n,P). Where PMT is the periodic payment, r is the interest rate, n is the number of amortisation periods, and P is the principal. In our example, the Excel function is =PMT(0.05,30,21,600,000). This gives $1,405,111, which is a blended payment of principal and interest. The amortisation schedule is easy to derive once the interest component is calculated in Year 1 from the *initial balance* of the loan: $21,600,000 × 0.05 = $1,080,000. Subtracting this figure from the fixed annual payment results in the principal payment in Year 1 and hence, the balance of the loan in Year 2. Repeat the calculation each year till Year 30 when the loan is fully amortised (goes to be zero). The foregoing can be written in the formulae:

$$\text{Principal}_t = \text{Fixed Payment}_t - \text{Interest}_t$$

$$\text{Interest}_t = r(\text{Loan Balance}_{t-1})$$

where *r* is the rate of interest and *t* goes from 1 to 30.

Alternatively, you can use a calculator and the formula of the fixed payment over "*n*" period:

$$\text{PMT} = P\frac{r(1+r)^n}{(1+r)^n - 1}$$

where

PMT  payment Amount per period,
P    initial Principal (loan amount)
r    interest rate per period (e.g. if the payment is monthly, the *r* is the annual rate divided by 12)
n    total number of payments or periods.

4. Of the many textbooks on property appraisal, these three are more than adequate as refresher and learning material. (1) W. B. Brueggeman and L. D. Stone (1981), *Real Estate Finance*, Richard D. Irwin, Chapter 10, Valuation of Income Properties; (2) A. Damodaran, A., (2012), *Investment Valuation*, 3rd Edition, John Wiley & Sons, Inc. Chapter 26; (3) Peter Wyatt, (2013), *Property Valuation*, 2nd Edition, John Wiley & Sons, Inc. The Wyatt textbook discusses three additional methods: (1) Profits Method, (2) Residual Method, and (3) Automated Valuation Models and Computer-Assisted Mass Appraisal (including regression analysis also discussed in the A. Darmodaran *Investment Valuation*, ibid.).

5. Property appraisal is part of a lender's collateral evaluation process to determine the desired loan exposure and the amount and type of credit enhancements for the loan. Effective collateral valuation is one of the pillars of a sound banking system. For this reason, government regulations govern minimum appraisal standards, appraiser independence, and the competency of the appraiser. Lenders come under strict regulations as well, such as having established controls to ensure the quality and independence of appraisals and evaluations. For example, banks need to maintain an updated list of *approved* appraisers. Mortgage lenders usually confirm their qualifications before placing them on the approved list.

6. Brueggeman and Stone (1981), op. cit., page 280 of Chapter 10.

7. Brueggeman and Stone (1981), op. cit., Section Approaches to valuation in Chapter 10.

8. Whether monetary policy can influence the *term structure of interest rates* has been an ongoing discussion in economics. The term "structure" is the familiar *yield curve*, a graph that depicts yields to maturity (*not* current yields) and time to maturity for bonds of the same asset class and credit quality. The theoretical argument for short-term rates affecting long-term rates is based on the equilibrium argument that *a **long-term** nominal interest rate is (approximately) the average of the current and expected nominal **short-term rates***. What is the economic logic underlying this result? Take two bonds with the same risk, for example. The return on a five-year bond should be comparable to the return on a one-year bond rolled over for an additional four years. If the yields on these two 5-year investments differed significantly, *arbitrage opportunity assures a positive profit at zero net cost* by selling short one investment and buying long into the other.

   But this amounts to a risk-free way of making money and thus unlikely to happen; hence, the stated result. With no arbitrage opportunity, the market's expectations about future changes in short-term rates (due to the stance in monetary policy) *and* certain risk premium will influence market rates of much longer maturities today. The major uncertainties are not only whether the changes are in the same direction (for the policy to be effective) but also the magnitude of the changes over the maturity spectrum in response to the change in monetary policy directly affecting overnight rates. It is worth noting that numerous econometric tests on US data of the "no arbitrage" hypothesis have shown otherwise, although this is not to say the expectation theory is invalid.

   Given the information imbedded in the curve, you can see why forecasters use it to predict the next phase of the economic cycle. Usually long-term rates exceed short-term rates, so an inverted curve means that longer-term rates are lower. The interpretation is that financial markets expect *future short-term rates* will fall in response to the anticipated economic slowdown when demand for loanable funds weakens. Conversely, an upward sloping curve means that financial markets expect growth to continue, so that future short-term rates are likely to rise in response to strong economic growth and increasing demand for loanable funds. Useful references: (1) For a refresher on arbitrage and bond pricing and the interpretation of the yield curve, Oliver Blanchard and David R. Johnson (2013), *Macroeconomics,* 6th edition, Pearson, Chapter 15, (2) Federal Reserve Bank of San Francisco (2005). *Can Monetary Policy Influence Long-term Interest Rates?* (authored by Òscar Jordà), and (3) Bank of Canada, *Monetary Policy: How It Works, and What It Takes,* Bank of Canada on the Bank's website.

9. Cap rates generally move with interest rates; however, there are periods when they diverge. By itself, this does not invalidate the theoretical relationship between the cap rate and risk-free rates that are a component in expected returns. Rather, it means in the periods when the rates diverge, other forces that influence cap rates dominate. Furthermore, there is no evidence of a decoupling.

10. Cushman and Wakefield provide the CRE Cap Rates Report quarterly and mid-year for the US and Canadian markets. There are pros and cons regarding the use of such survey data. See A. Damodaran, op. cit. Chapter 26.

11. Changing weights will require modification of the weighting procedure, but it does not affect the basic principles of the DCF model approach.

12. CAPM is like the linear equation model covered in introductory econometrics. To estimate the beta ($\beta$) in the equation using regression analysis, you need data series for (a) the property-type returns, (b) market returns (e.g., a stock market return, such as S&P 500, FTSE100, etc. serving as *a proxy* for the *market* portfolio, which should include *all assets including commercial real estate*), and (c) a risk-free return, e.g., government bond yields.

13. Fisher, I. (1930), *The Theory of Interest,* 1st edition, New York, Macmillan.

14. It is also common for lenders to set maximum loan to cost (construction) ratios by property type. The LTC ratio is another metric that CRE lenders consider to determine the risk of offering a construction loan. Although the LTC$^{Max}$ and LTV$^{Max}$ ratios are the same for a given property type, the loan amounts can often differ depending on the cost estimates and the appraised values. To control exposure risk, lenders offer the lower of the two.

15. United Nations Statistics Division, "Population density and urbanization." Note that population size is just one characteristic of an urban centre. There is no single definition of urban. The article states:

Urban/rural is a derived topic of high priority in a vital statistics system which is based on geographic information obtained from place of occurrence and place of usual residence. Because of national differences in the characteristics which distinguish urban from rural areas, *the distinction between urban and rural population is not amenable to a single definition applicable to all countries. For this reason, each country should decide which areas are to be classified as urban and which as rural, in accordance with their own circumstances.*

# 7

# Bank Credit Risk Analysis and Bank Credit Rating

## Chapter Objectives

1. Understand the importance of the banking system in a modern economy
2. Examine the special role commercial banks play in a modern economy and the reasons that banking is one of the most regulated industry
3. Discuss the unique features of a bank's financial statements
4. Perform bank credit risk analysis
5. Understand national and international (Basel) banking regulations
6. Identify the key risk factors that determine the creditworthiness of a commercial bank
7. Perform the analysis using the criteria-based approach to borrower risk rating (BRR) assessment

## 7.1 Introduction: Banking and the Banking System

Before we start analysing a bank's financial statements, it would be useful to understand the basics of banking and its regulatory environment. Indeed, an understanding of how a bank makes money opens the door to a better understanding of a bank's financial statements.[1] At the most fundamental level, Western-type banks are in the business of:

**Electronic Supplementary Material:** The online version of this chapter (https://doi.org/10.1007/978-3-030-32197-0_7) contains supplementary material, which is available to authorized users.

© The Author(s) 2020
T. M. Yhip, B. M. D. Alagheband, *The Practice of Lending*,
https://doi.org/10.1007/978-3-030-32197-0_7

- Accepting short-term deposits and making medium- to long-term interest-bearing loans—a function called *maturity transformation*—whereby short-term savings get *transformed* into long-lived productive assets (houses and plant and equipment for businesses). Banks, therefore, play a central role of financial intermediation and economic development at large.
- Supplying liquidity and processing payments to facilitate economic activity.
- Providing financial instruments to manage the risk and uncertainty in trade and commerce.
- Serving as the conduit for the government's monetary and fiscal policies that affect interest rates, the exchange rate, the price level, and employment. As we explain *the banking system essentially creates money (i.e., chequing deposits but not the actual fiat currency) through loan origination.*[2]

As you can see, these functions are vital to commerce and to an efficient economy. In return for these economic services and risk transformation, banks of the Western tradition earn income by charging interest, which is a margin over their funding costs, and also charging fees for financial services. A secured loan attracts lower interest than an unsecured loan, *ceteris paribus*. Because the stability of the banking system is so critical to an economy and its development, banks come under heavy regulations. They are intended to ensure public confidence in the banking system.[3] The Great Depression of the 1930s and Great Recession of 2008–2009 show how a modern economy is vulnerable to *systemic shocks*, where the collapse of one or a few financial institutions quickly spreads to other institutions and throughout the whole economy.

**Systemic Risk**

A risk of disruption to financial services that is caused by an impairment of all or parts of the financial system and has the potential for serious negative consequences for the real economy (definition based on the work by the International Monetary Fund, Financial Stability Board, and Bank of International Settlements for the Group of 20).

A banking crisis is something countries try to avoid. Today, national and international (Basel) banking regulations serve four purposes:

1. Financial stability: Regulators focus on macro-prudential supervision to prevent systemic risks.
2. Bank deposit protection: The deposit insurance schemes go by different names in countries. The basic practice is that the banks pay an insurance premium to the government in return for its guarantee to pay a defined amount per depositor per bank in the event of a bank's failing and going into liquidation.
3. Consumer protection: Customers are protected from unfair bank practices and are assured equal access to credit. Regulators audit bank deposit and lending operations and investigate consumer complaints. The penalties can be severe as in the case of Wells Fargo bank.[4]
4. Competition: The basic rationale is that a healthy banking system needs effective competition to ensure the availability and the fair pricing of banking services. Thus, regulators can deny bank mergers.

## 7.2    The Quality of the Business Environment

### 7.2.1  Legal and Financial Regulatory Framework

As we saw in Chap. 1 (Fig. 1.1), the operating environment of a bank consists largely of a country's legal and regulatory framework, the politics, and the economy. From the previous discussion on the economic contribution of banking, we gain insight into why banks in all countries are and should be regulated to the extent that they are. We also observe that both the structure of the banking system and the structure of the legal/regulatory framework differ from country to country. In this section, we look at what, at the minimum, an effective regulatory framework requires. A key measure of the effectiveness of the regulatory and supervisory framework is public trust and confidence, which is the bedrock of the banking business. A bank run is a perfect example of a total collapse of the trust and confidence that causes depositors to panic and withdraw their money. From Golin and Delhaise (2013),[5] we summarise some of the important attributes of a sound regulatory environment:

1. **The existence of an effective legal system:** An effective legal system is a precondition of an efficient and stable banking system. Such a system upholds and protects the rights of both creditors and debtors, and redresses legal issues without unnecessary delays and costs. An effective legal system is one

where the rule of law prevails. From the perspective of the credit analyst, an effective legal system is one that upholds the rights of creditors and the sanctity of contracts. As we discussed in Chap. 1, the Loan Agreement is one of the most important loan documents and its enforceability depends on the related jurisdiction's legal system. A source of useful information on the quality of a country's legal system can be obtained from the Worldwide Governance Indicators (WGI) Project supported by the World Bank.[6] The WGI Project reports an index consisting of six broad dimensions of governance, including the Rule of Law and Government Effectiveness.

2. **Independent structure of the regulatory regime:** The traditional structure is one where the central bank has responsibility for both monetary policy and financial regulation and supervision. Increasingly, countries are moving away from this structure to one with a separate financial regulator, called by various names such as Superintendence of Banks and Financial Institutions (SBFI) and Office of the Superintendent of Financial Institutions (OSFI). It is argued that the traditional structure might be best for developing countries with limited financial resources. It is, however, argued that the separate financial regulator is the best structure (a) to ensure funding for bank supervision is always available, (b) to shore up the independence of financial supervisors, and (c) to provide a centre of professional competence.[7] The WGI Project sheds light upon the regulatory regime in government effectiveness.

3. **The competence, independence, and authority of bank regulators:** These three relate to the quality of bank regulators. Like management competence that we examined in corporate credit analysis, the assessment of regulators' competence is also largely subjective, and good information on which to perform an appraisal is usually hard to find. Still, there are various sources of information. First, the WGI Project publishes a composite index on governance, and regulatory quality is a sub-index. Second, there are usually official documents that speak to the regulator's *de jure* independence from outside influence and their *de jure* authorities; however, press reports might contradict the official claims and this in itself is useful information. Third, for the countries that are members of the IMF (International Monetary Fund), the Working Papers are available to the public and they are full of banking and economic statistics that otherwise are not easily accessible. Finally, local media reports, like the IMF reports, may show a different picture than that of government documents.

4. **Supervision and enforcement:** Golin and Delhaise (2013)[8] make the point that regardless of the banking structure, supervision and enforcement are accomplished by similar measures that include:

a. Compulsory periodic reporting by the bank to the regulator
b. Ongoing monitoring and review of disclosed information
c. Regular onsite bank examinations
d. Consultative discussions between the regulator and the bank
e. Supervisory orders or penalties imposed upon the bank
f. The enforcement of regulator's orders administratively or through the judicial process by calling upon the power of the state to impose sanctions

## 7.2.2 The Economy

The financial performance of banks depends most importantly on the strength of the economy. The latter is a particularly important factor in assessing banks in *emerging markets*. Listed below are some of the characteristics of the operating environment in emerging markets:

- High level of corruption. It should be noted that no country is free of corruption and there are some goods sources of information on this. The WGI Project provides related information. Also, for a consistent record, the reader may look up the *Corruption Perception Index* published in Transparency International's website.[9] The data are available since 1995. For 2017, the organisation reported indices on a scale from 0 (highly corrupt) to 100 (clean) for 180 countries. The scores ranged from 9 to 89. The 75th percentile was a score of 57 (i.e., 75% of the scores were below 57), and most were from the developing regions of the world (low-middle-income countries), but many were from high-income countries in the Middle East, Asia, and Europe. The top-20th percentile was 60 (i.e., 20% of the scores were above 60).
- Weak governance
- The lack of transparency in the legal and regulatory systems
- Heavy reliance on a few industries and commodity exports for foreign exchange
- Small, highly open economies that are vulnerable to external economic shocks
- High likelihood of sovereign defaults
- High level of government borrowing through state-owned banks and from the commercial banks. In the assessment of bank creditworthiness, explicit or implicit government support is a positive for the BRR.

## 7.3    The Criteria-Based Approach to Bank Credit Risk Analysis

The criteria-based approach to assessing the creditworthiness of a bank builds on the CAMELS rating system that US regulators, such as the Federal Reserve, the FDIC (Federal Deposit Insurance Corporation), and the OCC (Office of the Comptroller of the Currency), use. The acronym CAMEL is a shorthand way of describing traditional bank analysis as the "Five Cs" is to describing credit analysis in general. The CAMEL stands for:

1. Capital adequacy
2. Asset quality
3. Management
4. Earnings
5. Liquidity

The CAMEL framework is an analytical way to decompose the risks that banking or credit entails. The fact that at all current methods of bank analysis, irrespective of the degree of sophistication, begin with the CAMEL speaks to the importance of this traditional framework. The CAMEL brings to the forefront the importance of two interrelated conditions: *solvency* and *liquidity* that are a big part of credit analysis. The former relates to the resources a bank has to absorb losses and, for this reason, is essential to a bank's ability to continue operations. The factors that contribute to insolvency are excessive debt (over leveraging), poor asset quality, low profits, and worsening profitability. Thus, capital adequacy risk combines leverage risk, asset risk, and earnings risk. The second, liquidity, relates the mismatch between the maturity of a bank's assets and its liabilities, the reliability of a bank's funding sources, all of which affect a bank's capacity to meet, on demand, cash outflows from liquid reserves. The liquidity strength of a bank depends on the confidence of customers in regard to their view of a bank's safety. From these examples, we see that whilst it is analytically useful and indeed necessary to compartmentalise the risks, which is essentially what a criteria-based scorecard also does, the credit analyst needs to keep an eye out for the interrelationships or the interactions.

A sixth component is a bank's sensitivity to market risk, which was added to the acronym in 1997 so that in the US banking supervision, CAMEL is synonymous with CAMELS.[10] Ratings are assigned for each component in addition to the overall rating of a bank's financial condition. The ratings are assigned on a scale of 1 to 5. Banks with ratings of 1 or 2 are considered to present few or no supervisory concerns, whereas 3, 4, or 5 present moderate to extreme degrees of supervisory concern. The FDIC and its two regulatory counterparts (the OCC and Federal Reserve) prohibit public disclosure of CAMEL ratings and warn that unauthorised disclosures are a criminal offence. Still, the information has ways of getting out to the public domain, sometimes unintentionally through other government reports, such as a US Senate investigation report on a particular bank, or (intentionally) through leaks.[11]

## 7.4    Risk Criteria: Qualitative Analysis

The overall BRR scorecard shown later in Table 7.1 comprises four sections:

1. Business Environment (10%)
2. Business Risk (15%)
3. Management Risk (25%)
4. Financial Risk (50%)

Under each criterion are risk factors and risk elements. The weights are in brackets. Financial Risk is considered the main driver in bank risk and is allotted a full half of the weight of the scorecard.

The first three criteria represent the qualitative part of the assessment, whose combined weight balances the weight of Financial Risk. Some lenders argue for more weight to Financial Risk but the recent financial scandals we mentioned briefly in passing may have dampened that view. Let us examine each Risk Criterion in turn. We already looked at Business Environment in Sect. 7.2. Management Risk, particularly corporate governance, is under increasing scrutiny and the criterion gets a relatively high weight of 25%. One can argue that the steady stream of banking scandals making the news this decade[12] justifies a relatively high weight to Management Risk. In the past, Financial Risk accounted for almost two-thirds of the total weight, but times have changed and lenders now have a close eye on emergent risk factors in management, such as fraud and other illegal practices and their effects on financial risk.

**Table 7.1** Template of a bank analysis risk rating scorecard

| RISK CRITERIA | W | RISK FACTORS | W | RISK ELEMENTS | W | AA | ... | ... | B | S | R |
|---|---|---|---|---|---|---|---|---|---|---|---|
| OPER. ENV. RISK | 10% | Economic | 50% | Economic | 50% | d | ... | ... | d | - | - |
| | | Regulatory | 50% | Regulatory | 50% | d | ... | ... | d | - | - |
| BUSINESS RISK | 15% | Competitiveness & Market Position | 100% | Competitiveness & Market Position | 100% | d | ... | ... | d | - | - |
| MANAGEMENT RISK | 25% | Business Plan & Operations | 34% | Business Plan & Operations | 34% | d | ... | ... | d | - | - |
| | | Risk Management & Internal Controls | 33% | Risk Management & Internal Controls | 33% | d | ... | ... | d | - | - |
| | | Corporate Governance | 33% | Corporate Governance | 33% | d | ... | ... | d | - | - |
| FINANCIAL RISK | 50% | Capitalisation | 25% | Tier 1 Ratio | 30% | d | ... | ... | d | - | - |
| | | | | Total Capital ratio | 30% | d | ... | ... | d | - | - |
| | | | | Capital Quality | 40% | d | ... | ... | d | - | - |
| | | Asset Quality | 25% | NPL/ Gross Loans | 15% | d | ... | ... | d | - | - |
| | | | | LLPs/PPI | 15% | d | ... | ... | d | - | - |
| | | | | ALL/NPL | 20% | d | ... | ... | d | - | - |
| | | | | Loan Quality | 50% | d | ... | ... | d | - | - |
| | | Earnings: Profit & Profitability | 15% | NIM (Net Interest Margin) | 20% | d | ... | ... | d | - | - |
| | | | | ROA (Return on Avg Assets) | 20% | d | ... | ... | d | - | - |
| | | | | ROE (Return on Avg Equity) | 20% | d | ... | ... | d | - | - |
| | | | | Cost-Income Ratio | 15% | d | ... | ... | d | - | - |
| | | | | Earnings Quality | 25% | d | ... | ... | d | - | - |
| | | Liquidity | 35% | Liquid Assets/ Total Assets | 15% | d | ... | ... | d | - | - |
| | | | | Customer Deposits/ Total Funding | 20% | d | ... | ... | d | - | - |
| | | | | Loans/ Customer Deposits + S/T Funding | 15% | d | ... | ... | d | - | - |
| | | | | Access to Liquidity | 25% | d | ... | ... | d | - | - |
| | | | | Liquidity Quality | 25% | d | ... | ... | d | - | - |

CRITERIA-BASED CRR (COUNTERPARTY RISK RATING):

CRR ADJUSTED FOR EXTERNAL SUPPORT:

CRR AFTER COUNTRY RISK/ SOVEREIGN RISK OVERRIDE (AS APPLICABLE):

W: Weight, S: Score, R: Rating

## 7.4.1 Business Risk

**Competitiveness and Market Position: Franchise and Franchise Value**

In competitiveness and market position, we analyse a bank's *franchises*,[13] which refers to the business lines that a bank differentiates or is attempting to differentiate itself as a leader regionally, nationally, or internationally. As part of their marketing strategy, banks tout their core franchises such as being or wanting to be leaders in all, or a good many, of the ones listed below:

- Retail mortgages
- Treasury and trade
- Fixed income markets
- Global credit card
- Investment banking
- Wealth management
- Commercial or business lending

- Investment banking
- Investor and treasury services
- Global credit cards

Consumers may show a stronger preference for a particular bank and its offerings over its competitor "across the street". The advantages of the preferred bank make its "demand curve" more price inelastic than those of its rivals. On the supply side, the bank may have certain advantages deriving from the bank's infrastructure and organisational structure (i.e., its extensive branch network, superior technology, efficient management information systems, the speed, and efficiency by which managers make and implement decisions).

All these factors determine the ability of a bank to maintain or attain the franchise goals like profitability, market shares, and volume of transactions (which could be deposits, loans, trades, and so on). The higher is the profitability, the higher the franchise value, and the stronger the bank to defend market shares. From the perspective of the credit analyst, the important information on which to assess the strength of a bank's franchise value would include the following:

- Knowledge of the businesses in which the bank is a leader or competitive
- The bank's market shares in the lines of business
- The demand/supply factors that contribute to the bank's franchise value
- The potential threats to the bank's franchise value

## 7.4.2  Management and Governance Risk

In any given time, management and many other factors account for the success of a company, but any reckoning of repeated success over a long period would give high credit to the management factor. Management means *operations*, which, broadly speaking, include planning, organising, staffing, leading, implementing, controlling, and motivating. Corporate governance relates to *oversight and control* aimed at ensuring that business, planning, and activities pursuant to the plan are conducted effectively, and that risk is managed properly. In this sense, corporate governance overlaps with management in the areas of planning and controlling.

The question is: how does the analyst assess management and governance? The biggest challenge is information and the problem of information asymmetry. There is a view in American banking circles—and sympathy from similar groups in other countries—that regulators ought to make public the findings of their bank examinations. This would help solve the information asymmetry problem and ensure that banking supervisors adopt prompt measures to avert risk to the financial system.[14] In the absence of reports made available by regulators, a bank credit analyst garners management information from three main sources: the newspapers, rating agency reports, and the audited annual reports. The bank credit analyst employed in a bank has the benefit of the call reports prepared by relationship managers. Newspaper reports are an indispensable information source. For example, the *Los Angeles Times* started to publish articles about Wells Fargo's improper sales-related conduct as early as December 21, 2013.[15] But it was not until 2016 that the rating agencies started to react and not before the regulators imposed a hefty fine of $185 million. Noteworthy is a Fitch Ratings Inc. report of the bank's sales practice that dated back to 2011.[16]

The rating agencies are an additional source of useful information but, as we know from experience, their credit ratings and their conclusions are often wide off the mark. Still, ratings do matter and credit analysts need to be aware of two issues. First, the rating agencies have a conflict of interest because the corporations they rate are also their clients who pay them to be rated. This is an old criticism that resonated strongly during the 2007–2008 subprime crisis.[17] The second is the problem of information asymmetry that occurs when management fails to provide full information—because it might be incriminating or unethical—to the risk assessor. For example, management might not want to give out information on certain transactions. Golin and Delhaise (2013) make a prescient observation concerning the quality of information that the rating agencies obtain in the course of site visits by their credit analyst:

> There also is a danger in agreeing – sometimes for want of a better option – to let the bank put forward a specially trained representative to handle questions on behalf of management. Nevertheless, familiarity can create comfort. Consequently, most rating agencies send a minimum of two analysts when performing a full rating of a bank. *It is also possible that the analysts may also face the opposite situation – one in which management appears to be reluctant to provide information to the analyst, and will disclose comparatively little about operations or strategy* [sic].[18]

This brings us to the audited annual reports. They are also indispensable because they are the primary source of financial and management information. The value from reading the reports, however, comes from not taking them at face value.[19] For example, banks go to great length to discuss their risk management practices to assure investors and the shareholders of their corporate governance. For example, Wells Fargo's 2014 Annual Report stated:

> The key elements of our risk management framework and culture include the following:
>
> - We strongly believe in managing risk as close to the source as possible. We manage risk through three lines of defense, and the first line of defense is our team members in our lines of business who are responsible for identifying, assessing, monitoring, managing, mitigating, and owning the risks in their businesses. All of our team members have accountability for risk management.
> - We recognize the importance of strong oversight. Our Corporate Risk group, led by our Chief Risk Officer who reports to the Board's Risk Committee, as well as other corporate functions such as the Law Department, Corporate Controllers, and the Human Resources Department serve as the second line of defense and provide company-wide leadership, oversight, an enterprise view, and appropriate challenge to help ensure effective and consistent understanding and management of all risks by our lines of business. Wells Fargo Audit Services, led by our chief auditor who reports to the Board's Audit and Examination Committee, serves as the third line of defense and through its audit, assurance, and advisory work evaluates and helps improve the effectiveness of the governance, risk management, and control processes across the enterprise.

Pronouncements similar to these appeared in the 2015 and 2016 annual reports. But an investigation initiated by the bank's Board of Directors—but not before US regulators fined the bank $185 million in 2016–cast doubt on the stated assurances. The Board identified a litany of major gaps in the bank's risk management and internal controls, and, in its report of April 2017, stated:

> Wells Fargo, with its successful Community Bank, had a long history of strong performance as a self-identified sales organization with a decentralized corporate structure guided by its Vision & Values statement. While there is nothing necessarily pernicious about sales goals, a sales-oriented culture or a decentralized corporate structure, these same cultural and structural characteristics unfortunately coalesced and failed dramatically here. There was a growing conflict over time in the Community Bank between Wells Fargo's Vision & Values and the Community Bank's emphasis on sales goals. *Aided by a culture of strong deference to management of the lines of business (embodied in the oft-repeated "run it like you own it" mantra), the Community Bank's senior leaders distorted the sales model and performance management system, fostering an atmosphere that prompted low quality sales and improper and unethical behavior [sic].*[20]

The following downgrade statement by Standard and Poor's on February 7, 2018 is noteworthy for the agency's "diagnosis" and the "prognosis":

> Following this punitive something called action, our downgrade reflects our view that regulatory risk for Wells is *more severe than we previously expected* [sic] and the process for improving its governance and operational risk policies may take longer than we previously expected. At the same time, the company may be subject to prolonged reputational issues. The company also announced that it will replace four additional members *of its Board of* Directors, signalling that the Board continues to be in transition.[21]

It is clear from the examination of these cases that an assessment of Management Risk should address three key areas:

- The existence or the lack thereof of a business plan, and the articulation of clear goals and strategies
- The effectiveness or the lack thereof of risk management and internal controls
- The effectiveness or the lack thereof of corporate governance or oversight
- Information transparency

The way we propose dealing with information transparency issues is the Information Asymmetry Override in the BRR scorecard discussed in Chap. 3. In Sect. 7.6.2, we use the discussion of Sect. 7.4.2 to identify predictors and to create descriptors for Management Risk.

## 7.4.3 The Enterprise-Wide Business Plan and Operations

Any successful bank is expected to have a written plan that establishes clearly and in detail the organisation's goals, strategies, and the roles and responsibilities of all stakeholders. The plan is the product of the Board of Directors, the lines of business, and risk management collaborating. The business needs the mandate of the Board and support from risk management. Risk management is an integral part of the planning process of determining risk appetites and risk tolerance levels. Banks do not share the details of their business plan with outside bank credit analysts, and the information they release is usually very general. Banks usually devote a section of risk management where they present the objectives, guiding principles, and the governance structure to ensure compliance and oversight. But as we saw earlier with Well Fargo bank, the risk management structure can be deficient in some critical areas and still remain unattended for many years until a major crisis erupts. Banks are expected to inform shareholders about their investitures and divestures, loan loss provisions, and the restructuring of operations. All these give credit and equity analysts information to assess a bank's growth strategy against their public statements.

The bank credit analyst assesses whether the goals are attainable and whether the strategies relative to the bank's franchises are aggressive. Again, the Wells Fargo sales scandal involving false accounts is instructive because it shows that the pursuit of aggressive tactics and targets poses business, operational, and reputational risks. In its report of April 2017, the bank's Board of Directors blamed management's "aggressive sales culture" that emphasised sales volume and relied heavily on consistent year-over-year sales growth. The report goes on to say: "In many instances, Community Bank leadership recognized that their plans were unattainable—they were commonly referred to as 50/50 plans, meaning that there was an expectation that only half the regions would be able to meet them."[22]

Sales and market share objectives must be measurable and clearly defined by the appropriate metrics that can be closely monitored periodically to ensure the bank's compliance with its self-imposed limits and those set by the regulators. Where limits and targets are in breach, a well-managed bank will have effective internal controls to monitor, identify, and correct deviations from targets. Obviously, the bank analyst will not have confidential information about specific breaches, but he or she can find reports on losses and loan concentration, which are windows into the effectiveness of a bank's controls.

A key requirement of a plan is *accurate and timely* reporting, which is necessary for transparency, data integrity, and accountability. Effective reporting means that a bank has a dedicated unit, which reports to risk management, monitors compliance, gathers the necessary information from the business segments, and prepares an enterprise risk report on a regular schedule. The report would normally contain discussion and explanation of missed targets, in particular, the self-imposed and regulatory limits. The Board and risk management usually approve the final draft of these reports before they go to press. As we noted earlier, the analyst does not usually get to learn about the lapses and deficiencies until disaster unfolds; however, in many cases, red flags go up well before the crisis erupts.

To recap, the bank analyst needs to assess the strengths and weaknesses of the business plan. The focus must be on these areas:

- The goals, the risk tolerance, and the strategies
- The clarity and feasibility of the business plan

- Risk management controls
- The oversight or governance structure

Usually, the outside bank credit analyst (who often is a financial reporter of a newspaper) has limited information to work with. In contrast, inside bank credit analysts have the benefit of call reports prepared by relationship managers.

## 7.4.4 Risk Management and Internal Controls

Banks usually devote a section in their annual reports to describe their risk governance and risk management framework and practices. Many banks use the three lines of defence model to manage risks (exposures) across the bank. The business units, which own the risks, are the first line of defence. The second is risk management and compliance, which provide oversight over the business and set risk management practice. The third is internal audit, which provides independent assurance to management and the Board of Directors on the effectiveness of risk management practices. Unlike the business units, the others do not own or manage balance sheets.

All banks have controls in place. They are the processes designed to ensure that the business units comply with approved bank policies and risk appetite, and with the laws and regulations of the country. The key function of a bank's internal audit is to assure management and report to the Board that the controls and the systems in place are effective. To assess the effectiveness of a bank's risk management the credit analyst needs to determine:

- The risk management culture starting with the Board—tone at the top
- The effectiveness of the controls and systems in place
- The effectiveness of Internal Audit, the third line of defence.

As we saw in previous sections, an outside credit analyst has no window into the quality of a bank's risk management practices, as does an internal auditor who is mandated to audit Risk Management functions periodically. One source of "red flags" is the newspaper (as in the case of Wells Fargo)—print and digital—but the problem with financial scandals, as we recall from Chaps. 1 and 2, is that the public gets to learn about them much too late when damage is already done. It is for this very reason that many in financial circles want the CAMEL ratings of bank regulators to be made public.

**Three Lines of Defence Model**

*Board of Directors*: The Board of Directors (the Board) of a bank establishes the "tone at the top" (essentially the credit culture discussed in Chap. 1), approves risk appetite, and provides general oversight of risk management policies and procedures, and the internal controls that keep risks within established risk appetite. The Board functions through committees, such as Finance Committee, Risk Committee, and the Audit Committee. The Board ensures that Risk Management is adequately independent of the businesses, which own the risks. The Audit Committee oversees the integrity of financial reporting, the performance of Internal Audit functions, the qualifications, performance and independence of external auditors, and compliance with legal and regulatory requirements.

*First Line*: The business units and their support functions are responsible for monitoring, identifying, evaluating, and reporting risks against approved policies and risk appetite. Because the businesses originate credit and own the risk, they are not authorised to assign credit ratings and approve credit transactions at the same time.

*Second Line:* Risk Management & Group Compliance provides risk oversight. They establish risk management policies and procedures, provide risk guidance and oversight of the effectiveness of First Line risk management practices, and monitor and independently report on the level of risk against the risk appetite. Where credit is concerned, Risk Management "owns" the risk ratings and approves all credit transactions.

*Third Line:* Internal Audit provides independent assurance to Management and the Board on the effectiveness of risk management policies and procedures and the internal controls. Internal Audit reports directly to the Audit Committee. Where credit is concerned, Internal Audit provides assurance through its periodic audits of the businesses, their supporting functions, and Risk Management that policies and procedures are being followed, reports the audit findings to Management and the Board, and ensures that Management satisfactorily resolves the reported deficiencies.

## 7.4.5  Corporate Governance

To introduce this section we quote Investopedia's definition of "corporate governance":

Corporate governance is the system of rules, practices and processes by which a company is directed and controlled. Corporate governance essentially involves balancing the interests of a company's many stakeholders, such as shareholders, management, customers, suppliers, financiers, government and the community. Since corporate governance also provides the framework for attaining a company's objectives, it encompasses practically every sphere of management, from action plans and internal controls to performance measurement and corporate disclosure.[23]

The Federal Reserve's indictment of Wells Fargo Bank called into question the bank's corporate governance. Golin and Delhaise (2013)[24] identify three requirements [sic] of good corporate governance:

1. An *independent and effective board of directors*, having sufficient experience, knowledge, judgement, and integrity to safeguard shareholders' interests.
2. *Independent auditors*
3. Adequate *disclosure to enable those stakeholders to evaluate management performance.*

As you can judge, the information requirements for a satisfactory assessment of Business Risk and Management Risk are daunting.

## 7.5   Risk Criteria: Quantitative Financial Analysis

In this section, we examine the six parts of the CAMELS rating system:

(C) Capital adequacy
(A) Assets
(M) Management capability
(E) Earnings
(L) Liquidity (also called asset liability management)
(S) Sensitivity (sensitivity to market/interest rate risks)

The quantitative analysis is essentially the financial analysis based on the bank's financial statements and material information pertinent to the analysis. Before we start delving into financial ratios, it would be productive to invest a bit of time reviewing a bank's financial statements in order to gain familiarly with a bank's basic operations and prepare you for the CAMELS framework, where the "S" is subsumed under Asset Quality in this book.

Because of the unique nature of the banking business, the analyst must take a different approach from the way he/she would assess the creditworthiness of a non-financial business, as we showed in Chaps. 5 and 6 for an airline and commercial real estate, respectively. Let us start with the three financial statements of Laurentian Bank of Canada, a chartered bank whose shares are traded on the Toronto Stock Exchange, with its head office in Montreal, Quebec. We use this bank's historical data because the bank's presentation of the line items is very easy to follow and captures the essential operations of a modern commercial bank, which is what we want to illustrate.

1. Income Statement (Table 7.2)
2. Statement of Cash Flows (Table 7.3)
3. Balance Sheet (Table 7.4)

From the vantage point of the external bank credit analyst, only the first two are relevant. This leads to the question: why is the cash-flow statement largely irrelevant to assessing a bank's performance. Recall that the cash flow

**Table 7.2** Laurentian Bank of Canada, income statement 2014–2016

| For the years ended October 31 (in thousands of Canadian dollars) | 2016 | 2015 | 2014 |
|---|---|---|---|
| **Interest income** | | | |
| Loans | 1,066,245 | 1,034,117 | 1,056,637 |
| Securities | 35,265 | 40,144 | 40,753 |
| Deposits with other banks | 1740 | 793 | 751 |
| Other, including derivatives | 63,630 | 66,104 | 47,080 |
| | **1,166,880** | **1,141,158** | **1,145,221** |
| **Interest expense** | | | |
| Deposits | 454,862 | 435,533 | 449,101 |
| Debt related to securitisation activities | 114,346 | 113,102 | 118,269 |
| Subordinated debt | 6433 | 16,094 | 16,071 |
| Other | 1595 | 1346 | 800 |
| | **577,236** | **566,075** | **584,241** |
| **Net interest income** | **589,644** | **575,083** | **560,980** |
| Other income | | | |
| Fees and commissions on loans and deposits | 145,690 | 141,589 | 141,849 |
| Income from brokerage operations | 71,435 | 63,294 | 63,640 |
| Income from sales of mutual funds | 40,299 | 38,811 | 29,228 |
| Income from investment accounts | 30,271 | 30,202 | 31,658 |
| Insurance income, net | 17,527 | 16,903 | 19,246 |
| Income from treasury | 12,782 | 23,365 | 16,138 |
| Other | 7803 | 7879 | 11,326 |
| | **325,807** | **322,043** | **313,085** |
| **Total revenue** | **915,451** | **897,126** | **874,065** |
| Amortisation of net premium on purchased financial instruments | 5190 | 5999 | 9653 |
| Provision for credit losses | 33,350 | 34,900 | 42,000 |
| Non-interest expenses | | | |
| Salaries and employee benefits | 334,903 | 342,269 | 340,394 |
| Premises and technology | 187,696 | 197,778 | 186,671 |
| Other | 114,197 | 104,368 | 101,383 |
| Impairment and restructuring charges | 38,344 | 78,409 | – |
| Costs related to business combinations | 4409 | – | 12,861 |
| | **679,549** | **722,824** | **641,309** |
| Income before income taxes | 197,362 | 133,403 | 181,103 |
| Income taxes | 45,452 | 30,933 | 40,738 |
| **Net income** | **151,910** | **102,470** | **140,365** |
| **Adjusted net income** | **187,013** | **172,199** | **163,582** |

Source: Company reports

**Table 7.3** Laurentian Bank of Canada, consolidated statement of cash flows 2014–2016

| For the years ended October 31 (in thousands of Canadian dollars) | 2016 | 2015 | 2014 |
|---|---|---|---|
| **Cash flows relating to operating activities** | | | |
| **Net income** | **151,910** | **102,470** | **140,365** |
| Adjustments to determine net cash flows relating to operating activities: | | | |
| Provision for credit losses | 33,350 | 34,900 | 42,000 |
| Net gains (losses) on disposal of available-for-sale securities | 2391 | −8253 | −8290 |
| Deferred income taxes | −6441 | −9077 | 2681 |
| Impairment of goodwill, software and intangible assets, and premises and equipment | 22,113 | 72,226 | − |
| Depreciation of premises and equipment | 9798 | 14,125 | 16,107 |
| Amortisation of software and other intangible assets | 28,771 | 38,657 | 39,509 |
| Gain on sale of commercial mortgage loans | − | − | −3686 |
| Revaluation of contingent consideration | − | − | 4100 |
| Change in operating assets and liabilities: | | | |
| Loans | −2,399,614 | −2,090,419 | −340,032 |
| Change in acceptances | 156,281 | 108,087 | − |
| Securities at fair value through profit and loss | −709,129 | 255,058 | 172,148 |
| Securities purchased under reverse repurchase agreements | 1,031,453 | −714,658 | −964,728 |
| Accrued interest receivable | −5504 | 5276 | −3740 |
| Derivative assets | 49,546 | −143,792 | −6192 |
| Deposits | 969,041 | 2,081,278 | 595,676 |
| Obligations related to securities sold short | −132,544 | 277,360 | 98,208 |
| Obligations related to securities sold under repurchase agreements | 228,551 | 80,925 | 862,565 |
| Accrued interest payable | 15,747 | −54,394 | −13,424 |
| Derivative liabilities | 24,816 | 34,843 | −11,201 |
| Change in debt related to securitisation activities | 1,750,852 | 629,754 | − |
| Other, net | 224,835 | −173,416 | 802 |
| | **1,446,223** | **540,950** | **622,868** |
| **Cash flows relating to financing activities** | | | |
| Change in acceptances | − | − | 94,408 |
| Repurchase of subordinated debt | −250,000 | − | − |
| Change in debt related to securitisation activities | − | − | −110,866 |
| Repurchase of preferred shares | − | − | −110,000 |
| Net proceeds from issuance of preferred shares | 121,967 | − | 122,071 |
| Net proceeds from issuance of common shares | 215,633 | 387 | 72 |
| Dividends | −55,209 | −73,025 | −60,803 |
| | **32,391** | **−72,638** | **−65,118** |

(continued)

**Table 7.3** (continued)

| For the years ended October 31 (in thousands of Canadian dollars) | 2016 | 2015 | 2014 |
|---|---|---|---|
| **Cash flows relating to investing activities** | | | |
| Change in available-for-sale securities | | | |
| Acquisitions | −2,229,090 | −1,970,989 | −3,339,421 |
| Proceeds on sale and at maturity | 1,885,770 | 2,152,640 | 2,454,227 |
| Change in held-to-maturity securities | −307,354 | −272,403 | −336,335 |
| Acquisitions | 198,344 | 202,188 | 662,202 |
| Proceeds on sale of commercial mortgage loans | – | – | 106,084 |
| Acquisition of a portfolio of investment loans | – | −613,120 | – |
| Additions to premises and equipment and intangible assets | −43,549 | −14,619 | −64,490 |
| Cash paid for business combinations | −996,500 | – | – |
| Change in interest-bearing deposits with other banks | 28,426 | 30,799 | 3394 |
| | −1,463,953 | −485,504 | −514,339 |
| Net change in cash and non-interest-bearing deposits with other banks | 14,661 | −17,192 | 43,411 |
| Cash and non-interest-bearing deposits with other banks at beginning of year | 109,055 | 126,247 | 82,836 |
| **Cash and non-interest-bearing deposits with other banks at end of year** | **123,716** | **109,055** | **126,247** |
| Supplemental disclosure about cash flows relating to operating activities: | | | |
| Interest paid during the year | 561,770 | 619,108 | 603,473 |
| Interest received during the year | 1,161,519 | 1,129,223 | 1,129,180 |
| Dividends received during the year | 11,436 | 15,111 | 8985 |
| Income taxes paid during the year | 35,561 | 45,041 | 19,884 |

statement records the movement of cash into and out of a firm to show the net cash flow for the reporting period. For non-financial companies, the cash flow statement is indispensable to assess creditworthiness because it gives a more accurate accounting for the cash flows than does the income statement because of the accrual accounting method. Thus, for both financial and non-financial enterprises, net income (loss) will almost never equate to the net increase (decrease) in cash earned over the same period. In the case of Laurentian Bank, net income for each year in the 2014–2016 period is not the same as the net change in cash and non-interest-bearing assets for the same period (compare Tables 7.2 and 7.3).

Whereas this result is the same for non-financial firms, the big difference is that the bank's production function is unique: cash is both input (deposits and other funding) and output (interest from lending and fees), so that movements in cash do not carry the same interpretation of performance as they do

**Table 7.4** Laurentian Bank of Canada, consolidated balance sheet 2014–2016

| For the years ended October 31 (in thousands of Canadian dollars) | 2016 | 2015 | 2014 |
|---|---|---|---|
| **Assets** | | | |
| Cash and non-interest bearing deposits with other banks | 123,716 | 109,055 | 126,247 |
| Interest-bearing deposits with other banks | **63,383** | **91,809** | **122,608** |
| **Securities** | | | |
| Available-for-sale | 2,723,693 | 2,368,757 | 2,577,017 |
| Held-to-maturity | 502,232 | 393,222 | 323,007 |
| Held-for-trading | 2,434,507 | 1,725,378 | 1,980,436 |
| | 5,660,432 | 4,487,357 | 4,880,460 |
| Securities purchased under reverse repurchase agreements | **2,879,986** | **3,911,439** | **3,196,781** |
| **Loans** | | | |
| Personal | 6,613,392 | 7,063,229 | 6,793,078 |
| Residential mortgage | 16,749,387 | 14,998,867 | 14,825,541 |
| Commercial mortgage | 4,658,734 | 4,248,761 | 2,651,271 |
| Commercial and other | 4,727,385 | 3,308,144 | 2,794,232 |
| Customers' liabilities under acceptances | 629,825 | 473,544 | 365,457 |
| | 33,378,723 | 30,092,545 | 27,429,579 |
| Allowances for loan losses | −105,009 | −111,153 | −119,371 |
| | 33,273,714 | 29,981,392 | 27,310,208 |
| Other | | | |
| Derivatives | 232,791 | 276,601 | 132,809 |
| Premises and equipment | 32,989 | 45,562 | 68,750 |
| Software and other intangible assets | 150,490 | 147,135 | 207,188 |
| Goodwill | 55,812 | 34,853 | 64,077 |
| Deferred tax assets | 36,495 | 17,450 | 7936 |
| Other assets | 496,532 | 556,851 | 365,721 |
| | 1,005,109 | 1,078,452 | 846,481 |
| | 43,006,340 | 39,659,504 | 36,482,785 |
| **Liabilities and shareholders' equity** | | | |
| Deposits | | | |
| Personal | 21,001,578 | 19,377,716 | 18,741,981 |
| Business, banks and other | 6,571,767 | 7,226,588 | 5,781,045 |
| | 27,573,345 | 26,604,304 | 24,523,026 |
| Other | | | |
| Obligations related to securities sold short | 1,707,293 | 1,839,837 | 1,562,477 |
| Obligations related to securities sold under repurchase agreements | 2,525,441 | 2,296,890 | 2,215,965 |
| Acceptances | 629,825 | 473,544 | 365,457 |
| Derivatives | 150,499 | 125,683 | 90,840 |
| Deferred tax liabilities | 32,755 | 8294 | 10 |
| Other liabilities | 968,077 | 780,682 | 869,029 |
| | 6,013,890 | 5,524,930 | 5,103,778 |
| Debt related to securitisation activities | 7,244,454 | 5,493,602 | 4,863,848 |
| Subordinated debt | 199,824 | 449,641 | 447,523 |

(continued)

**Table 7.4** (continued)

| For the years ended October 31 (in thousands of Canadian dollars) | 2016 | 2015 | 2014 |
|---|---|---|---|
| Shareholders' equity | | | |
| Preferred shares | 341,600 | 219,633 | 219,633 |
| Common shares | 696,493 | 466,336 | 465,854 |
| Retained earnings | 924,861 | 886,656 | 848,905 |
| Accumulated other comprehensive income | 11,873 | 14,366 | 10,127 |
| Share-based payment reserve | – | 36 | 91 |
| | **1,974,827** | **1,587,027** | **1,544,610** |
| | **43,006,340** | **39,659,504** | **36,482,785** |
| Total exposure (non-risk based) | 43,094,377 | 39,557,300 | N.A[a] |
| Exposure (risk weighted assets) | 17,922,653 | 15,422,282 | 13,844,014 |

[a]Not available: Under Office of the Superintendent of Financial Institutions (OSFI) Leverage Requirements Guideline issued in October 2014, the previous Asset to Capital Multiple (ACM) was replaced with a new leverage ratio as of January 1, 2015
Source: Company reports

for a non-financial enterprise. Another difference is that a bank's inflows (mainly deposits and other funding) add to its liabilities; outflows (advances and loans) add to assets. Therefore, a steady net cash inflow is not necessarily a positive for performance because it may mean the bank is not converting the liabilities into productive assets that would later lead to cash inflows. That said, the cash flow statement is relevant for treasury operations such as managing the bank's liquidity. From the perspective of the *external* credit analyst, however, the cash flow statement is largely irrelevant to assess bank creditworthiness and performance.

## 7.5.1 The Income Statement

A bank's stock in trade is money, as we noted earlier. Traditionally it does this by offering interest on various savings accounts and making loans from the same deposits, charging a higher interest rate. The bank makes a profit called *interest margin* from the difference between what it pays out and what it receives in interest, called the *interest spread*. In Table 7.2, we see that Laurentian Bank earned $1.1 billion in loan interest and paid interest of almost $454 million to depositors. The bank earned $612 million interest margin from its loan book. You can see the size of its loan book by examining the Balance Sheet reported in Table 7.4. The average of the bank' loans for 2015–2016 was almost $32,735 million. This implies an *average* interest rate spread of 1.92% ($612/$31,735).

In developed markets, banking has become less and less traditional over the years and the trend is reflected in the increasing share of non-interest income in total income. In Table 7.2, the non-interest income comprises essentially fees and commissions. Non-interest income accounted for 40% of the bank's total income in 2016, compared to 26% in 2002. Still, we find that loans continue to be the mainstay of the banking business. In the case of Laurentian Bank, loans account for over three-quarters (77%) of the bank's total assets on 31 October 2016 (fiscal year end). The growing share of non-interest income is a positive for a bank balance sheet. It means a bank's reliance on loans to generate income is diminishing, and the need for supporting the asset with capital is lower.

A modern bank earns income or cash from securities. For most banks, the securities portfolio is significant. Some 13% of Laurentian Bank's assets were securities at end-FY 2016. Securities for trading, investment, and available for sale are shown in the balance sheet reported in Table 7.4. The income that these activities generate is substantial and is listed under other income in the income statement. Banks hold securities for the following purposes:

1. Liquidity or asset liability management. Liquidity is a major determinant of the strength of a bank, and is determined by the maturity profile of a bank's assets and funding, and its ability to access cash. Access to funding reduces the precautionary demand for large holdings of liquid assets or cash. Banks hold the securities of various maturities as part of asset–liability management to mitigate interest rate risk due to maturity mismatch.
2. Sale of securities and repurchase (called repo for short) to reduce funding cost.
3. Proprietary trading occurs when a bank trades on its own behalf, using the organisation's own capital and balance sheet to conduct financial transactions. Proprietary trading has been meeting disapproval with regulators since the financial crisis in 2007–2008, when banks took heavy losses.
4. Strategic investment where a bank, as the investor, holds equity securities of stocks and preferred shares of a target or affiliated company.

## 7.5.2 The Balance Sheet

How does a bank put its cash (deposits and borrowed funds) to work? Fundamentally banking is the transformation of short-dated liabilities into longer-dated assets—"borrowing short lending long" in common parlance. The average maturity of loans normally exceeds that of deposits and because of the mismatch—loans maturing at a different dates than the deposit—a bank is exposed to interest rates risk (IRR). Banks assume some of this risk but attempt to mitigate the risk to avoid losses. Although deposit-taking institutions have ways to manage IRR, things can go awry. The Savings and Loans (S&L) Crisis in the United States is the extreme example of failed IRR management, although there were other contributing factors like "deregulation, insider fraud, and unchecked massive real estate lending".[25]

In 1985, there were 3246 S&Ls. By 1995, the number dropped to just over 1000.[26] The core business of the S&Ls was *fixed-rate* mortgages, funded by core savings deposits, then increasingly by short-dated brokered deposits after financial deregulation in the 1980s that allowed the owners of S&Ls to borrow money on a large scale to fund real estate loans. This type of funding was highly interest rate sensitive and more costly than ordinary savings and chequing accounts. As market interest spiked up due to tighter monetary policy, rates on brokered deposits rose in sympathy, but long-term mortgage rates remained fixed (for 15 years) or on average saw little change. The CDs (Certificates of Deposit) came due every six months at which point they were re-priced at the higher rates. The result was a severe contraction in NIMs (net interest margins) that carried over into huge losses across the entire S&L industry.

For good reason, the CAMEL approach emphasises liquidity strength in credit evaluation. As an analytical concept, liquidity is not something discrete or categorical but, to be accurate, a continuum that goes from liquid to illiquid. From simple intuition, people have no trouble recognising cash as the most liquid and at other end of the continuum, things like fixed assets are illiquid. In between are various types of assets varying in their liquidity, or the ease with which the asset is convertible into cash with little or no discount. In the finance lingo, the loss in value is referred to as a *haircut*.

The liquidity of an asset depends on market conditions, the volumes brought to market, and the time frame, all making it difficult to declare, *a priori*, that a particular asset is liquid or, for that matter, illiquid. Still, there are certain securities such as T-bills that generate funds without incurring large discounts in the repo (repurchase agreement) markets. For the purposes of measurement and the calculation of CAMEL liquidity ratios, the bank analyst needs to identify the liquid assets reported in the balance sheet. As Table 7.4 shows, the order in which a bank lists its assets on the balance sheet mimics the liquidity continuum, starting with the most liquid and ending with the least liquid. Liquid assets comprise cash, cash equivalents, and securities. Loans are considered illiquid assets. Note, however, that in developed capital markets, banks securitise their loans routinely, so loans are not, technically speaking, illiquid.

Earlier, we looked at loans and the funding through customers' deposits (referred to as *retail funding*), which is the cheapest and most stable source of funding gathered through a bank's branch network. A second source of funding is grouped under *commercial or wholesale* and includes interest rate sensitive wholesale funding, fed funds, large foreign deposits, and brokered deposits. Wholesale funding is more vulnerable to disruptions in financial markets as we saw in the 2007–2008 global financial crisis; however, wholesale funding fills an important gap in times of sluggish growth in core savings and current account deposits. The higher is the ratio of loans to retail or personal deposit, the higher the dependence on relatively unstable wholesale funding. This ratio is therefore the mirror image of a bank's dependence on wholesale funds. In the case of Laurentian Bank, the ratios in the 2014–2016 period averaged 1.54:1.00 (or 154%). Ratios below 1:1 indicate low dependence on wholesale funds; conversely, ratios above 1.25 indicate relatively high dependence.

In the footnotes of the annual reports, a bank provides a breakdown of its total interest-bearing liabilities. This information is important to assess a bank's exposure to interest rate risk. The interest rate sensitivity is not the same for all such liabilities. Those that are highly sensitive are brokered deposits and time deposits with balances of a certain amount. A bank that relies heavily on such funding would be more exposed to IRR as rates rise. From the perspective of the bank analyst, the important information is not only the aggregate amounts, as shown in Table 7.4, but the book value breakdown (i.e., the carrying amounts), which are not reported on the consolidated balance sheet, but listed as demand, notice, term, subordinated debt, and securitisation activities deposit in the footnotes of the annual report.

Banks need money for different maturity buckets, and the mix is determined by the asset liability, maturity profile, and the funding cost. *Ceteris paribus*, the longer is the tenor the higher the interest rate, and the higher the funding cost reflecting the higher uncertainty. Low funding costs, *ceteris paribus*, translate into wider interest margins and higher profit. Savings deposits pay low interest rates and are relatively stable. All things being equal, the shorter the tenor of a deposit, the lower the interest rate. In the case of Laurentian Bank, the footnotes in the 2016 Annual Report give a breakdown of the loans and the interest-bearing liabilities. This is useful information on maturity mismatch and, thus, for assessing IRR.

Capital, the assessment of capital adequacy, and CAR (capital adequacy ratios), feature prominently in the CAMEL framework. It should be clear in our minds what we mean by capital in our definitions of the capital ratios. For both banks and non-banks, capital refers to stockholders' (or shareholders') equity. We may refer to it as *accounting* capital to differentiate it from *regulatory capital* and *economic capital*. Regulatory capital has come to be synonymous with the Basel Committee on Banking Supervision (BCBS). Its capital adequacy guidelines are known as Basel Accords.[27]

**Economic Capital**

1. A measure of risk (difference between some given percentile of the loss distribution and the expected loss) derived from an economic capital model.
2. Not the same as accounting and regulatory capital reported in financial statements.
3. Model outputs are expressed as the amount of money necessary to absorb the unexpected losses. There is no requirement for banks actually to set aside this capital, but prudent banks use the calculations to determine whether they have adequate risk capital.

The economic capital of a bank is derived from an economic capital model that does not require assets as inputs (refer to Chap. 1 for the equation). Figure 7.1 depicts the concept of economic capital, where the smooth curve represents the loss distribution. The predetermined confidence level (the vertical line)[28] demarcates the unexpected loss (UL) that is *not* covered by economic capital from the expected loss (covered by reserves) plus the unexpected loss (covered by economic capital). The greater is the *confidence level* the lower the probability of insolvency. This is the area in the tail of the curve for that chosen level of confidence. As you can see, dragging the vertical line farther to the right increases the level of confidence so that the area in the tail gets smaller and smaller.

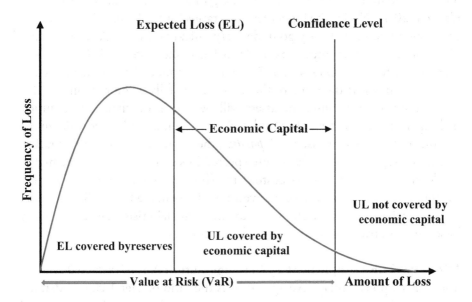

**Fig. 7.1** Economic capital

Consider a one-year default rate of 0.01 (99.99% equivalent to "AAA" rating). Most prudent banks use economic capital (model) calculations to determine how much *risk* capital to set aside.[29] The sum of EL and UL is called value at risk (VaR), which is the likely loss at the $X^{th}$ percentile of the distribution, in this case the confidence level $X = 99.99$. The 99.99th percentile in Fig. 7.1 holds 99.99% of the losses below it and 0.01% of the losses above it in the tail. This means that the bank is accepting 1 in 10,000 becoming insolvent in the next 12 months. J. C. Hull (2015) and P. Embrechts and R. Wang (2015) look at a better or coherent risk measure, known as Expected Shortfall (ES) or Expected Tail Loss, to determine capital requirements for a financial institution.[30] ES is the area beyond the tail of the distribution in Fig. 7.1 (see Hull).

We saw earlier that a bank finances its assets mainly with retail deposits but, in addition, borrowed funds (wholesale funds) and bank capital, that is, money raised by selling shares or earned by doing business. We discussed in Chap. 2 that the higher the use of debt rather than shareholders' equity to fund assets, the higher the leverage. In this sense, banks, in particular, are highly leveraged. Thus, in bank analysis, the leverage ratio is an important indicator of capital strength, measured by the ratio of bank capital to the total assets, including the off-balance sheet ones. Compared to non-financial businesses, leverage, measured by the ratio of liabilities to shareholders' equity, is higher for banks as a group.

For example, consider actual ratios for the Wal-Mart in retailing (1:5), Suncor in manufacturing (1:1), Wells Fargo Bank (9:1), and Royal Bank of Canada (20:1). Notice the higher leverage ratios for the banks. Because banks are so highly leveraged, they go under very quickly if assets take a significant hit. Consider this example: Bank A's balance sheet shows $100 in assets financed with $3 of capital and $97 of borrowed money (savings deposits and wholesale funds). If the value of the bank's assets falls by more than 3% due to some unforeseen cause, the assets will be worth less than the liabilities, making the bank insolvent. The bank lacks sufficient capital to write down the loss due to the shock. Thus, *ceteris paribus*, the stronger a bank's capital ratios, the more prepared it is to absorb unexpected losses and, therefore, the higher the level of confidence of its customers. This was not the case of Lehman Brothers. It was the fourth-largest investment bank in the United States before it filed for bankruptcy in 2008 due to the financial crisis that led to heavy losses in its portfolio of mortgage-backed securities.

### Minimum SLR (Supplementary Leverage Ratio): Not Risk-Based

The SLR (supplementary leverage ratio) is the ratio of Tier 1 capital defined as shareholders' equity (consisting of common stock, retained earnings, and non-redeemable preferred shares) to total assets (consisting of unweighted on-balance sheet assets and off-balance sheet commitments, derivatives, and securities financing transactions). Three percent is the *minimum SLR (supplementary leverage ratio)* for all banks under the Basel III Accord.[31] The example just examined serves to show why US bank regulators tightened the ratio for the biggest US bank holding companies to 5%, officially called e-SLR (enhanced minimum leverage ratio). These big banks are designated G-SIBS (global systemically important banks) by Basel. Three percent is the standard minimum leverage limit for all banks. The US G-SIBS have been looking for capital relief from regulators.

From the vantage point of these banks, any reduction from 5% represents less need to raise capital to fund growth. To see this, consider what a leverage ratio of 5% means: Given $20 of risk-weighted assets, the bank puts aside $1 of Tier 1 capital support. A reduction to 4% means that $25 of risk-weighted assets is supported by the same $1 of Tier 1 capital. Clearly, higher minimum capital ratio restricts lending, *ceteris paribus*. A sign of capital strength are ratios that exceed the minimum requirement. Looking at financial report for Laurentian Bank at FY-end 2016, we see the ratio was 4.1, based on Tier 1 capital of $1.8 billion and total assets of $43.1 billion (see Table 7.5).

**Table 7.5** Laurentian Bank, regulatory capital 2014–2016

| For the years ended October 31 (in thousands of Canadian dollars) | 2016 | 2015 | 2014 |
|---|---|---|---|
| Common shares | 696,493 | 466,336 | 465,854 |
| Share-based payment reserve | – | 36 | 91 |
| Retained earnings | 924,861 | 886,656 | 848,905 |
| Accumulated other comprehensive income, excluding cash flow hedge reserve | 203 | –11,391 | 13,337 |
| Deductions from common equity tier 1 capital | –182,181 | –166,399 | –240,963 |
| **Common equity tier 1 capital** | **1,439,376** | **1,175,238** | **1,087,224** |
| Non-qualifying preferred shares | 97,562 | 97,562 | 97,562 |
| Qualifying preferred shares | 244,038 | 122,071 | 122,071 |
| Additional tier 1 capital | 341,600 | 219,633 | 219,633 |
| **Tier 1 capital** | **1,780,976** | **1,394,871** | **1,306,857** |
| Subordinated debt | 199,824 | 199,641 | 355,048 |
| Collective allowances | 75,380 | 73,904 | 87,546 |
| Deductions from tier 2 capital | – | – | –1925 |
| **Tier 2 capital** | **275,204** | **273,545** | **440,669** |
| **Total capital** | **2,056,180** | **1,668,416** | **1,747,526** |
| Notes: | | | |
| Common equity tier 1 capital ratio | 8.0% | 7.6% | 7.9% |
| Tier 1 capital ratio | 9.9% | 9.0% | 9.4% |
| Total capital ratio | 11.5% | 10.8% | 12.6% |
| Tier 1 Capital/Total | 86.6% | 83.6% | 74.8% |

Source: Company reports

**Leverage Ratios: Risk Based**

The second leverage ratio is risk-based leverage ratio and is defined by the following metrics.

1. CET 1 (Common Equity Tier 1 capital ratio): Common Equity Tier 1 capital/Risk-Weighted Assets (RWA)
2. Tier 1 capital ratio: Tier 1 regulatory capital/RWA
3. Total capital ratio: Total regulatory capital/RWA

From the figures reported in Table 7.5, we see the corresponding ratios for Laurentian Bank at FY-end 2016 were 8.0%, 9.9%, and 11.5%, compared to regulatory requirements of 7.0%, 8.5%, and 10.5%, respectively. They went into effect on 1 January 2019. *Ceteris paribus*, the higher is the overachievement in regularity prudential requirements the higher the risk rating.

## 7.6  Creating the Descriptors

For the rest of the chapter we will be using the material of the previous discussion to create the descriptors. To recap, the BRR scorecard combines these four weighted Risk Criteria:

1. Operating Environment (10%)
2. Business Risk (15%)
3. Management Risk (25%)
4. Financial Risk (50%)

For each criterion, we follow the same method explained in Chap. 3.

### 7.6.1  Operating Environment

**The Important Predicators**

We examine the key features comprising a country's regulatory framework and the economy. You would notice that the operating environment and country risk/sovereign risk analysis overlap to some degree, which is to be expected. We look into the following predictors:

1. **Strength and stability of the economy:** Although there are numerous indicators of economic strength and stability, only a few are needed for a reasonably comprehensive picture:

a. **The structure of production in the economy:** The information is derived from looking at the goods and services that the country produces for domestic consumption and for exports (including tourism). The more economically dependent the country is on a limited number of economic activities and exports, the more exposed it is to internal and external economic shocks. The vulnerability increases for commodity export whose prices tend to be volatile.

b. **The rate of economic growth:** Relatively high rates of real GDP (Gross Domestic Product) or GNI (Gross National Income) growth per capita *indicate* improving living standards reflected in the higher incomes. GDP/GNI growth is only one measure of economic progress; it is silent on the issue of income distribution, which is also a measure of economic progress.

c. **Macroeconomic stability:** This condition boils down to assessing whether the country is pursuing sound macroeconomic policies—monetary, fiscal, and balance of payments—to maintain low inflation, sustainable economic growth, and a stable exchange rate. Some useful indicators of macroeconomic imbalances would include:

   i. The external debt/GDP ratio. Studies indicate that countries with external debts greater than 50% of GDP are more likely to default.[32]
   
   ii. The inflation rate, gross public-sector debt/GDP ratio (a key measure of solvency), the external current account balance/GDP ratio (a measure of external financing requirements), overall fiscal balance/GDP ratio (measures government sector financing requirements). The evidence from past debt defaults suggests high readings of these indicators *together with* high and rising external debt/GDP ratios are associated with higher default probability.

   - Total foreign reserves in months as a key measure of liquidity: In a liquidity crunch, a government might have no choice but to default rather than deplete its reserves to repay foreign loans. Countries typically try to maintain at least 3 months of import coverage; 12 months and more are strong, but the trending is also important.
   - The introduction of foreign exchange controls or the tightening of existing controls, and a parallel exchange rate market are all *red flags* of debt-servicing problems.

2. **Strength and stability of the banking sector:** The common indicators include the following:

a. **Size of the banking sector:** The larger the banking system, both absolutely and relatively to the economy, the more resilient it is to economic shocks. One useful measure of the size of the banking sector is the ratio of bank deposits to GDP. In the vast economic development literature,[33] we learn that the development of the financial system and the development of the broader economy closely intertwine in a process called *financial deepening.* This process occurs through the *financial intermediation* of commercial banks, credit unions, and trust companies.

The scatter points in Fig. 7.2 approximate a positive relationship between GDP per capita (proxy for the level of economic development) and the ratio of bank deposits to GDP across countries of different stages of economic maturity. The curve slopes up but starts to flattening out as *financial deepening* takes root and spreads.

This pattern occurs as an economy transitions from underdevelopment to full-blown economic maturity. With economic maturity and the emergence of a capital market comes *financial disintermediation.* Rather than investing in bank deposit, savers may now buy securities directly through security exchanges or the stock exchange. In the graph, we see evidence of the relative decline in the deposit ratios for France, Germany, Denmark, and the United States. In contrast, the ratios (shown in brackets) for emerging economies such as Barbados (97%), Thailand (116%), and Malaysia (123%) are higher, as expected, because the level of financial disintermediation is lower. Japan (216%),[34] though a

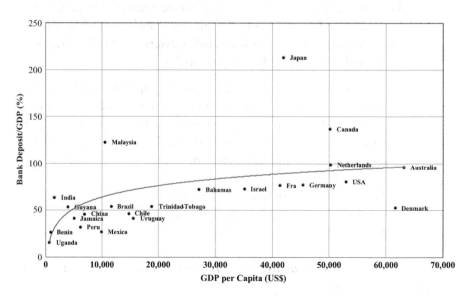

**Fig. 7.2** Bank deposits in percent of GDP (Avg. 2011–2015)

mature economy, does not invalidate the pattern because it is a unique case of savers overwhelmingly preferring bank deposits or cash to securities. The explanation has to do with preserving old cultural habits.

b. **Financial soundness of the banking sector:** The main predictors are the following:

- **Solvency risk:** The commonly used metrics are the capital adequacy ratios, such as regulatory capital/risk-weighted assets and regulatory Tier 1 capital to risk-weighted assets.
- **Liquidity risk:** The key indicators are customers' deposits/total loans, and liquid assets/total deposits.
- **Credit risk indicators:** The commonly used metrics are non-performing loans/total loans, and provisions/non-performing loans (NPLs). A non-performing loan is one that is in default for a specified period, which varies according to the loan term. Periods of 60, 90, and 180 days are typical.
- **Concentration risks:** Sectorial concentration risk is measured by the distribution of the banking sector's credit exposure across industries. Loan portfolio concentration is a negative in bank risk analysis. To determine the concentration, one looks at distribution of the banking sector's credit exposure across industries. Asset concentration risk is measured by the largest bank's share of the total assets of the banking sector.
- **Degree of competition:** A fragmented banking system of many small banks competing in a limited market, like the US Savings and Loans industry, poses prudential risk, as does a highly concentrated banking structure.
- **Profitability:** From the perspective of the bank risk analyst, the focus is on the trending of sector-wide return on assets, return on equity, and interest margin, for a general picture.

The sources of information include central bank data, IMF (International Monetary Fund) country reports, rating agencies' country reports, and newspapers.

c. **Structure of the regulatory regime:** The assessment of the legal, regulatory, and supervisory frameworks across the banking sector includes the following:

- Corruption in government and in the private sector: The main indicators are *Control of Corruption* (World Bank), *Corruption Perception Index* (Transparency International), and the WGI project (World Bank).
- The strength and reliability of a country's institutions. This attribute includes the quality and timeliness of financial reporting by banks.
- The competence, independence, and authority of bank regulators
- Enforcement of regulations

The sources of information include those mentioned previously.

## 7.6.2 The Descriptors

The previous discussion provides the theoretical and empirical groundwork for the descriptors. For qualitative descriptors, a reasonable approach is to try to define the mid-grades of the scale, provided the data exist. Following this method and using the empirical and theoretical information presented in previous sections, we define descriptors for each of the three comprising "Mid", "+/high", "–/low".

### Descriptors: Operating Environment
We start with Operating Environment and use a few BRR ratings for illustration. Table 7.6 gives the descriptors. In terms of building the BRR scorecard, the tricky part is to create definitions from the observed characteristics to differentiate effectively the BRR grades. For example, an "AA" grade is defined by the attributes shown in Table 7.6. We follow the same principle to complete the remaining sections of the scorecard and the results of this procedure are shown in Tables 7.7 and 7.8.

### Descriptors: Business Risk
Table 7.7 reports the descriptors for Business Risk.

### Descriptors: Management Risk
Table 7.8 reports the descriptors for Management Risk. We discussed the notions of "integrity" and "conduct" in discussing the "Five Cs". In this table, we create the descriptors for these attributes in order to differentiate the risk grades.

**Table 7.6** Descriptors of the operating environment

| Risk rating | Descriptors: one or more for each risk rating category |
|---|---|
| AA | Economic fundamentals are strong, with a stable outlook for growth and inflation over the medium term. Some internal and external risks exist but strong economic policies are in place. |
| | Stable financial system, with strong safety nets, for example, crisis management, provision of emergency liquidity, deposit insurance, and so on. |
| | High likelihood of government support. |
| | Strong legal, regulatory and supervisory frameworks: Independent banking supervision, effective enforcement of regulations, and so on. Banks conform to international GAAP. |
| A | High likelihood of government support. |
| | Economic fundamentals are in good shape with a fairly stable outlook for growth and inflation over the medium term. |
| | Stable financial system but improvements are needed in various areas, for example, consolidation of many regulatory agencies, emergency liquidity support, deposit insurance coverage, and so on. |
| | Strong legal, regulatory and supervisory frameworks. Bank supervisors are independent and empowered to enforce regulations. The banks conform to international GAAP. |
| BBB | Economic fundamentals are sound overall, but pockets of vulnerabilities threaten the medium-term outlook. |
| | Fairly stable financial system but with weaknesses in various areas, for example, need for banking consolidation, emergency liquidity support, deposit insurance, and so on. |
| | Likelihood of government support. |
| | Weak legal, regulatory and supervisory frameworks. Bank supervisors lack independence and power to enforce regulations. |
| | Banks conform to GAAP for the most part. Timeliness of reporting is a problem. |
| BB | Economic fundamentals are weak overall. Economic reforms are overdue. The country is vulnerable to both domestic and external economic shocks. |
| | Unstable banking sector. The economy is either overbanked and too competitive, or underbanked and not competitive enough for stability. |
| | No likelihood of government support |
| | Financial system lacks effective prudential and supervisory oversight due to lack of operational independence and adequate funding. |
| | Weak financial disclosure |
| | Weak legal system tainted by bribery and corruption |
| B | Economic fundamentals are either extremely weak or deteriorating, reflected in high inflation, depreciating exchange rate, stagnant growth, and so on. |
| | Very unstable banking sector. The economy is either overbanked and too competitive, or underbanked and not competitive enough for stability. |
| | No likelihood of government support |
| | Financial system lacks prudential and supervisory frameworks. |
| | Legal system is dysfunctional. |
| | Corruption is endemic. |
| D | The economy is failing to meet basic needs. |
| | Fragile banking system, lacking in prudential and supervisory frameworks, and vulnerable to systemic risk triggered by internal and external shocks. |
| | No likelihood of government support |
| | Legal system is dysfunctional. |
| | Corruption is endemic. |

**Table 7.7** Descriptors of business risk

| Risk rating | Descriptors: one or more for each risk rating category |
|---|---|
| AA | Leader in many lines of businesses. |
| | Bank's brand or franchise commands superior popularity nationally or regionally. Strong customer loyalty. |
| A | Amongst market leaders in important lines of businesses. |
| | Bank's brand or franchise commands strong popularity nationally or regionally. Strong customer loyalty. |
| BBB | Leads in a few lines of businesses in which it has pricing power. |
| | Competitive regional bank offering differentiated products. |
| | Ability to defend its brand or franchise not in question. |
| BB | Uncompetitive in many lines of business (national or regional bank). |
| | Faces tough competition, losing market shares, but still viable. |
| B | Uncompetitive national or regional bank. |
| | Minimal franchise value. |
| D | Not viable |

**Table 7.8** Descriptors of management risk

| Risk rating | Descriptors: one or more for each risk rating category |
|---|---|
| AA | A well-developed business plan with feasible goals, appropriate strategies, analysis of the risks and risk mitigants, and measurable targets for periodic monitoring and review by all stakeholders including the Board of Directors. |
| | An effective risk management framework is in place, staffed by competent people, and guided by a complete library of policies and procedures. There have been no negative reports since the last review to suggest otherwise. |
| | Effective corporate governance seems to exist. There have been no reports that negatively impact reputational, operational, credit, people, and other risks since the last review to suggest otherwise. |
| A | A sound business plan with defined goal, strategies, analysis of the risks to achieving targets that are measurable and to be monitored at regular periods. |
| | An effective risk management framework is in place, staffed by competent people. There have been no negative reports since the last review to suggest otherwise. |
| | Effective corporate governance seems to exist. There have been no negative reports since the last review to suggest otherwise. |
| BBB | A reasonable business plan with defined goal and strategies, and measurable and to be monitored at regular periods. There is insufficient analysis of the risks to achieving the targets. |
| | A risk management framework is in place. Whereas there have been no negative reports since the last review to suggest otherwise. |
| | A corporate governance framework exits. There have been no negative reports since the last review to suggest otherwise. |
| BB | Could be a national or regional bank. |
| | Generally uncompetitive. |
| | Faces fierce competition, continuing to lose market shares, but still viable. |
| B | Could be a national or regional bank. |
| | Uncompetitive. |
| | Minimal franchise value. |
| D | Not viable |

## Descriptors: Financial Risk
### Global Bank Data and Ratio Analysis

In this book we analyse banks globally, which means synthesising the financial information in the form of ratios for thousands of banks to identify and confirm patterns. The first task of the analyst is collecting the numerical data and making order of the statistics. The rating agencies, such as S&P and Moody's, as well as Bureau Van Dijk are the best sources because of their big databases. We use World Bank data[35] and, for our purposes, the information is sufficient. The same data are available in FRED (Federal Reserve Bank of St. Louis) website: https://fred.stlouisfed.org/. Table 7.9 gives the predictors used for the CAMEL analysis.

The second task is determining whether "one size fits all" so that one scorecard is just sufficient to rate banks regardless of size. We think size matters for bank risk rating. Of the many reasons for this is the notion of too big to fail. Therefore, it makes analytical sense to design separate scorecards for small, medium, and large banks to account for their unique attributes. The criteria-based method easily accommodates this refinement, and one may use asset size to create three groups. In this book, we are more interested in techniques, so we may ignore the conceptual refinements and pretend we are designing a BRR scorecard to an "average" bank. The third task is bucketing or binning the data into discrete intervals to differentiate effectively the BRRs of the rating system.

Let us turn to banking data from World Bank to review some important points. Banking is cyclical and so we expect the ratios to behave the same way. In order to smooth out the cyclicality in the data, we averaged the ratios for each predictor over a long period, 2008–2015, which comes close to a period of global economic expansion. Post-2015 data were not available on a world-

**Table 7.9** Financial ratios for banks worldwide (average of 2008–2015)

| Ratios | Mean | Median | Standard deviation | Number of countries |
|---|---|---|---|---|
| Regulatory capital to RWA | 16.69 | 16.04 | 4.29 | 110 |
| Bank capital to total assets | 9.94 | 9.56 | 3.80 | 89 |
| Loan loss provisions to NPLs | 69.48 | 59.38 | 40.92 | 109 |
| NPLs to gross loans | 6.52 | 4.14 | 6.57 | 70 |
| Liquid assets to deposits and S/T funding | 32.67 | 27.63 | 17.68 | 132 |
| Net interest margin (NIM) | 3.93 | 3.41 | 2.45 | 95 |
| Cost to income | 61.80 | 61.16 | 7.30 | 187 |
| Return on equity (ROE) | 11.44 | 12.40 | 15.23 | 154 |
| Return on assets (ROA) | 1.04 | 1.10 | 1.29 | 109 |

Source: Federal Reserve Bank of St Louis, https://fred.stlouisfed.org/

wide basis. Table 7.9 gives the summary of statistics based on the period. As you can see from the differences between the mean and median values, the observations for the key predictors are skewed. Only ROE (Return on Equity) and ROA (Return on Assets) show positive skewness. We use a statistical technique to fit the observations to a normal distribution (see Appendix 7.2 for the explanation).

**Bank Ratio Analysis**

A few preliminary observations and caveats are worth keeping in mind regarding financial ratios and analysis, and they are as follows:

1. **Universal benchmarks:** There are no universal benchmarks or standards but, instead, rules of thumb derived from best practices.
2. **Consistency on a cross-border basis and within markets:** Different ways of defining and measuring the numerator and the denominator severely limit comparative analysis. The analyst needs to dig deeper for the causes. Usually, they are differences in accounting policies and application, and differences in national banking regulations.
3. **Cyclicality of the banking business:** Bank ratios are sensitive to the phase of the business cycle. Since the current and future business conditions will vary, this calls for greater caution in comparative analysis of banks worldwide.
4. **Bank ratios are sensitive to company business plan and strategy:** For example, a relatively high ratio of non-performing loans to total gross loans (NPL ratio) may not necessarily be an indication of poor loan quality.
5. **The *ceteris paribus* ("other things being equal") argument:** This clause is an indispensable and a useful analytical device. It is akin to the *partial derivative* of a long equation—when trying to isolate causes and make sense of complexity of the real world.[36] We have used this time-honoured device throughout this book though in real life things are always changing or in motion and unequal.

## 7.6.3 Defining Descriptors of Financial Risk

**Capitalisation: Capital Adequacy**

Let us start with the "C" of CAMEL, capitalisation—a key solvency metric that we discussed previously and the Basel capitalisation ratios reported in Table 7.10. Regulatory CARs are defined in terms of risk-weighted assets (RWAs). These are the values of the assets for any given category (on- and off-balance sheet) multiplied by their risk weights.

**Table 7.10** Basel III minimum capital ratios

| Capitalisation ratios | Components | Requirement 2018 | Requirement Jan 1, 2019 onwards with mandatory capital conservation buffer | Requirement Jan 1, 2019 with optional counter cyclical buffer |
|---|---|---|---|---|
| CET1 (common equity capital 1) ratio | Shareholders' equity Retained earnings | 4.5% | 6.0% (4.5% + 2.5% mandatory capital conservation buffer buffer) | 7.0–9.5% = 4.5% + 2.5% mandatory capital conservation buffer buffer + up to 2.5% discretionary counter-cyclical buffer |
| Tier 1 ratio | Shareholders' equity Retained earnings Non-cumulative, non-redeemable preferred stock | 6.5% | 8.5% (6.5% + 2.5% mandatory capital conservation buffer buffer) | 8.5% – 11.0% (6.5% + 2.5% mandatory capital conservation buffer buffer + up to 2.5% discretionary counter-cyclical buffer |
| Total capital ratio | Tier 1 + tier 2[a] | 8.0% | 10.5% (8% + 2.5% mandatory capital conservation buffer buffer) | 10.5% – 12.5% (8% + 2.5% mandatory capital conservation buffer buffer + up to 2.5% discretionary counter-cyclical buffer) |
| Minimum leverage ratio[b] | CET1 + AT1 (additional tier 1) | ≥3.0% | ≥3.0% | |

[a]Also called supplementary capital, comprises undisclosed reserves, revaluation reserves, general provisions, hybrid instruments, and subordinated debt

[b]Non-risk-based measure (Tier 1 Capital/Average Total Consolidated Assets) introduced in 2013 and extended to March 2019

Source: BCBS, A global regulatory framework for more resilient banks and banking systems, Dec 2010, Annex 4

Adding the weighted values across all categories together yields a bank's total RWAs, which serves as the denominator of the risk-based capital ratios. In assessing a bank's capital strength or adequacy, an important reminder is that the Basel ratios are the *minimum* requirements. National regulators determine the standards, which in most cases are higher. It is worth noting that banks have been exceeding the minimum ratios since 2015, as we illustrated previously for Laurentian Bank. The big US banks are leading in terms of CET 1. The six largest reported CET 1 ratios above 10% compared to 9.5% including the 2.5% counter-cyclical buffer according to recent data.[37] A bank that just meets the minimum requirements is at a severe borrowing disadvantage against its rivals reporting higher ratios. Rating agencies base their credit ratings on a bank's capital adequacy (and other factors), so there is a strong market incentive for banks of similar size to do at least better than the regulatory minimum and exceed the average.

The bank analyst needs to assess capital adequacy from different angles:

1. The bank's major income earning assets, the potential risks to the quality of the assets, and the adequacy of the capital base—its absolute size—to absorb losses.
2. The trend in the capital ratios.
3. The quality of regulatory capital, separating Tier 1 from Tier 2 capital. The former is called *core* capital, which are the disclosed reserves, consisting of common equity, retained earnings, and non-redeemable non-cumulative preferred stock. Tier 1 excludes treasury shares and intangibles like goodwill, which can be a significant asset component of many banks. A write-down in goodwill through an impairment charge against income directly reduces capital by the decrease in the carrying value of the goodwill. Tier 2 *supplements*—not a substitute for Tier 1, hence referred to as supplementary capital. It includes revaluation reserves, undisclosed reserves, subordinated term debt, and hybrid instruments with subordination features. Tier 1 is of a higher quality than Tier 2, because Tier 1 types of capital are more liquid and have a lower degree of redemption priority. Tier 1 capital represents the amount of capital that allows a bank to cover losses so that depositors in the bank may recover their deposits. The key CARs (capital adequacy ratios) used to assess capital adequacy are the following:

- **Tier 1 Ratio:** Ratio of Tier 1 regulatory capital[38] to RWAs. Tier 1 capital comprises CET1 (common equity Tier 1 capital) and, as we saw with Laurentian Bank, this ratio cannot be calculated by just looking for the relevant line items in a bank's balance sheet, because the numerator of the ratio is calculated internally by banks per regulatory guidelines. Under Basel III rules that went into effect in January 2019, the minimum ratio increased to 8.5%, from 4% in the wake of the 2007–2008 global financial crisis.

- **Total Regulatory Capital Ratio:** Ratio of total regulatory capital to RWAs per regulatory guidelines. For this same reason stated earlier, the ratio also cannot be calculated from the balance sheet and the footnotes of the annual report. Under new Basel III rules that went into effect on 1 January 2019, the minimum ratio increased to 10.5%, from 8% in the wake of the 2008–2009 global financial crisis (see Table 7.10).

- **Tangible Common Equity Ratio:** This is another measure of capitalisation defined as the ratio of common equity—the highest quality of tangible capital—to total tangible assets (total assets minus intangible assets). There are two reasons for considering only the tangible component of equity for capital adequacy. First, intangible assets cannot be used to repay creditors. Second, the presence of intangible assets means that the book value of capital may indicate relatively little about a bank's ability to absorb unexpected losses on its assets (on- and off-balance sheet) without becoming insolvent. The TCE (Total Common Equity) measure treats all assets as equally risky, although in reality the risks vary. However, the metric is commonly used because (a) it is simple to calculate from the balance sheet, which is not possible with the other Basel metrics that involve RWAs, and (b) it serves as a check against unscrupulous calculation of RWAs designed to make the ratio higher than it really is. It is well to remember that the regulatory risk weightings are an *internal calculation*.

Table 7.11 gives examples of quantitative definitions of the rating scale for three key leverage ratios: Tier 1 Capital Ratio, Total Regulatory Capital Ratio, and Tangible Common Equity Ratio. In addition, the table presents examples of qualitative definitions of the Quality of Capital. Based on external rating agency reports and the 2017 annual reports for a sample of banks in mature and emerging markets worldwide, Tier 1 Ratios ranged from as low as 8.15% for Burgan Bank A.S. (Turkey) to as high as 17.4% for Morgan Stanley (United States). As an approximation of the median and standard deviation for the universe of banks, we used 12.50 and 3.46%, respectively, to construct the discrete ranges reported in Table 7.11. The qualitative predictors add essential complementarities to the quantitative predictors. They give further definition to the makeup of the capital and thus its quality.

**Table 7.11** Descriptors of capitalisation

| Risk rating | Tier 1 ratio | TRC ratio | TEQ ratio | Quality of capital |
|---|---|---|---|---|
| AA+ | ≥22.2 | ≥28.1 | ≥20.3 | Capital is nearly all common and |
| AA | 20.8–22.1 | 26.4–28.0 | 18.7–20.2 | preferred stock (equity). |
| AA– | 19.4–20.7 | 24.7–26.3 | 17.2–18.6 | Very low percentage of goodwill and other intangibles in total capital |
| | | | | Very low percentage of revaluation reserves, undisclosed reserves, hybrid instruments, and subordinated term debt in supplementary capital |
| A+ | 18.0–19.3 | 22.9–24.6 | 15.7–17.1 | Capital is nearly all common and |
| A | 16.7–17.9 | 21.2–22.8 | 14.1–15.6 | preferred stock (equity). |
| A– | 15.3–16.6 | 19.5–21.1 | 12.6–14.0 | Relatively low percentage of goodwill and other intangibles in total capital |
| | | | | Relatively low percentage of revaluation reserves, undisclosed reserves, hybrid instruments, and subordinated term debt in supplementary capital |
| BBB+ | 13.9–15.2 | 17.7–19.4 | 11.1–12.5 | Capital is substantially common and |
| BBB | 12.5–13.8 | 16.0–17.6 | 9.6–11.0 | preferred stock (equity). |
| BBB– | 11.1–12.4 | 14.3–15.9 | 8.0–9.5 | Moderate percentage of goodwill and other intangibles in total capital |
| | | | | Moderate percentage of revaluation reserves, undisclosed reserves, hybrid instruments, and subordinated term debt in supplementary capital |
| BB+ | 9.7–11.1 | 12.5–14.2 | 6.5–7.9 | High percentage of hybrid capital |
| BB | 8.3–9.6 | 10.8–12.4 | 5.0–6.4 | (with both debt and equity features) |
| BB–– | 7.0–8.2 | 9.1–10.7 | 3.4–4.9 | Relatively high percentage of goodwill and other intangibles in total capital |
| | | | | Relatively high percentage of revaluation reserves, undisclosed reserves, hybrid instruments, and subordinated term debt in supplementary capital |
| | | | | Potentially inadequately capitalised |
| B+ | 5.6–6.9 | 7.3–9.0 | 1.9–3.3 | High percentage of goodwill and other intangibles in total capital |
| B | 4.2–5.5 | 5.6–7.2 | 0.4–1.8 | |
| B– | 2.8–4.1 | 3.9–5.5 | −1.1–0.3 | High percentage of revaluation reserves, undisclosed reserves, hybrid instruments, and subordinated term debt in supplementary capital |
| | | | | Below regulatory requirements; recapitalisation needed |
| D | ≤2.7 | ≤3.8 | ≤−1.0 | Negative capital |

**Asset Quality**

We focus on these three ratios because they measure asset quality from different angles:

1. NPL (non-performing loans) to gross loans (NPL ratio)
2. Loan loss provisions to pre-provisions income
3. ALL (Allowance for Loan Loss) to NPLs (NPL or reserve coverage ratio)

Let us examine each in the order as they are presented. The NPL ratio is a basic indicator of asset quality commonly used to assess asset quality. It is easy to explain and easy to calculate:

$$\text{NPL Ratio}\,(\%) = \frac{\textbf{Total Nonperforming Loans}}{\textbf{Total or Gross Loans}}$$

The higher the ratio, the poorer the asset quality, subject to all the caveats noted earlier; in particular, the fact that (a) there are many definitions for non-performing but there exists no common or universal definition, and (b) banks determine internally whether a loan may be classified as formally non-performing for regulatory prudential reporting and monitoring. Not surprisingly, impaired loans, delinquent loans, defaulted loans, non-accrual loans, and special mention, all fall under the rubric of problem loans. The BCBS (Basel Committee for Banking Supervision) offers a harmonised definition of non-performing exposures.[39]

Assessing a bank's asset quality is the most difficult part of bank risk assessment and the root of the problem is the lack of information on the loan book. For example, the common practice of *evergreening* masks actual loan defaults with fresh loans provided to help delinquent borrowers repay old loans. Credit analysts must find an effective way to include the risk in the composite BRR. They may account for this in the quality of banking supervision in Operating Environment, quality of risk management and internal controls in Management Risk, or in the Information Asymmetry Override in the scorecard. There is no fixed approach in the criteria-based methodology but one that works best in the circumstance.

The following exposures are considered as non-performing:

(i) All exposures 'defaulted' under the Basel framework (e.g., paragraphs 452 and following of the Basel II rules text and their subsequent amendments); or

(ii) All exposures impaired (in the meaning of exposures having experienced a downward adjustment to their valuation due to deterioration of their creditworthiness) in accordance with the applicable accounting framework; or

(iii) All other exposures that are not defaulted or impaired but nevertheless are:

(a) Material exposures that are more than 90 days past due; or

(b) where there is evidence that full repayment of principal and interest without realisation of collateral is unlikely, regardless of the number of days past due.

A widely accepted analytical definition of an NPL is one that meets two criteria:

1. The loan is considered in *default*, meaning that the borrower is 90 days past due in interest (or principal), and/or is unlikely to repay all of the related principal and interest payments.
2. The loan is impaired (meaning, it is probable that not all principal and interest payments will be collected, so the original value of the loan is reduced according to the accounting framework).

All this amounts to saying an NPL is one that is *actually* in default or *expected* to be in default. A loan is *impaired* if, based on current information and events, the bank determines it will not be able to collect all contractual amounts due, including scheduled interest payments. Impaired loans include non-accrual loans.

The second metric looks at asset quality from another angle: a bank's capacity, represented by the income generated before provisioning, to absorb problem loans. The indicator is defined as follows:

$$\textbf{LLP to Pre-provision Income}\,(\%) = \frac{\textbf{LLP}\,(\textbf{Loan Loss Provisions})}{\textbf{Pre-provision Income}}$$

Provisioning for loan losses eats into a bank's profits. The numerator includes loan loss provisions *and* charges for securities impairment. The latter is a material number for the banks that hold large securities portfolios. As an example, let us look at Royal Bank of Scotland (RBS),[40] which made the headlines in the aftermath of the 2008–2009 financial crisis that spread from the United States to Europe. RBS was highly exposed to debt and equity derivatives, CMBS (Commercial Mortgage-Backed Securities), RMBS (Residential Mortgage-Backed securities), and CDO (Collateralised Debt Obligations), suffered huge losses from securities impairment charges.

**Table 7.12** Royal Bank of Scotland impairment charges (MM Pounds)–the 2008 financial crisis

|  | 2006 | 2007 | 2008 | 2009 | 2010 |
|---|---|---|---|---|---|
| Total income before impairment | £28,002 | £30,366 | £25,868 | £38,690 | £31,868 |
| Total impairment losses charged to the income statement: | £1878 | £1968 | £7439 | £13,908 | £9256 |
| Loans and advances | £1877 | £1946 | £6478 | £13,099 | £9144 |
| Securities | £1 | £22 | £961 | £809 | £112 |
| (Loss)/profit for the year | £6497 | £7712 | −£34,542 | −£2323 | −£1666 |
| Total impairment/Total income before impairment charges | 7% | 6% | 29% | 36% | 29% |

Source: RBS Annual Reports

Table 7.12 reports this ratio for RBS for the period covering two years before and after the crisis in October 2008. We see a stable ratio in 2006 and 2007 when banks did not foresee a major financial crisis coming. RBS reported a loss of £34.5 billion in 2008 due significantly to impairment charges of almost £1 billion for impaired securities. Total impairment charges jumped from 6% of pre-provisioning income in 2007 to 29% in 2008, and continued to increase in 2009, eating into profit for two more years.

The third indicator of asset quality, the NPL or reserve coverage ratio, measures the degree of protection a bank has built up through loan loss provisioning in the balance sheet, contra-asset account called ALL (allowance for loan losses). The reserve shields a bank's net worth or equity against non-performance, including actual default. The ratio is calculated as follows:

$$\textbf{NPL Coverage Ratio}\,(\%) = \frac{\textbf{Allowance for Loan Losses}}{\textbf{Total Nonperforming Loans}}$$

The numerator of this ratio includes leases. This NPL coverage ratio conveys more intuitive information than the NPL ratio. First, it compares a good number (ALL), also called reserve for bad debts, with a bad number (NPLs). Second, unlike total loans, a measure that does not differentiate the good from the bad, the denominator of the NPL coverage ratio is specific. Finally, a bank with 100% coverage is well reserved and higher ratios, *ceteris paribus*, are even better. The NPL coverage ratio supplements the NPL ratio. Take two banks, A and B. A has a lower NPL ratio than Bank B; however, Bank B has higher NPL coverage. Clearly, Bank A's lower NPL ratio does not necessarily mean higher asset quality than Bank B. But it would if, at the same time, Bank B's coverage ratio were lower than Bank A's. Another useful ratio measures the burden of impairment charges on operating income before the charges. The metric is PLL (provision for loan loss) divided by PPI (pre-provision operating income/profit). The higher the ratio, the lower the asset quality, *ceteris paribus*.

Table 7.13 gives examples of the quantitative descriptors for the predictors of asset quality. We supplement the ratios with qualitative descriptors for a more comprehensive profile of asset quality. For example, one of the weaknesses of the NPL ratio is that it does not provide information on the collateral strength of loan portfolios. Another weakness of quantitative descriptors is that they cannot capture the sensitivity of exposures to market risk (the potential *mark-to-market* losses resulting from revaluation of asset prices, e.g., Lehman

**Table 7.13** Descriptors of asset quality

| Risk rating | NPL to total gross loans ratio | ALL to NPL ratio | PLL to PPI ratio | Quality of assets |
|---|---|---|---|---|
| AA+ | ≤0.9 | ≥161.2 | ≤ 1.3 | Strong credit culture. |
| AA | 1.0–1.7 | 150.7–161.1 | 1.4–3.2 | In virtually all cases the bank |
| AA– | 1.8–2.5 | 140.1–150.6 | 3.3–5.2 | requires obligors to pledge collateral as security before advancing credit. |
| | | | | More than 90 percent of non-loan assets are high quality deposits and securities. |
| | | | | Earning assets well diversified by industry and product. |
| | | | | Loans well diversified globally. |
| | | | | Loans well diversified by client (business and public sector). |
| A+ | 2.6–3.3 | 118.9–140.0 | 5.3–7.2 | In most cases the bank requires |
| A | 3.4–4.1 | 108.4–118.8 | 7.3–9.1 | obligors to pledge collateral as |
| A– | 4.2–4.9 | 97.8–108.3 | 9.2–11.1 | security before advancing credit. |
| | | | | More than 75 percent of non-loan assets are high quality deposits and securities. |
| | | | | Earning assets diversified by industry and product. |
| | | | | Loans diversified globally. |
| | | | | Loans diversified by client (business and public sector). |
| BBB+ | 5.0–5.7 | 87.2–97.7 | 11.2–13.0 | The bank often requires |
| BBB | 5.8–6.6 | 76.6–87.1 | 13.1–15.0 | obligors to pledge collateral as |
| BBB– | 6.7–7.4 | 66.0–76.5 | 15.1–17.0 | security to advance credit. |
| | | | | Moderate credit losses. |
| | | | | More than 50 percent of non-loan assets are high quality deposits and securities. |
| | | | | Earning assets moderately diversified by industry, product, geography, and client. |

(*continued*)

**Table 7.13** (continued)

| Risk rating | NPL to total gross loans ratio | ALL to NPL ratio | PLL to PPI ratio | Quality of assets |
|---|---|---|---|---|
| BB+ | 7.4–8.2 | 55.5–65.9 | 17.1–18.9 | Above-average credit loss. |
| BB | 8.3–9.0 | 44.8–55.4 | 19.0–20.9 | Material amount of loans that |
| BB–– | 9.1–9.8 | 34.2–44.7 | 21.0–22.8 | are unsecured. |
| | | | | Less than 50 percent of non-loan assets are high quality deposits and securities. |
| | | | | Significant asset concentration by industry, product, geography, and client. |
| B+ | 9.9–10.5 | 23.6–34.1 | 22.9–24.8 | Weak credit culture. |
| B | 10.6–11.3 | 13.0–23.5 | 24.9–26.8 | High credit losses. |
| B- | 11.4–12.2 | 7.7–12.9 | 26.9–28.7 | Most loans are of poor quality (below investment grade). |
| | | | | Concentration by industry, product, geography, and client. |
| | | | | Significant under-collateralisation of the loan portfolio. |
| | | | | Poor quality of non-loan assets. |
| D | ≥12.3 | ≤7.6 | ≥28.8 | Very weak credit culture. |
| | | | | Extremely poor loan book, evidenced by large write-offs and low recoveries. |
| | | | | Extremely poor quality of non-loan assets. |

Brothers' bankruptcy in 2008 due to the financial crisis). For example, in the 2007–2008 financial crisis, the local and foreign financial institutions that suffered the most held large portfolios of ABS (Asset-Backed Securities), also called derivative securities.[41] These financial instruments were exposed to the US mortgage market, in particular, the subprime segment. When the subprime mortgages went under with the collapse of the US housing market in 2007, the banks that invested heavily in the ABS and bought "protection" from monoline insurers[42] experienced heavy losses. All of this comes down to a bank's credit culture and appetite for risk taking. A strong credit culture is a positive because it checks excessive risk taking.

**Earnings: Profit, Profitability, and Earnings Quality**
In the CAMEL framework, earnings include both the profits and the profitability of a bank. Profit measures, such as net income and gross margin, are

absolute values, whereas profitability measure such as ROE and ROA are ratios/percentages or growth rates. Although profit and profitability are related they are not identical in meaning: Bank A may have the same profit as Bank B, but Bank B is more profitable if NIM, ROE, and ROA are higher. Let us examine the following predictors and define descriptors for the scorecard:

1. NIM (net interest margin)
2. ROA (return on assets)
3. ROE (return on equity)
4. Cost-income ratio
5. Earnings quality

**Net Interest Margin**

Let us examine the return-type ratios in the order as they are listed. NIM is an indicator of the profitability of a particular line of business. For a conventional bank, loans and securities are the main sources of interest income, which account for well over half of total income as the graph in Fig. 7.3 shows. Interest income in mature markets represents on average about 60% of total interest and non-interest income. In emerging markets, the share of interest income is a bit higher. NIM is calculated as net interest income divided by average earning assets. If historical data are used (in contrast to a forecast), a three-year average, current year plus two previous years, is desirable than one year's ratio.

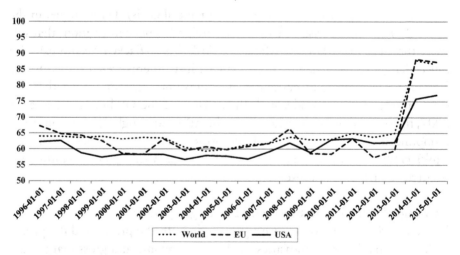

**Fig. 7.3** Interest income to total income (%)—1996–2015. (Source: World Bank)

$$\text{NIM}\left(\%\right) = \frac{\textbf{Net Interest Income}}{\textbf{Average Earning Assets}}$$

$$\textbf{AEA}\left(\textbf{Average Earning Assets}\right) = \frac{\textbf{AEA}\left(\textbf{Year 1}\right) + \textbf{AEA}\left(\textbf{Year 2}\right)}{2}$$

Earning assets account for the largest portion of a bank's balance sheet and include loans, assets purchased under repurchase agreements, securities (including securities borrowed), and deposits with other banks. Banks usually provide a breakdown of their earning assets in the footnotes of the financial statements. The denominator of this ratio is the average of the current year and the previous year because one year's figures for balance sheet items are, by definition, only a snapshot taken at a point-in-time. Another reason for the averaging is to iron out the year-to-year dips or spikes.

In the United States, the average NIM for all banks was 3.12% in the fourth quarter of 2017, down from a peak of 4.91% in Q2:1994 (see Fig. 7.4). During the same period, the average NIM fluctuated between a minimum of 2.95% (Q1:2015) and a maximum of 4.91% (Q1:1994). Data for 2018 (not captured in the graph) show an average of 3.3%, which was a slight rebound from a

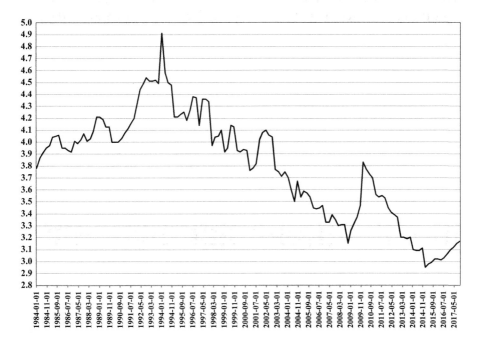

**Fig. 7.4** NIM (%) of all US banks Q1:1984–Q2:2017. (Source: Federal Reserve Economic Data)

30-year low of 2.95% in 2015. Still, average NIMs have been trending almost steadily downward and current average NIMs remain well below the 1994 peak. The graph implies that low interest rates in the last decade have squeezed interest margins, with lending rates declining more than the cost of funds.

For more than a decade now we have witnessed historically low longer-term interest rates, and the puzzling question is: will they remain low?[43] There is no satisfactory theory but some plausible theses.[44] One thing we know for sure is that inflation is a major determinant of market interest rates. Inflation rates in the industrialised world have fallen sharply since the mid-1980 and have stayed low for more than a decade. But subdued inflation only partly explains the puzzle of "low for long" interest rates because it is a global phenomenon. To explain the behaviour of longer-term rates, think of a long-dated bond. We know it has three components: the expected inflation, the expected path of real (future) short-term interest rates, and a term premium. This last is the extra return that lenders demand to compensate them for the risk associated with a long-term bond. To put it another way, the term premium is the extra return to hold a longer-dated bond rather than investing in a series of short-dated bonds. At this time of writing, all three components are keeping longer-term interest rates down, but, in particular, the steep drop in term premiums has exacerbated the trend. Figure 7.5 shows negative premium as of the first quarter of 2019. This may be due to (1) a decrease in the per-

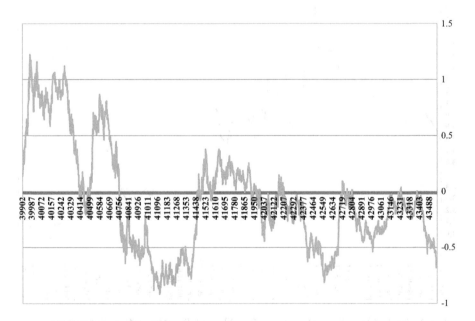

**Fig. 7.5**  Term premium on a 10-year zero coupon bond. (Source: FRED)

ceived riskiness of longer-dated securities (as inflationary expectations remain tame) and (2) an increase in demand for longer-term securities relative to the supply. The problem with the latter explanation is that the Federal Reserve and the EU Central Bank have ended QE (Quantitative Easing) and started the reverse process of siphoning money directly from the economy by buying back the long-dated government bonds previously sold.

It is hard to argue, however, that the declining NIM is not the result of the interest rate environment and, significantly, the increased competition from non-bank financial intermediaries that provide loans and mortgages. The data for the EU area show that 2% appears to be the upper bound, with average NIM of around 1% quite common. NIMs for emerging markets such as China, India, Brazil, and South Africa tend to be higher, exceeding 4% and consistently higher than in the mature economies as one would expect because in developing markets the banks are the main providers of financing while inter-bank competition is weak.

### Return on Assets
As an indicator of financial performance, ROA (return on assets) measures a bank's return on total assets employed. The ROA is calculated as:

$$ROA(\%) = \frac{Net\ Income}{Average\ Total\ Assets}$$

### Return on Equity
ROE (return on shareholders' equity) is another measure of performance calculated as follows:

$$ROE(\%) = \frac{Net\ Income}{Average\ Common\ Equity}$$

The denominators of these two ratios are calculated as averages just like average earning assets and for the same reason. It is worth remembering that a positive ROE could be the result of negative net income and negative equity—something to be aware of when using a computer spreadsheet to calculate ratios or accepting calculated ratios from a spreadsheet at face value. Some banks prefer to report ROE than ROA as their best measure of profitability or performance, but the bank analyst assesses both because they contain different information. To illustrate this point, let us turn our attention to the components of ROA and ROE applying the *DuPont Model.*

$$\text{ROE} = \frac{\text{Income}}{\text{Revenue}} \times \frac{\text{Revenue}}{\text{Assets}} \times \frac{\text{Assets}}{\text{Equity}}$$

ROE is the result of profitability, efficiency, *and* leverage (represented by asset to equity), or the interaction of all three. Notice that the leverage ratio is always greater than 1; therefore, with ROA unchanged, a bank can boost its ROE by just increasing assets—make more loans by wholesale funding or borrowing—without adding equity or capital. Thus, a high and rising ROE is not an unqualified positive indicator of creditworthiness because it does not take into view the possibility that the bank might be undercapitalised. This is a perfect example where the *ceteris paribus* device proves its analytical usefulness. ROA is the result of a bank's efficient use of all assets (represented by revenue to assets) and its ability to drive profitability (represented by income to revenue) or the interaction of both.

$$\text{ROA} = \frac{\text{Revenue}}{\text{Assets}} \times \frac{\text{Income}}{\text{Revenue}}$$

By definition, the ROA ratio does not directly involve a bank's capital structure or its leverage in the calculation and the result is a purer measure of a return relative to the base.

It is worth repeating that all the financial ratios that we have discussed, including the ones for bank performance, have no absolute standards for weak, normal, and strong performance. Still, based on observation and experience, credit practitioners generally agree on some broad ranges, essentially rules of thumb, to categorise the ratios. For example, Golin and Delhaise (2013)[45] suggest these ranges for ROE:

- Strong: Exceeds 20%
- Normal: Between 10 and 20%
- Weak: Below 10%

For ROA, the cut-off points are:

- Strong: Exceeds 2%
- Healthy: Between 1 and 2%
- Mediocre: Between 0.5 and 1%
- Weak: Below 0.5%

We use these ranges to create descriptor for the scorecard.

## Cost-to-Income Ratio

The cost-to-income ratio (CIR) is often touted in the management-discussion section of a bank's annual report as a metric of *bank efficiency* or *bank productivity*. The question is: what does efficiency/productivity exactly mean for a service provider and, furthermore, can one compare the measure across countries? To be clear, efficiency/productivity is an operational input-output relation, and productivity is something measured in quantities.[46] But this is not what the CIR is measuring, or is intended to measure, in bank analysis. Even if this were the case, it would still be a challenge to quantify productivity in services, let alone compare it across banks worldwide. Nor is productivity synonymous with efficiency, which has no precise definition and no benchmarks. The motivation for referring to it as an efficiency/productivity metric is, presumably, that the higher the ratio of non-interest expense to total income, the more costly it is for the bank to generate the same one dollar of interest income from its lending operations. Therefore, it is more accurate to say that CIR measures profitability looking from the expense side of the ledger.

Panel data (cross-sectional data for banks within a country and across countries and over a period) show significant variation in the CIR. Because of cross-country factors, comparing CIRs—and, for that matter, practically all financial ratios—is always a tricky task. In Fig. 7.6, the data are for the period 1996–2014; more recent data were not available from the same source. The data depict the variation ranging from 37% for Singapore to 77% for Germany. The median ratio was 60%, a close tie between Canada and the United States. Reviewing online data from *Statistica* that are more recent, we see a continuation of the pattern with the highest ratios recorded for France and Germany.[47] The latter serves as a good example of the influence of industry structure on the CIR and the profitability of the industry.[48] The high CIR for Germany is the mirror image of its lower profitability compared to the rest of Europe and North America. This performance is the result of three conditions of its banking system: fragmented, overbanked, and overbranched. The country boasts some 1800 banks (there is no up-to-date figure) from a three-tier banking system of private banks, savings banks, and credit unions. In addition to the three tiers are specialised banks (building societies, real estate, and development).[49]

Generally, large commercial banks in mature markets aim for a CIR of 60% or less. Indeed, some aim for and achieve even lower ratios. Based on a sample of 13 largest US banks, the ratio ranged between 52% for Capital One Financial Corp and 73% for Morgan Stanley in 2017. The median ratio was 63.3%. The five large Canadian banks consistently have been reporting ratios in the mid-50s for the last seven years.

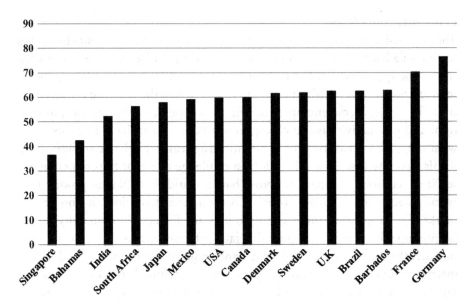

**Fig. 7.6** Cost to income ratio (%) 1996–2014. (Source: FRED)

The CIR is a commonly used ratio and is insightful if properly interpreted as a measure of profitability (looking from the expense side of the ledger). From the vantage point of the credit analyst, the measure is intuitively easy to interpret because the numerator of the ratio represents a "bad" number whereas the denominator represents a "good" number. The measure looks at the cost of running the operations relative to the income coming in. Lower ratios mean that a bank is operating more profitably, whereas a higher CIR signal indicates the reverse. The CIR is calculated as follows:

$$\text{Cost-Income Ratio}\,(\%) = \frac{\text{Non-Interest Expense}}{\text{Net Interest Income} + \text{Non-interest Income}}$$

Non-interest expense comprises mostly compensation and benefits for employees, and some other G&A (General and Administrative) expenses. Since the bulk of non-interest expense is employees' compensation, a bank can become more "efficient/productive" by employing less labour and employing more capital in the form of labour-saving technology (e.g., ATMs and online banking) and labour-saving processing systems. Indeed, this has been the trend worldwide.

**Earnings Quality**
As we saw with capital, the qualitative predictors add essential complementarities to the quantitative predictors. Earnings quality focuses on the market

factors that determine the sustainability and stability of a bank's total revenue and its rate of growth. Earnings quality is a structural attribute and it derives from a bank's franchise strengths. An important factor is the degree of diversification of a bank's income and thus the stability of the earnings. Revenue diversification is the result of the geographical reach of a bank's operations (the footprint) and a diversified balance sheet. One important class of assets is government securities and, in emerging markets, banks tend to have a disproportionate share of these assets, which exposes them to sovereign debt defaults. That said, the exposure benefits the banks because they can count on government liquidity support in times of economic stress.

The lesson is that banks whose earnings and operations are highly concentrated in one or two businesses or activity are at a severe risk of failing when the favourable conditions end or reverse course. Recent example is the 2007–2008 banking crisis, and before that, the savings and loans crisis in the United States. These qualitative descriptors, along with the quantitative directors, are shown in Table 7.14.

**Table 7.14** Descriptors of earnings: profits, profitability, and earnings quality

| Risk rating | NIM (net interest margin) | ROA (return on assets) | ROE (return on equity) | Cost-income ratio | Earnings quality |
|---|---|---|---|---|---|
| AA+ | ≥4.0 | ≥2.9 | ≥25.0 | ≤32.0 | A leader in the industry |
| AA | 3.4–3.9 | 2.6–2.8 | 23.3–24.9 | 33.0–36.0 | in most of its |
| AA– | 3.1–3.3 | 2.4–2.5 | 21.3–23.2 | 37.0–40.0 | businesses. Highly diversified business model. Earnings are solid, very stable and diversified by geography, economic sectors, business franchise, and customers. |
| A+ | 2.8–3.0 | 2.1–2.3 | 19.8–21.2 | 41.0–44.0 | Well diversified business |
| A | 2.6–2.7 | 1.9–2.0 | 18.0–19.7 | 45.0–48.0 | model. |
| A– | 2.3–2.5 | 1.6–1.8 | 16.2–17.9 | 49.0–52.0 | Earnings are diversified by geography, economic sectors, business franchise, and customers. Earnings are solid and stable. |

(continued)

**Table 7.14** (continued)

| Risk rating | NIM (net interest margin) | ROA (return on assets) | ROE (return on equity) | Cost-income ratio | Earnings quality |
|---|---|---|---|---|---|
| BBB+ | 2.0–2.2 | 1.4–1.5 | 14.4–16.1 | 53.0–56.0 | Earnings are vulnerable |
| BBB | 1.7–1.9 | 1.1–1.3 | 12.6–14.3 | 57.0–60.0 | to moderate |
| BBB– | 1.7–1.6 | 0.8–1.0 | 10.8–12.5 | 61.0–64.0 | concentration risk in one or more areas: Geography, economic sectors, business franchise, and customers. Earnings are relatively solid and stable. |
| BB+ | 1.4–1.6 | 0.6–0.7 | 9.0–10.7 | 65.0–68.0 | Earnings profile shows significantly |
| BB | 1.2–1.3 | 0.3–0.5 | 7.2–8.9 | 69.0–72.0 | concentration in one or |
| BB–– | 0.9–1.1 | 0.1–0.2 | 5.4–7.1 | 73.0–76.0 | more areas: Geography, economic sectors, business franchise, and customers. Earnings are fairly unstable. Income and profitability ratios reflect creative accounting at times. |
| B+ | 0.6–0.8 | −0.2–0.0 | 3.7–5.3 | 75.0–80.0 | Earnings are highly |
| B | 0.3–0.5 | −4.0–3.0 | 1.9–3.6 | 81.0–84.0 | concentrated in one or |
| B– | 0.0–0.2 | −7.0–5.0 | −0.02–1.8 | 85.0–88.0 | more areas: Geography, economic sectors, business franchise, and customers. Earnings are unstable. Income and profitability ratios often reflect creative accounting. Unprofitable. |
| D | ≤ −0.1 | ≤ −8.0 | ≤ −0.03 | ≥89.0 | Earnings are highly vulnerable to economic shocks. Income and profitability ratios often reflect creative accounting. Earnings and profits are unstable and the bank is or may be losing money. |

## Liquidity and Liquidity Quality

Liquidity and funding risk, or simply liquidity risk, is the risk that a bank may be unable to generate sufficient cash or its equivalents to meet its commitments in a timely and cost-effective manner. The cost includes (a) forgoing yield and profits for liquidity and (b) the direct cost of arranging and funding. First, let us look at what might be at the bottom of liquidity risks. As we discussed earlier, one reason is the possibility of bank runs. If depositors lose trust and confidence in their bank and withdraw their money, and if the bank has no alternative than to sell off illiquid loans at fire sale prices, *insolvency* results. The decline in asset value means an equal reduction in equity, with liabilities remaining unchanged. Capital strength, liquidity strength, and solvency are entwined. Let us examine this further. First, stronger capitalisation increases the confidence of lenders and reduces the risk of a bank run. Second, more liquid assets on the books combined with good access to liquidity helps to ensure solvency because a bank is less likely to unload illiquid assets at a loss in the event of a funding problem.

A funding problem can easily become a banking crisis, so the central bank plays an extremely vital role in this regard. As an example, let us look briefly at the array of measures that US Federal Reserve took to deal with the 2008 financial crisis, which was unprecedented in US history.

The Federal Reserve initially used the traditional tool of discount window lending and the lowering of the federal funds rate, but these proved inadequate to stabilise the financial institutions and the financial markets. The Fed had to employ a mix of *systemic* policies that included (a) Quantitative Easing through Fed purchases of Treasury bonds, (b) CPFF (Commercial Paper Funding Facility), and (c) TSLF (Term Securities Lending Facility), and (d) TALF (Term Asset-Backed Securities Loan Facility). QE had the effect of injecting money directly into the economy, whereas the other measures had the effect of preventing short- and long-term liquidity from drying up with the support of the Fed (see the note on *flight to quality* below). In addition, other government agencies worked in concert with the Fed. The agencies included the Treasury, the FDIC (Federal Deposit Insurance Corporation), Fannie Mae, and Freddie Mac. Finally, expansionary fiscal policy (the Recovery Act) helped the economy recover.

Apart from what the authorities can or cannot do, the credit analyst also needs to know a bank's strategies to mitigate the risks. The annual reports usually provide information on liquidity-management practices. The bank credit analyst also needs to assess the quality of the liquidity. The ultimate test of the liquidity quality of an asset is that it can be easily and immediately converted into cash with minimal loss in value, even in periods of shocks or market stress. The Basel Committee outlines "fundamental characteristics" of HQLA (High Quality Liquid Assets).[50] They include:

1. Low risk: The higher the credit standing of the issuer and the lower the degree of subordination, the higher the asset's liquidity
2. Ease and certainty of valuation
3. Low correlation with risky assets
4. Listed on a developed and recognised exchange
5. Active and sizable market
6. Low volatility
7. Flight to quality: In times of systemic shocks, the market tends to move to assets of the highest quality. The measurement of quality or liquidity is therefore crucial. There are a host of liquidity proxies and benchmarks. (The subject of measuring these metrics and determining which are the best is subject that will fill a book.)

Another important consideration in assessing liquidity is access to significant sources of cash to fill a bank's *funding gap*, which is the residual after subtracting the value of the assets the bank desires from the sum of customer deposits and the equity or capital. Like any borrower, a bank's credit standing is an important factor in its access to the money market[51] at favourable terms. The banks that are externally rated and have investment grade and higher are more likely to experience easier and quicker access than private banks that are not in this position. In a mature financial system, the markets in which commercial banks routinely buy money include all, or a combination, of:

- Inter-bank market or the Euro-market
- Federal funds market (in the United States)
- The CD market
- The Repo market

We use this background information to create the liquidity descriptors shown in Table 7.15. The scorecard consists of three quantitative and two qualitative factors:

**Table 7.15** Descriptors of liquidity

| Risk rating | Liquid assets to deposits and S/T funding | Loans to deposits | Customer deposits to total funding | Access to liquidity | Quality of liquidity |
|---|---|---|---|---|---|
| AA+ | ≥48.9 | ≤13.4 | ≥91.9 | Able to raise more than it needs and at all times in capital markets. Large and growing retail deposit base. Externally rated (lowest risk, highest quality). | Holds a sizeable portfolio of HQLA (high quality liquid assets). Minimal maturity mismatch. Assets could be sold with minimal discount, or used for repo transactions. |
| AA | 46.1–48.8 | 13.5 21.3 | 87.4–91.8 | | |
| AA– | 43.2–44.0 | 21.4–31.0 | 82.8–87.3 | | |
| A+ | 40.4–43.1 | 31.1–40.8 | 78.2–82.7 | Able to raise all that it needs at all times in capital markets. Large retail deposit base. Externally rated (above medium grade ratings). | Securities portfolio consists mostly of HQLA. Most of the securities could be sold with minimal discount, or used for repos. |
| A | 37.6–40.3 | 40.9–50.6 | 73.7–78.1 | | |
| A– | 34.8–37.5 | 50.7–60.5 | 69.1–73.6 | | |
| BBB+ | 31.9–34.7 | 60.6–70.2 | 64.6–69.0 | Favourable access to capital markets. Modest deposit base Externally rated (above medium grade ratings) | Adequate portfolio of HQLA More than half of the securities could be sold with minimal discount, or used for repos. |
| BBB | 29.8–31.8 | 70.3–80.0 | 60.0–64.5 | | |
| BBB– | 26.2–29.7 | 80.1–89.8 | 59.4–59.9 | | |
| BB+ | 23.3–26.1 | 89.9–99.6 | 50.9–59.3 | Limited access to capital markets. Narrow deposit base. Externally rated (below investment grade ratings). | Inadequate portfolio of HQLA. Only a small fraction of the portfolio could be sold with minimal discount, or used for repos. |
| BB | 20.5–23.2 | 99.7–109.5 | 46.3–50.8 | | |
| BB–– | 17.7–20.4 | 109.6–119.2 | 41.8–46.2 | | |
| B+ | 14.9–17.6 | 119.3–129.0 | 37.2–41.7 | Relies mainly on wholesale deposits. Unrated, privately owned. | Small and illiquid securities portfolio for the most part. Liquid assets less than short-term deposits. Significant maturity mismatch. |
| B | 12.0–14.8 | 129.1–138.8 | 32.6–37.1 | | |
| B– | 9.2–11.9 | 138.9–148.6 | 28.1–32.5 | | |
| D | ≤9.1 | ≥148.7 | ≤28.0 | No access to funds | No securities available for sale or repos. |

1. **Liquid Assets to Total Assets or Liquid Asset Ratio:** This basic ratio is the counterpart to the current ratio for a non-financial business. For both banks and non-bank enterprises, the ratio answers the same question: what proportion of the current liabilities (customer deposits and short-term funding) is covered by current assets (cash and cash equivalent assets) without risking insolvency from having to sell off illiquid, long-term assets at fire sale prices. The loss from such selling means a reduction in capital, as we discussed before. If the capital base is weak, the illiquidity can lead to bank failure.

2. **Loans to Customer Deposits + S/T Funding:** This metric, also known as the LDR (loan-to-deposit ratio) is an indicator of mismatch between asset and liability. Loans (net of loan loss reserves), which are relatively illiquid, are compared to relatively stable funding. The higher the ratio, the more dependent the bank on less stable funding. We note, however, that banks in mature economies with liquid capital markets can and do manage higher ratios than those of their counterparts in emerging economies where short-term funding is limited or unavailable. A ratio of 100% indicates that a bank lends a dollar for every dollar that it receives as deposits, indicating that the bank lacks sufficient cash to meet precautionary demand. What is considered a prudent ratio is an unsettled question. In the United States, the LTD ratio for large and small banks has been trending up over the last three decades. The rise reflects (a) a declining ratio of core deposits to assets since 1990 and (b) an increasing ability by the small banks to obtain funding from Federal Home Loan Banks (FHLBs). Prudent banking, banking supervision, and access to funding together suggest that the "new normal" for the LDR is around 80% for both small and large US banks. The median LTD used to be around 60% for small banks in the early 1980s.[52]

3. **Customer Deposits to Total Funding:** This metric is an indicator of the strength and stability of a bank's customer deposit base. The higher the ratio the less dependent the bank on commercial funding, which is more unstable than retail deposits. Large banks with strong retail franchises and national branch network tend to have higher ratios than small, local banks.

4. **Access to Liquidity:** The degree of liquidity access ranging from zero to nearly unlimited depends on whether the bank is privately owned and unrated, or widely owned by individuals and rated, the relative size and stability of the bank's customer base, and the bank's dependence on money markets to fill its funding gap.

5. **Liquidity Quality:** See HQLA characteristics.

The qualitative predictors further define the quantitative predictors. The qualitative attributes are the HQLA attributes we examine later under Liquidity and Liquidity Quality. The qualitative descriptors address the size of a bank's retail deposit base and, thus, the relative importance of low-cost funding and high-cost funding in the wholesale market.

## 7.7   Putting It All Together

Let us use the scorecard shown in Table 7.16 as the template for analysing a commercial bank and determining its BRR. The scorecard comprises four blocks, each defined by Risk Criteria, Risk Factors, Risk Element, and the weights. Note that the weights are shown in one column to save space, but it makes no difference for the computation. For example, financial risk is weighted 50%, the liquidity factor is weighted 35%, and the liquidity quality risk element is weighted 25%. The combined weight is 4.38% (0.50 × 0.35 × 0.25). The cells of the scorecard would be populated with the descriptors we went through in the previous sections. We list below the four building blocks: risk criteria, risk factors, and risk elements and the weights of the full scorecard:

1. **Operating environment risk (10%)**

    i.  Economic (50%)
    ii. Regulatory (50%)

2. **Business risk (15%)**

    i.  Competitiveness & market position (100%)

3. **Management risk (25%)**

    i.   Business plan & operations (34%)
    ii.  Risk management & internal controls (33%)
    iii. Corporate governance (33%)

4. **Financial risk (50%)**

    i.  **Capitalisation (25%)**

    - Tier 1 ratio (30%)
    - Total capital ratio (30%)
    - Capital quality (40%)

**Table 7.16** Template of a bank analysis risk rating scorecard

| RISK CRITERIA | RISK FACTORS | RISK ELEMENTS | W | AA+ | AA | AA- | A+ | A | A- | BBB+ | BBB | BBB- | BB+ | BB | BB- | D |
|---|---|---|---|---|---|---|---|---|---|---|---|---|---|---|---|---|
| OPER. ENV RISK | Economic | Economic | 5.00% | | | | | | | | | | | x | | |
| | Regulatory | Regulatory | 5.00% | | | | | | | | | | | x | | |
| BUSINESS RISK | Comp. & Mkt Position | Comp. & Mkt Position | 15.00% | | | | | | | | x | | | | | |
| MANAGEMENT RISK | Business Plan & Operations | Business Plan & Operations | 8.50% | | | | | x | | | | | | | | |
| | RM & Internal Controls | RM & Internal Controls | 8.25% | | | | | x | | | | | | | | |
| | Corporate Governance | Corporate Governance | 8.25% | | | | | x | | | | | | | | |
| FINANCIAL RISK | Capitalisation | Tier 1 Ratio | 3.75% | | | | | | x | | | | | | | |
| | | Total Capital ratio | 3.75% | | | | | | x | | | | | | | |
| | | Capital Quality | 5.00% | | | | | | x | | | | | | | |
| | Asset Quality | NPL/Gross Loans | 1.88% | | | | x | | | | | | | | | |
| | | LLPs/PPI | 1.88% | | | | | x | | | | | | | | |
| | | ALL/NPL | 2.50% | | | | | | x | | | | | | | |
| | | Loan Quality | 6.25% | | | | | x | | | | | | | | |
| | Earnings: Profit & Profitability | NIM (Net Interest Margin) | 1.50% | | | | | x | | | | | | | | |
| | | ROA (Return on Avg Assets) | 1.50% | | | | | | x | | | | | | | |
| | | ROE (Return on Avg Equity) | 1.50% | | | | | | x | | | | | | | |
| | | Cost-Income Ratio | 1.13% | | | | | x | | | | | | | | |
| | | Earnings Quality | 1.88% | | | | x | | | | | | | | | |
| | Liquidity | Liquid Assets/ Total Assets | 2.63% | | | | | | | x | | | | | | |
| | | Customer Dep./ Total Fund. | 3.50% | | | | | | | x | | | | | | |
| | | Loans/ Cust. Dep. + S/T Fund. | 2.63% | | | | | | x | | | | | | | |
| | | Access to Liquidity | 4.38% | | | | | | | x | | | | | | |
| | | Liquidity Quality | 4.38% | | | | | | | x | | | | | | |
| CRITERIA BASED BRR | 10.5 ("B+") | | | | | | | | | | | | | | | |
| CRR/SRR OVERRIDE | BBB | | | | | | | | | | | | | | | |
| INFORMATION ASYMMETRY OVERRIDE (YES/NO) | NO | | | | | | | | | | | | | | | |
| FINAL BRR | B+ | | | | | | | | | | | | | | | |

W: Weight, S: Score, R: Rating

ii. **Asset quality (25%)**

- NPL/gross loans (15%)
- LLPs/PPI (15%)
- ALL/NPL (20%)
- Loan quality (50%)

iii. **Earnings: profit & profitability (15%)**

- Net interest margin (20%)
- Return on average assets (20%)
- ROE (return on average equity) (20%)
- Cost-income ratio (15%)
- Earnings quality (25%)

iv. **Liquidity (35%)**

- Liquid assets/total assets (15%)
- Customer deposits/total funding (20%)
- Loans/customer deposits + S/T funding (15%)
- Access to liquidity (25%)
- Liquidity quality (25%)

The descriptor placements are highlighted in the scorecard. Based on the placements for the descriptors, the scorecard calculates a composite score of 10.48, which maps to "A–". Country risk override may or may not be applicable. If applicable, let us assume that the bank we are rating is a foreign bank and the country and sovereign risk rating is "B+". Furthermore, if we assume no Information Asymmetry Override, the final BRR is the lesser of the criteria-based risk rating and the country/sovereign risk rating, which is "B+".

# Appendix 7.1: A Note on Bank Size

Bank size is an important consideration in designing a scorecard. First, small banks with limited and unstable funding base and heavily dependent on NIM income for bottom-line profit, hence, are more likely to fail than big banks when economic adversity strikes. The larger diversified banks, with their more varied business, are generally in a stronger position to recover from external shocks. Data from the US FDIC (Federal Deposit Insurance Corporation)[53] provide supporting evidence of the high failure rate, as shown in Table 7.17.

**Table 7.17** US bank failures and assistance 1984–2017

| Transaction | ≤ 10BN | 10BN ≤ Assets < 25 BN | 25BN ≤ Assets < 50 BN | Assets ≥ 50 BN | All asset size |
|---|---|---|---|---|---|
| Failure | 2822 | 12 | 1 | 1 | 2836 |
| Assistance | 400 | 6 | 3 | 3 | 412 |
| Total | 3222 | 18 | 4 | 4 | 3248 |

Source: Federal Deposit Insurance Corporation

Banking is pro-cyclical and the period covers four recessions or periods of depressed economic activity to observe the behaviour of banks.

The data support the following tendencies:

- Small banks are more likely to fail than big banks. Of the 2835 banks that *failed*, 95.5% were small, local, or community banks with assets of less than $10 billion. The figure includes the 1000+ S&Ls that failed between 1986 and 1995. Throughout the period, only one big bank, Washington Mutual Bank, with total assets of $307 billion, failed on 25 September 2008 in the aftermath of the financial crisis and the Great Recession.
- The high rate of small bank failures was evident in the aftermath of the Great Recession. The number of total bank failures jumped from 25 in 2008 to 147 in 2009 and continued to climb to 157 in 2010. Still, few large banks failed. The largest bank failure in 2008 was Washington Mutual Bank (mentioned before); in 2009, Colonial Bank, Montgomery, Alabama, with approximately $25 billion in assets; in 2010, Westernbank Puerto Rico, with approximately $12 billion in assets.[54]
- The bigger the bank the more likely it would seek and obtain government assistance rather than fail.[55] We observe that of the 3222 small banks with assets ≤$10 billion, 14.2% of them (400 banks) received assistance, whereas for the larger banks, assistance rather than failing was more prevalent. Six of the 18 banks were in the $10–$25MM category, and three of the bigger four banks were in the assistance group.

In regard to balance sheet size, the classification of bank size is arbitrary. The US Federal Reserve defines "large banks" as those with consolidated assets of $300 million or more.[56] In contrast, a prudential definition of a big bank size was based on the $50 billion threshold, which came about in the aftermath of the 2008–2009 financial crisis and the 2010 Dodd-Frank Act, also known as the Systemic Risk Designation Improvement Act. The law required bank holding companies with more than $50 billion in assets to be subject to enhanced prudential regulations. In May 2018, Congress approved a bill to dismantle key parts of the 2010 Dodd-Frank act that decided which banks were designated "too big to fail". Under the new rules, a bank is *systematically important* if it has $250 billion or more in assets. That covers 13 G-SIBs (global systemically important banks), compared to 44 in 2008 in the aftermath of the financial crisis. These banks face the strictest banking regulations. As we said before, we ignore the question of bank size, though it is an important rationale for having separate scorecards.

The second consideration is that the Basel capital ratios are just the *minimum* international requirements, regardless of bank size. At the national level, regulators use their own discretions, and usually impose tougher rules than Basel. Data for the G-7 countries and China, shown in Fig. 7.7, show that average capital ratios exceeded the Basel minimum requirement of 10.5%. One explanation for this behaviour of banks worldwide is that the cost of higher capital requirements is offset by the lower risk premium for funding. A bank with a bigger capital buffer is stronger and better able to attract cheaper capital, thus enabling it to maintain its level of lending. Inasmuch as the market drives capital buffering, we would expect that the average bank's capital ratios would exceed the regulatory minimum and would be closer to the midpoint of the rating scale. In other words, a bank must do even better than the minimum just to be in the upper 50 percentile. We incorporated this second consideration in creating the ranges for capitalisation in Table 7.11.

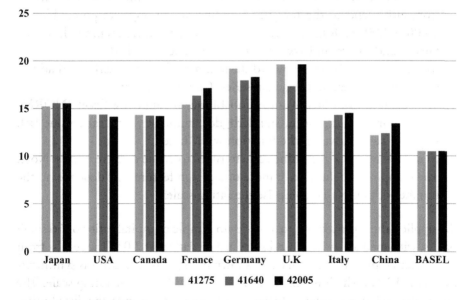

**Fig. 7.7** Regulatory capital to risk weighted assets. (Source: Federal Reserve Economic Data)

# Appendix 7.2: Bell Curve for Three Standard Deviations from the Mean

Grading on the curve starts with the *assumption* that financial ratios come from a normally distributed population with unknown mean (μ) and unknown standard deviation (σ). The normal distribution/Gaussian/Laplacian distribution, which is a probability density function with mean (μ) and variance (σ²):

$$P(x) = \frac{1}{\sigma\sqrt{2\pi}} e^{-(x-\mu)^2/2\sigma^2}$$

on the domain x ∈(−∞, +∞).

We want to create a normal distribution using the *sample* mean and *sample* standard deviation. Follow these steps in Excel:

1. Download the data on the spreadsheet. The larger is the sample size (*N*) the better.
2. Locate the median value (representing the mean) and calculate the standard deviation of the sample data using the appropriate Excel functions.
3. Divide the range of −3 to +3 into smaller deviations, a procedure that makes the curve smoother. For example, use increments of 0.1 starting from either end of the range and ending at the opposite point. Hence, ±3.00, ±2.90, ±2.80,…,0,…, ±2.80, ±2.90, ±3.00. (Remember, however, tails extend to −∞ and +∞). Let the latter series be called $y_i$.
4. Multiply each $y_i$ by the standard deviation of the actual series and add to the result the mean of the actual series. Call the result $x_i$.
5. Transform $x_i$ from Step 4 into probabilities by applying Excel "NORM. DIST" function (x, mean, standard_dev, cumulative) to each value ($x_i$). Replace "cumulative" in the function with "false".
6. Map each rating of the rating scale to the $x_i$ to create discrete ranges. Note: The mapping is definitional, more of a design feature that depends on the number of points that comprise the rating scale.

We applied these procedures to a made-up sample of capital ratios of 66 small banks, with median of 12.10 and standard deviation of 2.03. The results from Steps 5 and 6 produce the bell curve shown in Fig. 7.8. The curve is symmetrical about 12.10, which is defined as BBB, the middle of the rating scale. The cumulative relative frequency below is another way to depict the distribution (Table 7.18).

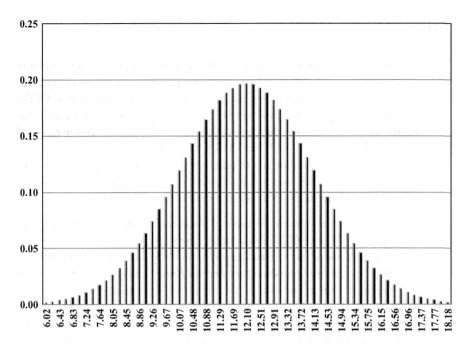

**Fig. 7.8**  Normal curve of total capital ratios for all banks in the world

**Table 7.18**  Cumulative normal frequency

| BRR | Total capital ratio (%) | Cumulative relative frequency (%) | BRR | Total capital ratio (%) | Cumulative relative frequency (%) |
|-----|-----|-----|-----|-----|-----|
| D | 6.0 | 0.1 | BBB | 12.1 | 50.0 |
| B– | 6.4 | 0.3 | BBB+ | 12.9 | 65.5 |
| B | 7.2 | 0.8 | A– | 13.7 | 78.8 |
| B+ | 8.0 | 2.3 | A | 14.5 | 88.5 |
| BB– | 8.9 | 5.5 | A+ | 15.3 | 94.5 |
| BB | 9.7 | 11.5 | AA– | 16.2 | 97.7 |
| BB+ | 10.5 | 21.2 | AA | 17.0 | 99.2 |
| BBB– | 11.3 | 34.5 | AA+ | 17.8 | 99.7 |

Note: The 100th percentile includes 18.2% (the upper end of the AA+ range)

We see that about 99.4 (99.7–0.3)% of the observations lie within three standard deviations of the mean, which is close to normal probability in this regard. The cumulative normal frequency gives the percentile for the BRRs. For example, "BBB" rating is in the 50th percentile, meaning that 50% of the total capital ratios are 12.1% ("BBB") and less, as expected for the median. In the following graph, the cumulative probability for the total capital ratio to be at least 8.0 is measured as the area under the curve from $-\infty$ to 8.0.

# Notes

1. The money supply of a modern economy includes currency (coins and bank notes), cheques, and electronic transfer of bank deposits for everyday business. As a store of value, money includes currency and bank accounts. Of the total money supply, currency represents *just a small fraction* in advanced economies. Take, for example, the United States. The US Federal reserve reported that at the end-2017, M2 was $13,836.1MM; currency in circulation, $1612.12MM, which translates to only 12% of the money supply at that day. Thus, 90% or so of the money supply is not actual cash. On their website, the US Board of Governors of the Federal Reserve System states:

   > *There are several standard measures of the money supply, including the monetary base, M1, and M2. The monetary base is defined as the sum of currency in circulation and reserve balances (deposits held by banks and other depository institutions in their accounts at the Federal Reserve). M1 is defined as the sum of currency held by the public and transaction deposits at depository institutions (which are financial institutions that obtain their funds mainly through deposits from the public, such as commercial banks, savings and loan associations, savings banks, and credit unions). M2 is defined as M1 plus savings deposits, small-denomination time deposits (those issued in amounts of less than $100,000), and retail money market mutual fund shares.* (https://www.federalreserve.gov/faqs/money_12845.htm)

2. In a *fractional reserve banking system* banks accept deposits but are not allowed to lend the whole amount. They are required to hold a certain fraction as *required reserve* at the central bank. The remainder, called *excess reserves*, can be loaned out and the process of the banks making loans ends up creating new money in the form of chequing accounts to pay bills. This simple example explains how deposits lead to monetary creation. Let's assume that there are no leakages in the economy that would cause money to be held idle (buried or hidden somewhere, for example), the *reserve ratio* is 10%, which means that for every dollar of deposit, the bank must retain 10 cents in reserves, and there are $N$ number of banks. Suppose that you make a deposit $100 such as opening an account with Bank A. Now, the bank has $100 to add to the liability side of its balance sheet. If the first bank does not lend, no *new money* is created; it just stays as an idle deposit. This is a very important point to grasp because it is **not** correct that deposits in themselves create money. If Bank A lends $90, however, its balance sheet will show a deposit (a liability) of $100 balanced by a loan (an asset) of $90 and required reserve (an asset) of $10. The $90 loan works its way in the economy and, eventually, becomes a deposit in another bank, Bank B, which accepts the $90 and makes a loan to earn interest over what it pays as interest on the deposit. Following fractional reserve requirement, Bank B lends $81 ($90 × (1–0.10). As you would have

correctly anticipated, the process continues up to $N^{th}$ bank in the system that receives a deposit, each time the sum getting smaller and smaller (like a snowball rolling down a hill). A neat way to find the final amount of money, including the initial deposit, is to multiply the $100 by the *money multiplier*—the reciprocal of the required ratio. If there are no leakages, as we assumed, the number is 10 (1 divided by 0.10). The amount of *new or additional* money in the economy is, therefore, $900 ($1000–$100). Note an important qualification in the case of *open market operations* where the central bank buys $100 in government securities (notes, bills, or bonds) that is already on a commercial bank's balance sheet (an asset). All $100 from the central bank is loaned out to earn interest (recall that idle cash earns no interest and will even lose purchasing power due to inflation). The new money created in open market purchases of government securities is thus the full $1000 ($100 × 10).

3. The classic textbook case is the Great Depression that started in the fall of 1930 with a wave of bank panics in the United States. The contraction lasted ten years. A major financial crisis triggered the Great Recession of 2008–2009. It required new tools and policies and concerted actions by the Federal Reserve and other federal agencies because the financial system on the eve of the crisis was much more complex and the systemic risks were so much greater.

4. Well Fargo was charged for various misconduct including opening as many as 3.5 million fraudulent accounts in order to meet sales quotas, and forcing up to 570,000 customers into unwanted auto insurance. For the illicit accounts, the bank paid a fine of $185 million to regulators and settled a class-action suit for $142 million in 2016. Investigations into misconduct continued during 2017 and, on February 2, 2018, the Federal Reserve imposed a cap on the entire assets of the bank, effectively freezing the bank's growth until it can prove it has improved its internal controls. The external rating agencies subsequently downgraded Wells Fargo credit rating. For example, S&P lowered the long-term rating to A- from A on February 7, 2018. The agency stated, "Regulatory risk for Wells is more severe than previously expected and the process for improving its governance and operational risk policies may take longer than previously expected."

5. Golin, J., and P. Delhaise (2013), *The Bank Credit Analysis Handbook, A Guide for Analysis, Bankers, and Investors*, Wiley Financial Series, 2nd Edition, 2013, Chapter 13. See also OECD (2010), *Policy Framework for Effective and Efficient Financial Regulation, General Guidance and High-Level Checklist.*

6. The World Bank Group, *The Worldwide Governance Indicators (WGI) project*, https://info.worldbank.org/governance/wgi/#home. The WGI project reports aggregate and individual governance indicators for more than 200 countries and territories from the period 1996 for six dimensions of governance: (1) Voice and Accountability Political, (2) Stability and Absence of Violence, (3) Government Effectiveness, (4) Regulatory Quality, (5) Rule of Law, (6) Control of Corruption.

7. Goodhart, C (2000), *The Organizational Structure of Banking Supervision*, Financial Stability Institute, Bank for International Settlements, Basel, Switzerland.

8. Golin, J., P. Delhaise (2013), ibid. page 753.

9. Transparency International, a non-profit, international, non-governmental organisation headquartered in Germany and based in more than 100 countries, has been publishing the *Corruption Perception Index* on a scale of 0 (highly corrupt) to 100 (very clean) since 1995. No country has scored 100 in all the years the organisation has been collecting data. Various other international organisations publish report on government and private sector corruption. The World Bank publishes the CPIA (Country Policy and Institutional Assessment) rating on transparency, accountability, and corruption in the public sector (1 = *low* to 6 = *high*).

10. See various Federal Reserve banks articles such as Ron J. Feldman and Jason Schmidt (1999), *What are CAMELS and who should know*, Federal Reserve Bank of Minneapolis, January 1, 1999, and another article by Jose A. Lopez (1999), *Using CAMELS Ratings to Monitor Bank Conditions,* FRBSF (Federal Reserve Bank of San Francisco) Economic Letter, June 11, 1999. The News Letter states that confidential supervisory material "filter into the financial markets". For example, on January 5 the *Wall Street Journal* reported, "banking regulators in mid-2017 downgraded the management component of the CAMELS rating for Wells Fargo Bank to a '3', which means that the capabilities of management or the board of directors "may be insufficient for the type, size or condition of the institution." The rating made business headlines, and fueled speculation that further enforcement action was coming.

11. Kane, J. M (2018), *Wells Fargo CAMELS rating leaked,* The twenty-first Century Banker, January 17, 2018.

12. There has been a string of bank scandals since the 2000s. They include mortgage frauds, insider trading, the illegal fixing of global interest rates or what is known as Libor (London Interbank Offered Rate), money laundering, the rigging of the US Treasury bond market, and the opening of false bank accounts, to name a few. But none of the scandals have captured the attention of the public quite the way that the Libor scandal and the Wells Fargo scandal have. On the Libor scandal, Wikipedia (see https://en.wikipedia.org/wiki/Liborscandal) states, "the banks were falsely inflating or deflating their rates so as to profit from trades, or to give the impression that they were more creditworthy than they were." In 2012, Barclays PLC, the United Kingdom's second largest bank with US$983 billion assets at end-2016, agreed to pay nearly half a billion dollars to regulators for its manipulations. Numerous other big banks came under investigation for similar misdeeds. Because of the investigations, oversight responsibility of Libor was moved from the British Bankers' Association to the UK regulators. On February 12, 2018, Barclays Bank Plc made the headlines again when it was reported that the SFO (Serious

Fraud Office) of the United Kingdom charged the bank over a £2.2MM loan to Qatari investors who used the funds to buy bank shares to prop it up at the peak of the financial crisis. Wells Fargo, third largest US bank with $1.93 trillion assets at end-2016, admitted to opening of as many as 1.5 million illicit accounts and charging more than 800,000 of the bank's auto-loan customers unwanted insurance. The revelation of misdeeds started to emerge in late-2016. See Wells Fargo account fraud scandal in https://en.wikipedia.org/wiki/Wells_Fargo_account_fraud_scandal. On February 15, 2018, newspapers reported that US regulators fined US Bancorp, America's fifth biggest by assets, $613 million "for two criminal violations of the Bank Secrecy Act over 'wilful' failings in its anti-money laundering programme over a period of more than five years. US Bancorp was well aware that these practices were improper, and resulted in the bank missing "substantial numbers" of suspicious transactions from 2009 to 2014, said the DoJ." See Ben McLannahan, *Financial Times*, New York, February 15, 2018.

13. Note that we are not using the term *franchise* in the legal sense of franchising, where a franchisor licenses its know-how procedures, intellectual property, and the use of its business model.

14. See a recent article, K. S. Petrou, *Make Camels Ratings Public Already*, American Banker, May 17, 2016. Criticisms of the secrecy of the CAMELS ratings go as far back as 1999; for example, see Jose A. Lopez, Using CAMELS Ratings to Monitor Bank Conditions, FRBSF Economic Letter, June 11, 1999. Analysts have argued that making the ratings public could improve market assessments, and discipline risk taking. Despite the potential benefits, the CAMELS ratings remain non-public information because of three potential costs. First, it could make bankers more sensitive to the ratings and less open to sharing of information. Second, depositors might lose confidence and trust in a bank after a downgrade, thereby triggering a run on the bank. Finally, the examiners might be sensitive to criticisms against a downgrade and would be slower to act.

15. The *Los Angeles Times* uncovered the illegal practices in December 2013. The Independent Directors of the Board of Wells Fargo & Company (2017), *Sales Practices Investigation Report*, April 10, 2017. The 110-page reports stated: "Wells Fargo's sales practice issues first came to public attention through articles in the *Los Angeles Times* that spotlighted troubling practices engaged in by some employees in Los Angeles."

16. Fitch Ratings Inc. (2016), *Fitch Affirms Wells Fargo & Company IDRs at 'AA-/ F1+'; Outlook Revised to Negative*, October 4, 2016.

17. The Washington Post (2011), *Moody's managers pressured analysts, former executive says*, August 19, 2011. The report stated, "According to Harrington, a fundamental conflict of interest permeated the firm's culture: Like other credit rating agencies, Moody's is paid by the very companies whose securities it is supposed to grade objectively."

18. Golin, J., and Delhaise, P. (2013), ibid., page 428–427.

19. See Fridson, M. and Alvarez, Fernando (2011), *Financial Statements Analysis*, ibid., Chapter 1, The Adversarial Nature of Financial Reporting. Other chapters on financial are well worth reading.

20. Independent Directors of the Board of Wells Fargo & Company (2017), ibid. Under the heading "Principal Findings", the 110-page report stated:

> The root cause of sales practice failures was the distortion of the Community Bank's sales culture and performance management system, which, when combined with aggressive sales management, created pressure on employees to sell unwanted or unneeded products to customers and, in some cases, to open unauthorized accounts. Wells Fargo's decentralized corporate structure gave too much autonomy to the Community Bank's senior leadership, who were unwilling to change the sales model or even recognize it as the root cause of the problem. Community Bank leadership resisted and impeded outside scrutiny or oversight and, when forced to report, minimized the scale and nature of the problem.

21. S&P downgraded Wells Fargo & Co.. to 'A−/A-2' from 'A/A-1' on "Prolonged Regulatory and Governance Issues", on February 7, 2018.

22. Independent Directors of the Board of Wells Fargo & Company (2017), ibid. page 4.

23. Investopedia, Corporate Governance, https://www.investopedia.com/terms/c/corporategovernance.Asp

24. Golin. J., & P. Delhaise (2013), ibid., page 434.

25. Newdorf, David. B (1993), *Inside Fraud, Outside Negligence and the Savings & Loan Crisis: When Does Management Wrongdoing Excuse Professional Malpractice*, 26 Loy. L.A. L. Rev. 1165

26. Congressional Budget Study (1993), *Resolving the thrift crisis*, April 1993; Federal Homes Loan Board, *Moral hazard and the thrift crisis; an analysis of the 1988 resolutions*, May 1989.

27. For more information about Basel, see Golin. J, & Delhaise. P, (2013), ibid., Chapter 9.

28. How does a bank come up with a VaR? As an illustration, it would calculate the value of its portfolio under say 350 scenarios (using the previous year consisting of 350 business days) based on historical markets data such as stock prices, volatilities, interest rates, foreign exchange rates. The results are ordered from best to worst. The third last value of the range is the 99th percentile loss [(350 × 0.99) = 346.5, rounded to 347]. The 99% serves as the predetermined confidence level.

29. FDIC (2004), *Economic Capital and the Assessment of Capital Adequacy*, Winter 2004.

30. Hull, John. C (2015), *Risk Management and Financial Institutions*, Wiley, 4th Edition, Chapter 12. Paul Embrechts and Ruodu Wang, *Seven Proofs for the*

*Subadditivity of Expected Shortfall,* https://people.math.ethz.ch/~embrecht/ftp/Seven_Proofs.pdf. VAR answers the question of what value of a given portfolio is at risk, or how bad can things get. It cannot answer what is the expected loss if things do get bad. The measure that answers the second question is Expected Shortfall (ES) or Expected Tail Loss. There are four properties any risk measure must have: (a) monotonicity, (b) translation invariance, (c) homogeneity, and (d) subadditivity, but the fourth is a key property that distinguishes any coherent risk measure. The subadditivity condition states that the risk measure for two portfolios after they have been merged, as in portfolio diversification, should be no greater than the sum of their risk measures before they were merged (see Hull). More precisely, a subadditive risk measure $\rho$ satisfies that for any two risks X and Y, $\rho(X + Y) \leq \rho(X) + \rho(Y)$ always holds (see Embrechts and Wang). Hull illustrates by numerical examples that VAR does not satisfy the fourth condition whereas ES satisfies all four. Embrechts and Wang provide formal mathematical proofs.

31. See the Board of Governors of the Federal Reserve press release of February 2, 2018, ibid. The Fed Chairman said in his first appearance before Congress on Tuesday, February 27, 2018 that the supplementary leverage ratio was an important backstop to the current Basel risk-based capital framework. Some Congressmen were concerned that the ratio was too punitive on lending.

32. Manasse, P., Roubini, N., Schimmelpfennig, A (2003), Predicting Sovereign Debt Crises, IMF Working Paper, WP/03/221.

33. The ideas behind the connections between financial development and economic development go back to Adam Smith (1776), *The Wealth of Nations.* The ideas have blossomed into a body of theories that has its beginnings in the earlier works of Raymond R. Goldsmith, *Financial Structure and Development* (Yale University Press, 1969), Ronald L. McKinnon, *Money and Capital in Economic Development* (Washington, DC: Brookings Institution, 1973), and Edward S. Shaw, *Financial Deepening in Economic Development* (New York: Oxford University Press, 1973).

34. Japanese are compulsive savers, partly due to the culture. At a young age, children learn to save. A unique feature of Japan is that the public prefers cash to credit for transactions. Compared to other industrialised Western economies, the use of the debit card rather than credit cards is much higher in Japan. This partly explains the prominence of bank deposits.

35. World Bank, Financial Soundness Indicators (Bank Non-Performing Loans to Gross Loans; Bank Regulatory Capital to Risk-Weighted Assets; Bank Deposits to GDP; Bank's Net Interest Margin; Bank's Return on Equity; Bank's Return on Assets; Liquid Assets to Deposits and Short Term Funding) retrieved from FRED (Federal Reserve Bank of St. Louis): https://fred.stlouisfed.org/series/DDSI02CNA156NWDB, March 25, 2018.

36. Stanford Encyclopedia of Philosophy, Ceteris Paribus *Laws,* available on the website: https://plato.stanford.edu/entries/ceteris-paribus/. Partial derivative

is a precise mathematical method of describing the *Ceteris Paribus* approach used in science (principally economics).

37. Khan, M. (2018), *Capital and RWA for Tier 1 US Banks—2Q 2018*, Clarus Financial Technology. The six are JP Morgan, Bank of America, Citigroup, Wells Fargo, The Goldman Sachs Group, and Morgan Stanley. https://www.clarusft.com/capital-and-rwa-for-tier-1-us-banks-2q-2018/

38. Regulatory capital is the minimum amount of capital that the *bank regulator* of a country determines is necessary to cover unexpected credit, market, and operational risks or losses so that depositors can get back their money. Economic capital, on the other hand, is based on the bank's own experience and business objectives, and is calculated internally by the bank. Unlike regulatory capital, Basel does not define economic capital. Whereas each bank has a unique way of defining capital, paragraph 528 of 2006 Revised Framework states that "banks' overall risk management practices used to manage their banking book equity investments are expected to be consistent with the evolving *sound practice guidelines* issued by the Committee and national supervisors."

39. Bank for International Settlements, Basel Committee on Banking Supervision (2016), *Prudential treatment of problem assets—definitions of non-performing exposures and forbearance*, July 15, 2016. Impairment is an accounting concept whereas non-performing is a regulatory prudential concept and the two are not interchangeable. From Paragraph 24, an impaired loan is non-performing but the inverse may not hold. The loan *may not be impaired* (in the accounting sense that the bank recognised the potential loss on the balance sheet) but in a regulatory sense, the loan is still considered non-performing because the obligor is unlikely to make all interest (and principal) payments.

40. Royal Bank of Scotland (RBS) is one of the oldest banks, founded five years before the first American president, George Washington, was born in 1727. RBS rose from being a local Scottish bank to becoming the fifth largest bank in the world after a dizzying pace of acquisitions and further investment in an array of high-risk US securities. Because of the 2008–2009 financial crisis originating in the United States, RBC reported its first loss, since its founding, in 2008. The UK government stepped in and bailed out the bank.

41. In finance, a *derivative* is a financial instrument *derived from* an underlying real asset, in this case, residential and commercial mortgages.

42. The derivative securities were insured (or to use the financial lingo, "wrapped") by bond insurers, called *monoline insurers*, whose business was to guarantee payment of principal and interest when a debt-security issuer defaulted. The banks took out insurance on the monolines such as AIG (American International Group), Ambac Financial, and MBIA (Municipal Bond Insurance Association) Inc. These contracts are called CDS (Credit Default Swap). These insurers did not plan for the collapse of the US housing bubble 2008 and they took heavy losses, essentially writing down their capital that provided the support to the initial "AAA" ratings. The downgrades in 2008

rapidly cascaded to the derivative securities that the monolines had insured. The financial house of cards collapsed because the structure rested on two faulty assumptions: (1) The "AAA" ratings, assigned by the rating agencies, were valid (or recession-proof) and (b) zero to negligible risk of *cascading failure* facilitated by interlinkages and interdependencies in the financial system. Ambac Financial and MBIA Inc. went bankrupt, whereas AIG received bailout assistance. The banks that bought CDS "wasted" hundreds of millions from the premiums they had been paying out when things were going well so that the "AAA" credit ratings held up. In addition, after the monolines filed for bankruptcy, the "insured" were left holding worthless insurance, so they had to write down billions in assets against their capital base, which proved inadequate. Royal Bank of Scotland was rescued by the UK taxpayers. No similar lifeline was thrown at Lehman Brothers, the dominant player in US subprime mortgage origination, as well as the securitisation of the mortgage loans. Lehman Brothers filed for bankruptcy on September 15, 2008.

43. Claessens, Stijn, Nicholas Coleman, and Michael Donnelly (2017). *"Low-For-Long" Interest Rates and Banks' Interest Margins and Profitability: Cross-Country Evidence*. International Finance Discussion Papers 117.

44. For an overview, see the three-part series by Ben Bernanke, *Why are interest rates so low?* in the Brookings Institution, Monday, March 30, 2015.

45. Golin, J., and P. Delhaise (2013), ibid., Chapter 6.

46. Daraio, C., and L. Simar (2007), *Advanced Robust and Nonparametric Methods in Efficiency Analysis, Methodology and Applications*, Springer. See Chapter 2, The Measurement of Efficiency.

47. Statistica, *Average cost-to-income ratios for banks in selected European countries as of December 2018*, https://www.statista.com/statistics/728483/cost-to-income-ratios-for-banks-in-europe-by-country/

48. *The Economist* uses the phrase "structural unprofitability of German retail" in its April 14–20 in the article, *Deutsche Bank Unravelling*, in the 2018 issue of the newspaper.

49. McKinsey and Company, *The road ahead Perspectives on German banking*, authored by: Philipp Koch, Max Flötotto, Ursula Weigl, Gerhard Schröck German Banking Practice March 2016.

50. Basel Committee on Banking Supervision (2013), *Basel III: The Liquidity Coverage Ratio and liquidity risk monitoring tools*, January 2013.

51. See Marcia Stigum, *The Money Market*, McGraw-Hill, 3rd edition (Dec 11, 1989) ibid.

52. Federal Deposit Insurance Corporation (FDIC), Industry Analysis, Failed Banks, *Failures and Assistance Transactions—Historical Statistics on Banking*. website: https://www.fdic.gov/

53. Disalvo, J., and Ryan Johnston (2017), *The Rise in Loan-to-Deposit Ratios: Is 80 the New 60?* Federal Reserve Bank of Philadelphia, Q3—2017. The article discusses the LDR trends for small and large US banks from the early 1980s

onwards. The study noted: "Over the past three decades, the median LTD ratio at small banks increased from about 60 percent to close to 80 percent at the end of 2016. Whilst LTDs were already higher at large banks, they increased less rapidly, from around 80 percent to over 85 percent during the same period." Small banks include independent commercial banks and thrifts with assets less than $1 billion, and banks and thrifts that are subsidiaries of holding companies with total banking assets less than $1 billion. Large or big banks include all other commercial banks and thrifts.

54. FDIC, Deposit Insurance, *Bank Failures in Brief*, ibid.

55. For example, in the wake of 2008 financial crisis in the United States, many weak banks turned to TARP (Troubled Asset Relief Program) for assistance, which involved the Federal government purchasing their toxic assets and equity to strengthen their balance sheet.

56. Board of Governors of the Federal Reserve System, List of Large Commercial Banks on website, https://www.federalreserve.gov/releases/lbr/

# Part II

## Statistical Methods on Credit Scoring

# 8

# Statistical Methods of Credit Risk Analysis

**Chapter Objectives**

1. Present probability models: linear and non-linear (probit and logit)
2. Apply estimation strategies to obtain the best statistical fit to a model
3. Learn to apply the model (using real data)
4. Learn to calculate probabilities using logit analysis
5. Understand the differences and the similarities of the three econometric approaches to decide which model to use
6. Briefly explore credit scorecard, and where the logit model fits in
7. Understand the limitations of credit scorecards

## 8.1  Introduction

In Part I of the book, we looked at various examples of the criteria-based approach to credit assessment, and we illustrated its versatility by applying it to three different industries: passenger airline, commercial real estate, and commercial banking. To recall, this hybrid model *subjectively* determines an *implicit* probability of default to any number of quantitative and qualitative factors through the assignment of weights. In contrast, the class of statistical models presented in this chapter *explicitly* determines the probability of default based on the empirical data set. Lenders rely not only on hybrid/

**Electronic Supplementary Material:** The online version of this chapter (https://doi.org/10.1007/978-3-030-32197-0_8) contains supplementary material, which is available to authorized users.

expert-judgement models, but also on statistical models to discriminate between good and bad loans.

This chapter extends the coverage to statistical methods of credit assessment, which every credit analyst's *toolbox* should contain for a couple of reasons. First, statistical models are objective, as we noted earlier. Second, statistical models tend to have relatively greater discriminatory power and thus serve to complement expert-judgement and hybrid models. We will be examining probability models and performing a case study on real company data. For simplicity, we start by describing the *basic* idea in the context of linear probability model. Then we extend the presentation to probit and logit models explained in Pindyck and Rubinfeld (1976).[1] After discussing the models, we perform a case study and its main purpose is to illustrate the link between probability of default and a set of financial ratios or predicators. We also discuss differences in the results obtained from the different approaches.

## 8.2 Probability Models

### 8.2.1 Linear Probability Model

Without loss in generality, consider a single variable or simple *linear probability model*, a term used to denote a regression model in which the dependent variable $y$ takes on a binary value of 1 if an event (e.g., default) occurs and 0 otherwise:

$$y_i = \alpha + \beta x_i + \varepsilon_i \tag{8.1}$$

where $x_i$ is the value of attribute, for example, last year's current ratio for $i$th firm, and

$$y_i = \begin{cases} 1 \text{ if the firm has defaulted in the current year,} \\ 0 \text{ if the firm is active in the current year.} \end{cases}$$

The randomness is captured in the error term, $\varepsilon_i$.

We can define probability distribution of default according to the values that $y_i$ can take. Define:

$$p_i = \text{Prob}(y_i = 1), \text{ and } 1 - p_i = \text{Prob}(y_i = 0).$$

Hence, the expected value of the dependent variable, $y_i$, is

$$E(y_i|x_i) = 1(p_i) + 0(1 - p_i) = p_i \qquad (8.2)$$

If $E(\varepsilon_i) = 0$, we have

$$E(y_i|x_i) = \alpha + \beta x_i + E(\varepsilon_i) = \alpha + \beta x_i \qquad (8.3)$$

From Eqs. (8.2 and 8.3), we can conclude that

$$p_i = \alpha + \beta x_i \qquad (8.4)$$

**Problem 1: Probability Values Are Not Bounded in the (0, 1) Range**
Probability has a restricted range of $[0, 1]$. Thus, the most important weakness of the linear probability model is that there is no guarantee that $\alpha + \beta x_i$ would be bounded in the admissible range of $[0, 1]$. We can, however, impose some rules on the linear probability function (8.4) to restrict its range not to be below 0 or exceed 1. The piecewise formulation is as follows:

$$p_i = \begin{cases} \alpha + \beta x_i, \text{when } 0 < \alpha + \beta x_i < 1 \\ 1, \text{when } \alpha + \beta x_i \geq 1 \\ 0, \text{when } \alpha + \beta x_i \leq 0. \end{cases}$$

Thus, we are interpreting $p_i$ as a probability and, as such, we are limiting the value of $p_i$ to be between 0 and 1. As for the error term, $\varepsilon_i$, when $y_i = 1$, Eq. 8.1 implies that $\varepsilon_i = 1 - \alpha - \beta x_i$ with probability $p_i$ and when $y_i = 0$, $\varepsilon_i = -\alpha - \beta x_i$ with probability $1 - p_i$. This has an important implication for the variance of the error term as discussed in the following section.

**Problem 2: Non-constant Variance of the Errors Term**
Heteroscedasticity is another severe shortcoming of the model. It can be shown that the error term $\varepsilon_i$ has zero mean and variance $p_i(1 - p_i)$.[2] Consequently, the variance of the error term is not constant but varies across firms. Equivalently, the error term varies with each $i^{th}$ value of the independent variable and, thus, the predicted value; this is what the term "heteroscedasticity" means. It is a major problem because the model will not yield efficient estimates and predictions. In other words, the estimates and predictions would not be as precise as they could be in the absence of heteroscedasticity.

To correct the heteroscedasticity, we can apply the following procedure:

- First, estimate the original model using ordinary least squares (OLS) estimation method, which yields unbiased estimates of model coefficients.
- Second, calculate predicted dependent variable $\hat{y}_i$, and estimated variance $w_i = \hat{y}_i \left(1 - \hat{y}_i\right)$, since $\hat{y}_i$ is the estimated probability, $p_i$. The estimated standard error is $\sqrt{w}_i$.
- Apply weighted OLS estimation using the *inverse* of the estimated standard error as weight to scale $\hat{y}_i$, model constant, and $x_i$. Following this step, we then apply OLS to the weighted model.

The drawbacks with this procedure, however, are threefold.

First, variance cannot be zero or negative, so $\hat{y}_i$ must not be less than or equal to zero, nor greater than or equal to 1. In practice, however, $\hat{y}_i \left(1 - \hat{y}_i\right)$ can be negative or zero. For example, for $\hat{y}_i = 1$, the variance is zero. To avoid this problem, we may exclude such observations, or set predictions that are zero or negative to 0.01 and those greater than or equal to 1 to 0.99. In either case the weighted least squares method will not be efficient. Moreover, the weighted least squares are sensitive to specification error. Consequently, the use of weighted least squares is not recommended.

Second, if there are too many extreme (small) values for $X$, we would under-(over)estimate the slope coefficient represented by $\beta$.

Finally, even if the linear relationship is correct, the probability values predicted by a linear probability model can fall outside the admissible range of [0, 1]. The third weakness comes under more criticism. One solution, as we saw before, is to impose rules to constrain the predicted values—the outputs of the function—within the [0, 1] range: negative values are set to 0, whereas values greater than 1 are set to 1. The drawback to this procedure, however, is that the restriction will result in biased predictions. An example of linear probability model will be discussed later on in this chapter.

With this background understanding of the weaknesses of the linear probability model, let us explore alternatives formulations for modelling probability of default in relation to one or more numerical predictor variables, including categorical variables. Specifically, we will be estimating the probit model and the logit model using actual data on a random sample of companies that can be classified as active (coded 0) or bankrupt (coded 1).

## 8.2.2 Alternative Formulation: Probit Model

We need to transform the linear model in such a way that its prediction is bounded between 0 and 1. One solution is using an apparatus called a *link function.*[3] A commonly used link function is the *cumulative normal probability function*[4]:

$$p_i = F\left(\alpha + \beta x_i\right) = F\left(z_i\right) = \frac{1}{\sqrt{2\pi}}\int_{-\infty}^{z_i}\exp\left[-\frac{s^2}{2}\right]ds \qquad (8.5)$$

**What the Function $F(z_i)$ Is Doing**

Simply stated, this probit model assigns a probability of default ($p_i$) to firm $i$ based on a quantitative measure ($x_i$), e.g. current ratio.

The cumulative normal distribution takes any real number and returns probability between 0 and 1. Define a cut-off point $Z^*$ below which $Y$ is zero (e.g., firm would not default) and above which $Y$ is 1 (firm would default). A natural choice in this regard is 0.5. Then $p_i$ is an estimate of the conditional probability or expectation that a firm will default, given that the firm's current ratio is $x_i$, i.e. $E(y_i|x_i) = 1$. Such conditional probability is equivalent to the probability that a standard normal variable will be less than or equal to $\alpha + \beta x_i$.

The main advantage of the probit model, compared to linear probability model, is that the predicted probabilities will never fall outside the admissible probability range of [0, 1]. As we noted earlier, this is not so in the case of linear probability model. As a result, predicted values above 1 are manually set equal to 1; those below 0, set to 0. A graphical comparison of the cumulative probability curves of the two models is presented in Fig. 8.1. As you can see, the probability implied by the probit curve is in the [0, 1] range, whereas this is not so for the linear curve without the manual adjustments noted earlier, so we can have values that fall outside the range.

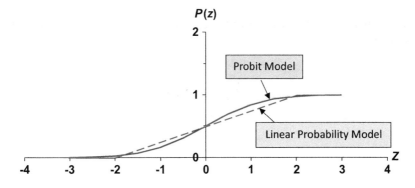

**Fig. 8.1** Prediction with probit model

Although it is clear that the probit model is more appealing than the linear model, the estimation of the curve is not as simple as OLS and involves non-linear Maximum Likelihood estimation.[5] But, with the availability of regression software and high-speed computers available today, estimation is no longer the daunting task that it was many years ago. Back then, the hardware and software technologies were unavailable. A rather more fundamental issue is that the use of cumulative normal distribution to limit probabilities to fall between 0 and 1 has limited theoretical justification. In the following section, we consider an alternative way of doing so based on the *cumulative logistic probability function*.

## 8.2.3  Alternative Formulation: Logit Model

In the probit regression, the link function is the *cumulative normal distribution*. The logit regression uses a *logit link function*, that is, the *cumulative logistic probability function*, which is also bounded in the [0, 1] range:

$$p_i = F(z_i) = F(\alpha + \beta x_i) = \frac{1}{\left[1 + \exp(-z_i)\right]} \tag{8.6}$$

Equally,

$$p_i = \frac{1}{\left[1 + \exp(-\alpha - \beta x_i)\right]} \tag{8.7}$$

In contrast with the log linear model (Eq. 8.4 above):

$$p_i = \alpha + \beta x_i$$

The logit model uses the natural log of the odds that $Y$ equals one of the categories:

$$\ln \frac{p_i}{1 - p_i} = \alpha + \beta x_i \tag{8.8}$$

> ### What the Logit Model (8.8) Means
> Simply put, this logit model assigns log-odds of default $\left(\dfrac{p_i}{1-p_i}\right)$ to firm i based on a quantitative measure ($x_i$), e.g. current ratio.

where $\dfrac{p_i}{1-p_i}$ is the odds ratio of default. As we will discuss later, the function takes the value of the estimated linear equation and converts it to a probability derived from a non-linear function.[6] The logistic link clearly leads to more intuitive coefficients than those of the probit regression. Each unit or marginal change in $x_i$ leads to a $\beta_i$ change in the *log-odds*, which we can restate into odds ratios that most people understand. The marginal effect could be interpreted just like linear regression coefficients, but, as we will see with a probit link, that is not the case.

The logistic function has a fatter tail compared to the normal as shown in Fig. 8.2, which means that it can handle cases of more extreme values than does the normal distribution.

The slopes of both the cumulative logistic and normal distributions are greatest at $p_i = 0.5$. This implies that changes in $X$ have their maximum impact on the odds at the mid-point of distribution and their lowest impact at its tails. In other words, at mid-point, small changes in $X$ are enough to change the odds whereas, at the tails, relatively larger changes in $X$ are needed to change the odds by the same amount. For example, if a company's current ratio approaches a value that implies a 50% chance of bankruptcy, a little improvement in it can prevent the firm from going bankrupt, whereas a little decrease would tip the firm over into bankruptcy.

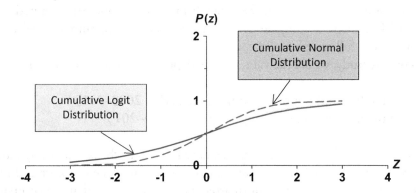

**Fig. 8.2** Cumulative logit vs. cumulative normal

Linear approximation can also be used to estimate the logit model. However, direct estimation method of the logit model is available in most regression software. In the following two sections, we use EViews software to estimate the probability models noted earlier.

## 8.3    Case Study: Probit Model to Predict Default

So far, we explored different probability models using a single explanatory variable, namely, the current ratio, to predict the likelihood of default. In practice, the decision to lend to individuals and corporations requires more than one explanatory variable. For example, to estimate the probability of default or bankruptcy, one needs at least a few financial ratios that ideally are not multi-collinear. From the vantage point of the credit analyst, the difficult question is the *a priori* selection of the financial ratios for the regression. Unfortunately, there is no theoretical basis for choosing one set of explanatory variables over another, or for including and excluding variables. The decision is essentially a pragmatic one, based largely on experience in credit practice, and the result is strong evidence of the statistical association between the chosen variables and default. In this section, we start with probit analysis to model the probability of default. A review of the relevant literature shows that extensive work by numerous authors has been done in the field of default prediction, using financial ratios in statistical models that employ binary dependent variables.[7]

We examine financial data of an initial sample of 37 randomly selected firms that defaulted in the period between 2009 and 2015. The data source is Wharton Research Data Services. To test the model, one needs a complete data set. Therefore, we excluded the companies for which observations of financial ratios were unavailable, leaving 19 firms with a complete set of observations. Similarly, from the active firms during same period noted earlier, 19 firms with a complete set of financial ratios were randomly selected, bringing the full sample to 38 companies.

For this study, we set the values of the dependent variable as follows:

$y = 0$ if the firm did not default during the period 2009–2015
$y = 1$ if the firm defaulted during the period 2009–2015

Financial ratios for companies that defaulted represent the last quarterly ratios for which all financial ratios were available before the default occurred. In all cases, the ratios are within four quarters before the period that the company entered default. "The public date" for the defaulted firms range between 2009 and 2015 with the middle-year being 2012. For active firms, there was no

**Table 8.1**  Variables used in the regressions

| Financial Ratio | Expected sign | Risk category |
|---|---|---|
| Current ratio (X1) | −ve | Liquidity |
| Quick ratio (acid test) (X2) | −ve | Liquidity |
| Cash ratio (X3) | −ve | Liquidity |
| Sales/Working capital (X4) | −ve | Efficiency |
| Interest coverage (after tax) (X5) | −ve | Solvency |
| Interest coverage ratio (X6) | −ve | Solvency |
| Total debt/Equity (X7) | +ve | Leverage |
| Total debt/EBITDA (X8) | +ve | Leverage |
| Net profit margin (X9) | −ve | Profitability |
| Operating Profit Margin (before depreciation) (X10) | −ve | Profitability |
| Operating Profit Margin (after depreciation) (X11) | −ve | Profitability |
| Gross Profit Margin (X12) | −ve | Profitability |
| Profit Margin (pre-tax) (X13) | −ve | Profitability |

Source: Wharton Research Data Services

default date (by definition). To have a similar systematic (economic) risk for the firms, the last complete quarterly result for the 2012 fiscal year-end was selected, which coincides with middle-year for the defaulted firms.

We present the complete set of financial ratio selected for this study in Table 8.1. The ratios represent five risk categories:

1. Liquidity
2. Efficiency
3. Solvency
4. Leverage
5. Profitability

From each risk category, we selected one financial ratio as the predictor or explanatory variable. To demonstrate model building in this context, we discuss different trials needed to arrive at the best probit model for this case as follows. The first model links probability of default to current ratio, sales over working capital, cash ratio, total debt over equity, and gross profit margin. We used EViews, a proprietary statistical package for Windows to estimate the equation. The regression results, with "C" representing the model constant (or intercept), are presented in Table 8.2.

The software produces the following fitted probit equation:

$$\text{Probit}\,(Y) = -0.08 - 0.59X_1 + 1.13X_3 + 0.06X_4 - 0.01X_7 - 0.67X_{12} \qquad \text{(P1)}$$

where $X_1$ = current ratio, $X_3$ = cash ratio, $X_4$ = sales/working capital, $X_7$ = total debt/equity, and $X_{12}$ = gross profit margin.

**Table 8.2** Results for P1

| Variable | Coefficient | Std. error | Z-statistic | Prob. |
|---|---|---|---|---|
| C | −0.07875 | 1.300614 | −0.060548 | 0.9517 |
| CURRENT_RATIO | −0.58885 | 0.613808 | −0.959341 | 0.3374 |
| SALES_OVER_WORKING_CAPITAL | 0.056851 | 0.030545 | 1.86123 | 0.0627 |
| CASH_RATIO | 1.133275 | 0.709049 | 1.598304 | 0.11 |
| TOTAL_DEBT_OVER_EQUITY | −0.01223 | 0.013971 | −0.875586 | 0.3813 |
| GROSS_PROFIT_MARGIN | −0.66764 | 1.331795 | −0.501306 | 0.6162 |
| McFadden R-squared | 0.315614 | Mean dependent var | | 0.5 |
| S.D. dependent var | 0.506712 | S.E. of regression | | 0.441141 |
| Akaike info criterion | 1.264551 | Sum squared resid | | 6.227368 |
| Schwarz criterion | 1.523117 | Log likelihood | | −18.0265 |
| Hannan-Quinn criter. | 1.356546 | Deviance | | 36.05292 |
| Restr. deviance | 52.67919 | Restr. log likelihood | | −26.3396 |
| LR statistic | 16.62626 | Avg. log likelihood | | −0.47438 |
| Prob(LR statistic) | 0.005266 | | | |
| Model prediction: | | | | |
| Actual | Active | | Bankrupt | |
| Active | 17 | | 2 | |
| Bankrupt | 6 | | 13 | |

### Interpreting the Fitted Equation

Before discussing the estimated equations for the probit model, it is impor-tant that we understand how a fitted equation is to be interpreted. In the case of the probit model, the marginal impact on a change in a particular variable is its coefficient weighted by a factor that depends on the values of all other regressors in the equation due to the non-linear form of the model (see Eq. 8.5).[8] However, the direction of the impact of a change in $X_{ij}$ depends only on the sign of its coefficient, $\beta_j$: positive (negative) values of $\beta_j$ imply that increasing $X_{ij}$ will increase (decrease) the probability of the response or default.

### Analysis of the Results

We can see from Eq. (P1) that the coefficients for current ratio and gross profit margin have the expected negative signs. The signs for the cash ratio, sales/working capital ratio, and the debt/equity ratio are counter-intuitive. For example, the negative sign for the debt/equity ratio means that a firm's probability of default will decrease with increasing indebtedness. The Z-statistics indicate that none of the regressors is statistically significant. The Z-statistic is the ratio of the coefficient to standard error, and an absolute value of 2 or more is the approximate yardstick for significance. The McFadden R-squared, which we will refer to as simply R-squared, is the analogue of $R^2$ that gets reported in linear regression models, has the property that it is bounded between 0 and 1. The R-squared value of 0.31 is low, indicating that the data are not close to the fitted regression.

Now, let us turn to the predictive ability of Eq. (P1). In Table 8.2, we see that the model predicts two firms that were actually active as defaulted. It also predicts that six firms were active when in fact they had defaulted.

**Testing Other Variables**

Using quick ratio in place of current ratio in (P1), the fitted regression is:

$$\text{Probit}(Y) = -1.59 + 0.37X_2 + 0.39X_3 + 0.08X_4 - 0.01X_7 - 0.24X_{12} \quad \text{(P2)}$$

where $X_2$ = quick ratio, $X_3$ = cash ratio, $X_4$ = sales/working capital, $X_7$ = total debt/equity, and $X_{12}$ = gross profit margin.

**Analysis of the Results**

The quick ratio (unlike the current ratio) has a positive coefficient, which is counter-intuitive, and the overall goodness-of-fit does not improve with $R$-squared at 0.31 (see Table 8.3). The model performs more poorly in terms of its predictive power. It incorrectly predicts that five of the actual active firms will default, compared to two in (P1).

Given that the quick ratio weakens the performance of what we are trying to model, we keep using the current ratio in the following regressions and try interest coverage ratio in place of cash ratio. We obtain the following estimated equation:

**Table 8.3** Results for P2

| Variable | Coefficient | Std. error | Z-statistic | Prob. |
|---|---|---|---|---|
| C | −1.5919 | 1.004237 | −1.585188 | 0.1129 |
| QUICK_RATIO | 0.372396 | 0.566044 | 0.657893 | 0.5106 |
| SALES_OVER_WORKING_CAPITAL | 0.075783 | 0.032619 | 2.323281 | 0.0202 |
| CASH_RATIO | 0.390421 | 0.715597 | 0.545588 | 0.5853 |
| TOTAL_DEBT_OVER_EQUITY | −0.01121 | 0.012989 | −0.863139 | 0.3881 |
| GROSS_PROFIT_MARGIN | −0.23698 | 1.289847 | −0.183728 | 0.8542 |
| McFadden R-squared | 0.305472 | Mean dependent var | | 0.5 |
| S.D. dependent var | 0.506712 | S.E. of regression | | 0.446492 |
| Akaike info criterion | 1.27861 | Sum squared resid | | 6.379363 |
| Schwarz criterion | 1.537176 | Log likelihood | | −18.2936 |
| Hannan-Quinn criter. | 1.370606 | Deviance | | 36.58719 |
| Restr. deviance | 52.67919 | Restr. log likelihood | | −26.3396 |
| LR statistic | 16.092 | Avg. log likelihood | | −0.48141 |
| Prob(LR statistic) | 0.006586 | | | |
| Model prediction: | | | | |
| Actual | Active | | Bankrupt | |
| Active | 14 | | 5 | |
| Bankrupt | 6 | | 13 | |

$$\text{Probit}(Y) = -0.92 + 0.63X_1 + 0.05X_4 - 0.26X_6 - 0.02X_7 + 0.82X_{12} \quad \text{(P3)}$$

where $X_1$ = current ratio, $X_4$ = sales/working capital, $X_6$ = interest coverage ratio, $X_7$ = total debt/equity, and $X_{12}$ = gross profit margin.

Notice that in (P1), (P2), and (P3), each of the five risk categories is represented by its risk measure.

As Table 8.4 shows, the new model improves the results. First, $R$-squared has more than doubled to 0.70. Second, model predictions have drastically improved. However, the *sign test* shows mixed results. Contrary to our expectation, the estimated coefficients of current ratio, gross profit margin, and sales over working capital are positive, and that for total debt/equity is negative. Replacing total debt/equity with total debt/EBITDA yields the expected positive estimated coefficient for the latter (Table 8.5). The estimated regression is:

$$\text{Probit}(Y) = -2.78 + 1.31X_1 + 0.07X_4 - 0.31X_6 + 0.03X_8 + 1.40X_{12} \quad \text{(P4)}$$

where $X_1$ = current ratio, $X_4$ = sales/working capital, $X_6$ = interest coverage ratio, $X_8$ = total debt/EBITDA, and $X_{12}$ = gross profit margin.

Clearly, there is room for improvement over (P4). We retain total debt/EBITDA as our measure of leverage because the sign confirms with *a priori*

**Table 8.4** Results for P3

| Variable | Coefficient | Std. error | Z-statistic | Prob. |
|---|---|---|---|---|
| C | −0.9239 | 1.80281 | −0.512476 | 0.6083 |
| CURRENT_RATIO | 0.631391 | 0.812945 | 0.776671 | 0.4374 |
| SALES_OVER_WORKING_CAPITAL | 0.045355 | 0.035787 | 1.267348 | 0.205 |
| INTEREST_COVERAGE_RATIO | −0.26542 | 0.116392 | −2.280354 | 0.0226 |
| TOTAL_DEBT_OVER_EQUITY | −0.01613 | 0.027332 | −0.590094 | 0.5551 |
| GROSS_PROFIT_MARGIN | 0.825586 | 2.729105 | 0.302512 | 0.7623 |
| McFadden R-squared | 0.701439 | Mean dependent var | | 0.5 |
| S.D. dependent var | 0.506712 | S.E. of regression | | 0.261766 |
| Akaike info criterion | 0.729683 | Sum squared resid | | 2.192686 |
| Schwarz criterion | 0.988249 | Log likelihood | | −7.86398 |
| Hannan-Quinn criter. | 0.821679 | Deviance | | 15.72795 |
| Restr. deviance | 52.67919 | Restr. log likelihood | | −26.3396 |
| LR statistic | 36.95123 | Avg. log likelihood | | −0.20695 |
| Prob(LR statistic) | 0.000001 | | | |
| Model prediction: | | | | |
| Actual | Active | | Bankrupt | |
| Active | 18 | | 1 | |
| Bankrupt | 1 | | 18 | |

**Table 8.5** Results for P4

| Variable | Coefficient | Std. error | Z-statistic | Prob. |
|---|---|---|---|---|
| C | −2.78417 | 2.409922 | −1.155293 | 0.248 |
| CURRENT_RATIO | 1.310579 | 1.111383 | 1.179232 | 0.2383 |
| SALES_OVER_WORKING_CAPITAL | 0.071604 | 0.041887 | 1.709433 | 0.0874 |
| INTEREST_COVERAGE_RATIO | −0.3164 | 0.148879 | −2.12524 | 0.0336 |
| TOTAL_DEBT_OVER_EBITDA | 0.032951 | 0.032569 | 1.011724 | 0.3117 |
| GROSS_PROFIT_MARGIN | 1.402656 | 3.089722 | 0.453975 | 0.6498 |
| McFadden R-squared | 0.676699 | Mean dependent var | | 0.5 |
| S.D. dependent var | 0.506712 | S.E. of regression | | 0.275239 |
| Akaike info criterion | 0.76398 | Sum squared resid | | 2.424209 |
| Schwarz criterion | 1.022546 | Log likelihood | | −8.51561 |
| Hannan-Quinn criter. | 0.855975 | Deviance | | 17.03122 |
| Restr. deviance | 52.67919 | Restr. log likelihood | | −26.3396 |
| LR statistic | 35.64796 | Avg. log likelihood | | −0.2241 |
| Prob(LR statistic) | 0.000001 | | | |
| Model prediction: | | | | |
| Actual | Active | | Bankrupt | |
| Active | 18 | | 1 | |
| Bankrupt | 1 | | 18 | |

expectation. Next, we exclude $X_{12}$ (gross profit margin), which has the wrong sign in (P4) and replace it with $X_{11}$ (operating profit margin after depreciation). The estimated regression is:

$$\text{Probit}(Y) = -2.15 + 1.12X_1 + 0.07X_4 - 0.25X_6 + 0.04X_8 - 2.90X_{11} \qquad \text{(P5)}$$

where $X_1$ = current ratio, $X_4$ = sales/working capital, $X_6$ = interest coverage ratio, $X_8$ = total debt/EBITDA, and $X_{11}$ = operating profit margin after depreciation.

As Table 8.6 shows, the results have improved. Now, only two coefficients (for current ratio and sales over working capital) have counter-intuitive signs. In search for a solution to this problem, we tried two formulations. In the first, we deleted the sales to working capital. In the second, we retained the efficiency metric of sales to working capital but in its inverted form. The coefficient will have the expected positive sign. Both approaches resulted in the expected signs for all the estimated coefficients, as follows (Table 8.7).

## Model Excluding $X_4$ (Sales to Working Capital)

$$\text{Probit}(Y) = 0.63 - 0.02X_1 - 0.20X_6 + 0.07X_8 - 8.36X_{11} \qquad \text{(P6)}$$

where $X_1$ = current ratio, $X_6$ = interest coverage ratio, $X_8$ = total debt/EBITDA, and $X_{12}$ = operating profit margin after depreciation.

**Table 8.6** Results for P5

| Variable | Coefficient | Std. error | Z-statistic | Prob. |
|---|---|---|---|---|
| C | −2.154118 | 2.026616 | −1.062914 | 0.2878 |
| CURRENT RATIO | 1.122895 | 1.007409 | 1.114637 | 0.265 |
| SALES OVER WORKING CAPITAL | 0.069464 | 0.045024 | 1.542811 | 0.1229 |
| INTEREST COVERAGE RATIO | −0.248218 | 0.129142 | −1.922055 | 0.0546 |
| TOTAL DEBT OVER EBITDA | 0.038899 | 0.046976 | 0.828076 | 0.4076 |
| OPERATING PROFIT MARGIN AFTER DEPRECIATION | −2.899273 | 6.367493 | −0.455324 | 0.6489 |
| McFadden R-squared | 0.67732 | Mean dependent var | | 0.5 |
| S.D. dependent var | 0.506712 | S.E. of regression | | 0.2811 |
| Akaike info criterion | 0.763118 | Sum squared resid | | 2.528543 |
| Schwarz criterion | 1.021685 | Log likelihood | | −8.49925 |
| Hannan-Quinn criter. | 0.855114 | Deviance | | 16.99849 |
| Restr. deviance | 52.67919 | Restr. log likelihood | | −26.3396 |
| LR statistic | 35.68069 | Avg. log likelihood | | −0.22366 |
| Prob(LR statistic) | 0.000001 | | | |
| Model prediction: | | | | |
| Actual | Active | | Bankrupt | |
| Active | 18 | | 1 | |
| Bankrupt | 1 | | 18 | |

**Table 8.7** Results for P6

| Variable | Coefficient | Std. error | Z-statistic | Prob. |
|---|---|---|---|---|
| C | 0.628065 | 1.082676 | 0.580104 | 0.5618 |
| CURRENT RATIO | −0.020095 | 0.700019 | −0.028707 | 0.9771 |
| INTEREST COVERAGE RATIO | −0.201009 | 0.107215 | −1.874812 | 0.0608 |
| TOTAL DEBT OVER EBITDA | 0.070399 | 0.06987 | 1.007573 | 0.3137 |
| OPERATING PROFIT MARGIN AFTER DEPRECIATION | −8.361114 | 8.006761 | −1.044257 | 0.2964 |
| McFadden R-squared | 0.626296 | Mean dependent var | | 0.5 |
| S.D. dependent var | 0.506712 | S.E. of regression | | 0.312994 |
| Akaike info criterion | 0.781222 | Sum squared resid | | 3.232846 |
| Schwarz criterion | 0.996694 | Log likelihood | | −9.84321 |
| Hannan-Quinn criter. | 0.857885 | Deviance | | 19.68642 |
| Restr. deviance | 52.67919 | Restr. log likelihood | | −26.3396 |
| LR statistic | 32.99276 | Avg. log likelihood | | −0.25903 |
| Prob(LR statistic) | 0.000001 | | | |
| Model prediction: | | | | |
| Actual | Active | | Bankrupt | |
| Active | 16 | | 3 | |
| Bankrupt | 1 | | 18 | |

## Model Including $X_4^{-1}$ (Inverted Sales/Working Capital)

The fitted equation using inverted sales/working capital is (Table 8.8):

$$\text{Probit}(Y) = 1.16 - 0.73X_1 + 5.08X_4^{-1} - 0.17X_6 + 0.09X_8 - 12.11X_{11} \qquad \text{(P7)}$$

**Table 8.8** Results for P7

| Variable | Coefficient | Std. error | Z-statistic | Prob. |
|---|---|---|---|---|
| C | 1.157065 | 1.392854 | 0.830715 | 0.4061 |
| CURRENT RATIO | −0.730489 | 1.321368 | −0.552828 | 0.8504 |
| I/SALES OVER WORKING CAPITAL | 5.078403 | 7.943507 | 0.639315 | 0.5226 |
| INTEREST COVERAGE RATIO | −0.172974 | 0.111862 | −1.546313 | 0.122 |
| TOTAL DEBT OVER EBITDA | 0.085067 | 0.078372 | 1.085429 | 0.2777 |
| OPERATING PROFIT MARGIN AFTER DEPRECIATION | −12.11929 | 10.44974 | −1.15977 | 0.2461 |
| McFadden R-squared | 0.634041 | Mean dependent var | | 0.5 |
| S.D. dependent var | 0.506712 | S.E. of regression | | 0.315879 |
| Akaike info criterion | 0.823116 | Sum squared resid | | 3.192943 |
| Schwarz criterion | 1.081682 | Log likelihood | | −9.63921 |
| Hannan-Quinn criter. | 0.915112 | Deviance | | 19.27842 |
| Restr. deviance | 52.67919 | Restr. log likelihood | | −26.3396 |
| LR statistic | 33.40077 | Avg. log likelihood | | −0.25366 |
| Prob(LR statistic) | 0 | | | |

| Model prediction: | | | |
|---|---|---|---|
| Actual | Active | | Bankrupt |
| Active | 16 | | 3 |
| Bankrupt | 2 | | 17 |

where $X_1$ = current ratio, $X_4^{-1}$ = inverted sales/working capital, $X_6$ = interest coverage ratio, $X_8$ = total debt/EBITDA, and $X_{11}$ = operating profit margin after depreciation.

**Analyses of the Results of (P6) and (P7)**

The last two formulations P6 and P7 yielded similar $R$-squared and nearly identical predictions. The second model is richer from a theoretical point of view. The question is which of the two a credit analyst would choose on statistical basis. The diagnostic tests are the Schwarz criterion and the Akaike information criterion, which is a close relative. Thus, one may use, for example, the Schwarz criterion or the Schwarz Bayesian information criterion (SBIC or BIC for short) for selecting or favouring a particular model amongst a finite set of models. To put it in simple terms, given any two estimated models, the model with the lower value of SBIC is the one to be preferred. We see that the Schwarz criterion of (P6) is less than that of (P7), thus favouring the smaller model. In both cases, the probability of likelihood ratio (LR) statistic is close to 0, indicating that not all the explanatory variables have zero coefficients.

We observe that the $Z$-statistics are very low, and this is because the explanatory variables that we are using to predict default are highly correlated with each other. Where there is high correlation among explanatory variables, a subset of them can pick up the impact of the others. Therefore, we may delete one or more explanatory variables from the model without changing the goodness of fit (e.g., R-squared) significantly.

**Omitting Statistically Insignificant Variables**

If we delete the most statistically insignificant variables, one at a time, the following model would finally result:

$$\text{Probit}(Y) = 0.82 - 0.30X_6 \qquad (P8)$$

where $X_6$ = interest coverage ratio.

We end up with one statistically significant explanatory variable. Notice also that the predictions are reasonable. Three out of 19 active firms are incorrectly classified as defaulted, and 1 out of 19 defaulted firms is classified as active. The Schwarz criterion is clearly in favour of (P8). The R-squared drops to 0.58 (from 0.63), but the predictive ability of the model improves for bankrupt cases compared to (P7), the "rich model" with all five default risk categories represented by their corresponding ratios (Table 8.9).

## 8.4   Example of Linear Probability (LP) and Logit Models

Let us now turn to the linear probability model. As we noted earlier, we can use ordinary least squares to estimate linear probability model and the estimates will be unbiased. The estimated linear probability equation is (Table 8.10):

**Table 8.9** Results for P8

| Variable | Coefficient | Std. error | Z-statistic | Prob. |
|---|---|---|---|---|
| C | 0.820081 | 0.333936 | 2.455807 | 0.0141 |
| INTEREST_COVERAGE_RATIO | −0.30013 | 0.106831 | −2.809409 | 0.005 |
| McFadden R-squared | 0.579492 | Mean dependent var | | 0.5 |
| S.D. dependent var | 0.506712 | S.E. of regression | | 0.309818 |
| Akaike info criterion | 0.688212 | Sum squared resid | | 3.455547 |
| Schwarz criterion | 0.7744 | Log likelihood | | −11.076 |
| Hannan-Quinn criter. | 0.718877 | Deviance | | 22.15204 |
| Restr. deviance | 52.67919 | Restr. log likelihood | | −26.3396 |
| LR statistic | 30.52714 | Avg. log likelihood | | −0.29147 |
| Prob(LR statistic) | 0 | | | |
| Model prediction: | | | | |
| Actual | Active | | Bankrupt | |
| Active | 16 | | 3 | |
| Bankrupt | 1 | | 18 | |

**Table 8.10** Results for LP1

| Variable | Coefficient | Std. error | Z-statistic | Prob. |
|---|---|---|---|---|
| C | 0.849822 | 0.260793 | 3.258607 | 0.0027 |
| CURRENT RATIO | −0.250068 | 0.201887 | −1.238656 | 0.2245 |
| I/SALES OVER WORKING CAPITAL | 0.718692 | 0.701636 | 1.024308 | 0.3134 |
| INTEREST COVERAGE RATIO | −0.00672 | 0.003089 | −2.175761 | 0.0371 |
| TOTAL DEBT OVER EBITDA | 0.004469 | 0.004285 | 1.042863 | 0.3048 |
| OPERATING PROFIT MARGIN AFTER DEPRECIATION | −1.085663 | 0.503357 | −2.156846 | 0.0386 |
| R-squared | 0.441574 | Mean dependent var | | 0.5 |
| Adjusted R-squared | 0.35432 | S.D. dependent var. | | 0.506712 |
| S.E. of regression | 0.407164 | Akaike info criterion | | 1.184739 |
| Sum squared resid | 5.305048 | Schwarz criterion | | 1.443305 |
| Log likelihood | −16.51004 | Hannan-Quinn criter. | | 1.276735 |
| F-statistic | 5.060782 | Durbin-Watson stat | | 1.097114 |
| Prob(F-statistic) | 0.001577 | | | |
| Model prediction: | | | | |
| Actual | Active | | Bankrupt | |
| Active | 17 | | 2 | |
| Bankrupt | 3 | | 16 | |

$$LP(Y) = 0.84 - 0.25X_1 + 0.72X_4^{-1} - 0.007X_6 + 0.004X_8 - 1.09X_{11} \qquad \text{(LP1)}$$

where $X_1$ = current ratio, $X_4^{-1}$ = inverted sales/working capital, $X_6$ = interest coverage ratio, $X_8$ = total debt/EBITDA, and $X_{11}$ = operating profit margin after depreciation.

It can be observed that all the estimated coefficients have correct signs and that three coefficients are statistically significant at least at the 96% probability level (with prob. <0.04). However, the linear probability model predictions are marginally different from the corresponding probit model. In contrast, the results for logit model are very similar to those for the probit model. For the logit function, we use the same explanatory variables of (P7) (Table 8.11).

$$\ln\left(\frac{p}{1-p}\right) = 2.09 - 1.23X_1 + 7.85X_4^{-1} - 0.31X_6 + 0.14X_8 - 19.85X_{11} \qquad \text{(L1)}$$

where $X_1$ = current ratio, $X_4^{-1}$ = inverted sales/working capital, $X_6$ = interest coverage ratio, $X_8$ = total debt/EBITDA, and $X_{11}$ = operating profit margin after depreciation.

Let us revisit the interpretation of the coefficients, focusing now on the estimated logit model (L1). In the probit model, the coefficients cannot be

**Table 8.11** Results for L1

| Variable | Coefficient | Std. error | Z-statistic | Prob. |
|---|---|---|---|---|
| C | 2.096466 | 2.388986 | 0.877555 | 0.3802 |
| CURRENT RATIO | −1.232748 | 2.218996 | −0.555543 | 0.5785 |
| I/SALES OVER WORKING CAPITAL | 7.851344 | 13.46257 | 0.583198 | 0.5598 |
| INTEREST COVERAGE RATIO | −0.3114 | 0.212904 | −1.462633 | 0.1436 |
| TOTAL DEBT OVER EBITDA | 0.143902 | 0.137802 | 1.044266 | 0.2964 |
| OPERATING PROFIT MARGIN AFTER DEPRECIATION | −19.85252 | 18.54147 | −1.070709 | 0.2843 |
| McFadden R-squared | 0.6313 | Mean dependent var | | 0.5 |
| S.D. dependent var | 0.506712 | S.E. of regression | | 0.314641 |
| Akaike info criterion | 0.826916 | Sum squared resid | | 3.167973 |
| Schwarz criterion | 1.085482 | Log likelihood | | −9.71141 |
| Hannan-Quinn criter. | 0.918912 | Deviance | | 19.42281 |
| Restr. deviance | 52.67919 | Restr. log likelihood | | −26.3396 |
| LR statistic | 33.25638 | Avg. log likelihood | | 0.25556 |
| Prob(LR statistic) | 0.000033 | | | |
| Model prediction: | | | | |
| Actual | Active | | Bankrupt | |
| Active | 16 | | 3 | |
| Bankrupt | 2 | | 17 | |

**Table 8.12** Linear probability model, probit model, and logit model

| Explanatory variable | Linear probability model[a] | Probit model[b] | Logit model[b] |
|---|---|---|---|
| Current ratio | −0.25 (−1.24) | −0.73 (−0.55) | −1.23 (−0.56) |
| Inverted sales/working capital | 0.72 (1.02) | 5.08 (0.64) | 7.85 (0.58) |
| Interest coverage ratio | −0.007 (−2.18) | −0.17 (−1.55) | −0.31 (1.46) |
| Total debt/EBITDA | 0.004 (1.04) | 0.09 (1.09) | 0.14 (1.04) |
| Operating profit margin after depreciation | −1.09 (−2.16) | −12.11 (−1.16) | −19.85 (−1.07) |
| Constant | 0.84 | 1.16 | 2.09 |
| **Predictive performance compared** | | | |
| Percent of active firms correctly predicted | 15/19 | 16/19 | 16/19 |
| Percent of defaulted firms correctly predicted | 16/19 | 17/19 | 17/19 |

Note: Total number of firms = 38. Half of them (19) actually defaulted and the rest were active firms.
[a] t- ratios in parentheses, [b] Z-statistic in parentheses

interpreted as the marginal effect because the latter is not a constant but depends on all other variables in the function. In the logit model, the coefficients reflect the impact of a unit change in explanatory variables on the logarithm of relative odds of bankruptcy. A comparison of the performance of three models is shown in Table 8.12:

## 8.5  Choice Between Probit and Logit Models

As you can see from Table 8.12 and earlier results, the difference between logit and probit is either very slight or non-existent on a practical level. This means that the logit and probit models tend to produce similar predictions. The choice comes down mainly to interpretation. At the intuitive level, the logit model is easier than the probit model to grasp. Most people—especially those of the betting type—are familiar with the concept of odds—expressed as the number of occurrences of a certain event as a proportion of the number of non-occurrences of that event—so it is relatively easy to understand the log-odds function, which is transformable to yield the odds ratio.

In the case of a probit model, we are working backward from an S-shaped cumulative normal distribution (or probability values) to a corresponding $Z$-value on the bell-shaped probability curve (or the probability density function). Thus, the coefficients for a probit model are the difference in the $Z$-score associated with each one-unit difference in a predictor, but the interpretation is less intuitive than that for a logit model.

The choice may also be determined by discipline convention, so that the audience plays an important role in the choice. In economics, probit analysis is frequently used. However, in some social sciences, such as psychology, logit seems to be a preferred method to model binary response variables. Finally, at the theoretical level, some researchers would prefer to use the logit model because the logistic function has a fatter tail compared to the normal, as we noted earlier. It means that logit can handle cases of more extreme values than would the normal distribution.

## 8.6  Interpretation of the Estimated Coefficients

We covered a lot of ground in the previous sections, so in this closing section, we present the main elements of probability models. We started out with a problem one often encounters in finance and that is the question of analysing categorical variables. In credit analysis and lending, we have to decide whether to grant a loan or decline a loan. One useful decision tool is the application of probability models to forecast the probability of default. From experience, the credit analyst knows that there are certain reliable predicators of default and he or she wishes to put the variables in an equation, estimate the parameters of the predetermined form of the equation, and use the estimated regression. As we showed, all this sounds relatively easy and straightforward until we start the estimation procedure and analyse the goodness of fit and the model's productive power. The final model is usually not the one we had in mind at the outset. We introduced three probability models:

1. Linear probability model
2. Probit Model
3. Logit Model

**Simple Linear Probability Model**

We presented a simple model, Eq. 8.1, with one predictor:

$$y_i = \alpha + \beta x_i + \varepsilon_i \qquad (8.9)$$

In the general case with many independent variables, the equation takes this form:

$$y_i = \alpha + \beta_1 X_{1i} + \beta_2 X_{2i} + \beta_3 X_{3i} + \cdots + \beta_k X_{ki} + \varepsilon_i \qquad (8.10)$$

where the binary feature includes:

$y$ = Firm defaults ($y$ = 1) or not ($y$ = 0)
Or: $y$ = Country defaults ($y$ = 1) or not ($y$ = 0)
Or: $y$ = A mortgage is approved ($y$ = 1) or not ($y$ = 0)

The coefficients of the equation are interpreted as the change in $y$ associated with a unit change in, for example, $X_{ki}$. In the language of calculus, we write the *partial derivatives* as:

$$\frac{\partial y_i}{\partial x_{ki}} = \beta_k \qquad (8.11)$$

Note that these marginal effects are constants, unlike the coefficients for the non-linear models that depend on what the values of the $X_{1i}, \ldots, X_{ki}$ are. We showed that the reasons that the linear probability model is unsatisfactory are twofold:

1. The predicted probabilities can be above 1 or below 0, but probability must be bounded in the (0, 1) range.
2. The variance of the error term is not a constant but varies with the values of the explanatory variables, resulting in the estimated coefficient being imprecise. We say the error terms are heteroskedastic.

We therefore looked at two alternative models and in both of these non-linear specifications, we introduced something called link function that does two things: (1) It converts the probability into a value that runs from $-\infty$ to $+\infty$ and (2) it has a *linear* relationship with the explanatory variables, which have a *non-linear* or sigmoidal relationship with the probabilities. The probit and logit functions do both.

**Probit Model**
We introduce the link function $F(Z)$ in Eq. 8.5, here stated for $k$ variables:

$$Z_i = \alpha + \beta_1 X_{1i} + \beta_2 X_{2i} + \beta_3 X_{3i} + \cdots + \beta_k X_{ki} + \varepsilon_i \qquad (8.12)$$

The inputs of the *linear Z* function are the values of $X$ and the output is $Z$-values. The cumulative normal distribution function, the *non-linear* link function $F(Z)$, takes these values and returns predicted probability values between 0 and 1.

**Logit Model**
We introduce the link function $F(Z)$ in Eq. 8.6, the cumulative standard logistic distribution function and derive Eq. 8.8 for the general case of more than one explanatory variable.

$$\ln \frac{p_i}{1 - p_i} = \alpha + \beta_1 X_{1i} + \beta_2 X_{2i} + \beta_3 X_{3i} + \cdots + \beta_k X_{ki} + \varepsilon_i \qquad (8.13)$$

We evaluate at $Z(x)$ and using Eq. 8.7, we obtain the log-odds ratio. Taking exponential of the log-odds gives the odds ratio $\left( \dfrac{p}{1-p} \right)$. The probability $(p)$ is calculated from Eq. 8.6, alternatively, by calculating it from the odds ratio.

**Marginal Effects Are Not Constant. Logit Model as an Example**
The coefficients are needed for prediction. Let us suppose that we have these two estimated probit and logit equations:

$$Z = -3.50 + 1.16X$$

$$\ln \left( \frac{p}{1-p} \right) = -6.44 + 1.86X$$

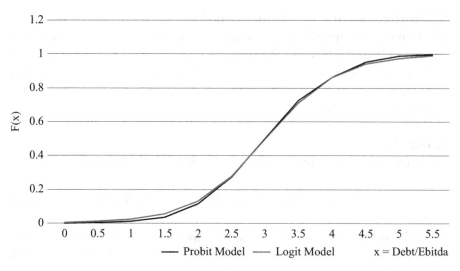

**Fig. 8.3** Predictions of logit and probit models

where the higher is $Z$ the higher probability of default, and $X$ represents debt/EBITDA. The predicted probabilities are shown in Fig. 8.3. As expected, the predicted values are very close.

Let us now illustrate the effect of a change in the probability that $y = 1$ associated with a unit change in $\dfrac{\text{Debt}}{\text{Ebitda}}$ ratio. The results for the probit and logit models are tabulated in Table 8.13.

Notice the following important results:

1. The marginal effects of the unit changes in $\dfrac{\text{Debt}}{\text{Ebitda}}$ ratio are not constant but change with the value of the independent variable. This result holds for more than one explanatory variable, reflecting the non-linearity (see the following part). A unit change from 1.5 to 2.5 yields an increase in the probability of default of 0.235 for the probit model and 0.222 for the logit model, whereas a unit change from 3.0 to 4.0 yields a bigger increase in the probability of 0.381 for the probit model and 0.368 for the logit model.
2. The changes in $\dfrac{\text{Debt}}{\text{Ebitda}}$ ratio have maximum impact on the odds at the mid-point of distribution than at the tails.
3. If the $\dfrac{\text{Debt}}{\text{Ebitda}}$ ratio approaches a value that implies a 50% chance of bankruptcy, even a small deterioration raises the odds of the company going bankrupt. We discussed this in Sect. 8.2 and this result is corroborative.

**Table 8.13** Effect of unit changes in debt/EBITDA on the probability $y = 1$

|  | Probability (Probit) | Probability (Logit) | Odds (Logit) |
|---|---|---|---|
| From: 1.5 | 0.039 | 0.057 | 0.060 |
| To: 2.5 | 0.274 | 0.279 | 0.387 |
| Change in probability/odds | 0.235 | 0.222 | 0.327 |
| From: 3.0 | 0.492 | 0.495 | 0.980 |
| To: 4.0 | 0.873 | 0.863 | 6.297 |
| Change in probability/odds | 0.381 | 0.368 | 5.316 |

## Multivariate Probit and Logit Models

Let us consider the impact of a change in an explanatory variable on the probability whilst the other variables are held constant in the context of the multivariate logit and probit model that we fitted (see Table 8.13). To demonstrate the process, we start with the probit model, using actual data of one active firm. Let us call this a base forecast. The set of base values are as follows (Table 8.14):

Now we want to calculate the impact of one unit increase in the interest coverage ratio on the probability of default, holding other explanatory variables constant. Using the model's estimated coefficients, we calculate $Z$, and thereby, the probability for the probit model using the base data. Then we do the same after changing the interest coverage ratio to 2.749 (i.e., increase it by 1 unit). The difference between the two probabilities measures the impact of increasing the interest coverage ratio by one unit. The results are presented in Table 8.15.

Thus, the impact of increasing the interest coverage ratio by one unit is a 3.3% reduction in the probability of default. Here, to calculate the Probability ($Z$), we find the cumulative probability of normal distribution for Z. In Excel sheet, this result is easily obtained by using the function NORM.DIST(Z,0,1,TRUE), where TRUE stands for cumulative probability option, and figures 0 and 1 are the mean and standard deviation of standard normal distribution, respectively.

Of course, the change in probability depends on the set of values of all explanatory variables measured at the start. This is what we call the base case. For example, if the interest coverage ratio at the start is 0.1, and we increase it by 1 unit to 1.1, the probability reduces by 4.5%, as shown in Table 8.16.

Now, let us turn to the logit model, where we evaluate the logarithm of the odds, $\ln \frac{P}{(1-p)}$, using the estimated coefficient times the corresponding values for explanatory variables. Next, we take exponentials of the result to obtain the odds ratio, $\frac{p}{(1-p)}$. Suppose that the later ratio has the value $b$, then the probability $p = \frac{b}{(1+b)}$. Following the procedure we used for the probit model, we obtain the following results for the logit model (Table 8.17):

**Table 8.14** Base forecast

| Explanatory variable | Value |
|---|---|
| Current ratio | 1.654 |
| Inverted sales/Working capital | 1/9.573 |
| Interest coverage ratio | 1.749 |
| Total debt/ EBITDA | 5.138 |
| Operating profit margin after depreciation | 0.144 |

**Table 8.15** Impact of a unit increase in interest coverage ratio from 1.749, using probit model

| | Before change | After change |
|---|---|---|
| Z | −1.131 | −1.304 |
| Probability (Z) | 0.129 | 0.096 |
| Change in probability | | −0.033 |

**Table 8.16** Impact of a unit increase in interest coverage ratio from 0.1, using probit model

| | Before change | After change |
|---|---|---|
| Z | −0.846 | −1.019 |
| Probability (Z) | 0.199 | 0.154 |
| Change in probability | | −0.045 |

**Table 8.17** Impact of a unit increase in interest coverage ratio from 1.749, using logit model

| | Before change | After change |
|---|---|---|
| $\text{Ln}[p/(1-p)]$ | −1.786 | −2.098 |
| Odds ratio: $p/(1-p)$ | 0.168 | 0.123 |
| Change in odds ratio | | −0.045 |
| Probability: $p$ | 0.144 | 0.109 |
| Change in probability | | −0.034 |

Again, we observe that the change in probability depends on the value of all explanatory variables in the base case. We follow the procedure we use for the probit model: Suppose that the base value for interest coverage ratio is 0.1 and we increase it by 1, then the probability of default reduces from 3.4% as shown in the previous table to 4.9% as shown in Table 8.18.

In the cases considered earlier, the changes in probability of a unit increase in the interest coverage ratio on the probability of default are slightly higher for the logit model compared to the probit model. This is not a general result regarding probit and logit models so that the opposite may be true in different cases, such as the case considered in Table 8.13.

**Table 8.18** Impact of a unit increase in interest coverage ratio from 0.1, using logit model

|                          | Before change | After change |
|--------------------------|---------------|--------------|
| $Ln[p/(1 - p)]$          | −1.273        | −1.584       |
| Odds Ratio: $p/(1 - p)$  | 0.28          | 0.205        |
| Change in odds Ratio     |               | −0.075       |
| Probability: $p$         | 0.219         | 0.17         |
| Change in probability    |               | −0.049       |

We have shown that in general for the multivariable case, the marginal changes are not constant but depend on the base values of all variables.

## 8.7 Practical Applications of the Logit Function

### 8.7.1 Predicting the Probability of Default

Let us assume we select logit Model L1 presented in Table 8.11 and we want to use it to predict the probability of default for a new firm that is outside the sample. To do this, we need to measure the value of current ratio and other explanatory variables in that model for the new firm and simply input the values in the right-hand-side of the equation. Such input values times the corresponding estimated coefficients would result in the probability of default for the new firm. If this probability is greater than, say, 0.5, then we can conclude that there is more than 50% chance that the new firm will experience default.

### 8.7.2 Scaling the Log-Odds Ratio

The estimated logit function is perfectly suitable to supplement credit assessment using a hybrid model, which we presented in Chap. 3. But, for business application, it may be important not to use the natural output of the logit function, that is, the *log-odds*, but a different measure of *discrete numbers* that is intuitive to clients, users, and sales staff, the majority of whom tend to be non-experts. The question becomes how we create an application scorecard to predict the probability that a borrower will default or not default.

Let us revisit the logit Eq. 8.6.

$$p_i = \frac{1}{1 + e^{-z_i}}$$

where $z_i = \alpha + \beta x_i$ the estimated linear logit regression. Suppose we evaluate the $z_i$ function at 0.35 and 3.70. One might ask what appears or is psychologically more significant: going from 0.35 to 3.70 or, alternatively, from 35 to 370 if we multiple the original $Z$-values by 100. Non-experts are more likely to choose the second. More confusing would be negative $Z$-scores. Clearly, a major reason for modifying the logit score is for easier understanding. The three properties of a scale are the following:

1. Total score is positive.
2. There is one reference or anchor score.
3. Differences in score have constant meaning throughout the scale.

## 8.7.3 Scaling Calculation

In this section, we introduce the basics of scaling calculations following the works of N. Siddiqi (2006) and L. Thomas (2009).[9] The process of rescaling involves applying a linear transformation to the log-odds score to obtain this general form:

$$\text{Scaled score} = \alpha + \beta * \ln(\text{odds}) \tag{8.14}$$

In Eq. 8.14, we have to figure out the value of the intercept ($\alpha$) called the offset and the slope ($\beta$) called the factor. The odds come from the estimated logit function. Note that we are not estimating a linear regression because this is an exact equation, akin to rescaling the Fahrenheit temperature scale to Celsius and vice versa.

In credit scoring, one would choose a baseline or centred score. Let us suppose that we want or decide that 600 is going to be the baseline score when the good-bad odds are 15:1. This means that 6.7% (1/15) of application with a score of 600 will go delinquent on their loan. We also want the odds to double with an increase of 20 in the scaled score. The increase in the scaled score that doubles the odds is called the *pdo* (points to double the odds) and 20 is commonly used in the credit scoring business.

$$600 = \alpha + \beta * \ln(15) \tag{8.15}$$

$$620 = \alpha + \beta * \ln(30) \tag{8.16}$$

Subtracting Eqs. 8.15 from 8.16 gives

$$20 = \beta * \ln(2) \tag{8.17}$$

Hence, the general formulae for $\beta$ (using 8.17) and $\alpha$ (using 8.15) are

$$\beta = \frac{pdo}{\ln(2)} \tag{8.18}$$

$$\alpha = \text{Scaled score} - (pdo / \ln(2)) * \ln(15) \tag{8.19}$$

Plug the values $pdo$ = 20 and scaled score = 600 into 8.19 to calculate the value of the intercept:

$$\alpha = 600 - 28.85 * \ln(15) = 521.86 \tag{8.20}$$

Hence, the linear transformation to the log-odds score is:

$$\text{Scaled score} = 521.85 + 28.85 \ln(\text{odds}) \tag{8.21}$$

Notice that when the odds are 15:1, the scaled score is 600. Double the odds to 30:1 and 60:1, the scaled score increases to 620 and 640, respectively. The increase in score stays constant at 20. Therefore, a 20-point increase has a consistent meaning of the odds doubling throughout the scale, and thus easier to understand.

## 8.7.4 Cautionary Notes on the Reliance on Credit Scorecard in Credit Decisions

Three important points about scorecards are worth bearing in mind:

- The scores derived from the scaling serve the function of ranking the subject (e.g., borrowers).
- The predictive power of the scorecard derives from the strength of the logit model and the accuracy of the log-odds score to begin with; not the other way around. If the log-odds ratios are inaccurate, so would be the probabilities and, hence, the scorecard.

- The reliability of the cut-off point of a scorecard is very sensitive to the stability of the probability distribution as well as the log-odds. *This observation holds in general for all models that define cut-off point or thresholds for decision-making,*

It is clear from the above that validating or testing the predictive power of a scorecard is vital to making accurate credit decisions. The estimated parameters of the underlying analytical model, such as the logit model, can become unstable due to changes in applicants' risk profile. For example, after the 2008 financial crisis, the probability distribution of the scores might have likely shifted to the left reflecting the structural change, as Fig. 8.4 illustrates.

Various econometric procedures may be applied to test for the shift.[10]

For illustration, let us assume that the scores are graded on a normal distribution. The mean score of the Expected Distribution is 629. A bank has set the *minimum* score at 475 at which the approval rate is about 84%, and the rejection rate is 16%, the area to the left of 475 under the Expected Distribution curve. Assume also that at the 475 threshold, the expected target bad rate is 2%. If the distribution stays stable, the bank would achieve the target bad rate and the approval rate. But what if the distribution were to become unstable after a severe economic crisis hits, causing financial behaviour to change significantly. This can be represented by a shift of the distribution to the left to a mean of 603. With no change in lending policy, at the same minimum score, credit-application approvals will drop. This is depicted by a larger rejection area under the new distribution after the crisis. At the same time, the target bad rate will rise because the quality of the credit applications deteriorated.

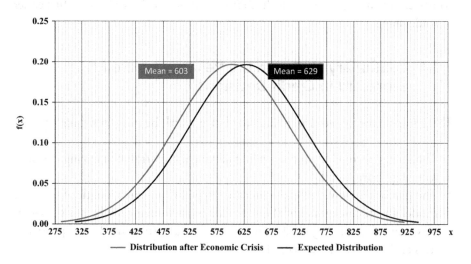

**Fig. 8.4** Shift in the distribution of credit scores

A change in the risk profile of a population from which the data sample for estimation originated requires model redevelopment and update of the estimated parameters[11] of the logit model that generated the log-odds output for the function have changed. Recall that the input for the Credit Scorecard was the output of the logit model (see Eq. 8.16). Alternatively, if the redevelopment is not feasible due to the lack of data, then the credit policy must adjust. For example, with a target bad rate of 2%, the minimum score has to increase. Short of redevelopment, there are various "fixes" discussed in Siddiqi (2006).[12]

## Notes

1. Pindyck. Robert, Rubinfeld. Daniel (1976), *Econometric Models and Economic Forecasts,* 4th Edition, Irwin/McGraw-Hill. Refer to Chapter 11 for a full discussion of these probability models. For a more theoretical discussion, the interested reader may also benefit from consultation. Chapters 1 and 2 of G. S. Maddala, *Limited-Dependent and Qualitative Variables in Econometrics,* Cambridge University Press, 1983.
2. For proof, see Pindyck and Rubinfeld (1976).
3. There are other candidates for the link function but the normal probability function is the most common.
4. Recall that a function is a mechanism that takes an input (or many inputs for that matter) and produces a *unique* output. For example, take a practical example we do every day on a road trip without even thinking about it, such as $Y = f(x) = 100X$, where $X$ is hour, 100 is the speed limit in kilometres per hour, and $Y$ is distance travelled in kilometres. The inputs in this function are the various values of $X$, and the output is distance. For example, after 2 hours, distance travelled is 200 km. Sometimes, however, we want to know how long it will take to cover 200 km, so in this case, the input is distance and the output is time in hours. Hence, we need a rule to work backwards and this is the inverse function. Since we are *multiplying* $X$ by 100, we now have to do the opposite of *dividing* $Y$ by 100 and we get the inverse function: $f^{-1}(Y) = \dfrac{Y}{100}$. Plug $Y = 200$ km into the inverse function (denoted by the $^{-}1$ sign) and the answer is 2 hours.
5. Maximum likelihood estimation is finding the values of the parameters of a likelihood function that produces the maximum likelihood. It involves differentiating the *log* of the likelihood function with respect to $p_i$ and setting the equation to zero. The log translation simplifies the calculus by transforming the likelihood function, which is a product of terms, into a simpler linear form that is easier to differentiate.

6. The logit function is written as:

$$F(z) = \frac{\exp(z)}{1 + \exp(z)}$$

where $z$, the input, is any real number, and $F(z)$ produces a value in the (0,1) range. We know this is the range because if we examine the limiting property of the $F(z)$, as $z$ goes to $-\infty$, the numerator approaches 0, whilst the denominator approaches 1; hence, $F(z)$ approaches 0. As $z$ goes to $+\infty$, the numerator and the denominator get larger and larger (so the 1 in the denominator can be ignored); hence, $F(z)$ approaches 1. Therefore, we can restate the above expression as a

$$p = \frac{\exp(z)}{1 + \exp(z)}$$

$$1 - p = \frac{1 + \exp(z) - \exp(z)}{1 + \exp(z)} = \frac{1}{1 + \exp(z)}$$

Hence, the *odds ratio* is

$$\left(\frac{p}{1-p}\right) = \exp(z)$$

Taking the natural log on both sides results in

$$\ln\left(\frac{p}{1-p}\right) = z$$

In our case, $Z_i$ is the estimated $i^{th}$ value derived from the equation, $\alpha + \beta_j x_{ij}$. Given the values of $Z_i$, the probability and the odds ratio are easy to calculate.

7. Going back over the last half a century. The pioneers in this field of bankruptcy prediction were William Beaver (1967), who applied $t$ tests to evaluate the importance of individual accounting ratios, and Edward I. Altman (1968), who applied multiple discriminant analysis within a pair-matched sample. Indeed, the widely known and used Altman $Z$-score is named after the author of this influential paper, "Financial Ratios and Discriminant Analysis and Prediction of Corporate Bankruptcy", published in the *Journal of Finance*, 23, pp. 189–209. Since the Altman study, numerous other authors have extended and dug field deeper and extended by numerous authors over the last half a century.

8. The derivative of linear probability model given by Eq. (8.1) is constant, $\frac{\partial y_i}{\partial x_i} = \beta$.

   The model is generalised for more than one explanatory variable, $X_{ij}$. In contrast, in the probit and logit model, the derivatives are not constant and cannot be interpreted as the marginal effects on the dependent variable. The marginal impact of a change in $X_{i1}$ is not only $\beta_{i1}$, a constant in the linear model, but $\beta_{i1}$ is weighted by a function whose value depends on $X_{i1}$ and all other variables in the function.

9. Siddiqi, N (2006), *Credit Risk Scorecards, Developing and Implementing Intelligent Credit Scoring*, John Wiley & Sons. Lyn. C. Thomas (2009), *Consumer Credit Models, Pricing, Profit, Portfolios*, Oxford University Press, Oxford, UK.

10. The tests may include the $t$ test for the difference in the means of the two populations or the $F$ test for difference in the variance of the two populations.

11. Parameters are the most important features of a function. Put simply, these are the numbers in the model (such as the econometric models presented in the book) that have to be estimated. They are not fed into the model as input (like the values for the explanatory variables). Parameters are important because they determine the output for given values of the predictors.

12. Siddiqi, N. (2006), Chapter 8, ibid.

# 9

# Statistical Methods of Predicting Country Debt Crisis

## Chapter Objectives

1. Understand logit analysis and discriminant analysis
2. Learn to apply the models to predict sovereign debt crisis
3. Compare the two statistical approaches

## 9.1 Introduction

Figure 9.1 shows the rapid rise in cross-border lending. The volume of cross-border claims has grown from US$1 trillion in the fourth quarter of 1983 to US$17 trillion in the fourth quarter of 2018. The non-bank private sector, the fastest growing segment that includes investment funds, accounted for US$10 trillion. The total stock of cross-border lending was about the same as the combined assets of US$17.1 trillion for all US commercial banks at year-end 2018. Cross-border or international lending poses all the risks that domestic lending entails, plus additional risks that fall under country risk and sovereign risk. Regardless, we have learned in these past chapters that there are three basic principles that underpin lending:

**Electronic Supplementary Material:** The online version of this chapter (https://doi.org/10.1007/978-3-030-32197-0_9) contains supplementary material, which is available to authorized users.

© The Author(s) 2020
T. M. Yhip, B. M. D. Alagheband, *The Practice of Lending*,
https://doi.org/10.1007/978-3-030-32197-0_9

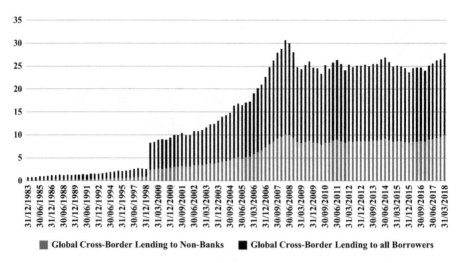

**Fig. 9.1** Cross-border lending (US dollars, trillion). (Source: BIS Consolidated Banking Statistics)

- Safety: ability and willingness of the borrower to repay interest and principal on time
- Profitability: sufficient return on the investment
- Suitability: the term and structure of the loan best suits (a) the purpose of the loan, (b) the needs of the borrower, and (c) the borrower's repayment ability

In the 1970s and 1980s, commercial banks played the leading role in recycling the current account surpluses of Organisation of Petroleum-Exporting Countries (OPEC) by providing syndicated term loans (loans provided by a group of lenders) and trade financing to sovereign borrowers. LDC (less developed country)-syndicated lending was very profitable in the 1970s. But the following decade saw a wave of debt crises in the emerging markets and, during the 1990s, recurrent crisis Latin America and Africa. As the lines in Fig. 9.2 for multilateral (comprising governments, World Bank, and International Monetary Fund [IMF]) and private creditors (includes mostly commercial banks) depict. The virtual collapse of LDC lending, combined with the deterioration in bank creditworthiness and tighter prudential banking regulations, brought a virtual end to syndicated bank lending to sovereign borrowers. Sovereign defaults dominated Western banks' lending woes throughout most of the 1980s, and receded after the banks withdrew altogether from emerging markets. Still, the market for emerging market bonds has remained active and is growing, offsetting the decline in syndicated loans.

Returns to sovereign bonds from emerging markets are several percentage points higher than generic government bonds of mature markets to compensate

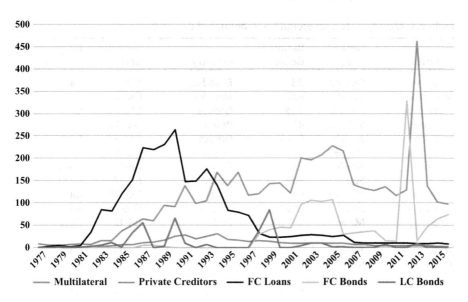

**Fig. 9.2**   Sovereign defaults (US$ millions). (Source: Bank of Canada, CRAG)

for default and restructuring risks.[1] According to a Moody's periodic report on sovereign defaults and restructuring, there have been 24 bond defaults in the period 1983–2016. The year 2017 saw a spike of four rated defaults (Belize, Mozambique, Republic of Congo, and Venezuela). In June 2018, Barbados defaulted on its foreign debt. Table 9.1 shows that all the ratings at default were below investment grade of BBB. The correlation is no coincidence. Although country ratings are not perfect predictors of sovereign default, over long periods they have been reasonably successful in warning which countries are at risk or more a risk than others are. Another observation worth noting from Table 9.1 is the relatively high rate of serial or repeated defaults. Argentina, Belize, Greece, Jamaica, and Venezuela have defaulted at least two times since 1980.

Debt restructuring includes extension of maturities, reduced interest, and haircuts. They are remedies at hand for a temporary liquidity problem, but if the diagnosis is insolvency, the problem is structural and more severe. In this type of situation, the countries usually seek long-term financial support from IMF and, in exchange for the assistance, they agree with the IMF to follow an economic stabilisation programme and achieve certain macroeconomic targets for continued financial support. As we noted before, the history of sovereign defaults is full of cases of serial defaulters. Based on Moody's, the average of bond recovery rates in 2017 was 57% and in line with the 55% for the period 1983–2017. The recovery rates vary widely, however, between 18% and 95%. Another interesting feature of sovereign defaults is that maturity extension is more common

**Table 9.1** Moody' rated sovereign bond default 1983–2018

| Country | Default date | Rating at default | Country | Default date | Rating at default |
|---|---|---|---|---|---|
| Argentina | Dec-89 | B3 | Ecuador | Mar-12 | Caa1 |
| Venezuela | Jul-98 | Ba2 | Jamaica | Feb-10 | Caa1 |
| Russia | Aig-98 | Caa1 | Greece | Mar-12 | C |
| Ukraine | Sep-98 | B3 | Belize | Sep-12 | Ca |
| Pakistan | Jul-99 | Caa1 | Greece | Dec-12 | C |
| Ecuador | Aug-99 | B3 | Jamaica | Feb-13 | B3 |
| Ukraine | Jan-00 | Caa3 | Cyprus | Jul-13 | Caa3 |
| Peru | Sep-00 | Ba3 | Argentina | Jul-14 | Caa2 |
| Argentina | Nov-01 | Caa3 | Ukraine | Oct-15 | Ca |
| Moldovia | Jun-02 | Caa1 | Mozambique | Oct-16 | B3 |
| Uruguay | Maw-03 | B3 | Republic of Congo | Jul-17 | Caa2 |
| Nicaragua | Jul-03 | Caa1 | Mozambique | Jul-17 | Caa3 |
| Dominican Republic | May-05 | B3 | Venezuela | Jul-17 | C |
| Belize | Dec-08 | Caa3 | Belize | Jul-17 | B3 |
| Nicaragua | Feb-10 | Caa1 | Barbados | Jun-18 | Caa3 |

Source: Moody's Investors Service

feature than nominal haircuts on principal. Since 1997, "all but one sovereign restructurings involved a maturity extension, while 81% involved coupon reduction and 48% involved nominal haircut on principal".[2]

# 9.2    Country and Sovereign Risk

### Don't Conflate Country Credit Risk and Sovereign Credit Risk

The former captures a *country's* economic and socio-political prospects; the latter captures narrowly the risk of the *governments* becoming unwilling or unable to meet its loan obligations. Sovereign risk ratings are usually used as proxies for the CRR, but this is not strictly correct. At the height of the Greek debt crisis in 2009–2015, the collapse of sovereign credit risk was not accompanied by an equivalent collapse in country risk, so the gap widened. The use of sovereign risk rating as a proxy for CRR for modelling corporate default would therefore be unsuitable when the two risks exhibit significant divergence.

As we have seen in previous chapters, the CRR (country risk rating) serves as a ceiling on the counterparty risk rating. Sovereign risk is the risk of a government being unable or unwilling to honour its debt obligations. In addition, there is a broader risk called country risk. Pancras Nagy (1984),[3] one of the pioneers in the development of country risk analyses in the 1980s, provides this definition of country risk:

> Country risk is exposure to a loss in ***cross-border lending*** (emphasis added), caused by events in a particular country. The events must be, at least to some extent, be under the control of the government of that country; they are definitely not under the control of a private enterprise or individual.

Risk is the potential or the possibility of both gain and loss, but in the everyday usage of the term, we usually focus on downside risk. This broad definition of county risk is from *Investopedia* and bit includes sovereign risk, economic risk, and political risk:

> Country risk refers to a set of risks associated with investing in a particular country. Country risk varies from one country to the next, and can include political risk, exchange-rate risk, economic risk, and transfer risk. In particular, country risk denotes the risk that a foreign government will default on its bonds or other financial commitments. In a broader sense, country risk is the degree to which political and economic unrest affect the securities of issuers doing business in a particular country.

In particular, a CRR or SRR (Sovereign Risk Rating) override is only relevant in credit rating in so far as the entity that is being assessed meets one of these two conditions. First, the entity is a *foreign* borrower, for example, a government, a private firm, or a bank. Second, the CRR/SRR override may also be relevant to rating a *domestic* borrower whose only source of repayment comes from its operations in the foreign country. In this case, the firm faces a gamut of risks such as country risk, sovereign risk, economic risk, and political risk. For example, the repatriation of profits might be vulnerable to nationalisation.

## 9.2.1 Approaches to Country Risk Assessment

There is no such thing as comprehensive quantitative model of country risk but various approaches to analyse, quantify, and predict some feature of it. The short and simple answer for the lack of a general theory is that country risk is multi-dimensional and too complex to describe mathematically. We do not imply that mathematics is the *only* language that makes ideas precise. In certain situations, the use of technical vocabulary can achieve the same result or minimise imprecision. But, as you see from the definitions, the explanation of country risk is confined not only to economic and financial factors but also to social and political factors.

There are various methodologies on country risk analysis with different levels of formalisation and quantification.

- Expert opinion
- Statistical/mathematical models
- Scorecard combined with expert opinion

**Expert Opinion Approach**
On a scale that goes from the lowest level of formalisation to the highest level of formalisation, *qualitative* methods would occupy the lowest end. Essential to the qualitative approach is expert knowledge and opinion. But even as country expertise is crucial in country risk analysis, its biggest drawback is inherent subjectivity. Thus, it is open to the criticism that a qualitative analysis is just another opinion. Nevertheless, a robust qualitative approach to country risk still leads to an assessment of the economic, financial, regulatory, and socio-political framework and their inter-connections. The analysis will still provide an evaluation of the profitability and repayment of a loan to foreign country, or the return prospects on a capital investment in a foreign country.

**Statistical/Mathematical Models**
As we move towards the other end of the scale, formalisation increases until at the opposite end are the highly theoretical works done mainly by academics. In between the extremes, we have a variety of econometric and mathematical approaches. We will be looking in detail at discriminant analysis and logit analysis. These are examples of parametric models where we restrict the relation between the dependent and independent variables to a specific form and estimate the regression coefficients—the parameters of the model—by some estimation procedure. The restriction on the form of the function is itself a criticism for using such models. As a result, parametric methods with non-constant (heteroscedastic) variance, and non-parametric methods to model the non-linearity, which is a characteristic property of complex and non-linear systems,[4] have become part of the credit analyst's toolbox.

It suffices to mention some of the methods although they are outside the scope of this book. They include ARCH (autoregressive conditional heteroscedasticity) model, GARCH (general autoregressive conditional heteroscedasticity) model, fractal analysis, and Markov-switching models. Since the severe 2007–2008 global financial crisis, a variety of "cutting-edge" non-linear or non-parametric models have been adapted to financial risk analysis. They include the application of *graph theory* and *chaos theory* to social network analysis, neural network, and non-linear dynamics.

Whilst all these methods are useful, the users must be mindful of their limitations. First, methodologically speaking, in regard to statistical/econometric models of single equations and systems of equations, there is the old problem of causality. Our *assumed* exogenous variables may be endogenous, or just a handful of variables may be truly exogenous to the system. Second, even with the cutting-edge models based on chaos theory (non-linear dynamical systems), getting accurate predictions of financial outcomes is all but impossible. The problem is that the behaviour of such systems is sensitive to the initial conditions, and the longer the forecast horizon, the more imprecise the predictions (think of going on a very long journey and relying on a long-range weather forecast).

## Scorecard Approach Plus Expert Opinion

This is a hybrid model with both qualitative and quantitative features, and it is essentially the same as that of the criterion-based approach. Thus, one can map the country risk ratings produced by such a model to sovereign default probabilities, as we see in Table 9.2, which summarises S&P estimates[5] of cumulative default rates for bonds for each point of their rating scale for the 1981–2018 period. A triple-A rated country has 0.4 probability of defaulting

**Table 9.2** Summary of S&P default rates (1981–2018)

| Rating | Year 1 | Year 5 | Year 10 | Year 15 |
|---|---|---|---|---|
| AAA | 0.0 | 0.4 | 0.7 | 0.9 |
| AA+ | 0.0 | 0.2 | 0.4 | 0.8 |
| AA | 0.0 | 0.4 | 0.9 | 1.3 |
| AA− | 0.0 | 0.3 | 0.7 | 0.9 |
| A+ | 0.1 | 0.4 | 1.0 | 1.8 |
| A | 0.1 | 0.5 | 1.4 | 2.1 |
| A− | 0.1 | 0.5 | 1.3 | 1.9 |
| BBB+ | 0.1 | 1.0 | 2.2 | 3.4 |
| BBB | 0.2 | 1.4 | 3.1 | 4.3 |
| BBB− | 0.2 | 2.8 | 5.4 | 7.4 |
| BB+ | 0.3 | 3.7 | 7.0 | 9.3 |
| BB | 0.5 | 6.2 | 11.0 | 13.5 |
| BB− | 1.0 | 9.3 | 16.5 | 20.2 |
| B+ | 2.0 | 14.2 | 21.5 | 25.1 |
| B | 3.4 | 17.1 | 23.7 | 26.9 |
| B− | 6.8 | 25.4 | 31.4 | 33.5 |
| CCC/C | 26.9 | 46.1 | 50.4 | 52.8 |
| Investment grade | 0.1 | 0.9 | 2.0 | 2.8 |
| Speculative grade | 3.7 | 14.6 | 20.6 | 23.7 |
| All rated | 1.5 | 6.1 | 8.9 | 10.4 |

Source: S&P, 2018 Annual Global Corporate Default All rated Transition Study
Table 26: Global Corporate Average Cumulative Default Rates By Rating Modifier (1981–2018)

over the next five years, whereas a triple-B rated country has a 1.4% cumulative average probability of defaulting in Year 5. Speculative grades are more highly correlated with defaults than investment.

## 9.3  Providers of Country Risk Ratings and Sovereign Risk Ratings

Since the 1990s many banks have done away with in-house country risk rating (and industry risk rating) through outsourcing the same information to external providers who specialise in these areas. For example, the Economist Intelligence Unit (EIU) provides country risk scores on a scale 0–100 for 131 countries, based on a simple average of sovereign risk, currency risk, and banking sector risk. The EIU model is updated three times a year. Euromoney[6] provides country risk scores, also on a scale 0–100, derived from surveys of 400 economists. The scores are updated at regular intervals. Another service, Political Risk Service,[7] provides forecasts of country risk scores on a scale 0–100 for 140 countries, derived from a set of 22 components representing three major categories of risk: political, financial, and economic, with political risk comprising 12 components (and 15 subcomponents), and financial and economic risk each comprising five components. The scores are then grouped into discrete ranges:

- Very high risk: 0.0–49.9 points
- High risk: 50.0–59.9 points
- Moderate risk: 60.0–69.9 points
- Low risk: 70.0–79.9 points
- Very low risk: 80.0–100 points

The rating agencies, Moody's, S&P, and Fitch have their own versions of country/sovereign risk analysis for more than 100 ratings apiece. They provide two ratings for each country—a local currency rating (for domestic currency debt or bonds) and a foreign currency rating (for government borrowings in a foreign currency). Their list of countries now includes emerging economies as the market for sovereign bonds has expanded over the years. Standard and Poor's methodology[8] comprises an assessment of five risk categories: institutional, economic, external, fiscal, and monetary. Moody's methodology[9] is based on four "broad risk factors": economic strength, institutional strength, fiscal strength, and susceptibility to event risk.

Depending on the rating services that develop and fine-tune their models, there are differences in the categorisation of risk classes, their sub-factors, and in the number of variables. Nonetheless, they follow a criteria-based methodology and therefore they share some common characteristics:

1. A breakdown of the overall country risk into its broad risk categories.
2. The application of theory and practice to decide which quantitative and qualitative predictors to use.
3. Specification of quantitative and qualitative descriptors to differentiate risk ratings.
4. Weighting or not weighting the predictors.
5. Provision for an override functionally in the scorecard.
6. The calculation of a composite score based on a simple average (where no weights are assigned), or a weighted average.
7. The scores provide an *ordinal* or a relative ranking or rating. For example, take two scores: 80 for country A and 20 for country B. An ordinal ranking means that A is better than B but not four times better than B (which is a cardinal rating).

Also, depending on the service vendor, the models provide "point-in-time" and "through-the-cycle" ratings. Table 9.3 summarises the indicators for the four categories of Moody's sovereign rating methodology. The methodologies of other external rating agencies and the EIU (Economist Intelligence Unit) are not strikingly different.

Other services use the same predictors, albeit measured differently. For example, the EVI (External Vulnerability Indicator) is an indicator of *liquidity* strength and is measured by the ratio of residual maturity short-term debt (including original maturity short-term debt and principal payments on long-term debt) falling due in the *current year* to official foreign reserves at the end of the *previous year*. The ratio compares a "bad" number with a "good" number. Therefore, a high ratio signals vulnerability because of high short-term debt or a bunching of repayments on long-term debt coming due relative to the level of reserves that may be low to begin out with. The higher is the ratio, the higher the vulnerability.

## 9.4 Applying Logit Analysis to Predict Sovereign Debt Crisis

Both the CRR and SRR are useful to compare risk across countries. In addition, because the ratings are reasonably correlated with sovereign debt crisis (see Table 9.2), they are useful composite indicators of sovereign default 12 months out. However, suppose that we wanted a timelier heads up. This is where an in-house early warning model of sovereign debt crises is advantageous because, as we will address in detail later, many of the predictors of sovereign debt crisis are different from those of the CRR and SRR in their theoretical constructs and measurements.

**Table 9.3** Indicators of sovereign rating methodology

| Broad rating factors | Indicators |
|---|---|
| Economic strength | |
| | Average Real GDP Growth (t–4 to t+5) |
| | Volatility in Real GDP Growth (t–9 to t) |
| | WEF Global Competitiveness Index |
| | Nominal GDP (US$ bn) t |
| | GDP per capita (PPP, US$) t |
| Institutional strength | |
| | Worldwide Government Effectiveness Index |
| | Worldwide Rule of Law Index |
| | Worldwide Control of Corruption Index |
| | Inflation Level (t–4 to t+5) |
| | Inflation Volatility(t–9 to t) |
| Fiscal strength | |
| | General Government Debt/GDP (%) |
| | General Government Debt/Revenues (%) |
| | General Government Interest Payments/Revenue (%) |
| | General Government Interest Payments/GDP (%) |
| | Debt Trend (t–4 to t+1) |
| | General Government Foreign Currency Debt/General Government Debt (%) |
| | Other Public Sector Debt |
| Susceptibility to event risk | |
| | Domestic Political Risk |
| | Geopolitical Risk |
| | Market Funding Stress |
| | Strength and Size of Banking System |
| | Funding Vulnerabilities |
| | (Current Account Balance + FDI Inflows)/GDP |
| | External Vulnerability Indicator (EVI) |
| | Net International Investment Position |

Source: Moody's Ratings Methodology Sovereign Bond Ratings December 2016

In this section, our aim is to show how the methodology of the logit model applies to predict the probability of *sovereign debt crisis,* a procedure akin to predicting corporate bankruptcy that we showed in Chap. 8. We use "sovereign" and "country" interchangeably since a *sovereign* debt crisis is the inability of a *country* to pay the bills owing to foreign creditors. We begin by defining what we mean by a country in debt crisis and we choose a simple but serviceable definition to describe such a situation: *A country in external debt crisis is one that has defaulted on its foreign debt or is unable to meet contractual payments on its foreign debt and is seeking IMF bailout.*

The entire aim of this chapter is *application* using actual country data. As part of the learning exercise, we will introduce the use of dummy independent variables, or binary variables, in a logit model. As you go through the various formulation of the models we present, it will become clear that estimation is not like following a *magic* recipe. In practice, one often estimates and tests many formulations of the function based on certain important criteria, not all of which are met satisfactorily. The choice of the final model involves theoretical and statistical trade-offs, as you will see from the forthcoming examples.

The literature on sovereign debt crisis covers four broad areas:

1. Theories of sovereign default
2. Empirical studies of the determinants of payments crisis
3. Empirical studies of the predictive power of credit ratings of the rating agencies
4. Empirical studies of the determination of spreads on emerging market debt

Although there is no comprehensive theory of debt crisis, taken together, the literature suggests certain economic and non-economic regularities of countries that have experienced sovereign default and payments crisis. Numerous indicators, such as the ones shown in Table 9.3, have been developed. We use some of these in the examples to illustrate the application of statistical models to analyse binary and categorical response variables.

We apply the logit model to a sample of 40 LDCs (less developed countries), of which 24 defaulted during 1980–1985. This period is famously known as the *1980s Debt Crisis* that followed the recycling of "petrodollars" in the 1970s. During this period, oil prices spiked up and OPEC countries were depositing the excess oil revenues in foreign commercial banks (this, by the way, is an example of a wholesale deposit). Until the start of the debt crisis in the early 1980s, syndicated bank lending to LDCs was more profitable than domestic lending. Most of the countries that defaulted in this first wave of the debt crisis were from Latin America crippled by economic stagnation, hyperinflation, and political crises. However, the region was not unique in these respects because Turkey, the Philippines, and countries in Africa also defaulted. The sample is a cross-section of developing countries.

To illustrate the application of the logit model, we look at six broad factors and their sub-factors for the 40 LDCs noted above (see Appendix 9.1 for the country list and debt crisis episodes). These are the metrics used to describe the risk categories. Not surprisingly, some of the measurements for insolvency, illiquidity, and debt structure resemble the financial ratios that we use as the bellwethers for corporate bankruptcy in Chap. 8. The other metrics capture macroeconomic imbalance, openness of the economy, and political uncertainty. Table 9.4 shows the expected sign for the impact of the variable on the probability of default (PD).

**Table 9.4**  Predictors of sovereign debt default

| Risk categories/Sub-factors | Logit coefficient signs | Mnemonics |
|---|---|---|
| 1. Macroeconomic imbalance | | |
| *Real GDP Growth (%)* | −ve | GDP |
| *Inflation Rate, CPI based (%)* | +ve | INF |
| *Current Account Balance/GDP (%)* | +ve | CABpGDP |
| 2. Insolvency | | |
| *Total External Debt/GDP (%)* | +ve | ExtDpGDP |
| *Total Debt Service/Foreign Reserves (%)* | +ve | DSpFR |
| *Total Debt Service/Exports of G&S and Primary Income (%)* | +ve | DSpE |
| 3. Illiquidity | | |
| *Short-Term Debt/Foreign Reserves (%)* | +ve | STDpFR |
| *Total Foreign Reserves (months import cover)* | −ve | RMICov |
| 4. Debt structure | | |
| *Concessional Debt/Total External Debt (%)* | −ve | CDpExtD |
| *Short-term Debt/Total External Debt (%)* | +ve | STDpTED |
| 5. Openness | | |
| *(Export + Import of G&S)/GDP* | −ve | EpIpGDP |
| 6. Political uncertainty | | |
| *Political shock or disruption before default (e.g., military coup, general elections)* | +ve | PI |

In logit analysis, the independent variables cannot take on any signs but the expected signs to be of any meaning. Conversely, in discriminant analysis (which we will cover later) the linear combination of the independent variables is important rather than the signs of the coefficients. This distinction is important to bear in mind. For example, the higher "Total External Debt/ GDP" the higher would be the probability of default so it must have a positive (+ve) impact on that probability if we are estimating a logit model. From each category of risk, one measurement was selected as an explanatory variable. Alternative measures of the same risk category were also tested to obtain the best possible fit.

## 9.4.1  Rationale for the Expected Signs of the Predictors

1. Inverse of Nominal GDP Growth (1/GDP+INF)

Declining production coupled with high and rising inflation indicates macroeconomic imbalance. According to the empirical literature, real growth weakens or declines in the years before crisis entry whilst inflation spikes. Therefore, the likelihood of a payments and debt crisis is less likely in a growing economy and, conversely, more likely with inflation, which causes overvaluation of the nominal exchange rate. In various specifications that we tried, the logistic equation could not measure the separate effects in a sensible way due to the correlation amongst the explanatory variables. However, the combined effect, or nominal GDP, turns out to be a statistically significant predictor with the expected sign. It is as if the model does not need to distinguish between the INF and GDP, but their combined effect. We find that the best measure of macroeconomic imbalance is the inverse of nominal GDP growth. Depending on which component of it (INF or GDP) dominates, the metric takes the *opposite* sign of that factor. We find that inflation overwhelms nominal GDP growth for the countries in the sample. For those that defaulted, the median GDP growth was −1.0% and the median inflation rate was 21.5%, whereas, for those that did not default in the same period, the corresponding rates were 5.3 and 10.7%.

## 2.  Debt Service Payments as a Percentage of Total Foreign Reserves (DSpFR)

Sovereign default results from insolvency, which is the inability to repay interest and principal payments. We expect the coefficient of this variable to be positive.

## 3.  Short-Term Debt as Percentage of Total Foreign Debt (STDpFR)

Sovereign default results from illiquidity, an acute shortage of foreign exchange. Short-term debt is debt coming due in 1 year. If properly structured, a country can avoid a bunching of maturities that pushes up short-term debt, but often that is not the case. In addition, countries that borrow heavily for trade financing build up high levels of short-term debt. When all these short-term payments come due at the same time, whilst the country's foreign reserves can barely cover necessary merchandise imports like food, medicines, machinery, and agricultural supplies, a debt crisis erupts. The country either undertakes pre-emptive debt restructuring usually with an IMF-supported programme to avoid arrears and minimise any reduction in net capital inflow, or halts repayments on its external debt.[10] For example, Barbados declared in June 2018 that it would not pay the 26th coupon on Eurobonds maturing in 2035, and its Sovereign Risk rating tumbled. The country's foreign reserves had dwindled to less than 2 months' import cover. Barbados' problem of inadequate reserves against severe domestic and external economic shocks is not just a liquidity problem but also a solvency problem requiring structural or longer-term solutions. As far as the probability model is concerned, we would expect the coefficient of short-term debt/total foreign debt to be positive.

### 4. Concessional Debt as a Percentage of Total External Debt (CDpExtD)

By definition, concessional loans have longer maturities, lower interest rates, and longer grace period than commercial loans, so debt servicing is more manageable. We expect the coefficient of this variable to be negative because the higher the share of concessional financing the lower the likelihood of default or a payments crisis.

### 5. Trade Openness (EpIpGDP)

The openness of a country to international trade, measured by the sum of exports and imports as a percent of GDP, influences default. The higher is the openness or the dependence of a country on foreign trade, the higher the costs of default and hence, the lower the likelihood the country would choose to default. Therefore, we expect the coefficient for Trade Openness to be negative.

### 6. Political Uncertainty/Instability (PI)

Economic uncertainty and political uncertainty feed on each other in a vicious circle and determining the cause is not easy, but one can argue on the basis of history that economic uncertainty arises from political uncertainty. The defaults in many LDCs, particularly countries in Latin America in the late 1970s and 1980s, were preceded by military coup and general elections. We capture the instability or political shock by a dummy variable, which takes the values of 0 for stable countries, 0.5 for countries that have cross-border and domestic political tensions, and 1 for those experiencing political upheavals such as military coup. We expect the sign of the dummy variable to be positive.

## 9.4.2  The Estimated Logistic Function: Key Criteria for Choosing the Best Fit

The model selection is based on the standard regression criteria including high (adjusted) R-squared, high likelihood ratio (LR), and estimated coefficients having the expected sign and reasonable magnitude. To demonstrate this point, we present two estimated models below. Here, the dependent variable is the probability of default (PD). For the historical period, PD equals 1 if the country defaulted; 0 otherwise. The first model includes one measurement for each of the risk categories shown in Table 9.4. We can think of this formulation as the "full model". Below is the SAS output (Table 9.5).

**Table 9.5** Estimated logistic function – model A (full model)

| Variable | Coefficient | Std. error | Z-statistic | Prob. |
|---|---|---|---|---|
| Constant | 6.992616 | 7.2904 | 0.959154 | 0.3375 |
| 1/(GDP+INF) | −82.22669 | 65.30002 | −1.259214 | 0.208 |
| DSpFR | 0.025015 | 0.016608 | 1.163097 | 0.2448 |
| STDpTED | 0.019192 | 0.014347 | 1.337741 | 0.181 |
| CDpExtD | −0.069354 | 0.062439 | −1.110753 | 0.2667 |
| EPIpGDP | −0.147352 | 0.167257 | −0.880991 | 0.3783 |
| PI | 1.4854 | 2.319566 | 0.640379 | 0.5219 |
| McFadden R-squared | 0.81852 | Mean dependent var | | 0.6 |
| S.D. dependent var. | 0.496139 | S.E. of regression | | 0.224169 |
| Akaike info criterion | 0.594277 | Sum squared resid | | 1.658304 |
| Schwarz criterion | 0.88983 | Log likelihood | | −4.88553 |
| Hannan–Quinn criter. | 0.701139 | Deviance | | 9.771061 |
| Restr. deviance | 53.84093 | Restr. log likelihood | | −26.9205 |
| LR statistic | 44.06987 | Avg. log likelihood | | −0.12214 |
| Prob(LR statistic) | 0 | | | |
| Model prediction: | | | | |
| Actual | Active | | Bankrupt | |
| Active | 14 | | 2 | |
| Bankrupt | 1 | | 23 | |

The $R$-squared is high and all estimated coefficients have the expected signs. The model also predicts default for 23 (out of 24) defaulted countries (bankrupt for short) reflecting 96% accuracy in this regard. Notice, however, that the standard errors are about as large as the coefficients, so the $Z$-statistics are too low to declare statistical significance.

In contrast with the "full model", the following has lower $R$-squared without the variable for macroeconomic imbalance, marginally worse performance in predicting default, but marginally better performance in predicting non-default. All predictors have the expected signs; however, as with the full model, the $Z$-statistics are too low to support statistical significance (Table 9.6).

The first model would be our selected model if we want to account for one factor per risk category. However, despite high $R$-squared and statistically significant likelihood ratio, the $Z$-statistics (which have asymptotic standard normal distribution) in the full model are not statistically significant. The result reflects the presence of multicollinearity amongst the included explanatory variables rather than the variables lacking theoretical importance.

In order to obtain a functional specification for which all variables are statistically significant, a common practice is to delete statistically insignificant variables one at a time so that, at each step, one deletes the explanatory variable with the lowest $Z$-statistic. Doing so yields model C (Table 9.7).

**Table 9.6** Estimated logistic function – model B

| Variable | Coefficient | Std. error | Z-statistic | Prob. |
|---|---|---|---|---|
| Constant | 1.01712 | 2.394268 | 0.424815 | 0.671 |
| DSpFR | 0.016281 | 0.016644 | 0.978139 | 0.328 |
| STDFR | 0.005612 | 0.00498 | 1.126844 | 0.2598 |
| CDpExtD | −0.051374 | 0.035611 | −1.442662 | 0.1491 |
| EPIpGDP | −0.075007 | 0.079773 | −0.940264 | 0.3471 |
| PI | 2.337528 | 1.847536 | 1.265214 | 0.2058 |
| McFadden R-squared | 0.752152 | Mean dependent var | | 0.6 |
| S.D. dependent var. | 0.496139 | S.E. of regression | | 0.258215 |
| Akaike info criterion | 0.633609 | Sum squared resid | | 2.266957 |
| Schwarz criterion | 0.886941 | Log likelihood | | −6.672179 |
| Hannan–Quinn criter. | 0.646838 | Deviance | | 13.34436 |
| Restr. deviance | 53.84093 | Restr. log likelihood | | −26.92047 |
| LR statistic | 40.49658 | Avg. log likelihood | | −0.166804 |
| Prob(LR statistic) | 0 | | | |
| Model prediction: | | | | |
| Actual | Active | | Bankrupt | |
| Active | 15 | | 1 | |
| Bankrupt | 2 | | 22 | |

**Table 9.7** Estimated logistic function – model C

| Variable | Coefficient | Std. error | Z-statistic | Prob. |
|---|---|---|---|---|
| Constant | −0.089413 | 0.894124 | −0.100001 | 0.9203 |
| 1/(GDP+INF) | −55.27349 | 23.87394 | −2.315223 | 0.0206 |
| STDpTED | 0.025523 | 0.009434 | 2.705391 | 0.0068 |
| McFadden R-squared | 0.684796 | Mean dependent var | | 0.6 |
| S.D. dependent var. | 0.496139 | S.E. of regression | | 0.276108 |
| Akaike info criterion | 0.574272 | Sum squared resid | | 2.820714 |
| Schwarz criterion | 0.700938 | Log likelihood | | −8.485448 |
| Hannan–Quinn criter. | 0.620071 | Deviance | | 16.9709 |
| Restr. deviance | 36.87004 | Restr. log likelihood | | −26.92047 |
| LR statistic | 40.49658 | Avg. log likelihood | | −0.212136 |
| Prob(LR statistic) | 0 | | | |
| Model prediction: | | | | |
| Actual | Active | | Bankrupt | |
| Active | 14 | | 2 | |
| Bankrupt | 2 | | 22 | |

Model C is simpler with only two explanatory variables, which are statistically significant. Not surprisingly, the simple model has a lower $R$-squared, compared to the full model. $R$-squared tends to decrease as one or more explanatory variable are deleted from the model, regardless of their theoretically relevance. The asymptotic likelihood ratio (LR) obtained from deleting three variables from the full model to arrive at the small model is not statistically significant at 5% level. The related calculations are presented below using the regression results for models A and C:

$$LR = -2 \times \big( \log - \text{likelihood for the unrestricted} \, (\text{larger}) \, \text{model}$$
$$- \log - \text{likelihood for the restricted} \, (\text{smaller}) \, \text{model} \big)$$
$$= 2 \times \big[ (-4.885531) - (-8.485448) \big] = 7.199834$$

We compare the latter figure with chi-square value with 3 (which is the number of deleted variables) degrees of freedom at 5% significance, which is 9.488. Since 7.1998 < 9.488, we cannot reject the deleted variables had zero coefficients; however, the prediction performance of the smaller model is marginally worse compared to the earlier models.

In practice, a regression model normally includes the intercept. This ensures that the error term would have zero mean. However, we may delete the intercept since the estimated coefficient is statistically insignificant. The prediction results remain unchanged without the intercept. It should be noted that in a linear model without intercept, $R$-squared is known not to be bounded between 0 and 1 (and is not shown by the EViews software used to estimate it). The regression results for the latter case are presented below. The $Z$-statistics for both Model C (except for intercept) and Model D are greater than 2, signifying that the variables are estimated with greater precision (Table 9.8).

**Practical Application of a Logit Model**

Let us assume we select Model D and we want to use it to predict the probability of default for a new country that is outside the sample. To do this, we need to measure the value of 1/(GDP+INF) and STDpFR for the new country and simply use the values as inputs in the right-hand side of the equation. These values times the corresponding estimated coefficients result in the prob-

**Table 9.8** Estimated logistic function – model D

| Variable | Coefficient | Std. error | Z-statistic | Prob. |
|---|---|---|---|---|
| 1/(GDP+INF) | −33.1847 | 11.37429 | −2.917517 | 0.0035 |
| STDpFR | 0.015229 | 0.00498 | 3.057881 | 0.0022 |
| Mean dependent var | 0.6 | S.D. dependent var | | 0.496139 |
| S.E. of regression | 0.27141 | Akaike info criterion | | 0.516309 |
| Sum squared resid | 2.799217 | Schwarz criterion | | 0.600753 |
| Log likelihood | −8.326173 | Hannan–Quinn criter. | | 0.546841 |
| Deviance | 16.65235 | Restr. deviance | | 53.84093 |
| Avg. log likelihood | −0.208154 | | | |
| Model prediction: | | | | |
| Actual | Active | | Bankrupt | |
| Active | 14 | | 2 | |
| Bankrupt | 2 | | 22 | |

ability of default for the new country. If this probability is greater than, say, 0.5, then we can conclude that there is more than 50% chance that the new country will experience default.

# 9.5    Introduction to Discriminant Analysis

Like logit analysis, discriminant analysis is a statistical method for handling classification problem (see W.W. Cooley and P. R. Lohnes (1971), B. Efron (1975), D. J. Hand (1981)).[11] It is used to classify one or more new cases into one of the population groups whose characteristics are known. This procedure is performed by matching characteristics of the new case(s) with those of the population groups. The best match is selected on the basis of probability analysis. Altman (1968) and Altman et al. (1977),[12] for example, used the technique to predict firm bankruptcy. In the case of sovereign risk analysis, the idea is to classify countries according to whether or not they are likely to default. Discriminant analysis has application in credit analysis as well as in many other fields (see W.R. Klecka (1980)).[13]

## 9.5.1  Forming Population Groups

Multivariate regression method is used to link measured characteristics of population groups to a categorical variable representing the groups' labels so that each category corresponds to one population group. In general, the error term is assumed to be normally distributed. If the error terms for all groups share the same variance-covariance matrix, then a *linear* discriminant model is used to assign a new case to one of the groups. In contrast, if the variance-covariance matrix differs across groups, then a *quadratic* discriminant model is used. In either case, the model is estimated by taking into account the variance-covariance matrix of the error terms, using a computer software such as Statistical Analysis System (SAS), MINITAB, and R. The procedure yields an estimated discriminant model for each group, also known as discriminant function. Maximum likelihood method is used to estimate the models.

For simplicity, consider the case where five variables (see Table 9.9) are used to discriminate between two types of companies—those with poor performance and those with strong performance. Knowing the financial status of the companies would help to explore if the discriminant analysis method would work the way it is supposed to do so. Each of the five independent variables reflects a particular aspect of financial strength of the company, as follows (Table 9.9).

**Table 9.9** Definition of the variables used in the model

| Variable | As a measure of: | Mnemonics |
|---|---|---|
| Current rate | Liquidity | LIQ |
| Net sales to receivables (days) | Efficiency | EFF |
| EBIT/Interest | Cash flow | CSH |
| Total liability/TNW | Leverage | LEV |
| Net income before tax/TNW (%) | Profitability | PRO |

Notes: TNW (total net worth) and EBIT (earnings before interest and tax)

Table 9.10 reports the data, which represent simulated financial ratios for two sets of companies, with the first set performing better than the other does.

## 9.5.2 Classification Test

To examine to which group a new case would belong, the measured character-istics for the new case are used to determine the probabilities that the new observation would belong to each group. Thus, a likelihood function for each group is used for that purpose. Accordingly, the new case is considered to belong to the group that corresponds to the highest likelihood. Some details in this regard follow.

Let $\Sigma_j$ be the variance-covariance matrix for group $j$. We can estimate $\Sigma_j$ using information of group $j$, denoted by $\hat{\Sigma}_j$, or if they are considered to be identical by $\hat{\Sigma}_p$ using all sample information. We refer to the former as within-group variance-covariance matrix and the latter, the pooled variance-covariance matrix and is calculated as

$$\hat{\Sigma}_p = \frac{\sum_{j=1}^{g}(n_j - 1)\hat{\Sigma}_j}{\sum_{j=1}^{g}(n_j - 1)} \tag{9.1}$$

where $n_j$ is the number of observations in group $j$ and $g$ is the total number of groups. Thus $\hat{\Sigma}_p$ estimates a common variance-covariance matrix, say, $\Sigma_p$. Conventionally, we use bold font to represent vectors and matrices (e.g., $\Sigma$ is a square matrix) and normal font for scalars and integers.

We can test whether the within-group variance-covariance matrices, or the pooled variance-covariance matrices should be used using a chi-square test (D. F. Morrison, 1976).[14] Using SAS for the problem at hand, the hypothesis of homogeneity of the variance-covariance matrix is rejected, so within-group variance-covariance matrices are to be used to perform the analysis (Table 9.11). The SAS software produces the following output:

**Table 9.10** Simulated ratios for two groups

| Group | LIQ | EFF | CSH | LEV | PRO |
|---|---|---|---|---|---|
| 1 | 1.8 | 78.0 | 17.0 | 1.1 | 43.6 |
| 1 | 3.0 | 51.3 | 50.3 | 0.5 | 90.5 |
| 1 | 2.3 | 77.0 | 34.0 | 0.8 | 84.0 |
| 1 | 1.9 | 72.0 | 23.0 | 0.6 | 78.0 |
| 1 | 2.1 | 77.0 | 30.0 | 0.8 | 87.0 |
| 1 | 2.4 | 66.0 | 49.0 | 0.7 | 80.0 |
| 1 | 2.1 | 62.0 | 44.0 | 0.7 | 57.0 |
| 1 | 1.9 | 76.0 | 26.0 | 1.0 | 46.0 |
| 1 | 2.4 | 59.0 | 39.0 | 0.8 | 77.0 |
| 1 | 2.4 | 57.0 | 50.0 | 1.1 | 87.0 |
| 1 | 2.0 | 56.0 | 27.0 | 0.5 | 46.0 |
| 1 | 2.0 | 74.0 | 24.0 | 0.6 | 79.0 |
| 1 | 3.0 | 78.0 | 46.0 | 0.9 | 79.0 |
| 1 | 2.2 | 54.0 | 47.0 | 0.8 | 75.0 |
| 1 | 2.9 | 65.0 | 35.0 | 0.6 | 72.0 |
| 1 | 2.3 | 63.0 | 47.0 | 0.7 | 59.0 |
| 2 | 1.7 | 82.2 | 14.7 | 1.2 | 0.4 |
| 2 | 1.1 | 113.4 | 3.8 | 2.3 | 0.1 |
| 2 | 1.6 | 85.0 | 7.1 | 1.2 | 0.2 |
| 2 | 1.2 | 102.0 | 9.2 | 1.4 | 0.3 |
| 2 | 1.6 | 101.0 | 10.6 | 2.0 | 0.1 |
| 2 | 1.2 | 110.0 | 13.2 | 1.6 | 0.2 |
| 2 | 1.5 | 95.0 | 11.8 | 1.4 | 0.3 |
| 2 | 1.7 | 91.0 | 6.8 | 2.0 | 0.2 |
| 2 | 1.4 | 113.0 | 7.8 | 1.8 | 0.3 |
| 2 | 1.6 | 85.0 | 7.1 | 1.4 | 0.2 |
| 2 | 1.2 | 108.0 | 13.6 | 2.2 | 0.3 |
| 2 | 1.2 | 89.0 | 14.4 | 2.3 | 0.3 |
| 2 | 1.5 | 106.0 | 10.5 | 1.6 | 0.2 |
| 2 | 1.6 | 91.0 | 4.0 | 1.6 | 0.3 |
| 2 | 1.6 | 93.0 | 4.8 | 1.5 | 0.1 |
| 2 | 1.4 | 91.0 | 14.3 | 1.6 | 0.1 |

**Table 9.11** Test results for homogeneity of variance-covariance matrix

| $\chi^2$ | Degrees of freedom | Prob. |
|---|---|---|
| 141.169421 | 15 | <0.0001 |

Now, let $x$ represent measurements for a *new case or company*. The squared Mahalanobis generalised distance from $\mathbf{x}$ to group $j$ is given by

$$d_j^2(x) = (x - m_j)' \Sigma_j (x - m_j) \tag{9.2}$$

where $m_j$ represents a vector consisting of population mean values for group $j$ that is estimated by the sample mean measurements for group $j$, denoted by $\hat{m}_j$. Also, $\Sigma_j = \Sigma_p$ if a common variance-covariance matrix is assumed for all groups. The corresponding group-specific probability density is then given by

$$f_j(x) = (2\pi)^{-1/n_j} \left| \Sigma_j^{-1} \right|^{-1/2} \exp\left( -\frac{1}{2} d_j^2(x) \right) \tag{9.3}$$

where $\left| \Sigma_j^{-1} \right|$ is the determinant of $\Sigma_j^{-1}$. If $\Sigma_p$ is used in place of $\Sigma_j$ and all groups have an equal number of observations, then only $d_j^2(x)$ is a variable term amongst groups. In this case, the larger the Mahalanobis distance from $x$ to group $j$, the smaller is $f_j(x)$ and, therefore, the lower is the likelihood that the new case would belong to group $j$. Take the simple case of two groups. The Mahalanobis distance measures the square of the distance from $x$ to the means of two groups. In the case of two groups (e.g., group 1: default, and group 2: no default), Eq. (9.2) simplifies to

$$d_1^2(x) = (x - m_1)' \Sigma_1 (x - m_1) \text{ for group 1 and,}$$

$$d_2^2(x) = (x - m_2)' \Sigma_2 (x - m_2) \text{ for group 2.}$$

The corresponding likelihood values are

$$f_1(x) = (2\pi)^{-1/n_1} \left| \Sigma_1^{-1} \right|^{-1/2} \exp\left( -\frac{1}{2} d_1^2(x) \right)$$

and

$$f_2(x) = (2\pi)^{-1/n_2} \left| \Sigma_2^{-1} \right|^{-1/2} \exp\left( -\frac{1}{2} d_2^2(x) \right)$$

The basic rationale in **discriminant analysis** is rather simple: The larger the difference between the new case measurements $x$ and those of group $j$ (as measured by Mahalanobis distance $d_j^2(x)$, the lower the likelihood that the new case would belong to group $j$ (as measured by $f_j(x)$), here $j = 1, 2$.

Thus, for a new case or in-sample observation, if $f_1(x) > f_2(x)$, we can conclude that this particular case belongs to group 1. In practice, one does not need to work through these calculations and comparison because the work would be done by the software that one is using, such as SAS.

## 9.5.3 Accounting for Prior Information

Sometimes, the relative frequency or the probability by which each group may occur is known. For example, in a two-group analysis, if the probability by which group 1 may occur is three times more compared to group 2, we may want to take that information into account. Thus, these probabilities would imply that a new case is three times more probable to belong to group 1. In this case, we may assign prior probability of 0.75 to the first group and 0.25 to the second. More generally, there are three options to incorporate the prior probabilities into the analysis as follows.

(a) Equal probabilities: Assigns equal probability to all classes (in SAS the corresponding priors statement is "PRIORS equal"; and this is the default priors).
(b) Proportional: Assigns probabilities in proportion to sample size (in SAS: "PRIORS proportional").
(c) Assign probabilities: Here, one would assign a probability to each group such as 0.6 to group 1 and 0.4 to group 2 (in SAS: "priors 1 = 0.6, 2 = 0.4").

Suppose $p_j$ is the prior probability for a new observation belonging to group $j$ and that $f_j(x)$ is its unconditional probability. Applying Bayes' theorem, the *posterior probability* of the new observation to belong to group $j$ is

$$p(j|x) = \frac{p_j f_j(x)}{\sum_{j=1}^{g} p_j f_j(x)} \tag{9.4}$$

where $x$ represents measurements for the new case. These posterior probabilities are computed by SAS software and would be too complicated to handle using calculators. Since the denominator is constant amongst groups, one would assign the new case to the group for which $p_j f_j(x)$ or its logarithm is the highest. In logarithmic form, we have

$$\ln p_j f_j(x) = \ln p_j + \ln f_j(x). \tag{9.5}$$

The $\ln f_j(x)$ is the value of log-likelihood that can be calculated for the new case measurements $(x)$ for group $j$. Replacing for $f_j(x)$ from Eq. (9.3), we have

$$\ln p_j f_j(x) = \ln p_j + \ln\left[(2\pi)^{-\frac{1}{n_j}}\left|\Sigma_j^{-1}\right|^{-\frac{1}{2}}\exp\left(-\frac{1}{2}d_j^2(x)\right)\right]$$

yielding the quadratic discriminant function:

$$\ln p_j f_j(x) = \ln p_j - \frac{1}{n_j}\ln 2\pi - \frac{1}{2}\ln\left|\Sigma_j^{-1}\right| - \frac{1}{2}d_j^2(x)$$

Equally,

$$\ln p_j f_j(x) = c_j - \frac{1}{2}d_j^2(x) + \ln p_j \tag{9.6}$$

where $c_j = -\frac{1}{n_j}\ln 2\pi - \frac{1}{2}\ln\left|\Sigma_j^{-1}\right|$.

If the prior probabilities are equal, the value of $\ln p_j$ is constant for all $j$ so, effectively, we are adding a constant to the log-likelihood function. Consequently, in this case, the resulting likelihood for all cases would increase by the same amount. This implies that the new case would be assigned to the same group with or without accounting for the prior probabilities. However, if the prior probabilities vary for different groups, then the assignment would be affected.

In the example used earlier, the priors were selected to be in proportion to sample size for each case. However, since the sample size for both groups is 16, this simplifies to equal probabilities. As discussed earlier, equal probabilities do not affect the assignment of the new case to a group. When a common variance-covariance matrix is used, the aforementioned equation can be simplified; replacing $\Sigma_j^{-1}$ by $\Sigma_p^{-1}$, and using Eq. (9.2):

$$d_j^2(x) = x'\Sigma_p^{-1}x - 2m_j'\Sigma_p^{-1}x + m_j'\Sigma_p^{-1}m_j$$

Now, $x'\Sigma_p^{-1}x$ remains the same across equations, so that it does not affect the assignment of a new case to one of the groups. Using the remainder of $d_j^2(x)$ in Eq. (9.6), yields

$$s_j^L = c_j - \frac{1}{2}\left[-2m_j'\Sigma_p^{-1}x + m_j'\Sigma_p^{-1}m_j\right] + \ln p_j,$$

Or, equally,

$$s_j^L = c_j - \frac{1}{2}m_j'\Sigma_p^{-1}m_j + m_j'\Sigma_p^{-1}x + \ln p_j \qquad (9.7)$$

The latter equation is known as the linear discriminant function and is referred to as the linear score function. The scalar $c_j - \frac{1}{2}m_j'\Sigma_p^{-1}m_j$ is considered as the intercept of the linear model ($c_{j0}$) and the 1 by $q$ vector $m_j'\Sigma_p^{-1}$ represents the coefficients of the $q$ measurements in $x$ so that the equation is written as

$$s_j^L = c_{j0} + \sum_{i=1}^{q} c_{ji}x_i + \ln p_j \qquad (9.8)$$

Again, all the calculations and comparison are done by software such as SAS. In SAS output, if prior probabilities are identified, they would be reflected in the intercept for the resulting log-likelihood for each group because they do not depend on $x$. Also, SAS provides estimated linear discriminant function even for the case that the quadratic version is used for discriminant analysis (Table 9.12).

As for the new case, the measurements (i.e., the $x$ values) for the five variables defined earlier are presented in Table 9.13. Plugging the measurements into each of the quadratic discriminant functions yields the highest value for group 1 so we can conclude that the new case belongs to group 1 (Table 9.14). (The definition of abbreviations used in the following tables are provide in Table 9.9.):

**Table 9.12** Estimated linear discriminant functions

| Variable | 1 | 2 |
|---|---|---|
| Constant | −89.29418 | −108.63969 |
| LIQ | 32.40816 | 39.98398 |
| EFF | 1.18341 | 1.40626 |
| CSH | 0.42129 | 0.36516 |
| LEV | 2.31002 | 11.01798 |
| PRO | 0.09877 | −0.52587 |

**Table 9.13** Measurements related to the new case

| LIQ | EFF | CSH | LEV | PRO |
|---|---|---|---|---|
| 2.4 | 57 | 24 | 1.1 | 68 |

**Table 9.14** Number of observations and percent classified into groups

|  | 1 | 2 | Total |
|---|---|---|---|
| Total | 1 | 0 | 1 |
|  | 100 | 0 | 100 |
| Priors | 0.5 | 0.5 |  |

## 9.5.4  Misclassification

The discriminant rule for allocating an observation into one of the known groups is a statistical process, so random factors may adversely affect the classification. To measure the probability of misclassification, we may use the following methods.

**Confusion Table**

In this method, the discriminant functions that are already estimated from the full sample are used to classify each sample observation into a group. The number of times that the observations are mapped into the known groups correctly or incorrectly are then counted and reported is a table. This table would reflect how good the classification rule works, and the probability of misclassification is calculated as the corresponding relative frequency. However, we always need to bear in mind that the results of discriminant functions that are based on incorrectly classified groups could be biased. The SAS output for the case in question is shown in the Table 9.15, where the "percent classified into group" reflects posterior probability of correct classification. For incorrect classification, the posterior probability is (1—probability of correct classification). It turned out that the classifications were correct for all the observations (Table 9.16).

**Table 9.15** Confusion table; number of observations and percent classified into groups

| From group | 1 | 2 | Total |
|---|---|---|---|
| 1 | 16 | 0 | 16 |
|   | 100 | 0 | 100 |
| 2 | 0 | 16 | 16 |
|   | 0 | 100 | 100 |
| Total | 16 | 16 | 32 |
|   | 50 | 50 | 100 |
| Priors | 0.5 | 0.5 | |

**Table 9.16** Error count estimates for groups

| | 1 | 2 | Total |
|---|---|---|---|
| Rate | 0 | 0 | 0 |
| Priors | 0.5 | 0.5 | |

## Set Aside Method

In this method, half of the observations are randomly set aside and the rest are used to estimate discriminant function for each group. The functions are then used to classify the remainder of observations and, thereby, calculate the proportion of misclassified. The advantage of this method is that it yields unbiased estimates of misclassification probability, that is, there is no systematic deviation of estimates from the corresponding true parameters. The disadvantage is in not using all the available information, so the estimates are not efficient, that is, they could be subject to big deviation from the true parameters due to the large variance associated with the estimates. In short, although there is no systematic under- or over-estimation of the parameters, the actual estimates could deviate significantly from true parameters on the high or low side.

## Cross Validation

In this method, one observation is deleted from the sample and the remaining observations are used to estimate the discriminant functions. The functions are then used to classify the deleted observation. This process is repeated for all observations one at the time. Finally, the proportion of misclassified observations is calculated to estimate misclassification probability.

Another source of misclassification arises when the new case does not belong to any of the groups included in the study at hand. Clearly, the latter case cannot occur if the groups are exhaustive (e.g., default or no default). The discriminant rule would assign such new case into one of the groups that yields the highest probability. In other words, the discriminant rule assumes that the new case would belong to one of the groups included in the study.

Here one needs to look for possible groups that may have been missing from the study. Validating the groups is further discussed in the following section.

## 9.5.5 Related Statistics

So far, the assumption was that the groups are well identified. In practice, we may want to check for this before performing discriminant analysis. The following statistics may be used in this regard.

**Univariate Test Statistics**
Using $F$-statistics, for one variable at a time, we can test if the mean of measurements is different across the groups (see William H. Greene, 2012).[15] Continuing the example noted earlier, the SAS output for these tests is presented later, indicating that each variable has different means across the two groups (Table 9.17).

**Multivariate Statistics**
The following four measures in multivariate analysis of variance (MANOVA) are also used to validate statistical significance of the grouping (see Gregory Carey (1998)[16]):

1. Wilks' lambda
2. Pillai's trace
3. Hotelling's trace
4. Roy's largest root

These statistics are for testing whether the means of the variables in different groups are different from each other. For the example noted earlier, the SAS

**Table 9.17** Univariate test statistics

| Variable | F statistics, Total SD | Pooled SD | Between SD | Num DF = 1, Den DF = 30 $R^2$ | $R^2 / (1 - R^2)$ | F Value | Pr > F |
|---|---|---|---|---|---|---|---|
| LIQ | 0.53 | 0.3074 | 0.6059 | 0.6745 | 2.0721 | 62.16 | <0.0001 |
| EFF | 18.3921 | 9.9581 | 21.6671 | 0.7163 | 2.5249 | 75.75 | <0.0001 |
| CSH | 16.0562 | 8.3445 | 19.2077 | 0.7386 | 2.8259 | 84.78 | <0.0001 |
| LEV | 0.5489 | 0.2841 | 0.6576 | 0.7407 | 2.8569 | 85.71 | <0.0001 |
| PRO | 37.7062 | 11.1208 | 50.2271 | 0.9158 | 10.8794 | 326.38 | <0.0001 |
| | | | Average $R^2$ | | | | |
| | Unweighted | | | 0.7571912 | | | |
| | Weighted by variance | | | 0.859691 | | | |

**Table 9.18** Multivariate statistics and exact $F$ statistics

| Statistic | $S = 1, M = 1.5, N = 12$ | | | | |
| | Value | $F$ Value | Num DF | Den DF | Pr > F |
|---|---|---|---|---|---|
| Wilks' lambda | 0.06456653 | 75.34 | 5 | 26 | <0.0001 |
| Pillai's trace | 0.93543347 | 75.34 | 5 | 26 | <0.0001 |
| Hotelling-Lawley trace | 14.48790081 | 75.34 | 5 | 26 | <0.0001 |
| Roy's greatest root | 14.48790081 | 75.34 | 5 | 26 | <0.0001 |

**Table 9.19** Generalised squared distance to groups

| From group | 1 | 2 |
|---|---|---|
| 1 | 1.38629 | 55.71592 |
| 2 | 55.71592 | 1.38629 |

output for these tests is presented above, indicating that the groups were significantly different amongst each other (Table 9.18).

### Pairwise Generalised Squared Distances Between Groups
This is a measure of how much the difference is between the means of the variables across the groups, taking into account the variance-covariance matrix (Table 9.19).

### Altman's $Z$-Score
Altman (1968)[17] used multiple discriminant analysis to develop a predictor for the likelihood of bankruptcy. The predictor, known as Altman's $Z$-score, is a linear function of five financial ratios as follows:

$$Z = 0.717x_1 + 0.847x_2 + 3.107x_3 + 0.42x_4 + 0.998x_5,$$

where $x_1$: working capital/total assets, $x_2$: retained earnings/total assets, $x_3$: earnings before tax and interest/total assets, $x_4$: shareholders equity/total liability, and $x_5$: sales/total assets.

We can interpret $x_1$ to $x_5$ as reflecting liquidity, firm age and cumulative profitability, profitability, financial structure, and capital turnover rate, respectively. As noted earlier, the discriminant function is simply a linear combination of independent predictors that discriminate between the categories of the dependent variable; furthermore, the signs of the estimated coefficients do not necessarily have to conform to the hypotheses (although it would be more intuitive if they do). In contrast, probit and logit models must have correct signs for estimated coefficient to be consistent with economic theory.

**Table 9.20** Predictions of Altman's Z-score

| Z-score | Prediction |
|---|---|
| Less than 1.20 | High probability of bankruptcy |
| Greater than 2.90 | Low probability of bankruptcy |
| Between 1.20 and 2.90 | The grey or undetermined area |

This is how the Altman's Z-score can be used in practice to identify the probability of default for a firm. The user inputs the values of the predictor variables into the Z-equation, which gives a corresponding Z-score. Next, the score is compared to different cases (ranges) presented in Table 9.20.

There are currently different versions of Z-score in different applications (see Burt Edwards, 2004).[18] Experience suggests that Z-score is a useful screening, monitoring, and attention-directing device (see Leopold A. Bernstein and John J. Wild, 1993).[19]

## 9.6 Applying Discriminant Analysis to Predict Sovereign Debt Crisis

In this part, we apply discriminant analysis to the country data introduced in Sect. 9.4. The objective is to classify countries for their risk of default based on a set of predictors (e.g., political shock) of such countries. The predictors or characteristics used are the same that we used in the previous logit probability analysis and are summarised below for ease of reference (Table 9.21).

We also examine how the discriminant analysis classifies a new case, based on matching the characteristics of the new case with those of the population groups already examined. To do so, we keep data for one defaulted country aside as the new case and use the remaining data (for 23 defaulted and 16 active countries) to estimate the model. The SAS software performs a probability analysis and selects the best match.

**Linear Discriminant Results**
As noted in the previous section, one may use linear or a quadratic form of the discriminant function. Although our intention is to use the quadratic discriminant model, by default the SAS programme also estimates the linear model, which we refer to as Model A presented later. It is a linear function of the predictors and thus resembles the Altman Z-score shown earlier. It is important to be aware, however, that Altman Z-score is not the statistical counterpart to Model

**Table 9.21** Predictors used in discriminant analysis

| Characteristic | Measurement | Mnemonics |
|---|---|---|
| Macroeconomic imbalance | 1/(real GDP growth + inflation rate) | 1/(GDP + INF) |
| Insolvency | Total debt service/foreign reserves | DSpFR |
| Illiquidity | Short-term debt/foreign reserves | STDpFR |
| Debt structure | Concessional debt (% of total external debt) | CDpExtD |
| Trade openness (proxy for the cost of default) | (export + import of G&S)/GDP | EpIpGDP |
| Political instability | Political shock (categorical variable) | PI |

**Table 9.22** Discriminant model A

| Variable | 0 | 1 |
|---|---|---|
| Constant | −5.91772 | −6.13969 |
| 1/(GDP+INF) | 3.48232 | −11.62581 |
| DSpFR | −0.0008202 | 0.01034 |
| STDpFR | −0.00125 | −0.0003512 |
| CDpExtD | 0.10359 | 0.06776 |
| EpIpGDP | 0.07109 | 0.04396 |
| PI | 3.05654 | 6.75357 |

A. The difference is that Model A is a final output, whereas the Z-score includes certain refinements that Altman judged necessary in order to come up with a final linear formulation. To classify which group a new case belongs to, its measured characteristics are used in the likelihood function such as Model A (Table 9.22). The classification is explained in detail in Sect. 9.5.2. In the case of Model A, for example, if the likelihood value of a new case is greater under group 1, the new case belongs to group 1.

## 9.6.1 Classification Test

As we showed in the previous sections, discriminant analysis is a powerful technique to discriminate between the categories of the dependent variable, given the measurements for a set of predictors. In this section, we look at a practical application where we are presented with a new case and our interest is to determine to which of two groups the new case belongs. The procedure that we use here is to compare the measured characteristics of the new case with the population and, thereby, determine the probabilities that the new observation would belong to each group. In Sect. 9.5.3, we introduced the notion of *prior probability*, which is the probability or the relative frequency of an observation coming from a particular group in a simple random sample with replacement, and we looked at three options used to assign the prior

**Table 9.23** Measured characteristics of the new country

| Measurement | Value |
|---|---|
| 1/(real GDP growth + inflation rate) | 0.088 |
| Total debt service/foreign reserves | 90.396 |
| Short-term debt/foreign reserves | 223.582 |
| Concessional debt (% of total external debt) | 0.289 |
| (export + import of G&S)/GDP | 48.769 |
| Political shock (categorical variable) | 1 |

**Table 9.24** Observation profile for test data

| Number of observations read | 1 |
|---|---|
| Number of observations used | 1 |

**Table 9.25** Number of observations and percent classified into groups—new case

|  | 0 | 1 | Total |
|---|---|---|---|
| Total | 0 | 1 | 1 |
|  | 100 | 0 | 100 |
| Priors | 0.5 | 0.5 | |

probabilities. In this study, for simplicity, we use the option of *equal probabilities*, which is SAS default option "PRIORS equal". The results shown below are based on the quadratic discriminant model described in the previous section. For the new country, the measured characteristics are presented in the following Table 9.23.

Plugging these values into each of the likelihood functions yields the highest value for group 1 so we can conclude the new case belongs to group 1 (Tables 9.24 and 9.25).

The results indicate that the new case has been correctly mapped to group 1.

## 9.6.2 Checking the Group Assumptions

We may also check if the groups were formed correctly using the Generalised Squared Distance Function described in the previous section (Tables 9.26 and 9.27).

The results indicate that there is less than 5% chance that a country in group 1 would be misclassified in group 0.

**Table 9.26** Number of observations and percent classified into groups

| From group | 0 | 1 | Total |
|---|---|---|---|
| 0 | 16 | 0 | 16 |
| | 100 | 0 | 100 |
| 1 | 1 | 22 | 23 |
| | 4.35 | 95.65 | 100 |
| Total | 17 | 22 | 39 |
| | 43.59 | 56.41 | 100 |
| Priors | 0.5 | 0.5 | |

**Table 9.27** Error count estimates for groups

| | 0 | 1 | Total |
|---|---|---|---|
| Rate | 0 | 0.0435 | 0.0217 |
| Priors | 0.5 | 0.5 | |

## 9.7  Choosing Between Probit, Logi, and Discriminant Analysis

We have shown that probit and logit are alternatives for modelling dichotomous variables, which are variables that take a value of 1 or 0. Moreover, we discussed discriminant analysis, which is a useful tool for classifying entities (e.g., firms, countries) based on their characteristics. As a practical consideration, it would be helpful to know which methodology one should use for classification problems. As we saw in the previous chapter, the probit model is very similar to the logit model, except that it assumes the error terms are normally distributed. In the logit model, the distribution of errors has fatter tails compared to normal so that it can accommodate cases involving more extreme values compared to logit. The discriminant model assumes the errors for each category (or group) are normally distributed or may have a joint normal distribution across the categories. G.S. Maddala (1983)[20] states:

> If the independent variables are normally distributed, the discriminant-analysis estimator is the true maximum-likelihood estimator and is asymptotically more efficient than the logit maximum likelihood estimator (MLE). However, if the independent variables are not normal, the discriminant analysis estimator is not even consistent, whereas the logit MLE is consistent and therefore more robust.

Recall that the linear discriminant model requires the assumption of homogenous variance-covariance matrix across the populations in question. However, this assumption does not apply to all cases. As we explained earlier, for heterogeneous variance-covariance matrices, quadratic discriminant analysis must be used.

## 9.7.1   Practical Uses of the Discriminant Analysis in Credit Assessment

Let us assume that Model A is Bank ABC's in-house discriminant model, and the bank is contemplating a US$25 million loan to Country D. To see if Country D is statistically likely to default or reschedule over the life of the loan, the analyst assigned to Country D uses the bank's model to classify the new country. He finds that the model classifies Country D into the default group. From the vantage point of the credit analyst, this result of the discriminant analyses is useful, for it serves as a check on the BRR that a hybrid model such as the criteria-based model assigns. If the discriminant (statistical) model has been doing a fairly good job at signalling debt crises, then the result forces the analyst to review the BRR rating of the hybrid model.

Another practical use of the discriminant analysis is in credit scoring for corporations. The outputs of the discriminant model also can be used to check the reliability of the criteria-based ratings.

# Appendix 9.1: Countries and Debt Crisis Episodes

| Country | External debt crisis episodes |
| --- | --- |
| Argentina | 1982 |
| Belize | No debt crisis |
| Bolivia | 1980–1981 |
| Botswana | No debt crisis |
| Brazil | 1983 |
| Cameroon | 1985 |
| China | No debt crisis |
| Colombia | 1982, 1983 |
| Costa Rica | 1981, 1984 |
| Dominican Republic | 1982, 1983 |
| Ecuador | 1982, 1983 |
| El Salvador | 1981 |
| Ethiopia | No debt crisis |
| Gabon | No debt crisis |
| Ghana | 1981, 1982 |
| Guyana | 1982 |
| India | No debt crisis |
| Indonesia | No debt crisis |
| Jamaica | 1981 |
| Jordan | No debt crisis |
| Kenya | No debt crisis |
| Malaysia | No debt crisis |

(*continued*)

(continued)

| Country | External debt crisis episodes |
|---------|-------------------------------|
| Lesotho | No debt crisis |
| Mexico | 1982 |
| Morocco | 1983 |
| Nepal | No debt crisis |
| Nicaragua | 1979 |
| Nigeria | 1983 |
| Panama | 1983 |
| Peru | 1984 |
| Pakistan | No debt crisis |
| Philippines | 1983, 1984 |
| Senegal | 1981 |
| Sierra Leone | 1980 |
| Sri Lanka | No debt crisis |
| Sudan | 1981 |
| Thailand | No debt crisis |
| Tunisia | No debt crisis |
| Turkey | 1980, 1981 |
| Venezuela | 1983 |

# Notes

1. The yield spread between the Emerging Market Local Credit Index and the US Generic Government 5 Year Index was more than 5.50% during the 2008 financial crisis. The spread has narrowed after the recovery to around 2.85% in July 2018.
2. Refer to Moody's Investors Services, *Sovereign Default and Recovery Rates, 1983–2016,* 30 June 2017; and Moody's Investors Service, *Sovereign Defaults and Restructurings,* October 2013.
3. Nagy, Pancras. J, (1984), *Country Risk: How to Assess, Quantify, and Monitor It* (London, Euromoney Publications, 1984). Country risk analysis and forecasting country default are a relatively new area of study that grew out of commercial banks' recycling of the current account surpluses of OPEC countries in the 1970s. See P. J. Nagy (1984), ibid.; M. H. Bouchet, Ephraim Clark and Bertrand Groslambert (2002), *Country Risk Assessment, A guide to Global Investment Strategy,* Wiley Finance, 2002. In this textbook, you find a comprehensive survey of the qualitative and quantitative method to country risk analysis.
4. There is no concise definition of a complex system, so it is more instructive to list the essential features of the system. A complex system includes many everyday examples such as a truck, a sports team, banking, an economy, and the human body. The common thread is that they all have goals, which drive

their behaviour. A complex system comprises many individual pieces but it is not so much the number of individual pieces that is important for complexity but how they connect with each other. Thus, linkages are a necessary feature of all complex systems. Complex systems exhibit non-linearity (changes in input lead to disproportionate changes in output), feedback loops, and adaptiveness in their behaviour.

5. Standard and Poor's (2017), 2016 Annual Sovereign Default Study and Rating Transitions, April 2017.
6. Euromoney, Currency Risk Methodology. https://www.euromoney.com
7. The PRS Group Inc., *International Country Risk Guide Methodology.*
8. Standard and Poor's (2017), Sovereign Rating Methodology, December 18, 2017.
9. Moody's Investors' Service (2016), *Ratings Methodology – Sovereign Bond Ratings,* December 22, 2016.
10. A strictly pre-emptive (sovereign) debt restructuring occurs when default risk is high *ex ante* and restructuring takes place pre-emptively without missing **any** payments to creditors. In practice, pre-emptive debt restructurings involve some missed payments but only temporarily. In contrast, in post-default debt restructuring, the borrower defaults unilaterally before it starts to renegotiate its debt. Most debt rescheduling are pre-emptive because the cost to the country due to a cessation of foreign credit is high in terms of lower real GDP. Various IMF studies suggest "severe credit and net capital inflow declines occur more likely following post-default restructurings than weakly or strictly pre-emptive restructurings." See IMF (2019), *Costs of Sovereign Defaults: Restructuring Strategies* by Tamon Asonuma, Marcos Chamon, Aitor Erce, and Akira Sasahara, WP/19/69. Bank Distress and the Capital Inflow-Credit Channel.
11. See these authors: W. W. Cooley, and P. R. Lohnes (1971), *Multivariate Data Analysis*, New York, John Wiley & Sons. B. Efron (1975), *The Efficiency of Logistic Regression Compared to Normal Discriminant Analysis*, Journal of the American Statistical Association, 70, 892–898. D. J. Hand (1981), *Discrimination and Classification*, New York, John Wiley & Sons; and D. J. Hand (1982), *Kernel Discriminant Analysis*, New York: Research Studies Press.
12. Altman, E. I. (1968), *Financial Ratios, Discriminant Analysis, and the Prediction of Corporate Bankruptcy*, Journal of Finance 22 (September), pp. 589–609.
13. Klecka, W. R. (1980), *Discriminant Analysis*, Sage University Paper Series on Quantitative Applications in the Social Sciences, 07–019, Beverly Hills and London: Sage Publications.
14. Morrison, D. F., (2005), *Multivariate Statistical Methods*, Thomson/Brooks/Cole.
15. Greene, W. H., (2012), *Econometric Analysis*, 7th edition, Prentice Hall.
16. Carey, G. (1998), *Multivariate Analysis of Variance (MANOVA): I. Theory*, pdf file.

17. Altman, E. I., (1968). *Financial Ratios, Discriminant Analysis, and the Prediction of Corporate Bankruptcy*, Journal of Finance 22 (September), pp. 589–609. Edward I. Altman (1993) Corporate Financial Distress and Bankruptcy: *A Complete Guide to Predicting & Avoiding Distress and Profiting from Bankruptcy*, Wiley.
18. Edwards, B., (2004), *Credit Management Handbook*, fifth edition, Gower.
19. Bernstein, L. A., and John J. Wild (1993), ibid.
20. G. S. Maddala, ibid.

# Part III

## Credit Management

# 10

# Credit Monitoring and Compliance

**Chapter Objectives**

1. Understand why monitoring is as important as origination in the life cycle of a loan
2. Examine best practices in credit monitoring
3. Identify the requirements of a robust monitoring system
4. Explore the benefits of automation in credit monitoring

## 10.1 Introduction

In Part I and Part II, we focused on credit origination, essentially the process of getting a loan on the books. In this final Part III, we discuss credit administration under the rubric of loan monitoring and problem loan management. Credit administration does not have the glamour of origination/underwriting presumably because it is mainly the back office function of a bank, but it is equally important in the profitability and full repayment of a loan. After a loan is paid out, the bank has to ensure that the obligor will repay the loan, and the waiting period might be many years. During this time, the risk profile of the obligor can be expected to change due to a host of reasons that we can classify into four broad groups: management decisions, competitive conditions in the market, industry trends, and the economic environment. In most

**Electronic Supplementary Material:** The online version of this chapter (https://doi.org/10.1007/978-3-030-32197-0_10) contains supplementary material, which is available to authorized users.

© The Author(s) 2020
T. M. Yhip, B. M. D. Alagheband, *The Practice of Lending*,
https://doi.org/10.1007/978-3-030-32197-0_10

cases, borrowers repay their debts, but as we pointed out in Chap. 1, it is a statistical certainty that many deals that were initially high fliers and promised huge returns, based on the lender's profitability model, will go sour.

## 10.2  Reasons for Loan Monitoring

The most obvious reason a lender regularly monitors credit quality throughout the life of a loan is that it wants to avoid loan losses. These may arise from deterioration in the credit worthiness of borrowers, deficiencies in risk mitigation such as the value of collateral, and loan documentation that are "out of order". This last lapse, if not remedied, could negatively affect the lender's ability to realise on the collateral security in case the obligor defaults. There is also a regulatory oversight aspect of the monitoring process. Banks are facing regulatory pressure to have in place strong management processes in credit data. Supervisors including central banks are requesting timelier and more detailed reporting from commercial banks, and want to ensure that they are up to the task. System capabilities include data availability, aggregation, calculation, calibration, reconciliation, and quality control. The purpose of the more stringent reporting requirements is to ensure the soundness of the banking system. Therefore, supervisors have started monitoring closely the banks' efforts to reduce non-performing loans and maintain high underwriting standards.

> **What the Reporting Requirements Mean for Lenders?**
>
> Banks will be spending enormous sums over the next few years on their data infrastructures to ensure they have timely access to credit underwriting and monitoring data at sufficient levels of quality and granularity.

To become a Basel II-compliant institution, a bank must implement a set of banking regulations under the AIRB approach, one of which is risk rating system operations. These three paragraphs from BCBS, International Convergence of Capital Measurement and Capital Standards (June 2006)[1] drive home the point:

424. Rating assignments and periodic rating reviews must be completed or approved by a party that does not directly stand to benefit from the extension of credit. Independence of the rating assignment process can be achieved through a range of practices that will be carefully reviewed by supervisors. These operational processes must be documented in the bank's procedures and incorporated into bank policies. Credit policy and underwriting procedures must reinforce and foster the independence of the rating process.

425. Borrowers and facilities must have their ratings refreshed at least on an annual basis. Certain credits, especially higher risk borrowers or problem exposures, must be subject to more frequent review. In addition, banks must initiate a new rating if material information on the borrower or facility comes to light.

426. The bank must have an effective process to obtain and update relevant and material information on the borrower's financial condition, and on facility characteristics that affect LGDs and EADs (such as the condition of collateral). Upon receipt, the bank needs to have a procedure to update the borrower's rating in a timely fashion.

## 10.3  Best Practices of Loan Monitoring

### 10.3.1  Covenant Monitoring

The transaction request (TR) that we introduced in Chap. 1 is the main organising document for the credit monitoring process. Banks employ a variety of policies and procedures for monitoring on two fronts: (1) credit quality and (2) loan documentation and collateral. First, let us look at credit quality. In order to perform the monitoring effectively, a lender puts in place covenants and other protective requirements in the Loan Agreement. A bank's commercial Loan Agreement incorporates numerous clauses or terms. The following are the important ones for monitoring.

- **Representations and warranties of the borrower:** This provision assures a bank that the legal, financial and regulatory requirements of the borrower are met each time funds are advanced under a facility.
- **Material adverse change:** An event of default is triggered if the lender believes that the condition of the borrower makes it unable to perform its obligations under the Loan Agreement.
- **Covenants:** Covenants can be affirmative (promises to do) or negative (promises to refrain from doing).
- **Events of default:** Includes payment default, breach of covenant, breach of representation or warranty, cross-default, material adverse change, material adverse change in the borrower's financial condition, collateral shortfall, and non-filling of financial statements. A lender includes events of default to force the borrower to renegotiate the loan in an attempt to strengthen the collateral and the borrower's cash flow.
- **Cross-default:** The provision gives the lender the ability to trigger a default under one loan agreement if the borrower is in default under another agreement with the same bank or another lender. This provision has serious

consequences for a borrower with multiple facilities, since it can result in the borrower facing repayment on all loans at the same time. Banks prefer this arrangement to cross-acceleration because it enables them to escalate their position against the borrower against other creditors.

- **Cross-acceleration:** A cross-acceleration provides the bank the ability to declare an event of default, but only after another creditor accelerates its loan. It is less creditor friendly.
- **Remedies in the event of default:** This clause sets out the rights and measures the bank can adopt to remedy an event of default that exists.

In addition to the Loan Agreement, the Transaction Request that we discussed in Chap. 1 has a section on Monitoring and Compliance. The Loan Agreement serves as the primary monitoring tool for the lender because it contains all the promises that the borrower must fulfil—including negative and affirmative covenants—until the loan is fully repaid. The three important covenants for monitoring are (a) Financial Covenants, (b) Affirmative Covenants, and (c) Negative Covenants. Through these covenants or promises, the lender can monitor the performance of the borrower's operation, identify operational risks, and raise timely red flags. There are numerous financial covenants. Listed below are the ones that a loan administrator sees in most commercial Loan Agreements.

1. Minimum Current Ratio (Current Assets divided by Current Liabilities) specified for given times of the year
2. Maximum borrowing base (X% of eligible Accounts Receivable) for drawings from a Line of Credit
3. Minimum Tangible Net Worth of $X at any time
4. Maximum capital expenditure of $X in any fiscal year
5. Maximum debt service ratio (e.g., (Principal + Interest)/EBITDA) of X% measured at some specified time of the year
6. Maximum Total Liabilities to Tangible Net Worth of X% at any time

The values are determined at the loan structuring stage and they depend on the borrower's business, the balance sheet, the types of credit facilities, and the collateral held.

In addition to the financial covenants are affirmative and negative covenants. The affirmative loan covenants require the borrower to do certain things, such as paying all taxes, maintaining adequate insurance policies, maintaining current financial records, and delivering to the lender for review. Financial disclosure is critical to monitoring financial covenants. Lenders typically require quarterly (unaudited) and annual (audited) financial statements within a certain period. For some types of facilities, prompt monthly reporting of eligible accounts receivables and inventory are required.

The negative loan covenants require the borrower to refrain from certain actions, and obtain the lender's approval. Negative covenants include:

1. Financial covenants such as limiting the total amount of indebtedness for the business and/or shareholders (e.g., a specific Total Liabilities/Tangible Net Worth ratio or a specific Debt Service Coverage)
2. Restriction on or forbidding distributions and dividends to the owners of private companies and to shareholders of public companies
3. Prevention of the sale of assets without the lender's approval
4. Prevention of a merger or acquisition without the lender's permission
5. Restriction on or forbidding management fees paid to related parties

As you would have noticed in going through this list, the covenants are all working in the same direction: ensuring that the cash flow from the operation is always available to repay the lender. In some Loan Agreements, a lender night require a "cash sweep" clause, which enables the lender to use excess free cash flows to pay down outstanding debt rather than for distribution to the owners and shareholders of a company.

**Breach of Loan Covenants**

Banks use various remedies in the event the borrower violates one or more of the loan covenants. The *severity of the breach* is a key consideration in the lender's response. For example, failure to submit financial statements on time for the first time is a minor breach, and the bank may simply waive the right to enforce the event of default by extending the deadline. Serious violations such as exceeding indebtedness or distributions, or acquiring a company without the lender's permission, could cause the bank to demand early repayment regardless of the maturity of the debt, halt any additional lending, and take legal actions. As you can see, effective monitoring and the timely reporting of the breaches are the critical factors to avoid delayed actions.

## 10.3.2  Periodic Credit Review Process

Banks review the borrowers at least annually and even continually if their BRRs are slipping. Weak borrowers, whose ratings have dropped to or breached a certain cut-off rating (at the low end of the scale), are usually candidates for continuous risk assessment. The annual review is a full credit risk assessment, and the tools are the BRR scorecard that we discussed in previous chapters and the statistical models as may be necessary. The credit officer is essentially refreshing the BRR based on new information, and is looking for changes in credit quality that may signal repayment problems over the next year or over a three-year time horizon, depending on whether the BRR is a point-in-time or through-the-cycle.

Additionally, the credit officer reviews the credit facilities and the collateral security. In reviewing a facility, the credit officer checks the accuracy of certain mandatory information on the Transaction Request, such as the template in Chap. 1, that includes:

1. Facility type: Committed or uncommitted
2. Facility Risk Rating (FRR)
3. Committed expiry date (CED), which is the last disbursement date on which the lender is required to pay out funds
4. Final maturity date (FMD), which is the final payment date, at which point the principal and all remaining interest on a loan or other facilities are due to be paid. Note that loan term and amortisation period are not the same. For example, a mortgage may have a five-year term with a 25-year amortisation period. It takes 25 years to pay off the entire mortgage, but for 5 years, the borrower is committed to the Mortgage Agreement. At the end of the term, the borrower may decide to renegotiate the mortgage with the same lender.

## 10.3.3  Watch List Process

A common practice of all banks is to place accounts that require increased or more frequent monitoring on a Watch List. These borrowers are usually identified at the annual review process, or they through the monitoring process as material information becomes available:

1. Deteriorating financial performance (evidenced by late payments and delinquency)
2. Breaches of financial covenants
3. Breaches of negative covenants (e.g., asset sale, mergers/acquisitions, restructuring)
4. Breaches of affirmative covenants (not submitting financial information and late reporting)

The Watch List process varies across lenders but there are a few commonalities. The process requires regular meetings involving the business units and Risk Management, timely and accurate information on the Watch Listed accounts, and the plan to deal with each account and monitor progress.

## 10.3.4  Monitoring Loan Documentation and Collateral

Inaccurate, incomplete, and out-of-order loan documentation and collateral can cause impairment in the value of the collateral and lead to loan losses. It is worth noting that security impairment is often included as an event of default in a Loan Agreement. *A common strategy of a bankrupt borrower is to attack the documentation of the credit.*[2] For monitoring loan documents, a typical list of duties would include many seemingly prosaic examples but the consequences from failure to perform the right tasks can turn out to be very costly. The checklist of questions includes the following:

1. Are the borrower's and guarantor's names accurate and correctly spelled?
2. If your borrower is an entity, is it registered as a corporation, limited liability company, or is a fictitious name?
3. If it is a corporation or limited liability company, do you have an up-to-date list of signing officers or members and their personal addresses (pertinent information for collecting the obligation), and their signatures?
4. If individual guarantors or sureties or any other type of obligors are part of the transaction, are their personal addresses (not the corporate debtor's address) available on the documents they execute in their individual capacity?
5. Do the loan documents accurately describe the collateral?
6. Is there proper documentation confirming the holder of the loan?

> **Effective Management of Loan Documentation**
>
> Loan documentation is legal evidence of the transaction between a lender and the obligor. Deficiencies in the documentation can cause a lender to incur unnecessary losses or prevent the lender from recovering a loan in situations such as foreclosures.

For the collateral, the checklist would include the following:

1. Do you have a documented list of all required collateral? Take a simple residential mortgage: do you have the two critical pieces of document in good order: the deed of trust and the promissory note?
2. Do you have a description of the type of collateral?
3. Do you have the address of the collateral's location?
4. Who owns the collateral? (Never *assume* that the borrower has possession).

5. Is there proof of ownership of the collateral?
6. Are there scanned copies of the collateral, including serial numbers or other identifiers, and the location of the collateral?
7. Are the collateral values refreshed and adequate (according to policy)?
8. Are the real estate appraisals performed by professionals? Are they on the current, "approved list"?
9. What are the lien positions? As we noted in Chap. 1, a lender needs to be aware of structural subordination and find avenues to mitigate the risks of lending to a holdco.
10. Are liens accurately *registered* to the correct collateral? Note: Incorrect registration affects the lender in two ways: recovering the collateral and being sued.[3]
11. Are liens accurately *recorded* and described in sufficient detail in the systems?
12. How is the collateral recorded in public records? (Lender needs to know this for consistency or correction).

## 10.4 Compliance Status

It is usual at the Annual Review process for the credit officer who is preparing the Annual TR (for submission to Risk Management) to report on the borrower's compliance status. Typically, this section of the TR would include a table listing the requirements that the borrower must fulfil and other actions that the lender must undertake. Alongside the list, the credit officer would check the appropriate box: "yes", "no", or "not applicable" in regard to compliance status. For the "no" check marks, the officer provides details and the amounts in another column. In another column, the officer states the date the problem will be resolved. Examples of the items include:

1. Covenants
2. Security
3. Margins
4. Principal payments
5. Interest payments
6. Environment
7. Non-performing loans
8. Provision for loan loss
9. Overdue debt written off

# 10.5  Requirements of an Effective Monitoring System

It is clear from the forgoing discussion that for the monitoring system to be effective in identifying and resolving repayment problems, it ideally has these five capabilities with the benefit of new technologies:

1. Centralised data: An enterprise-wide database is a critical component of the management information system (MIS). Such a database provides more accurate and timely information, speeds up information gathering and processing, and contributes to lowering cost. A centralised database fits neatly with the new technologies that allow people to work anywhere and everywhere. For example, remote rather than onsite auditing is now common practice in many banks because cost is the major factor. The cost of onsite audits could easily run into hundreds of thousands of dollars, depending on the location, the size of the team, and the time spent onsite.
2. Tracking capability: A robust system must be able to monitor and test covenants, and track out-of-order documentation.
3. Reporting capability: The system must be able to generate a detailed report of the out-of-order documentation and covenant violations.
4. Timeliness: Timeliness is critical in addressing loan problems, such as taking immediate actions to prevent loss or further loss. Timely monitoring ensures that the bank is complying with prudential regulations *and* quantifying its risk, accurately calculating its capital, and making provisions.
5. Accuracy capability: Automated systems are more reliable and accurate than manual systems that rely on manual inputting of information and individual spreadsheets or word documents to test financial covenants and reporting breaches.

## 10.5.1  Automation of the Monitoring Process

Although banks use manual systems to monitor loans, more and more banks have been switching to automated processes in the last decade. The main reasons are that automated systems are faster, more efficient, and more accurate. From a management information perspective, an automated monitoring system is more effective in detecting deteriorating credit trends at the individual borrower level and at the portfolio level. Automation works best for public companies where the required financial data can be easily downloaded from a vendor. The monitoring system does the rest of the functions.

The scope for automation is, however, more limited for borrowers that are private companies whose data are not easily accessible. Whilst there is still the need for manual inputting of raw data into the system, once this is done, the system completes the rest of the functions automatically.

---

### Advantages of Onsite Bank Audits

Traditionally, internal auditing has been a very manual and person-to-person activity involving, at its core, sample-based testing and intensive interviews with the auditee. With the application of big data and data analysis, an analyst can gather evidence from a high percentage of a population, or all of it offsite (e.g., working at home). Consequently, the traditional testing methods, the role of the auditor, and the required skills are changing. The assurance role of Internal Audit will stay the same, of course, but the methods that the internal auditor uses to gather evidence of irregularities or incongruities are getting more sophisticated and automated. For example, artificial intelligence or machine learning is being applied to detect fraud in accounting transactions in real time. All this means that the onsite bank audit for various operations is quickly becoming a thing of the past as banks rely more and more on big data applications and systems. Clearly, this is a cost-effective way to manage the internal audit department; however, there are staunch defenders of the traditional audit. The arguments for its continued practice include the advantages not found in big data analysis:

1. Additional documentation can be readily obtained onsite.
2. Direct observation of practice is possible.
3. Face-to-face interviews with staff and senior managers.
4. Insight gained on working conditions and staff morale.

---

## Notes

1. Basel Committee on Banking Supervision (June 2006). Page 95, ibid.
2. Johnson, S. L. (2014), *Proactive steps for the secured lender in the world of bankruptcy*, Illinois Banker, October 2014.
3. There was a recent case in Vancouver, Canada, where a man sued Royal Bank of Canada for seizing his car. The bank admitted it was an error and explained the lien was registered to the incorrect vehicle. The CBC (Joan Marshall of the Canada Broadcasting Corporation) reported the news on October 25, 2018, "*'I was in utter disbelief': Man sues RBC after high-performance car seized.*"

# 11

# Problem Loan Management

## Chapter Objectives

1. Understand why problem loans are costly to a lender
2. Describe the organisational structure for managing problem loan
3. Discuss the types of loan loss provisioning
4. Review the pros and cons of loan recovery strategies

## 11.1 Introduction

In Chap. 3, we looked at the business or economic cycle (see Table 3.1) and its direct effect on borrower risk rating (BRRs). Not surprisingly, a bank's experience with problem loans tracts closely the cycle as it goes through one complete expansion, measured from trough to peak. We observe a clear pattern in Fig. 11.1: non-performing loans (NPL) as a percentage of total loans of all US banks tend to fall during the recovery and expansion phases (1990–2007 and 2009–2019), then rise sharply during the contraction phases (e.g., 2008–2009). The US economy was not in a recession in the 1980s, but the graph shows a rise in the NPL ratio. This is not an anomaly but a reflection of the Savings and Loans crisis when thousands of small US banks failed. Without question, the deterioration in the NPL/Gross Loans ratio in the 2008–2009 recession was the worst since the Great Depression

**Electronic Supplementary Material:** The online version of this chapter (https://doi.org/10.1007/978-3-030-32197-0_11) contains supplementary material, which is available to authorized users.

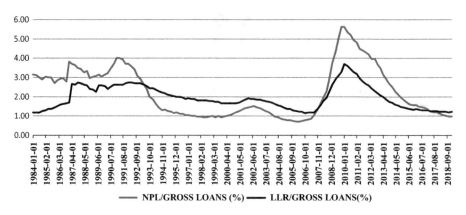

**Fig. 11.1** NPLs and LLR to Gross Loans for all US banks

when bankruptcies and defaults soared, causing widespread bank failure, with more than 1000 US banks closing each year from 1930 to 1933.[1]

The NPL ratio is almost where it was at the peak of the previous expansion, and the question uppermost in the minds of market observers, given the length of this economic cycle, is when it will reverse direction. A related concern is whether the deterioration will be moderate or severe. We also notice in the graph that the two ratios tend to converge in the *late stage of the business cycle* as banks increase provisioning faster than they are putting new loans on the books. As a result, the LLR/Gross Loans measure starts to exceed NPLs/Gross Loans. However, the gap is not nearly as wide as in the last expansion, which is not comforting given the age of the current economic cycle. We know from history that all expansions end at some point.

Banks do not like to write off loans; after all, as we saw in Chap. 7, loans are the main income earning assets on a bank's balance sheet. Problem loans are costly to a lending institution and mainly for this reason a commercial bank, for instance, closely monitors the credit quality of its borrowers and attempts to identify problem loans to avert default. It is a very labour-intensive but indispensable operation of a bank. Without question, lending is an expensive way of earning income in contrast to earning fees from investment services and wealth management, activities that expose the institution to minimal or virtually no credit risk. The direct costs of problem loans include the following:

- Lost principal
- Lost interest income

- Administrative expenses (such as a specialised group and the resources to manage and recover the problem loans)
- Recovery expenses such as legal and transactional
- Interest expense
- The costs of time delays in collecting principal and/or interest (see below for more details).

In addition, there are indirect costs to the lender that include:

---

**Debt Written Off Is Not Debt Forgiven/Forgotten**

Debt write-off is just an accounting procedure to remove a bad asset, the unpaid loan, from the books. Otherwise, the financial position of the bank is misleading. But rarely is debt forgiven; the defaulter still legally owes the money unless the obligor receives a letter from the lender confirming the debt has been forgiven. Note also that the expiration of the statute of limitations for a debt does not erase the obligation. Some debts do not have statute of limitations.

---

- Opportunity. The bank has forgone an alternative and profitable use of its scarce capital.
- Reputation. Bad management and resolution of a file could tar a bank's corporate image.

Adopting the right strategy is critical to recovering any losses or, ideally, rehabilitating a borrower to make it profitable and self-sustaining. We noted earlier that a bank does not like to write off loans, yet after it does the debt remains unpaid and lenders usually exhaust all possible means to recover the loans.

## 11.2  Management Structure

In Chap. 10, we examined the processes that a bank has established to identify early borrowers in financial difficulty. Once a borrower is in default or is in imminent default, a prudent lender would deal promptly with the account because time delays could lead to bigger losses. A bank would typically have a specialised group to manage delinquent or defaulted borrowers. This set-up is a straight application of the principle of division of labour, which is premised on efficiency. It is also an application of the principle of separation of duties to prevent fraud due to conflict of interest. Imagine what the outcome would be if the business unit that originated the loans was also responsible for managing the credit risks, including BRR assessment, and dealing with covenant breaches. However, once the loans move to the impaired loan portfolio, the business unit hands over control of the accounts to the Problem Loans Unit.

This specialised structure is typically a part of a bank's overall risk management framework. Remember: the function of Risk Management is to support the business units, balancing risk for the return, but it is supposed to remain *independent* of the businesses. It means Risk Management does not have a balance sheet to manage. It is worth noting that this specialised structure is relatively recent in the history of commercial banking. It got started in the aftermath of the Less developed country (LDC) debt crisis and energy bad debt in the early 1980s when banks were overwhelmed by debt restructurings. These developments argued for a specialised unit to manage the loans.

In banks that adhere to proper risk management practices, the Problem Loans Unit operates under strict credit policy and guidelines and furthermore, the group is subject to periodic audits by the internal auditors (as are all operations in the organisation). The problem loans unit has the authority to modify loan terms in order to improve loan recovery and to avoid foreclosure, repossession, or other legal remedies. The restructuring of bad debts often involves concessions such as rate reduction, principal forgiveness, and term extensions. As a result, the original terms of loan agreements or contracts have to be modified, requiring changes to the original covenants. Although the recovery avenue that a bank takes and the techniques it applies depend on internal credit policy and a borrower's financial situation, the customer's cooperation is crucial to success or failure of the strategy.

## 11.3 Provisioning for Problem Loans

In Chap. 10 on credit monitoring, we saw that financial institutions employ various ways to assess and track credit quality. The principal ones are the annual and more frequent credit reviews, the Watch List, and the Early Warning System. A bank makes three types of provisions for impaired loans:

1. Specific provision
2. General provision
3. Bad debt write-off (or charge-off)

The cross-default and cross-acceleration clauses in a Loan Agreement enable the bank to declare an account is in default. A bank prefers cross-default to cross-acceleration, as we noted earlier. The cross-default gives the lender the ability to trigger a default under one loan agreement if the borrower defaults under another agreement, whereas cross-acceleration gives the lender the ability to declare an event of default only after another lender accelerates its loan. Furthermore, regulators consider that if a borrower has multiple facilities and one becomes impaired, then all facilities are treated as impaired.

## 11.3.1  Specific Provision

When a bank determines that a particular loan is impaired, it reduces the book or carrying value to an estimated realisable value by recording a specific provision for credit loss (PCL). This provision incorporates two components: (1) the expected amount of the loan that will not be recovered and (2) the costs of time delays in collecting principal and/or interest, referred to as the time value of money (TVM) component, for the recoverable part of the loan. The TVM component is the difference between the estimated value of the future cash flow over a specific period and the present value of the cash flow over the same time horizon:

$$\text{TVM} = \sum_{t=1}^{N} \text{EV}_t - \text{PV}_t$$

where:

TVM = Time value of money component
EV = The *estimated* value of the future cash flow for period $N$
PV = The present value of the estimated cash flows

The factors driving the EV component are the loan loss provisioning, the amount of gross impaired loan, and write-offs. The higher the amount of impaired loans, the higher is EV; whereas the higher the write-offs and loan loss provision, the lower is EV, *ceteris paribus*. The discount rate is usually the interest rate of the segment with the largest expected loss at the time of impairment. As you can see from this equation, the higher the interest rate, the lower the PV and the greater the TVM, or alternatively, the higher the cost of time delays in receiving payments. We also see that if a lender writes off the entire amount of the impaired loan, the EV goes to zero, as there will be no future repayment cash flows to "present value". Likewise, the TVM component also goes to zero.

In making a specific provision, the lending institution debits the expense account and credits Loan Loss Reserves (LLR) or Allowance for Loan Losses (ALL), which is *contra asset* account. These accounting entries result in an increase in the (credit) balance of the LLR account, thereby reducing net loan amount (gross loans minus LLR). Specific provision, an expense, is an income statement account.

### 11.3.2 General Provision

Unlike a specific provision, a general provision is held against future, *unidentified* losses and the lender creates the provision from the time it approves the loan. This method is in keeping with regulatory requirements. In making a general provision, the bank debits Bad Debts Expense and credits LLR. Just as with a specific provision, these entries increase the (credit) balance of the LLR account and reduce the net loan amount (gross loans minus LLR). As we noted in Chap. 1, general provision qualifies as Tier 2 or supplementary capital of a bank.

### 11.3.3 Bad Debt Write-Off (or Charge-Off)

Unlike specific and general provisions that pass through the Income Statement, a charge-off flows through the Balance Sheet. This means the lender credits loans (thereby removing it from the performing loan book) and debits LLR (thereby reducing the credit balance). Since LLR is a "contra asset", the write-off against LLR reduces the amount of net loans by the same amount.

It is a misconception that the borrower automatically receives debt forgiveness when the lender writes off a debt. The provisioning and charge-off fulfil accounting and regulatory requirements, but, as far as the bank is concerned, the unpaid debt is still collectible and it is not unusual for a bank to hire a collection agency or pursue other legal recourse to recover the loans. However, in jurisdictions where Statute of Limitations apply, a borrower may have protection from the collection of old debt. This common law sets a maximum time after an event within which legal proceedings may be initiated.

## 11.4 Problem Loan Management Process and Policies

In most banks, problem loan management is integrated into the overall risk management process. The following are some of the commonalties of the structure of problem loans management across banks:

- Banks have a specialised unit to manage problem loans. Let us call it the Problem Loans Unit.
- Banks have formal problem loans management programmes. Their degree of centralisation varies across banks but most banks prefer a centralised head office structure.
- Banks have adopted credit policy and procedures for problem loans management within the overall risk management structure. Internal bank policy specifies the *minimum* risk rating for an account to be treated as a problem loan and to be managed by the Problem Loans Unit and not the business unit.
- For the day-to-day operations, banks have formal internal mechanisms for the monitoring and reporting, involving the problem loan officers, various levels of senior management and their joint accountability to the board of directors.
- Problem loan managers are responsible for recommending specific loan recovery strategies and risk tolerances. Special loans managers perform the dual roles of relationship manager and risk managers.
- Senior management of the Problem Loans Unit approves transactions and strategies according to their delegated lending limits.

The transfer of non-performing and impaired accounts to the Problem Loans Unit does not happen suddenly. The accounts would have been on the Watch List for some time and the Watch List process involves the Problem Loans Unit, so that there are few surprises at the transition. For most banks, the routes to loan recoveries include three main strategies:

1. Remarket (find another lender)
2. Rehabilitation (continue with the borrower)
3. Compulsory liquidation (realising on the collateral)

## 11.4.1 Problem Loans Documentation

As we have seen in Chap. 10, proper loan documentation is crucial to the repayment of a loan and this applies regardless of whether a loan is performing or non-performing. Consider a strategy such as rehabilitation. It usually takes many years to bear fruit, as much as five years or more, and it costs the lender significant resources. A key decision is which strategy is optimal. The path to the final resolution of a non-performing account is hardly ever straight so that a bank's strategy could change along the way. For each strategy, authorisations by senior management are required for various purposes including provisioning, write-off, and credit transactions. A lender may reach a point where legal remedies, such as liquidation or foreclosure, may be the only feasible recovery avenues after exhausting a cooperative strategy. All of these must adhere to a formalised documentation process. The organising document is the counterpart to the Transaction Request that you saw in Chap. 1 for a performing account. That document contains all pertinent information like gross amount of impaired loans, the provisioning, current and projected allowance for loan loss, the write-offs, history of covenant breaches, a description of the work out plan, and the related authorisations. The document serves as the primary vehicle for periodic credit review, approving credit transaction requests, monitoring progress, and documenting all deliberations and actions to return the account to the business unit upon successful rehabilitation, or to remarket or liquidate.

## 11.4.2  Remarketing the Loan

Under this strategy, the bank encourages or forces the borrower to seek another lender. The approach works only if through its monitoring process the lender uncovers the financial problem in the early stages before the loan goes delinquent. The *information asymmetry* problem that we discussed in Chap. 1 can easily occur here because the borrower has more information than the lender about the company, and is likely to withhold bad information about its current and future performance. Early detection gives the lender the time to tighten the pressure on the borrower to bank elsewhere by increasing the interest rate charged on the loans, imposing more restrictive covenants, and toughening up the monitoring requirements. The majority of problem loans are not so quickly resolved by remarketing, however, because a bank may be reluctant to adopt "pressure tactics" for fear of tarnishing its image, so that it must choose between rehabilitating the borrower and initiating liquidation.

## 11.4.3  Rehabilitation

The lender evaluates the feasibility to rehabilitate a borrower by assisting the company to becoming profitable again to repay the loan. The appraisal requires the following steps that include discussions with the borrower especially in the development of a *work out plan*:

- Identify the causes of the problem
- Develop alternative solutions
- Model the alternatives for a sensitivity analysis of the critical key variables and the outcomes
- Compare the alternatives
- Decide on the most feasible and practical alternative
- Develop and implement the plan
- Monitor the results

The benefits of rehabilitation are: (a) the bank preserves the customer relationship, and (b) the expected return is likely to be higher than liquidation because the borrower is able to repay the loan in full, whereas compulsory liquidation depends on the assets to begin with and recovery is partial. If the rehabilitation succeeds, the account returns to the business with an updated risk rating. The Loan Agreement will usually have new covenants.

## 11.4.4 Troubled Debt Restructure (TDR)

Because rehabilitation often involves the restructuring of debt, it can result in an accounting (Financial Accounting Standard 15) and regulatory classification known as **Troubled Debt Restructure (TDR)**. To be considered a TDR, (a) the creditor before and after the restructuring must be the same, (b) the obligor is experiencing financial distress – evidenced by operating losses, delinquency, overdrafts, and default – and (c) the creditor must grant a concession. Concessions include:

1. Reduction in interest rate
2. Reduction in principal due
3. Extension of the maturity date
4. Forbearance
5. Forgiveness of a portion of debt in exchange for assets or an equity interest in the debtor.

The loan continues as a TDR until it is repaid in full, or until it becomes substantially performing. Loans classified as a TDR must be tested for impairment using the present value (PV) of the future cash flows. The discount rate is the contract rate, which is the interest rate that will be paid on the principal balance for the life of the loan. The impairment test measures whether the liability is worth the amount reported on the balance sheet. The balance sheet amount is reduced if the impairment test indicates a lower value.

## 11.4.5 Compulsory Liquidation of Collateral

Sometimes rehabilitation might not be the optimal or least cost recovery route. Alternatively, a court-ordered liquidation, which the creditor initiates, is the final and most drastic step a bank can take against a company that has failed to repay its debts. The liquidation of the company gives the lender the best chance of recovering some of the loans from the sale of assets. The advantages of liquidation over rehabilitation are:

- Faster recovery of funds
- Shorter time involved
- Easier to execute (assuming no bankruptcy)
- No further credit risk due to extending additional credit, reducing interest, and stretching out amortisation to reduce principal payments.

However, compared to rehabilitation, the legal costs of liquidation are much higher, and the lender pays initially with the hope of recouping the costs from the sale of the insolvent company's assets.

In a liquidation, various options are available to the lender including:

- Sale as a going concern
- Sale of major segments
- Sale of assets (in whole or in part)
- Auction
- Foreclosure followed by Repossession. The foreclosure process could drag out for years before the lender may repossess the asset.

Upon the compulsory liquidation of a company, the distribution of the proceeds follows the creditor ranking set out by law. If we are talking about Western law, at the top of the heap are the secured creditors such as banks and asset-based lenders and, at the very bottom, are the shareholders. Right above them are the unsecured creditors such as suppliers and contractors. The creditor ranking means that an unsecured creditor is only likely to initiate a liquidation if the entity is sure the company has assets of significant value.

## Note

1. Wheelock, David. C., (2007), *An Overview of the Great Depression*, Federal Reserve Bank of St Louis, Sept 20, 2007.

# Index[1]

---

[1] Note: Page numbers followed by 'n' refer to notes.

© The Author(s) 2020
T. M. Yhip, B. M. D. Alagheband, *The Practice of Lending*,
https://doi.org/10.1007/978-3-030-32197-0